Supply Chain Management and Transport Logistics

The enterprise-focused framework of supply chain, which an overwhelming majority of books on supply chain management (SCM) have adopted, falls short in explaining recent developments in the real world, especially the so-called Wal-Mart model, in which a "factory" is a virtual logistics network of multiple international manufacturing firms. This book fills the gap and examines supply chain and transport logistics.

The book also includes the development of a unified methodological framework which underpins all the characteristics of the interrelationship between supply chain management and logistics. It covers many aspects of the important and innovative developments well. The book offers a unique coverage of integrated logistics of navigation, aviation and transportation.

The book not only answers the urgent need for a book on supply chain management and transport logistics but also highlights the central role of supply chain logistics in the emerging fields of sustainable (green), humanitarian, and maritime supply chains and the importance of studying supply chain management together with transport logistics. It also explains the difference between supply chain logistics and manufacturing logistics. It is a useful reference for those in the industry as well as for those taking related courses.

John J. Liu has more than twenty years of extensive teaching, research and consultancy experience in risk and decision analysis of logistics, supply chain and maritime services. He has very distinctive experiences in leading and designing executive development programs for senior executives and professionals. His publications are frequently found in refereed journals such as *OR* and *Management Science*, receiving different teaching and research awards. He has served on the Engineering Panel of Research Grant Council, HKSAR (2005–2011). He serves on the Advisory Board for Journal of Maritime Policy and Management (2008–2010), and on the Human Resource Taskforce of Maritime Industry Council, HKSAR (2006–2010).

Supply Chain Management and Transport Logistics

John J. Liu

Routledge
Taylor & Francis Group

LONDON AND NEW YORK

First published 2012
by Routledge
2 Park Square, Milton Park, Abingdon, Oxon OX14 4RN

Simultaneously published in the USA and Canada
by Routledge
711 Third Avenue, New York, NY 10017

Routledge is an imprint of the Taylor & Francis Group, an informa business

British Library Cataloguing in Publication Data
A catalogue record for this book is available from the British Library

Library of Congress Cataloging in Publication Data
A catalog record for this book has been requested

ISBN: 978–0–415–61895–3 (hbk)
ISBN: 978–0–415–61896–0 (pbk)
ISBN: 978–0–203–80586–2 (ebk)

Typeset in Bembo
by Book Now Ltd, London

MIX
Paper from
responsible sources
FSC
www.fsc.org FSC® C004839

Printed and bound in Great Britain by
CPI Antony Rowe, Chippenham, Wiltshire

Dedicated to the contributing editors on the latest developments in the integration of all-mode transport logistics:

Tsz-Leung Yip, Adolf Ng, Zhou Xu, Xiaowen Fu, Meifeng Luo

Contents

PART III
Integrated supply chain and transport logistics: integration
of all-mode supply chain logistics   375

Illustrations

Figures

Tables

Preface

Why supply chain management and transport logistics?

The urgent need for a book on *supply chain management and transport logistics* (or simply *supply chain logistics*) can be illustrated with a number of questions regarding state-of-the-art developments in the field of logistics and supply chain management (SCM).

- Are you aware that over 90 percent of international trade volume is carried across seas and waterways, and consequently over 90 percent of supply chains involve *port and transport logistics*?
- Are you aware that **manufacturing** and **transportation** each generated the same average of 14 percent of global greenhouse gas emissions in 2006?
- Do you understand why it is important to study *supply chain management* together with *transport logistics*? What is the difference between *supply chain logistics* and *manufacturing logistics*?
- Do you know the difference between *firm-focal* and *port-focal logistics*? (Note: Economic globalization is bringing about an inevitable trend toward port/airport-focused logistics, with firm-based logistics/SCM as building blocks.)
- Are *supply chain logistics* and *supply chain management* the same thing?

Although complete answers to these questions are still being explored, the most important and innovative developments in this regard are embedded throughout this book. In short, the answers are based on the following findings:

- Globalization is not a prediction; it is an inevitable reality.
- Globalization is underpinned by two technological innovations: containerization and the Internet, on which the "World's Factory" and the Wal-Mart Economy are founded.
- Globalization consists of two dimensions: global manufacturing and global services, with logistics as the vital link between the two.

For the sake of reference, we will begin with a brief introduction to the relevant terminologies. *Logistics* refers to the provision of supplies, which not only includes shipping and the transportation of supplies (物流, the Chinese translation of logistics), but also the relevant services and support (后勤, such as maintenance and insurance, etc.). In terms of professional content and academic terminology, shipping encompasses all modes of navigation, aviation, and transportation, whereas logistics services are wide-ranging, including finance, insurance, technology, and infrastructure. *Supply chain management* (SCM) has so far been referred to by both researchers and practitioners as the management of supply chains within a business organization, and most existing textbooks on SCM are based on enterprise-focused manufacturing settings and applications. In this connection, two categories have emerged in supply chain and transport logistics: *industrial logistics* and the *logistics industry*. *Industrial logistics* is enterprise focused (e.g., typical business logistics and manufacturing logistics), whereas the *logistics industry* is enterprise crossing (e.g., third-party logistics and the shipping industry). Specifically, *industrial logistics* is a necessary logistical function of individual enterprises and firms, whereas the *logistics industry* refers to industrial organizations that specialize in SCM and transport logistics. For example, logistics is geared around a *focal factory* as described in the mainstream SCM literature (e.g., La Londe 1998) and is a specific form of *industrial logistics*, whereas third-party logistics firms serving the automobile industry represent a specific *logistics industry* in the form of *nested* industrial supply chains.

Nevertheless, the interrelationship between logistics and SCM has been both striking and intriguing. On the one hand, when the supply chain is viewed as a business platform for the acquisition and provision of supplies and goods, industrial *logistics* is inseparable from SCM, and at the same time supply chain operations contain logistics. On the other hand, when viewed as a service industry, *logistics* is enterprise crossing rather than enterprise focused, according to the conventional definition of SCM. In this regard, logistics can be clearly distinguished from SCM.

The motivation for writing a book on *supply chain and transport logistics* arises from the observation that the enterprise-focused framework of SCM, which an overwhelming majority of books on SCM have adopted, falls short of explaining recent real-world developments, especially the so-called Wal-Mart model in which a "factory" is a virtual logistics network of multiple international manufacturing firms. The success of the Wal-Mart model rests on two dynamic innovations: all-mode logistics service facilitation and the industrial organization of supply chains, which are inadequately covered by existing SCM textbooks. For example, the management of transport utilities and facilities, such as seaports and airports, has become an expected part of logistics and SCM, especially from an international perspective, yet is seldom covered in textbooks on SCM and logistics. *Supply chain and transport logistics*, as termed in this book, is based on this intriguing interrelationship, referring to supply-chain centered logistics with enterprise-crossing characteristics, including both the service facilitation and the industrial organization (IO) aspects of logistics. The true challenge in writing a book on *supply chain and transport logistics* is the development of a unified methodological framework that underpins all of the characteristics of the intriguing interrelationship between firm-focal and port-focal SCM and logistics.

Winning-before-doing methodology for supply chain and transport logistics

> A winner secures victory before engaging in a fight, whereas a loser engages a fight and then seeks victory. 是故胜兵先胜而后求战败兵先战而后求胜.
>
> *The Art of War*, Chapter 4, Verse 4.15 (500 BC, by Sun Zi)

In modern language, Sun Zi's words from 500 BC mean "winning before doing," which I sincerely believe in, especially because I have realized how well it still applies in modern times. In *The Art of War*, Sun Zi wrote "兵马未到, 粮草先行", which translates as, "a vital secret to *winning-before-doing* (WBD) is the efficient and timely *provision of supplies*," which is undeniably the earliest reference to the concept of *supply chain* and *logistics*. Sun Zi went on to say that the world is constantly *changing* in an extremely precise yet seemingly uncertain manner. The inevitable challenge in WBD is to deal with changes that are often unpredictable and to identify and then solve the seemingly unsolvable problems that arise from such changes. The key to winning-before-doing lies in flawless planning and adaptation. It is astonishing how these 1,000-year-old words sound just like lecture notes for a modern management class in a business school. It is no wonder that *The Art of War* has been referred to in Japan as "the bible of business competition" since the 1950s. The term "logistics" in this book is broadly defined in the sense of Sun Zi's portrayal.

When it comes to modern management, the six-sigma principle cannot be ignored by researchers and practitioners. An easy test for someone who claims to know six-sigma is to check if he/she can spell out the five-letter golden rule of the six-sigma principle: D-M-A-I-C: Define–Measure–Analysis–Improve–Control. To demonstrate how great Chinese culture is, I need only quote Sun Zi's *The Art of War*: "兵法: 一曰度 (define), 二曰量 (measure), 三曰数 (count), 四曰称 (balance), 五曰胜 (win)." The five-word rule of war defined by Sun Zi over 2,500 years ago is virtually identical to the D-M-A-I-C of modern enterprise management. I was astonished to find this identical translation in 1999 when I was preparing lectures for a SCM course at the University of Wisconsin, Milwaukee.

Supply Chain Management and Transport Logistics is written particularly for senior undergraduate and postgraduate students in general management and decision sciences, especially with a major or specialization in SCM and logistics. For example, the book could be used for a compulsory MBA course with a specialization or "track" in SCM and logistics. The book is expected to be particularly useful for MBA curricula in Asia. In addition to SCM- and OM-oriented programs, the book will also be useful for shipping and maritime logistics programs, at both the undergraduate and postgraduate levels.

This book focuses on the system dynamics and solution tools that are essential to WBD, streamlined into three parts (modules). Parts I and II are devoted to the basics of SCM and transport logistics, and Part III offers unique coverage of the integrated all-mode logistics of navigation, aviation, and transportation. Part III is written by five contributing editors who are specialized in different aspects of transport logistics. The three parts are organized as follows.

- **Part I. Business supplies and logistics: theories and methodologies** are covered in Chapters 1, 2, 3, and 4.
- **Part II. Supply chain management: sourcing and outsourcing** are covered in Chapters 5, 6, and 7.
- **Part III. Integrated supply chain and transport logistics: integration of all-mode supply chain logistics** is covered in Chapters 8, 9, 10, 11, and 12, which are authored by five contributing editors: Tzs-Leung Yip (Chapter 8 on shipping and navigation logistics), Adolf Ng (Chapter 9 on global port logistics facilitation), Zhou Xu (Chapter 10 on logistics information technology), Xiaowen Fu (Chapter 11 on aviation logistics), and Meifeng Luo (Chapter 12 on environment logistics).

Parts I and II are related to operational economics and the management of logistics and supply chains, with Part I devoted to the fundamentals of operational economics and management in the context of supply chain logistics and Part II to the management of firm-focal SCM and logistics. The first two parts were largely developed from my lecture notes compiled over the past 20 years of teaching operations management and business logistics, and particularly from two redesigned courses—*Logistics and Supply Chain Management* and *Manufacturing Technology and Simulation*. Part III offers unique coverage of the integration of port-focal supply chain and transport logistics, with firm-focal logistics and SCM as the building blocks. Part III contains collective teaching notes developed by my colleagues at the Department of Logistics and Maritime Studies at Hong Kong PolyU, including Dr. Tsz-Leung Yip on "shipping and navigation logistics" (Chapter 8), Dr. Adolf Ng on "global ports/airports and logistics facilitation" (Chapter 9), Dr. Zhou Xu on "information technology in supply chain and transport logistics" (Chapter 10), Dr. Xiaowen Fu on "aviation logistics management" (Chapter 11), and Dr. Meifeng Luo on "environment logistics" (Chapter 12).

System dynamics are introduced and then explained with reference to the three modules, with emphasis given to *descriptive* models, such as time-series, queuing, and simulation models, because these have fared better for solving persistent and complex management problems, compared with *prescriptive* models. The descriptive models are selected in conjunction with methodological tools and topics that are pertinent to both firm-focal and port-focal SCM and transport logistics: time-series forecasting, inventory systems, efficiency assessment (statistical and econometrical), and Purchasing-Manager-Indexing (PMI) techniques. Because simulation is nonanalytical and visually interactive, and thus applicable to a wide range of complex problems, most chapters include a simulation-lab session where appropriate.

Part I, *Business supplies and logistics: theories and methodologies*, starts with how to deal with fundamental changes in logistics and supply chain operations, especially the revolutionary changes that have been brought about by computer and information technology (Chapter 1). Such changes have instigated all recent innovative advances and technologies, such as enterprise resource planning (ERP), manufacturing data warehousing, and business-to-business (B2B) logistics, to name just a few. Nevertheless, any change involves uncertainty and risk, which makes accurate calculation and planning seemingly impossible. Principles and useful models are then described according to three basic aspects of a supply chain—the operational core of a company. Logistical activities are explained in the context of a supply order fulfillment system, a descriptive flow network model of capacitated resources plus transitional inventory. Chapter 2 is devoted to the planning and control of production capacity. Basic repetitive supply management is discussed in Chapter 3. Demand management in supply chain and transport logistics is covered in Chapter 4, including time-series forecasting in the main part of the chapter, and the preliminaries of time-series demand with first-order time-series processes in the supplement (Chapter S4).

Part II, *Supply chain management: sourcing and outsourcing*, covers issues and developments in managing a supply chain. It consists of three chapters (Chapters 5–7), which are particularly suited for corporate buyers who are specialized in contract production and supply chain and logistics operations, including supply outsourcing. Chapter 5 provides unique coverage of supply chain efficiency and quality management, which represents the latest advances in SCM. Chapter 6 focuses on basic coverage of transportation and distribution problems. Chapter 7 is devoted to the newly emerging topics of maintenance and contingent supply chains, including production maintenance supply chains, post-sale service supply chains, and humanitarian supply chains.

Part III, "Integrated supply chain and transport logistics", is concerned with the study of port- and airport-focused networks of global logistics and supply chain management. Chapter 8 covers the analysis of "shipping and navigation logistics", Chapter 9 focuses on "global ports and logistics facilitation", and Chapter 10 on "information technology in supply chain and transport logistics". The book concludes with two unique and important chapters, Chapter 11 on "aviation logistics management" and Chapter 12 on "environment logistics".

This book is intended to provide an integrated coverage of both subjects with a modular structure, so that it can be easily customized to fit a particular pedagogical focus and style. There is no separate coverage of computer simulation; rather, it is covered through case studies and projects incorporated throughout the text. Most chapters include a designated simulation case, and each of the core subjects ends with a simulation project. Thus, to fully utilize the book, it is important to ensure that students have access to simulation software installed in a lab environment.

Professor John J. Liu
Director, Center for Transport, Trade and Financial Studies
College of Business
City University of Hong Kong
February 10, 2011 (in Hong Kong)

Reference

La Londe, B.J. 1998. "Supply Chain Evolution in Numbers," *Supply Chain Management Review* 2, No. 1, 7–8.

Part I

Business supplies and logistics

Theories and methodologies

Part 1

1 The art of winning in supply chain logistics

Key items:

- *Industry logistics versus the logistics industry*
- *Supply chain logistics and supply chain management: What's the difference?*
- *Sun Zi's winning-before-doing (WBD) philosophy*
- *Two elements of WBD: win-with-speed and win-by-singularity*

Firm-focal supply chain logistics: advancements and trends

Firm-focal versus port-focal logistics and supply chain management

Until the beginning of the twenty-first century, the theory and methodology of supply chain management (SCM) was centered on manufacturing, whereas logistics was centered on firm-focused shipping and transport. With increasing economic globalization, port-focal production systems have drawn increasing attention from academic research, industrial practices, and government policy agendas. Emerging evidence indicates a global trend suggesting that SCM has become increasingly service based (e.g., logistics and trade services), as opposed to manufacturing based. Consequently, port-focal logistics, as opposed to typical firm-focal logistics, play an increasingly important role in the global economy and have generated increasing interest in the study of trade-based supply chain logistics with a special focus on transport and maritime services, from both theoretical and empirical perspectives.

There are key differences between port-focal and firm-focal production, which can be summarized as follows:

- Port production technology is typically nonmanufacturing based, whereas firm production technology is mostly suited to manufacturing.
- In terms of organizational structure, port production is engaged in a single-seller (port) multibuyer (carriers) service system, whereas firm production

can be characterized as a single-buyer (firm) multisupplier manufacturing system.

- In terms of market and risk structure, port production faces idiosyncratic demands from the oligopolistic shipping market, whereas firm production is assumed to face systemic demands from a competitive market. It should be noted that due to the high entrance barrier in international shipping markets, the number of international carriers is quite limited compared with the number of manufacturers worldwide.
- Compared with firm-focal logistics, which is underpinned by a framework that consists of an inbound-factory-outbound logistics chain, port-focal logistics integrates all modes of supply chain and transport logistics, including navigation, aviation, and transportation.

Parts I and II of this textbook are devoted to firm-focal logistics, and Part III provides unique coverage of port-focal logistics and SCM.

Logistics versus supply chain management

Logistics refers to the provision of supplies, which includes not only the shipping and transportation of supplies (e.g., 物流, the Chinese translation of logistics), but also the related services and support systems (e.g., 后勤, such as maintenance and insurance, etc.). In terms of professional content and academic terminology, shipping encompasses all modes of navigation, aviation, and transportation, whereas logistics services cover all aspects, including finance, insurance, technology, and infrastructure. *Supply chain management* (SCM), a separate but related discipline, is generally referred to by both researchers and practitioners as the management of supply chains within business organizations. Most existing textbooks suggest that SCM has so far been production based, typically in terms of manufacturing and service operations management. Logistics activities that are associated with a production-based supply chain, such as the shipping and transportation of supplies, are enterprise focused. For example, in a manufacturing-based supply chain, inbound and outbound logistics are centered on the firm as a production function. Production-based SCM and its associated enterprise-focused logistics represent the primary focus of this book. In addition, in Part III we will examine trade-based SCM and the associated port-focused logistics, as outlined in the following paragraphs.

As globalization becomes a reality rather than a prediction, global supply chains are evolving from production based to trade based, and the associated logistics from enterprise focused to port/airport focused (simply referred to as port based).

The interrelationship between enterprise-focused logistics and production-based SCM has been striking and intriguing. On the one hand, if a supply chain is regarded as a business platform for the acquisition and provision of supplies and goods, then enterprise-focused industrial *logistics* is inseparable from SCM. On the other hand, SCM contains production operations that are exclusive from logistics, such as manufacturing operations. In this regard, logistics can be clearly distinguished from SCM.

The production-based framework of SCM, however, falls short in explaining recent developments in the real world, especially the so-called Wal-Mart model, in which a "factory" is a virtual global logistics network of multiple international manufacturing and service firms. This network of global logistics is indeed a prototype of a trade-based global supply chain. The success of the Wal-Mart model rests on dynamic innovations in two key dimensions, namely, global sourcing and contract manufacturing, and integrated multimode transport logistics. For example, the management of transport utilities and facilities, such as seaports and airports, has become an inevitable part of trade-based SCM and port-focused logistics, especially from an international perspective. *Supply chain logistics*, as defined in this book, is based on these intriguing interrelationships between production-based and trade-based supply chains, and between enterprise-focused and port-focused logistics. Following the convention adopted by both practitioners and academics, *logistics* is simply referred to in this book as enterprise focused and SCM as production based, unless otherwise specified.

The definition of *logistics* that was produced by the Council of Logistics Management in 1998 will help to explain the interrelationship between logistics and SCM:

> Logistics is that part of the supply chain process that plans, implements, and controls the efficient, effective flow and storage, services, and related information from the point-of-origin to the point-of-consumption in order to meet customers' requirements.

The point-of-origin herein is understood as a reference point after the inbound stage of a firm. When logistics is viewed as a subset of SCM, the production-based functions of SCM that are not considered a part of logistics are:

* inbound flow management: strategic supplier alliances, outsourcing;
* integrated supply chain operations: adaptive planning, competitive coordination;
* supply chain design concurrent with product development; and
* customer relationship management.

Industrial logistics versus logistics industry

Two categories have emerged in supply chain logistics: *industrial logistics* and the *logistics industry*. *Industrial logistics* is enterprise focused (e.g., typical business logistics and manufacturing logistics), whereas the *logistics industry* is enterprise crossing (e.g., third-party logistics and the shipping industry). An essential characteristic of the *logistics industry* is the nature of its trade-based cross-industry service. Specifically, *industrial logistics* is a necessary logistical function of individual enterprises and firms, whereas the *logistics industry* refers to industrial organizations that specialize in supply chain logistics. For example, logistics geared around a *focal factory*, as termed in the SCM literature (e.g., La Londe 1998), is a specific form of *industrial logistics*, and freight forwarders and shipping lines represent a specific port/airport-focused *logistics industry* in trade-based supply chains. This book will begin with the study of *industrial logistics*, and then proceed to study aspects of the *logistics industry* in the context of supply chains.

Firm-focal logistics and supply chain management

A basic firm-focal logistics and SCM system can be considered as a three-stage supply order fulfilling system, including inbound, factory (work-in-progress, WIP), and outbound stages of order fulfillment, as depicted in Figure 1.1.

Each of the three stages—inbound, factory, and outbound—operates in the form of a *supply order fulfillment* system. **Supply order fulfillment** (SOF) is broadly referred to as a contract production process engaged in the fulfillment of order contracts for supplies and goods, including supply provision, inventory control, manufacturing, and delivery of orders. The SOF activities at each stage are functionally differentiated as follows.

> **Inbound stage:** Purchasing, procurement, and supply/service acquisition. Regular measures of inbound logistics include pricing, on-time supply, and quality of supply/service.
> **Factory/WIP stage:** Enterprise resource planning (ERP), especially capacity and inventory management, production planning and control. Regular measures of the factory stage are production costs, on-time order fulfillment, and product/process quality.
> **Outbound stage:** Distribution, delivery, and transportation. Regular measures are concerned with distribution costs, on-time delivery, and customer service.

The interfaces and transactions among the three stages are normally relayed sequentially, as depicted in Figure 1.1. However, there are some situations in which orders are transferred or contracted to so-called third parties (either suppliers and/or distributors), in which case the middle stages may be partially or even fully bypassed to increase efficiency.

Specific third-party logistics cases are discussed in depth by Simchi-Levi *et al.* (2000). With advances in IT, innovative practices such as *transferred channel assembly* (TCA) and *value-added distribution* (VAD) have become common in SCM. For example, to fulfill and deliver an order from a CT-scanner plant located in the United States to a customer in Europe under a TCA arrangement, the main scanner unit will be made and delivered by the CT plant in the United States, but accessories such as gauges and plug-ins will be delivered directly from the supplier (say, in Japan) to a distributor for final assembly in Europe, as indicated by the double-lined arrow in Figure 1.1. The interface and transactions between stages are facilitated via an order fulfillment mechanism, which unavoidably

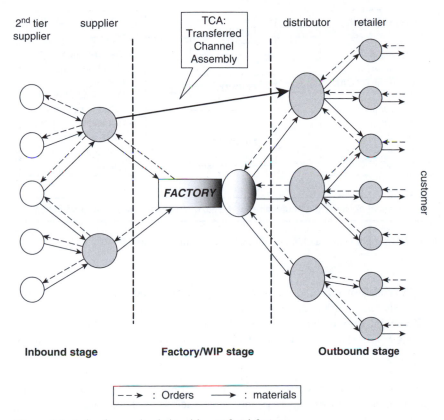

Figure 1.1 A simple supply chain with one focal factory.

incurs transaction costs. In other words, the final, future market demand is divided in advance into numerous SOF contracts between various pairs of buyers and suppliers across the whole supply chain. A firm may play different roles in different contracts—as a buyer in one contract but as a supplier (seller) in another contract. In sum, transaction cost economics (TCE), as described by Williamson (2002), plays a vital role in SCM and logistics.

THREE FORMS OF FLOW IN A SUPPLY CHAIN

A supply chain consists of multiple stages of operations, connected by three types of "flow": information flow, material flow, and financial flow.

> **Information flow** refers to informational interactions between supply chain stages, such as information regarding orders and requests for supplies and products.

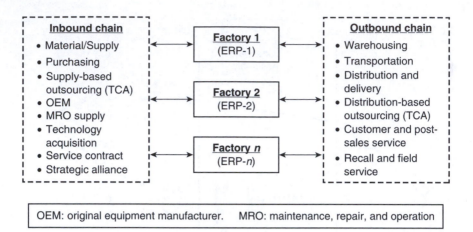

OEM: original equipment manufacturer.   MRO: maintenance, repair, and operation

Figure 1.2 Supply chain: a chain of competitive selling and buying.

Material flow refers to the flow of supplies and products that are delivered in response to orders and requests.

Financial flow includes all of the financial transactions that are associated with supply chain operations, which represent the core economics of supply chains.

A striking trend in modern SCM is that the flows in a supply chain become Unbounded: across firms, across countries, and across markets worldwide.

Firm-focal logistics industry and nested supply chains

From a functional viewpoint, a factory can be symbolically represented by a specific ERP system, which is engaged with both the inbound and outbound stages. It is interesting to note that an ERP system, by nature, is not shared among factories, especially among competitive factories. In contrast, inbound or outbound chains are, by nature, meant to be shared. Thus, a real-world supply chain is usually nested, as depicted in Figure 1.2. We can see from Figure 1.2 that a supply chain can be viewed as a chain of competitive selling and buying.

In general, the factories in Figure 1.2 are competing firms. Each competitive firm will maintain an independent and unique ERP system as its operational and informational engine. In this regard, supply chains are the battlefield on which competition is regularly engaged in, in lieu of ERP technology. In other words, ERP represents a regularity and commonality among competing firms. The theory of win-by-singularity, which will be described later in this chapter, states that a firm can only win by nonregular means and measures. Thus, the winning secret for a company must be something other than ERP technology itself.

In fact, the secret lies in how a firm can uniquely operate and compete given the same set of publicly available viable technologies, which is why not all companies using the same ERP system enjoy the same success. For example, an ERP system consists of interfaces for third-party logistics, which include both supply-based and distribution-based outsourcing, as depicted in Figure 1.2. With the same interfacing technology, supplier and/or customer relationships may differ drastically among firms that produce the same products.

It is important to note that although the ERP systems in a supply chain are not suited for sharing with other competing firms, the inbound and outbound resources are, by definition, shared by competing firms.

Supply chain management

Since its introduction in the early 1980s, the term *supply chain management* has gained tremendous popularity (La Londe 1998). Especially since the late 1980s, academics have pursued rigorous studies of SCM (Stock and Lambert 2000). The SCM of a focal company (see Figure 1.1) has been conceptualized as a dynamic process of integrating and managing the "triple flows" in a focal supply chain— the information, material, and financial flows that were described earlier.

MANAGE TO WIN: ADAPTATION

A supply chain is a chain of order fulfillment in terms of inventory acquisition, production, and supply provision, and managing the chain entails a network of logistics contract services. Most of the recent adaptive innovations in the field of SCM have been related to advances in information and computer technology. For example, the latest developments in *third-party logistics* and *maintenance supply chain*, as illustrated in Figure 1.3, have been made possible by advances in IT systems.

Although the subcontracting of logistics operations began in the 1980s, it really only started to increase in prevalence as a result of new developments in information and computer technology for electronic business transactions.

Because managers are obligated to "manage to win," the winning-before-doing (WBD) principle is naturally important in the management of manufacturing and supply chains. Having mentioned "adaptation" in the area of manufacturing and supply chains in previous sections, we will now rigorously characterize the adaptation process in the context of business competition. An abstract characterization of this process was established by Holland (1992), in line with Arrow's insightful statement on evolution:

> Adaptation by natural selection has many analogies with adaptive learning to the environment in the higher animals and in human individuals and society.
>
> Kenneth J. Arrow, Joan Kennedy Professor of Economics and
> Professor of Operations Research,
> Stanford University (Nobel Laureate)

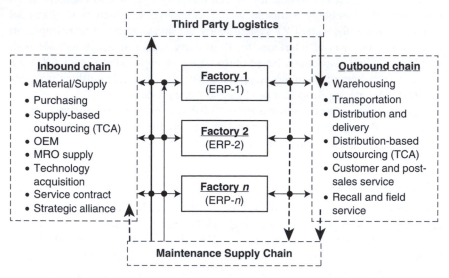

Figure 1.3 Supply chain logistics: a network of competitive contract services.

According to Holland (1992), adaptation and learning is a dynamic planning process, centered around three factors:

1   The environment: a system with certain structures and purposes, where adaptation takes place.
2   The adaptive plan: a sequence of operations and transformations in response to the environment.
3   The performance measure: a measure of performance in terms of the structures and purposes within the environment.

Within this framework, adaptation is conceptualized as a dynamic transformation process containing sequences of transformational operations and actions, termed adaptive plans, directed toward certain purposes within the environment. The dynamics of an adaptive system, as proposed by Holland (1992), are governed by four components.

1   Strategy set: the set of attainable strategies (or structures) that constitutes the domain of the adaptive system.
2   Transformation set: the set of operations and functions that transforms objects and modifies strategies in physical and abstract forms.
3   Data set: the information that is entered into or is available in the system at time *t*. The data set increases over time. An example of a subset of the data set is the demand data, which can be dynamically observed as time progresses.

4   Plan set: the set of plans generated on the basis of the input and the strategy. Each plan determines which operations and functions should be applied at time *t*, which, in turn, will determine the realizable level of output.

In general, the dynamics of an adaptive system are complex and difficult to express in a closed analytical form. Studies of adaptive systems, therefore, usually resort to descriptive tools and methods, leading to simulations and numerical solutions. This concept will be further elaborated throughout the book, using numerous examples such as capacity planning in Chapter 2.

Winning-before-doing (WBD): adaptation and simulation

Taoist strategy versus disciplined tactics

The Art of War (500 BC) by Sun Zi, an ancient Chinese military strategist and philosopher, has long been established as one of the world's greatest martial classics. It has been studied by Japanese and Korean military commanders for over 1,500 years, and has been known to European military leaders since the eighteenth century. More recently, its appeal and principles have spread across many nonmilitary situations, especially in the world of business. It has been referred to in Japanese business as the "Bible of Business Competition." The applicability of *The Art of War* is rooted in the fact that *management means competition, and the ultimate goal of management is "manage to win."*

The essence of *The Art of War*, as Sun Zi wrote, is the Taoism in general, and the *ying-yang* doctrine in particular, of "Uncertain disorder postulates perfect discipline, 乱生于治." (Sun Zi, Chapter 5, Verse 5.17). In other words, the world's "order" is constantly changing in a seemingly uncertain manner, without reference to the likes or dislikes of human beings. Thus, "disorder" is the inevitable way that "order" is disciplined. The "order" is comprehensible but not definable. Based on this doctrine, Sun Zi established his philosophy of *winning-before-doing* (WBD), a philosophy of calculation and adaptation in the changing world. The essence of WBD philosophy can be best characterized by his famous saying:

> A winner secures victory before engaging in a fight, whereas a loser engages a fight and then seeks victory 胜兵先胜而后求战，败兵先战而后求胜.
>
> *The Art of War*, Chapter 4, Verse 4.15 (500 BC, by Sun Zi)

Sun Zi founded his *winning-before-doing* philosophy on a universal, adaptive Taoist (道略) system that consists of the so-called "three Fives," namely, *five essences* (五经), *five secrets* (五诀), and *five tactics* (五策). The **five essences** are:

1   *Moral law,* 道: A belief or a mission that people of all ranks are devoted to.
2   *The Heavens,* 天: An uncertain, mighty world that everyone must endure, such as yin/yang, the weather, and the seasons.

3   *The Earth,* 地: The inevitable physical environment in which the mission takes place, such as mountains and plains, rivers and lakes, and birth and death.
4   *Commanders,* 将: Leaders and executives who are specialized and proven in specific area(s).
5   *Disciplines,* 法: Rules and codes that must be followed.

To ensure victory the **five secrets** must be acquired. According to Sun Zi's saying:

> Thus, there are five secrets for victory: 1) He will win who knows when to fight and when not to fight; 2) He will win who knows how to handle both superior and inferior forces; 3) He will win whose army is animated by the same spirit throughout all its ranks; 4) He will win who is prepared himself, while he waits to take the enemy unprepared; 5) He will win who has military capacity and is not interfered with by the sovereign.

The Art of War *of Sun Zi and the six sigma*

According to Sun Zi, the five essences are universal and invariant, whereas the implementation of the five-essence Taoist system is all but invariant. We will therefore describe Sun Zi's "five-tactics" method of WBD (Sun Zi, Chapter 4), which should be applied according to specific situations. The **five-tactics** method of WBD is summarized by Sun Zi with five words: targeting (measuring), assessing, calculating, balancing, and executing (TACBE), elaborated as follows.

1   *Targeting (measuring),* 度: Setting up a goal or a series of carefully measured objectives that everyone will strive to attain together. The target should be dynamically defined and established, in accordance with changing needs and varying situations.
2   *Assessing,* 量: Identifying the criteria and metrics by which the performance and outcomes are evaluated and assessed, and the rewards and penalties are devised.
3   *Calculating,* 数: Gathering and analyzing information and data, and simulating all possible scenarios and outcomes.
4   *Balancing,* 称: Balancing the chance of winning by adjusting and adapting according to advantages versus disadvantages, and strengths versus weaknesses.
5   *Execute (to win),* 胜: Implementing and executing the winning plan that contains winning strategies and actions.

It is interesting to note that the five ancient tactics described by Sun Zi are remarkably similar to the six sigma of modern times, which have been referred to as "the most powerful breakthrough management tool ever devised" in the modern corporate world (Mikel and Schroeder 2000). Although we cover the technical details of six sigma in Chapter 2, a brief mention of the five core phases of six sigma (what we call D-M-A-I-C) illustrates how closely the two are related:

Six sigma: Define–Measure–Analyze–Improve–Control (DMAIC)
Sun Zi: Target–Assess–Calculate–Balance–Execute (TACBE)

Although volumes of literature have been written on the tactical (法术) aspects of Sun Zi's *The Art of War* (e.g., rules and tricks 法和计), much less attention has been given to the Taoism (道略) of Sun Zi. This book focuses on the Taoism of Sun Zi in the context of innovative manufacturing and SCM.

The WBD creed advocates acting-by-adaptation as opposed to acting-on-expectation. It involves an adaptive process of learning: *learning-before-doing*, *learning-while-doing*, and *learning-after-doing*. Surprisingly, the Toyota production system (TPS) has much in common with Sun Zi's WBD philosophy. The TPS (Ohno 1978) appears to be a modern version of Sun Zi's saying, "What matters in battle is winning, not lengthy campaigning, 兵贵胜, 不贵久." (Chapter 2, Verse 2.14). According to Ohno, Toyota began the innovation of the TPS in 1945 when Kiichiro Toyoda, then president of Toyota, determined that Toyota must "… catch up with America in three years. Otherwise, the automobile industry of Japan will not survive." Although Toyota did not succeed in this goal, the ambitious campaign of Kiichiro Toyoda sparked the most influential innovation in the world of manufacturing, namely the birth of the TPS. The TPS rests on two pillars, as described by Ohno:

1   **Just in Time (JIT).**
2   **Jidoka** (autonomous adaptation or automation with a human touch).

An early implementation of JIT at Toyota is the well-known Kanban production system. Unlike JIT, the Jidoka mentioned in Ohno (1978) has received little attention. This is, in part, because Jidoka represents a unique culture or tradition that was developed at Toyota, and is therefore not as easily recognizable as JIT. The concept of Jidoka originated from the design of an automated loom that was invented in 1902 at Sakichi Toyoda, which subsequently developed into the Toyota group. With this design, the automated loom would immediately stop whenever a thread broke. Several decades later, Taiichi Ohno, a production engineer at the Toyota Motor Company in the 1970s, formalized the idea of stopping production in response to every defect as "Jidoka." An early implementation of Jidoka at Toyota was the self-activated stopping policy: a production unit or team at any stage of a manufacturing process is authorized to interrupt and stop the entire production line if a problem or failure occurs at that stage. Later, Jidoka came to refer to any mechanism of pre-authorized internal/local ruling and control. However, the concept of Jidoka goes far beyond the self-stopping policy, just as the concept of JIT goes far beyond the Kanban system.

Both pillars can be traced to Sun Zi's rule of WBD: the theory of win-with-speed (速胜, "Su Sheng" in Chinese) and the theory of win-by-singularity (奇胜,

"Qi-Sheng" in Chinese). In relation to Sun Zi's WBD, Jidoka is regarded as the singularity in a TPS. The principle of JIT, popularly known in the field of manufacturing and SCM, is considered to be the counterpart of win-with-speed. To this end, we quote Sun Zi as saying:

> There is no instance of a country having benefited from prolonged warfare. 夫兵久而国利者，未之有也.
>
> *The Art of War,* Chapter 2, Verse 2.5 (500 BC, by Sun Zi)

Let us take a closer look at the win-by-singularity (Qi-Sheng) rule, which is not as easily explained as the win-with-speed (Su-Sheng) rule.

Theory of win-by-singularity: the Qi-Sheng rule

According to Sun Zi, adaptation is a dynamic process of interaction between regularity and singularity. Regularity refers to the common knowledge, principles, and protocols that can be effectively documented and taught, whereas singularity involves talent and wisdom that are almost impossible to teach in a textbook setting. In manufacturing, regular operations and reactive measures such as the production process and inventory policy are related to the regularity principle, whereas aspects such as the corporate culture and human capital are more of a singular nature. In the TPS, "countermeasures" such as Kanban (which means *visual card* in Japanese) and quality circle, are related to *regularity*. Although it may be argued that these are unique innovations by Toyota and should therefore be considered singular, Kanban can, in fact, be considered under the regularity principle rather than the singularity principle. Following an in-depth field study of Toyota factories, Spear and Bowen at Harvard Business School reported:

> Toyota does not consider any of the tools or practices—such as Kanbans or andon cords, which so many outsiders have observed and copied—as fundamental to the Toyota Production System. Toyota uses them … as "countermeasures," rather than "solutions."
>
> (Spear and Brown 1999)

A striking difference between the two is that regularity can be taught, whereas singularity can only be cultivated. A metaphor can perhaps explain it better: *A professional (such as a competent manager) can be trained, but a talent (such as a topflight CEO) can only be found.* However, to master singularity, one must understand how to deal with regularity, just as a general must know how his soldiers fight a battle. This book is intended for those who need to acquire the basics of manufacturing and supply chain operations to become a top-notch CEO, rather than someone who already has a grasp of the basics.

Although regularity and singularity are polar opposites, one cannot exist without the other. A secret to WBD is the theory of win-by-singularity:

Any battle is to be engaged by regularity, but is to be won by singularity. 凡战者, 以正合, 以奇胜. Singularity and regularity engage with each other, as if forming a circle with no ends. Who can exhaust the possibilities of their combination? 奇正相生, 如环之无端, 孰能穷之.

> *The Art of War*, Chapter 5, Verses 5.5 and 5.6 (500 BC, by Sun Zi)

The theory of win-by-singularity can also help to explain why many US firms have failed in their attempts to copy the Toyota JIT production system. The reason is that outsiders have copied only one part of the secret to success, yet the irony is that what can be copied alone cannot lead to success. This explains why other Japanese companies, such as Nissan, have also achieved lackluster results in copying the TPS system (Spear and Bowen 1999).

The other part of the secret to Toyota's success is a unique adaptive process that has been incorporated into the company's culture, such as the behavioral capacity of Jidoka (which means *autonomous adaptation* in Japanese). In addition, the interaction between regularity and singularity is dynamic and constantly changing, thus winning today does not assure winning in the future. Hence the saying: *An undefeated general wins every single battle differently*. The regularity and singularity aspects of TPS will be covered in greater depth in Chapters 2 and 3, but first we will consider some other WBD strategies.

Example 1.1 Competitive clustering (the bandwagon effect)

The *bandwagon effect* is best presented in the Beer-Vendors Location game included in Reflection 1.1. Here, regularity is considered in a scenario in which you imagine yourself selling beer to sunbathers on a beach in a free market environment. Suppose you are one of the vendors, Ms. Bud. Regardless of where your competitor, Ms. Weiser, selects her location, the best strategy for you (Ms. Bud) is to locate your stall in the middle of the beach. Why? Because, if Ms. Weiser is smart, she will also locate herself in the middle right next to you so that the sales are equally split.

Can you think of other real-world examples that use such a clustering strategy (or bandwagon effect)? A list of examples would presumably include gas stations, fast-food restaurants, and more, although it is interesting to note that the *bandwagon effect* also occurs in many less obvious business applications, such as product positioning and supply-chain location decisions. Many consumer products, including soft drinks, are almost always positioned identically in terms of price, flavor, and packaging.

Reflection 1.1 Beer-vendor location

Two beer vendors, Ms. Bud and Ms. Weiser, operate on a beach. They are required to charge the same price, but they can choose where to locate themselves on the beach. Their customers, sunbathers, do not like to be near each other, so they are spread evenly along the beach. Sunbathers also are averse to walking, so they purchase one can of beer from the vendor closest to them.

The Game

Where on the beach (which can be simplified as a straight line) will the vendors (B and W), seeking large sales, locate themselves?

Example 1.2 Competitive concession (maximin principle)

Let us use a classical game, as presented in Reflection 1.2, to demonstrate the logical difference between act-by-adaptation and act-on-expectation. This is a typical case of applying the maximin (or minimax) principle: accept the best outcome out of the worst possibilities. The minimax principle is pervasive in many areas, especially in military operations. It is interesting to note that it can also be found in Darwin's concept of adaptation by natural selection in his theory of evolution. In contrast to Reflection 1.1, Reflection 1.2 involves two stages of action. Similar situations can be found in many business applications, such as negotiations between a corporate buyer and his/her supplier, where multiple rounds of price negotiations are common.

Reflection 1.2 Winning by calculated concession

BG (big general) and SS (small soldier) have just received rewards of $3,000 and $1,000, respectively, and both have bet their rewards on the right to divide $1 million between themselves. Each of the parties must at least recover the bet (i.e., the reward) and both are trying to obtain the maximum possible share. Each also knows that the game has the following structure.

Stage 1: SS proposes how much of the $1 million he gets. Then either BG accepts it, in which case the game ends and BG receives the remainder of the $1 million; or BG rejects it, in which case the game continues.

Stage 2: The sum to be divided has now shrunk by 10 percent to $900,000. Now, BG makes a proposal for his share of the $900K. Then SS either accepts it and gets the remainder; or rejects it, in which case each receives nothing and the game ends.

The game

1 *What should SS offer at the first stage?*
2 *What similar examples can you think of (or know of) that also incur the* **maximin principle**?

Another unique feature of Reflection 1.2 is its asymmetric structure: the two players, general and soldier, are not simultaneously and independently making decisions. Rather, there is a "first mover" (the soldier) who will make the first move, and then there is a "second mover" (the general) who can only react to the move made by the first mover. The soldier knows all of the general's possible reactions, but the general does not know what the soldier's first move will be. Such asymmetry is also common in business competition (e.g., the price-offer and counter-offer dynamic between a supplier and a corporate buyer).

WBD integration: the concept of the supply chain ring

Intuitively, the supply chain, by its name, is an open system that starts at the supply end, goes through transformation, and ends at distribution and delivery. There has been a trend in SCM toward continued after-sales management, such as customer relations management (CRM) and reverse logistics. Effective management of the complete supply chain system requires a great deal of adaptive integration. Supply chain quality improvement is developing into an effective method of adaptive integration. As a result of this WBD integration of the complete supply chain, the concept of a supply chain ring is emerging, as depicted in Figure 1.4.

Supply chain operations

Supply order fulfillment (SOF)

Although ways of doing business have changed, the business fundamentals remain the same. From an industrial organization perspective, the same fundamentals have embodied the mechanism of a *supply order fulfillment* (SOF) system as shown in Figure 1.5: resources are utilized to fulfill an order triggered by demand. Nevertheless, innovative ways of producing a product or running a company have continued to emerge, especially with developments in Internet technology.

One of the most significant innovations is the so-called Wal-Mart model of megaretailing, in which a "factory" is a virtual network of SOF systems, especially

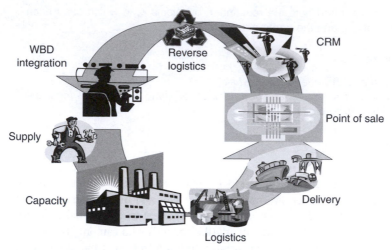

Figure 1.4 Supply chain: a chain of competitive selling and buying.

Figure 1.5 Supply order fulfillment (SOF) system.

in terms of contract manufacturing and outsourcing. According to the theory of economic growth, which we will study in the next section, economic growth can only arise from *technological developments*, such as the invention of electricity, the telephone, and more recently the Internet.

Two production principles

If we compare the TPS with typical US industrial systems, two manufacturing principles can be identified: Just in Time (JIT) from Japan, and just-in-case (JIC) from the United States. JIT, stemming from Toyota's Kanban system (Ohno 1978), strives to win with speed, while JIC, based on the so-called MRP (material, requirements, planning) systems, endeavors to win with safety. According to the JIT principle, the key to a quick win is to eliminate production waste. Therefore, JIT stresses reducing waste in the inventory, setup, and quality management, and promotes direct and strong links with all parties in the supply chain. The crusade against waste also entails greater speed and accuracy, and engages *quality* as a unified and ultimate measure of performance. To win safely, the JIC model focuses on integrated (or centralized) planning ahead of

Table 1.1 Characteristics of JIT and JIC

Category	JIT	JIC
Philosophy	Quick-win, reactive	Safe-win, proactive
Strategy	Pull: eliminating waste	Push: planning in advance
Approach	Make-to-order	Make-to-stock
Planning and control	Kanban	MRP
Critical measures	Reduction: inventory, setup, lead-time, delivery time	Accuracy: Forecast, safety stock, lot sizing, service level
Competitive edge	Robust, IT simplistic, close-looped	Integrated, IT advanced, open-looped

time, which in turn relies on forecasting and precautionary measures such as safety stock. Just as mass production is associated with the US automobile industry, the term "lean production," coined by Womack *et al.* (1990), is used to characterize the TPS. Table 1.1 presents a list of the two systems' contrasting characteristics.

As indicated in Table 1.1, the two production principles underpin two different operational strategies: a pull strategy under JIT, and a push strategy under JIC. In short, production in a pull system is triggered (i.e., pulled) by demand (e.g., customer orders), while production in a push system is planned in advance (e.g., planned order release in MRP). The two strategies result in two different manufacturing approaches: make-to-order for JIT, and make-to-stock for JIC. These manufacturing methods will be covered in more detail in Chapter 2.

It is interesting to note that the term JIT did not originate from Toyota. Rather, it is a term invented by outsiders to describe TPS, although Toyota itself has now adopted the acronym JIT for its own system. Perhaps there is truth in the analogy that JIT is to the TPS what the fortune cookie is to Chinese restaurants. As we know, the fortune cookie was invented outside China but is now popularly adopted by almost all Chinese restaurants in China. We should point out that copied and modified tools and measures alone will not lead to success, and that adopting new ways and means of doing business does not necessarily change the fundamental basis of a business. Ultimately, success depends on how a business copes with the fundamentals and adapts to the changing world: to *win by singularity*.

Although the two principles contrast significantly in their philosophical focus, both allow the use of common countermeasures, as mentioned earlier. Today, it is just as easy to find a JIT system that contains safety stock, as it is to find a JIC system that uses Kanbans. There is nevertheless a convergence on Sun Zi's theory of winning and, more precisely, the theory of winning before doing, in the general context of cost minimization and profit maximization. A simple but practical method of minimizing costs is to use break-even analysis, as illustrated in the following example.

Example 1.3   Make-or-buy decision at Alex Clothing

Alex Clothing is considering opening a new plant in Taiwan to produce silk shirts. The plant will cost the firm $10 million in capital. The plant will be able to produce the shirts for $4.70 each. However, Alex can subcontract the production of the shirts and pay $6.30 each. How many shirts will Alex have to sell worldwide to break even on its investment in the new plant? The total cost for producing a given quantity Q of shirts by a plant is $C_1 = F_1 + v_1 \times Q$, where $F_1 = \$10$ million, and $v_1 = \$4.70$ (per shirt). For the same output Q, the cost of subcontracting is

$$C_2 = F_2 + v_2 \times Q = 6.3 \times Q,$$

with zero capital investment (i.e., $F_2 = 0$). Both C_1 and C_2 depend on the output quantity Q, as shown in Figure 1.6.

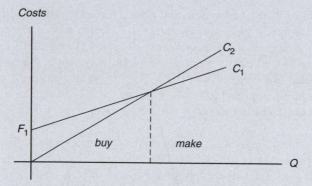

Figure 1.6 Make-or-buy by break-even.

A break-even quantity Q^* is defined as the cumulative output that makes $C_1 = C_2$, that is:

$$F_1 + v_1 \times Q^* = F_2 + v_2 \times Q^*.$$

It is then easy to obtain that:

$$Q^* = \frac{F_1 - F_2}{v_2 - v_1} = \frac{10,000,000 - 0}{6.3 - 4.7} = 6,250,000.$$

Thus, the cost of building a new plant or buying from a subcontractor will be the same if Alex can sell a total of 6.25 million shirts. If the expected output level is below Q^*, then Alex is better off subcontracting the shirt manufacturing, otherwise it would be better to build a new plant.

Manufacturing innovations

The manufacturing and transformation stages of supply chain operations have always been dynamic pioneers in the adoption of technological innovations. Manufacturing has responded to recognized advances in technology and science with the development of innovative products and processes. This can be witnessed from the history of manufacturing innovations, from spinning machines to transfer lines, and from mass production to SCM. Manufacturing innovation can be categorized into two types: product and process innovations. Product innovation represents new technological developments in the form of industrial products or consumer goods, such as AGVs (automatic-guided vehicles) and DVD players. Process innovation involves new production methods resulting from advances in science and technology, such as e-commerce, JIT production, and ERP. The ever-growing list of manufacturing innovations continues to change the face of business. We refer to this dynamic field as *innovative manufacturing. Innovative manufacturing* is rooted in the continuous adoption of product and process innovations. Technology adoption is *discrete* by nature, and requires significant capital investment. Decisions regarding technology adoption include strategic issues such as what and when to adopt. These issues are of extreme long-term importance to a firm, and involve quite complex decision-making processes. The adoption of innovative technology has become a textbook subject in the fields of economics and marketing science.

To illustrate the adoption process without going into too much detail, let us consider a simplified example in which a firm is planning to expand its production capacity to meet a projected increase in demand over a given time period (say, the next 5 years). With a fixed level of aggregate labor input, the expansion capacity of a factory is based on the anticipated increase in equilibrium output Y. The capacity expansion is to acquire cost-minimized technology that is capable of producing an output quantity of Y. The cost of technology acquisition, denoted by K (capital cost), can be derived from a Cobb–Douglas production function in the form of:

$$K = K_c \times Y^a,$$

where K_c is a capital cost coefficient and a is a capacity scaling factor. A list of all possible expansion plans (or options) must then be compiled.

Because capital investments are long-term compared with variable costs, technology adoption often involves computing *present value*. The concept of *present value* is based on the *interest rate*, denoted by r, and the cash flow. For example, a deposit of $1 million today with a 10 percent fixed interest rate will generate a total of $1.1 million—the principle plus interest—in 1 year. In this case, we can state that a 1-year future fund of $1.1 million has a present value of $1 million given an interest rate of 10 percent (i.e., $r = 0.1$). The following relevant notation will be used in this book:

$$PV = \frac{F_n}{(1+r)^n},$$

where PV stands for the present value, and F_n is the amount of future funds incurred in the nth year from now. A specific example can help to explain capacity expansion.

Example 1.4   Capacity expansion by incremental adoption

A community clinic expects that the number of annual visits will increase at a rate of 500 visits/year for the next 6 years, and is considering a proposal for incremental expansion to acquire an additional CT scanner with the capacity to treat a maximum of 1,000 people (visits/year) every 2 years (the expansion interval) over a 6-year span. The acquisition cost of the CT scanner is given as $K = K_c \times Y^a = 0.0107Y^{0.62}$ (in million dollars) by the industrial engineers. A fixed interest rate of $r = 16$ percent is assumed for the next 6 years. One option is to purchase one CT scanner with a capacity of 1,000 maximum visits per year immediately, and then follow with two additional expansions every 2 years. The proposed option is depicted in Figure 1.7.

Question 1: Compute the PV (present value) of the investment for the next expansion.
Question 2: Compute the PV of the total investments for the proposed expansion option.

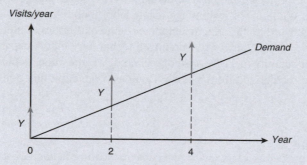

Figure 1.7 A capacity expansion option.

The required expansion capacity can be determined as $Y = 1,000$ visits per year, and the cost of acquiring the scanner with this capacity is given as:

$$K = 0.0107 \times (1000^{0.62}) = \$0.7751 (\text{million dollars}).$$

Thus, to acquire the scanner immediately will cost $775,100. The first expansion, which will cost another $775,100, is scheduled in 2 years' time.

With a fixed interest rate of 16 percent, the present value of the first expansion cost, that is, today's value of $775,100 spent 2 years from now, is computed as:

$$PV_1 = \frac{F_n}{(1+r)^n} = \frac{0.7751}{(1+0.16)^2} = \$0.576 \text{ (million dollars)}.$$

Similarly, the present value of the second expansion in the fourth year is:

$$PV_2 = \frac{F_4}{(1+r)^4} = \frac{0.7751}{(1+0.16)^4} = \$0.4281 \text{ (million dollars)}.$$

Thus, the total present value of the cost of the proposed option, denoted by TC, can be computed as:

$$TC = PV_0 + PV_1 + PV_2 = 0.7751 + 0.5760 + 0.4281$$
$$= \$1.7792 \text{ (million dollars)}.$$

For all of the other viable options, the above analysis can be repeated and the total cost (in present value) can be obtained. A final selection can then be determined by choosing a cost-minimizing option.

We can see from the above example that a capacity expansion plan (or option) contains two crucial decision-making components: when and how much to expand. A common practice is to schedule capacity expansion under an incremental scheme, in which an equal time interval—termed the expansion interval, denoted by τ—is specified between consecutive expansions. In the proposed option given in Example 1.4, the expansion interval is specified as $\tau = 2$ (years). With the specified expansion interval, the necessary size of the capacity expansion Y can be determined from the forecasts of the demand over a given planning horizon. For Example 1.4, the expansion size is determined from the demand forecast as $Y = 1,000$ visits per year. Clearly, capacity expansion decisions are critically dependent on accurate forecasting of the demand, which will be discussed in Chapter 2. In summary, a typical capacity *incremental expansion* procedure contains the following steps.

1   Select a planning horizon for the expansion.
2   Obtain forecasts of the demand over the planning horizon.
3   Compile a set of all possible expansion plans (or options), each of which must contain a specific expansion schedule given in terms of the expansion interval τ, and the corresponding expansion size Y. Note that the expansion size Y is determined from the demand forecasts with a given value of τ.
4   Compute the total cost in present value for each of the plans. Select the plan with the lowest total cost.

Supply chain logistics

According to the flow of demand, supply orders can be classified into two groups: repetitive and nonrepetitive. A repetitive order is usually associated with existing products and markets, whereas a nonrepetitive order is typically related to innovation of products and processes.

Prototype example: Packers' Yearbook production

Production orders: quantity and lead-time

A manufacturing order is in fact a forward-contract that will either be fulfilled (fully or partially) or defaulted within a finite time period. The order is forward in the sense that it is designated for future needs and uses. The total time elapsed from the release of an order to the delivery of the order is termed the total manufacturing lead-time, or simply the *lead-time*, denoted as L. The total manufacturing lead-time includes the time to acquire the necessary supplies, to fill the order, and to transport and deliver the order. Thus, the manufacturing lead-time is the time lag between the release and delivery of an order.

A manufacturing system differs from a service system in how production is triggered by demand. For example, television sets can be made before actual buyers are known, but a doctor cannot treat anyone before the arrival of a patient who needs treatment. In an MRP manufacturing system, production orders are released in advance of a demand order arriving, whereas a Kanban order can only be released upon or after a demand order arrives. However, for a service order (e.g., a clinic visit) the service operations can be performed either upon or after a customer's arrival. It should be noted that the preparation of raw materials for production in both manufacturing and service systems can begin before the demand order, but the two processes differ in terms of their execution.

A manufacturing order Q can be specified by (or converted to) its required workload. A manufacturing order in general is expressed in terms of the *base order* and *safety stock*, in a linear form of $Q = q + \text{ss}$, where q represents a base order and ss denotes the safety stock that is allowed to be negative. The base order is determined by expectation (e.g., average demand over average lead-time), whereas the safety stock is used as a countermeasure against uncertainty in demand. In manufacturing, safety stock is based on consideration of the *service level. A common definition of service level is the probability of demand being met on time*. Intuitively, a higher service level implies a higher level of satisfying customers' needs, which requires higher levels of safety stock. It can also be recognized that a higher degree of variability in demand will require a higher level of safety stock to achieve a given service level. JIT production aims to eliminate or minimize the use of safety stock, but with the condition that the service level should not be undermined. Consider the following example.

Example 1.5   Packers' Yearbook production

In August each year, the *Milwaukee Sports Journal* must decide the production order for the Packers' Yearbook for the next NFL football season. Each yearbook costs $2.00 and is sold for $9.50. After December 1, any unsold yearbooks are sold to the Dollar-a-Book used bookstore for $0.75 per book. The *Milwaukee Sports Journal* believes that the number of books sold by December 1 follows the probability distribution (extremely simplified) shown in Table 1.2. It wishes to maximize the expected net annual profit from Packers' Yearbook production.

Question (newsboy problem): Determine the production order size (i.e., how many yearbooks) that the *Milwaukee Sports Journal* should release in August.

Keywords: *uncertain demand, production order release, safety stock, overstock and understock, service level (in-stock probability).*

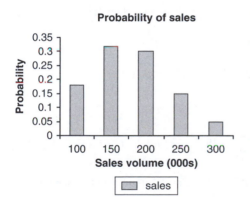

Probability of sales

Table 1.2 Packers' Yearbook annual sales distribution

Demand (000s)	Probability
100	0.18
150	0.32
200	0.30
250	0.15
300	0.05

Characteristics of uncertain demand

Mean and variance of demand

Let D denote the annual demand as given in Table 1.2. The mean, $E(D)$ and variance, $\mathrm{var}(D)$ of the demand can be calculated as follows:

$$E(D) = \sum_k k \times \Pr(D = k)$$

$$= \left[0.18(100) + 0.32(150) + 0.30(200) + 0.15(250) + 0.05(300)\right] = 178.5$$

$$\mathrm{var}(D) = E\left((D - E(D))^2\right)$$
$$= \left[0.18(100 - 178.5)^2 + \cdots + 0.05(300 - 178.5)^2\right] = 3,012.75$$

$$\sigma_d = \sqrt{\mathrm{var}(D)} = 54.9$$

An immediate solution would be to set the base order equal to the mean demand, that is, $q = 178.5$ (in thousands). For the sake of comparison, let us consider the expected profit if the *Milwaukee Sports Journal* only plans to produce the base order quantity without any safety stock. Because demand can only take integer values, as listed in Table 1.2, for the sake of exposition let us set the production order to the closest integer value below the mean, that is, $Q = 150$. Clearly, the unit sales profit on each yearbook sold is

$$r = \$9.50 - \$2.00 = \$7.50,$$

and the loss on each overstocked yearbook is

$$c_o = \$2.00 - \$.75 = \$1.25.$$

The expected profit under production order $Q = 150$ can then be computed as follows:

$$E(\text{net profit} \mid Q) = E(\text{sales profit} \mid Q) - E(\text{overstock cost} \mid Q)$$

$$= r \sum_{k=100}^{Q} k \times \mathrm{Pr}(D = k) + r \sum_{k=Q+1}^{300} Q \times \mathrm{Pr}(D = k)$$

$$- c_o \sum_{k=100}^{Q} (Q - k)\mathrm{Pr}(D = k) = r \sum_{k=100}^{150} k \times \mathrm{Pr}(D = k) + r \sum_{k=200}^{300} Q \times \mathrm{Pr}(D = k)$$

$$- c_o \sum_{k=100}^{150} (Q - k)\mathrm{Pr}(D = k) = \{1057.5 - 11.25\} = \$1,046.25\,(\text{in thousands}).$$

Production quantity, actual sales, and inventory status

As the production quantity Q must be determined before realization of next year's demand, the actual sales of the yearbook during the next season will depend on the actual demand D for the next season. It is important to note that actual sales in the next year may differ from actual demand in the next year. To illustrate this, let us repeat the analysis for a production order of $Q = 200,000$. The number of actual sales is clearly a function of both production quantity Q and actual demand D. Specifically, the number of actual sales in the next season would be the smaller of either production quantity or demand volume, that is:

$$\text{Actual sales} = \min\{Q, D\}.$$

For example, suppose that 200 thousand yearbooks have been produced, and that the actual demand turns out to be 150 thousand for the coming season. Then, the actual sales for the next season would be (when $Q = 200$ and $D = 150$):

Actual sales $= \min\{Q, D\} = \min\{200, 150\} = 150.$

In this case, there will be a total of 50 thousand yearbooks unsold (over produced) by the end of the season. For convenience, we write **overstock** as:

$$(Q - D)^+ = \max\{0, Q - D\}.$$

If, for example, the actual demand turns out to be 250 thousand, the actual sales would be (when $Q = 200$ and $D = 250$):

Actual sales $= \min\{Q, D\} = \min\{200, 250\} = 200.$

Overstock when $Q = 200$ and $D = 250$:

$$(Q - D)^+ = (200 - 250)^+ = 0.$$

However, there would be 50 thousand out of stock (i.e., short), expressed as **stockout** quantity when $Q = 200$ and $D = 250$:

$$(D - Q)^+ = (250 - 200)^+ = 50 \,(\text{thousand}).$$

Given the production quantity $Q = 200$, actual sales, overstock, and stockout can be computed in a similar fashion for all possible demand scenarios, as summarized in Table 1.3. Expected values of actual sales, overstock, and stockout can then be computed accordingly, as follows:

$$E(\text{sales}) = \left[0.18(100) + 0.32(150) + 0.30(200) + 0.15(200) + 0.05(200)\right]$$
$$= 166 \,(\text{thousand}).$$

$$E(Q - D)^+ = \left[0.18(100) + 0.32(50) + 0.30(0) + 0.15(0) + 0.05(0)\right]$$
$$= 34 \,(\text{thousand}).$$

$$E(D - Q)^+ = \left[0.18(0) + 0.32(0) + 0.30(0) + 0.15(50) + 0.05(100)\right]$$
$$= 12.5 \,(\text{thousand}).$$

Under the production plan of $Q = 200$ thousand yearbooks, the expected sales profit and expected overstock cost can be obtained as:

$$E(\text{revenue}|Q = 200) = r \times E(\text{sales}) = (7.50 \times 166) = \$1,245 \,(\text{thousand}).$$

$$E(\text{overstock cost}|Q = 200) = c_o \times E(Q - D)^+ = (1.25 \times 34) = \$42.5 \,(\text{thousand}).$$

Table 1.3 Actual sales and inventory status with $Q = 200,000$

Actual demand (000s)	Probability	Actual sales (000s)	Overstock (000s)	Stockout (000s)
100	0.18	100	100	0
150	0.32	150	50	0
200	0.30	200	0	0
250	0.15	200	0	50
300	0.05	200	0	100

Probabilistic profits and costs

If the service level (SL) is defined as the probability of next year's demand being met, that is, $SL = Pr(D \leq Q)$, then the service level achieved under production volume $Q = 150$ thousand can be computed as:

$$SL = Pr(D \leq 150) = Pr(D = 100) + Pr(D = 150) = 0.5.$$

A 50 percent service level seems to be too low to the management at the *Milwaukee Sports Journal*. To increase the service level, the base order of $Q = 150$ thousand must be amended with extra production volume (termed safety stock). Suppose that a safety stock of 50 thousand is introduced so that the total production quantity is increased to $Q = 200$ thousand, with which a more acceptable service level of 80 percent can be achieved:

$$SL = Pr(D \leq 200) = Pr(D = 100) + Pr(D = 150) + Pr(D = 200) = 0.8.$$

Intuitively, however, additional costs must be incurred to increase the service level. To this end, we compute the expected profit based on $Q = 200$ thousand:

$$E(\text{profit} \mid Q = 200) = E(\text{sales profit} \mid Q = 200) - E(\text{overstock cost} \mid Q = 200)$$
$$= \{1245 - 42.5\} = \$1,202.5 \, (\text{thousand}).$$

Recall that the expected profit when $Q = 150$ thousand is \$1,046,250. Clearly, a production order of 200 thousand yearbooks next year is superior to that of 150 thousand both in terms of expected profit and service level. To find an order quantity that maximizes the expected profit, we can repeat the above computation by amending the base order with different safety stock considerations. We leave the rest of the analysis for you to complete as an assignment.

Now is a good time to refresh your knowledge of basic probability theory. The demand in the previous example is referred to as a discrete random variable, as it only takes a set of discrete values, such as $X = \{\ldots, x_1, x_2, \ldots\} = \{x_k\}_{k=-\infty}^{\infty}$. The probability measure of each possible demand realization is given by a *probability mass function*:

$$f(x_k) = Pr(D = x_k), \quad \text{for all} \quad x_k \in X.$$

A cumulative distribution function is then defined as:

$$F(x_k) = \Pr(D \le x_k) = \sum_{i=-\infty}^{k} f(x_i), \quad \text{with} \quad F(x_\infty) = \sum_{i=-\infty}^{\infty} f(x_i) = 1.$$

Note that the definitions introduced above can be considered merely for notational convenience. It may be a useful exercise to match the notation with the corresponding items in Example 1.5. With the notation just introduced, the expected profit under a given order quantity Q can be generally expressed as follows:

$$E(\text{net profit} \mid Q) = E(\text{sales profit} \mid Q) - E(\text{overstock cost} \mid Q)$$

$$= r \sum_{k=-\infty}^{Q-1} k \times \Pr(D = k) + r \sum_{k=Q}^{\infty} Q \times \Pr(D = k) - c_o \sum_{k=-\infty}^{Q-1} (Q - k) \Pr(D = k)$$

$$= (r + c_o) \sum_{k=-\infty}^{Q-1} k \times f(k) + rQ(1 - F(Q-1)) - c_o QF(Q-1).$$

The profit-maximizing solution of Example 1.5, Q^*, can be derived from the principle of *marginal equilibrium*: the expected marginal sales profit and savings should be equal to the expected marginal overstock inventory cost. That is:

$$r \times \Pr(\text{marginal sales profit} \mid Q^*) = c_o \times \Pr(\text{overstock cost} \mid Q^*).$$

The "marginal revenue" is the additional revenue generated by producing one extra yearbook (i.e., a total of $Q^* + 1$ yearbooks produced). It can be verified that:

$$\Pr(\text{marginal revenue} \mid Q^*) = \Pr(\text{selling one extra yearbook}) = \Pr(D > Q^*)$$

$$= \Pr(\text{selling one extra yearbook given } Q^* + 1 \text{ yearbooks produced})$$

$$= \Pr(D \ge Q^* + 1) = 1 - F(Q^*).$$

Similarly, we can verify for overstock that:

$$\Pr(\text{overstock} \mid Q^*) = \Pr(\text{one extra overstocked given } Q^* \text{ yearbook produced})$$

$$= \Pr(D < Q^* + 1) = \Pr(D \le Q^*) = F(Q^*).$$

Thus, the marginal equilibrium can be equivalently expressed as:

$$r(1 - F(Q^*)) = c_o F(Q^*).$$

Then we can obtain the following condition for Q^*:

$$\Pr(D \le Q^*) = F(Q^*) = \frac{r}{r + c_o}.$$

Recall from Example 1.5 that $r = \$7.50$ and $c_o = \$1.25$, thus we can compute:

$$\frac{r}{r + c_o} = \frac{7.50}{1.25 + 7.50} = 0.857.$$

We can then determine from Table 1.2 that:

$$Pr(D \leq 200,000) = 0.80, \text{and } Pr(D \leq 250,000) = 0.95.$$

The expected profit under $Q = 200,000$ was previously obtained as:

$$E(\text{profit} \mid Q = 200,000) = \$1,202,500.$$

Similarly, we obtain:

$$E(\text{profit} \mid Q = 250,000) = \$1,227,500.$$

The profit-maximizing order quantity for the Packers' Yearbook production can thus be determined as: $Q^* = 250,000$.

In reality, demand can be, and usually will be, realized continuously. For example, next year's demand for the Packers' Yearbook could be anywhere between 100,000 and 300,000. That is, the set X, on which a random variable is valued, consists of continuous intervals. In this case, we introduce a *continuous* random variable, which takes a value on a continuous interval on the real axis.

Newsboy problem: service level and safety stock

A generalized version of the production problem in Example 1.5 is the newsboy problem, referred to by operations researchers as the prototype for stochastic inventory theory (Nahmias 2001). A newsboy is faced with an uncertain demand D of newspapers for the next period (e.g., daily, weekly, etc.). The demand D can take any value on a real axis $(-\infty, \infty)$, with a certain probability distribution $F(x)$, a mean μ, and a variance σ^2, which are defined respectively as:

$$F(x) = Pr(D \leq x), \mu = E(x), \text{and } var(x) \equiv E\left(x - E(x)\right)^2.$$

A brief review of probability terminology is provided for reference in Appendix 1A at the end of this chapter.

Normal demand

To obtain more accurate results, one approach is to refine the characterization of demand. For example, Figure 1.8 illustrates the refined demand data for the Packers' Yearbook with a closer study of the current database.

Based on the refined data, statistics for the annual demand can be updated as having a mean of 176,500 and a standard deviation of 49,910, which we present in the spreadsheet depicted in Figure 1.9.

A continuous representation of the annual demand will lead to a normal random variable D following a normal distribution with the same demand mean $\mu = 176,750$ and the same standard deviation $\sigma = 49,910$, denoted as:

$$D \sim N(\mu, \sigma^2) = N(176,750, 49,910^2).$$

Demand (1000s)	Probability
25	0.03
100	0.08
125	0.12
150	0.17
175	0.18
200	0.15
225	0.12
250	0.08
275	0.05
300	0.02

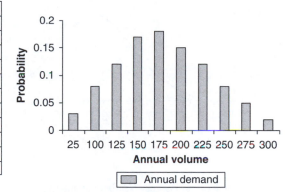

Figure 1.8 Refined annual demand data of Packers' Yearbook.

	Demand (1000s)	Probability	weighted demand	weighted (D - mu)^2
5	25	0.03	0.75	690.8
6	100	0.08	8.00	471.2
7	125	0.12	15.00	321.4
8	150	0.17	25.50	121.6
9	175	0.18	31.50	0.6
10	200	0.15	30.00	81.1
11	225	0.12	27.00	279.4
12	250	0.08	20.00	429.2
13	275	0.05	13.75	482.7
14	300	0.02	6.00	303.8
15		mean =	176.75	
16	sum(p) = 1		VAR =	2490.97
17			STDEV =	49.91

Figure 1.9 Refined statistics of annual Packers' Yearbook demand.

The distribution of the normal yearbook demand is illustrated in Figure 1.10.

SERVICE LEVEL VERSUS SAFETY STOCK

In inventory theory, the distribution function $F(x)$ coincides with the concept of *service level*, which is defined as the probability of *in-stock* inventory, that is,

Pr(adequate inventory to meet the demand) = $Pr(D \le S)$,

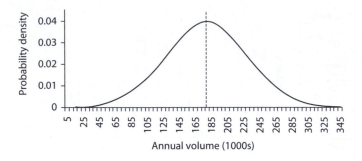

Figure 1.10 Normal Packers' Yearbook demand.

where S is the on-hand inventory available at the time demand D occurs. Thus, under a planned inventory level (a decision variable) S, the resulting service level is measured by the distribution function with $x = S$, that is,

$$\Pr(D \leq S) = F(S).$$

The newsboy needs to determine the quantity of newspapers to purchase from the publisher for the next period. In addition to the unit revenue r and the over-stock cost c_o, we allow an intangible understock cost of c_u for each sale that is lost due to insufficient stock. If the demand for the next period is known for certain, then the newsboy can avoid both costs c_o and c_u. However, because the demand is uncertain, the actual overstock and understock costs will depend on the order quantity Q. A larger Q tends to reduce the possible understock costs, and at the same time tends to increase the probability of being over-stocked. Thus, it is difficult to avoid overstock and understock at the same time. How much should the newsboy order for the next period, to maximize the expected net profit? For continuous demand, the profit-maximizing order quantity Q^* can be obtained from the following optimal service level equation (see Appendix 1B for details):

$$F(Q^*) = \frac{r + c_u}{r + c_o + c_u}.$$

When $c_u = 0$, the above equality becomes identical to the one we obtained previously for the case of discrete demand.

Example 1.6   Packers' Yearbook production under normal demand

Let us consider the same Packers' Yearbook production at the *Milwaukee Sports Journal*, except that the annual demand D is normally distributed with a mean of $\mu = 185{,}000$ and standard deviation of $\sigma = 27{,}000$. For convenience, we denote a normally distributed variable as $D \sim N(\mu, \sigma)$. A *normal* variable with $\mu = 0$ and $\sigma = 1$ is termed as *standard normal* variable, denoted as $Z \sim N(0,1)$. For any normal random variable D, a standard normal variable Z can be constructed as follows:

$$Z = \frac{D - \mu}{\sigma}.$$

For a given Q, the in-stock probability (i.e., service level) $F(Q) = \Pr(D \leq Q)$ can be expressed in terms of standard normal Z as follows:

$$F(Q) = \Pr(D \leq Q) = \Pr\left(\frac{D - \mu}{\sigma} \leq \frac{Q - \mu}{\sigma}\right) = \Pr(Z \leq z),$$

where $z = (Q - \mu)/\sigma$ represents the standardized decision variable Q, termed the safety factor. Given the optimal service level of $F(Q^*) = 0.857$, we can see from the Standard Normal Table (e.g., in Microsoft Excel) that:

$$F(Q^*) = \Pr(Z \leq 1.07) = 0.857, \text{i.e.,} z = 1.07.$$

Note that each given value of service level $F(Q)$ corresponds to a unique safety factor z. The Standard Normal Table can be found in Microsoft Excel (see more in the Simulation lab section of this chapter). Thus, the profit-maximizing quantity can be determined from $z = (Q - \mu)/\sigma$ as:

$$Q^* = \mu + z\sigma = 185{,}000 + (1.07)(27{,}000) = 213{,}890.$$

As can be seen from Example 1.6, if there is no variability in demand, then it is logical for the base order to be set to equal the expected demand with no safety stock, which would incur a 100 percent service level. However, in an ever-changing world the challenge lies in responding to uncertainty and variability. Variability in demand tends to lower the service level (i.e., the probability of meeting the demand), thus the level of safety stock is amended "just in case," to maintain a desirable service level. Clearly, consideration of the safety

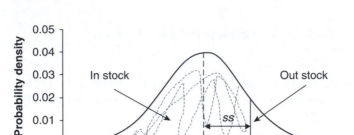

Figure 1.11 Packers' Yearbook example: service level versus safety stock.

stock level is related to the variability of underlying processes and the desirable service level.

Thus, the safety stock in this case can be quantified as:

$$ss = \text{safety stock} = z \times \sigma_e = \text{the amount in access of the mean,}$$

where z is a safety factor that can be determined from any given service level, and σ_e is a variability measure, usually the standard deviation of the forecast error (or the standard deviation of the demand σ if the forecast error is not viable). If demand stays as a constant, there will be no variability ($\sigma_e = 0$), and the safety stock will vanish (i.e., $ss = z \times \sigma_e = 0$). The relationship between service level and safety stock is illustrated in Figure 1.11.

In summary, safety stock is proportionally associated with demand variability, such that for a given service level, a higher safety stock is needed when demand variability is higher. However, given the same demand variability, a higher safety stock is needed if a higher service level is required. If service level is taken as a common measure of manufacturing process quality, the ultimate challenge in modern manufacturing is to maintain a desirable quality level while using the minimum possible level of safety stock. In fact, the concept of JIT manufacturing centers on the challenge of achieving the highest possible service level with zero or minimum safety stock.

Order fulfillment and performance

Order fulfillment schemes

Figure 1.5 depicts a typical SOF system, including three fundamental considerations—quantity, capacity, and lead-time (i.e., the time needed to fulfill the order), which in turn entails the functions of order arrival/generation, supply acquisition/order-filling, and delivery/distribution. There are two basic order-fulfillment schemes: push (i.e., make-to-stock) versus pull (i.e., make-to-order).

Make-to-stock (MTS) production. A make-to-stock production order calls for a stock of standardized products to be produced before customer orders for the products occur (or arrive). A typical US firm using an MRP system would operate under an MTS scheme.

Make-to-order (MTO) production. In contrast, pure make-to-order production occurs only in response to customer (or upstream) orders in a JIT manner. The well-known Toyota Kanban system is a classic example of make-to-order production, in which work at any workstation must be triggered (pulled) by a Kanban signal that signifies the arrival of a new upstream order.

Note that the key reason for having two different production policies is because manufacturing capacity is always limited. That is, it always takes time to fill an order, unless an infinite production capacity can be maintained. Therefore, to meet the demand in a timely fashion a manufacturer must either produce in advance (MTS) or produce in time (MTO). Although not yet scientifically proven, MTS is generally characterized as being better suited to "selling old products to new customers," while MTO is better suited to "selling new products to old customers." Due to revolutionary advances in IT and constant innovations in manufacturing, there has been an increasing trend toward MTO production, as adopted, for instance, by Dell Computers.

Manufacturing capacity is measured in terms of the production rate (i.e., volume produced per unit time), or unit production time (i.e., the reciprocal of production rate), because production always involves labor, and production capacity is influenced by behavior such as learning.

Learning curves

The concept of learning in the context of production capacity has been studied since the 1920s, and is referred to as the *learning curve* or *experience curve*. The term **learning curve** was adopted to describe the observation in the aircraft industry that the number of labor hours needed to produce a unit of output declined in a particular pattern as a function of the cumulative number of units produced. The term **experience curve** is used when direct labor costs are considered instead of labor hours. According to the theory of production outlined in the section on "Supply chain operations," the cost is interdependent of other factors, such as demand level and capital input. Because labor hours can be treated as a pure independent variable, we will focus on learning curves.

The key to the learning curve is the concept of a percentage learning factor, denoted by P, which is defined as the ratio of the production time (i.e., labor hours) that a worker spends on the first and second unit of tasks. Intuitively, P gives the percentage of time spent on the first unit that is needed to repeat the job a second time. The learning factor P characterizes, on an aggregate scale, the learning that occurs in any specific situation, by theorizing that the same ratio P will be preserved whenever the cumulative volume doubles. That is,

$$P = \frac{T_2}{T_1} = \frac{T_4}{T_2} = \cdots = \frac{T_{2k}}{T_k}, k = 1, 2, 3, \ldots,$$

where T_k is the time needed to produce the kth unit. For a worker with an 80 percent learning factor who spends 10 h on the first job, the unit production time on subsequent jobs is expected to be:

$$T_1 = 10; T_2 = 0.8T_1 = 8; T_4 = 0.8T_2 = 6.4; \text{ and so on.}$$

With any given learning factor P, a learning curve determines the time to produce an nth unit (or job) in the form of:

$$T_n = T_1 \times n^b = \frac{T_1}{n^{-b}}, \text{ with } b = \frac{\ln(P)}{\ln(2)},$$

where $b \leq 0$ is a scaled learning factor that is solely determined by the percentage learning factor P.

Example 1.7   Application of learning while doing

The G-tech company is recruiting an AutoCad grapher. The company has established a time standard of 2 h per new job (i.e., be able to complete a new AutoCad design drawing within 2 h). The managers at G-tech have determined that an individual's performance can be considered to have reached his/her "steady level" after ten repetitions. Mr. Luck has just been interviewed, during which he was tested on two new drawings. He took 2 h 45 min on the first drawing and 2 h 36.75 min on the second. Can Mr. Luck meet the company's time standard requirement and thus be hired? Given that the time spent on the first and the second drawings was recorded as $T_1 = 165 \text{ min}$ and $T_2 = 156.75 \text{ min}$, respectively, the percentage learning factor can be determined as:

$$P = \frac{156.75}{165} = 0.95.$$

Thus, the scaled learning factor is $b = \ln(0.95)/\ln(2) = -0.074$. With a 95 percent learning curve, the time that Mr. Luck will need to complete the tenth drawing can be projected as:

$$T_{10} = \frac{T_1}{n^{-b}} = \frac{165}{10^{0.074}} = 139.15 \text{ (min)}.$$

Unfortunately, Mr. Luck will not be able to meet the standard of 120 min per drawing, and therefore cannot be hired.

Many applications of learning curves require an estimation of the cumulative production time. Let Y_n be the total cumulative time to perform the first n tasks. That is,

$$Y_n = T_1 + T_2 + \cdots + T_n = \sum_{i=1}^{n} T_1 \times i^b.$$

For Mr. Luck in Example 1.7, the cumulative time for completing the first ten drawings can be estimated as:

$$Y_{10} = 165\left(1 + \frac{1}{2^{0.074}} + \cdots + \frac{1}{10^{0.704}}\right) = 165(8.95) = 1477.5\,(\text{min})$$

In reality, of course, learning involves a much more complex process of adaptation and simulation.

Simulation lab: Learning curves and the newsboy problem

Assignment 1.1: Exercise conducted in Excel

A Example 1.3 conducted in Excel.
- Specify the parameters F_1, F_2, v_1, and v_2 in a "worksheet."
- Compute the break-even point, making "absolute reference" to the parameters specified above.
- Let quantity Q be measured in millions, and set up "ranges" in the same "worksheet," in a format similar to the following:

Q (million)	C_1	C_2
0.2	$= F_1 + v_1 \times (0.2)$	$= F_2 + v_2 \times (0.2)$
0.4		
0.6		

- Plot the cost lines C_1 and C_2 in the same graph, and verify with the theoretical results.

B Example 1.4 calculated in Excel.
- Specify the parameters: r, K, and Y.
- Set up a "range" for year n as 0, 1, ..., 15, then compute PV(n) (present value) for each value of n.
- Let the capacity expansion plan in Example 1.4 be Plan-1: expansions in year 0, 2, and 4 with an expansion capacity of $Y = 1,000$. Compute the total cost (in PVs) of Plan-1.
- Consider another plan, called Plan-2: expansions in year 0, 1, 2, 3, 4, and 5, with an expansion capacity of $Y = 500$. Compute the total cost in PV of Plan-2.

Assignment 1.2: Newsboy problem—Packers' Yearbook production

A Basic elements for simulation in Excel.
- Random numbers =RAND( ): independently generated and uniformly distributed between (0,1).
- Discrete random variables (e.g., demand):
  - ex. Given distribution of weekly demand: $\Pr\{d = 100\} = 0.3$; $\Pr\{d = 200\} = 0.7$
    → generate random variable in Excel
  - =IF(B3 < 0.3, 100, 200)
  - repeated trials: simulate the weekly demand for 52 weeks.
- Statistics: = average(B1:B52); = stdev(B1:B52)

B Modified Example 1.5.
- Develop a direct Excel newsboy solution model for the Packers' Yearbook production with a modified discrete random demand as given in the following table.

Demand (thousands)	Probability
25	0.03
100	0.08
125	0.12
150	0.17
175	0.18
200	0.15
225	0.12
250	0.08
275	0.05
300	0.02

- Compute the demand mean, variance, and standard deviation. Produce a bar-chart for the demand distribution.
- Given the cost data and other input data as "absolute references," your solution model should be able to determine the following, using the marginal equilibrium equation: optimal service level (i.e., in-stock probability), optimal order quantity Q^*, and optimal expected net profit.
- Develop a random generator with Excel that will generate demand samples according to the probability distribution as given in the table above.
- Generate 20 samples for next year's demand for yearbooks. Then, conduct a simulation analysis using the 20 sample demand data sets, as

follows: for each possible Q between 100,000 and 300,000, compute the revenues generated, overstock costs incurred, and actual net profits for each of the sample demands. Compute an average net profit over the 20 samples for each Q.

- Identify the order quantity and the associated safety stock that generate the highest average net profit. Obtain an estimate of service level (i.e., in-stock probability) from the 20 simulated samples under the best order quantity just identified.

C Modified Example 1.6.

- Develop a direct Excel newsboy solution model for the Packers' Yearbook production when the demand is normal and with the same mean and variance that were obtained in B. Now, the solution model will determine the optimal order quantity Q^*, using the Normal Tables (e.g., the tables in Excel are given by "=NORMSDIST(z)" and "=NORMSINV(probability)").

- Generate 20 samples for next year's demand for yearbooks. Then, with a fixed Q^* as obtained above, simulate the yearbook production for each of the sample demands (i.e., conduct 20 simulation runs). Note: your simulation should include realized revenues, overstock costs incurred, and actual net profits. Compute the average net profit for the given Q^*.

- Tally the frequency for in-stock inventory (i.e., the number of simulation runs in which enough yearbooks are produced). Obtain an estimate for the service level, using the following:

$$\Pr(D \le Q^*) \approx \frac{\text{frequency of in-stock inventory}}{\text{total number of simulation runs}}.$$

Assignment 1.3: Learning curves

A Generate a learning curve table with P (learning percentage) and T_1 as inputs:

$$T_n = T_1\, n^b, n = 1, 2, \ldots (T_n : \text{production time on the } n\text{th unit}).$$

$$b = \frac{\ln(P)}{\ln(2)}, P : \text{learning-curve percentage} \left(\text{e.g.,} 0.9 \text{ for } 90 \text{ percent}\right).$$

B Mini-case: develop an Excel simulation program for the following learning curve application.

- A group of 36 skilled workers is scheduled for a project to make a new receiver for a global satellite positioning system (GSPS). The skill level of the workers is estimated as: 50 percent are on a 90 percent learning curve, 20 percent are on a 95 percent curve, and the remaining 30 percent are on an 84 percent curve (i.e., each worker has a probability of 0.5 of being on a 90 percent learning curve, a 0.2 probability of being on a 95 percent curve, and a 0.3 probability of being on an 84 percent curve).
- Suppose that all 36 workers spend 0.5 h on the first unit. Calculate the average number of units produced per person on the first day (assuming a 10 h shift per day). Collect other statistics, such as the standard deviation.

Problems

Basic exercises

1   The InstChem company is considering adding a new cement plant in Thailand to fulfill a regional demand of 60,000 tons per year. The plant will cost the firm $11 million in capital. It will cost the plant $490 to produce 1 ton of cement. Alternatively, they could subcontract the production of the cement to Alecs and pay $650 per ton. Should InstChem invest in the new plant, if the company wants to at least break even within the first year? Why?

2   According to a careful study of past data, a food flavoring company estimates that the cost of adding new capacity follows the law:

$$f(y) = 0.019y^{0.69},$$

where y represents tons per year and $f(y)$ denotes millions of dollars. Demand is growing at the rate of 2,000 tons per year and the interest rate can be fixed at 16 percent. Suppose that an expansion plan calls for additional annual capacity in increments of 2,000 tons every 3 years for the next 9 years, including an initial increase immediately.

(a) Calculate the present value of the first addition (the first addition only, excluding the initial addition).

(b) Calculate the total cost of the 9-year plan at its present value.

3   The XYZ company is recruiting an AutoCad grapher. The company has established a time standard of 2 h per new job (i.e., being able to complete a new AutoCad design drawing within 2 h). Industrial engineering managers at XYZ have determined that an individual's performance can be considered to be at his/her "steady level" after ten repetitions. Mr. Luck has just been interviewed, during which he was tested on two new drawings. He took 4 h and 30 min on the first job and 3 h and 27.9 min on the second. Can Mr. Luck meet the company's time standard requirement and thus be hired?

4 A retail outlet sells a seasonal product for $95 per unit. The cost of the product to the retailer is $79 per unit. All units not sold during the regular season are sold with 65 percent off the retail price in the after-season clearance sale. Assume that demand for the product is normal, with $\mu = 500$ and $\sigma^2 = 100^2$.

  (a) What quantity should be ordered for the season?
  (b) What is the probability of stockout, using the quantity suggested in (a)?
  (c) (Optional) Determine the expected number of products that will be stocked out in the regular season, if the quantity suggested in (a) is ordered. (*Hint*: To calculate (c), you will need to use the Loss Function Table (e.g., from MS Excel). Find the unit loss $L(z)$ from the Loss Function Table first. Then, compute the expected stockout: $E(D-Q)^+ = \sigma \times L(z)$.)

5 A seafood store sells fresh lobsters for $25 per pound. Each week the store buys lobster from local fishermen at $12 per pound. Any unsold lobsters at the end of each week are sold to a pet food company for $1.50 per pound. The holding cost is $7.5/unit/week, and the shortage cost is $9/unit. The weekly lobster demand is given in the following table.

Weekly demand	Probability
85	0.020
90	0.132
95	0.312
100	0.260
105	0.131
110	0.103
115	0.032
120	0.010

  (a) Determine the weekly quantity (in pounds) that the store should order.
  (b) Using the order quantity determined in (a), calculate the expected loss (in dollars) due to overstock.
  (c) Determine the expected number of products stocked out in the regular season, if the quantity suggested in (a) is ordered.
  (d) What *fill rate* will be incurred? Note:

$$\text{fill rate} = \frac{E\{\text{actual sales}\}}{Q} = \frac{E\{\min(\text{demand}, Q)\}}{Q}.$$

Additional exercises

6 SmartVal Inc., a high-pressure pump manufacturer, currently buys bearing rings from a supplier in Asia for $9 each. Each pump consists of four bearing rings. Due to the economic crisis in Asia the price is scheduled to increase to $18 each, so SmartVal is considering producing the rings itself, which would require an additional production facility at a cost of $2 million. The production cost (as opposed to the purchase price) is estimated to be $7.50 per ring. Current annual sales of pumps are running at 30,000 units.

(a) Assuming the purchase price indeed increases to $18 each, should SmartVal decide to produce the rings itself, and would it be able to break even in the first year?

(b) At the current sales rate, how long would it take for the savings (between "make" versus "buy") to pay back the investment required for the additional production facility?

7   Hanseng, a cigarette lighter producer in Hong Kong, buys plastic cases from suppliers in Guang Dong, China. The cases currently cost $2.25 each, and Hanseng is considering the option of producing the cases in the north suburb of Hong Kong, which will require a capital investment of $1,250,000. The production cost at the new Hong Kong facility will be $0.75 per item. Hanseng currently sells 90,000 lighters a year.

(a) Assume that the sales rate will remain the same. How many years would it take for Hanseng to pay back the capital investment if the cases are produced in Hong Kong?

(b) If sales are expected to decrease by 5 percent per year, how many years would it take to pay back the investment?

8   According to a careful study of past data, a company estimates that the cost of adding new capacity follows the law:

$$f(y) = 0.021y^{0.70},$$

where y represents tons per year and $f(y)$ represents millions of dollars. Demand is growing at the rate of 2,500 tons per year and the interest rate can be fixed at 12 percent.

(a) Suppose that a new facility of 5,000 tons/year capacity has just been purchased, and the same increase in capacity will be needed every 2 years. Determine the cost of each increase.

(b) Compute the present value of the cost for the first two additions, excluding the current capacity. Then, compute the present value of the total costs, including the current capacity plus the first two additions.

9   (Continued from Problem 3.) The XYZ company has purchased a new AutoCad machine. The company has established a time standard of 2 h per new job (i.e., being able to complete a new AutoCad design drawing within 2 h). The IE managers at XYZ have determined that an individual's performance can be considered to have reached his/her "steady level" after ten repetitions. Mrs. Noluck has just finished her interview. Due to a fire alarm interruption, her first drawing time was not properly recorded. The manager decides to use the times on her second and third drawings, which were recorded as 3 h 27 min 54 s for the second and 2 h 58 min 25 s for the third drawing. Should Mrs. Noluck be hired?

10   An IT engineering firm has just started a contract to replace a new electronic order-processing system at five distribution centers for a medical supply

distributor. The contract specifies that the five jobs must be completed within 75 days. The past data indicate that the software engineers at the firm would entail an 87 percent learning curve with an average of 21 days for the first job.

(a) How many days would be needed for the final job (i.e., replacing the fifth system)?
(b) A $3,000 bonus is offered for each day that the contract is completed before the 75th day, with a $1,500 penalty for each day that completion exceeds the deadline. How much bonus or penalty will the IT firm receive from the contract for the five jobs?

11 Job applicants are interviewed for a project to produce a new receiver for a GSPS (global satellite positioning system). Each applicant will be given a short training session for a specific job order, and will then be asked to perform the job order twice. The learning ability of the next applicant is estimated as having a probability of 0.5 with a 90 percent learning curve for the job, a 0.2 probability of a 95 percent curve, and a 0.3 probability of an 84 percent curve.

(a) Suppose that everyone takes 0.5 h to perform the job order for the first time. What is the expected time the next applicant will spend on the second job order?
(b) What would be the expected total time that the next applicant would need to complete ten job orders (i.e., repeat the same job ten times)?

Appendix 1A   Review of probability

Probability distribution, mean, and variance

Suppose that a demand variable D can take any value over a real axis $(-\infty, \infty)$, and it follows a certain probability distribution characterized by a distribution function $F(x)$ given as:

$$F(x) = \Pr(D \le x) = \int_{-\infty}^{x} dF(s) = \int_{-\infty}^{x} f(s)ds,$$

where $f(x) = dF(x)/dx$ is the probability density function (pdf) associated with D. We shall note that the distribution function $F(x) = \Pr(D \le x)$ is generally defined for any random variable, discrete as well as continuous. With such notation, the **expectation** and **variance** of any random variable x can be then written as:

$$\mu = E(x) = \int_{-\infty}^{\infty} x \, dF(x) = \int_{-\infty}^{\infty} x \times f(x)dx$$

$$\mathrm{var}(x) \equiv E\left(x - E(x)\right)^2 = \int_{-\infty}^{\infty} (x - \mu)^2 \, dF(x) = \int_{-\infty}^{\infty} (x - \mu)^2 f(x)dx.$$

Useful probability formulas and equalities

Let x and y be two random variables defined in a probability space (Ω, F, ρ). Suppose that both x and y posses finite expectation and second moment. Then, it holds the following equalities:

1 $E(cx) = cE(x)$, where c is a constant.
2 $E(x \pm y) = E(x) \pm E(y)$.
3 $\operatorname{var}(x) = E\left(x - E(x)\right) = E(x^2) - \left(E(x)\right)^2$.
4 $\operatorname{var}(cx) = c^2 \operatorname{var}(x)$, where c is a constant.
5 $\operatorname{var}(x \pm y) = \operatorname{var}(x) + \operatorname{var}(y) \pm \operatorname{cov}(x, y)$, where
   $\operatorname{cov}(x, y) \equiv E\left((x - E(x))(y - E(y))\right)$.
6 $\operatorname{var}(x \pm y) = \operatorname{var}(x) + \operatorname{var}(y)$, where x and y are independent.

Appendix 1B Newsboy solution under continuous demand

For the continuous demand of a newsboy problem, the expected profit under a given Q can be expressed as follows:

$$E(\text{profit} \mid Q) = r \int_{-\infty}^{Q} xf(x)dx + r \int_{Q}^{\infty} Qf(x)dx - c_o \int_{-\infty}^{Q} (Q - x)f(x)dx$$

$$-c_u \int_{Q}^{\infty} (x - Q)f(x)dx = (r + c_o) \int_{-\infty}^{Q} xf(x)dx - c_u \int_{Q}^{\infty} xf(x)dx$$

$$+(r + c_u)Q \int_{Q}^{\infty} f(x)dx - c_o Q \int_{-\infty}^{Q} f(x)dx.$$

Applying the principle of marginal equilibrium, we obtain the following equality under the profit-maximizing order quantity Q^*:

$$(r + c_u) \int_{Q^*}^{\infty} f(x)dx = c_o \int_{-\infty}^{Q^*} f(x)dx.$$

A rigorous proof of the above equality can be obtained by solving the derivative equation:

$$\frac{\partial E(\text{profit} \mid Q)}{\partial Q} = 0,$$

which conforms to the marginal equilibrium equation. Then, it is straightforward to obtain the optimal service level equation:

$$F(Q^*) = \frac{r + c_u}{r + c_o + c_u}.$$

Bibliography

Ash, R.B. 1972. *Real Analysis and Probability*, New York: Academic Press.

Feller, W. 1971. *An Introduction to Probability Theory and its Applications*, Vol 2, New York: John Wiley and Sons.

Holland, J. 1992. *Adaptation in Natural and Artificial Systems*, Cambridge, MA: The MIT Press.

La Londe, B.J. 1998. "Supply Chain Evolution in Numbers," *Supply Chain Management Review*, 2(1), 7–8.

Mikel, H. and R. Schroeder. 2000. *Six Sigma: The Breakthrough Management Strategy Revolutionizing the World's Top Corporations*, New York: Currency and Doubleday, Random House, Inc.

Nahmias, S. 2001. *Production and Operations Analysis*, 4th Edition, Boston, MA: McGraw Hill.

Ohno, T. 1978. *Toyota Production Systems* (in Japanese), Tokyo: Diamond-Sha.

Romer, P. 1990. "Technical Change and the Aggregate Production Function," *Review of Economics and Statistics*, 39, 312–320.

Simchi-Levi, D., P. Kaminsky, and E. Simchi-Levi. 2000. *Designing and Managing the Supply Chain: Concept, Strategies, and Case Studies*, Chicago, IL: McGraw-Hill/Irwin.

Solow, R.M. 1956. "A Contribution to the Theory of Economic Growth," *Quarterly Journal of Economics*, 70 (February), 65–94.

Spear, S. and H.K. Bowen. 1999. "Decoding the DNA of the Toyota Production System," *Harvard Business Review*, September–October, 96–106.

Stock, J.R. and D.M. Lambert. 2000. *Strategic Logistics Management*, 4th Edition, Chicago, IL: McGraw-Hill/Irwin.

Swan, T. 1956. "Economic Growth and Capital Accumulation," *Economics Record*, 32 (November), 334–361.

Williamson, O.E. 2008. "Outsourcing: Transaction Cost Economics and Supply Chain Management," *International Journal of Supply Chain Management*, 44(2), 1559–1576.

Womack, J.P., D.T. Jones, and D. Roos. 1990. *The Machine That Changed the World: The Story of Lean Production*, New York: Harper Perennial.

2 Capacity and productivity of supply chain logistics

Key items:

- *Institute for Supply Management (ISM) index and theory of supply*
- *Supply capacity and facility*
- *TPS: a process-driven pull system focusing on "lean"*
- *MRP: an inventory-driven push system geared for computer integration*
- *SOF: an order-driven interactive system underpinned with contracts and incentives*
- *What is the difference between six-sigma and lean?*

As described in Chapter 1, the winning-before-doing (WBD) theory embraces two key rules: the win-with-speed (Su-Sheng, 速胜) rule of agile and quick response, and the win-by-singularity (Qi-Sheng, 奇胜) rule of adaptation and innovation. WBD operations are guided by the five tactics (TACBE): targeting (度), assessing (量), calculating (数), balancing (称), and executing (胜), and their modern six-sigma equivalent: D-M-A-I-C—define, measure, analyze, improve, and control. In this connection, the key to building a WBD supply chain is to acquire WBD conformant capacity systems that are both agile and adaptive. According to Sun Zi's five tactics, the process starts with *measuring* and *monitoring*.

Measuring supply capacity: the Institute for Supply Management index

In the 1920s, the Institute for Supply Management (ISM) started to collect data on manufacturing supplies, and since 1931 has regularly published the *Manufacturing ISM Report on Business* (for more details, see the ISM website http://www.ism.ws). The ISM reports consist of a monthly survey based on a set of ISM indices that have been developed and amended over decades, including the Supplier Deliveries index added in 1971, and the Purchasing Managers' index (PMI) developed in the early 1980s. Since then, the ISM indices and reports have become an important source of supply and logistics survey data for macro-economic conditions. Professor Joseph E. Stiglitz recently commented, "The Manufacturing ISM Report on Business has one of the shortest reporting lags of any macro-economic series and gives an important early look at the economy," as quoted by Mr. Norbert J. Ore (2005), the Chair of ISM Business Survey Committee. By popular demand, the *Non-Manufacturing ISM Report on Business* was launched in 1998, including data starting from July 1997.

Manufacturing ISM indices

The current manufacturing ISM reports include a set of nine indices.

1 production (output in units);
2 new orders (production orders in units);
3 inventories [raw; maintenance, repair, and operations (MRO); intermediates; and purchased finished goods];
4 employment;
5 supplier deliveries (order completion and delivery time);
6 prices (weighted average price for purchased commodities);
7 new export orders;
8 imports (including raw, MRO, parts, intermediates, and purchased finished goods);
9 backlog of orders.

In the early 1980s, the PMI was developed as a composite index of the weighted average of the first five ISM indices (i.e., production, new orders, inventories, employment, and supplier deliveries) specifically for the purchasing and logistics professions. Directly participated in by the US Department of Commerce, the PMI assigns weights to the five ISM indices as follows (as of 2005, by the ISM Business Survey Committee):

Production	0.25
New orders	0.30
Inventories	0.10
Employment	0.20
Supplier deliveries	0.15

The ISM indices are nonmodel-based survey indicators, primarily for supply capacity and capability, and are applicable both to the overall economy and to

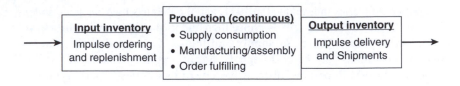

Figure 2.1 SOF system: an ISM-compatible prototype.

specific economic sectors and industries. The ISM indices can be grouped into four categories of supply capacity indicators:

1   capital: production (technology and systems);
2   labor: employment (education, training);
3   investment: inventory (insurance, risk management, and speculation); and
4   market: price and new orders (demand, conditions).

A basic supply order fulfillment (SOF) system represents an ISM-compatible prototype of a supply chain, as illustrated in Figure 2.1.

A key structural feature of an SOF prototype is the separation of the input inventory from the output inventory, which makes an SOF system compatible with and applicable to ISM indices that provide separate measures for incoming orders (specified by quantity and price), input inventory, output inventory, order delivery, and production control (capacity and workforce). The SOF prototype is a basic unit (e.g., an enterprise) of the supply chain, which is interactive with both upstream and downstream units via input and output inventories. The interaction is triggered by a purchase order (i.e., a buying–selling contract), consisting of order quantity and price. The interaction is competitive, as the buying and selling parties always have contrasting objectives. An SOF system, the logistical prototype of a supply chain, is based on an established contractual relationship, termed *competitive equilibrium* in industrial organization (IO) theory. Broadly speaking, IO theory is concerned with interenterprise relationships and structure and is clearly enterprise crossing.

Supply production capacity and facility

Sun Zi's five essentials are clearly applicable to today's modern business operations. For example, to operate a manufacturing firm successfully, a factory manager must know when to produce and when not to. The center of a production/manufacturing system is the production facility (i.e., the factory). In business, the art of winning rests on how to master and operate a production facility in the face of uncertain changes and unexpected disturbances. In fact, the study of production facilities has become a scientific subject (see *Factory Physics* by Hopp and Spearman 2000).

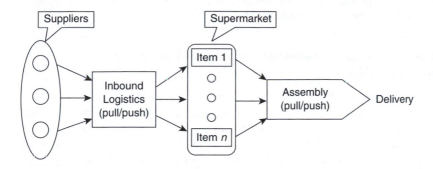

Figure 2.2 Mixed layout in supermarket manufacturing.

Layout and production scheme

Recall from Chapter 1 that the two manufacturing principles, Just in Time (JIT) versus just-in-case, underpin two basic manufacturing strategies: pull (make-to-order) and push (make-to-stock) systems. A practical way to differentiate between make-to-order manufacturing and make-to-stock manufacturing is whether production starts with the arrival of a customer order, or starts before an order is placed. Although each of the three process layouts can operate under either of the two strategies, a specific layout type may be particularly suitable for a specific type of manufacturing strategy. For example, material requirement planning (MRP)-type push control would be better suited for a make-to-stock batch system with a fairly wide range of products, whereas a Kanban-style make-to-order manufacturing strategy would typically be used for a stable flow system.

In today's manufacturing, it is common to find a mixture of push and pull controls incorporated in the same factory. A good example of such a combination is the recent development of "supermarket" manufacturing, as has been adopted by GE-Medical Systems and Harley-Davidson. Figure 2.2 depicts a schematic layout of a typical supermarket production system.

The output end of the assembly line in Figure 2.2 operates in a push manner: produce a certain amount of stock for delivery that is established in advance (e.g., via forecasting). The input materials for the assembly line are pulled from the "supermarket," where all necessary materials for the assembly are acquired and maintained. The operator(s) at the input station to the assembly line will check out (i.e., pull out) the materials needed, just like shopping in a supermarket.

Stocks at the supermarket are managed and maintained by a functional unit for inbound logistics, which can operate under either push (make-to-stock) or pull (make-to-order) schemes. Typically, a logistics department linked to the manufacturing supermarket operates as a transit link between a pull scheme with the supplier(s) and a push scheme with the assembly line.

Prototype example: production capacity at Diagnostic Equipment (DE)

A manufacturing facility (or factory) is a capacity system. We consider three basic capacity systems: the Toyota production system (TPS), the SOF, and the MRP systems. The **TPS** system is suited for **pull** production with a stable flow; the **SOF** is structured with PMI indices, focusing on the fulfillment and delivery of supply orders; and **MRP** is by definition concerned with materials planning and releasing in a **push** manner. All three are real-world manufacturing systems, although none of them can be regarded as universally successful. Before we examine each of the three capacity systems in the subsections of this chapter, let us consider an example of manufacturing order fulfillment.

> ### Example 2.1　Computer topography scanner assembly plant at DE
>
> The computer topography (CT) plant at DE, a manufacturer of medical diagnostic equipment, is a worldwide leading provider of CT scanners. Figure 2.3 depicts the CT plant and its relative position in its supply chain. Customer orders are received in the form of a purchase contract between the customer (hospital) and the sales representative(s) of DE. In addition to technical specifications, the contract contains the site foundation drawings for installation at the acquiring hospital and the delivery date (ready-to-use date). The delivery date quoted by DE is computed from the total order cycle time as depicted in Figure 2.3. A typical order cycle time is 90 days, which includes a 1-month supply response time, 1-month assembly time at the plant, and a 1-month delivery and installation time.

A CT scanner is a highly tech-intensive product, and most components are outsourced from designated suppliers. The main operation at the CT plant is the final assembly of the CT scanner, consisting of three major subassemblies: gantry, control console, and movable table, as illustrated in Figure 2.4.

Bill of material for the CT scanner

A scanner is specified by a "tree" of all its lower-level items (e.g., parts, components, and subassemblies). This technical profile for each end item, termed a bill of material (BOM), is designed to be a "permanent" data record. Figure 2.4 gives an illustrative BOM for a CT-100 model.

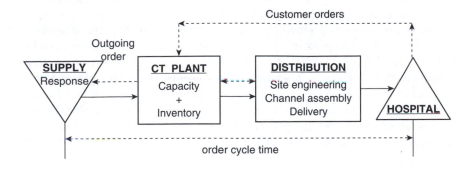

Figure 2.3 Manufacturing and delivery of CT scanner.

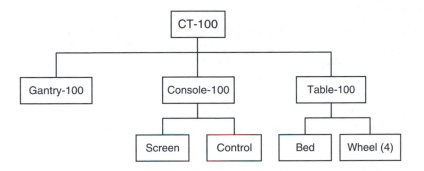

Figure 2.4 A schematic BOM of CT-100 model.

The end item is the Model CT-100, and its BOM contains details of every part and the quantity required to build a Model CT-100 scanner. For example, each CT-100 consists of four wheels. In terms of supply of materials, a production order of 10 CT-100 units will require 10 sets (or copies) of the BOM, which includes 40 wheels.

Also note that there will be a certain lead-time (supply response time) for those materials that are provided by outside sources. For example, the Table-100 (movable table assembly) is acquired from an overseas supplier who requires a 1-month lead-time. In reality, the parts are usually procured separately without strict accordance to the BOM, and therefore there are usually additional part inventories that do not constitute a complete set(s) of BOM. The largest number of BOM sets contained in the current inventory of parts, termed the *aggregate supply status*, indicates the number of units of end items that can be produced using the inventory on-hand. For example, if the current accounts of three subassemblies specify 100 gantries, 80 consoles, and 120 tables, the largest number of complete BOM sets is then 80. That is, the current inventory will be adequate for producing 80 final CT-100 scanners, with 20 extra gantries and 40 extra tables, but short on consoles.

Because demand is usually uncertain, whereas production capacity is largely fixed (at least for the current planning period), one of the challenges for DE is how to develop a monthly capacity plan in terms of planned production orders (e.g., units produced per month), such that promised orders can be fulfilled and delivered on time (i.e., in 90 days) and on target (i.e., meeting actual monthly demands). Manufacturing capacity is usually planned and adjusted at certain discrete points in time (e.g., weekly or monthly), whereas order fulfillment is a continuous process under the given capacity plan. Based on this CT production prototype, we will examine three operational systems currently practiced in the field of manufacturing: the TPS, SOF, and MRP systems.

TPS: the origin of lean manufacturing

The house of TPS

The authentic TPS can be best characterized by the *house of TPS*, as introduced by the Shigijutsu Group, a student of TPS from the school of Dr. Ohno's JIT manufacturing philosophy. According to the Shigijutsu Group, the house of TPS consists of three elements: the left pillar (JIT), the right pillar (Jidoka), and the foundation (Heijunka), as depicted in Figure 2.5.

The three elements are based on a single operational doctrine: to eliminate or minimize any waste incurred in the manufacturing process. Specifically, the three elements can be described briefly as follows:

1   JIT (及時化加工). To complete a task or meet a target in the timeliest fashion, neither too early nor too late. This is consistent with Sun Zi's *win-with-speed* (速勝) principle. The JIT pillar of TPS consists of three key elements: (1) pull production; (2) single piece flow, which is intended to detect and remove defective parts as soon as possible by adhering to three "*dont's*," namely, *don't* produce a defect, *don't* pass along a defect, and *don't* accept a defect; and (3) takt time production. We will elaborate on the takt time concept later in this section.
2   Jidoka (自働化). The original definition of Jidoka was to empower each production unit or team with the autonomous authority to halt the entire production flow when an error or flaw was identified. The expanded and generalized essence of Jidoka is to devise special rules and schemes that are uniquely suited for specific companies and situations. This is consistent with Sun Zi's win-with-singularity (奇勝) principle.
3   Heijunka (平準化). To balance production flow across all stages by planning level workloads in advance. Any unexpected fluctuation or interruption will cause waste and must be dealt with by a carefully planned course of action to eliminate or minimize its effect. This is a realization of Sun Zi's winning-before-doing.

The chemistry that "glues" the three pillars together is the TPS theory of *waste elimination*. That is, the key to a perfect TPS is to eliminate, or at least minimize, any

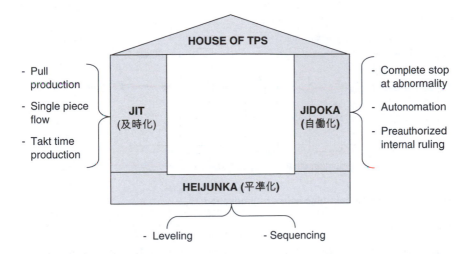

Figure 2.5 The house of TPS.

waste in each of the three pillars. *Waste* (i.e., "muda" in Japanese) is broadly defined as anything that should not be done, as opposed to value-added work. According to TPS theory, there are *seven* types of waste in manufacturing; they are as follows:

1   defective parts
2   overproduction
3   inventory
4   motion
5   processing transactions
6   transportation
7   waiting.

Some types of waste can be eliminated, such as defects and inventory, whereas others (e.g., motion and transportation) are virtually impossible to eliminate, in which case they should be minimized.

Takt time of JIT manufacturing

The concept of takt time, which is fundamental to lean manufacturing, is based on the principle of striving for the most balanced and fastest paced production. In a typical multistage production line, the takt time is defined as follows:

$$\text{Takt time} = \frac{\text{Total production time available}}{\text{Demand target}}$$
$$= \frac{\text{Total minutes available per week}}{\text{Demand quantity per week}}.$$

Minute

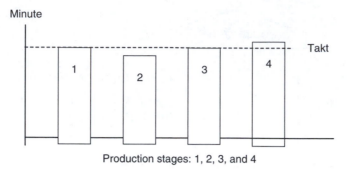

Production stages: 1, 2, 3, and 4

Figure 2.6 Strive for takt-time balanced production.

JIT manufacturing strives for each production stage to be balanced as closely as possible to the "beat" of takt time, as illustrated in Figure 2.6.

Stages that are slower than the takt time (e.g., stage 4) will incur waste by holding up the other, faster stages, whereas if stages run faster than the takt time they will incur waste by being idle. Those stages that are synchronized with the takt time (e.g., stages 1 and 3 in Figure 2.6) fulfill the JIT principle. TPS has developed a systematic program of *continuous improvement* ("Kaizen" in Japanese), which is intended to eliminate all possible waste in a manufacturing process by continuously repeating the so-called Kaizen sessions, with each session focusing on a specific set of priorities. The TPS Kaizen system aims to identify waste and conducts Kaizen sessions as soon as specific areas of waste are identified. TPS has also developed skills and accumulated experience in how to identify and prioritize waste and potential waste in a supply capacity system.

Queuing analysis of a Heijunka flow in TPS

A **queuing system** is a descriptive model of a class of stochastic processes, which is a well-established subject in the field of applied probability (Gross and Harris 1974). By referring to a descriptive model, as opposed to a prescriptive one, we mean a system that is not characterized by prescribed analytical expressions and optimization structures. When applied to manufacturing, a **queuing system** can be viewed as a pull type of make-to-order production, because production in a queuing system only starts when customer orders arrive. This view will become clear as we proceed in this section.

As depicted in Figure 2.7, a queuing system consists of a stationary capacitated facility (e.g., a bank teller) with a type of queuing mechanism, which is designed to deliver services to customers. Customers arrive, usually in an unpredictable way, to queue for services that can be subject to random disturbance, and will depart after receiving the service. Furthermore, the service process may be subject to disturbance and also incur internal variation. Typical examples of queuing

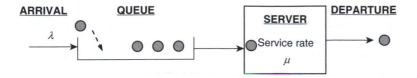

Figure 2.7 A queuing system.

include ATM banking machines, traffic toll stations, and outpatient clinics. At an aggregate level, a manufacturing facility can be viewed as a queuing system, with random orders arriving that need to be fulfilled by variable manufacturing capacities.

Queuing processes

A queuing system can be characterized by its arrival and service processes. In the context of manufacturing, the average arrival rate λ (e.g., number of order arrivals per unit time) represents the input rate of supply, which reflects the rate of throughput, and the average service rate μ average processing rate (or production rate). Both the interarrival time and the service time can be uncertain. As both the arrival and departure processes are determined by the same flow of customers, the actual output generated cannot be more than the input (i.e., $\lambda \leq \mu$).

It is also important to note that the service cannot be performed without a customer being present, therefore a queuing system will have certain limits when applied to manufacturing orders that are issued on forecasts that are made before actual customer demand. Nevertheless, the queuing system is applicable to certain manufacturing situations, especially for aggregate production. The most notable and relevant concept regarding the *steady state* of a queuing system is known as **Little's Law**.

Little's Law

In the context of manufacturing, the average work-in-process (WIP), L (i.e., total average number of customers in the system), is related to the total time W (i.e., average time that a customer stays in the system, between arrival and departure), according to the following rule:

Average WIP = Average arrivals while waiting, or equivalently

$$L = \lambda W,$$

where λ is the average arrival rate, representing the average throughput in manufacturing. Note that in a queuing system L denotes the average number of customers in the system, which should not be confused with the lead-time L in a manufacturing system. The interpretation of Little's Law is that the WIP per unit of total lead-time equates to the throughput rate. It is known from queuing theory that an accurate realization of Little's Law is the so-called $M/M/1$ queuing system, in which the first letter ("M" in this case) represents the type of arrival process, the second letter specifies the type of service process, and the third indicates the number of parallel servers for the queuing system.

The application of a queuing system is illustrated here using a simple CT scanner example. Suppose that customer orders for CT-100 scanners arrive according to a Poisson process with an average rate of 25 orders per month ($\lambda = 25$), and that the CT assembly plant exhibits a Poisson aggregate processing rate of 30 orders per month on average ($\mu = 30$). We can see that the capacity of the assembly plant is adequate (i.e., $\lambda < \mu$). Thus, over time, the average cycle time to put out a CT-100 scanner should settle at (see Appendix 2A for details):

$$W = \frac{1}{\mu - \lambda} = \frac{1}{30 - 25} = 0.2 \,(\text{month}) = 0.2 \times 30 = 6 \,(\text{days}).$$

The resulting average WIP can be obtained as:

$$\text{WIP} = \lambda W = \frac{\lambda}{\mu - \lambda} = \frac{25}{5} = 5 \,(\text{orders}).$$

Thus, the average WIP inventory in the system is expected to be five CT-100 scanner orders. In a Kanban system, the average WIP is the basis for determining the total number of Kanban cards to be released into the system:

$$\text{Number of Kanbans} = \frac{(1 + r)\text{WIP}}{c},$$

where c is the container size, and r is a safety factor $(r \geq 0)$. If the system is of $M/M/1$ with $c = 1$ and $r = 0$, then the number of Kanbans can be computed as:

$$\text{Number of Kanbans for } M/M/1 \text{ system} = \frac{(1 + r)\text{WIP}}{c} = \frac{(1 + r)\lambda}{c(\mu - \lambda)}$$
$$= \frac{1.15 \times 25}{5} = 5.75.$$

MRP system

MRP grew out of the material explosion problem, first reported by Orlicky (1975). MRP involves detailed planning of all necessary materials according to a **master production schedule** (MPS) for end items, as illustrated in Figure 2.8. The MPS is an aggregate forecast-based production plan over a fixed time window (or horizon) regarding a specific end product. For example, an MPS may contain the projected monthly requirement for an end item over the next 6 months. The MPS usually follows a rolling planning scheme; for instance, a

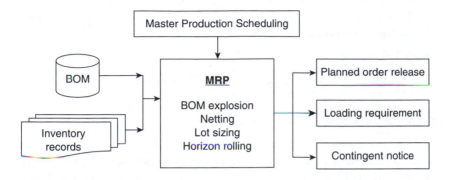

Figure 2.8 An MRP system.

6-month MPS window can be updated and revised on a monthly forward basis. Each end item (or final product) is profiled by a "tree" of lower-level items, described in the *bill of material* **(BOM)**. As explained earlier, the BOM is a "permanent" data record and any change to it will involve redesigning or re-engineering of the product. As illustrated in Figure 2.8, based on an MPS, the MRP will compute the requirements for all necessary materials, such as parts and components, according to the associated BOMs and current inventory records.

Beginning with the end items that are specified in the MPS, the MRP typically follows a repetitive procedure for each item (including all items at all levels):

1   *BOM explosion*: Determine the **gross requirements** (GRs) passed on from an upper level; the GRs for end items at the top level are given in the MPS.
2   *Netting*: Compute **net requirements** (NRs) by subtracting the inventory [on-hand stock plus scheduled receipts (SRs)] from the GRs.
3   *Lot sizing*: Divide the NRs into appropriate lots (or batches) of jobs (or orders), and schedule the timing of the job release, taking the **lead-time** into consideration.
4   *Horizon rolling*: Update and repeat the planning process.

Next, we will illustrate how the MRP procedure works using a simplified CT-100 scanner production example. Before getting into the MRP details, which can be quite complicated and tedious, we present a general algorithmic structure for a typical MRP procedure as follows:

Step 0. Begin with an MPS and all input data (BOM, inventory records).
Step 1. Start from the BOM top level and proceed one level at a time until the bottom level is reached.

For each item within the same level, do the following:
BOM explosion (compute GRs);
Netting (compute NRs);

　　　Lot sizing (determine the size and the timing of planned order release, POR); and
　　　Subsummary (update inventory transition status)

Step 2. Summarize and update MRP output.
Step 3. Roll to the next planning window, and repeat from step 0.

Example 2.2　MRP for CT-100 scanner

Suppose that a 6-month MPS for CT-100 scanner production has just been released, as detailed in Table 2.1. We now describe an MRP procedure triggered by the MPS given above, including the following repetitive steps in order: BOM explosion, netting, lot sizing, and timing.

BOM explosion

Let us consider applying BOM explosion to the first level of the BOM shown in Figure 2.4. With the given MPS, the GRs for each item at the first level can be computed as shown in Table 2.2.

　　Staying with the first-level items, iteration of the next two steps, *netting* and *lot sizing,* must be completed before moving to the next lower-level items (see Figure 2.4). Continue the MRP procedure with the item Table-100. Note that the input data for the BOM explosion at the next lowest level are derived from the MRP output schedules generated at the upper level, unlike the first-level BOM explosion where the MPS is used as the input data.

Netting

The results of *netting* are the **net requirements** for each item in the current BOM level. The NR of an item is defined as the demand beyond what the projected on-hand inventory can cover, in which the projected on-hand inventory includes two parts: the inventory positive carryover and the SR initiated from outside the current MPS horizon. To further explain, we introduce the following notation:

NR_t = NR for period $t = \max\{0, -I_t\}$
I_t = projected on-hand inventory at the end of period $t = \max\{0, I_{t-1}\} + SR_t - d_t$,
　　given the initial inventory (on-hand) I_0
SR_t, SRs for period t, which were initiated prior to the current planning window

　　A positive projected on-hand inventory means that the on-hand inventory is adequate to cover the demand, and thus the NR is zero (i.e., $NR_t = 0$ if $I_t \geq 0$). Otherwise, a negative value for projected on-hand inventory I_t indicates an inventory shortage (i.e., the demand in period t is beyond the on-hand inventory), which, by definition, constitutes the NRs for period t (i.e., $NR_t = -I_t$ if $I_t < 0$).

Table 2.1 An MPS

CT-100	Month					
	1	2	3	4	5	6
GRs	25	25	45	35	35	75

Table 2.2 BOM explosion of the first-level items

CT-100	Month					
	1	2	3	4	5	6
Gantry-100: GRs	25	25	45	35	35	75
Console-100: GR	25	25	45	35	35	75
Table-100: GR	25	25	45	35	35	75

Combining the two cases, we write $NR_t = \max\{0, -I_t\}$. It should also be noted that a negative projected on-hand inventory is not carried over to the next period, that is, the inventory carried over to period t equals $\max\{0, I_{t-1}\}$. For the sake of illustration, let us focus on the *netting* for the Table-100. Suppose that we are given some additional input data: $I_0 = 20$, $SR_1 = 10$ (i.e., 10 units of Table-100 are scheduled to arrive in month 1), $SR_2 = 20$, and $SR_3 = \ldots = SR_6 = 0$ (i.e., no other SRs). With the input data, the BOM explosion for the Table-100 can be updated in a typical MRP format, as in Table 2.3, where a column numbered 0 is inserted for the initial time reference. The new input data are typed in bold in Table 2.3.

Note that the last three rows in Table 2.3 contain three important MRP output items—scheduled completion (SC), POR, and ending on-hand—for which we denote and define as follows:

Scheduled completion, SC_t, planned order completed in period t.
Planned order release, POR_t, planned production order to be started in period t.
Ending on-hand inventory, EI_t, actual on-hand inventory by the end of period t.

We will discuss these three items as we proceed with the example. For now, let us return to the *netting* example. Carrying out the computation for month 1, we obtain:

Projected on-hand: $I_1 = \max\{0, I_0\} + SR_1 - d_1 = 20 + 10 - 25 = 5$, and

Net requirement: $NR_1 = \max\{0, -5\} = 0$.

As the total inventory available for month 1 is 30 (initial 20, plus SR 10), the on-hand inventory is sufficient to meet the demand for 25 units in month 1, thus

Table 2.3 Input data for netting

Table-100	Month						
	0	1	2	3	4	5	6
GRs		25	25	45	35	35	75
SRs		10	20				
Projected on-hand	20						
NRs							
SC							
POR							
Ending on-hand	20						

Table 2.4 Netting result

Table-100	Month						
	0	1	2	3	4	5	6
GRs		25	25	45	35	35	75
SRs		10	20	0	0	0	0
Projected on-hand	20	5	0	−45	−35	−35	−75
NRs		0	0	45	35	35	75
SC							
POR							
Ending on-hand	20						

the NR for month 1 is zero. Repeating the computation for each subsequent month will produce the *netting* result, printed in bold in Table 2.4. In this example, there is sufficient on-hand inventory to cover the demand in the first 2 months. For the remaining 4 months, additional production must be scheduled to satisfy the unmet demand.

Lot sizing

Given the netting result obtained thus far, the quantity and timing of production orders must be planned to meet the NRs, which is referred to as lot sizing in MRP. The output of lot sizing is represented by POR_t and SC_t for each period t. Lot sizing is also a two-level decision-making process: first, lot-sizing rules need to be selected, and lot-sizing actions can then be determined accordingly. Common lot-sizing rules include **fixed order quantity** (i.e., equal order size) and **fixed order period** (i.e., equal time between orders) policies.

The simplest lot-sizing rule is the so-called **lot-for-lot** rule, under which the amount to be produced in a period is set to equal the NRs for that period. To continue with the example, let us use a lot-for-lot policy, assuming a 1-month production cycle time (i.e., 1 month needed for completing a planned order, $L = 1$).

Table 2.5 Lot sizing output

Table-100	Month						
	0	*1*	*2*	*3*	*4*	*5*	*6*
GRs		25	25	45	35	35	75
SRs		10	20	0	0	0	0
Projected on-hand	20	5	0	−45	−35	−35	−75
NRs		0	0	45	35	35	75
SC				45	35	35	75
POR		**0**	**45**	**35**	**35**	**75**	
Ending on-hand	20						

Because the first period that shows a positive NR is month 3, according to the lot-for-lot rule, the first-order quantity available for month 3 will be 45. As it takes 1 month to fill an order $(L = 1)$, the order will be released in month 2, so that it can be completed for use in month 3. That is, the first POR is scheduled as: $POR_2 = 45$ and $SC_3 = 45$. Such lot-for-lot lot sizing can be expressed in a general form with a given production cycle time L as follows:

$$POR_t = NR_{t+L} \text{ and } SC_{t+L} = POR_t.$$

Repeating the computation for each subsequent period will produce the figures in Table 2.5. The output of lot sizing is printed in bold. Note that the lot-sizing results are dependent on the lot-sizing rule, some of which can produce quite complicated results.

Subsummary

The subsummary for the example only contains an **ending on-hand inventory**. By definition, we compute:

$$EI_t = \max(0, I_t) + SC_t - NR_t.$$

For the first month, we obtain $EI_1 = 5 + 0 - 0 = 5$. For the remaining periods, we obtain a complete output report for the iteration, as shown in Table 2.6.

When applying the MRP procedure to the lower-level items (say, to the item **Leg** for Table-100), the planned orders for Table-100 given in Table 2.6 will be the GRs for the item **Leg**. Remember, before moving to the lower level, the MRP procedure must be completed for all of the items at the current level. In this case, the computation shown above must be repeated for Gantry-100 and Console-100.

MRP under the make-by-promise planning scheme

The MRP we have studied so far is based on the implicit assumption of a make-by-forecast (MBF) planning scheme, with forecasts represented in the form of an

Table 2.6 Output report of one iteration

Table-100	Month						
	0	*1*	*2*	*3*	*4*	*5*	*6*
GRs		25	25	45	35	35	75
SRs		10	20	0	0	0	0
Projected on-hand	20	5	0	−45	−35	−35	−75
NRs		0	0	45	35	35	75
SC				45	35	35	75
POR		0	45	35	35	75	
Ending on-hand	20	**5**	**0**	**0**	**0**	**0**	**0**

MPS. For example, the MPS given in Table 2.1 represents the demand forecast over the next 6 months. Thus, the production order release under an MBF planning scheme is based on the forecasts provided by the MPS. The production orders can also be planned on the basis of a make-by-promise (MBP) scheme. In this case, the MRP is generated based on the schedule of promised delivery, as illustrated in Table 2.7, assuming a 1-month production cycle time.

Thus, the MRP under an MBP planning scheme will be based on *promised delivery*, as opposed to the GRs that are used in a regular MRP system.

A dilemma in MRP

As we can see from the examples above, MRP is a complex procedure involving every detail of materials planning and is driven by the inventory, especially the end-product inventory, which relies on a fixed MPS and builds powerful "inertia" into the entire system against any changes. However, there is an apparent dilemma in MRP. Whereas MRP requires a deterministic MPS as its input, the MPS, which relies on assessment of market demand, cannot be deterministic. In general, demand is a stochastic process and forecasts of future demand will always be subject to error. Thus, an MPS such as the one in Table 2.1, which represents a projected sample demand path for the next 6 months, can never be perfect. A process called **horizon rolling** is therefore incorporated into MRP, to rectify planning errors retroactively. In short, horizon rolling requires that planned orders are executed and then updated in a period-by-period fashion. To demonstrate how horizon rolling is carried out in MRP, consider the planning output given in Table 2.6. First, the POR for month 1 (i.e., $POR_1 = 0$) will be firmed and executed. As a result, zero units of Table-100 are produced in month 1. However, by the end of month 1, the actual demand for that month is recorded and the ending inventory on-hand is updated. For example, suppose the actual demand in month 1 is for 30 units (i.e., $d_1 = 30$), as indicated in the last row of Table 2.8.

In this case, the actual ending inventory on-hand is zero, as opposed to five as originally projected. With the updated inventory status at the beginning of month 2, the MRP will be repeated for another 6 months from month 2 through month 7 (assuming the GR for month 7 is projected to be 60). Because there is

Table 2.7 Example schedule of promised delivery schedule with 1-month cycle

CT-100	Month						
	1	*2*	*3*	*4*	*5*	*6*	*7*
GRs	25	25	45	35	35	75	
Promised delivery		25	25	45	35	35	75

Table 2.8 One-period rolling with a given demand for month 1 $(d_1 = 30)$

Table-100	Month						
	1	*2*	*3*	*4*	*5*	*6*	*7*
GRs	**25**	25	45	35	35	75	**60**
SRs	10	20		0	0	0	0
Projected on-hand	0	0					
NRs	0						
SC							
POR	0						
Ending on-hand	**0**	**0**					
Backlog		5					
Actual demand	**30**						

a 1-month lead-time $(L = 1)$, the production order released in month 2 will not be fulfilled until month 3. Thus, the available on-hand inventory for month 2 is the 20 units of SRs, which will be 5 units short of the GRs for month 2. This will result in a backlog of five units as the initial inventory status for the next MRP iteration, as summarized in Table 2.8. With the initial status given in Table 2.8, the same MRP procedure will be repeated, starting from month 2 through month 7.

As we can see from this illustration, the MRP actually bases its execution on a strategy of "missing it now and catching up later." Most manufacturing systems are too complex to be characterized by deterministic models. It is almost inevitable that nonanalytical and nondeterministic solution methods, such as adaptive planning and simulation, should be applied to manufacturing capacity systems. Adaptive planning follows a generic adaptation process in complex dynamic settings that cannot usually be characterized in analytical terms, and allows nonanalytical solution methods and tools, including simulation and visual interaction. The next subsection is devoted to the methodology of *adaptive planning* as applied to manufacturing capacity systems.

SOF system

Example of SOF: CT-100 production with a US supplier of Table-100

The production process for the CT-100 scanner at DE, similar to the one shown in Figure 2.3, represents a SOF system with a production cycle time of 2 weeks

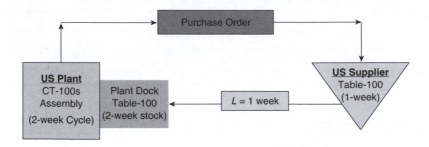

Figure 2.9 CT-100s SOF system with Table-100 supplied in the United States.

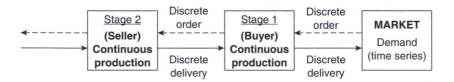

Figure 2.10 SOF system.

at DE's assembly plant, with a US supplier of Table-100s for CT-100 assembly. For the purpose of illustration, let us consider DE's SOF system with a US supplier of Table-100s as shown in Figure 2.4, with a normal cycle time (takt time) of 2 weeks (Figure 2.9).

A general SOF system

A general **supply order fulfillment** system refers to a capacitated production facility (or a factory) that transforms the input of supply, with a time lag, into product output to fulfill demand orders, as illustrated in Figure 2.10. Incoming customer orders are taken as moving targets, and the repetitive target orders are fulfilled by a capacitated production facility. Because capacity is always limited, there is an inevitable time lag between starting to fill an order and its fulfillment.

A basic SOF system consists of two stages of order-filling operations, with a known order-fulfillment capacity at each stage. Each stage requires a certain order-fulfillment time to fill and then deliver an order. A SOF is primarily suited for fulfilling repetitive orders. For the CT-100 SOF system in Figure 2.9, orders are issued, fulfilled, and dispatched every 2 weeks. Note that the lead-time can differ between stages in a SOF system.

A SOF system, which is engaged in a two-stage pursuit of target orders with a delayed start, is analogous to a multistage group *pursuit game*, an advanced and well-established subject in *game theory*. It will become clear throughout the book that the theory of *pursuit games* plays a vital role in solving SOF problems.

However, the focus in this chapter is on the description and characterization of a SOF system, rather than its solutions. The study of solutions using game theory is covered in Chapters 6 and 10.

Comparisons of TPS, MRP, and SOF

Readers are encouraged to consider their own justifications for the differing characteristics of each of the three capacity systems, summarized as follows.

1   TPS is a process-driven pull system with a particular focus on waste elimination. It is often referred to as the origin of "lean manufacturing." It achieves winning-with-speed by maintaining "lean" production (i.e., eliminating waste) and achieves winning-with-singularity by developing a unique environment, culture, and behavior in individual firms. Perhaps due to the cultural and behavioral nature of the system, the success of TPS is highly company specific, in the sense that it is hard to "copy" and "repeat" the success of another TPS.

2   MRP is an inventory-driven push system particularly suited for computer integration. In fact, enterprise resource planning (ERP) systems such as SAP and Oracle are integrated and developed from an MRP system. The MRP dilemma—the inventory "inertia" problem mentioned in the section "TPS: the origin of lean manufacturing"—is a major factor that hinders and limits the advance of ERP technology.

3   SOF is an order-driven interactive incentive system, which is underpinned by supply contracts. It represents a basic prototype of a supply chain that is widely observable and applicable in any economic system. Because it is based on contracts, an SOF system is engaged in a game-theory setting. SOF systems have been well studied from an economics perspective under contract and incentive theory, although they have not been considered much from the operations management (OM) perspective.

Adaptive capacity planning: a hybrid of MRP and SOF

The adaptive planning method is intended to resolve or reduce the inventory "inertia" problem of MRP by incorporating WBD mechanisms into ERP technology, such as the computerized adjustment of ERP plans with simulated market changes and disturbances. In the context of capacity planning, a solution plan must be based on a scientific study of the past and must be easy to adjust in response to changes.

Basics of adaptive planning

Manufacturing capacity is measured by the output rate (e.g., the number of parts produced per month). Associated with each manufacturing system is a *design capacity*, which specifies the maximum output rate that the system can generate within given technical and engineering design terms. Design capacity is a measure of limiting capability, which does not take into account labor skills and other operational factors. The capacity expansion case (Example 1.4) is concerned with the design capacity. However, there is an *effective capacity*, which represents the actual output rate realized under certain production conditions and configurations. Capacity management herein is mainly concerned with *effective capacity* decisions in the operational short term, as opposed to strategic long-term capital decisions. Clearly, effective capacity (or simply capacity for short) depends on the underlying production scheme and schedule, including production structures and strategies. Typical production structures include make-to-stock and make-to-order, and typical production strategies include actions that affect the production rate (e.g., the workforce and the process rate), and production schedule (e.g., work shifts, overtime, and subcontracting). We have shown that the capacity of a given system behaves quite differently under an MRP system in comparison to other capacity systems. The capacity planning to be studied in this section describes a short-term planning and control process, outlined as follows:

> **Capacity planning** is used to determine a *plan* that specifies the sequence of actions that should take place under a given set of viable *strategies*, to achieve the most *effective capacity* to meet a *target* (e.g., demand or order).

As most capacity systems in manufacturing cannot be characterized by simple analytical models, we need to apply adaptive planning solutions to a manufacturing capacity system. The outcome of capacity planning is in the form of a capacity plan that contains a sequence of structures, under which actions are to take place. To select the best plan, there is a performance measure associated with each capacity plan. As illustrated in Figure 2.11, the process of capacity planning is an adaptive system in pursuit of a given target. As studied in Chapter 1, an adaptive system consists of three basic elements: the environment, an adaptive plan, and a performance measure. A framework for adaptive planning is constructed and proposed by Holland (1992), as follows:

> **Strategy set**: the set of attainable strategies (structures) that constitutes the domain of capacity planning actions.
> **Transformation set**: the set of operations and functions that transforms objects and modifies strategies (structures) in physical and abstract forms.
> **Data set**: the set of input and observable information to the system available at time t. The data set increases over time. An example of a subset of the data could be, for instance, the demand samples on which production orders are based.
> **Plan set**: the set of plans that are generated on the basis of the input and the strategy. Each plan determines which operations and functions are to be applied at time t under a selected set of strategies, which in turn will generate output strategies (e.g., realized capacity structures).

The *strategy set* in capacity planning is understood to contain a wide range of structures, options, and policies. For example, a strategy may contain a detailed

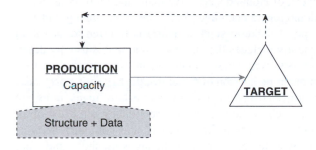

Figure 2.11 Framework for capacity planning.

production schedule that specifies details about the regular and temporary work-force, and regular and overtime shifts for the next 6 months of production. A strategy might also consist of a series of changes in action over time, or even a continuous variable over time.

A strategy set can be characterized as one of three types: *pure, mixed,* or *behavioral*. The practical definitions of the three types of strategies are given as follows.

1   A **pure strategy** is pre-specified and deterministic. A pure strategy can be static (e.g., a one-time single action), or dynamic (e.g., a sequence of actions), but the strategy must be specified in advance.

2   A **mixed strategy** is randomly selected from a set of pure strategies. A mixed strategy is applicable in situations with a given pure strategy set and an uncertain target, in which capacity planning must be exercised repeatedly, such as every 10 weeks. At first glance, randomly selecting a capacity plan does not seem to be a feasible strategy. However, a simple example can help to explain how a mixed strategy can be implemented. Suppose a production capacity manager faces an unpredictable weekly demand, which could be either *high* or *low,* with a certain probability distribution. The manager has two options, plan A and plan B, in which plan A works best if demand is high, whereas plan B works best if demand is low. Because the uncertain demand keeps the manager guessing from week to week, it may be better for him to mimic the random pattern of demand to determine which plan to adopt for the following week. To mimic the random demand, different implementation mechanisms can be devised, such as flipping a coin or throwing a dart. In this case, the pure strategy set has two elements—plan A and plan B—and a mixed strategy is generated by randomly mixing these two pure strategies.

3   A **behavior strategy** is an *adaptive* mixed strategy. A behavior strategy is a mixed strategy that is randomly selected from a pure strategy set, but in this case the set of pure strategies may differ from period to period. That is, the set of pure strategies to be used for planning of week 2 can be updated, and therefore differ from the set of pure strategies used for week 1. The word "behavioral" reflects the adaptive nature of this type of strategy.

To illustrate the framework of Holland's adaptive planning, let us consider an example of manufacturing aggregate planning (AP). Capacity planning under an MRP structure (a push type of make-to-stock scheme) is referred to as AP, in which input information mainly includes the target demand that is usually determined by time-series forecasts over a fixed planning horizon, as required by MPS. For example, with a planning horizon of 6 months, the MPS for a particular product will contain six projected orders that determine how many units are scheduled for production in each of the 6 months. The strategy set, a list of all possible operations and options, needs to be identified and compiled, such as increasing or decreasing the workforce, adding or reducing work shifts, and other viable capacity planning actions. Transformations in AP represent the effective capacity output functions, such as a particular combination of viable strategies, a specific production function, or a probability distribution for the entire set of strategies. Each capacity plan represents successive selections of capacity output functions, which will generate a specific sequence of production schedules (including workforce, capacity, and inventory schedules). The best possible capacity plan can then be determined using a preselected objective measure, such as total cost or minimum service level.

Simulation-facilitated adaptive capacity planning

Thus, an adaptive plan produces a sequence of strategies (or mixture of strategies), by successively selecting from a set of transformations. According to the WBD philosophy, optimal adaptation must be achieved. Optimal adaptation means obtaining an optimal plan according to the performance measure. The actual realized performance depends on the successive selection of transformations. Because the selections are critically influenced by information obtained from the environment, optimal adaptive planning must be **learned**. In particular, the data set must be **filtered** and the effective transformations must be **characterized** using information obtained from the past and the present.

Because the transformations in most complex adaptive systems cannot be characterized in *prescriptive* terms, the methodology of adaptive planning is in general *descriptive*, like that of adaptive learning. As is typical in adaptive learning, characteristics fitting has been found to be the most appropriate and effective method. With this methodology, patterns of characteristics (i.e., characteristic models) are first established by retrospectively studying the objects or systems of interest. The outcome paths and trajectories that are associated with each of the patterns are also researched and theorized. The specific adaptive plan can be formulated by fitting the specific objects and instances with established patterns or models.

Simulation, especially *computer simulation*, has been shown to be an effective tool for adaptive learning. The behavior and characteristics of an adaptive system can be emulated via simulated analysis of the past. This approach to studying adaptive systems is termed simulation-facilitated adaptive planning (SIM-AP). The following is a list of typical steps in SIM-AP.

Step 1. Define the environment of the adaptive system under study.

Step 2. Define the performance measure to evaluate the adaptive plans.

Step 3. Obtain and update the data set.

Step 4. Define and update the strategy set.

Step 5. Establish and update the set of characteristic models and patterns. Conduct a retrospective study using the most up-to-date information regarding the adaptive system, including strategy sets, transformation sets, data sets, and adaptive plans. Simulation will be used to validate and enhance the characteristic models.

Step 6. Simulate and evaluate the system trajectory and performance for each selection (i.e., each plan) with a given data set and system settings.

Step 7. Determine the best-performing adaptive plan.

Note that SIM-AP does not solely rely on analytical modeling and is heuristic and adaptive. This point is illustrated in the following examples using simulation-facilitated AP in a push system.

Example 2.3   AP for CT-100 scanner under a fixed MPS

An MPS for the next 6 months' production of CT-100 scanners is outlined in Table 2.1. The initial inventory contains two units, ten workers are currently assigned to produce the scanner, and an inventory of two units is required at the end of the 6th month. The number of aggregate units produced by one worker per day is 0.15. The number of regular working days for the next 6 months is 22, 25, 20, 26, 25, and 16. Suppose that production for each month can be consumed within the same month (i.e., $L = 0$), and that there are other viable options, such as overtime and workforce adjustment by hiring or firing. The cost data are given as follows:

Cost of hiring one worker = $750
Cost of laying off one worker = $1,500
Cost of holding one unit of inventory for 1 month = $125
Cost of backordering one unit of inventory for 1 month = $215
Regular production cost = $47 per unit produced
Overtime production cost = $62 per unit produced in overtime (maximum 3 days per week allowable for overtime production)
Subcontracting cost = $50 per unit produced by outside contractors, plus a fixed setup cost of $175 per contract.

In this case, an aggregate plan contains a complete set of monthly decisions on the workforce level (i.e., hiring and laying-off decisions) and PORs.

We note that an aggregate plan can be viewed as a special type of adaptive plan. To further justify this viewpoint, let us first describe the above example within the framework of an adaptive system.

The **strategy set** in Example 2.3 consists of combinations of viable capacity actions and options, such as level production and lot-for-lot production. Level production involves employing a regular workforce at a consistent level each month, with product capacity adjusted through overtime and subcontracting. Lot-for-lot production (also termed a chase strategy) sets the production capacity month by month, strictly in accordance with the demand requirements of the MPS. Each strategy is represented by a specific combination of capacity actions. The strategy set contains all possible combinations of actions and options.

The **transformation set** for the example represents the complete set of output effects generated by capacity actions. For example, with level production there will be no fluctuation in the regular workforce, but there will be a noticeable variation in inventory (both overstock and shortage). In contrast, lot-to-lot production usually assures zero or little inventory build-up, but with significant workforce adjustment. Thus, the underlying inventory transition equations and production throughput rates comprise the transformation set in this case. The **data set** in this example consists of MPS, technical data, and cost data.

Although with highly restrictive assumptions an aggregate plan can be formulated as a linear programming model, real-world AP is too complex to be modeled in a closed analytical form. Therefore, simulation is usually used to facilitate planning. To illustrate the SIM-AP model as applied to capacity planning, we will simulate Example 2.3 using a specific capacity plan that adopts a lot-for-lot production strategy with regular production only (i.e., no overtime shifts or subcontracting are allowed).

Under this strategy, the regular workforce (currently ten workers) must be adjusted monthly to generate a monthly output that exactly meets the monthly requirement given by the MPS. For example, let us consider the number of workers needed to produce the GR for month 1, 25 units, as given in Table 2.1. With an initial on-hand inventory of two units and a required EI of two units, the NR for month 1 is 23 units, computed as follows:

$$NR_1 = GR_1 - (\text{initial on-hand}) - (\text{initial backlog}) = 25 - 2 - 0 = 23.$$

As each worker produces 0.15 units per day and there are 22 working days in month 1, the monthly throughput rate per worker can be computed as follows:

$$\text{Monthly output per worker} = 0.15 \times 22 = 3.3 \, (\text{units/month/worker}).$$

It is now easy to determine that the number of workers needed to produce a net of 23 units of CT-100 in month 1 will be:

$$\text{Workforce for month 1} = \frac{23}{3.3} = 6.97 \approx 7 \, (\text{workers}).$$

Table 2.9 Simulation of CT-100 production with lot-for-lot aggregate plan ($L = 0$)

CT-100	Month										
	0	*1*	*2*	*3*	*4*	*5*	*6*	*7*	*Total*	*Cost ($)*	
GR		25	25	45	35	35	75		240		
NR		23	24.9	43.7	33.7	33.6	74.8				
Working days/ month		22	25	20	26	25	16		134		
No. workers											
Used	10	7	7	15	9	9	32		79		
Hired		0	0	8	0	0	23		31	23,250	
Removed		3	0	0	6	0	0		9	13,500	
Planned throughput		23.1	26.3	45	35.1	33.8	76.8		240.0	11,280	
Projected beginning on-hand		2	0.1	1.4	1.35	1.45	0.2	2.0	6.4		
Projected ending on-hand	2	0.1	1.4	1.35	1.45	0.2	2.0		6.4	806.25	
Projected backorder		0	0	0	0	0	0		0	0	
									Total =	48,836.25	

As the current level of workforce for CT-100 scanner production is ten, three workers must be removed from the production team. With a production team of seven, the actual output (i.e., planned throughput) for month 1 will be $3.3 \times 7 = 23.1$ (units of CT-100). Including the initial two units on-hand, after satisfying the NR of 23 units ($NR_1 = 23$) there will be 0.1 unit(s) on-hand at the end of the month. Then, the NR for month 2 can be computed as follows:

$$NR_2 = GR_2 - (\text{beginning on-hand}) - (\text{month 1 backlog}) = 25 - 0.1 - 0 = 24.9.$$

The same planning process is then repeated for month 2, and so on. The transformation for month $t(t = 1, 2, \ldots, 6)$ can be expressed by a set of equations, using the same notation as introduced for MRP:

$$SC_t = \text{throughput in month } t = 0.15(\text{workforce in } t)(\text{working days in } t),$$

$$EI_t = \text{ending on-hand by month } t = SC_t - NR_t.$$

Table 2.9 presents the simulation results for all 6 months. The outcome of the plan is measured by the total cost—$48,836.25 in this case.

Given a fixed MPS (i.e., GRs), the lot-for-lot aggregate plan allows for frequent adjustments in the workforce so that there is zero backordering inventory and near-zero on-hand inventory at the end of the period. Alternative capacity plans can be constructed by selecting different strategy combinations, each of which can be evaluated according to its total cost. The plan with the best performance measure will then be adopted for implementation. The planning process is adaptive; that is, dynamic changes and modifications can be made to the system structures over subsequent planning horizons. Note that in this example a deterministic MPS is assumed.

In reality, however, an MPS contains stochastic fluctuations that reflect the underlying demand process that is always subject to uncertainty. In such a case, the MPS is said to be stochastic. The next example represents a more realistic AP situation.

Example 2.4 Lot-for-lot AP under stochastic demand ($L = 0$)

Suppose that the average monthly demands for the CT-100 for the next 6 months are normally distributed, as given in Table 2.1, but each with the same standard deviation of 5.0. All other data are the same as given in Example 2.3 above. How would the aggregate plan that was obtained in Example 2.3 perform in terms of meeting the actual demand?

Because the actual demand is stochastic, the planned orders generated from the standard MRP approach, which assumes a deterministic MPS, will be erroneous when compared with the realizations of the demand process. Thus, a natural way to evaluate the performance of the given aggregate plan is to simulate the system transitions (e.g., inventory status) under the given AP, but only replace the GRs with the random demand. The SIM-AP approach is naturally suited to achieving this. As previously noted, because the SIM-AP is heuristic and adaptive, multiple solution methods and plans can be generated for each specific application. We leave it as a simulation assignment for the reader to develop a specific SIM-AP solution for Example 2.4. To illustrate this point, let us consider five simple computer-simulated paths of the demand process given in Example 2.4, as listed in Table 2.10.

Because demand is confined to integers, the simulated samples are rounded to integers. For example, the first simulated path (i.e., the first row of the table) of sample demands for the following months would be (rounded to integer): 31, 26, 51, 35, 31, and 81. With the AP fixed, as shown in Table 2.9, the inventory transition of CT-100 scanners under sample path 1 can be simulated, as depicted in Table 2.11, in which the shaded area contains the specifications of the original AP.

Note that the given AP would incur a significant backlog inventory if the demand process is actually realized as in sample path 1, resulting in a higher total cost of $59,098.80 compared to the original projection of $48,836.25.

Table 2.10 Computer-generated five demand sample paths for Example 2.4

Sample path	Month					
	d_1	d_2	d_3	d_4	d_5	d_6
1	30.77	25.80	51.18	35.40	31.13	80.77
2	23.39	20.67	48.19	34.55	32.14	73.39
3	28.31	29.37	45.54	31.05	32.05	78.31
4	30.06	26.07	51.40	34.67	31.05	80.06
5	33.71	24.75	46.26	30.77	37.91	83.71

Table 2.11 Performance of the AP under the first sample path in Table 2.10 ($L = 0$)

	Month								Total	Cost
	0	1	2	3	4	5	6	7		
Sample demand		31	26	51	35	31	81		255	
GR		25	25	45	35	35	75		240	
NR		23	24.9	43.7	33.7	33.6	74.8			
Working days/month		22	25	20	26	25	16		134	
No. workers										
Used	10	7	7	15	9	9	32		79	
Hired		0	0	8	0	0	23		31	23,250
Removed		3	0	0	6	0	0		9	13,500
Planned throughput		23.1	26.3	45	35.1	33.8	76.8		240.0	11,280
Projected beginning on-hand		2	0.1	1.4	1.35	1.45	0.2	2.0		
Projected ending on-hand	2	0.1	1.4	1.35	1.45	0.2	2.0			
Actual beginning on-hand		2	0	0	0	0	0	0	2	
Actual ending on-hand	2	0	0	0	0	0	0		0	0
Backorder	0	5.9	5.7	11.7	11.6	8.8	13.0		56.6	12,158.25
									Total =	60,188.25

Also note that the actual EI is 0, which is different from the original estimate shown in Table 2.9.

Let us elaborate on the details of the computation for the updates in month 1. According to the original AP, planned production is for 23.1 units, which is computed at the beginning of month 1, assuming the GR (i.e., demand forecast for month 1) is 25, as shown in the shaded area of Table 2.11.

However, the actual sample demand for month 1 turns out to be 31, which becomes available by the end of month 1. According to the actual sample demand of $d_1 = 31$, the inventory status is then updated as follows:

$$EI_1 = \text{ending on-hand inventory by month 1} = \max\{0, I_1 + POR_1 - d_1 - B_0\}$$
$$= \max\{0, 2 + 23.1 - 31 - 0\} = \max\{0, -5.9\} = 0,$$

$$B_1 = \text{backorders in month 1} = \max\{0, d_1 + B_0 - I_1 - POR_1\}$$
$$= \max\{0, 31 + 0 - 2 - 23.1\} = \max\{0, 5.9\} = 5.9,$$

where I_1 is the *beginning* on-hand inventory in month 1, POR_1 represents the POR (i.e., planned throughput) in month 1, and B_1 is the backorders in month 1.

For any period $t(t = 1, 2, ...)$, the iterative updating of the inventory status can be similarly carried out for a given sample path, using the following formulas:

$$EI_t = \text{ending on-hand inventory by period } t = \max\{0, I_t + POR_t - d_t - B_{t-1}\},$$

$$B_t = \text{backorders in period } t = \max\{0, d_t + B_{t-1} - I_t - POR_t\}.$$

Table 2.11 contains complete updates following the first sample path given in Table 2.10. Repeating the simulation with a number of different sample paths, simulated statistics can be collected regarding performance measures, such as the total cost. The performance statistics for a given AP can then be analyzed and evaluated. The simulation analysis can then be conducted on a complete set of viable alternative APs, so that the best AP can be identified.

Six-sigma quality versus TPS quality

Six-sigma quality

It is clear from the discussions so far that the feasibility and effectiveness of an MRP are based on the stability of the GRs at each level of the MRP system. Thus, the key to making MRP work is to minimize the variability in the underlying operation process. To this end, six-sigma quality management is a business strategy that is solely intended to achieve this goal; that is, to minimize or reduce the process variability before a defective product is produced.

Because the cause and the form of variability are application specific, six-sigma quality can only be attained by devising specific winning methods in accordance with a specific situation at a specific point in time; that is, the win-by-singularity approach of Sun Zi. In this regard, Sun Zi is quoted as saying:

> Do not repeat the tactics which have gained you one victory, but let your methods be regulated by the infinite variety of circumstances. 故其战胜不复, 而应形于无穷.

> *The Art of War*, Chapter 6, Verse 6.26 (500 BC, by Sun Zi)

The pioneers of *six-sigma production* were US firms such as Motorola, Allied Signal, and GE (Hoerl 1998). Since then, many six-sigma training materials and seminar presentations have been developed. It is beyond the scope of this book to introduce specific six-sigma processes. Rather, we shall describe the basic concept of six-sigma manufacturing.

The concept of six-sigma manufacturing: shrink the variability

In a nutshell, six-sigma manufacturing is all about "shrinking variability in a manufacturing process," as phrased by GE. In the terminology of six-sigma manufacturing, the quality of each manufacturing process is measured with a target (T), a lower limit (LL), and an upper limit (UL). The target is given as the design specifications, which a "perfect" manufacturing output must conform to. For example, the target could be the design length of Table-100. However, the actual output of a manufacturing process will generally deviate from the target, sometimes below and sometimes above it. The output is acceptable if it falls around the target T within LL and UL, otherwise it will be rejected as defective. Manufacturing quality (output) is typically assumed to follow a normal distribution, as illustrated in Figure 2.12.

Suppose, for example, that the design length of Table-100 is 1.00 m (i.e., $T = 1.0$), with both the LL and UL as 6.0 cm (i.e., $LL = UL = 0.06$). Thus, it is acceptable if a table is produced with a length between 0.94 and 1.06 m. Assume that the current manufacturing process follows a normal distribution with a mean of 1.0 m and a standard deviation of 0.03 m (i.e., $\sigma_{old} = 0.03$). It is easy to verify that twice the old sigma equals the deviation limit:

$$2 \times \sigma_{old} = 2 \times 0.03 = 0.06 = LL = UL.$$

Thus, the current manufacturing process is considered to be a two-sigma process (i.e., a deviation limit contains twice the standard deviation of the process.). Because the standard deviation (i.e., sigma σ) measures the variability of a process against the mean, it is generally desirable to minimize

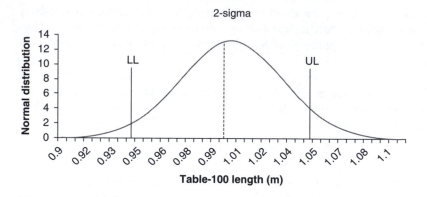

Figure 2.12 Manufacturing process: target, LL, and UL.

or reduce the variability of the process, which is reflected by a smaller sigma (σ).

What would then produce a six-sigma process? Six-sigma manufacturing requires the variability of the current manufacturing process be reduced to 0.01 (i.e., $\sigma_{improved} = 0.01$, so that

$$6 \times \sigma_{improved} = 6 \times 0.01 = 0.06 = LL = UL.$$

Intuitively, the length of the finished Table-100 must be very close to the target almost all the time. Statistically, a six-sigma manufacturing process will generate no more than 3.4 defects per one million parts produced (termed 3.4 DPM for short). In a nutshell, in six-sigma terminology the standard deviation, or "sigma," of a manufacturing process is considered an intrinsic metric of its variability and is then used to measure (or estimate) the quality level of the process. The six-sigma quality measure is constructed as the ratio relative to the technical allowance. A three-sigma quality level means that the allowance range is three times the "sigma." An improved six-sigma Table-100 manufacturing process is shown in Figure 2.13, together with the two-sigma process against the same target, LL, and UL.

TPS quality: elimination of waste

In terms of its approach to quality, the TPS advocates that excellent quality can only be achieved through a continuous improvement process that focuses on the elimination of waste in the production process. As outlined in the section on "The house of TPS," there are seven forms of waste in a production system. TPS quality is to be achieved by continuously improving the quality

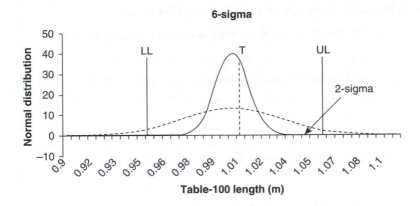

Figure 2.13 Improved six-sigma Table-100 production.

of the process, which is typically implemented in the form of Kaizen sessions (or projects). A typical Kaizen session would start with identifying critical waste(s) in the system, and then devising plans to improve by eliminating or minimizing the identified waste. This improvement process is carried out dynamically by conducting repeated Kaizen sessions.

In the TPS, the seven forms of waste, such as defects, waiting, and inventory, are the enemy of winning with speed. In response to the ever-changing market, a business must be as agile as it can be in order to be successful. The only way to be agile is to eliminate, or minimize, waste. A system that has little or no waste is considered to be a "lean" system. We can see that the concept of TPS quality with lean manufacturing is in total accord with Sun Zi's win-with-speed.

Note that the only purpose of waste elimination is to gain speed, which is in total agreement with Sun Zi's win-with-speed strategy. To this end, we quote:

> It is only one who is thoroughly acquainted with the evils of war that can thoroughly understand the profitable way of carrying it on. 故不尽知用兵之害者, 则不能尽知用兵之利也.

> *The Art of War*, Chapter 2, Verses 2.5 and 2.6 (500 BC, by Sun Zi)

Now let us examine how Sun Zi's "evils of war" are reflected in JIT manufacturing. According to the TPS, waste is the primary "evil" of JIT manufacturing. The seven well-known types of waste are universally identified in manufacturing systems and need to be removed or minimized to be JIT compliant. The *lean* concept, which is an American extension of Japanese JIT, is now applicable to a much wider range of industrial situations, such as *lean enterprise* and *lean logistics*.

Simulation lab: Manufacturing capacity planning

Assignment 2.1: Traffic toll station at the Wisconsin–Illinois border

Historical data indicate that in the morning, the interarrival time of traffic traveling in the Illinois direction follows an exponential distribution with a mean of 3.5 min. The service time at the toll station is also exponential with a mean of 1.2 min.

A   Simulation of an exponential arrival process. Let Y_t be an exponential interarrival time with a mean of $1/\lambda$; that is, its distribution function is given as:

$$F(\tau) = \Pr(Y_t \leq \tau) = 1 - e^{-\lambda\tau} \ (\tau \geq 0).$$

Its probability density function is then given as:

$$f(\tau) = \lambda e^{-\lambda\tau}.$$

Generate samples of exponentially distributed random variable Y_t.

- Let U be uniformly distributed over $[0,1]$, which can be simulated using "=RAND()."
- Then, an exponential random variable Y_t can be obtained using the following expression:

$$Y_t = -\frac{\ln(U)}{\lambda}.$$

- *Hint*: Verify that $-\dfrac{\ln(U)}{\lambda}$ has the same distribution function of Y_t.

$$\Pr\left(-\frac{\ln(U)}{\lambda} \leq \tau\right) = \Pr\left(\ln(U) \geq -\lambda\tau\right) = \Pr(U \geq e^{-\lambda\tau})$$

$$= \Pr(e^{-\lambda\tau} \leq U \leq 1) = 1 - e^{-\lambda\tau}.$$

B   Let X_t be the cumulative arrivals per minute at time t. Then, X_t follows a Poisson distribution with a mean of λ in units per minute. Let W_t be the cumulative arrivals per hour starting at time t (i.e., $W_t = X_{t+1} + X_{t+2} + \ldots + X_{t+60} = \sum_{i=1}^{60} X_{t+i}$). W_t is also a Poisson random variable with a mean of 60λ. Using Excel, generate ten sample paths for W_t for the hours between 6:00 am and 12:00 noon (i.e., for $t \in [6.0, 12.0]$).

C   Compute the average number of arrivals during these hours and compare it with the theoretical mean number of arrivals.

Assignment 2.2: MRP for CT-100 scanners

A Reproduce the MRP computations for Example 2.2, using an Excel spreadsheet. Recall that there is a 1-month lead-time (i.e., $L = 1$). That is, use the MPS given in Table 2.1, start with Table 2.3, and reproduce Table 2.6.

B Repeat Example 2.2 with an initial inventory cut by half, i.e., $I_0 = 10$. The new input data are now summarized in Table 2.12. Complete the MRP netting computation in Excel.

Table 2.12 Input data with new initial inventory $(I_0 = 10, L=1)$

Table-100	Month						
	0	1	2	3	4	5	6
GRs		25	25	45	35	35	75
SRs		10	20				
Projected on-hand	10						
NRs							
SC							
POR							
Ending on-hand	10						
Backlog inventory							

Assignment 2.3: Rolling MRP for CT-100

A Continue with Assignment 2.2. Suppose that the production is scheduled according to the MRP you determined in item B of Assignment 2.2. That is, the orders are actually released according to the "POR" determined in Assignment 2.2B. The initial input data are the same as in Table 2.12. Suppose that by the end of month 6 the actual realizations of demand are recorded as given in Table 2.13. Recalculate the inventory status (ending on-hand and backlog inventory) for each of the 6 months under the actual demand.

Table 2.13 Demand samples for Assignment 2.3

	Month					
	d_1	d_2	d_3	d_4	d_5	d_6
Sample path	31	26	51	35	31	81

Assignment 2.4: MBP policy at CT-100 at DE, Inc.

Mr. BB (big buyer) at DE faces a monthly demand (d_t) for the CT-100 scanner. Suppose that the MPS is still the same as given in Table 2.1, reprinted below for your reference.

Table 2.1 An MPS

CT-100	Month					
	1	*2*	*3*	*4*	*5*	*6*
GRs	25	25	45	35	35	75

The production of CT-100 scanners is planned according to a per-month MBP system with a fixed manufacturing lead-time of 2 months (including manufacturing time and on-site installation time). Under the MBP target system, Mr. BB will assess, at the beginning of each month, the pending orders for CT-100 scanners that can be promised for delivery in 2 months, and then determine a monthly capacity plan. That is, the released production order has a GR for month t, and a due date within 2 months. The initial inventory is assumed to be zero, i.e., $I_0 = 0$.

A   Help Mr BB to develop an AP plan under the per-month MBF planning scheme (i.e., determine a monthly planned capacity level u_t such that the MBP target is met on time). Note that the forecasts are given by monthly GR, and that the inventory status is updated monthly.

B   Generate an AP plan, but now under a per-month MBP planning scheme with a 2-month cycle. Note: (1) MBP planning is based on "promised delivery," as illustrated in Table 2.14; and (2) the PORs within each promised delivery cycle should be leveled out, so that the level of monthly production is smooth.

Table 2.14 Promised delivery schedule derived from the same MPS

CT-100	Month							
	1	*2*	*3*	*4*	*5*	*6*	*7*	*8*
GRs	25	25	45	35	35	75		
Promised delivery		25	25	45	35	35	35	75

Assignment 2.5: CT-100 AP under variable MPS

This assignment simulates the performance of the aggregate plan obtained in Assignment 2.4, when the actual demand follows an i.i.d. (independent and identically distributed) normal process as follows:

A Using a random number generator, generate five sample paths for the next 6 months' demand, similar to Table 2.15 above.

B For each of the five sample paths just generated and for the given AP obtained in Assignment 2.4 without rolling updates, compute the following averages (over the five simulation runs): average total cost, average on-hand inventory cost, and average backordering cost. Use the same cost data as given in Example 2.3.

C Can you suggest a revised MPS, so that the AP generated will turn in a better average performance under the five sample paths used in B above? (No rolling updates are allowed.)

Table 2.15 Normal demand distributions for Assignment 2.5

Normal	Month					
	d_1	d_2	d_3	d_4	d_5	d_6
Mean	25	25	45	35	35	75
Standard deviation	5.0	5.0	5.0	5.0	5.0	5.0

Problems

Basic exercises

1 Historical data indicate that the interarrival time of job orders to a Kanban system for precision-motor assembly follows an exponential distribution with a mean of 1.25 h. The cycle time for the Kanban system to fill each job order is exponential with a mean of 1.10 h.

   (a) Compute the probability of a total of 15 job orders in progress in the Kanban system (including those being processed, and those waiting in buffers).
   (b) Compute the expected total number of job orders in progress (i.e., WIP) in the system, and the expected flow-time of each car (queuing time plus service time).
   (c) Given a 10 percent safety factor and a container size of 1, calculate the number of Kanbans to be launched into the system.

2 Consider the same input data and cost data as given in Example 2.3, but with a 1-month lead-time and the shortage fully backordered with a

Table 2.16 (For Problem 2): CT-100 AP with lead-time $(L = 1)$

CT-100	Month								Total	Cost
	0	1	2	3	4	5	6	7		
GRs		25	25	45	35	35	75		240	
NRs										
Working days/ month		22	25	20	26	25	16		134	
No. workers										
Used	**10**									
Hired										
Removed										
Planned throughput										
Beginning on-hand		2								
Ending on-hand	2						≥ 2			
Backlog inventory										
									Total =	

backordering cost of $215 per unit backlog. That is, the "planned throughput" in month 1 can only be delivered to meet the requirements in month 2, and so on. The shortage in month 1 (i.e., unmet demand in month 1) will be backlogged by 1 month (i.e., will be made up in month 2). Generate a lot-for-lot AP plan for this case in the format shown in Table 2.16.

3   Continue with Problem 2. Suppose that the actual monthly demand is uncertain, and one sample path of the demand for the next 6 months is obtained by simulation, given in Table 2.17. Given the AP plan obtained in Problem 2, develop a monthly adjusted AP with rolling monthly update with the demand given in the sample path.

Additional exercises

4   Roger Hansen, materials handling manager at the Valley Foundry Company, is considering how many heavy-duty forklift trucks to purchase for transporting heavy foundry materials for the company's newly expanded foundry shop. The foundry orders arrive at random and call the material-handling unit to move a load, at a mean rate of four per hour. The total time for a forklift truck to move a load has an exponential distribution with an average of 9 min. The total hourly operation cost (including capital recovery) is $150 per truck. The estimated idle (or waiting) cost because of increased WIP is $20 per load per hour.

   Roger has established certain criteria for the performance of the material-handling unit at the Valley Foundry. These criteria are: (1) an average of no more than 25 min for completing each material-handling order (i.e., moving

Table 2.17 (For Problem 3): sample demands for the next 6 months

	Month					
	d_1	d_2	d_3	d_4	d_5	d_6
Sample path	28	29	46	31	32	78

a load); (2) a material-handling order completion time of 45 min should be maintained 80 percent of the time; (3) there should be no more than two loads (orders) waiting to be moved 80 percent of the time (i.e., an average of no more than three loads in the system).

(a) Suppose that one forklift truck is purchased. Evaluate how well the three performance criteria can be met.
(b) Repeat part (a) if two forklift trucks are to be purchased.
(c) Compare the two alternatives in terms of their expected total cost per hour (including the idle cost).
(d) Which alternative do you suggest Roger should choose?

5 Consider a Kanban controlled two-line assembly system for PM-x1 motors at Precision-Motor, as depicted in Figure 2.14. Job orders arrive at a Kanban controlled dispatching station at a rate of λ (e.g., number of jobs per day). When a job arrives at the dispatching station, if there is an idle Kanban container of assembly material available, the job is dispatched along with the Kanban container to the first available assembly line (either line 1 or line 2) for processing. Otherwise, if no container is available, the job will be queued at the dispatch station until a Kanban container is available. As soon as the job order is filled at one of the two assembly lines, an idle Kanban container is returned to the dispatching station and is available for the next job in the queue (Figure 2.14).

(a) Given a Kanban safety factor of $r = 10$ percent, determine the total number of Kanbans to be issued at the dispatch station that will be adequate for the long-term operation of the two-line assembly system.
(b) Under the total number of Kanbans you determined in (a), compute the resulting service level for the two-line assembly system, where the service level is defined as the in-stock probability, that is:

Pr(zero job waiting at the dispatching station in steady state).

(c) If the management requires a 95 percent probability that no more than three jobs are waiting at the dispatch station, how many Kanbans are needed?

Appendix 2A *M/M* **queues**

Now, let us briefly review how a queuing system is analyzed. Queuing analysis starts with the *state* of the system at any time t, denoted by $X(t)$ and defined as the number of customers in the system observed at t. For any time interval $[0,T]$ (say,

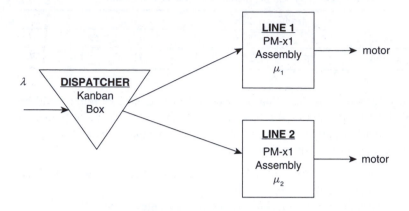

Figure 2.14 (For Problem 5): two assembly lines at Precision-Motor, Inc.

a week), $X(t)$ is a **stochastic process**, and a single realization of it (e.g., for a particular week) is termed a **sample path** of $X(t)$ over $[0,T]$. Figure 2.15 illustrates three sample paths of $X(t)$ (e.g., volume of cars at a highway toll station over a typical summer week), denoted as $X_1(t)$, $X_2(t)$, and $X_3(t)$, respectively.

Time average and ensemble average

In reality, what we usually have available is a single sample path over a certain time interval, say, $X(t)$ for $t \in [0,T]$. Let us consider, for example, the number of daily visits to a highway toll station over a 1-week period, Monday through Sunday. Suppose that the set of observations during the first week are recorded as $\{X(1), X(2), \ldots, X(7)\}$, where $X(k)$ represents the number of visits observed on day k in the first week. Then the data set $\{X(k) : k = 1, 2, \ldots, 7\}$ forms a sample path of the daily visit process $X(t)$ over a 1-week period.

For a sample path $X(t)$ over $[0,T]$, a **time average** (i.e., a *sample mean* taken over time), can be computed as follows:

$$\tilde{X}_T = \frac{1}{T} \int_0^T X(t)\,dt \quad \left(\text{or in discrete time} : \tilde{X}_T = \frac{1}{T} \sum_{t=1}^{T} X(t) \right).$$

On the other hand, we can repeat the experiment for a specific number of times, say, for n times. Back to the toll station example, suppose that the sample path for the ith time is recorded as $\{X_i(t) : t = 1, 2, \ldots, 7\}$ $(i = 1, 2, \ldots, n)$. Note that for a fixed t (say, for Sunday, $t = 7$), the process $X(t)$ gives a random variable. That is, fixed at Sunday, $X(7)$ represents the number of visits to the station on Sunday, which is a random variable. With the set of n sample paths, we have n samples for each fixed t.

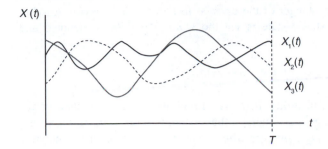

Figure 2.15 Sample paths, time average, and ensemble average.

Thus, for each fixed time t, there can be defined an expectation, $E(X(t))$, termed **ensemble average** (not a time average), as follows:

$$E(X(t)) = \lim_{n \to \infty} \frac{1}{n} \sum_{i=1}^{n} X_i(t), \text{ for every fixed } t,$$

where $X_i(t)$ is the ith sample observed at a fixed time t. The process $X(t)$ is said to be *ergodic* for the *mean* if

$$\lim_{T \to \infty} \tilde{X}_T = \lim_{t \to \infty} E(X(t)) = \mu \text{ (a constant)}.$$

Similarly, the process $X(t)$ is ergodic with respect to its second moment if

$$\lim_{T \to \infty} N_T^2 = \lim_{t \to \infty} E(X^2(t)) = m^2 \text{ (a constant)},$$

where N_T^2 is the **time average** of squared realization, and $E(X^2(t))$ is **ensemble average** $X^2(t)$ with a fixed t, computed respectively as follows:

$$N_T^2 = \frac{1}{T} \int_0^T X^2(t) dt, \text{ or in discrete time}: N_T^2 = \frac{1}{T} \sum_{t=1}^{T} X^2(t),$$

$$E\left(X^2(t)\right) = \lim_{n \to \infty} \frac{1}{n} \sum_{i=1}^{n} X_i^2(t).$$

Steady state

Therefore, we say that a process $X(t)$ possesses a steady state if it is ergodic for all its moments (i.e., ergodic in distribution function), and that each moment possesses a limit that is independent of time. That is, a queuing system reaches a steady state if time is no longer of the essence in a system's behavior. Another way of characterizing steady state is via the *state probabilities*, denoted and defined as follows:

$$p_n(t) = \Pr\{\text{observing } n \text{ customers in system at time } t\} .$$

In general, the state probability $p_n(t)$ is a function of time t. In other words, the probability of finding n customers in the system will differ when observing at different points in time. However, after a steady state is reached, the state probability is no longer a function of time, denoted as p_n. Thus, if a process $X(t)$ possesses a steady state, there is a unique steady-state probability p_n such that

$$\sum_{n=0}^{\infty} p_n = 1.$$

M/M/1 queue

The arrival process is Poisson with the average rate λ (e.g., five customers per hour), and the service process is also Poisson with the average service rate μ (e.g., ten customers served per hour). Since the rate of arrival reflects the time between consecutive arrivals, the average interarrival time (time between arrivals) can be equivalently determined from the arrival rate as $1/\lambda$ (e.g., $1/5 = 0.2$ h between arrivals), and the interservice completion time (time between service completions) is $1/\mu$ (e.g., $1/10 = 0.1$ h between completions). We have learned in Appendix 2A that the interarrival time is exponential if the number of arrivals per unit time is of a Poisson (see Assignment 1.4). An exponential process is well known for its property of no-memory for the past (also termed Markov property). Hence, the first letter M indicates that the arrivals are Markovian, and so are the services according to the second letter M. Thus in an $M/M/1$ queue, the interarrival time exhibits an exponential process with mean $1/\lambda$, and the intercompletion time is also exponential with mean $1/\mu$. It is useful to present the steady state of an $M/M/1$ queue by a steady-state flow diagram as follows:

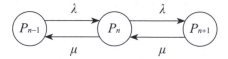

The diagram translates to the so-called steady-state flow balance equations; that is, the expected flow into each state is equal to the expected flow out of that state:

$$\begin{cases} (\lambda+\mu)p_n = \lambda p_{n-1} + \mu p_{n+1} & (n \geq 1) \\ \lambda p_0 = \mu p_1 \end{cases} .$$

This is a set of difference equations, and the solutions can be expressed in terms of an initial probability p_0. For example, using $p_1 = \frac{\lambda}{\mu} p_0$, it is easy to derive from the flow balance equations the following equalities:

$$(\lambda + \mu)p_1 = (\lambda + \mu)\frac{\lambda}{\mu} p_0 = \lambda p_0 + \mu p_2,$$

which then immediately leads to the expression:

$$p_2 = \left(\frac{\lambda}{\mu}\right)^2 p_0 = \rho^2 \times p_0, \text{ where } \rho = \frac{\lambda}{\mu} < 1.$$

Continuing with the successive substitution will yield the solution for steady-state probabilities as:

$$p_n = \rho^n(1 - \rho), \left(\rho = \frac{\lambda}{\mu}\right).$$

Then, in steady state we have

$$L = E(\text{number of customers in the system}) = \frac{\lambda}{\mu - \lambda},$$

$$W = E(\text{time customers are in the system}) = \frac{1}{\mu - \lambda},$$

$$L_q = E(\text{number of customers in the queue}) = \frac{\lambda^2}{\mu(\mu - \lambda)},$$

$$W_q = E(\text{time in the queue}) = \frac{\lambda}{\mu(\mu - \lambda)}.$$

It is easy to verify that Little's Law applies to both pairs for the *M/M/*1 queues, namely, $L = \lambda W$ and $L_q = \lambda W_q$.

M/M/k queue

An immediate extension of the *M/M/*1 queue is to allow more than one identical servers. It is common to encounter multiserver queues. The toll stations, for example, usually have parallel pay booths (servers). Let k be the number of identical servers and denote such queuing system as an *M/M/k* queue. Note that each of the k servers has an average service rate of μ. The combined average service rate will depend on the number of customers in the system at the steady state, namely, either $n < k$ (more servers than customers) or $n \geq k$ (otherwise). It is easy to verify that the average service rate is $n\mu$ if $n < k$, while average service rate is $k\mu$ if $n \geq k$, as illustrated as follows:

(a) $n < k$ case:

(b) $n \geq k$ case:

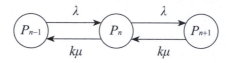

Thus the steady-state flow balance equations for a multiple-server queue can be derived as follows:

$$\begin{cases} (\lambda + k\mu)p_n = \lambda p_{n-1} + k\mu p_{n+1} & (n \geq k) \\ (\lambda + n\mu)p_n = \lambda p_{n-1} + (n+1)\mu p_{n+1} & (n < k) \\ \lambda p_0 = \mu p_1 \end{cases}.$$

By successive substitution in a similar manner, we can obtain:

$$p_n = \begin{cases} \dfrac{\rho^n}{n!}p_0, & (n < k) \\[2ex] \dfrac{\rho^n}{k!k^{n-k}}p_0, & (n \geq k) \end{cases},$$

where $\rho = \lambda/\mu$, and $n! = n(n-1),\ldots,2 \times 1$ (with $0! = 1$ by definition). Setting $\sum\limits_{n=0}^{\infty} p_n = 1$ (as all probabilities must sum up to (1)), we can then derive:

$$p_0 = \frac{1}{\left(\sum\limits_{n=0}^{k-1} \dfrac{\rho^n}{n!} + \dfrac{\rho^k k}{k!(k-\rho)} \right)}, \quad \left(\rho = \frac{\lambda}{\mu} \right).$$

It can be verified that Little's Law applies to the average waiting (excluding the ones being served), that is,

$$L_q = \lambda W_q, \text{ and } L_q = \frac{\rho^{k+1}}{(k-1)!(k-\rho)^2}.$$

For total average measures, we have

$$L = L_q + \frac{\lambda}{\mu}, \text{ and } W_q = W_q + \frac{1}{\mu}.$$

Bibliography

Gross, D. and C.M. Harris. 1974. *Fundamentals of Queuing Theory*, New York: John Wiley & Sons.

Hoerl, R.W. 1998. "Six Sigma and the Future of the Quality Profession," *Quality Process*, June, 35–42.

Holland, J. 1992. *Adaptation in Natural and Artificial Systems*, Cambridge, MA: The MIT Press.

Hopp, W. and M. Spearman. 2000. *Factory Physics*, Boston, MA: McGraw Hill.

Liu, J. 2001. "A Real Beer Game: Make-to-Order Incentive Problems," *Working Paper Series*, School of Business Administration, University of Wisconsin–Milwaukee.

Ore, N.J. 2005. "Now There Are Two," *Proceedings of the 14th International Federation of Purchasing and Supply Management World Congress*, Beijing, October 17–18.

Orlicky, J. 1975. *Material Requirement Planning: The New Way of Life in Production and Inventory Management*, New York: McGraw Hill.

3   Inventory and reserve systems

> **Key items:**
>
> - *The micro/macro paradox of inventories*
> - *Simple repetitive inventory decisions*
> - *Statistical inventory models*
>   *Demand over lead-time*
>   *Variability reduction: bundling, risk pooling*
>   *Reorder systems*
> - *Multiple-item order systems*

The micro/macro paradox of inventories

According to Sun Zi, becoming undefeatable is the prelude to defeating opponents. According to the *art of war* as applied to *business operations*, managing capacity can be considered an analogy for defeating opponents, and managing inventory as an analogy for not being defeated by opponents. Therefore, a rule of the *art of war in business* is that to win, one must first successfully manage the inventories of supplies and goods, at both an operational (micro) level and an aggregate (macro) level.

Inventory models have been developed using the methodology of Operations Research (OR), and are founded on the principle of stabilization of production at an operational level of individual products and firms. However, the microeconomic view that inventory should stabilize production output seems to be in sharp contrast with the macro-economic characteristics of business cycle theory (as summarized in Blinder and Maccini 1991), which states that: (1) variance in production exceeds variance in sales (i.e., the bullwhip effect, as it is termed in the supply chain literature); (2) sales and inventory investments are positively correlated; and (3) aggregate outputs are typically associated with cyclic fluctuations and disequilibrium (e.g., annual inventory clearance of durable goods as common practice). An apparent paradox emerges, because the aggregate effect of inventories, which are supposed to stabilize production at a micro level, apparently destabilizes the system at the macro level, thus serving the opposite purpose (Blinder 1982; Kydland and Prescott 1982).

Since the late 1970s, a great deal of intellectual resources and attention has been devoted to reconciling the discrepancies between theoretical micro-analysis and empirical macro-characterization. In this regard, researchers typically initiate inventory analysis with a static, single-product model and then aggregate it over time, products, and firms, allowing it to be verified according to the macro-characteristics that are always presented in an aggregated manner. To date, the micro/macro paradox remains largely unsolved, and the search for solutions to the paradox is still ongoing. It is still a critical problem that aggregation of these inventory models can neither adequately explain nor confirm the empirical aggregate characteristics. For example, the following contradiction remains unexplained:

- Inventory theory: optimal safety stock is proportional to demand variability; inventory investment and production output are positively correlated.
- Business cycle theory: aggregate inventory investment is negatively (reversely) correlated with the system output; adequate finished goods available lead to less investment in inventory (e.g., reduced production capacity allocation and safety stock reserve).

For specificity, let us compare the OR view with the aggregate view of inventory.

OR view of inventory: cost minimization

- *Inventory problem*: Determine when and how much to produce orders of goods and supplies so that desirable inventory stocks can be maintained to best meet demand and smoothly support production.
- *Inventory system*: Demand (d), order quantity (q), inventory position (y), lead-time (L). Inventory stock transition equation: $x_{t+1} = x_t + q_{t-L} - d_t$.
- *System parameters*: costs (holding, shortage, ordering), prices (selling, purchasing) (Figure 3.1).

Economic views of inventory

- *Inventory problem*: Production facilitation, risk management, and market speculation.
- *Inventory system*: Price–quantity equilibrium production.
- *System parameters*: Macro-economic series that constitutes fundamental economic indicators, for example, the purchasing manager index (PMI), including measures of production (output), new orders (demand), inventories (input supplies), labor and production capacity (u_t), supplier deliveries (finished inventory), and prices (purchasing) (Figure 3.2).

The rest of this chapter is devoted to the basic inventory models that underpin the micro-economic characteristics of production stabilization.

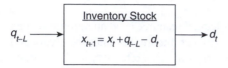

Figure 3.1 OR views of inventory.

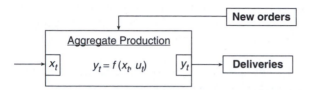

Figure 3.2 Aggregate views of inventory.

Prototype example: repetitive order systems at Quick-Engine

An order-fulfillment system involves planning and controlling the flow of materials, supplies, and work-in-process (WIP) on a repetitive basis. The planning and control of production generate a series of inventory orders. The system of order generation and execution is referred to as an inventory order system (or simply inventory system). An example will help to explain this concept.

Example 3.1   Reorder-point inventory system for pistons at Quick-Engine

Quick-Engine makes commercial and residential stand-by generators. Generator QE-1, the best-selling commercial model, has drawn an average annual demand of 90,000 units. The engine manufacturing cell at Q-E fabricates complete engine assembly of the QE-1 model. Each engine requires four pistons, which are purchased from a single supplier with a 3-day response time (i.e., the time needed by the supplier to provide ordered pistons). The engine cell operates under a periodic-review reorder-point system as follows. Every Monday, the buyer reviews the on-hand stock of pistons and will place an order for more pistons if the current on-hand inventory of pistons falls on, or below, a pre-determined level (termed a reorder point). Otherwise, the buyer will not place any orders until Monday of the next week. The buyer needs to determine the quantity level of the reorder point, and the order quantity if an order needs to be placed.

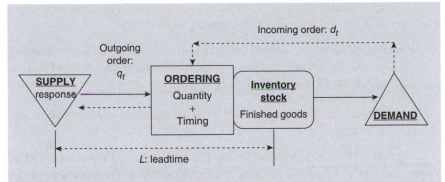

Figure 3.3 Repetitive inventory system.

Figure 3.3 depicts a typical model of a repetitive inventory system in the general context of a manufacturing supply chain. The system contains two streams of directed orders: the flow of order release, represented by dotted lines, and the flow of order delivery, represented by solid lines. According to Zipkin (2000), a general inventory system can be viewed as a directed flow network. The **demand** herein is broadly understood to be any requirement to consume or utilize materials and supply. An inventory system is designed to acquire the supplies needed to fulfill the demand orders.

There are two important exogenous (or input) variables in an inventory order system – target demand and lead-time – which are two of the basic components of the SOF (supply order fulfillment) model we studied in Chapter 2. If there is no demand then there would be no need to produce. Whenever there is a demand order, it inevitably takes time for a supplier to fulfill the order. Clearly, the inventory system is an intrinsic part of the SOF system, as depicted in Figures 3.3 and 2.10. Incorporating and regulating these two variables require a suitable operational scheme to be applied to the underlying inventory system. For example, given a fixed lead-time (e.g., 3 weeks), a suitable inventory operational scheme will differ considerably depending on whether demand is stable (and therefore predicable) or not. If demand is known for certain and is therefore predictable, there will be no need for safety stock and a pure make-to-order JIT system would be a natural choice. However, if demand is variable and uncertain, as in most realistic situations, some safety measures must be incorporated to cope with the variability. However, if there was no lead-time (i.e., products could be delivered in no time – a hypothetical scenario), then it would not matter whether demand was predictable or not. In this case, an instant, made-to-order system would be adequate to cope with the situation. In reality, it is impossible to eliminate lead-time and there is always room for managing demand, which is where managerial priorities are typically focused. Nevertheless, we assume in this chapter that the lead-time is given and fixed. For convenience, let us denote:

> **Demand process**, d_t: demand realization in period t (e.g., in months). Suppose the current time is t (e.g., in months), and the past demand realizations are observed and obtained as $D_t = \{d_t, d_{t-1}, \ldots\}$, where d_t is the underlying time-series demand; and
>
> **Lead-time**, L: the time elapsed from the issuance of an order until the receipt (or fulfillment) of it.

In contrast with the newsboy problem studied in Chapter 1, a repetitive inventory system involves the repetitive ordering of supplies and WIP inventories, to meet a repetitive time-lagged *target* (e.g., weekly demand). Because a supplier will inevitably take a certain time (i.e., **lead-time** L) to respond to inventory orders, the realization of demand is lagged in time following the issuance of the inventory order.

System dynamics

Given the demand and lead-time as input variables, a repetitive inventory system engages regulatory actions regarding three system dynamic variables: *inventory transition*, *inventory review*, and *inventory ordering*. Note that these three variables are considered to be *endogenous* and *controllable*, in contrast to the input variables, *demand* and *lead-time*. Typical measures of **inventory transition** include the on-hand inventory and the inventory position (i.e., the on-hand plus the on-order inventory incurred at time t, including the backorder inventory if any). There are, in general, two types of **inventory review**: *periodic review* as in Example 3.1, and *continuous review*, which continuously monitors the inventory status. **Inventory ordering** consists of two decision-making components: when and how many to order. Figure 3.4 illustrates the trajectory of inventory transitions under a reorder-point inventory system, similar to that in Example 3.1.

As depicted in Figure 3.4, the inventory is stocked by placing inventory orders, and the stock of inventory is then used to meet the demand. In other words, the inventory stock is depleted at the rate of demand realization. As seen from Figure 3.4, the **reorder point** R signifies the time it takes to issue a replenishment order, that is, an inventory replenishing order should be issued as soon as the actual inventory stock becomes equal to or below the reorder point.

Because there is a lead-time for the arrival of a replenishing order, the reorder point should be specified such that the on-hand inventory is adequate to meet the demand during the lead-time, while awaiting the replenishment inventory. It is often necessary to consider the total demand accumulated from time t over the lead-time, or simply the **lead-time demand** D_t^L, or D^L if time index t is irrelevant (i.e., for stationary cases). That is,

$$D_t^L = d_{t+1} + d_{t+2} + \cdots + d_{t+L} \text{ or } D^L = d_1 + d_2 + \cdots + d_L.$$

The determination of the *reorder point* will depend on input variables, i.e., *lead-time* and *demand*. For example, if there is no lead-time (i.e., $L = 0$) then the order

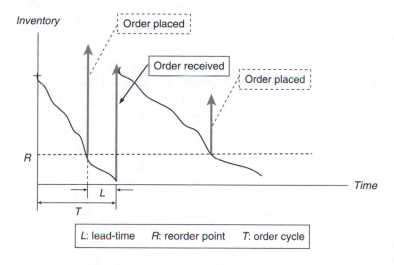

Figure 3.4 Inventory transition in reorder-point inventory system.

can be placed at the moment when the on-hand inventory becomes depleted. Or, if demand is stable over the lead-time interval, and the lead-time demand is a constant, say $D_t^L = \mu_L$ (constant), then the reorder point can be determined as $R = \mu_L$.

A deterministic inventory order system will be covered in detail in the section on "Simple repetitive inventory decisions." However, the demand process, and therefore the lead-time demand, often incur noticeable random fluctuations. In this case, the lead-time demand D_t^L is a random variable. Suppose that lead-time demand D_t^L is stationary with a constant mean of μ_L and a constant variance of σ_L^2. The reorder point with random lead-time demand must then include certain safety factors to accommodate the effect of demand variability. The statistical inventory system will be described in the section on "Variability and variability reduction."

Inventory ordering policy

Next, we define and denote specific endogenous variables that are commonly involved in an inventory system.

On-hand inventory, I_t: the amount of inventory on-hand at time t, which includes inventory carried over plus received replenishment inventory orders.

Inventory position, y_t: the amount of inventory on-hand plus on order (i.e., in the pipeline) at time t, including promised backorders, if any.

Inventory status (or state), x_t: the net amount of inventory; that is, the on-hand position minus demand, $x_t = I_t - d_t$.

Inventory order, q_t: the amount of replenishing inventory to be requested at time t.

Review cycle, τ: the time between consecutive reviews of the inventory status.
Order cycle, T: the time between consecutive replenishment inventory orders.

We will omit the time index in the above notation whenever it is appropriate (e.g., when the time index is irrelevant). There are two basic review schemes in an inventory system – periodic review and continuous review – and the selection of the review scheme is a typical managerial decision. Continuous review is generally used in systems where the inventory status always has to be known. When demand is in the form of a *time series*, continuous review entails reviewing the system status for every time period (i.e., $\tau = 1$). In practice, a continuous-review inventory system monitors the inventory status for every period, although it only reports when an inventory transaction takes place. It is important to note that there are situations where a continuous-review system is not a good choice. For instance, if the supplier of a daily-consumed item accepts orders only once a week, there is no reason why the buyer would review the stock of the item more often than weekly. In this case, a periodic review on a weekly basis would be a logical choice (i.e., $\tau = 7$, assuming seven working days a week).

Similar to a production order, as studied in the previous chapter, an inventory order q_t is determined according to a specific order policy. Below are some of the common inventory order policies practiced in the manufacturing supply chain.

Reorder-point policy, or (R,Q) policy: when the inventory position is equal to or less than the reorder point R, place an order for Q units.
Min-max policy, or (s,S) policy: when the inventory position is equal to or less than the reorder level s, place an order such that the inventory position is increased to the order-up-to level $S(s \leq S)$.
Lot-for-lot (L-4-L) order policy: the inventory stock is replenished on a period-by-period basis with the amount equal to a projected one-period requirement in a lead-time-length future. That is, a lot-for-lot order is placed in period t with the order size being equal to the current forecast for demand in period $t + L$ (i.e., in L-period future).

Inventory ordering policies can also be classified into two major types: **make-to-stock** and **make-to-order**. Reorder-point and min-max orders are of the make-to-stock type, whereas lot-for-lot ordering represents a make-to-order type. In terms of implementation, these inventory policies, just like the production policies studied before, are suited to two types of planning and control systems: MRP (make-to-stock) and Kanban (make-to-order).

To determine the most suitable order policy for a given inventory order system, some performance measures and objectives must be established, such as total cost, profit, and service level (SL). Thus, the key to inventory management is to select and implement the best order policy under a given set of performance measures.

Operational costs and service level

The challenge for managing the inventory is in the trade-off (or dilemma) between service quality and operational costs. Here is the notation of performance measures that will be used for the inventory systems:

SL = service level = Pr (demand is met on time);

P = purchase cost ($ per unit);

c_s = order cost, or setup cost ($ per order);

c_h = inventory holding cost due to overstock
     ($ per unit held for unit time period); and

c_b = backorder (or lost sales) cost due to shortage
     ($ per unit backordered or lost).

A common measure of service quality is the SL, defined by the probability of meeting the demand over the lead-time (in short, the in-stock probability). The in-stock probability is termed a type A measure of service quality, which is formally defined as follows.

Type A service level:

SL = Pr (on-hand inventory to meet demand for each cycle)

  = Pr (not stocking out during lead-time) = $\Pr(D^L \leq R)$,

where D^l represents the average lead-time demand, and R is a reorder point.

An alternative measure of SL is the FR (fill rate), termed a type B service measure that is formally defined as:

Type B service level (i.e., fill rate):

FR = ratio of in-stock units versus total demand per cycle

$$= 1 - \frac{\text{average units of stockout per cycle}}{\text{average inventory units ordered per cycle}}$$

$$= 1 - \frac{E\,(\text{stockouts per cycle})}{E\,(\text{order size per cycle})}.$$

Simple repetitive inventory decisions

The simplest case of a repetitive order system is the so-called *fixed* order system under constant demand. When demand is a known constant, production cost becomes the main concern, which is affected by short-term planning. There are two fixed-order scenarios under known demand, namely, fixed *delivery* quantity

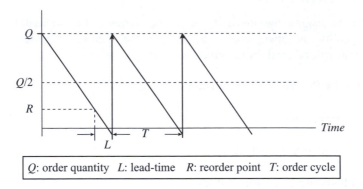

Q: order quantity   L: lead-time   R: reorder point   T: order cycle

Figure 3.5 Fixed delivery quantity system.

and fixed *production* quantity systems. In a fixed *delivery* quantity system, an order is produced in advance and delivered upon order completion, whereas in a fixed production quantity system, an order is gradually delivered while being produced. Let us first consider a fixed order quantity system. Figure 3.5 illustrates the trajectory of the inventory level in a fixed order quantity system.

Fixed delivery quantity model

A fixed quantity Q is repetitively ordered to meet annual demand (i.e., the target). Every time an order arrives, the inventory level is raised up to Q, and then starts to deplete as demand orders are filled. The lead-time is fixed at L periods, between the time of the order being placed and the time of order arrival. Thus, an order must be placed before the on-hand inventory runs out. The inventory level at which an order is placed is termed the reorder point, R. Clearly, the reorder point R is intended to cover the demand over lead-time L, that is, $R = L \times d$, where d is a demand rate consistent with lead-time L. For example, if L is given in weeks, then d represents the weekly demand.

Example 3.2   Economic order quantity (EOQ) of pistons at Quick-Engine

Quick-Engine makes commercial and residential stand-by generators. QE-1, the best-selling commercial model, has enjoyed a stable annual demand of 90,000 units, which has reached the current design capacity at Q-E. The engine manufacturing cell at Q-E fabricates complete engine assembly for the QE-1 model. Each engine requires four pistons, which are purchased from a single supplier for $25 each with a 3-day response time (i.e., the time needed by the supplier to provide the ordered pistons). The buyer for the engine cell at Q-E must decide how many equal-sized batches of pistons to acquire each year for the engine cell. The cost of setting up an order transaction with the supplier is estimated as $250 per purchase order. The cost of holding each piston for 1 year is given as 20 percent of the price when it was purchased.

Question: How many pistons should the Quick-Engine buyer order from the supplier each time to meet the annual demand?

The economic order quantity (EOQ)

In Example 3.2, the target is an annual demand of 360,000 pistons, as each engine requires four pistons. According to the cost data given, there are three cost components the buyer needs to consider: annual purchase cost, annual setup cost, and annual holding cost. The annual purchase cost is a constant, given as:

$$P \times D = 25(360,000) = \$9 \, (\text{million}),$$

where P = price, D = annual demand.

The remaining two cost components are not constant, depending on the order quantity, Q, that the buyer decides to order each time from the supplier. For example, if the buyer decides to buy a whole year's supply of pistons at once (i.e., $Q = 360,000$ pistons), then only a one-time setup cost of $250 is incurred at the beginning of the year. However, this is a large amount of piston inventory to carry throughout the year. Alternatively, if the buyer decides to purchase the pistons monthly, then to meet the annual demand the buyer will have to place 12 batch orders, each with a quantity of $Q = 360,000/12 = 30,000$ (pistons). In this case, the total setup cost will be 12 times higher, but the holding cost will be much lower because the inventory is now carried on a monthly basis. As we can see, the total inventory cost depends on the order quantity Q, with a proportional setup cost and the holding cost inversely related to Q. Specifically, as the order quantity increases, the annual setup cost decreases while the annual holding cost increases. This type of repetitive inventory system is referred to as a fixed order quantity inventory system, as depicted in Figure 3.5. The question the buyer faces is how to determine the order quantity such that the total annual inventory cost is minimized.

Let Q be a variable amount that a buyer needs to determine to minimize the total annual inventory cost, as described in Example 3.2. Then, the number of order batches needed to meet annual demand can be computed as:

$$n = \frac{D}{Q}.$$

With the order quantity Q, the annual setup cost can then be computed as:

$$(\text{setup cost per batch}) \times (\text{number of batches per year}) = c_s \times \frac{D}{Q},$$

where c_s = setup cost per batch.

As depicted in Figure 3.5, the average inventory is $Q/2$ over a year. Thus, the annual holding cost is:

$$(\text{unit holding cost}) \times (\text{average inventory per year}) = c_h \times \frac{Q}{2},$$

where c_h = unit holding cost (\$/unit/year).

The total annual inventory cost can then be written as:

$$TC = P \times D + c_s \times \frac{D}{Q} + c_h \times \frac{Q}{2}.$$

The fixed order inventory problem determines a cost-minimizing order quantity, which is also referred to as an EOQ. An EOQ can be determined by the principle of marginal equilibrium, which in this case translates to the following equality:

$$\text{Annual setup cost} = \text{Annual holding cost}.$$

That is, if Q^* generates a minimum total annual inventory cost TC, then the following equality holds:

$$c_s \times \frac{D}{Q^*} = c_h \times \frac{Q^*}{2}.$$

The above equality can also be obtained by setting the derivative of the total cost TC to zero with respect to order quantity Q, (i.e., $\partial TC / \partial Q = 0$). This then yields the well-known EOQ formula:

$$Q^* = \sqrt{\frac{2 c_s D}{c_h}}.$$

With the cost data given in Example 3.2, the cost-minimizing order quantity can be determined as:

$$Q^* = \sqrt{\frac{2 c_s D}{c_h}} = \sqrt{\frac{2(250)(360,000)}{0.2(25)}} = 6,000.$$

Reorder point under EOQ

The reorder point under EOQ is determined separately for two different cases, depending on whether or not the lead-time L exceeds the order cycle T.

Case 1 ($L \leq T$). This is the case represented in Figure 3.5. To confirm whether $L \leq T$, we first compute the number of orders per year under EOQ:

$$n = 360{,}000 / 6{,}000 = 60 \, (\text{times}),$$

which translates to five orders per month. Because the lead-time (i.e., response time) is 3 days (i.e., $L = 3$ days), we convert the order cycle into a daily scale. Assuming 30 working days in a month, the buyer will place an order every 6 days, roughly on a weekly basis (i.e., $T = 30/5 = 6$ days). This confirms that the order cycle T is greater than the lead-time L (i.e., $L < T$ in this case). The **reorder point** R is then calculated as demand over lead-time:

$$R = (\text{lead-time in days}) \times (\text{daily demand rate})$$

$$= L \times d = 3 \times \frac{360{,}000}{30 \times (12)} = 3{,}000 \, \text{pistons}.$$

Thus, the buyer can monitor the on-hand inventory, and place an order whenever the on-hand inventory of pistons drops to 3,000. In practice, the reorder point R is often given in time (e.g., in days), for example, as follows:

$$\text{Reorder point (in days)} = \frac{\text{reorder point in units}}{\text{daily demand}} = \frac{R}{d} = 3 \, (\text{days}).$$

As such, the reorder point is specified as 3-days' worth of demand (i.e., the lead-time worth demand).

Case 2 ($L > T$). To see why we need to consider this case separately, let us assume that the Quick-Engine firm in Example 3.2 has decided to switch to another piston supplier at a better price. As a result, the lead-time in Example 3.2 is extended from the original 3 days to 10 days (i.e., now $L = 10$). As all the cost data and demand data remain the same, the EOQ remains at 6,000 and thus the order cycle is still 6 days, the same as in Case 1 (i.e., $T = 6$). In this case, we have $L > T$, as depicted in Figure 3.6. Let us plan for the next order to arrive at the end of the second order cycle, indicated by the solid upward arrow in Figure 3.6. Because there is a 10-day lead-time, an order must be placed 10 days in advance, which is, in fact, one cycle (6 days) plus 4 days before the order arrival, as depicted in Figure 3.6. The first dotted upward arrow in Figure 3.6 indicates the arrival of an order that has already been placed 10 days earlier.

As far as the order arrival indicated by the solid arrow is concerned, the order must be placed when there are 4 days remaining in the first order cycle. In this case, the order point can be determined as:

$$R = (4 \, \text{days remaining}) \times (\text{daily demand rate}) = 4 \times \frac{360{,}000}{30 \times (12)} = 4{,}000 \, \text{pistons}.$$

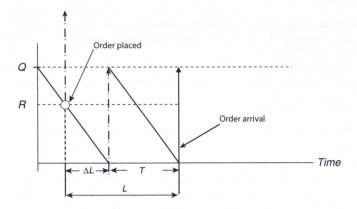

Figure 3.6 Fixed delivery quantity system with $L > T$.

That is, whenever the remaining stock of pistons drops to 4,000, an order for 6,000 pistons should be immediately issued, which will be delivered in 10 days' time to raise the stock level back up to 6,000.

In general, when $L > T$ we first determine the largest number of order cycles T contained in the lead-time L, which is denoted as INT(L/T) (i.e., the integer part of the division L/T). Thus, the remaining part of L after taking out the multiple cycles from the lead-time, denoted as ΔL in Figure 3.6, can be determined as:

$$\Delta L = L - \left(\text{multiples of cycle time } T\right) = L - \text{INT}(L/T) \times T.$$

The reorder point can then be calculated as follows:

For the case where $L > T$:

$$R = (\text{remaining time}) \times (\text{demand rate}) = \Delta L \times d = \left[L - \text{INT}\left(\frac{L}{T}\right) \times T\right] \times d$$

$$= \left[10 - \text{INT}\left(\frac{10}{6}\right) \times (6)\right] \times (1,000) = [10 - 1 \times (6)] \times (1,000)$$

$$= 4 \times (1,000) = 4,000,$$

where INT(L/T) gives the integer number of multiple cycle times T in L.

Fixed production quantity model

As mentioned earlier, the other scenario is a *fixed production quantity* system, in which an order is delivered while it is produced, say, at a production rate of p (e.g., units produced per month). The production order quantity system can be

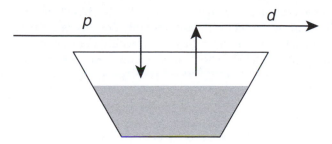

Figure 3.7 WIP accumulation during production.

considered a continuous flow system, with an inflow rate of p (e.g., monthly production rate) and an outflow rate of d (e.g., monthly demand rate), as depicted in Figure 3.7.

Example 3.3 Economic production quantity (EPQ) of pistons at Quick-Engine

The same Quick-Engine company as in Example 3.2 is now considering making the piston for model QE-1 in-house using the newly acquired flexible manufacturing cell (FMC), which has the capacity to produce 50,000 pistons per month. The cost data for the FMC operations are estimated as follows: $20 operational cost per piston made, $450 per FMC setup for each production run, and the same 20 percent of production cost for the holding cost.

Question: How many production runs of equal size should be scheduled to ensure that FMC produces enough pistons to keep pace with the engine manufacturing production rate?

Let us analyze the three cost components, as defined in the previous example, for the in-house production of the pistons. FMC can produce 50,000 pistons each month, and must make a total of 360,000 pistons annually as required for the production of the engine. As the unit operational cost is fixed at $20 per piston, the annual operational cost will amount to $7.2 million ($= \$20 \times 360,000$). The manager of FMC needs to determine the number of production runs (or batches) per year (say n runs per year). The size of each run is:

$$Q = \frac{D}{n}.$$

For example, if the manager decides to produce 12 runs per year on a monthly basis (i.e., $n = 12$), then each run must produce $Q = 360,000/12 = 30,000$ pistons to meet the annual requirement. For convenience, monthly demand is denoted by d, with D for the annual demand. Note that the monthly demand in the example is 30,000 (i.e., $d = 30,000$). The annual setup cost can then be computed as:

$$c_s \times \frac{D}{Q} = (450)(12) = \$5,400.$$

Now, let us examine how the WIP inventory is accumulated under the fixed quantity production schedule. With a given monthly production rate p (in this case, $p = 50,000$ per month), the time needed to produce each batch can be determined as:

$$\frac{Q}{p} = \frac{30,000}{50,000} = 0.6 \,(\text{month}).$$

That is, it would take about two-thirds of a month to produce a monthly demand of 30,000 pistons. In other words, the number of pistons produced in two-thirds of a month is enough for a whole month's demand. In terms of WIP, enough pistons are accumulated during the first two-thirds of a month, which will then be used to continue the engine production for the rest of the month, as illustrated in Figure 3.8. It can be verified that the monthly accumulation of piston inventory is $p - d$ (i.e., monthly production rate minus monthly demand rate). However, inventory accumulation occurs only during production in the first 0.6 month period. Therefore, by the time a batch of Q pistons is produced, the accumulation of inventory reaches its maximum level (I_{max}), which can be computed as:

$$I_{max} = (p - d) \times (\text{batch production time}) = (p - d) \times \frac{Q}{p}$$
$$= (50,000 - 30,000) \times (0.6) = 12,000 \,(\text{pistons}).$$

Recall that Q is defined as 30,000 pistons, whereas the maximum WIP inventory is 12,000. We can see that the maximum inventory is less than the order quantity. Compared with Figure 3.5, it is important to note the difference in the maximum inventory level between the two fixed-order systems. From Figure 3.8, the average inventory in a fixed quantity production system can be verified as $I_{max}/2$, and therefore the annual inventory cost is:

$$c_h \times (\text{average inventory}) = c_h \times \frac{I_{max}}{2} = c_h \times \left(1 - \frac{d}{p}\right)\frac{Q}{2}.$$

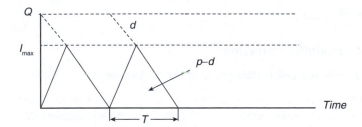

Figure 3.8 Fixed production quantity system.

Total annual production cost can then be written as:

$$TC_p = P \times D + c_s \times \frac{D}{Q} + c_h \times \left(1 - \frac{d}{p}\right) \times \frac{Q}{2}.$$

The marginal equilibrium equation for EPQ $\left(Q_p^*\right)$ can then be written as:

$$c_s \times \frac{D}{Q_p^*} = c_h \times \left(1 - \frac{d}{p}\right) \frac{Q_p^*}{2}.$$

Solving the above equality for order quantity, the EPQ can thus be obtained as:

$$Q_p^* = \sqrt{\frac{2c_s D}{c_h \left(1 - \frac{d}{p}\right)}}.$$

With the data given in Example 3.3, it is easy to compute the EPQ (also termed economic lot-sizing) as follows:

$$Q_p^* = \sqrt{\frac{2c_s D}{c_h \left(1 - \frac{d}{p}\right)}} = \sqrt{\frac{2(450)(360,000)}{(0.2)(20)\left(\frac{2}{5}\right)}} = 14,230 \,(\text{pistons}).$$

The time needed to produce a batch is $Q/p = 14,230/50,000 = 0.28 \,(\text{month})$ (i.e., it takes over a week to produce a batch). The time between orders can be obtained as:

$$T = \frac{Q_p^*}{D} = \frac{14,230}{360,000} \times 12 = 0.47 \,\text{month (i.e., around 2 weeks)}.$$

Thus, a production order must be released about every half of a month. The maximum level of inventory build-up during each half-month period can be determined as:

$$I_{max} = \left(1 - \frac{d}{p}\right) Q = \frac{2}{5}(14,230) = 5,692 \,(\text{pistons}).$$

Thus, the new FMC must be equipped with a storage facility that can hold up to 5,692 finished pistons.

Variability and variability reduction

Prototype example: safety stock management at Quick-Engine

As illustrated in the previous sections, lead-time demand plays an important role in inventory decision-making. For example, with both deterministic demand rate d (e.g., daily demand of 1,000 units) and lead-time L (e.g., 3 days), then the reorder point R can be calculated for the case of $L \le T$ as:

$$R = d \times L = 3,000 \, (\text{units}).$$

In this section, we study the lead-time demand when the demand in each period, d_t, is i.i.d. (independent and identically distributed) with a constant mean μ and constant variance σ^2. In short, we denote such stochastic demand as $d_t \sim \text{IID}(\mu, \sigma^2)$, and as $d_t \sim \text{IIDN}(\mu, \sigma^2)$ if the demand variable follows a normal distribution. In a more realistic setting, the Quick-Engine example can be described as follows.

Example 3.4   Lead-time demand for pistons at Quick-Engine

Suppose that daily demand for the QE-1 stand-by generator at Quick-Engine represents an i.i.d. normal variable with a mean of 250 and a variance of 64, with a 360 working-day annual schedule. Each QE-1 engine requires four pistons, which are purchased from a single supplier with a 3-day lead-time.

Question: What is the mean and variance of demand for pistons over the 3-day lead-time?

Given a stochastic demand process such as this, the lead-time demand D^L can be expressed as the aggregate demand over the lead-time L, that is:

$$D^L = d_1 + d_2 + \cdots + d_L = \sum_{i=1}^{L} d_i, \text{with each}, d_i \sim \text{IID}(\mu, \sigma^2).$$

For a fixed **constant lead-time** L, the mean and variance of the lead-time demand D^L can be calculated as follows:

$$\mu_L = E(D^L) = E(d_1) + E(d_2) + \cdots + E(d_L) = L \times \mu,$$

$$\sigma_L^2 = \text{var}(D^L) = \text{var}(d_1) + \text{var}(d_2) + \cdots + \text{var}(d_L) = L \times \sigma^2.$$

It is interesting to note that both the mean and variance of the sum of i.i.d. demand over L periods are L multiplied by the original mean and variance. Thus, we can denote the lead-time demand as $D^L \sim \left(\mu_L, \sigma_L^2\right) = (L\mu, L\sigma^2)$, with its mean and standard deviation given as:

$$\mu_L = L\mu \text{ and } \sigma_L^2 = L\sigma^2,$$

where μ and σ are the mean and standard deviation of the original demand (e.g., daily demand in this example). The mean of the aggregate demand over L periods is L times the original mean demand, and the standard deviation of the aggregate demand is $\sqrt{L}$ times the original standard deviation.

Note that an aggregate demand is in fact the **sum** of individual demand variables over a certain L number of periods. It is important to note that the sum of L i.i.d variables is different from the *multiplication* of an individual demand variable by L. For example, let us consider the reorder point R that is estimated by the multiplication of demand d_1, by a factor of L; that is:

$$R = \text{estimated lead-time demand} = L \times d_1.$$

Note that the variance of this estimate is fundamentally different, as demonstrated below:

$$E(R) = E(L \times d_1) = L \times \mu = \mu_L,$$

$$\text{var}(R) = \text{var}(L \times d_1) = L^2 \times \sigma^2 = L \times (L \times \sigma^2) = L \times \sigma_L^2.$$

We can see from the above that this estimate of lead-time demand (R) incurs a variance that is L times as large as the variance of the lead-time demand D^L.

Next, we consider lead-time demand D^L when the lead-time L is also a random variable. Suppose that the **variable lead-time** L is independent of the demand with a constant mean $E(L)$ and a constant variance $\text{var}(L)$. For the lead-time demand under **variable lead-time**, we have:

$$\mu_L = E\left(D^L\right) = E\left(\sum_{i=1}^{L} d_i\right) = E_L\left(E\left(\sum_{i=1}^{L} d_i \bigg| L\right)\right) = E_L\left(L \times \mu\right) = E(L) \times \mu,$$

$$\sigma_L^2 = \text{var}\left(D^L\right) = \text{var}\left(\sum_{i=1}^{L} d_i\right) = E(L) \times \sigma^2 + \text{var}(L) \times \mu^2.$$

The variance of lead-time demand under a variable lead-time contains an extra non-negative term, $\text{var}(L) \times \mu^2$. In summary, the variability of demand over lead-time is an increasing function of the length of the lead-time, and uncertainty in the lead-time will further increase the variability in lead-time demand. To appreciate the implications of such a property, let us revisit the piston inventory system at Quick-Engine under uncertain demand.

Returning to Example 3.4, the daily demand for the QE-1 engine is denoted by d^e, with $E(d^e) = 250$ and $var(d^e) = 64$. The daily engine demand is given as $d^e \sim IID(250, 8^2)$. As each engine requires four pistons, the daily demand for pistons can be expressed as:

$$d = \text{daily demand for pistons} = 4 \times d^e.$$

Thus, the mean and variance of the daily piston demand can be calculated as:

$$\mu = E(\text{daily piston demand}) = E(4 \times d^e) = 4 \times 250 = 1,000,$$

$$\sigma^2 = var(\text{daily piston demand}) = var(4 \times d^e) = 4^2 \times 64 = 1,024 = 32^2.$$

In short, we denote the daily piston demand as $d \sim N(1000, 32^2)$. Given a constant lead-time of 3 days, the lead-time demand is the sum of demand over 3 days:

$$D^L = d_1 + d_2 + d_3, d_i \sim IIDN(1000, 32^2) \text{ for } i = 1, 2, 3.$$

Then, we compute:

$$\mu_L = E(D^L) = 3 \times E(\text{daily piston demand}) = 3 \times 1,000 = 3,000,$$

$$\sigma_L^2 = var(D^L) = 3 \times var(\text{daily piston demand}) = 3 \times 1,024 = 3072 = 55.43^2,$$

$$\sigma_L = \sqrt{var(D^L)} = \sqrt{3 \times 1,024} = 55.43.$$

Assuming 360 working days a year, the mean and variance of the annual demand D can be obtained as:

$$\bar{D} = E(D) = 360 \times E(\text{daily piston demand}) = 360 \times 1,000 = 360,000,$$

$$var(D) = 360 \times var(\text{daily piston demand}) = 360 \times 1,024 = 368,640$$
$$= 607.16^2,$$

$$\sigma_D = \sqrt{var(D)} = \sqrt{360 \times 1,024} = 607.16.$$

For convenience, we summarize that given i.i.d. demand $d_t \sim (\mu, \sigma^2)$, then:
(1) n times d_t: $n \times d_t \sim n\mu, (n\sigma)^2$ and
(2) L sum of d_t: $(d_1 + d_2 + \cdots + d_L) \sim (L\mu, L\sigma^2)$.

Reorder point, demand over lead-time, and service level

We have learned that the reorder point R is intended to cover the demand over lead-time L. When demand is uncertain, so is the demand over lead-time $D^L \sim (\mu_L, \sigma_L^2)$. Clearly, it will become out of stock if the reorder point is insufficient to cover the lead-time demand (i.e., if $R < D^L$). The SL, i.e., the in-stock probability, can then be expressed as:

$$\text{SL} = \text{Pr(sufficient inventory to meet lead-time demand)} = \text{Pr}\left(D^L \leq R\right).$$

According to the newsboy analysis described in Chapter 1, the reorder point R can be determined in terms of safety stock (ss) as follows:

$$R = \mu_L + \text{ss} = \mu_L + z \times \sigma_L,$$

where z is uniquely determined from a desired SL. Again, reduced variability in lead-time demand will achieve the same SL with less safety stock.

Reducing variability by bundling

The variability of an exogenous demand process is not generally subject to direct control within an order system. However, demand variability can be reduced indirectly. As shown previously, because the aggregated variability in demand over a time interval is an increasing function of both the average length and the variability of that time interval, variability can be reduced along two general dimensions: **time-wise** and **item-wise** reduction. **Lead-time reduction** represents the key time-wise method of reducing variability, while **aggregation** is the typical item-wise reduction method.

The **lead-time reduction** method is based on the fact that demand variability increases as the lead-time increases. For example, suppose that Quick-Engine in Example 3.4 has worked with the supplier and found a way to reduce the lead-time from 3 days to 2 days. Then, under the same daily demand process, the variance in demand over a 2-day lead-time can be computed as:

$$\sigma_L^2 = \text{var}\left(D^L\right) = 2 \times \text{var(daily piston demand)} = 2 \times 1,024 = 2,048 = 45.25^2.$$

By reducing the lead-time by 1 day, the standard deviation of 55.43 with a 3-day lead-time is reduced by 18 percent to 45.25, as verified by:

$$\text{Variability reduction (by lead-time reduction)} = \frac{55.43 - 45.25}{55.43}$$
$$\approx 0.18 = 18 \text{ percent.}$$

Common **aggregation** methods for reducing variability include **bundling** and **risk pooling**. First we will illustrate **bundling**, again using Quick-Engine as an example. Suppose that Quick-Engine has decided to stop buying individual pistons from the supplier. Instead, Quick-Engine only releases its engine production plan to the supplier, and the supplier is asked to bundle four pistons into one kit, which corresponds to one QE-1 engine. That is, the daily usage of piston kits is equal to the daily demand for the QE-1 engine. With the order quantity now expressed as the number of kits, the variance in piston demand over the 3-day lead-time becomes:

$$\sigma_L^2 = 3 \times \text{var(daily piston demand in kits)} = 3 \times 64 = 192 = 13.86^2.$$

Given the same daily engine demand and 3-day lead-time, bundling will reduce the variability of piston demand over the lead-time by about 75 percent:

$$\text{Variability reduction} = \frac{55.43 - 13.86}{55.43} \approx 0.75 = 75\,\text{percent}.$$

Implementation of bundling strategy: VPM and VMI

There are two important methods for implementing a bundling strategy: vender-planned materials (**VPM**) and vender-managed inventory (**VMI**). Under a **VPM** program the manufacturer (e.g., Quick-Engine) issues its MPS (master production schedule) to the supplier(s) (e.g., the piston supplier) in advance to allow lead-time for supply delivery. The supplier(s) then plan and deliver the required supplies to meet the MPS. In a sense, VPM delegates the task of materials planning from the manufacturer to the supplier. In contrast, under a VMI arrangement, supplier(s) will manage the inventory at the manufacturer's facility according to the manufacturer's production schedule. In this case, the piston supplier will directly stock and replenish the piston inventory at Quick-Engine.

Bundling is implemented in both VPM and VMI; that is, both will "bundle" the materials into the end product by delegating the "material explosion" to the supplier(s). In Example 3.4, Quick-Engine only works on the master schedules for engine production, without exploding them into components such as pistons, under either VPM or VMI. Rather, the materials explosion from the MPS is conducted by the supplier(s) in both VPM and VMI. The key differences between VPM and VMI include:

1   With VPM, the inventory of supplies is held at the supplier's facility, whereas in a VMI system the inventory is directly held and managed at the manufacturer's facility.
2   With VPM, purchase orders must be issued before delivery of the needed supplies, whereas supplies are usually shipped to and used by the manufacturer before the bill for the used supplies is paid.

VMI is perceived to incur a higher risk of information leaking, due to the mixed working environment. Figure 3.9 illustrates the differences between VPM and VMI systems.

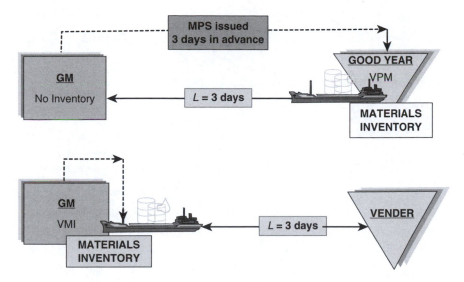

Figure 3.9 VPM versus VMI systems.

Reducing variability by risk pooling

If bundling is an aggregation across items, then risk pooling can be considered an aggregation across locations. Next, we illustrate risk pooling with an example.

Example 3.5   Risk pooling in inbound logistics at Quick-Engine

Consider two assembly plants for the QE-1 stand-by generator at Quick-Engine: plant 1 and plant 2, as depicted in Figure 3.10. Plant 1 is the original final assembly facility, and plant 2 is a facility newly acquired through a recent merger, which is located about 20 miles away from plant 1 and has an identical assembly capacity. Each of the two plants is designated to one half of the US market, each facing an i.i.d. normal daily demand with a mean of 125 and a variance of 32 (i.e., $d_i^e \sim N(125, 5.66^2)$, $i = 1, 2$). The pistons are supplied by the same supplier with a 3-day lead-time. As shown in Figure 3.10, each assembly plant has its own inbound piston stock (i.e., stock 1 or stock 2). The management at Quick-Engine requires an 87 percent SL (in-stock probability) across the two plants. Specifically, each plant needs to determine a minimum stock level for pistons, with which there is an 87 percent chance of meeting demand over the 3-day lead-time.

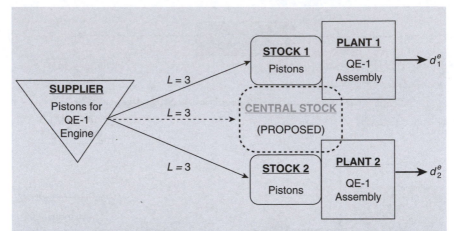

Figure 3.10 Inbound piston stock areas at Quick-Engine: (a) without risk pooling and (b) with risk pooling.

Question: Quick-Engine is considering a proposal to combine the two piston stock areas into one centralized inbound stock center. It will incur the same 3-day lead-time because it is to be located in-between the two current stock areas. With the same 87 percent SL requirement, compute the piston stock levels before and after centralizing the stock areas.

Let us start by computing the annual demand at each of the two plants. Suppose that the daily engine demand at plants 1 and 2 $\left(d_1^e \text{ and } d_2^e\right)$ are both $N(125, 5.66^2)$ and that each engine requires four pistons. The piston demand over the lead-time, denoted by D_1^L and D_2^L, respectively, can then be calculated as follows (assuming 360 working days in a year).

For plant i:

$$\bar{D}_i^L = E(D_i^L) = L \times E(4 \times d_i^e) = 3 \times (4 \times 125) = 1{,}500,$$

$$\mathrm{var}(D_i^L) = L \times \mathrm{var}(4 \times d_i^e) = 3 \times 16 \times 32 = 1{,}536 = 39.19^2.$$

Decentralized piston stocking

Denoting the **minimum stock level** (also termed the **reorder point**) at plants 1 and 2 by R_1 and R_2, respectively, the SL at each plant $i(i = 1, 2)$ can be expressed as:

$$\mathrm{SL} = \mathrm{Pr}\left(D_i^L \leq R_i\right), (i = 1, 2).$$

Imposing an 87 percent SL at each assembly plant, we can determine a z-value by setting:

$$\Pr(Z \leq z) = 0.87.$$

It can thus be determined from a Standard Normal Table that $z(0.87) = 1.13$ (i.e., $\Pr(Z \leq 1.13) = 0.87$). We can then compute the **reorder point** at each plant i in a similar way to the newsboy problem, as follows:

$$R_i = E(D_i^L) + z(0.87) \times \sqrt{\mathrm{var}(D_i^L)} = 1{,}500 + 1.13 \times 39.19 \approx 1{,}544 \, (i = 1, 2).$$

Note that each plant carries 44 pistons as safety stock, in addition to the average lead-time demand of 1,500. Therefore, at the aggregate level, a total of 88 units of safety stock and 3,000 units in total lead-time demand must be held to maintain an 87 percent SL across the board.

Centralized piston stocking

Now, let us consider the **reorder point** after the two piston stock areas are combined into one. The aggregate piston demand at the centralized stock area, denoted as D_c^L, will be the sum of the two piston demands, D_1^L and D_2^L. That is:

$$D_c^L = D_1^L + D_2^L \sim N(3000, 3072) = N(3000, 55.43^2).$$

With the same 87 percent SL, the **reorder point** at the central piston stock area, R_c, can be determined from $\Pr(D_c^L \leq R_c) = 0.87$ (with $z = 1.13$) as follows:

$$R_c = E(D_c^L) + z \times \sqrt{\mathrm{var}(D_c^L)} = 3{,}000 + 1.13 \times 55.43 \approx 3{,}063.$$

In this case, only 63 units of safety stock (in addition to the average lead-time demand of 3,000 pistons) are needed to achieve an 87 percent SL across the board, compared with the 88 units of safety stock that was needed before centralization of the stock area. By centralizing the stock area, it is possible to achieve the same level of service with a reduced safety stock. In fact, the percentage reduction in safety stock for Example 3.5 is actually 28.8 percent, computed as follows:

$$\frac{88 - 63}{88} = 0.288 = 28.8 \, \text{percent}.$$

Such a reduction in inventory stock is explained as the effect of **risk pooling**. By combining the two inbound inventory stocks, we can offset the fluctuations in separate market demands. Intuitively, it is more likely that the two demands are nonsynchronized, and it is often the case that one is upward and the other is downward. Thus, with combined safety stock, it is easy to allocate safety stock laterally to meet the aggregate demand. Figure 3.11 presents a comparison of piston stocking decisions with and without risk pooling.

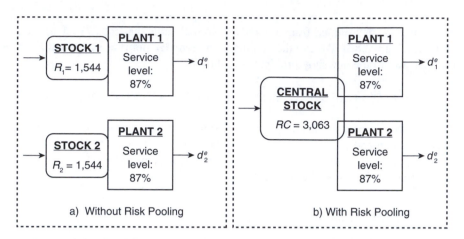

Figure 3.11 Comparison of piston stocks with versus without risk pooling.

Limitations of risk pooling

The major limitations of risk pooling are the constraints on the location of centralized stocking sites:

1   A feasible central location may be unavailable.
2   Centralization of the inventory stock may be too costly, and therefore not financially justified.
3   Centralization of inventory stock may result in uneven lead-times due to differing distances to the central stocking area, and in some cases may prolong lead-times and thereby increase the variability.

Implementation of risk pooling

Risk pooling by centralized inventory is not always plausible and feasible. It is therefore important to examine carefully the feasibility and merit of applying risk pooling to specific situations. There are some useful points for consideration in implementing risk pooling.

1   The effect of risk pooling should be examined and evaluated carefully before it is adopted.
2   The lead-times under risk pooling should be as balanced as possible.
3   In practice, virtual centralization of the inventory can be achieved using information technology. For example, the physical stocking of inventory items is decentralized, whereas the database and information system for inventory management are centralized.

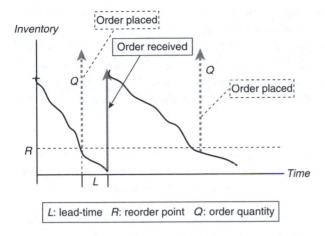

Figure 3.12 Reorder-point inventory system.

Repetitive order system under uncertain demand

Reorder-point fixed-order system with constant lead-time

When market demand fluctuates in an uncertain manner, safety stock will be needed when considering the reorder point because it is no longer possible to predict the inventory position with certainty. In the case of a fixed-order system, the reorder point must contain an element of safety stock that is solely determined by the variability in demand over the lead-time, as depicted in Figure 3.12.

Safety stock in the supply chain represents an extra inventory of goods and capacity to protect against uncertainty. As we proceed, it will become apparent that the backorder cost needs to be taken into account under uncertain demand. Let us continue with the reorder-point order system at Quick-Engine as introduced in Example 3.1, filling in the necessary demand and cost data.

Example 3.6 Reorder-point system for pistons at Quick-Engine with a given SL

Suppose that daily demand for the QE-1 stand-by generator at Quick-Engine presents an i.i.d. normal variable with a mean of 250 and a variance of 64. Each QE-1 engine requires four pistons, which are purchased from a single supplier with a 3-day response time. The engine cell operates under a reorder-point system for 360 working days per year. The cost data are given as follows: each piston costs $25 to purchase from the supplier; the cost of setting up an order transaction with the supplier is estimated as $250 per purchase order; and the cost of holding each piston for 1 year is given as 20 percent of the price when it was purchased.

Question: Suppose that the management requires an 87 percent SL (i.e., the in-stock probability). Determine what the reorder point R and order quantity Q for piston ordering at Quick-Engine should be, to minimize the expected annual cost while maintaining the required 87 percent SL.

Similar to a deterministic system, the annual inventory cost can be based on the average cost per order cycle, consisting of three cost components: **holding, setup,** and **stockout** costs. First, consider the **expected annual holding cost,** which is calculated by multiplying the expected average inventory by the unit holding cost c_h. Recall that in a deterministic order system, the average inventory is determined as $Q/2$. However, when demand is uncertain, safety stock (denoted as ss) will be used, which represents extra inventory in addition to the deterministic average inventory:

$$\text{Average inventory with safety stock} = \frac{Q}{2} + \text{ss}.$$

In a reorder-point system, the safety stock is included in the reorder-point calculation in the following manner:

$$R = E(\text{lead-time demand}) + \text{ss} = \mu_L + \text{ss}.$$

Thus, we can express the safety stock as:

$$\text{ss} = R - \mu_L.$$

The average inventory with safety stock can then be expressed as:

$$\frac{Q}{2} + \text{ss} = \frac{Q}{2} + (R - \mu_L).$$

Thus, the expected annual holding cost can be calculated as:

$$c_h \left(\frac{Q}{2} + \text{ss} \right) = c_h \left(\frac{Q}{2} + (R - \mu_L) \right).$$

Now, **consider the expected annual setup cost,** which is computed by multiplying the expected number of orders per year by the unit setup cost c_s. That is:

$$\text{Expected annual setup cost} = c_s \times E(\text{number of orders per year})$$

$$= c_s \frac{E(\text{annual demand})}{Q} = c_s \frac{\bar{D}}{Q},$$

where $\bar{D} = E(\text{annual demand})$. Lastly, we consider the **expected annual stock-out cost** by computing the expected units stocked out per cycle, which is equivalent to the expected units of shortage over the lead-time. Note that a shortage occurs when the reorder point is insufficient to cover the lead-time demand (i.e., $R < D^L$). Thus, the units stocked out per cycle can be expressed as:

$$\text{Units stocked out per cycle} = \max(0, D^L - R) \equiv (D^L - R)^+.$$

The average stockout level can therefore be obtained by dividing the amount of stockout by the expected cycle time. Note that the expected cycle time can be computed as $Q/\bar{D}$. Then, the expected annual stockout cost can be derived as:

$$E(\text{annual stockout cost}) = c_b \frac{E(D^L - R)^+}{E(\text{cycle time})} = c_b \frac{\bar{D} \times E(D^L - R)^+}{Q}$$

$$= c_b \frac{\bar{D} \times L(R)}{Q},$$

where c_b represents the backlog cost (in dollars per unit stocked out), and $L(R) = E(D^L - R)^+$ represents expected units stocked out during the lead-time, termed the **loss function** (or partial expectation). In general, the loss function $L(R)$ cannot be expressed in closed form, and therefore it is computed numerically according to the specific distribution of the underlying demand. The loss function for standard normal demand is defined as:

$$L(z) = E(Z - z)^+,$$

where $Z = D^L - \mu_L/\sigma_L$ represents the standardized lead-time demand, lead-time demand is i.i.d. across order cycles, $D^L \sim \text{IID}(\mu_L, \sigma_L^2)$, and $z = R - \mu_L/\sigma_L$ is a standardized reorder point. The loss function $L(R)$ is related to the standard loss function $L(z)$ by the following equality:

$$L(R) = \sigma_L \times L(z).$$

The proof of the above equality is included as an exercise in Problem 2 at the end of this chapter. The expected annual cost, denoted by $\text{TC}(R,Q)$, can then be expressed as a function of R and Q as follows:

$$\text{TC}(R,Q) = E(\text{holding cost}) + E(\text{setup cost}) + E(\text{stockout cost})$$

$$= c_h \left(\frac{Q}{2} + \text{ss} \right) + c_s \left(\frac{\bar{D}}{Q} \right) + c_b \frac{\bar{D} \times E(D^L - R)^+}{Q}$$

$$= c_h \left(\frac{Q}{2} + (R - \mu_L) \right) + c_s \left(\frac{\bar{D}}{Q} \right) + c_b \frac{\bar{D} \times L(R)}{Q}.$$

The objective is to choose R and Q so as to minimize $TC(R,Q)$. Applying a marginal analysis similar to the Newsboy problem with a fixed order quantity Q, a condition for the optimal reorder solution can be obtained as:

$$F(R) = 1 - \frac{c_h Q}{c_b \bar{D}}, \left(\text{or } 1 - F(R) = \frac{c_h Q}{c_b \bar{D}} \right),$$

where $F(R) = \Pr(D^L \leq R)$ is the in-stock probability (i.e., type A SL). Or, the stockout probability is $1 - F(R)$, which is determined by $c_h Q / c_b \bar{D}$. The above optimality condition can be rigorously obtained by taking the partial derivative of $TC(R,Q)$ with respect to R, in a similar way to the detailed analysis of the Newsboy problem in Chapter 1.

Note that the backlog cost c_b is given in dollars per unit stocked out (i.e., $/unit), and the holding cost is in dollars per unit per time period (i.e., $/unit/year). Given a SL of 87 percent (i.e., $SL = F(R) = 0.87$), we can determine from the optimal solution equations that:

$$Q^* = (1 - F(R)) \times \frac{c_b \bar{D}}{c_h} = (0.13) \times \frac{15 \times (360,000)}{5} = 140,400.$$

Similar to the Newsboy solution, with $SL = F(R) = 0.87$ we can determine from the Standard Normal Table that $z = 1.13$. Given a normal lead-time demand D^L with known $\mu_L = 3,000$ and $\sigma_L = 55.43$, the solution for the reorder point R^* can be determined as:

$$R^* = \mu_L + z \times \sigma_L = 3,000 + (1.13) \times (55.43) = 3062.6.$$

That is, the solution (R^*, Q^*) will ensure an 87 percent SL with a minimized total expected cost. Note that given a prescribed SL, the solution (R^*, Q^*) can be determined without computing the average backorder units during the lead-time, $L(R)$.

In cases where the SL is not prescribed, the backorder cost c_b (in dollars per unit backordered) is then needed and the loss function $L(R)$ must be computed to obtain an optimal solution (R^*, Q^*). When the SL is not prescribed, it can be shown that the optimal solution (R^*, Q^*) must solve the two equations simultaneously:

$$\begin{cases} Q = \sqrt{\dfrac{2\bar{D}\left(c_s + c_b L(R)\right)}{c_h}} \\ F(R) = 1 - \dfrac{c_h Q}{c_b \bar{D}} \end{cases}.$$

Because the loss function $L(R)$ cannot be expressed in closed form, nonanalytical methods, such as numerical iteration and simulation, need to be used to determine the optimal solution (R^*, Q^*), especially when the demand is not normally distributed. To illustrate the numerical iteration method, let us consider the same reorder-point system for QE-1 pistons but without a prescribed SL.

Example 3.7   Reorder-point system for QE-1 pistons with a given backorder cost

Consider the same system as in Example 3.6, except that the management does not require a specific SL but suggests a penalty of $10 for each unit stocked out (i.e., $c_b = \$10$ per unit stocked out).

The objective is to determine a solution (R^*, Q^*) that satisfies both equations simultaneously. To begin the numerical iteration, we first select an initial value of Q using an EOQ formula as follows:

$$Q_0 = \sqrt{\frac{2\bar{D}c_s}{c_h}} = \sqrt{\frac{2(360,000)(250)}{0.2(25)}} = 6,000.$$

Then we can compute the initial SL resulting from Q_0:

$$F(R_0) = 1 - \frac{c_h Q_0}{c_b \bar{D}} = 1 - \frac{5(6,000)}{10(360,000)} = 0.9917.$$

It can be determined from the Standard Normal Table that:

$$z_0 = 2.3940 \, (\text{i.e.,} \Pr(Z \leq 2.3940) \approx 0.9917),$$

and

$$R_0 = \mu_L + z_0 \times \sigma_L = 3,000 + (2.3940) \times (55.43) = 3,133.$$

It can then be determined from the *standard* loss function table that $L(z_0) = L(2.39) = 0.0028$. The regular loss function can then be computed as:

$$L(R_0) = \sigma_L \times L(z_0) = 55.43 \times (0.0028) = 0.1552.$$

This concludes the initial iteration with an initial iterative solution (R_0, Q_0). Now, we proceed to the next iteration (denoted by *iteration* 1), and obtain an *iteration* 1 solution (R_1, Q_1). We can complete iteration 1 with the following computations:

$$Q_1 = \sqrt{\frac{2\bar{D}\left(c_s + c_b L(R_0)\right)}{c_h}} = \sqrt{\frac{2(360,000)(250 + 10 \times 0.1552)}{0.2(25)}} = 6,019,$$

$$F(R_1) = 1 - \frac{c_h Q_1}{c_b \bar{D}} = 1 - \frac{5(6,019)}{10(360,000)} = 0.9916,$$

$$z_1 = 2.3928 \, (\text{i.e.,} \Pr(Z \leq 2.3928) \approx 0.9916),$$

$$R_1 = \mu_L + z_1 \times \sigma_L = 3,000 + (2.3938) \times (55.43) = 3,133.$$

Thus, the solution (R_1, Q_1) is obtained for iteration 1. Compared with the previous solution, we can see that the solutions are converging to (R_1, Q_1) if we continue the iterative computations. Therefore, we can conclude that the optimal solution is $R^* \approx 3,133$ and $Q^* \approx 6,019$. In general, such an iterative procedure can be continued until acceptable convergence is achieved. Note that safety stock (ss) is given as:

$$ss = z \times \sigma_L = 133 \, (\text{units}).$$

If the demand is deterministic (i.e., $\sigma = 0$), there is no need for safety stock (ss $= 0$). This can be further verified by comparison with the reorder point ($R = 3,000$) obtained in Example 3.2, in which demand is deterministic. If it is preferable to specify the reorder point and safety stock in time (e.g., in days), they can be computed as follows:

$$\text{Reorder point (in time)}: R^t = \frac{\text{reorder-point in units}}{\text{average demand rate}} = \frac{R}{E(d_t)}$$

$$= \frac{3,133}{1,000} = 3.1 \, (\text{days}),$$

$$\text{Safety stock (in time)}: ss^t = \frac{\text{safety stock in units}}{\text{average demand rate}} = \frac{ss}{E(d_t)}$$

$$= \frac{133}{1,000} = 0.1 \, (\text{days}).$$

Note that the above conversion to time measure is applicable when the average demand is stationary (i.e., the expected demand $E(d_t)$ is a constant).

Other common repetitive order systems

Min-max (s,S) order system

A min-max order system can be considered to be an immediate variant of the reorder-point (R,Q) system, by letting $s = R$ and $S = R + Q$. Both the reorder-point and min-max systems are make-to-stock, and only differ in their implementation schemes. Let us recap on the ordering mechanism of inventory systems. An inventory order decision q_t comprises two elements: time of order and size of order. The time to place an order is given by the reorder point R in a reorder-point system, and by a min-level s in a min-max system. The order size is given as Q

in a reorder-point system, and is determined from the max-level (i.e., order-up-to level) S.

Lot-for-lot order system

Recall from Chapter 2 that a lot-for-lot order system is of the make-to-order type, in the sense that orders are placed on a period-by-period basis. Given a fixed lead-time L, a lot-for-lot order q_t, which is to be released at the end of the current period t, is intended to meet the gross requirement (the demand) in a lead-time-length future, plus backorders, if any. Suppose that the demand in period t is realized as d_t and the actual ending inventory is recorded as x_t (a negative x_t indicates backorders pending). Due to the lead-time L, an order q_{t+1} that is released now (i.e., at the beginning of period $t+1$) will be due to arrive in L periods, by the beginning of period $t+L+1$, and therefore will be available for consumption in period $t+L+1$. Suppose that the ending inventory for the period $t+L$ is estimated as $\hat{x}_{t+L}$, and the demand in period $t+L+1$ is estimated as $\hat{d}_{t+L+1}$. Then, the current planned order release q_{t+1} can be determined as:

$$q_{t+1} = \max\left\{0, (\hat{d}_{t+L+1} - \hat{x}_{t+L})\right\} = \begin{cases} \hat{d}_{t+L+1} - \hat{x}_{t+L}, & \text{if } \hat{d}_{t+L+1} - \hat{x}_{t+L} > 0 \\ 0, & \text{otherwise} \end{cases}.$$

The estimate $\hat{x}_{t+L}$ is determined from the updates of inventory records and scheduled order receipts in the pipeline. A negative $\hat{x}_{t+L}$ means that projected backorders will be pending by the end of period $t+L$, which will be added on to the current order release q_{t+1}. To illustrate the transactions under lot-for-lot ordering, let us consider how the same QE-1 piston inventory system would work under a lot-for-lot ordering scheme.

Example 3.8   Lot-for-lot orders of pistons at Quick-Engine

Consider the same piston inventory system with the same cost data as given in Example 3.7, and given an updated forecast of daily piston demand of 1,030 pistons per day (i.e., $\hat{d}_{t+1} = \hat{d}_{t+2} = \cdots = 1,030$). Note that there is a 3-day lead-time. Now, the pistons are ordered under a lot-for-lot order policy. Suppose that an initial inventory of 133 pistons is available at the current time t (i.e., $x_t = 133$), and 1,000 pistons are scheduled to arrive on each of the following 3 days (lead-time) via previous orders. The initial conditions are summarized in Table 3.1.

Table 3.1 Lot-for-lot pistons order transactions ($L = 3$)

	L = 3				
	t	t+1	t+2	t+3	t+4
Daily requirement		$\hat{d}_{t+1}$	$\hat{d}_{t+2}$	$\hat{d}_{t+3}$	$\hat{d}_{t+4}$
		1,030	1,030	1,030	1,030
Scheduled receipt		1,000	1,000	1,000	[ ]
End inventory	133	$[\hat{x}_{t+1}]$	$[\hat{x}_{t+2}]$	$[\hat{x}_{t+3}]$	
Lot-for-lot order release		q_{t+1}			

Question: Determine a lot-for-lot order q_{t+1} released at the beginning of period $t+1$, which is due in 3 days.

First, we compute a projected ending inventory $\hat{x}_{t+L} = \hat{x}_{t+3}$ (i.e., the marked cell in Table 3.1). Given the initial inventory of $x_t = 133$, we can determine the projected on-hand inventory by the end of the lead-time interval as follows:

$$\hat{x}_{t+3} = x_t - (\text{total estimate of shortage over leadtime})$$
$$= 133 - (30 + 30 + 30) = 43.$$

Then, the lot-for-lot order q_{t+1}, which is to be released at the beginning of period $t+1$ and is due for receipt by the beginning of period $t+4$, can be calculated as:

$$q_{t+1} = \hat{d}_{t+4} - \hat{x}_{t+3} = 1,030 - 43 = 987.$$

This ordering process will then be repeated period by period. For example, the next day (i.e., the end of period $t+1$), the system status including the projected on-hand inventory will be updated and another order will be generated, and so on. Let us walk through a couple of iterations, starting with day 0 (i.e., $t+0$). For $t+0$, given the initial ending inventory x_0, the order release at the beginning of day 1 is $q_1 = 987$, which will arrive at the beginning of day 4, as depicted in Table 3.2.

Suppose that it is now the end of day 1, and the actual piston demand realized in day 1 is $d_1 = 1045$ (indicated with underlined boldface in Table 3.3). The ending inventory is updated at the end of day 1, as follows:

Table 3.2 Initial lot-for-lot order release ($t = 0$)

	L = 3				
	0	*1*	*2*	*3*	*4*
Daily requirement		$\hat{d}_{t+1}$	$\hat{d}_{t+2}$	$\hat{d}_{t+3}$	$\hat{d}_{t+4}$
		1,030	1,030	1,030	1030
Scheduled receipt		1,000	1,000	1,000 ⤑	[987]
End inventory	133	[103]	[73]	[43]	
Lot-for-lot order release		q_1			

$$x_1 = x_0 + SR_1 - d_1 = 133 + 1,000 - 1,045 = 88,$$

where $SR_1 = q_{-2} = 1,000$ is the scheduled receipt for day 1, which was released 3 days ago. The ending inventory was originally projected to be 103, as shown in Table 3.2. However, the actual ending inventory by day 1 is 88, thus the following inventory projections must be also updated accordingly, as shown in Table 3.3.

With the forecast $\hat{d}_5 = 1,030$, the next order release by day 1 can be determined: $q_2 = \hat{d}_5 - \hat{x}_4 = 1,030 - (-15) = 1,045$, as in Table 3.3 with all updates indicated in underlined boldface.

In general, a **lot-for-lot order procedure** can be summarized as follows:

At the end of each period t (given lead-time L):

- obtain sample demand d_t;
- update the actual ending inventory status:

$$x_t = x_{t-1} + SR_t - d_t, \text{ where } SR_t = q_{t-L};$$

- obtain forecasts for the following $L+1$ periods, that is, $\hat{d}_{t+1}, \hat{d}_{t+2}, \dots \hat{d}_{t+L+1}$, and update the projected ending inventory for the next L periods, as follows:

$$\hat{x}_{t+i} = \hat{x}_{t+i-1} + SR_{t+i} - \hat{x}_{t+i} \ (i = 1, 2, \dots, L, \text{ with } \hat{x}_t = x_t), \text{ and especially}$$

$$\hat{x}_{t+L} = \hat{x}_{t+L-1} + SR_{t+L} - \hat{x}_{t+L} = \left(\hat{x}_{t+L-2} + SR_{t+L-1} - \hat{x}_{t+L-1} \right) + SR_{t+L} - \hat{x}_{t+L}$$

$$= x_t + \left(SR_{t+1} + \dots + SR_{t+L} \right) - \left(\hat{d}_{t+1} + \dots + \hat{d}_{t+L} \right)$$

$$= x_t + \left(q_{t-L+1} + \dots + q_t \right) - \left(\hat{d}_{t+1} + \dots + \hat{d}_{t+L} \right)$$

$$= x_t + \sum_{i=1}^{L} q_{t-i+1} - \sum_{i=1}^{L} \hat{d}_{t+i}; \text{ and}$$

Table 3.3 Updates with demand actual by the end of day 1 ($t = 1$)

	L = 3					
	0	1	2	3	4	5
Daily requirement		$\hat{d}_{t+1}$	$\hat{d}_{t+2}$	$\hat{d}_{t+3}$	$\hat{d}_{t+4}$	$\hat{d}_{t+5}$
		1,030	1,030	1,030	1,030	1,030
Demand actual		**1,045**				
Scheduled rec.		1,000	1,000	1,000	[987]..➤	[1,045]
End inventory	133	**[88]**	**[58]**	**[28]**------	**[−15]**	
Lot-for-lot order release		q_1	1,045			

- Determine the lot-for-lot order release by the beginning of period $t+1$ as

$$q_{t+1} = \max\left\{0, \hat{d}_{t+L+1} - \hat{x}_{t+L}\right\}, \text{where } \hat{x}_{t+L} = x_t + \sum_{i=1}^{L} q_{t-i+1} - \sum_{i=1}^{L} \hat{d}_{t+1}.$$

Multiple-item repetitive order systems

ABC inventory classification by 80-20 rule

When there are large numbers of different items in a repetitive order system, it is suggested that an inventory manager classify the items into groups, according to certain classification criteria. A common classification criterion is the so-called 80-20 rule, which was first observed by Vilfredo Pareto in 1897 regarding the distribution of income and wealth in Italy. He concluded:

> A large percentage of the total income was concentrated in the hands of a small percentage of the population in a proportion of roughly 80 percent to 20 percent, respectively.

Since then, Pareto's law has found wide application in business and the 80-20 rule is often observed in business operations. That is, roughly 80 percent of a firm's sales are typically generated by 20 percent of the product line items. Applying the 80-20 rule to a multiple-item inventory system, the inventory items can be classified into A, B, and C groups:

> **Class A inventory**: the top 20 percent of items that generate about 80 percent of the sales.
> **Class B inventory**: the next 30 percent of items.
> **Class C inventory**: the bottom 50 percent of items.

The above three classes of inventory bear differing characteristics, and should therefore be dealt with according to different ordering policies. For instance, the inventory status of class A items should be closely monitored because they account for the major share of total revenue. If possible, a high turnover ratio should be established for the class A inventory, typically with a make-to-order production scheme. The class C items, however, need only a minimum level of control. For inexpensive C items with a moderate volume of demand, make-to-stock with a large lot size would be most suitable. For relatively expensive C items with low demand volume, make-to-order with a near-zero inventory stock is typically adopted.

Example 3.9   Managing inbound inventory by the 80-20 rule

Consider the top 20 outsourced parts for the QE-1 generator product line, as listed in Table 3.4. For convenience, the 20 items are renumbered in ascending order (marked as PT #). Quick-Engine decides to establish an ABC classification of these 20 items, and imposes requirements on the annual inventory turnover as follows: seven turns per year for A items, five turns for B items, and three turns for C items.

Table 3.4 Selected 20 parts for QE-1 line

Item ID	PT #	Price	Annual demand
QE-1101	1	22.50	26,000
QE-1102	2	28.00	470
QE-1103	3	17.50	2,500
QE-1110	4	7.50	40,000
QE-1201	5	44.50	6,500
QE-1205	6	61.00	22,000
QE-1208	7	31.00	12,500
QE-1212	8	13.20	78,000
QE-1305	9	128.00	1,400
QE-1310	10	249.95	30,000
QE-1312	11	77.50	2,400
QE-1315	12	6.75	7,000
QE-1317	13	2.50	5,500
QE-1401	14	38.90	57,500
QE-1405	15	77.00	6,500
QE-1413	16	62.25	8,000
QE-1420	17	8.50	12,500
QE-1440	18	7.75	60,000
QE-1511	19	12.30	5,000
QE-1520	20	40.50	1,200

First, applying the 80-20 rule, we establish an ABC inventory classification using the following procedure.

- Re-rank all the items in descending order according to the annual usage in dollars.
- Classify the top 20 percent of items as class A and compute the cumulative value of the group in dollars, which typically amounts to around 80 percent of the total value of annual sales.
- Identify the next 30 percent of items as class B, and compute the cumulative dollar value.
- Identify the bottom 50 percent of the item as the C-class group, and compute the value.

The results of the ABC classification are presented in Table 3.5, where the 20 items are now listed according to their dollar value in descending order. Each of the three classes can then be treated as a single "composite" item (or as a single group). The total value of annual sales for the 20 items is $15,831,560. As shown in Table 3.5, the top 20 percent of items (top four items) account for 76 percent of the total value. The B group (the next 30 percent of items) accounts for 18 percent of the total value. The C group (the remaining 50 percent of the items) accounts for only 6 percent of the total value.

Different inventory policies can then be created for different groups of items. For example, A items are closely monitored and are turned over more frequently, whereas C items are monitored and turned around less frequently.

Note that seven inventory turnovers per year need to be created for A items, five turnovers for B items, and three for C items. To ensure seven turnovers for the A group, the volume per turnover for each of the four items in the group can be determined by dividing the annual demand for each item by seven, as follows:

$$\text{Volume per turnover for QE-1310} = \frac{30,000}{7} \approx 4,286$$

$$\text{Volume per turnover for QE-1401} = \frac{57,500}{7} \approx 8,214$$

$$\text{Volume per turnover for QE-1205} = \frac{22,000}{7} \approx 3,143$$

$$\text{Volume per turnover for QE-1212} = \frac{78,000}{7} \approx 11,143.$$

Similarly, the volume per turnover for group B can be computed by dividing the annual demand by five, and dividing by three for group C. In general, the turnover of A items will be faster, and will therefore have a lower stock level, compared with the B or C items.

Table 3.5 ABC classification of the selected 20 parts for QE-1 line

Item ID	PT #	Price	Annual demand	$ value	$ cumulative	Grouping
QE-1310	10	249.95	30,000	7,498,500	7,498,500	**A group:**
QE-1401	14	38.90	57,500	2,236,750	9,735,250	**20% of items**
QE-1205	6	61.00	22,000	1,342,000	11,077,250	
QE-1212	8	13.20	78,000	1,029,600	12,106,850	**76% of value**
QE-1101	1	22.50	26,000	585,000	12,691,850	
QE-1405	15	77.00	6,500	500,500	13,192,350	**B group:**
QE-1413	16	62.25	8,000	498,000	13,690,350	**30% of items**
QE-1440	18	7.75	60,000	465,000	14,155,350	**18% of value**
QE-1208	7	31.00	12,500	387,500	14,542,850	
QE-1110	4	7.50	40,000	300,000	14,842,850	**94%**
QE-1201	5	44.50	6,500	289,250	15,132,100	
QE-1312	11	77.50	2,400	186,000	15,318,100	**C group:**
QE-1305	9	128.00	1,400	179,200	15,497,300	**50% of items**
QE-1420	17	8.50	12,500	106,250	15,603,550	**6% of value**
QE-1511	19	12.30	5,000	61,500	15,665,050	
QE1520	20	40.50	1,200	48,600	15,713,650	
QE-1315	12	6.75	7,000	47,250	15,760,900	
QE-1103	3	17.50	2,500	43,750	15,804,650	
QE-1317	13	2.50	5,500	13,750	15,818,400	
QE-1102	2	28.00	470	13,160	15,831,560	**100%**
			Annual total = 15,831,560			

Multi-item EOQ model

The ABC classification is applied at an aggregate level, so that proper inventory strategies can be created for different groups of items. At an operational level, however, it is still necessary to determine inventory orders for each item. A simple model for multiple-item ordering decisions is the multi-item EOQ model. First, we introduce proper notation for a multi-item inventory system, such as the one given in Table 3.4.

i: index of items, assuming a total of n items $(i = 1, \ldots, n)$.
D_i: annual demand for item i. For the example of items given in Table 3.4, the annual demand for the first item is 26,000, that is, $D_1 = 26,000$.
P_i: purchase price of item i ($\$$ per unit). From Table 3.4, we can write $P_1 = 22.50$.
c_{s_i}: setup (ordering) cost for item i ($\$$ per order).
c_{h_i}: holding cost for item i ($\$$ per unit per year).

Let Q_i be the **order quantity** for item i (a decision variable), and let r_i be the number of **runs per year** of item i to meet demand D_i. It can be seen that r_i is also the **turns per year** of item i. That is,

$$\text{Number of runs per year for item } i : r_i = \frac{D_i}{Q_i}.$$

We can then write the **total annual cost for item i** as follows:

$$TC_i = P_i \times D_i + c_{s_i} \times \frac{D_i}{Q_i} + c_{h_i} \times \frac{Q_i}{2}.$$

Following a similar argument as for the single-item EOQ model, we obtain EOQ for each item i as:

$$Q_i^* = \sqrt{\frac{2 c_{s_i} D_i}{c_{h_i}}}, (i = 1, 2, \ldots, n).$$

Let us apply the multi-item EOQ model to Example 3.9, with the cost data given in Table 3.6 and an inventory holding factor of 22 percent (i.e., $c_{h_i} = 0.22 \times P_i$).

The EOQ quantity for each item i, Q_i^*, can be computed for $i = 1, 2, \ldots, 20$, using the multi-item EOQ model, and these are shown in the right-hand column of Table 3.6. Note that under the multi-item EOQ model the inventory **runs per year** differ from item to item. For example, we can compute the runs per year for the first two items in Table 3.6 as:

$$r_1 = \frac{D_1}{Q_1} = \frac{26,000}{870} = 30 \,(\text{per year}); \quad r_2 = \frac{D_2}{Q_2} = \frac{470}{77} = 7 \,(\text{per year}).$$

Table 3.6 Cost data for selected 20 parts in Example 3.9

Item ID	Item i	P_i (price)	D_i	c_{s_i}	c_{h_i} (22%)	Q_i^*
QE-1101	1	22.50	26,000	72	4.95	870
QE-1102	2	28.00	470	39	6.16	77
QE-1103	3	17.50	2,500	81	3.85	324
QE-1110	4	7.50	40,000	24	1.65	1079
QE-1201	5	44.50	6,500	68	9.79	300
QE-1205	6	61.00	22,000	85	13.42	528
QE-1208	7	31.00	12,500	53	6.82	441
QE-1212	8	13.20	78,000	12	2.90	803
QE-1305	9	128.00	1,400	26	28.16	51
QE-1310	10	249.95	30,000	18	54.99	140
QE-1312	11	77.50	2,400	34	17.05	98
QE-1315	12	6.75	7,000	27	1.49	505
QE-1317	13	2.50	5,500	30	0.55	775
QE-1401	14	38.90	57,500	19	8.56	505
QE-1405	15	77.00	6,500	22	16.94	130
QE-1413	16	62.25	8,000	29	13.70	184
QE-1420	17	8.50	12,500	16	1.87	462
QE-1440	18	7.75	60,000	32	1.71	1501
QE-1511	19	12.30	5,000	13	2.71	219
QE-1520	20	40.50	1,200	42	8.91	106

Recall that the same number of turns per year is typically required for a given classified group of items using the ABC classification. In this case, the so-called **common-cycle EOQ model** can be considered.

Common-cycle EOQ model

Suppose that each item i in the same group is required to incur a common number of turns per year. Denote r number of turns per year for a group of items. For example, for group A in Example 3.9, we have $r = 7$ and for group B we have $r = 5$, as shown in Table 3.7.

This is referred to as **common-cycle** ordering, as illustrated in Figure 3.13. Common-cycle ordering differs from multi-item EOQ ordering because the order quantity for each item in the same group is subject to the requirement of r common cycles; that is:

$$\text{Order quantity for item } i \text{ with } r \text{ cycles} : Q_i = \frac{D_i}{r}\left(r = \frac{D_i}{Q_i}\right).$$

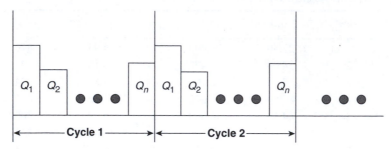

Figure 3.13 Common-cycle ordering systems.

Thus, the cost of a common-cycle order for item i can be derived as:

$$\text{TC}_i = P_i \times D_i + c_{s_i} \times \frac{D_i}{Q_i} + c_{h_i} \times \frac{Q_i}{2} = P_i \times D_i + C_{s_i} \times r + C_{h_i} \times \frac{D_i}{2r}.$$

The total cost across all the items in the same common cycle can then be derived as:

$$\text{TC} = \sum_i \text{TC}_i = \sum_i P_i \times D_i + r \sum_i c_{s_i} + \frac{1}{2r} \sum_i c_{h_i} \times D_i.$$

The common-cycle EOQ problem now becomes how to determine the optimum number of common cycles r^* so that the total cost TC is minimized. Note that the first sum $\sum_i P_i \times D_i$ is independent of the number of runs r (decision variable). According to the principle of marginal equilibrium, the total setup cost is equal to the total holding cost. That is, the following equality holds for r^*:

$$r^* \sum_i c_{s_i} = \frac{1}{2r^*} \sum_i c_{h_i} \times D_i.$$

The optimal number of common cycles can then be obtained as:

$$r^* = \sqrt{\frac{\sum_i c_{h_i} \times D_i}{2 \times \sum_i c_{s_i}}}.$$

Therefore, the common-cycle EOQ for each item i can be calculated as:

$$Q_i^* = \frac{D_i}{r^*} = \frac{D_i \sqrt{2 \times \sum_i c_{s_i}}}{\sqrt{\sum_i c_{h_i} \times D_i}}.$$

Table 3.7 Common-cycle EOQ analysis

Item i	D_i	c_{s_i}	c_{h_i}	$c_{h_i} \times D_i$	r^*	Q_i^*
10	30,000	18	54.99	1,649,670	**A-class:**	300
14	57,500	19	8.56	492,085	**100**	575
6	22,000	85	13.42	295,240		220
8	78,000	12	2.90	226,512		780
1	26,000	72	4.95	128,700	**B-class:**	604.7
15	6500	22	16.94	110,110	**43**	151.2
16	8000	29	13.70	109,560		186.0
18	60000	32	1.71	102,300		1395.3
7	12500	53	6.82	85,250		290.7
4	40000	24	1.65	66,000		930.2
5	6500	68	9.79	63,635	**C-class:**	382.4
11	2400	34	17.05	40,920	**18**	141.2
9	1400	26	28.16	39,424		82.4
17	12500	16	1.87	23,375		735.3
19	5000	13	2.71	13,530		294.1
20	1200	42	8.91	10,692		70.6
12	7000	27	1.49	10,395		411.8
3	2500	81	3.85	9,625		147.1
13	5500	30	0.55	3,025		323.5
2	470	39	6.16	2,895		27.6

Let us compute common-cycle EOQs for group A in Table 3.5, which consists of four items (item # 10, 14, 6, and 8). From the data given in Table 3.6, we can then compute:

$$\sum_i c_{s_i} = c_{s_{10}} + c_{s_{14}} + c_{s_6} + c_{s_8} = 18 + 19 + 85 + 12 = 134,$$

$$\sum_i c_{h_i} D_i = c_{h_{10}} D_{10} + c_{h_{14}} D_{14} + c_{h_6} D_6 + c_{h_8} D_8 = 2,663,507,$$

$$r^* = \sqrt{\frac{\sum_i c_{h_i} \times D_i}{2 \times \sum_i c_{s_i}}} = \sqrt{\frac{2,663,507}{2 \times (134)}} = 99.7 \approx 100.$$

Thus, the common-cycle total cost for group A is minimized when each A-class item turns over 100 times per year. It can be seen that setting the quantity as $Q_i^* = D_i/100$ for each A-class item will ensure 100 runs per year for item i. Given r^*, the common-cycle EOQ for each A-class item i can be determined as $Q_i^* = D_i/r^*$. Detailed calculations are included in Table 3.7.

Following a similar process, common cycle EOQs can be obtained for groups B and C, which are also included in Table 3.7. Briefly, they are summarized as follows:

For B-class items: $\sum_i c_{s_i} = 232,\ \sum_i c_{h_i} \times D_i = 828,432,\ r^* = 42.3 \approx 43$ (rounded up); and

For C-class items: $\sum_i c_{s_i} = 376,\ \sum_i c_{h_i} \times D_i = 217,516,\ r^* \approx 18$ (rounded up).

To conclude this chapter, we will summarize the EOQ ordering procedure for a multi-item inventory system. A two-step procedure is introduced in this section. First, an ABC classification is applied to the multiple items of interests, and the items are grouped into three classes—A, B, and C—according to the 80-20 rule. Next, an EOQ ordering analysis is applied to each of the three groups separately, and then the group-wise, cost-minimizing orders are determined.

Simulation lab: Repetitive order systems (project)

The simulation lab for Chapter 3 is a simulation project for repetitive ordering systems, consisting of four assignments.

Assignment 3.1: Make-by-promise (MBP) repetitive orders at Precision-Motor (PM)

Mr. BB (Big Buyer) at PM (Precision-Motor, Inc.) faces a weekly demand (d_t) for the PM-x1, a high precision AC motor made by Precision-Motor. Suppose that an MPS is given as in Table 3.8.

The production of PM-x1 is planned under a make-by-promise (MBP) system with a fixed manufacturing lead-time of 2 weeks (including manufacturing time and delivery time). Under the MBP target system, at the beginning of each week Mr. BB will assess the pending weekly orders for PM-x1 that are promised for delivery in 2 weeks, and then determine a weekly capacity plan. That is, the released production order is equal to the weekly gross requirements for week t, and is due within 2 weeks. The initial inventory for PM-x1 is assumed to be zero.

A   Help Mr. BB to develop an AP plan for PM-x1 under the MBP target (i.e., to determine a weekly planned capacity level u_t such that the MBP target is met on time). Note that the inventory status is updated weekly.

B   Mr. BB must then plan the ordering of Housing-x1 from an overseas supplier. Each unit costs \$1,200, and requires a one-month lead-time. The setup of each order costs \$2,000, and the weekly holding cost for each Housing-x1 is 30 percent of the purchase cost. The shortage cost is \$850 per unit short. Help Mr. BB to determine the most economical fixed order quantity Q for Housing-x1, which is also the required initial inventory for Housing-x1 (i.e., $I_0 = Q$).

Table 3.8 An MPS

PM-x1	Week					
	1	2	3	4	5	6
Gross requirements	350	350	650	250	250	700

Table 3.9 Demand samples for Assignment 3.1

Sample path	Week					
	d1	d2	d3	D4	d5	d6
1	410	362	621	205	301	781

C Suppose that the actual weekly demand is uncertain, and a sample path of the demand for the next 6 months is obtained by simulation, as shown in Table 3.9. Based on the AP plan for PM-x1 that was obtained in A, develop a weekly adjusted AP for PM-x1 by rolling weekly update against the demand samples given in Table 3.9. *Hint*: Update the AP six times, starting with the first sample d1. Each update propagates up to month 6 (i.e., stay within the 6-month horizon).

D Suppose that the production orders for Housing-x1 remain the same as was determined in B. Compute the actual total costs incurred under the rolling AP obtained in C. (Note: The total cost of Housing-x1 consists of purchasing, holding, setup, and shortage cost components).

Assignment 3.2: EPQ orders for Console-x1 production

Continue with the same situation as outlined in Assignment 3.1. Each PM-x1 consists of a control console (Console-x1), which is built in-house. Now, let us consider how to build the Console-x1 in-house to facilitate the AP plan for PM-x1 production as determined in Assignment 3.1A. The maximum in-house capacity for the console is 800 units per week. Each console costs $5,000 to build (including labor and other operational costs), and the production setup cost is $9,500 per order (or per batch). Weekly holding of each completed console will cost 35 percent of its variable cost (i.e., labor plus operational cost).

A Determine an EPQ for Console-x1 production.
B Use a spreadsheet to simulate the inventory transactions and costs of Console-x1 production under the EPQ orders.

(Continued)

(Continued)

Assignment 3.3 Stocking decision for brush contactor at Precision-Motor

Jerry Schmidt, a materials manager at the Precision-Motor company, needs to determine a "min" (i.e., reorder point) for a brush contactor used in the PM-x1, the best-selling precision motor at the moment. Each PM-x1 requires two brush contactors, which are purchased from a single supplier with a 3-week lead-time. Suppose that weekly demand for the PM-x1 motor is an i.i.d. normal variable with a mean of 600 and a variance of 75 (assume 52 working weeks a year). The company decides to establish a reorder purchasing system for the brush, so that an 85 percent in-stock probability over the lead-time can be achieved.

A   Determine a reorder point for brush stock that will ensure an 85 percent SL.
B   Simulate the reorder system under the reorder point that was obtained in A above. Generate 20 samples of lead-time demand (not weekly demand) and then compute an average percent in-stock over the 20 samples. *Hint*: Compare each lead-time demand sample with the "min."

Assignment 3.4 Risk pooling in inbound logistics at Precision-Motor

Consider two assembly plants for PM-x1 motors at Precision-Motor, as depicted in Figure 3.14. Plant 1 faces an IIDN (i.e., i.i.d. normal) weekly demand, $d_1^m \sim N(625, 25^2)$, and plant 2 faces an IIDN weekly demand, $d_2^m \sim N(375, 21^2)$. Suppose that each PM-x1 consists of two brush contactors, which are provided by a single supplier with a lead-time of 1.5 weeks (one and a half weeks). Currently, each of the two plants maintains its own inbound stock of brush contactors under an 82 percent SL (in-stock probability), as depicted in Figure 3.14.

A   With the same 82 percent SL requirement, compute the brush inbound reorder points (i.e., the "min's") for plants 1 and 2, respectively.
B   Precision-Motor is considering whether to combine the two brush-contactor stock areas into one centralized inbound stock center that will incur the same 1.5-week lead-time. What would be the "min" at the proposed central stock center, to maintain the 82 percent SL?
C   Determine the percentage reduction in safety stock, compared with the total sum of the safety stocks at the two plants before centralizing the stock areas.
D   Generate sample demands for the next 20 weeks for plants 1 and 2. Estimate the simulated SL at the central stock area with the "min" point fixed at the level you determined in B. Compare the simulated SL with the original SL (i.e., 82 percent).

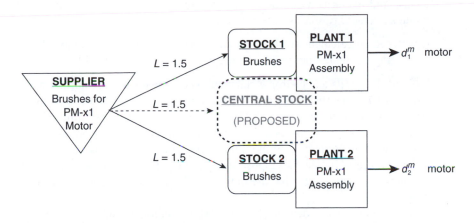

Figure 3.14 Inbound brush stock areas at Precision-Motor, Inc.

Problems

Basic exercises

1   Historical data indicate that the arrival rate of job orders to a Kanban system
    for precision-motor (PM) assembly follows a Poisson distribution with a
    mean of 24 orders per hour. The throughput rate of the Kanban system is also
    Poisson with a mean of 27 order completions per hour.

   (a) Suppose that each job order corresponds to a container that is allocated
       with a Kanban card. Determine the number of total Kanban cards to
       be released into the system, using a Kanban safety factor of 0.5 (i.e.,
       $r = 0.5$).
   (b) Suppose each job order (i.e., each container) for the motor assembly
       requires 120 pairs of stator brushes, which must be purchased from an
       outside supplier with 6 h of lead-time. Each pair of brushes costs $15,
       and it costs $42 to set up each purchase order with the stator supplier.
       The holding cost ($/pair/year) is 22 percent of the price. Assume a total
       of 2,000 working hours per year. Determine how the stators should be
       ordered for the Kanban system to ensure minimal annual inventory
       costs: both the order quantity and reorder point. *Hint*: Consider EOQ
       ordering, and determine a cost-minimizing order quantity (in pairs of
       stator brushes).

2   GlobalCom is considering switching to overseas suppliers for its PLC (pro-
    grammable logic control) board to reduce labor costs. In the United States,
    each PLC board costs $175, whereas overseas it costs $140. Holding costs
    per year are 20 percent of the inventory value, and the demand has been
    fairly steady at 200 units per week. Assume that order costs are $500 both

locally and overseas. Order lead-times are one half-month locally and two months overseas (use 52 weeks per year).

(a) Based on calculations of annual costs, which location is preferable?
(b) Compute the reorder points at the two locations, respectively.

3   Offistuf, Inc. sells an electronic calendar. The annual sales are normal with a mean of 1,000 units and standard deviation of 25. The calendar is ordered from a supplier at the cost of $95 each with a delivery lead-time of 2.5 months. The ordering cost is $750 per order and the inventory holding cost is estimated as 24 percent of the item value. The stockout cost is assumed to be $125 per unit short. Suppose the company is to implement an (Q,R) inventory system. Determine the optimal order quantity Q and the reorder point R.

4   Suppose that weekly demand for the PM-x1 motor, a high-precision AC motor made by Precision-Motor, is an i.i.d. normal variable with a mean of 600 and a variance of 75. (Assume 52 working weeks a year.) Each PM-x1 motor includes two brush contactors, which are purchased from a single supplier with a 3-week lead-time. The company decides to adopt a reorder purchasing system for the brush, and requires an 85 percent in-stock probability over the lead-time. Determine a reorder point for brush stock that will ensure an 85 percent SL.

5   Consider two assembly plants for PM-x1 motors at Precision-Motor, as depicted in Figure 3.15. plant 1 faces an IIDN (i.e., i.i.d. normal) weekly demand, $d_1^m \sim N(625, 25^2)$, and plant 2 faces an IIDN weekly demand, $d_2^m \sim N(375, 21^2)$. Suppose that each PM-x1 consists of two brush contactors, which are provided by a single supplier with a lead-time of 1.5 weeks (one and a half weeks). Currently, each of the two plants maintains its own inbound stock of brush contactors under an 82 percent SL (in-stock probability), as depicted in Figure 3.15.

(a) With the same 82 percent SL requirement, compute the brush inbound reorder points (i.e., the "min's") for plants 1 and 2, respectively.
(b) Precision-Motor is considering whether to combine the two brush-contactor stock areas into one centralized inbound stock center that will incur the same 1.5-week lead-time. What would be the "min" at the proposed central stock center, to maintain the 82 percent SL?
(c) Determine the percentage reduction in safety stock, compared to the total sum of the safety stocks at the two plants before centralizing the stock areas.

6   Consider the same two assembly plants for PM-x1 motors at Precision-Motor, but with a different supplier for the two brush contactors per motor, who requires a reduced lead-time of 1 week, as depicted in Figure 3.16. Under improved market conditions, plant 1 is now facing an IIDN weekly demand, $d_1^m \sim N(700, 35^2)$, and plant 2 is facing an IIDN weekly demand,

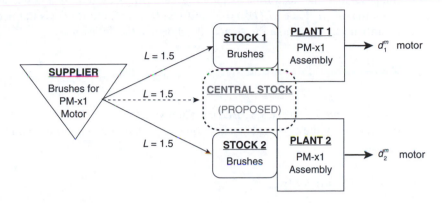

Figure 3.15 (For Problem 3.5): two plants at Precision-Motor, Inc.

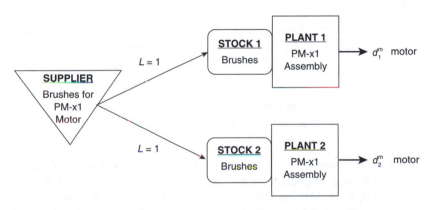

Figure 3.16 (For Problem 3.6): two assembly plants with VMI option.

$d_2^m \sim N(400, 25^2)$. Each of the two plants maintains its own inbound stock of brush contactors under a new 85 percent SL (in-stock probability).

(a) With the same 85 percent SL requirement, compute the brush inbound reorder points (i.e., the "min's") for plants 1 and 2, respectively.
(b) Precision-Motor has decided to adopt VMI for the supply of brush contractors, i.e., the supplier directly manages Stock 1 and 2 areas. With the same 85 percent SL required under VMI, compute the reorder points for VMI stocks at plants 1 and 2, respectively.
(c) Determine and compare the total sum of the safety stocks at the two plants before versus after adopting VMI.

7   Suppose that the lead-time demand in an (R,Q) system is known as: $D^L \sim \text{IID}\left(\mu_L, \sigma_L^2\right)$, i.e., $E(D^L) = \mu_L$ and $\text{var}(D^L) = \sigma_L^2$. (Note: D^L is not necessarily normal.) Denote the standardized demand as follows:

$$Z = \frac{D^L - \mu_L}{\sigma_L}.$$

(a) Show that $Z \sim (0,1)$, i.e., $E(Z) = 0$ and $\text{var}(Z) = 1$.

(b) Show that the expected stockout quantity under a given reorder point R is:

$$E(D^L - R)^+ = \sigma_L \times L(z),$$

where $z = (R - \mu_L)/\sigma_L$ and $L(z) = E(Z - z)^+$ is a standard loss function.

Additional exercises

8   TireTown sells 20,000 tires of a particular type per year. The ordering cost for each order is $40, and the holding cost is 20 percent of the price per year. The purchase price is $20/tire. There is a half-month lead-time for each order.

(a) How many tires should TireTown order each time?

(b) What is the minimum total cost?

(c) What is the reorder point?

9   VirTech faces an annual demand of 3,200 plastic templates for Virtual Prototyping. The templates are manufactured in-house with a production cost of $24 each. With the current capacity, the company can produce 202 templates per week with a setup cost of $52. The holding cost is 14 percent of the production cost. Assume 52 weeks a year.

(a) Compute the EPQ for VirTech.

(b) What is the total cost under the EPQ obtained in (a)?

(c) Compute the cycle time and production time under the EPQ.

10   Medget company, an X-ray image gauge producer, faces an annual demand for 3,000 gauges. Each gauge consists of two light sensors that can be either purchased from a local supplier at $28 each with a lead-time of 3 weeks, or manufactured in-house with a production cost of $25 each. With the current capacity, the company can produce 410 sensors per week with a setup cost of $40, while the ordering cost for purchase is $17. The holding cost is 28 percent of the respective costs of the item. Assume 52 weeks a year.

(a) Based on total costs, should the sensors be purchased or made?

(b) If the management decided to purchase, what reorder point would you recommend?

(c) When made in-house, the finished sensors require a special storage cabinet. The current cabinet can hold up to 200 finished sensors, which then feed into the final assembly of the gauge. Thus, production of the sensor must stop as soon as the finished sensors fill up the storage cabinet. Considering the capacity of the cabinet, should the sensors be purchased or made?

11   Suppose that weekly demand for PM-x1 motor, a high precision AC motor made by Precision-Motor, is an i.i.d. normal variable with a mean of 300 and a variance of 75 (assume 52 working weeks a year). Each PM-x1 motor includes two brush contactors, which are purchased from a single supplier with a 3-week lead-time. The company decides to adopt an (R,Q) inventory system for the brush. Each contactor costs $10, and the holding cost is based on a 40 percent annual rate of interest. The fixed cost of order setup is $28 per order, and the backorder cost is estimated as $9 per unit short.

(a) What are the optimal order size and reorder point for the brush contactor?

(b) What is the optimal safety stock for the contactor?

(c) Suppose that the management at Precision-Motor decides to bundle each pair of brush contactors. The cost for each pair of bundled contractors is $12.5 per pair. Determine the optimal order size, reorder point, and safety stock for the contactor after bundling.

(d) What savings will be made in expected total costs by bundling the contractors in pairs?

Appendix 3A   Loss function

Consider an (R,Q) inventory system under an i.i.d. lead-time demand $D^L \sim \text{IID}\left(\mu_L, \sigma_L^2\right)$, with its distribution function denoted as $F_{D^L}(x)$, and the probability density function as $f_{D^L}(x) = dF_{D^L}(x)/dx$. The loss function, denoted as $L(R)$, is defined to be the expected stockout units per cycle, as follows:

$$L(R) = E(D^L - R)^+ = \int_R^\infty (x - R)dF_{D^L}(x) = \int_R^\infty (x - R)f_{D^L}(x)dx \qquad (A3.1)$$

Then the $L(R)$ has the following properties:

1   $L(R) = \sigma_L L(z)$, where $z = R - \mu_L/\sigma_L$.
2   If demand D^L is normal, then $L(-z) = z + L(z)$.

Proof. Taking the derivative of $L(R)$ with respect to R yields the following:

$$\frac{\mathrm{d}L(R)}{\mathrm{d}R} = \frac{\mathrm{d}}{\mathrm{d}R}\left(\int_R^\infty (x-R)f_{D^L}(x)\mathrm{d}x\right)$$

$$= \left(\int_R^\infty \left(-f_{D^L}(x)\right)\mathrm{d}x - (R-R)f_{D^L}(R)\right)$$

$$= \left(-\int_R^\infty f_{D^L}(x)\mathrm{d}x - 0\right) = -\left(1 - F_{D^L}(R)\right). \tag{A3.2}$$

Let $Z = D^L - \mu_L/\sigma_L \sim (0,1)$ be the standardized lead-time demand, and $z = R - \mu_L/\sigma_L$ be the standardized reorder point. A standard loss function, denoted by $L(z)$ is defined as:

$$L(z) = E(Z-z)^+ = \int_z^\infty (x-z)f_Z(x)\mathrm{d}x,$$

where $f_Z(x)$ is the probability density function of Z. It is easy to show (see Problem 7) that

$$L(R) = E(D^L - R)^+ = \sigma_L \times L(z) = \sigma_L \times E(Z-z)^+ = \sigma_L \times L(z). \tag{A3.3}$$

This concludes the proof of property 1. Note the proof above does not require demand to be normally distributed.

Suppose the demand is also normal, i.e., $D^L \sim \mathrm{IIDN}(\mu_L, \sigma_L^2)$. As a closed-form expression of the loss function is not attainable, tabulated values of a normal standard loss function are provided, assuming that Z is a standard normal random variable with its probability density function, $f_Z(x)$, given as,

$$f_Z(x) = \frac{1}{\sqrt{2\pi}}\,e^{-\frac{x^2}{2}}.$$

It is easy to verify from the above equality that

$$f_Z'(x) = \frac{\mathrm{d}f_Z(x)}{\mathrm{d}x} = \frac{\mathrm{d}}{\mathrm{d}x}\left(\frac{1}{\sqrt{2\pi}}\,e^{-\frac{x^2}{2}}\right) = -x \times \frac{1}{\sqrt{2\pi}}\,e^{-\frac{x^2}{2}} = -x \times f_Z(x).$$

For numerical computation of standard normal loss function $L(z)$, the following equalities are particularly useful:

$$L(z) = \int_R^\infty (x-z)f_Z(x)\mathrm{d}x = \int_R^\infty xf_Z(x)\mathrm{d}x - z\int_R^\infty f_Z(x)\mathrm{d}x$$

$$= -f_Z(x)\big|_R^\infty - z\left(1 - F_Z(R)\right) = -\left(f_Z(\infty) - f_Z(z)\right) - z\left(1 - F_Z(z)\right)$$

$$= -\left(0 - f_Z(z)\right) - z\left(1 - F_Z(z)\right) = f_Z(z) - z\left(1 - F_Z(z)\right),$$

where $f_Z(z) = \left(1/\sqrt{2\pi}\right)e^{-z^2/2}$ and $F_Z(z) = \int_{-\infty}^{z} f_Z(x)dx$, which can be numerically obtained from built-in functions in spreadsheet software such as Excel.

For standardized normal lead-time demand Z, i.e., $Z \sim N(0,1)$, we also have

$$L(-z) = z + L(z). \tag{A3.4}$$

Next, we derive the equality (A3.4). First we note the following three equalities for standard normal distribution function:

$$E(Z) = \int_{-\infty}^{\infty} x f_Z(x)dx = 0, \int_{-\infty}^{\infty} f_Z(x)dx = 1, \text{and } f_Z(-x) = f_Z(x).$$

Then we derive the following

$$L(-z) = \int_{-z}^{\infty} \left(x - (-z)\right) f_Z(x)dx$$

$$= \int_{-\infty}^{-z} (x+z)f_Z(x)dx + \int_{-z}^{\infty} (x+z)f_Z(x)dx - \int_{-\infty}^{-z} (x+z)f_Z(x)dx$$

$$= \int_{-\infty}^{\infty} (x+z)f_Z(x)dx - \int_{-\infty}^{-z} (x+z)f_Z(x)dx$$

$$= 0 + z\int_{-\infty}^{\infty} f_Z(x)dx + \int_{-z}^{-\infty} (x+z)f_Z(x)dx$$

$$= z + \int_{z}^{\infty} (-x+z)f_Z(-x)d(-x).$$

Since $f_Z(-x) = f_Z(x)$, it is immediate to obtain,

$$L(-z) = z + \int_{z}^{\infty} (x-z)f_Z(x)dx = z + L(z).$$

This concludes the proof of the second property of the loss function.

Appendix 3B   Derivation of optimal (R,Q) order policy

The expected annual cost function for an (R,Q) inventory system is expressed as

$$TC(R,Q) = c_h\left(\frac{Q}{2} + (R - \mu_L)\right) + c_s\left(\frac{\bar{D}}{Q}\right) + c_b\frac{\bar{D} \times L(R)}{Q},$$

The derivative of $TC(R,Q)$ with respect to R can then be obtained, using (A3.2), as follows,

$$\frac{\partial}{\partial R}TC(R,Q) = c_h\left(\frac{\partial}{\partial R}(R-\mu_L)\right) + c_b\frac{\bar{D}}{Q}\times\frac{dL(R)}{dR}$$

$$= c_h - c_b\frac{\bar{D}}{Q}\times\left(1-F_{D^L}(R)\right). \tag{A3.5}$$

Letting

$$\frac{\partial}{\partial R}TC(R,Q) = 0,$$

we can then obtain the following equality,

$$c_h = c_b\frac{\bar{D}}{Q}\times\left(1-F_{D^L}(R)\right).$$

The above equality leads to one of the two optimality equations for (R,Q) policy, expressed as follows:

$$F_{D^L}(R) = 1 - \frac{c_h Q}{c_b\bar{D}}. \tag{A3.6}$$

Then setting $\dfrac{\partial}{\partial Q}TC(R,Q) = 0$,

we obtain the following equation,

$$\frac{c_h}{2} - c_s\left(\frac{\bar{D}}{Q^2}\right) - c_b\frac{\bar{D}\times L(R)}{Q^2} = 0.$$

Solving for Q from the above equality, we have

$$Q = \sqrt{\frac{2\bar{D}\left(c_s + c_b L(R)\right)}{c_h}}. \tag{A3.7}$$

In summary, an optimal (R,Q) inventory policy must solve the following system of two equations:

$$\begin{cases} Q = \sqrt{\dfrac{2\bar{D}\left(c_s + c_b L(R)\right)}{c_h}} \\[2ex] F(R) = 1 - \dfrac{c_h Q}{c_b\bar{D}} \end{cases} \tag{A3.8}$$

Bibliography

Blinder, Alan S. 1982. "Private Pensions and Public Pensions: Theory and Fact," NBER Working Papers 0902, Cambridge, MA: National Bureau of Economic Research.

Blinder, Alan S. and Louis J. Maccini. 1991. "The Resurgence of Inventory Research: What Have We Learned?," *Journal of Economic Surveys*, 5(4), 291–328.

Box, George E.P. and Gwilym M. Jenkins. 1976. *Time Series Analysis: Forecasting and Control*, San Francisco, CA: Holden-Day.

Hamilton, J.D. 1994. *Time Series Analysis*, Princeton, NJ: Princeton University Press.

Kydland, Finn E. and Edward C. Prescott. 1982. "Time to Build and Aggregate Fluctuations," *Econometrica*, 50(6), 1345–1370.

La Londe, B.J. 1998. "Supply Chain Evolution in Numbers," *Supply Chain Management Review*, 2(1), 7–8.

Zipkin, Paul. 2000. *Foundations of Inventory Management*, Boston, MA: Irwin/McGraw Hill.

4   Forecasting in supply chain and transport logistics

Key items:

- *Characterizing demand propagation in a supply chain*
- *Principles of time-series forecasting*
- *Least-mean squared error forecast*
- *General-purpose forecast methods*
- *Forecast-facilitated order planning and bullwhip effect*

Characterizing demand propagation in a supply chain

Prototype example: correlated demand for bottled beer

Demand processes in a supply chain typically appear in time-series of orders. For example, quarterly sales at a car dealer are initiated by series of customer orders, which then translate into purchase orders submitted by the dealer to automobile manufacturer(s) such as General Motors. Demand orders arriving at a downstream stage triggers purchase/production orders being released to its upstream stage(s), as depicted in Figure 4.1, where q_t represents the outgoing flow of orders, and d_t stands for incoming flow of demand. Figure 4.1 illustrates the relayed order flows in the most downward two stages of a supply chain, which can continue to expend further upward with outgoing orders viewed as incoming demands for the next upstream stage.

It is obvious that the interstage order/demand flows are correlated with each other. The interaction, however, is ultimately triggered by market demands at the most downward level of the chain. The market demand at the end-user level is considered exogenous. We refer to such upward relayed transition of demand/order flows as the demand *propagation* in a supply chain. Ultimately, all the ordering activities in a supply chain are motivated by exogenous demand, which is assumed to be independent of the order policies implemented at various stages in a supply chain. Thus, it is natural to focus on characterizing the market demand in a supply chain. We shall note that exogenous market demand is entailed in the form of time-series and is in general correlated across time. For example, there can be a certain degree of interdependency between sales of two consecutive

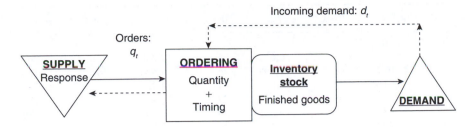

Figure 4.1 Demand/order flows in supply chain.

weeks. Such time-based interdependency within the same time-series process is termed **autocorrelation**.

The idea of demand characterization is to recognize and "model" the inherent pattern(s), if any, exhibited in an incoming demand process. Due to Box and Jenkins (1976), various types of time-series models have been developed to characterize a variety of demand patterns, such as autoregressive (AR) models. A typical procedure for demand characterization includes the following:

1   system specification: demand target, time dimension, and background settings;
2   data consideration and collection;
3   model specification: selection and evaluation;
4   monitoring, modification, and recharacterization.

Each of the four steps above involves advanced statistics and time-series analysis (Hamilton 1994), which again are beyond the scope of this book. In light of Sun Zi's winning-before-doing (WBD), we will examine operational aspects of demand characterization via simulation-based approaches rather than pure statistical methods. In this chapter, we will first study basic stationary time-series models such as first-order moving-average [MA(1)] and first-order autoregressive [AR(1)] processes, and then the nonstationary models including ARIMA(0,1,1). For each model in discussion, we will illustrate a simulation-based method for model specification and verification. Let us begin with an example of data analysis in a beer brewery supply chain.

Example 4.1   Demand in a brewery supply chain

A beer wholesaler (distributor in Figure 4.1) faces weekly demand from an existing market for bottled beer produced by a brewer (supplier in Figure 4.1). Suppose that there is no notable change in the market condition. All the sales data in the past are collected and recorded, from which it is ascertained that the mean of the weekly demand is 12,800 and the variance is $1,316^2$. Table 4.1 presents the sales data collected for the most recent 48 weeks. How can the underlying demand process be characterized (or modeled)?

Table 4.1 Sales data of weekly demand for bottled beer (in 24-bottle cases)

Week	$\hat{d}_t$	Week	$\hat{d}_t$	Week	$\hat{d}_t$	Week	$\hat{d}_t$
0	12,500						
1	11,327	13	9,617	25	12,295	37	13,864
2	12,087	14	9,958	26	14,444	38	13,110
3	13,613	15	8,835	27	14,734	39	13,759
4	14,527	16	9,655	28	16,433	40	11,979
5	15,656	17	10,351	29	14,507	41	11,419
6	12,473	18	11,343	30	15,571	42	10,381
7	12,353	19	11,488	31	12,989	43	10,865
8	13,604	20	11,620	32	13,462	44	11,510
9	12,236	21	11,663	33	14,132	45	11,989
10	11,743	22	13,403	34	15,585	46	11,950
11	10,423	23	13,107	35	14,526	47	14,442
12	9,408	24	12,813	36	13,398	48	12,125

Before we proceed with the example, we shall note that time-series analysis is based on one single realization of the underlying process that is originated from an infinitive past. Practically, this is to require "sufficiently large" samples collected from the past, and to continue data collection forever in the future. Then mathematical characteristics of the demand process, such as mean and variance, can be defined and then ascertained. We assume this is the case for Example 4.1 as well, namely, the weekly demand possesses a finite mean of 12,800 and a finite variance of $1,316^2$. In real-world application, the mean and variance need to be ascertained by statistical estimation, which, of course, would require a larger volume of data collection. For the purpose of illustration, we characterize the weekly beer demand using only the 48 data entries given in Table 4.1.

Table 4.1 contains a set of 48 consecutive samples of weekly demands, and each data entry, $\hat{d}_t$, represents a sample of weekly demand d_t realized in week t ($t = 1, 2, \ldots, 48$). Suppose that the demand history can be traced back into infinite past, and the time periods in the past can be marked with a negative index such as $t = \ldots, -2, -1, 0$. With such indexing, we can write the demand of j periods prior to the current period t as d_{t-j} and denote the collection of all demand observations prior to period t as $D_t = \{d_{t-j} : \ j = 0, 1, \ldots\}$. Thus, the infinite demand series $\{d_t : t = 0, \pm 1, \pm 2, \ldots\}$ is a stochastic process (Ref: Chapter 2), and the sample data given in Table 4.1 give a specific sample path of the demand process realized during the past 48 weeks. A plot of this segment of sample path is shown in Figure 4.2.

Characteristics of time-series processes

Time average versus ensemble average

Note that the segment presented in Figure 4.2 is a part of one single sample path up to time t. The total sample path would contain a complete collection of all the

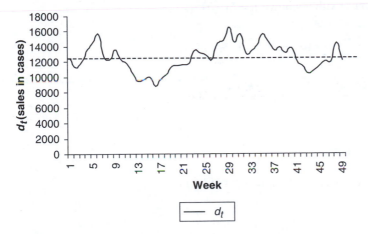

Figure 4.2 A segment of sample path of the beer demand.

samples back into an infinite past. Since multiple sample paths can hardly be obtained in reality, demand characterization has to be based on a single sample path (i.e., a single realization). The sample path in Figure 4.2 seems to indicate that the weekly demand fluctuates around a horizontal dotted (imaginary) line within a finite range of deviation from the line. Given a single realization, **time averages** can be computed to measure the mean (i.e., the horizontal line) and the squared deviation from the mean, which we will further discuss later in this section.

For the time being, let us switch to another angle and consider the demand in a given period. The demand d_t for any given week t is a random variable with the mean $\mu = E(d_t)$ and $\sigma^2 = \text{var}(d_t)$, of which samples can also be generated. An average of the samples for a given period t is termed an **ensemble average** (as opposed to the time average). For a given set of samples $\{\hat{d}_1, \hat{d}_2, \ldots, \hat{d}_n\}$, the sample (ensemble) mean and sample (ensemble) variance are defined as (with numeral example using the data in Table 4.1)

Sample mean:

$$\bar{d} = \frac{\hat{d}_1 + \cdots + \hat{d}_n}{n} = \frac{1}{n}\sum_{i=1}^{n}\hat{d}_i = \frac{\hat{d}_1 + \cdots \hat{d}_{48}}{48} = 12{,}558$$

Sample variance (with known $\mu = E(d_t)$):

$$S^2 = \frac{(\hat{d}_1 - \mu)^2 + \cdots + (\hat{d}_n - \mu)^2}{n} = \frac{1}{n}\sum_{i=1}^{n}(\hat{d}_i - \mu)^2$$

$$= \frac{(\hat{d}_1 - 12{,}800)^2 + \cdots + (\hat{d}_{48} - 12{,}800)^2}{48} = 1{,}798^2$$

Sample variance (with unknown $\mu = E(d_t)$):

$$S^2 = \frac{(\hat{d}_1 - \bar{d})^2 + \cdots + (\hat{d}_n - \bar{d})}{n-1} = \frac{1}{n-1}\sum_{i=1}^{n}(\hat{d}_i - \bar{d})^2 =$$
$$\frac{(\hat{d}_1 - 12,558)^2 + \cdots + (\hat{d}_{48} - 12,558)^2}{47} = 1,800^2$$

Sample standard deviation: $S = \sqrt{S^2}$

Sample jth covariance (with known $\mu = E(d_t)$):

$$\hat{\gamma}_j = \frac{\sum_{t=j+1}^{n}(\hat{d}_t - \mu)(\hat{d}_{t-j} - \mu)}{n-j}$$

Sample jth covariance (with unknown $\mu = E(d_t)$):

$$\hat{\gamma}_j = \frac{\sum_{t=j+1}^{n}(\hat{d}_t - \bar{d})(\hat{d}_{t-j} - \bar{d})}{n-j-1}$$

In short, a **time average** is taken over a single sample path as time elapses, while an **ensemble average** is taken over a set of samples observed at a given point in time. To formally characterize a demand process, we must answer further questions: Does such an imaginary line exist? If it does, does the line coincide with the long-term mean? If it does, how does the demand fluctuate around the mean? And so on. The answers to these questions have to do with the uniformity in the sense of ensemble average (stationarity), and with the convergence in the sense of time average (ergodicity) of the demand process. For reference, more details on the two are presented in Appendix 4A in the end of this chapter.

In fact, characterization of an ergodic stationary process $\{d_t\}_{t=-\infty}^{\infty}$ is concerned with the dynamics of transition and interrelation between d_t's across time t, given characteristics μ and σ^2 for each d_t. In this regard, *time-series analysis* (Box and Jenkins 1976; Hamilton 1994) has emerged as a primary method in modeling (characterizing) time-series processes. Time-series modeling, and stochastic modeling in general, is rooted on the conception of *drift* and *disturbance*, which we continue with in the next subsection.

Drift and disturbance in time-series

In classical stochastic modeling, such as Ito's diffusion process in continuous time and time-series analysis in discrete time, a stochastic process is presented as a system of dynamic stochastic equation(s), each consisting of two separable (or additive) time-variant components: an inherent transitional term (**drift**) and an exogenous noise term (**disturbance**). Back to the *theory of singularity* in *The Art of War* (Sun Zi), the *drift* term would be the corresponding part for the *regularity* (e.g., spring will come for sure right after the winter), and the *disturbance* term would be associated with the *singularity* (e.g., the uncertain weather conditions always affect how long the next winter will last). That is, the *drift* reflects regular patterns exhibited in the process that can be predicted, while the disturbance represents irregular deviations that are not predictable. Based on such theory, the WBD strategy devised by Sun Zi reads: calculation (of predictable) plus adaptation (in response to unpredictable). This WBD of Sun Zi's is well applicable nowadays in business operations, although it was invented more than 2000 years ago!

The **drift** (e.g., average sales rate per week) reflects intrinsic characteristics that can be expressed as a deterministic function of past observations (e.g., $D_t = \{d_{t-j} : j = 0,1,\ldots\}$) and system parameters (e.g., μ and σ^2), while the **disturbance** represents aggregate impact by exogenous random noises that are unpredictable. Note that the system parameters can be time variant. Let X_t be the set of all parameters currently contained in the system, and let $Z_t = \{X_{t-j} : j = 0,1,2,\ldots\}$ denote the complete collection of past system parameters. Then the total information set, denoted by $\mathbf{F}_t$, is defined as the union of observation set and parameter set, as follows:

$$\mathbf{F}_t = D_t \cup Z_t.$$

According to time-series theory, the demand in the next period, d_{t+1}, can be expressed as a **linear** set-to-point function superimposed with a *disturbance* term as follows:

$$d_{t+1} = f(\mathbf{F}_t) + \varepsilon_{t+1},$$

where $f(\cdot)$ represents the *drift*, which is a linear mapping from the information set $\mathbf{F}_t$ to real axis $R = (-\infty, \infty)$ (see more details as we proceed), and ε_{t+1} is a disturbance term (i.e., white noise) in period $t+1$. White noise is an unpredictable random time-series process, which we will further study in the next section.

Let us study some popular time-series models, through which we further illustrate the linear structure in time-series processes. Before we proceed with details of time-series models, it is useful to point out the similarity in continuous stochastic modeling and compare the continuous version of the linear structure:

$$\delta d_t = f(d_t, t)\delta t + \delta W_t,$$

where δd_t is the differential of d_t, and δW_t is the continuous version of random disturbance (termed Brownian motion).

Model structure of autoregressive moving average time-series

In what follows in this chapter, we will examine four stationary time-series models that belong to the autoregressive moving average (ARMA) class of time-series processes, first introduced by Box and Jenkins (1976). By stationary, we mean "stationary about mean and covariance" (i.e., constant mean and covariances across all lags, as defined previously). In terms of modeling structure, the stationary ARMA process is constructed with linear drift function of sample observations and/or sample errors. Before we proceed into the details of the time-series models, let us take a look at the model structure of each of the four ARMA processes.

1   Uncorrelated process (white noise with drift): $d_t = \mu + \varepsilon_t$, where μ is a constant, and $E(d_t) = \mu$.
2   Moving-average (MA) process

   - First-order MA process, MA(1): $d_t = \mu + \varepsilon_t + \theta \varepsilon_{t-1}$, where μ and θ are constants, and $E(d_t) = \mu$
   - qth-order MA process, MA(q): $d_t = \mu + \varepsilon_t + \theta_1 \varepsilon_{t-1} + \cdots + \theta_q \varepsilon_{t-q}$, where μ and $\theta_j (j = 1, \ldots, q)$ are constants, and $E(d_t) = \mu$.

3   AR process

   - First-order AR process, AR(1): $d_t = c + \phi d_{t-1} + \varepsilon_t$, where c and ϕ are constants. For $(|\phi| < 1)$, the mean exists (i.e., $\mu = E(d_t)$), and $c = (1 - \phi)\mu$
   - pth-order AR process, AR(p): $d_t = c + \phi_1 d_{t-1} + \cdots + \phi_p d_{t-p} + \varepsilon_t$, where c and $\phi_j (j = 1, \ldots, \phi)$ are constants.

4   ARMA process

   - First-order ARMA process, ARMA(1, 1): $d_t = c + \phi d_{t-1} + \varepsilon_t + \theta \varepsilon_{t-1}$.
   - ARMA (p, q) process: $d_t = c + \phi_1 d_{t-1} + \cdots + \phi_p d_{t-p} + \varepsilon_t + \theta_1 \varepsilon_{t-1} + \cdots + \theta_q \varepsilon_{t-q}$.

For the stationary ARMA processes, we will focus on first-order ARMA processes in this chapter. Later in this chapter, we will also study some basic non-stationary time-series processes that all consist of linear drift function but no longer possess stationary autocovariances.

Characterization of time-series demand

Characterization of time-series demand herein refers to specifying a time-series model that best characterizes an underlying demand process, given a sample path observed from the same demand process. For the example of the beer sales in Table 4.1, which gives the sample path in the past 48 weeks, $D_t = \{d_{t-j} : j = 0, 1, \ldots, 48\}$ (with current $t = 48$), the underlying beer sales process can be characterized by specifying a time-series model that best represents the characteristics of the beer sales process. The characterization is typically based on scientific study of sample paths of the concerned demand process. The **characterization of time-series demand** can be generally defined as follows:

Assuming that the demand process follows a certain time-series model structure (i.e., certain drift function and disturbance term), and that sample paths of the demand process are available, then characterize the demand process by specifying a drift function and disturbance term that best represent the characteristics of the concerned demand process.

There have been profound studies in the field of statistics devoted to specification and characterization of statistical processes. Application of advanced statistical methods is beyond the scope and the interests of this book, and therefore is omitted. Instead, we introduce a simulation-based characterization method that is most suited for applications in supply chain management. The proposed simulation characterization method is derived from the adaptive system of Holland's (1992), as we studied in Chapter 1. Here is a schematic description of the simulation-based characterization method:

- Obtain a set of sample path data, $D_t = \{d_{t-j} : j = 0,1,\ldots,t\}$, from the concerned demand process.
- Establish a finite set of feasible time-series model structures P, for example, $P = \{d_{t+1} = f(D_t) + \varepsilon_{t+1} : \text{MA}(1), \quad \text{AR}(1),\ldots,\text{ARMA}(p,q)\}$
- For each feasible model structure in P, compute (or simulate) sample residuals $\hat{e}_{t-j}$ for $j = 1,2,\ldots,t-1$, using the given sample data D_t, where a sample residual is defined as follows:

$$\hat{e}_{t-j} = d_{t-j} - f(D_{t-j-1}).$$

For example, for $j = t-1$ the sample residual based on the beer sales data in Table 4.1 is computed as $\hat{e}_1 = d_1 - f(D_0) = d_1 - f(d_0)$, where the values of d_0 and d_1 are given in Table 4.1.

- Verify if the sample residuals generated from the selected model structure match the characteristics of a simulated white noise. That is, if the underlying demand process (e.g., beer sales process) indeed follows the selected model structure, then the sample residuals under the selected model would be of white noise.

Next, we illustrate the proposed simulation characterization using the sample beer sales data given in Table 4.1. For the sake of exposition, we consider, in the following three sections, characterizing the beer sales process shown in Table 4.1 with one of the three basic time-series models listed previously: drifted white noise, MA(1), and AR(1).

Principle of time-series forecasting

So, no calculation, no victory! Of course, calculation requires numbers and measures, but it goes much beyond just the numbers and measures. According to Sun Zi, **thorough calculation** involves theorized prediction and verification in the

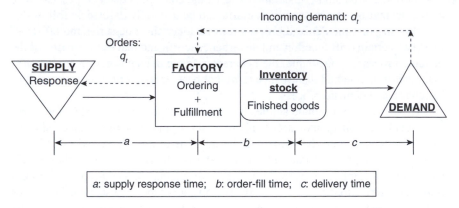

Figure 4.3 Time lags in supply chain.

face of an uncertain and changing world. Sun Zi's *thorough calculation* is founded on theorized patterns of variation, and is carried out in the form of simulation-facilitated prediction. Consistent with Sun Zi, forecasting in this chapter is viewed as an inevitable part of **thorough calculation**, and therefore is covered with a focus on theorized patterns in underlying processes. As we proceed in this chapter, we will see that the theorized patterns in time-series demand come naturally upon the simulation-based characterization as studied in Chapter S4.

The forecast is needed only when making decisions that depend on future unknown variable(s). As noted in the previous chapter, the unknown variable(s) in time-series modeling exist in terms of uncertain disturbance (e.g., white noise). There are two *musts* in forecasting, namely, reference to future and uncertainty. In manufacturing and supply chain, the *reference to future* is made via lead-time that is broadly defined as the time needed to fulfill and deliver an order. If it takes no time to execute manufacturing operations (e.g., zero lead-time), there would be no need to forecast the future. We have learned from previous chapters that factory and supply chain operate as a supply order fulfillment system, where nonzero lead-time is intrinsic as depicted in Figure 4.3.

As we can see there is always some time lag between order releasing and order delivery. In this view, forecasting has to be an intrinsic part of manufacturing and supply chain management, regardless of operational schemes, either make-to-order or make-to-stock.

As to *uncertainty*, the second *must* in forecasting, it leads to the saying: ***fore-casting is always wrong***, which is also referred to as the *practical principle of forecast*. The truth of it is entirely due to *uncertainty*. If one knows with certainty about sales in the future weeks, there would be no error in forecasts, and therefore there would be no inventory costs incurred.

As demand in the supply chain is presented in the form of time-series, the forecasts of time-series demand are also presented in the form of time-series.

Time-series forecasting is one of the quantitative forecasting methods, on which there are volumes of textbooks including those by Box and Jenkins (1976), Adams (1986), and Hamilton (1994). Another class of forecasting methods is of subjective and nonanalytical, including the Delphi method and jury of executive opinion as described in Wilson *et al.* (2002). We confine the study in this book to the forecast of time-series demand. A typical time-series forecast process is outlined as follows:

1   identify and define the forecast system:

    (a) variable(s) to forecast
    (b) time dimensions
    (c) objectives of forecast

2   data consideration and characterization
3   model specification and verification
4   forecast presentation and implementation
5   adaptation and modification.

Before we proceed with time-series forecasting, let us recap the analytical settings for the time-series models as studied in Chapter S4. The underlying demand d_t $(t = 0, \pm 1, \pm 2, \cdots)$ is supposed to follow a certain time-series process, and a set of observations up to time t, denoted as $D_t = \{d_{t-j} : j = 0, 1, \ldots\}$, is assumed to be available for the purpose of analysis. Let X_t be the set of all parameters currently (at time t) contained in the system including coefficients of time-series model such as θ's in an MA model and ϕ's in an AR model. Let $Z_t = \{X_{t-j} : j = 0, 1, 2, \ldots\}$ denote the complete collection of past system parameters. Then the total information set (or information filtration), denoted by $\mathbf{F}_t$, is defined as the union of observation sets and parameter set, as follows:

$$\mathbf{F}_t = D_t \bigcup Z_t.$$

(4.1)

Note that the information set $\mathbf{F}_t$ is increasing in time t, because additional information transpires as time elapses. According to time-series theory, the demand in the next period can be expressed by a linear set-to-point function plus a superimposed *disturbance* term as follows:

$$d_{t+1} = f(\mathbf{F}_t) + \varepsilon_{t+1},$$

(4.2)

where $f(\cdot)$ is a linear mapping from the information set $\mathbf{F}_t$ to real axis $R = (-\infty, \infty)$ (see more details in Chapter S4), and ε_{t+1} is a white disturbance in period $t+1$ that is unpredictable in nature. In the theory of stochastic process, the term $f(\cdot)$ of (4.2) is called a drift (function), which in fact represents the "theorized patterns" in Sun Zi's term. The drift function can be a nonlinear mapping. Nevertheless, time-series models we have studied so far adopt a linear drift function $f(\cdot)$. The forecast for d_{t+1} (i.e., the demand in the next period given a current period t), is denoted as $F_{t+1|t}$ (or simply F_{t+1}), and the forecast for d_{t+L} ($L \geq 1$), the demand in an L-period future, is denoted as $F_{t+L|t}$ (or simply F_{t+L}). Then a forecast process can be constructed in the form of time-series, expressed as $\{F_{t+L|t} : t = 0, 1, \ldots\}$.

Least-mean squared error forecasting

Since forecasting is never entirely accurate, it is natural to establish a principle of forecasting based on minimum error. Let us formally characterize such error-minimizing principle of forecasting. First, we define a forecast error for the next period $t+1$ as follows:

$$\text{Forecast error: } e_{t+1} = d_{t+1} - F_{t+1|t} \ (\text{or simply } e_{t+1} = d_{t+1} - F_{t+1}).$$

A positive (or negative) error indicates that demand is over (or under) the forecast. Then associated with each forecast $F_{t+1|t}$ the *mean squared error* (MSE) is defined:

$$\textbf{MSE of forecast: } \text{MSE}(F_{t+1|t}) = E\left(e_{t+1}\right)^2 = E\left(d_{t+1} - F_{t+1|t}\right)^2.$$

$$\textbf{Root-MSE (RMSE): } \text{RMSE}(F_{t+1|t}) = \sqrt{E\left(e_{t+1}\right)^2} = \sqrt{E\left(d_{t+1} - F_{t+1|t}\right)^2}.$$

When only finite observations are available, sample MSE needs to be obtained from a finite number of sample forecast errors, which is defined as:

$$\textbf{Sample MSE of forecast: } \overline{\text{MSE}}(F_{t+1|t}) = \frac{1}{t}(e_1^2 + e_2^2 + \cdots + e_t^2) = \frac{1}{t}\sum_{i=1}^{t} e_i^2.$$

$$\textbf{Sample RMSE of forecast: } \overline{\text{RMSE}}(F_{t+1|t}) = \sqrt{\frac{1}{t}(e_1^2 + e_2^2 + \cdots + e_t^2)} = \sqrt{\frac{1}{t}\sum_{i=1}^{t} e_i^2}.$$

where e_t denotes a sample forecast error in period t. Thus, the error-minimizing principle of forecast, termed **least-MSE** (or **least-square**) **forecast**, can now be stated as follows:

Choose a forecast $F_{t+1|t}$ for all t so that the associated MSE is minimized.

Theoretically, the least-MSE forecasting principle is applicable in continuous time (e.g., Brownian motion with drift) or discrete time (e.g., time-series). The forecast studied in this chapter is the least-MSE *time-series* forecast (i.e., in discrete time), since the underlying demand process is presented in the time-series model. Let us begin with the same example of weekly bottled beer sales.

Prototype example: forecasting weekly beer sales

Example 4.2   Intuitive forecasts for weekly beer sales

Consider the same weekly demand process as of Example 4.1. All the weekly sales data in the infinite past are assumed to have been observed, from which it is ascertained that the demand follows an AR(1): $d_t = (1-\phi)\mu + \phi \times d_{t-1} + \varepsilon_t$, with $\mu = 12{,}800$, $\phi = 0.65$, and error term $\varepsilon_t \sim N(0, \sigma_\varepsilon^2)$ where $\sigma_\varepsilon = 1{,}316$. Table 4.1 presents the annual sales data collected for the past 48 weeks (assuming 48 working weeks per year). Suppose that we are asked to produce least-MSE weekly forecasts, starting at the end of week 0 with a given initial data $d_0 = 12{,}500$.

Let us first illustrate the forecasting procedure adopted in this chapter, by applying two common forecasting methods to the beer sales data, namely, naïve forecasting and MA forecasting.

Naïve forecasting

By naïve forecasting, the forecast for the next period is set equal to the current demand realization. For the example of beer sales, starting at the end of period 0 with an initial value of d_0 (=12,500), the forecast for the next period $t+1$ is as follows:

$$F_{t+1|t} = d_t, \quad \text{for } t = 1, 2, \ldots$$

where d_t is the sales realized in period t, which is observed by the end of period t. For example, the naïve forecast for week 1 is computed at the beginning of week 1 when the actual sale in week 1 is unknown yet, as follows:

$$F_1 = F_{0+1|0} = d_0 = 12{,}500.$$

By the end of week 1, the actual week 1 sale is then observed as $d_1 = 11{,}327$, by which the week 1 forecast error can be determined as follows:

$$e_1 = d_1 - F_1 = 11{,}327 - 12{,}500 = -1{,}173.$$

The naïve forecast for week 2 is then computed as follows:

$$F_2 = F_{1+1|1} = d_1 = 11{,}327.$$

Table 4.2 Naïve forecast for weekly beer demand

Week	d_t	F_{t+1}	e_t	Week	d_t	F_{t+1}	e_t
0	12,500						
1	11,327	**12,500**	−1,173	25	12,295	**12,813**	−518
2	12,087	**11,327**	760	26	14,444	**12,295**	2,149
3	13,613	**12,087**	1,526	27	14,734	**14,444**	290
4	14,527	**13,613**	914	28	16,433	**14,734**	1,699
5	15,656	**14,527**	1,129	29	14,507	**16,433**	−1,926
6	12,473	**15,656**	−3,183	30	15,571	**14,507**	1,064
7	12,353	**12,473**	−120	31	12,989	**15,571**	−2,582
8	13,604	**12,353**	1,251	32	13,462	**12,989**	473
9	12,236	**13,604**	−1,368	33	14,132	**13,462**	670
10	11,743	**12,236**	−493	34	15,585	**14,132**	1,453
11	10,423	**11,743**	−1,320	35	14,526	**15,585**	−1,059
12	9,408	**10,423**	−1,015	36	13,398	**14,526**	−1,128
13	9,617	**9,408**	209	37	13,864	**13,398**	466
14	9,958	**9,617**	341	38	13,110	**13,864**	−754
15	8,835	**9,958**	−1,123	39	13,759	**13,110**	649
16	9,655	**8,835**	820	40	11,979	**13,759**	−1,780
17	10,351	**9,655**	696	41	11,419	**11,979**	−560
18	11,343	**10,351**	992	42	10,381	**11,419**	−1,038
19	11,488	**11,343**	145	43	10,865	**10,381**	484
20	11,620	**11,488**	132	44	11,510	**10,865**	645
21	11,663	**11,620**	43	45	11,989	**11,510**	479
22	13,403	**11,663**	1,740	46	11,950	**11,989**	−39
23	13,107	**13,403**	−296	47	14,442	**11,950**	2,492
24	12,813	**13,107**	−294	48	12,125	**14,442**	−2,317

After the actual sale in week 2 is observed, the forecast error in week 2 is then computed similarly, and so on. The results of naïve forecasting as applied to the beer sales data are presented in Table 4.2.

The errors of naïve forecast can be determined from the Table 4.2 as follows:

Sample RMSE of naïve forecast: $\overline{\text{RMSE}}(F_{t+1|t}) = 1,230$.

For comparison, the sample paths of both actual beer sales and naïve forecasts are presented in Figure 4.4. As we can see from Figure 4.4 the naïve forecasts tended to follow the demand, but always deviated from the demand. This confirms that "forecasting is always wrong," and that efforts must be devoted to minimizing forecast errors. For the beer sales, the naïve forecasts produced an average error of 1,230 (i.e., $\overline{\text{RMSE}}(F_{t+1|t}) = 1,230$.). Next, let us check if the other common forecast method would perform better in beer sales forecasting.

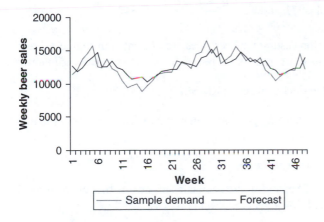

Figure 4.4 Sample paths of beer sales and naïve forecasts.

Lag-p MA forecasting

In this case, a lag-p MA forecast for the next period is determined as the average of realizations in the past p periods. For the example of beer sales, a lag-3 MA forecast for the next period $t+1$ is determined as follows:

$$\text{Lag-3 MA forecast}: F_{t+1} = F_{t+1|t} = \frac{d_t + d_{t-1} + d_{t-2}}{3}, \quad \text{for } t = 2,3,\ldots$$

$$\text{Lag-}p \text{ MA forecast}: F_{t+1} = F_{t+1|t} = \frac{d_t + d_{t-1} + \cdots + d_{t-p+1}}{p},$$

for $t = p-1, p, p+1,\ldots.$

For the periods that are before period $p-1$, the average has to be taken over less than p periods. In this case, the MA forecasts can be determined as follows:

$$F_{t+1} = F_{t+1|t} = \frac{d_0 + \cdots + d_t}{t+1}, \quad \text{for } 0 \le t < p-1.$$

For the example of the beer sales, the MA forecast for weeks 1 and 2 are computed as follows:

$$F_1 = F_{0+1|0} = \frac{d_0}{1} = d_0 = 12,500,$$

$$F_2 = F_{1+1|1} = \frac{d_0 + d_1}{2} = \frac{12,500 + 11,327}{2} = 11,914.$$

From F_3 and so on, lag-3 MA forecasts can then be obtained by averaging over the past three periods. For example, the lag-3 MA forecasts for weeks 3 and 4 are:

$$F_3 = \frac{d_0 + d_1 + d_2}{3} = 11,971, \text{ and } F_4 = \frac{d_1 + d_2 + d_3}{3} = 12,342.$$

The results of lag-3 MA forecasting for beer sales are presented in Figure 4.5 and Table 4.3. The lag-3 MA forecast error for the beer sales is then computed as follows:

Sample RMSE of lag-3 MA forecast: $\overline{\text{RMSE}}(F_{t+1|t}) = 1,359.$

For this case, lag-3 MA forecasting generates **larger** forecast errors as compared with the naïve forecasts.

Forecasting by conditional expectation

According to our study in Chapter S4, the beer sales process is best characterized as an AR(1) model. Recall that a general AR(1) process,

$$d_t = (1-\phi)\mu + \phi(d_{t-1} + \varepsilon_t), \text{ where } \varepsilon_t \sim (0, \sigma_\varepsilon^2) \text{ and } |\phi| < 1,$$

is covariance-stationary, with mean $E(d_t) = \mu$ for all t and variance $\text{var}(d_t) = \sigma_\varepsilon^2 / 1 - \phi^2$. The parameters are specified in Example 4.2 as, $\phi = 0.65$, and $\sigma_\varepsilon = 1,316$. To carry out the forecast process, we consider the same beer sales data. First, we illustrate the procedure of forecasting by conditional expectation, using the same beer sales example.

Example 4.3   Forecast by conditional expectation for beer sales

Let us continue with Example 4.2, and elaborate on how to generate forecasts by conditional expectation, using a given set of past data. Given a value of d_0 at the beginning of week 1, let us consider the forecast for week 1. With the AR(1) parameters specified in Example 4.2, the demand during week 1, given $d_0 = 12,500$, can be expressed as follows:

$$d_1 = (1-\phi)\mu + \phi(d_0 + \varepsilon_1) = 4,480 + 0.65(12,500) + \varepsilon_1,$$

where $\varepsilon_1 \sim (0, 1,000^2)$ represents the error term that will occur in week 1. Since $d_0 = 12,500$ is realized already, the uncertainty in d_1 at the moment is solely caused by the white noise, which cannot be forecasted. Intuitively, the least-MSE forecast for week 1, in this case, should be the deterministic part in d_1, leaving out only the unpredictable noise term. It is easy to see that the deterministic part of d_1 given d_0 can be determined as follows:

$$E(d_1 | d_0) = E\big((1-\phi)\mu + \phi(d_0 + \varepsilon_1 | d_0)\big) = (1-\phi)\mu + \phi d_0,$$

where $E(d_1 | d_0)$ is the expectation of demand in week 1 conditional on the realized demand in week 0 (i.e., $d_0 = 12,500$). Then we argue that a forecast by conditional expectation for week 1, F_1, can be obtained as follows:

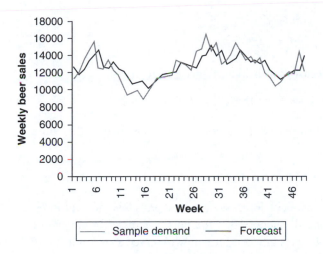

Figure 4.5 Sample paths of beer sales and lag-3 MA forecasts.

Table 4.3 Lag-3 MA forecast for weekly beer demand

Week	d_t	F_{t+1}	e_t	Week	d_t	F_{t+1}	e_t
0	12,500						
1	11,327	12,500	−1,173	25	12,295	13,108	−813
2	12,087	11,914	174	26	14,444	12,738	1,706
3	13,613	11,971	1,642	27	14,734	13,184	1,550
4	14,527	12,342	2,185	28	16,433	13,824	2,609
5	15,656	13,409	2,247	29	14,507	15,204	−697
6	12,473	14,599	−2,126	30	15,571	15,225	346
7	12,353	14,219	−1,866	31	12,989	15,504	−2,515
8	13,604	13,494	110	32	13,462	14,356	−894
9	12,236	12,810	−574	33	14,132	14,007	125
10	11,743	12,731	−988	34	15,585	13,528	2,057
11	10,423	12,528	−2,105	35	14,526	14,393	133
12	9,408	11,467	−2,059	36	13,398	14,748	−1,350
13	9,617	10,525	−908	37	13,864	14,503	−639
14	9,958	9,816	142	38	13,110	13,929	−819
15	8,835	9,661	−826	39	13,759	13,457	302
16	9,655	9,470	185	40	11,979	13,578	−1,599
17	10,351	9,483	868	41	11,419	12,949	−1,530
18	11,343	9,614	1,729	42	10,381	12,386	−2,005
19	11,488	10,450	1,038	43	10,865	11,260	−395
20	11,620	11,061	559	44	11,510	10,888	622
21	11,663	11,484	179	45	11,989	10,919	1,070
22	13,403	11,590	1,813	46	11,950	11,455	495
23	13,107	12,229	878	47	14,442	11,816	2,626
24	12,813	12,724	89	48	12,125	12,794	−669

$$F_1 = E(d_1 \mid d_0) = (1-\phi)\mu + \phi d_0$$
$$= 4,480 + 0.65(12,500) = 12,605.$$

Theoretically, the forecast error is indeed only a white noise:

$$e_1 = d_1 - F_1 = ((1-\phi)\mu + \phi(d_0 + \varepsilon_1)) - ((1-\phi)\mu + \phi d_0) = \varepsilon_1.$$

Therefore, the MSE of forecast F_1 is equal to the variance of the white noise:

$$\mathrm{MSE}(F_1) = E(F_1 - d_1)^2 = E(\varepsilon_1)^2 = \sigma_\varepsilon^2 = 1,000^2.$$

Since the white noise cannot be forecasted, this suggests that the error in F_1 cannot be further reduced. Suppose that the time progresses to the end of week 1, and the sample sales in week 1 are now observed as given in Table 4.1. Using the sample data for the sales in week 1, we can compute a sample forecast error for week 1 as follows:

$$e_1 = d_1 - F_1 = 11,327 - 12,605 = -1,278.$$

Along this line of argument, we can produce the forecasts by conditional expectation for each of the 48 weeks.

As we are to seek a least-MSE forecast, therefore the question is: how can the forecasting by conditional expectation be used to obtain the least-MSE forecast for every t? For a general class of stochastic models, a least-MSE forecast turns out to be attainable based on conditional expectation.

Least-MSE forecasts by conditional expectation

First, we claim that the forecasts generated by conditional expectation, as we did for the AR(1) beer sales process, are indeed least-MSE. Formally, we state, with the proof deferred to Appendix 4A at the end of this chapter, the following:

The forecast with the least MSE, denoted by $F^*_{t+1|t}$ (or simply F^*_{t+1}), turns out to be the expectation of d_{t+1} conditional on the total information set $\mathbf{F}_t$:

$$F^*_{t+1|t} = E(d_{t+1} \mid \mathbf{F}_t) \tag{4.3}$$

where $\mathbf{F}_t$ is total information set as defined in (4.1), which contains the complete set of realized demands and complete set of incurred system parameters. Consider, for example, an AR(1) process: $d_{t+1} = (1-\phi)\mu + \phi d_t + \varepsilon_{t+1}$, where $|\phi| < 1$ and μ are known parameters. In this case, the least-MSE forecast can be determined by conditional expectation as:

$$F^*_{t+1|t} = E(d_{t+1} \mid \mathbf{F}_t) = E((1-\phi)\mu + \phi d_t + \varepsilon_{t+1} \mid d_t)$$
$$= (1-\phi)\mu + \phi d_t + E(\varepsilon_{t+1} \mid d_t) = (1-\phi)\mu + \phi d_t. \tag{4.4}$$

Table 4.4 Least-MSE forecast for weekly beer demand

Week	d_t	F_{t+1}	e_t	Week	d_t	F_{t+1}	e_t
0	12,500						
1	11,327	12,605	−1,278	25	12,295	12,808	−513
2	12,087	11,843	244	26	14,444	12,472	1,972
3	13,613	12,337	1,276	27	14,734	13,869	865
4	14,527	13,328	1,199	28	16,433	14,057	2,376
5	15,656	13,923	1,733	29	14,507	15,161	−654
6	12,473	14,656	−2,183	30	15,571	13,910	1,661
7	12,353	12,587	−234	31	12,989	14,601	−1,612
8	13,604	12,509	1,095	32	13,462	12,923	539
9	12,236	13,323	−1,087	33	14,132	13,230	902
10	11,743	12,433	−690	34	15,585	13,666	1,919
11	10,423	12,113	−1,690	35	14,526	14,610	−84
12	9,408	11,255	−1,847	36	13,398	13,922	−524
13	9,617	10,595	−978	37	13,864	13,189	675
14	9,958	10,731	−773	38	13,110	13,492	−382
15	8,835	10,953	−2,118	39	13,759	13,002	758
16	9,655	10,223	−568	40	11,979	13,423	−1,444
17	10,351	10,756	−405	41	11,419	12,266	−847
18	11,343	11,208	135	42	10,381	11,902	−1,521
19	11,488	11,853	−365	43	10,865	11,228	−363
20	11,620	11,947	−327	44	11,510	11,542	−32
21	11,663	12,033	−370	45	11,989	11,962	28
22	13,403	12,061	1,342	46	11,950	12,273	−323
23	13,107	13,192	−85	47	14,442	12,248	2,195
24	12,813	13,000	−187	48	12,125	13,867	−1,742

With $\mu = 12,800$ and $\phi = 0.65$, it is easy to produce a least-MSE forecast for each of the 48 weeks, using the conditional expectation given by (4.4). Table 4.4 contains a complete list of resulting least-MSE forecasts, where forecasts are in bold, and sample error "e_t" gives the difference between the demand data and forecasts, that is, $e_t = d_t - F_t$ for all t. Note that the forecasts in Table 4.4 are produced at the beginning of each week without reference to the demand data in that week and thereafter.

An ideal forecast would incur no error, although it is practically impossible. Thus, the most desirable forecast is the one with the least error, and the least-MSE is the obvious choice of criterion. Figure 4.6 presents the trajectory of forecasts by conditional expectation as compared with actual beer sales data as given in Table 4.4.

Using the data of forecast errors given in Table 4.4, we can then compute the sample MSE of the forecasts for the beer sales:

$$\overline{\mathrm{MSE}}(F_t) = \frac{1}{t}(e_1^2 + e_2^2 + \cdots + e_t^2) = \frac{1}{t}\sum_{i=1}^{t} e_i^2 = \frac{1}{48}(e_1^2 + e_2^2 + \cdots + e_{48}^2)$$

$$= \frac{1}{48}\left((-1,278)^2 + (244)^2 + \cdots + (-1,742)^2\right) = 1,380,394.$$

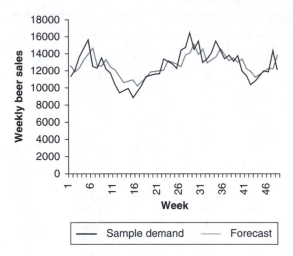

Figure 4.6 Forecast by conditional expectation for AR(1) beer demand.

Or it is often convenient to consider the root-MSE (RMSE):

$$\overline{\text{RMSE}} = \sqrt{\overline{\text{MSE}(F_t)}} = \sqrt{1,380,394} = 1,175.$$

We must note from Figure 4.6 that there can be identified a so-called mean-reverting behavior in an AR(1) process, namely, a behavior of meandering around but reverting toward the theoretical mean. We can also see from Figure 4.6 that the forecast by conditional expectation mimics the mean-reverting pattern quite well. Similarly, the least-MSE forecast by conditional expectation can be applied to other time-series models including general ARMA processes that all cast a sort of mean-reverting behavior.

We can see that least-MSE forecast by conditional expectation is quite robust, as long as the "patterns," such as the drift function, of the underlying process can be accurately identified. The "patterns" are in general presented as a function of realizations or observations, either a linear or a nonlinear function. By robust, we mean that the least-MSE forecast is applicable for both linear and nonlinear drift functions.

We shall note again that time-series models assume a linear combination of past observations. All in all, it is crucial to accurately identify the drift function (i.e., the pattern), and specify the correct model for the process that is to be forecasted. A **least-MSE forecasting procedure** can then be summarized as follows:

1   Determine the demand pattern by identifying statistically the time-series model of the underlying demand process.
2   Generate time-series forecasts by applying conditional expectation. The resulting forecasting has the least MSE.

In real-world situations, accurate identification of a time-series process often requires tremendous statistical resources and efforts, and can result in insurmountable computational difficulties. To face the challenge, a WBD approach has evolved in time-series forecasting, that is,

WBD time-series forecasting procedure:

1   *Collect patterns.* Categorize and construct representative "patterns" from all the existing time-series models, such as ARMA and ARIMA models.
2   *Derive pattern-based forecasting models.* For each "pattern," derive a pattern-based, general-purpose forecasting method that does not require statistical identification of an underlying demand process.
3   *Simulate.* Apply each of the pattern-based forecasting models to available sample demand data, and evaluate forecast performance for each forecasting model.
4   *Select and implement.* Select the best performing forecasting model, and implement it for real-time forecasting.

For example, the demand "patterns" can be collected from the time-series models that we have studied so far. The following **three** patterns are fairly representative of basic forecasting models and will be considered in this chapter:

1   **AR-pattern** is the drift function in an AR time-series model. For an AR(1) model, $d_{t+1} = (1-\phi)\mu + \phi d_t + \varepsilon_{t+1}$, the AR-pattern is $\mu + \phi(d_t - \mu)$.
2   **MA-pattern** is the function of past observations in a MA time-series model. For an MA(1) model, $d_{t+1} = \mu + \varepsilon_{t+1} + \theta\varepsilon_t$, where ε_t is the error observed in the past period, the MA-pattern is $\mu + \theta\varepsilon_t$.
3   **IMA-pattern** is the drift function in an integrate MA time-series model. For an IMA(1,1) model, $d_{t+1} = d_t + \varepsilon_{t+1} + \theta\varepsilon_t$, the IMA-pattern is $d_t + \theta\varepsilon_t$.

Forecasting first-order stationary ARMA process

As we have confined the time-series analysis to first-order processes, the forecast models considered herein are also limited to the first-order ARMA models. In what follows, we consider, in the correct order, forecasts for an AR(1), MA(1), and then ARMA(1,1) process.

Forecasting AR(1) process

Least-MSE forecast for AR(1) process

Suppose that the demand follows an AR(1) process of the following form:

$$d_{t+1} - \mu = \phi(d_t - \mu) + \varepsilon_{t+1}, \text{ or } d_{t+1} = (1-\phi)\mu + \phi d_t + \varepsilon_{t+1},$$

where $\varepsilon_t \sim (0, \sigma_\varepsilon^2)$ and $|\phi| < 1$. It is known that such an AR(1) process is covariance-stationary with

$$E(d_t) = \mu < \infty, \text{ and } \mathrm{var}(d_t) = \frac{\sigma_\varepsilon^2}{1-\phi^2} = \sigma^2. \tag{4.5}$$

Given current demand term d_t, the one-step least-MSE forecast can be obtained by taking conditional expectation, as shown in (4.4):

$$F_{t+1|t}^* = E(d_{t+1} \mid d_t) = \mu + \phi(d_t - \mu) = (1-\phi)\mu + \phi d_t. \tag{4.6}$$

As mentioned earlier, an AR(1) process manifests a behavior of mean reverting. In this regard, the forecast given by (4.6) can be viewed as a mean-reverting smoothing (MRS). To see this point, let us rewrite (4.6) as follows:

$$F_{t+1|t}^* = \mu + \phi(d_t - \mu).$$

Noting that the term $d_t - \mu$ represents the current demand deviation away from the mean, we can see that the least-MSE forecast given by (4.6) is equal to the mean plus a proportion (ϕ) of the error. To see if the forecast $F_{t+1|t}^*$ is indeed mean reverting, let us consider the unconditional mean of the forecast. Given the unconditional expectation of demand $E(d_t) = \mu$, the unconditional mean of the least-MSE forecast by (4.6) is

$$E(F_{t+1|t}^*) = E\big(\mu + \phi(d_t - \mu)\big) = \mu + \phi(E(d_t) - \mu) = \mu + \phi(\mu - \mu) = \mu \tag{4.7}$$

With (4.7), we can see that the least-MSE forecast of (4.6) is mean reverting, in the sense that the forecast is expected to converge to the demand mean ultimately. Statistically, we call such a forecast *unbiased*. The parameter ϕ is called a smoothing constant in forecasting. In this case, the autocorrelation parameter ϕ of an AR(1) process is the MRS constant. The larger the value of ϕ is, the less proportion $(1-\phi)$ of the mean is included in the forecast, and therefore the less mean-reverting effect is the forecast. In short, the smoothing constant ϕ has a damping effect on the mean-reverting factor in the forecast. Now, we consider the L-step forecast given d_t. In this case, it is often useful to express an L-step future demand in term of current demand d_t:

$$\begin{aligned}
d_{t+L} &= (1-\phi)\mu + \phi d_{t+L-1} + \varepsilon_{t+L} = (1-\phi)\mu + \phi\big((1-\phi)\mu + \phi d_{t+L-2} + \varepsilon_{t+L-1}\big) \\
&+ \varepsilon_{t+L} = (1+\phi+\cdots+\phi_{L-1})(1-\phi)\mu + \phi_L d_t + \big(\phi_{L-1}\varepsilon_{t+1} + \cdots + \phi\varepsilon_{t+L-1} + \varepsilon_{t+L}\big) \\
&= \frac{1-\phi_L}{1-\phi}(1-\phi)\mu + \phi_L d_t + \sum_{j=1}^{L}\phi_{L-j}\varepsilon_{t+j} = (1-\phi_L)\mu + \phi_L d_t + \sum_{j=1}^{L}\phi_{L-j}\varepsilon_{t+j}.
\end{aligned}$$

In the derivation above, we need to use the following equality for the sum of an equal-ratio series,

$$1+\phi+\cdots+\phi^{L-1}=\frac{1-\phi^{L}}{1-\phi}.\tag{4.8}$$

A proof of the equality is included in Appendix 4D for reference. Note that $E(d_t)=\mu$ for all t and $E(\varepsilon_{t+j}\mid d_t)=0$ for all $j\geq 1$. Then, the L-step least-MSE forecast for AR(1) is

$$F_{t+L\mid t}^{*}=E\left(d_{t+L}\mid d_{t}\right)=E\left((1-\phi^{L})\mu+\phi^{L}d_{t}+\sum_{j=1}^{L}\phi^{L-j}\varepsilon_{t+j}\,\middle|\,d_{t}\right)$$

$$=(1-\phi^{L})\mu+\phi^{L}d_{t}.\tag{4.9}$$

In the case that the mean μ is unknown, then a sample mean, denoted as $\bar{m}_t$, can be used as an estimate of the mean in AR(1) forecasting, that is,

$$\mu\cong\bar{m}_{t}=\frac{d_{0}+d_{1}+\cdots+d_{t}}{t+1}.$$

It is easy to verify that $E(F_{t+L\mid t}^{*})$ is also unbiased, that is,

$$E(F_{t+L\mid t}^{*})=(1-\phi^{L})\mu+\phi^{L}E(d_{t})=\mu.$$

Thus, the forecast given in (4.9) is also generated from MRS, except now the smoothing constant is ϕ^{L}. In addition, given d_t the least-MSE forecast converges to the mean as lead-time L approaches infinity,

$$\lim_{L\to\infty}F_{t+L\mid t}^{*}=\lim_{L\to\infty}(1-\phi^{L})\mu+\phi^{L}d_{t}=\mu,\tag{4.10}$$

where $\lim_{L\to\infty}\phi^{L}=0$ for $|\phi|<1$. In this case, we call the forecast to be consistent (i.e., asymptotically approaches to the mean as L approaches infinity). This matches the intuition: Since the AR(1) demand is mean reverting (i.e., ultimately converges to the mean), the forecast for an infinite future ($L\to\infty$) would be the demand mean. In summary, an L-step least-MSE forecast for the AR(1) process is both *unbiased* and *consistent*, that is,

$$E(F_{t+L\mid t}^{*})=E(d_{t})=\mu,\text{ and }\lim_{L\to\infty}F_{t+L\mid t}^{*}=\mu.$$

Mean-reverting smoothing forecast derived from AR(1) process

Suppose we are to forecast an AR(1) demand, only with a given initial demand observation d_0. For the beer sales in Table 4.1, the initial data is $d_0=12,500$. Based on the analysis of the least-MSE forecast for the AR(1) process as discussed in the previous section, a general procedure of AR(1)-derived mean-reverting smoothing (AR-MRS) forecast can be derived as follows:

1   Given an initial value d_0 and an initial sample average demand $\bar{m}_0$, select a smoothing constant ϕ between −1 and 1 (i.e., $-1 < \phi < 1$). If an $\bar{m}_0$ is not available, compute the initial sample average as: $\bar{m}_0 = d_0$.

2   For any current time t $(t > 0)$ and a given realization d_t, update the sample average as follows:

$$\bar{m}_t = \frac{1}{t+1}\left(t\bar{m}_{t-1} + d_t\right).$$

3   Then, an L-lag forecast $(L \geq 1)$ can be obtained as

$$F_{t+L} = F_{t+L|t} = (1-\phi^L)\bar{m}_t + \phi^L d_t.$$

As a numerical experiment, let us apply the AR-MRS forecast procedure to the beer sales as given in Table 4.1, with a smoothing constant $\phi = 0.55$. For $t = 0$ with $d_0 = 12,500$ and $\bar{m}_0 = 12,500$, the forecast for the next week's sales can be computed as follows:

$$F_{1|0} = (1-\phi)\bar{m}_0 + \phi d_0 = (1-0.55)(12,500) + 0.55 \times 12,500 = 12,500.$$

Now, suppose we proceed to the end of the first week (i.e., $t = 1$), and observed the first week's demand as $d_1 = 11,327$. For $t = 1$, the sample average is first updated as

$$\bar{m}_1 = \frac{1}{1+1}\left(1 \times \bar{m}_0 + d_1\right) = \frac{1}{2}\left(1 \times 12,500 + 11,327\right) = 11,914.$$

Then, the forecast for the second week beer sales can be computed as follows:

$$F_{2|1} = (1-\phi)\bar{m}_1 + \phi d_1 = (1-0.55)(11,914) + 0.55 \times 11,327 = 11,591$$

$$F_{3|2} = (1-\phi)\bar{m}_2 + \phi d_2 = 12,035, \quad \text{where } \bar{m}_2 = \frac{1}{2+1}\left(2\bar{m}_1 + d_2\right)$$

and so on. For each period t, a forecast error can be recorded as $e_t = d_t - F_t$, and then a sample MSE can be computed as follows:

Sample MSE of forecast: $\overline{\mathrm{MSE}(F_t)} = \frac{1}{t}(e_1^2 + e_2^2 + \cdots + e_t^2) = \frac{1}{t}\sum_{i=1}^{t} e_i^2$.

If historical data are available, the smoothing constant can be selected as the one that would generate the least possible sample MSE. For comparison, Figure 4.7 contains the trajectories of MRS forecasts under three different values of

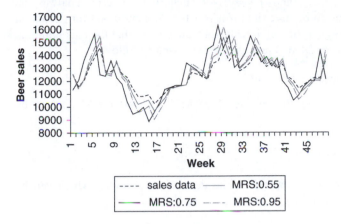

Figure 4.7 AR-MRS forecast with various smoothing constants.

smoothing constant ξ (for $\xi = 0.55$, $\phi = 0.75$, and $\phi = 0.95$), as compared with the original beer sales data presented in Table 4.1.

Comparing with the original sales data, we can compute and record the forecast errors for each of the three MRS forecasts. The numerical details of these sample errors are tedious, and therefore omitted. For comparison, we print out the square roots of the three sample MSEs as follows:

$$\text{For } \phi = 0.55 : \sqrt{\text{MSE}} = 1,273$$

$$\text{For } \phi = 0.75 : \sqrt{\text{MSE}} = 1,193$$

$$\text{For } \phi = 0.95 : \sqrt{\text{MSE}} = 1,209.$$

As the sample MSE is the smallest for $\phi = 0.75$ among the three, we would choose $\phi = 0.75$ for the MRS forecast in this case. Next, we consider the least-MSE forecast, which is derived from an MA(1) model (i.e., a first-order moving average model).

Forecasting MA(1) process

Least-MSE forecast for MA(1) process

Consider an invertible MA(1) process expressed as follows:

$$d_{t+1} = \mu + \theta \varepsilon_t + \varepsilon_{t+1},$$

where $\varepsilon_t \sim (0, \sigma_\varepsilon^2)$, $|\theta| < 1$, and $\mu < \infty$. Note that in time-series analysis, an MA(1) process is said to be invertible if $|\theta| < 1$ (see Appendix 4B for details on invertibility of an MA(1) process). Recall from Chapter S4 that the unconditional mean and variance of an MA(1) process are expressed as follows:

$$E(d_t) = \mu, \text{and } \mathrm{var}(d_t) = (1+\theta^2)\sigma_\varepsilon^2.$$

By conditional expectation, the one-step least-MSE forecast for MA(1) can be determined as follows:

$$F_{t+1|t}^* = E(d_{t+1}|\varepsilon_t) = \mu + \theta\varepsilon_t,$$

where ε_t is the white noise realized in the demand in period t, which can be expressed according to an MA(1) model as

$$d_t = \mu + \theta\varepsilon_{t-1} + \varepsilon_t.$$

Or equivalently, the error term ε_t can be obtained by the forecast error incurred in the last period t, derived as follows:

$$\varepsilon_t = d_t - \mu - \theta\varepsilon_{t-1} = d_t - (\mu + \theta\varepsilon_{t-1}) = d_t - F_{t|t-1}^*,$$

where $F_{t|t-1}^* = E(d_t|\varepsilon_{t-1}) = \mu + \theta\varepsilon_{t-1}$ is the one-step forecast made at the end of period $t-1$. Therefore, the forecast error for period t is

$$e_t = d_t - F_{t|t-1}^*.$$

Thus, the least-MSE forecast for MA(1) is also a modified demand mean with a proportion of error term. In this sense, it is also a forecast of MRS.

Now, we consider the forecasts more than one step into the future. By conditional expectation, an L-step least-MSE forecast for MA(1) with $L \geq 2$ can be determined as follows:

$$F_{t+L|t}^* = E(d_{t+L}|\varepsilon_t) = E\left(\mu + \theta\varepsilon_{t+L-1} + \varepsilon_{t+L}|\varepsilon_t\right)$$
$$= \mu + \theta E(\varepsilon_{t+L-1}) + E(\varepsilon_{t+L}) = \mu,$$

where $E(\varepsilon_{t+L-1}) = 0$ and $E(\varepsilon_{t+L}) = 0$ for $L \geq 2$. In summary, the L-step least-MSE forecast for MA(1) (with $L = 1, 2, \ldots$) can be determined as follows:

$$F_{t+L|t}^* = \begin{cases} \mu + \theta\varepsilon_t, & L = 1 \\ \mu, & L \geq 2 \end{cases}$$

where $\varepsilon_t = d_t - F_{t|t-1}^*$ is the one-step forecast error incurred in period t. Finally, it is easy to verify the unbiasness and consistence of the forecast for all $L = 1, 2, \ldots$, as summarized below:

$$E(F_{t+L|t}^*) = E(d_t) = \mu, \text{ and } \lim_{L \to \infty} F_{t+L|t}^* = \mu.$$

Mean-reverting smoothing forecast derived from MA(1) process

Similar to the forecast for AR(1) process, a general procedure for the MA(1)-derived mean-reverting smoothing (MA-MRS) forecast can be constructed.

1   Given an initial demand d_0 and an initial sample average demand $\bar{m}_0$, select a smoothing constant θ ($-1 < \theta < 1$). If an $\bar{m}_0$ is not available, compute the initial sample average: $\bar{m}_0 = d_0$. Then, let the initial forecast be $F_0 = \bar{m}_0$.

2   For any current time t ($t > 0$) and a given realization d_t, update the sample average as follows:

$$\bar{m}_t = \frac{1}{t+1}\left(t\bar{m}_{t-1} + d_t\right).$$

3   Then, an L-lag forecast ($L \geq 1$) can be obtained as

$$F_{t+L|t} = \begin{cases} \bar{m}_t + \theta(d_t - F_{t|t-1}), & L = 1 \\ \bar{m}_t, & L > 1 \end{cases}.$$

Next, let us apply the MA-MRS forecast to the beer sales as given in Table 4.1, with a smoothing constant $\theta = 0.55$. For $t = 0$ with $d_0 = 12,500$ and $\bar{m}_0 = 12,500$, the MA-MRS forecast for the next week's sales can be computed as follows:

$$F_{1|0} = \bar{m}_0 + \theta(d_0 - F_0) = 12,500 + 0.55(12,500 - 12,500) = 12,500.$$

Now, suppose we proceed to the end of the first week (i.e., $t = 1$), and observe the first week's demand as $d_1 = 11,327$. For $t = 1$, the sample average is updated using $d_1 = 11,327$ as

$$\bar{m}_1 = \frac{1}{t+1}\left(t\bar{m}_0 + d_t\right) = \frac{1}{2}\left(1 \times 12,500 + 11,327\right) = 11,914.$$

Then, the MA-MRS forecast for the second week beer sales can be computed as follows:

$$F_{2|1} = \bar{m}_1 + \theta(d_1 - F_{1|0}) = 11,914 + 0.55(11,327 - 12,500) = 11,268,$$

and so on.

To evaluate the performance of MA-MRS forecasts as applied to the beer sales data, we also consider the forecast under three different values of smoothing constant θ (for $\theta = 0.35$, $\theta = 0.55$, and $\theta = 0.75$). Numerical results of the three forecasts along with the original beer sales data are shown in Figure 4.8.

Comparing with AR-MRS forecasts in Figure 4.7, we can see that the performance of MA-MRS forecasts is not as good when applied to the beer sales data. This seems to suggest that AR(1) tends to be a better fit for the beer sales

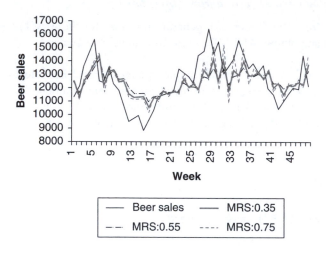

Figure 4.8 MA-MRS forecast with different smoothing constant.

data, which is consistent with the analysis conducted in the previous chapter. The square roots of the three sample MSEs are obtained as follows:

$$\text{For } \theta = 0.35: \quad \sqrt{\text{MSE}} = 1,510$$

$$\text{For } \theta = 0.55: \quad \sqrt{\text{MSE}} = 1,458$$

$$\text{For } \theta = 0.75: \quad \sqrt{\text{MSE}} = 1,596.$$

Among the three MA(1) MRS forecasts, the one under $\theta = 0.55$ generates the smallest forecast errors. However, the three MSEs of the MA(1) MRS forecasts are all larger than that of the AR(1) MRS forecasts. Thus, an AR(1) MRS forecast model is better suited for the beer sales.

So far, the forecasting models we have considered are of simple first order, either AR(1) or MA(1). By "simple," we mean it is not mixed. In the next subsection, we will consider a mixed first-order model, namely, an ARMA(1,1)-MRS forecast model, where ARMA(1,1) stands for mixed first-order autoregressive, first-order moving average. According to Box and Jenkins, a practical rule of selecting forecasting models is to keep the model as simple as possible. So, one would keep it to a first-order model (such as AR(1)), rather than a higher-order model (such as AR(2) or higher). Also, one would keep it to a simple model, rather than a mixed model. In this sense, the ARMA(1,1) model that is to be introduced next should be treated with lower priority in forecast model selection, although it is the simplest among the mixed models.

Forecasting ARMA(1,1) process

Least-MSE forecast for ARMA(1,1) process

Now, let us consider a forecast that is derived from a covariance-stationary ARMA(1,1) process of the following form:

$$d_{t+1} = (1-\phi)\mu + \phi d_t + \varepsilon_{t+1} + \theta\varepsilon_t = c + \phi d_t + \varepsilon_{t+1} + \theta\varepsilon_t, \tag{4.11}$$

with $c = (1-\phi)\mu$. Or, equivalently written in the form

$$d_{t+1} - \mu = \phi(d_t - \mu) + \theta\varepsilon_t + \varepsilon_{t+1},$$

that is stationary ($|\phi| < 1$) and invertible ($|\theta| < 1$). Both unconditional mean and variance exist, namely,

$$E(d_t) = \mu, \text{ and } \operatorname{var}(d_t) = \frac{(1+\theta^2)\sigma_\varepsilon^2}{1-\phi^2} = \sigma^2.$$

An ARMA(1,1) demand of (4.11) also has the aforementioned mean-reverting behavior, that is, a current demand realization d_t, which may have meandered away from the theoretical mean μ, would always intend to revert back toward the theoretical mean. Note that an ARMA(1,1) process represents an MA(1) process if $\phi = 0$ while it represents an AR(1) process if $\theta = 0$. Let us consider a least-MSE forecast for d_{t+1} that follows an ARMA(1,1), given realizations of the demand d_t and the error $\varepsilon_t \sim (0, \sigma_\varepsilon^2)$. Then a one-step least-MSE forecast for ARMA(1,1) demand can be obtained via conditional expectation as follows:

$$F_{t+1|t}^* = E(d_{t+1} \mid d_t, \varepsilon_t) = \mu + \phi(d_t - \mu) + \theta\varepsilon_t. \tag{4.12}$$

Since $d_t = \mu + \phi(d_{t-1} - \mu) + \theta\varepsilon_{t-1} + \varepsilon_t$, the noise term ε_t can be expressed as

$$\varepsilon_t = d_t - \mu - \phi(d_{t-1} - \mu) - \theta\varepsilon_{t-1} = d_t - \left(\mu + \phi(d_{t-1} - \mu) + \theta\varepsilon_{t-1}\right). \tag{4.13}$$

According to formula (4.12), the one-step least-MSE forecast made at the end of period $t-1$ can be expressed as

$$F_{t|t-1}^* = E(d_t \mid d_{t-1}, \varepsilon_{t-1}) = \mu + \phi(d_{t-1} - \mu) + \theta\varepsilon_{t-1}.$$

Using the above equality, Equation (4.13) can be written as

$$\theta = 0$$

Then, the one-step least-MSE forecast of (4.12) can be equivalently expressed as

$$F^*_{t+1|t} = \mu + \phi(d_t - \mu) + \theta(d_t - F^*_{t|t-1}) = \mu + \phi(d_t - \mu) + \theta(d_t - F^*_{t|t-1}). \tag{4.14}$$

The least-MSE forecast for the ARMA(1,1) process, given by (4.14), is also mean-reverting, combined with ϕ smoothing of demand deviation $(d_t - \mu)$ and θ smoothing of forecast error $(d_t - F^*_{t|t-1})$. For more than a one-step forecast for an ARMA(1,1) process (i.e., for $L = 2, 3, \cdots$), the following equality holds (with detailed derivation deferred to Appendix 4C):

$$F^*_{t+L|t} = \mu + \phi^{L-1}(F^*_{t+1|t} - \mu), \text{ for } L > 1. \tag{4.15}$$

In summary, the L-step least-MSE forecast for the ARMA(1,1) process, (with $L = 1, 2, \ldots$) can be determined as:

$$F^*_{t+L|t} = \begin{cases} (1-\phi)\mu + \phi d_t + \theta(d_t - F^*_{t|t-1}), & L = 1 \\ \mu + \phi^{L-1}(F^*_{t+1|t} - \mu), & L \geq 2 \end{cases}.$$

Mean-reverting smoothing (MRS) forecast derived from ARMA(1,1) process

Similarly, a general procedure of an ARMA(1,1)-derived mean-reverting smoothing (ARMA(1,1)-MRS) forecast can be constructed as follows:

1   Given an initial demand d_0 and an initial sample average demand $\bar{m}_0$, select smoothing constants ϕ and θ (with $|\phi| < 1$ and $|\theta| < 1$). If an $\bar{m}_0$ is not available, compute the initial sample average: $\bar{m}_0 = d_0$. Then, let the initial forecast be $F_0 = \bar{m}_0$.

2   For any current time t ($t > 0$) and a given realization d_t, update the sample average as follows:

$$\bar{m}_t = \frac{1}{t+1}(t\bar{m}_{t-1} + d_t).$$

3   Then, an L-lag forecast ($L \geq 1$) can be obtained as

$$F_{t+L|t} = \begin{cases} (1-\phi)\bar{m}_t + \phi d_t + \theta(d_t - F_{t|t-1}), & L = 1 \\ \bar{m}_t + \phi^{L-1}(F_{t+1|t} - \bar{m}_t), & L > 1 \end{cases}.$$

Let us consider the one-step ARMA-MRS forecast for the same beer sales as given in Table 4.1, with smoothing constants $\phi = 0.75$ and $\theta = 0.55$. For $t = 0$

with $d_0 = 12,500$ and $\bar{m}_0 = 12,500$, the ARMA-MRS forecast for the next week's sales can be easily computed as follows:

$$F_{1|0} = (1-\phi)\bar{m}_0 + \phi d_0 + \theta(d_0 - F_0) = (1-0.75)12,500$$
$$+ 0.75 \times 12,500 + 0.55(12,500 - 12,500) = 12,500.$$

For $t = 1$, the sample average is updated using $d_1 = 11,327$ as

$$\bar{m}_1 = \frac{1}{t+1}(t\bar{m}_0 + d_t) = \frac{1}{2}(1 \times 12,500 + 11,327) = 11,914.$$

Then, the ARMA-MRS forecast for the second week beer sales can be computed as follows:

$$F_{2|1} = (1-\phi)\bar{m}_1 + \phi d_1 + \theta(d_1 - F_{1|0}) = 10,828,$$

and so on. The results of an extensive numerical test with different combinations of ϕ and θ indicate that the sample MSE of a one-step ARMA(1,1)-derived forecast of beer sales is greater than that of AR(1) derived, except that the two sample MSEs are equal only when $\phi = 0.75$ and $\theta = 0$. Since an ARMA(1,1) is an AR(1) if $\theta = 0$, we shall conclude that an AR(1)-derived forecast is the most suitable for forecasting beer sales.

Forecasting first-order nonstationary ARIMA process

In this section, we will consider the forecast derived from an ARIMA(0,1,1) (termed IMA(1,1) for short), which is also known as a nonstationary unit-root process. The name "unit-root" reflects the fact that an ARIMA(0,1,1) process can be viewed as an ARMA(1,1) with $\phi = 1$. Recall from Chapter S4 that an ARIMA(0,1,1) process is modeled as:

$$d_{t+1} = c + d_t + \varepsilon_{t+1} + \theta\varepsilon_t, \text{ with } \varepsilon_t \sim (0, \sigma_\varepsilon^2) \text{ and } |\theta| < 1 \qquad (4.16)$$

where c is a constant (a drift). Comparing with the ARMA(1,1) given in (4.11), the only ARIMA(0,1,1) in (4.16) differs only in the coefficient ϕ, which becomes unit in (4.16). With $\phi = 1$, however, an ARIMA(0,1,1) process is no longer stationary, since the mean $E(d_t)$ and variance var(d_t) are not well determined. This can be easily verified from equalities in (4.12) that both $E(d_t)$ and var(d_t) become infinite as ϕ approaches 1. The equality $c = (1-\phi)\mu$ is no longer valid for the process given in (4.16), since $E(d_t) = \mu$ is no longer well defined.

Least-MSE forecast for ARIMA(0,1,1) process

The one-step least-MSE forecast for ARIMA(0,1,1) demand can be obtained via conditional expectation as follows:

$$F^*_{t+1|t} = E(d_{t+1} \mid d_t, \varepsilon_t) = c + d_t + \theta\varepsilon_t, \quad |\theta| < 1. \tag{4.17}$$

From (4.16) and (4.17), the forecast error is

$$d_{t+1} - F^*_{t+1|t} = (c + d_t + \varepsilon_{t+1} + \theta\varepsilon_t) - (c + d_t + \theta\varepsilon_t) = \varepsilon_{t+1}.$$

That is, the forecast error is a white noise that is unpredictable. An *L*-step least-MSE forecast for ARIMA(0,1,1) is then

$$F^*_{t+L|t} = E(d_{t+L} \mid d_t, \varepsilon_t) = E(c + d_{t+L-1} + \theta\varepsilon_{t+L-1} \mid d_t, \varepsilon_t)$$
$$= E\big(c + (c + d_{t+L-2} + \theta\varepsilon_{t+L-2}) \big| d_t, \varepsilon_t\big) = Lc + d_t + \theta\varepsilon_t.$$

Using the equality for the forecast error $\varepsilon_t = d_t - F^*_{t|t-1}$, a general *L*-step least-MSE forecast for ARIMA(0,1,1) can be written as:

$$F^*_{t+L|t} = Lc + d_t + \theta\varepsilon_t = Lc + d_t + \theta(d_t - F^*_{t|t-1})$$
$$= Lc + (1+\theta)d_t - \theta F^*_{t|t-1}. \tag{4.18}$$

Especially when there is no drift (i.e., $c = 0$) and assuming that $-1 < \theta < 0$, the ARIMA derived one-step forecast (4.18) is referred to as *exponential smoothing* (or adaptive expectation, Hamilton 1994):

$$F^*_{t+1|t} = (1 + \theta)d_t - \theta F^*_{t|t-1} = \alpha d_t + (1 - \alpha)F^*_{t|t-1}. \tag{4.19}$$

where $\alpha = 1 + \theta$ is an exponential smoothing constant ($0 < \alpha < 1$). Note that the exponential smoothing forecast is of least-MSE only for an ARIMA(0,1,1) process without drift. A general exponential smoothing forecast method, called exponentially weighted moving average (EWMA), has been derived for applications in general ARIMA forecasting. Perhaps, the EWMA forecast is the most popular method adopted in commercial forecasting software.

Exponential smoothing forecast derived from ARIMA(0,1,1) process

A general procedure of ARIMA(0,1,1)-derived exponential smoothing (ARIMA(0,1,1)-ES) forecast can be constructed as

1　Given an initial demand d_0, select a smoothing constants α ($0 < \alpha < 1$). Then, let the initial forecast be $F_0 = d_0$.

2 For any current time $t(t > 0)$ and a given realization d_t, the one-step EWMA forecast is determined as follows:

$$F_{t+1|t} = \alpha d_t + (1-\alpha)F_{t|t-1}.$$

3 Then, an L-lag forecast $(L \geq 1)$ can be obtained as

$$F_{t+L|t} = F_{t+1|t}.$$

To illustrate how exponential smoothing forecast is applied, let us consider a one-step EWMA forecast for the same beer sales as given in Table 4.1, with smoothing constants $\alpha = 0.7$. For $t = 0$ with $F_0 = d_0 = 12,500$, the EWMA forecast for the next week's sales can be easily computed as follows:

$$F_{1|0} = \alpha d_0 + (1-\alpha)F_0 = 0.7 \times 12,500 + 0.3 \times 12,500 = 12,500.$$

For $t = 1$, the EWMA forecast is updated using $d_1 = 11,327$ as

$$F_{2|1} = \alpha d_1 + (1-\alpha)F_{1|0} = 0.7 \times 11,327 + 0.3 \times 12,500 = 11,679$$

and so on. An extensive numerical test of EWMA forecast on the beer sales data, with different values of α, reveals that the smallest sample MSE is attained with $\alpha = 0.79$. According to the test results, the square root of the sample MSE with $\alpha = 0.79$ is found to be:

$$\text{For EWMA with } \alpha = 0.79: \quad \sqrt{\text{MSE}} = 1,202.$$

Recall that the smallest square root of sample MSE under AR-MRS is

$$\text{For AR-MRS with } \phi = 0.75: \quad \sqrt{\text{MSE}} = 1,193.$$

In the case of beer sales forecast, the AR-MRS is still the best performer in terms of minimum MSE criterion. In general, selection of the proper forecasting model critically depends on accurate characterization of the processes that are to be forecasted, by careful analysis of past data as studied in Chapter 4. In the next section we will further examine the selection and application of general-purpose forecast models.

General time-series forecast models

Guidelines for forecast model selection

As mentioned earlier, selection of a proper forecast model relies on accurate characterization of the behavior of the underlying processes. The characterization requires thorough calculations (in Sun Zi's sense) that are based on, and theorized

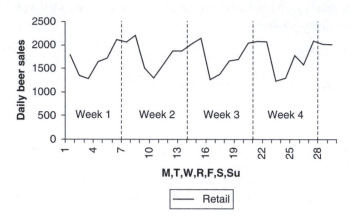

Figure 4.9 Daily beer retail sales with seasonality.

from, careful study of the "patterns" in the realizations of the demand processes. In the context of demand forecast, typical elements of the "patterns" (i.e., drift functions) that are of particular interest include the following:

- Stationarity: mean-stationary (i.e., mean-reverting), covariance-stationary (or in-control fluctuation), and so on.
- Correlation: autocorrelated versus uncorrelated, first-order versus higher-order correlation, and so on.
- Trend: linear time-line growth.
- Seasonality: cyclical patterns of fluctuation. For example, sales of winter coats typically experience a peak in the winter season, and a valley during the summer season.

Thus far, we have studied all of the above elements, except for seasonality. Analytical characterization of seasonality involves advanced mathematics, such as nonlinear time-series and stochastic integration, which are far beyond the scope of this book, and therefore omitted. Instead, let us illustrate the concept of seasonality via an example of seasonal data. Figure 4.9 shows daily sales of the bottled beer for the past 4 weeks (Monday through Sunday) at a retailer who purchases beer from the same wholesaler as in Example 4.2.

From the sample daily demand presented in Figure 4.9, we can see that there exists an obvious pattern of seasonality, where the sales tend to peak over the weekend, and tend to slow down during the weekdays. It is interesting to note that in the beer example, daily retail sales exhibit the pattern of seasonality, while the weekly wholesale, which is an aggregation of daily retail sales, is not necessarily seasonal. The wholesale demand, for example, may follow an $AR(1)$ process. Thus, the characterization of an unknown process is highly dependent of specific applications and situation, and so is model selection.

Table 4.5 Four-week daily beer consumption data

Week	Day	Daily s(i)	Week	Day	Daily s(i)
		3,147			
1	1	824	3	1	827
	2	1,130		2	666
	3	818		3	1,369
	4	1,340		4	901
	5	1,798		5	1,995
	6	2,703		6	2,870
	7	3,718		7	3,417
2	1	642	4	1	239
	2	446		2	1,153
	3	709		3	1,044
	4	684		4	1,146
	5	2,233		5	2,319
	6	2,327		6	2,767
	7	3,329		7	3,498

Prototype example: daily forecasting of beer demand with seasonality

Consider the same beer demand process as the one given in Table 4.1, which is known to be an $AR(1)$ time-series, except that now we have obtained a set of break-down daily demand data for the past 4 weeks (a month). The data are displayed in Table 4.5, and the sample path of the daily beer demand is plotted in Figure 4.10.

We can see from Figure 4.10 that a "seasonal" pattern appears in the sample path, namely, Monday demand tends to be lower than weekly average and week-end demand tends to be higher than weekly average. On the one hand, we know that the weekly beer demand follows an AR(1) process, $d_{t+1} = (1-\phi)\mu + \phi d_t + \varepsilon_{t+1}$ with $\phi = 0.65$, $\mu = 12,800$, and $\sigma_\varepsilon = 1,316$. While on the other hand, the daily beer consumption presents seasonality with a seasonal cycle of 7 days.

Disaggregated time-series demand

For ease of presentation, let us denote the seasonal cycle by L (in this case, $L = 7$), and denote daily demand in week t as $s_t(i)$, where i is the daily index with a seasonal cycle (i.e., $i = 1, 2, \ldots, L$). The weekly demand d_t can be thus disaggregated into daily demand as follows:

$$d_t = s_t(M) + s_t(T) + s_t(W) + s_t(Th) + s_t(F) + s_t(Sa) + s_t(Su)$$

$$= s_t(1) + \cdots + s_t(L) = \sum_{i=1}^{L} s_t(i).$$

Given an AR(1) aggregated weekly demand $d_t = c + \phi d_{t-1} + \varepsilon_t$ with white error $\varepsilon_t \sim (0, \sigma_\varepsilon^2)$, the disaggregated daily demand $s_t(i)$ can be constructed as another AR(1) process as follows:

$$s_t(i) = c_i + \phi s_{t-1}(i) + \tilde{\varepsilon}_t(i), \text{ with white error } \tilde{\varepsilon}_t(i) \sim (0, \tilde{\sigma}_\varepsilon^2)$$

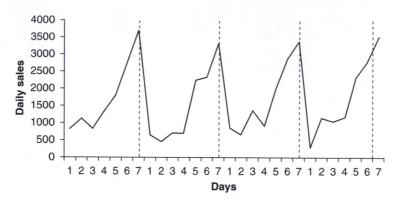

Figure 4.10 Sample path of daily beer consumption.

where $\sum_{i=1}^{L} c_i = c$, and $\sum_{i=1}^{L} \tilde{\varepsilon}_t(i) = \varepsilon_t$.

The mean and variance of the disaggregated AR(1) demand can be obtained as follows:

$$E\left(s_t(i)\right) = \frac{c_i}{1-\phi}, \text{and var}\left(s_t(i)\right) = \frac{\tilde{\sigma}_{\varepsilon}^2}{1-\phi^2}$$

It is easy to verify that

$$d_t = \sum_{i=1}^{L} s_t(i) = \sum_{i=1}^{L} c_i + \phi \sum_{i=1}^{L} s_{t-1}(i) + \sum_{i=1}^{L} \tilde{\varepsilon}_t(i) = c + \phi d_{t-1} + \varepsilon_t.$$

Obviously, the following statistical characteristics must be satisfied:

- $E(d_t) = E\left(\sum_{i=1}^{L} s_t(i)\right) = \sum_{i=1}^{L} E\left(s(i)\right) = \mu$

- $\text{var}\left(\varepsilon_t\right) = \text{var}\left(\sum_{i=1}^{L} \tilde{\varepsilon}_t(i)\right) = \sum_{i=1}^{L} \text{var}\left(\varepsilon_t(i)\right)$, that is, $\sigma_{\varepsilon}^2 = L\tilde{\sigma}_{\varepsilon}^2$

- Daily average over a week $= \dfrac{E\left(\text{weekly demand}\right)}{L} = \dfrac{\mu}{L}$.

Seasonality index

For each season t (e.g., week t), seasonal indices, $I_t(i)$ ($i = 1, \cdots, L$), are introduced to characterize seasonal averages as follows:

$$I_t(i) = \frac{\text{average } i\text{th season demand}}{\text{daily average of a week}} = \frac{E(s(i))}{\mu/L} = \frac{LE(s_t(i))}{\mu}$$

Since $\sum_{i=1}^{L} E(s(i)) = \mu$ by definition, the following equality must follow:

$$\sum_{i=1}^{L} I_t(i) = \frac{L}{\mu} \sum_{i=1}^{L} E(s_t(i)) = L$$

Using $E(s_t(i)) = \dfrac{c_i}{1-\phi}$ and $\mu = \dfrac{c}{1-\phi}$, the seasonal index can also be expressed as follows:

$$I_t(i) = \frac{Lc_i}{\mu(1-\phi)} = \frac{L}{c}c_i, \text{ or equivalently } c_i = \frac{c}{L}I_t(i)$$

From Figure 4.10, we observe the following:

- $L = 7$: seasonal cycle of 7 days.
- $s_t(i)$: demand of the ith day in a week t presents a cyclic pattern.
- $E(s_t(1))$: expected Monday demand in a week t tends to valley below daily average μ/L. That is, $I_t(1) < 1$.
- $E(s_t(7))$: expected Sunday demand in a week t tends to peak above daily average μ/L. That is, $I_t(7) > 1$.

Forecasting daily beer demand with seasonality

General AR-MRS forecasting with seasonality, without knowledge of weekly demand mean μ, can be derived as follows:

1   Set initial time $t \Leftarrow t_0$, and compute initial values: an initial weekly demand data $\bar{m}_t = d_t$, initial daily demand data set $\{s_t(i) : i = 1,\dots,L\}$, and initial disaggregated daily average $\bar{s}_t(i) = s_t(i)$ ($i = 1,\cdots,L$). Obtain initial set of seasonal indices, $I_t(i) = \dfrac{L\bar{s}_t(i)}{\bar{m}_t}$, for $i = 1,\dots,L$. Let $t \Leftarrow t+1$

2   At the beginning of a current week t, for $i = 1,\dots,L$, compute the constant $c_i = (c/L)I_{t-1}(i)$, and compute the AR-MRS daily forecasts for the current week t as follows:

$$F_{t(i)} = c_i + \phi \, s_{t-1}(i)$$

3   At the end of a current week t, collect the newly realized data set $\{s_t(i) : i = 1,\ldots,L\}$, and update the parameters as follows:

- $\bar{s}_t(i) = \dfrac{s_0(i)+\cdots+s_t(i)}{t+1}$, and $\bar{m}_t = \dfrac{d_0+\cdots+d_t}{t+1}$

- $I_t(i) = \dfrac{L\bar{s}_t(i)}{\bar{m}_t}$

- Let $t \Leftarrow t+1$, and go to step 2.

For the example data given in Table 4.5 with $\mu = 12,800$, let us take the week 1 data to compute initial seasonal indices:

$$I_1(1) = \frac{Ls_1(1)}{\mu} = \frac{7(824)}{12,800} = 0.45, \quad I_1(2) = \frac{Ls_1(2)}{\mu} = \frac{7(1,130)}{12,800} = 0.62$$

$$I_1(3) = \frac{Ls_1(3)}{\mu} = \frac{7(818)}{12,800} = 0.45, \quad I_1(4) = \frac{Ls_1(4)}{\mu} = \frac{7(1,340)}{12,800} = 0.73$$

$$I_1(5) = \frac{Ls_1(5)}{\mu} = \frac{7(1,798)}{12,800} = 0.98, \quad I_1(6) = \frac{Ls_1(6)}{\mu} = \frac{7(2,703)}{12,800} = 1.48$$

$$I_1(7) = \frac{Ls_1(7)}{\mu} = \frac{7(3,718)}{12,800} = 2.03 .$$

Now, let us generate forecasts for week 2 (i.e., for $t = 2$). First, the disaggregated constants c_i $(i = 1,2,\ldots,7)$ can be updated as follows:

$$c_1 = \frac{c}{L}I_{t-1}(1) = \frac{4,480}{7}I_1(1) = 289, \quad c_2 = \frac{c}{L}I_1(2)$$

$$= \frac{4,480}{7} \times 0.62 = 395$$

$$c_3 = \frac{c}{L}I_1(3) = \frac{4,480}{7} \times 0.45 = 286, \quad c_4 = \frac{c}{L}I_1(4) = \frac{4,480}{7} \times 0.73 = 469$$

$$c_5 = \frac{c}{L}I_1(5) = \frac{4,480}{7} \times 0.98 = 629, \quad c_6 = \frac{c}{L}I_1(6) = \frac{4,480}{7} \times 1.48 = 946$$

$$c_7 = \frac{c}{L}I_1(7) = \frac{4,480}{7} \times 2.03 = 1,301.$$

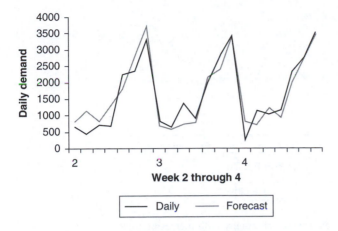

Figure 4.11 Forecasts of daily beer demand with seasonality.

We can then produce daily forecasts for week 2 as follows:

$$F_{2(1)} = c_1 + \phi s_1(1) = 289 + 0.65 \times 824 = 824,$$
$$F_{2(7)} = c_7 + \phi s_1(7) = 3,718.$$

By the end of week 2, we collect sample demand data $\{s_2(i), i = 1,\ldots,7\}$ and sample week 2 demand d_2, and update the following:

- $\bar{s}_2(i) = (s_1(i) + s_2(i))/2$ (for $i = 1,\ldots,7$), and if μ is not given, then $\bar{m}_2 = (d_1 + d_2)/2$

- $I_2(i) = L\bar{s}_2(i)/\mu$. If μ is not given, then $I_2(i) = L\bar{s}_2(i)/\bar{m}_2$.

Then, we continue and repeat the forecasting process for week 3, and so on. Figure 4.11 illustrates the forecasting trajectory from week 2 through 4, as compared with the actual demand data given in Table 4.5.

Forecast models with trend and seasonality

In reality, a seasonal demand process may well also exhibit a trend, as for the sample data shown in Figure 4.12. Although there can hardly be a single way that will guarantee the best model to be identified, the following considerations for a forecast model selection are usually recommended.

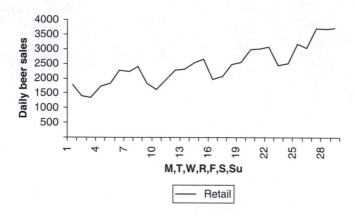

Figure 4.12 Daily beer retail sales: seasonality with increasing trend.

- Gather time-series data and observations.
- Graphical presentation and visual inspection: visually identify the elements of patterns (i.e., characteristics) of the time-series.
- Characterize the time-series: fit sample data with time-series models.
- Select, or construct if needed, forecast models according to the characterization obtained.
- Validate and verify the model selected by conducting simulation tests on the sample data.

Holt's trend-adjusted exponential smoothing (TAES) forecast

When a trend exists, which often appears in real-world data, the forecast may be improved by using the Holt's two-parameter exponential smoothing method. The Holt's method is also referred to as trend-adjusted double smoothing, which consists of two smoothing equations—one for demand forecast and the other for trend estimate.

Holt's trend-adjusted forecast model:

$$S_{t+1|t} = \alpha d_t + (1-\alpha)(S_{t|t-1} + T_{t|t-1})$$

$$T_{t+1|t} = \beta(S_{t+1|t} - S_{t|t-1}) + (1-\beta)T_{t|t-1}$$

$$F_{t+L|t} = S_{t+1|t} + LT_{t+1|t}$$

where

d_t = demand realization in period t

$S_{t+1|t}$ = smoothed base (i.e., intercept) for the trend line at the beginning of period $t+1$

α = smoothing constant for the base demand $(0 < \alpha < 1)$

$T_{t+1|t}$ = trend estimate for period $t+1$

β = smoothing constant for trend estimate $(0 < \beta < 1)$

$F_{t+L|t}$ = Holt's trend-adjusted forecast for period $t + L$.

Note that the forecast, $F_{t+L|t}$, in Holt's model is presented by a linear time trend line, with $S_{t+1|t}$ as the intercept, $T_{t+1|t}$ as the slope, and L as the time variable (i.e., independent variable). Also note that the most recent trend $(S_{t+1|t} - S_{t|t-1})$ is smoothed with β, and the last trend estimate is smoothed with $(1 - \beta)$. The sum of such weighted values represents an exponential smoothing, applied to adjust the trend.

Winters' trend-seasonal exponential smoothing forecast

For the situations where trended seasonality is identified in the data, the Winters' forecast method of trend-plus-seasonality exponential smoothing may be considered. It is an extension of Holt's double smoothing model, by amending with the third component of the exponential smoothing on seasonality estimate. The Winters' model of triple smoothing is constructed as follows:

Winters' trend-seasonal forecast model (with seasonal cycle C):

$$S_{t+1|t} = \alpha \frac{d_t}{I_{t|t-C}} + (1-\alpha)(S_{t|t-1} + T_{t|t-1})$$

$$T_{t+1|t} = \beta(S_{t+1|t} - S_{t|t-1}) + (1-\beta)T_{t|t-1}$$

$$I_{t|t} = \gamma \frac{d_t}{S_{t+1|t}}(S_{t+1|t} - S_{t|t-1}) + (1-\gamma)I_{t|t-C}$$

$$F_{t+L|t} = \left(S_{t+1|t} + LT_{t+1|t}\right) \times I_{t+L|t+L-C}$$

where

d_t = demand realization in period t (by the end of period t)

$S_{t+1|t}$ = smoothed base (i.e., intercept) for the trend line at the beginning of period $t+1$

α = smoothing constant for the base demand $(0 < \alpha < 1)$

$T_{t+1|t}$ = trend estimate for period $t+1$

β = smoothing constant for trend estimate $(0 < \beta < 1)$

$I_{t|t-C}$ = estimated of seasonality index.

γ = smoothing constant for seasonality estimate $(0 < \gamma < 1)$

$F_{t+L|t}$ = Holt's TAES forecast for period $t+L$.

Comparing with Holt's model, Winters' model differs only in the extension regarding seasonality, which is measured by the seasonality index. Seasonality index is defined as the ratio of actual demand versus the theoretical base (intercept), or symbolically expressed as d_{t-C}/S_{t-C}, where period $t-C$ is the same period of the last seasonal cycle. For example, if $t =$ March of this year, then $t-C$ represents March of last year. By S_{t-C}, we denoted the theoretical base (intercept) that can be assessed for period $t-C$. Since theoretical base is usually unknown, thus the seasonality index must be estimated. The symbol $I_{t|t-C}$ represents an estimate of the seasonality index for period t, but the estimate is obtained from the last season (i.e., in period $t-C$).

Forecast-facilitated order planning and bullwhip effect

Example 4.4   Forecast-facilitated lot-for-lot beer wholesale orders

Suppose that a wholesaler faces the same weekly demand for bottle beer as in Example 4.2. The wholesaler orders the bottled beer from a brewer with a 1-week lead-time, using a **lot-for-lot** order policy as described in Example 3.8. Specifically, every Monday morning the wholesaler submits orders to the brewer, who then delivers the ordered beer to the wholesaler by Sunday afternoon, so that the ordered beer will be ready for consumption starting the following Monday. Thus, the order released this Monday is intended for 1-week consumption starting the next Monday. During the implementation of such a lot-for-lot order, the wholesaler must involve forecasting, either a good or bad forecast, or even some wild guess. For example, in order to determine the order size for the Monday of week 1, the wholesaler needs to obtain some forecast for the weekly demand in week 2. The wholesaler decided to select a suitable forecast model for the lot-for-lot beer orders, by conducting a simulation test on the sample data as given in Table 4.1, starting at the Monday morning of week 0 with the initial demand data $d_0 = 12,500$, initial inventory $x_0 = 0$, and an order of 12,500 that was placed last week is scheduled to arrive at the beginning of week 1 (i.e., $q_0 = 12,500$). The initial conditions are summarized in Table 4.6.

Table 4.6 Initial wholesale beer stocks ($L = 1$)

	0	1	2	3	...
Weekly requirement	12,500	$\left[\hat{d}_1\right]$	$\left[\hat{d}_2\right]$		
Scheduled receive		12,500			
End inventory	0	$\left[\hat{x}_1\right]$			
Lot-for-lot order release	q_0	$\left[q_1\right]$			

To proceed with the simulation, the wholesaler first will select a forecast model. Since the analysis so far indicated that an AR-MRS model with $\phi = 0.75$ fits the beer sales data the best, let us consider an AR-MRS forecast for the simulation of the lot-for-lot beer orders.

With the initial values given in Table 4.6, the wholesaler needs to produce two forecasts, one for week 1 $\left(\hat{d}_1\right)$ and one for week 2 $\left(\hat{d}_2\right)$ based on initial sample data $d_0 = 12,500$. Note that the forecasts are made at the beginning of week 1 when demand in week 1 (d_1) is not realized yet. Without using the sample data d_1, the wholesaler needs to determine the lot-for-lot order q_1 that is to be released at the beginning of week 1. Since the order q_1 is intended for consumption in week 2, the quantity of q_1 is determined as follows:

$$q_1 = (\text{forecast for week 2}) - (\text{projected end inventory of week 1}) = \hat{d}_2 - \hat{x}_1,$$

where

$$\hat{x}_1 = \text{projected ending inventory of week 1} = x_0 + q_0 - \hat{d}_1$$
$$= (\text{begin inventory of week 0}) + (\text{order received in week 0}) - (\text{week 1 forecast})$$
$$= x_0 + q_0 - \hat{d}_1 = 0 + 12,500 - \hat{d}_1.$$

All the values that are to be determined by the wholesaler at the beginning of week 1 are shown in brackets in Table 4.6. We can see that the first-order decision q_1 are determined from the forecasts $\hat{d}_1$ and $\hat{d}_2$. By the AR-MRS forecast with $\phi = 0.75$ and $d_0 = 12,500$, the two forecasts can be determined as

$$d_{t+1} - \mu = \theta\varepsilon_t + \varepsilon_{t+1} = \theta\big((d_t - \mu) - \theta\varepsilon_{t-1}\big) + \varepsilon_{t+1}$$

$$= \theta\big((d_t - \mu) - \theta(d_{t-1} - \mu) + \theta^2(d_{t-2} - \mu) - \cdots\big) + \varepsilon_{t+1}$$

$$= \theta\sum_{i=1}^{\infty}(-\theta)^{i-1}(d_{t-i+1} - \mu) + \varepsilon_{t+1} = \sum_{i=1}^{\infty}\theta(-\theta)^{i-1}(d_{t-i+1} - \mu) + \varepsilon_{t+1}$$

$$\hat{d}_2 = F_{2|0} = (1-\phi^2)\bar{m}_0 + \phi^2 d_0 = (1-(0.75)^2)(12,500) + (0.75)^2$$

$$\times 12,500 = 12,500.$$

With the forecasts, the projected inventory and the order release can be determined as

$$\hat{x}_1 = x_0 + 12,500 - \hat{d}_1 = 0, \text{ and}$$

$$q_1 = \hat{d}_2 - \hat{x}_1 = 12,500.$$

The results are updated in Table 4.7. Now, let us consider the next iteration, with the sample demand of week 1 recorded as $d_1 = 11,327$. First, we updated the actual ending inventory of week 1 with the sample demand d_1, as follows:

$$x_1 = x_0 + q_0 - d_1 = 0 + 12,500 - 11,327 = 1,173$$

The actual ending inventory x_1 differs from the projected ending inventory $\hat{x}_1 = 0$ by an amount of 1,173. Using $d_1 = 11,327$, the forecasts for weeks 2 and 3 can be obtained as

$$\bar{m}_1 = (d_0 + d_1)/2 = (12,500 + 11,327)/2 = 11,914$$

$$\hat{d}_2 = F_{2|1} = (1-\phi)\bar{m}_1 + \phi d_1 = (1-0.75)(11,914) + 0.75 \times 11,327 = 11,474$$

$$\hat{d}_3 = F_{3|1} = (1-\phi^2)\bar{m}_1 + \phi^2 d_1 = (1-(0.75)^2)(11,914) + (0.75)^2 \times 11,327 = 11,584$$

Then the projected ending inventory $\hat{x}_2$ and the new order release q_2 can be calculated as

$$\hat{x}_2 = x_1 + q_1 - \hat{d}_2 = 1,173 + 12,500 - 11,474 = 2,199$$

$$q_2 = \max\{0, \hat{d}_3 - \hat{x}_2\} = 11,584 - 2,199 = 9,385.$$

Table 4.7 Initial wholesale beer stocks ($L = 1$)

	0	1	2	3	...
Weekly requirement	12,500	[12,500]	[12,500]		
Scheduled receive		12,500	12,500		
End inventory	0	[0]			
Lot-for-lot order release	q_0	q_1			

Table 4.8 Week 1 updates for wholesale beer stocks ($L = 1$)

	0	1	2	3	...
Weekly requirement	12,500	11,327	[11,474]	[11,584]	
Scheduled receive		12,500	12,500	[9,384]	
End inventory	0	1,173	[2,199]		
Lot-for-lot order release	q_0	q_1	q_2		

Note that the order q_2 is released at the beginning of week 2, after sample demand d_1 is realized. The wholesaler order transactions are updated in Table 4.8.

Forecast-facilitated lot-for-lot order planning

From the iterations carried out so far, we can see that forecasting plays a vital role in both inventory management and planned order release. Let us summarize these variations with an algorithmic procedure for **forecast-facilitated lot-for-lot order release**:

Given demand realization d_t by the end of period t (with fixed lead-time L):

- Update actual end inventory: $x_t = x_{t-1} + q_{t-L} - d_t$.
- Obtained forecasts for each of the next $L+1$ periods:

$$\left\{ \hat{d}_{t+i} : i = 1, 2, \cdots, L+1 \right\}.$$

Forecasts are generated by a preselected forecast model.

- Update projected end inventory for each of the next L periods:

$$\left\{ \hat{x}_{t+i} = \hat{x}_{t+i-1} + q_{t+i-L} - \hat{d}_{t+i} : i = 1, 2, \cdots, L \right\}, \text{ with } \hat{x}_t = x_t.$$

- Determine the order release by the beginning of period $L+1$:

$$q_{t+1} = \max\left\{ 0, \hat{d}_{t+L+1} - \hat{x}_{t+L} \right\}.$$

Applying the above algorithmic procedure with $L=1$ to the whole data set given in Table 4.1, a complete set of lot-for-lot orders can be determined, $\{q_1, q_2, \ldots, q_{48}\}$ under AR-MRS forecasting with $\phi = 0.75$. Figure 4.13 presents the sample path of the lot-for-lot orders, as compared with original sample data. The last order release is made at the beginning of week 48, which is scheduled for delivery by the beginning of week 49, per the 1-week lead-time.

Note that the lot-for-lot order-release procedure described above is generic, and is applicable under forecasting models other than AR-MRS. As we can see from the order-release procedure, order-release planning is based on the forecasts over lead-time. Clearly, the bottom line for order release is to match it with the demand realization as closely as possible. This is consistent with the objective of minimizing MSE, namely, minimizing deviation of the order process $\{q_t\}$ from the demand process $\{d_t\}$. Since the measure of MSE reflects the accuracy of the underlying forecast method, forecast models must be carefully selected in production order planning. The comparative simulation, as we have engaged in in this book, would be useful in evaluating and selecting a forecast model for production order planning.

Forecasting and bullwhip effect in production order planning

In reality, it is impossible to make the sequence of order release follow exactly the sample path of the demand. Obviously, the best we can do is to minimize the deviation of order process from the demand process. We can examine fluctuations incurred in the orders generated under a specific forecasting scheme. Then, the most suitable forecast model can be selected by comparing the resulting values of least-MSE under different forecast methods. For example, based on the simulation outputs of released orders, we can compute the sample mean and sample variance of the lot-for-lot orders:

Sample mean: $\bar{q} = \dfrac{q_1 + \cdots + q_{48}}{48} = 12,548$

Sample variance: $S^2(q_t) = \dfrac{(q_1 - \bar{q})^2 + \cdots + (q_{48} - \bar{q})}{48 - 1} = 8,392,692$

Sample standard deviation: $S(q_t) = \sqrt{S^2(q_t)} = 2,897.$

For comparison, we recalculate the sample mean and variance for the demand data given in Table 4.1 as follows:

$\bar{d} = \dfrac{d_1 + \cdots + d_{48}}{48} = 12,558$, and $S(d_t) = \sqrt{S^2(d_t)} = 1,800.$

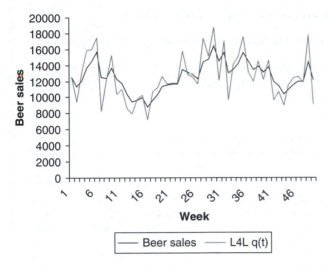

Figure 4.13 Sample path of lot-for-lot orders under AR-MRS forecasting.

Then, the ratio of the variance between the planned orders versus the demand is termed bullwhip ratio, which is defined as

$$\text{Bullwhip ratio (BR)}: \text{BR} = \frac{\text{var}(q_t)}{\text{var}(d_t)}, \text{ and sample BR}: \overline{\text{BR}} = \frac{S^2(q_t)}{S^2(d_t)}.$$

The bullwhip effect is then said to exist in the ordering process if $\text{BR} > 1$ (or $\overline{\text{BR}} > 1$), otherwise it is referred to as no-bullwhip effect. For the case of a lot-for-lot order under AR-MRS forecast, the bullwhip ratio is

$$\overline{\text{BR}}(\text{L4L-AR}) = \frac{2879^2}{1,800^2} = 2.59 (> 1).$$

As the bullwhip ratio is greater than 1, the bullwhip effect exists in the lot-for-lot orders under *AR*-MRS forecasting. For illustrative purposes, we repeated the simulation to the beer data of Table 4.1, but EWMA is used in the order-planning process instead. For the case of lot-for-lot under EWMA forecast, the bullwhip ratio computed from the simulation results is:

$$\overline{\text{BR}}(\text{L4L-EWMA}) = \frac{3,122^2}{1,800^2} = 3.01.$$

By comparison, we can see that bullwhip effect is incurred in both the L4L-AR and L4L-EWMA order-planning processes. However, the best model choice remains the L4L-AR method, as it gives a smaller bullwhip ratio (or equivalently, a smaller measure of MSE).

Simulation lab: Forecast-facilitated order release

Assignment 4.1: Forecasting piston daily demand at Quick-Engine

Daily piston sales for the past 60 days at Quick-Engine (QE) are shown in Table 4.4 (reprinted below for convenience). Suppose that the market condition has remained the same.

Table 4.4 Least-MSE forecast for weekly beer demand

Week	d_t	F_{t+1}	e_t	Week	d_t	F_{t+1}	e_t
0	12,500						
1	11,327	12,605	−1,278	25	12,295	12,808	−513
2	12,087	11,843	244	26	14,444	12,472	1,972
3	13,613	12,337	1,276	27	14,734	13,869	865
4	14,527	13,328	1,199	28	16,433	14,057	2,376
5	15,656	13,923	1,733	29	14,507	15,161	−654
6	12,473	14,656	−2,183	30	15,571	13,910	1,661
7	12,353	12,587	−234	31	12,989	14,601	−1,612
8	13,604	12,509	1,095	32	13,462	12,923	539
9	12,236	13,323	−1,087	33	14,132	13,230	902
10	11,743	12,433	−690	34	15,585	13,666	1,919
11	10,423	12,113	−1,690	35	14,526	14,610	−84
12	9,408	11,255	−1,847	36	13,398	13,922	−524
13	9,617	10,595	−978	37	13,864	13,189	675
14	9,958	10,731	−773	38	13,110	13,492	−382
15	8,835	10,953	−2,118	39	13,759	13,002	758
16	9,655	10,223	−568	40	11,979	13,423	−1,444
17	10,351	10,756	−405	41	11,419	12,266	−847
18	11,343	11,208	135	42	10,381	11,902	−1,521
19	11,488	11,853	−365	43	10,865	11,228	−363
20	11,620	11,947	−327	44	11,510	11,542	−32
21	11,663	12,033	−370	45	11,989	11,962	28
22	13,403	12,061	1,342	46	11,950	12,273	−323
23	13,107	13,192	−85	47	14,442	12,248	2,195
24	12,813	13,000	−187	48	12,125	13,867	−1,742

A　Apply *MA*-MRS forecasting to the piston sales data, and record the forecast error for each of the past 60 days. Determine a smoothing constant that would generate the smallest sample MSE. Compute the sample mean and sample variance of forecast error under the best smoothing constant you just determined. *Hint*: Given a set of samples $\{d_1, d_2, \ldots, d_n\}$ with unknown theoretical mean $\mu = E(d_t)$, the sample mean and variance are defined as follows:

Sample mean: $\bar{d} = \dfrac{d_1 + \cdots + d_n}{n} = \dfrac{1}{n}\sum_{i=1}^{n} d_i$

Sample variance: $S^2 = \dfrac{(d_1 - \bar{d})^2 + \cdots + (d_n - \bar{d})}{n-1} = \dfrac{1}{n-1}\sum_{i=1}^{n}(d_i - \bar{d})^2$

Sample standard deviation: $S = \sqrt{\dfrac{1}{n-1}\sum_{i=1}^{n}(d_i - \bar{d})^2}$.

B Instead, apply AR-MRS forecasting to the piston sales data, and record the forecast error for each of the past 60 days. Repeat the analysis as you did in A.

C Now apply the EWMA forecast to the data, and repeat the analysis as you did in A and B.

D Compare the performance of the three forecasting methods, and recommend a forecasting method for the piston sales forecast. Then use the recommended forecasting method to generate forecasts for the next 10 days, namely, the forecasts for day 61 through day 70.

Assignment 4.2: Forecast-facilitated lot-for-lot orders of pistons at QE

Consider the same piston inventory system with the same past data as given in Table 4.4. Suppose that daily piston demand follows an AR(1) time-series model with mean $\mu = 2{,}927$ and $\phi = 0.59$. The piston is purchased from a designated supplier with a 3-day lead-time. The piston orders are placed by QE under a lot-for-lot order policy. Suppose that initial conditions are given as in Table 4.9.

Table 4.9 Lot-for-lot pistons order transactions ($L = 3$)

	0	1	2	3	4
Daily requirement	3,200	$\hat{d}_1$	$\hat{d}_2$	$\hat{d}_3$	$\hat{d}_4$
Scheduled receive		3,000	3,000	3,000	[ ]
End inventory	133	$\left[\hat{x}_1\right]$	$\left[\hat{x}_2\right]$	$\left[\hat{x}_3\right]$	
Lot-for-lot order release		q_1			

A Using the lot-for-lot ordering policy, determine q_1 that is released at the beginning of day 1, given initial conditions in Table 4.9. *Hint*: To determine q_1 at the beginning of day 1, you need to obtain demand forecasts of $\hat{d}_1, \hat{d}_2, \hat{d}_3,$ and $\hat{d}_4$, and then obtain estimated ending inventory status $\hat{x}_1, \hat{x}_2,$ and $\hat{x}_3$. Finally, the lot-for-lot order released at the beginning of day 1 can be determined as: $q_1 = \max\{0, \hat{d}_4 - \hat{x}_3\}$.

B Now, proceed to the next period (i.e., at the beginning of week 2) as follows: First, replace the forecast $\hat{d}_1$ with the realized demand in day 1 given in Table 4.4, that is, $d_1 = 3,108$; second, update the actual ending inventory for day 1 (i.e., x_1); third, using the updated d_1 and x_1, determine the next order release q_2 in the same way as you did in step A above.

C Using the data given in Assignment 4.1, repeat the lot-for-lot ordering procedure and determine all the rest order release, namely, $q_3, q_4, \ldots, q_{60}$.

D Compute sample average and sample variance of the order:

$$\bar{q} = \frac{q_1 + \cdots + q_{60}}{60}, \text{ and } S^2 = \frac{(q_1 - \bar{q})^2 + \cdots + (q_{60} - \bar{q})^2}{60 - 1}.$$

E Compute sample average and sample variance of the demand data (d_t) you obtained in Assignment 4.1. Then, compute the sample variance ratio defined as follows:

$$\text{Variance ratio} = \frac{\text{var}(q_t)}{\text{var}(d_t)}.$$

(Note if the variance ratio is greater than 1, then it is said there is a bullwhip effect in an order system.)

F Compute average ending inventory stock and average backorder. *Hint*: Ending inventory stock for period t = actual ending inventory x_t, if $x_t \geq 0$. Backorder for period $t = -x_t$, if $x_t \leq 0$.

Problems

Basic exercises

1   Daily sales of bottled beer (in thousands) for the past 30 days at B&D beverage wholesaler are shown in Table 4.10. Suppose that the market condition will remain the same.

Table 4.10 (For Problem 1): B&D daily beer sales

Day	d_t	Day	d_t	Day	d_t
0	9.810				
1	11.624	11	8.158	21	5.504
2	8.623	12	11.960	22	4.854
3	8.045	13	9.381	23	7.606
4	7.566	14	8.261	24	8.519
5	7.663	15	8.762	25	6.838
6	6.013	16	7.052	26	6.454
7	8.481	17	9.402	27	7.070
8	10.094	18	10.019	28	5.904
9	8.364	19	8.577	29	6.801
10	9.924	20	6.007	30	8.966

Table 4.11 (For Problem 2): lot-for-lot beer order transactions ($L = 3$)

		Day			
	30	31	32	33	34
Daily requirement	8.966	$\hat{d}_{31}$	$\hat{d}_{32}$	$\hat{d}_{33}$	$\hat{d}_{34}$
Scheduled receive		9	9	9	$[\quad]$
End inventory	0	$[\hat{x}_1]$	$[\hat{x}_2]$	$[\hat{x}_3]$	
Lot-for-lot order release		q_{31}			

(a) Analyze the data: generate a time-series plot of the data in Table 4.10, and characterize the identifiable patterns (e.g., trend and seasonal) by visual inspection.

(b) Determine a lag-1 time-series forecasting model that you believe is the most appropriate.

(c) Produce forecasts for the next 10 days, from day 31 to day 40.

2   Consider the same beer sales as given in Problem 1 above, assuming a 3-day lead-time. Using the forecasting model you selected in Problem 1, determine forecast-facilitated lot-for-lot MRP records for day 31 through day 40. Suppose that initial conditions are given as follows:

(a) Using the lot-for-lot ordering policy, determine q_{31} that is released at the beginning of day 31 and scheduled to arrive in 3 days by the beginning of day 34, as depicted in Table 4.11 where $\hat{d}_{31}$ denotes the forecast for day 31.

(b) Repeat (a), and obtain planned orders q_{31} through q_{37} that are to arrive on day 34 through day 40.

(c) Compute projected inventory status for day 31 through day 40.

Appendix 4A Derivations in least-MSE time-series forecasting

Let F_{t+1} denote a forecast for the next period demand d_{t+1}, based on the information set $\mathbf{F}_t$, a set of demand variables and inputs observed by date t. For each forecast F_{t+1}, there is associated the MSE, which is defined and denoted as:

MSE of forecast F_{t+1} : $\quad \mathrm{MSE}(F_{t+1}) \equiv E(d_{t+1} - F_{t+1})^2.$

Next, we show the claim that the expectation of d_{t+1} conditional on $\mathbf{F}_t$ is indeed the forecast with the minimum MSE. To proceed with the proof, let us consider a forecast that is based on any function other than the conditional expectation:

$$F_{t+1} = g(\mathbf{F}_t),$$

(A4.1)

where $g : \mathbf{F}_t \rightarrow (-\infty, \infty)$ is a general set-to-point real mapping other than the conditional expectation. Then, the MSE of the forecast F_{t+1}, which is defined by (A4.1), would be

$$
\begin{aligned}
\mathrm{MSE}(F_{t+1}) &= E(d_{t+1} - F_{t+1})^2 = E\big(d_{t+1} - g(\mathbf{F}_t)\big)^2 \\
&= E\big(d_{t+1} - E(d_{t+1} \mid \mathbf{F}_t) + E(d_{t+1} \mid \mathbf{F}_t) - g(\mathbf{F}_t)\big)^2 \\
&= E\big(d_{t+1} - E(d_{t+1} \mid \mathbf{F}_t)\big)^2 + E\big(E(d_{t+1} \mid \mathbf{F}_t) - g(\mathbf{F}_t)\big)^2 \\
&\quad + 2E(\Delta_{t+1}),
\end{aligned}
$$

(A4.2)

where

$$\Delta_{t+1} \equiv \big(d_{t+1} - E(d_{t+1} \mid \mathbf{F}_t)\big)\big(E(d_{t+1} \mid \mathbf{F}_t) - g(\mathbf{F}_t)\big).$$

Let us consider first the conditional expectation of Δ_{t+1}, that is,

$$
\begin{aligned}
E(\Delta_{t+1} \mid \mathbf{F}_t) &= E\big((d_{t+1} - E(d_{t+1} \mid \mathbf{F}_t)) \mid \mathbf{F}_t\big) \\
&\quad E\big((E(d_{t+1} \mid \mathbf{F}_t) - g(\mathbf{F}_t)) \mid \mathbf{F}_t\big) \\
&= \big(E(d_{t+1} \mid \mathbf{F}_t) - E(d_{t+1} \mid \mathbf{F}_t)\big) \\
&\quad \big(E(d_{t+1} \mid \mathbf{F}_t) - g(\mathbf{F}_t)\big) \\
&= 0\big(E(d_{t+1} \mid \mathbf{F}_t) - g(\mathbf{F}_t)\big) = 0.
\end{aligned}
$$

Thus, the third term in the right-hand side of Equation (A4.2) vanishes. Noting that the first term in the r.h.s. of (A4.2) does not depend on $g(\mathbf{F}_t)$, it is easy to verify that the r.h.s of (A4.2) is minimized only when the second term is set to zero,

$$g(\mathbf{F}_t) = E(d_{t+1} \mid \mathbf{F}_t).$$

As such, we conclude that the least-MSE forecast, F_{t+1}^*, is attained by conditional expectation,

$$F_{t+1}^* = E(d_{t+1} \mid \mathbf{F}_t).$$

The least MSE is

$$\mathrm{MSE}(F_{t+1}^*) = E\big(d_{t+1} - E(d_{t+1} \mid \mathbf{F}_t)\big)^2.$$

This completes the proof.

Appendix 4B Invertibility of MA(1) process

Consider an MA(1) process in the following form:

$$d_{t+1} = \mu + \theta\varepsilon_t + \varepsilon_{t+1} \text{ with } \varepsilon_t \sim (0, \sigma_\varepsilon^2) \text{ for all } t$$

or,

$$d_{t+1} - \mu = \theta\varepsilon_t + \varepsilon_{t+1}. \tag{A4.3}$$

Note that a general MA(1) process allows the parameter θ to be arbitrary (i.e., $-\infty < \theta < \infty$). An MA(1) process is said to be invertible if it can be expressed as an $AR(\infty)$. Recall from Chapter S4 that an $AR(p)$ can be presented in the following form:

$$AR(p)\,\text{process}: d_{t+1} - \mu = \phi_1(d_t - \mu) + \cdots + \phi_p(d_{t-p+1} - \mu) = \sum_{i=1}^{p}\phi_i(d_{t+1-i} - \mu).$$

Thus, the $AR(\infty)$ here can be expressed as:

$$AR(\infty)\,\text{process}: d_{t+1} - \mu = \phi_1(d_t - \mu) + \phi_2(d_{t-1} - \mu) + \cdots$$

$$= \sum_{i=1}^{\infty}\phi_i(d_{t+1-i} - \mu).$$

Next, let us rewrite an MA(1) process in recursive terms of deviations $(d_t - \mu)$. To do this, first we note that for any t, the deviation in an MA(1) process is:

$$d_t - \mu = \theta\varepsilon_{t-1} + \varepsilon_t.$$

That is, the error term ε_t can be expressed as:

$$\varepsilon_t = (d_t - \mu) - \theta\varepsilon_{t-1}.$$

By recursive substitution, the MA(1) process of (A4.3) can be rewritten as follows:

$$
\begin{aligned}
d_{t+1} - \mu &= \theta\varepsilon_t + \varepsilon_{t+1} = \theta\big((d_t - \mu) - \theta\varepsilon_{t-1}\big) + \varepsilon_{t+1} \\
&= \theta\big((d_t - \mu) - \theta(d_{t-1} - \mu) + \theta^2(d_{t-2} - \mu) - \cdots\big) + \varepsilon_{t+1} \\
&= \theta\sum_{i=1}^{\infty}(-\theta)^{i-1}(d_{t-i+1} - \mu) + \varepsilon_{t+1} = \sum_{i=1}^{\infty}\theta(-\theta)^{i-1}(d_{t-i+1} - \mu) + \varepsilon_{t+1} \qquad \text{(A4.4)} \\
&= \sum_{i=1}^{\infty}\phi_i(d_{t-i+1} - \mu) + \varepsilon_{t+1}
\end{aligned}
$$

where $\phi_i = \theta(-\theta)^{i-1}$ $(i = 1, 2, \ldots)$. Indeed, the right-hand side of Equation (A4.4) is a representation of $AR(\infty)$ provided $|\theta| < 1$. Otherwise if $|\theta| > 1$, the infinite sequence in the right-hand side of Equation (A4.4) would not be well defined. Thus, we conclude that the invertibility of an $MA(1)$ process requires $|\theta| < 1$.

Appendix 4C   L-Step least-MSE forecast for ARMA(1,1) process

Consider an ARMA(1,1) process in the following form:

$$d_{t+1} - \mu = \phi(d_t - \mu) + \theta\varepsilon_t + \varepsilon_{t+1}, \text{ with } \varepsilon_t \sim (0, \sigma_\varepsilon^2) \text{ for all } t.$$

For the ARMA(1,1) process given above, the one-step least-MSE forecast is determined as

$$F_{t+1|t}^* = \mu + \phi(d_t - \phi) + \theta(d_t - F_{t|t-1}^*).$$

First, we show that for $L = 2, 3, \ldots$, the L-step least-MSE forecast obeys the recursion:

$$F_{t+L|t}^* = \mu + \phi(F_{t+L-1|t}^* - \mu).$$

This equality is proved through the following derivation:

$$
\begin{aligned}
F_{t+L|t}^* &= E\big(d_{t+L} \,\big|\, d_t, \varepsilon_t\big) = E\big(\mu + \phi(d_{t+L-1} - \mu) + \theta\varepsilon_{t+L-1} + \varepsilon_{t+L} \,\big|\, d_t, \varepsilon_t\big) \\
&= \mu + E\big(\phi(d_{t+L-1} - \mu) \,\big|\, d_t, \varepsilon_t\big) = \mu + \phi\big(E(d_{t+L-1} \,|\, d_t, \varepsilon_t) - \mu\big) \\
&= \mu + \phi(F_{t+L-1|t}^* - \mu).
\end{aligned}
\qquad \text{(A4.5)}
$$

Then, by recursive substitution, we obtain for $L > 1$ that

$$F^*_{t+L|t} = \mu + \phi^{L-1}(F^*_{t+1|t} - \mu).$$

This coincides with (4.15).

Appendix 4D   The sum of an equal-ratio series

Consider a finite series

$$\{a_n\}_{n=0}^{L-1} = \{a_0, a_1, \ldots, a_{L-1}\}.$$

The above series is called equal-ratio, if the ratios a_n/a_{n-1} are equal for all n. For example, the series,

$$\{a_n\}_{n=0}^{L-1} = \{1, \phi, \phi^2, \cdots, \phi^{L-1}\}, \text{ with } a_n = \phi^n \text{ and } |\phi| < 1, \tag{A4.6}$$

is an equal-ratio series, since the ratio is $a_n/a_{n-1} = \phi$ for all $n = 1, 2, \ldots, L-1$. Now, let us consider the sum of such series given in (A4.6). Denoting the sum by Y, we are to derive a formula for the sum

$$Y = 1 + \phi + \phi^2 + \cdots + \phi^{L-1}. \tag{A4.7}$$

Multiplying both sides of (A4.7) with $(1-\phi)$ yields

$$\begin{aligned}
(1-\phi)Y &= (1-\phi)\left(1 + \phi + \phi^2 + \cdots + \phi^{L-1}\right) \\
&= (1 + \phi + \phi^2 + \cdots + \phi^{L-1}) - \phi(1 + \phi + \phi^2 + \cdots + \phi^{L-1}) \\
&= (1 + \phi + \phi^2 + \cdots + \phi^{L-1}) - (\phi + \phi^2 + \phi^3 + \cdots + \phi^L) \\
&= (1 - \phi^L)
\end{aligned}$$

Then, it is easy to derive the sum of the equal-ratio series

$$Y = \frac{1-\phi^L}{1-\phi} = 1 + \phi + \cdots + \phi^L \tag{A4.8}$$

The finite sum in (A4.8) is well determined if $\phi \neq 1$. Furthermore, If $|\phi| < 1$, then the equality of (A4.8) holds as $L \to \infty$, that is,

$$Y = 1 + \phi + \cdots = \lim_{L \to \infty} \frac{1-\phi^L}{1-\phi} = \frac{1}{1-\phi}.$$

This concludes the derivation for the sum of an equal-ratio series, either finite or infinite.

Bibliography

Adams, F.G. 1986. *The Business Forecasting Revolution*, New York: Oxford University Press.

Box, G.E.P. and G.M. Jenkins. 1976. *Time-series Analysis: Forecasting and Control*, San Francisco, CA: Holden-Day.

Hamilton, J.D. 1994. *Time-series Analysis*, Princeton, NJ: Princeton University Press.

Holland, J. 1992. *Adaptation in Natural and Artificial Systems*, Cambridge, MA: The MIT Press.

Holt, C.C. 1957. "Forecasting Seasonals and Trends by Exponentially Weighted Moving Average." *Office of Naval Research Memorandum*, No. 52, Pittsburg, PA: Carnegie Institute of Technology.

Wilson, J.H., B. Keating, and J.G. Solutions. 2002. *Business Forecasting*, New York: McGraw Hill.

Winters, P.R. 1960. "Forecasting Sales by Exponentially Weighted Moving Averages," *Management Science*, 6, 324–342.

S4 Supplement to Chapter 4

Review of time-series demand

Key items:

- *Uncorrelated demand: white noise*
- *Stationary first-order time-series: MA(1), AR(1), and ARMA(1,1)*
- *Nonstationary time-series: ARIMA(0,1,1)*

Uncorrelated time-series

For sake of exposition, we will use the following example and sample data taken from Chapter 4, whenever appropriate, to elaborate the topics covered in this chapter.

Example S4.1   Demand in a brewery supply chain

A beer wholesaler (distributor in Figure S4.1) faces weekly demand from an existing market for bottled beer produced by a brewer (supplier in Figure S4.1). Suppose that there is no notable change in the market condition. All the sales data in the past are collected and recorded, from which it is ascertained that the mean of the weekly demand is 12,800 and the variance is $1,316^2$. Table S4.1 presents the sales data collected for the most recent 48 weeks. How can the underlying demand process be characterized (or modeled)?

White noise with drift

The simplest uncorrelated time-series is the white-noise process with a constant drift, generally expressed in the following form:

$$d_t = \mu + \varepsilon_t, \quad t \in (-\infty, \infty) \tag{S4.1}$$

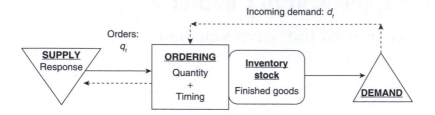

Figure S4.1 Demand/order flows in supply chain.

Table S4.1 Sales data of weekly demand for bottled beer (in 24-bottle cases)

Week	$\hat{d}_t$	Week	$\hat{d}_t$	Week	$\hat{d}_t$	Week	$\hat{d}_t$
0	12,500						
1	11,327	13	9,617	25	12,295	37	13,864
2	12,087	14	9,958	26	14,444	38	13,110
3	13,613	15	8,835	27	14,734	39	13,759
4	14,527	16	9,655	28	16,433	40	11,979
5	15,656	17	10,351	29	14,507	41	11,419
6	12,473	18	11,343	30	15,571	42	10,381
7	12,353	19	11,488	31	12,989	43	10,865
8	13,604	20	11,620	32	13,462	44	11,510
9	12,236	21	11,663	33	14,132	45	11,989
10	11,743	22	13,403	34	15,585	46	11,950
11	10,423	23	13,107	35	14,526	47	14,442
12	9,408	24	12,813	36	13,398	48	12,125

or

$$d_t - \mu = \varepsilon_t$$

where μ represents a drift (constant), and $\varepsilon_t \sim (0, \sigma_\varepsilon^2)$ is a random error term (not necessarily normal) with

$$E(\varepsilon_t) = 0 \text{ and } E(\varepsilon_t^2) = \sigma_\varepsilon^2 \tag{S4.2}$$

$$E(\varepsilon_t \varepsilon_\tau) = 0 \text{ for } t \neq \tau. \tag{S4.3}$$

With (S4.3), the error ε_t is said to be uncorrelated across time. A process satisfying (S4.2) and (S4.3) is called a *white-noise* process. A process is *independent* across time, if the joint probability $P(e_t, e_\tau) = \Pr(\varepsilon_t = e_t, \varepsilon_\tau = e_\tau)$ satisfies the following:

$$P(e_t, e_\tau) = P(e_t)P(e_\tau) \text{ for } t \neq \tau. \tag{S4.4}$$

We shall note that condition (S4.4) is stronger than that of (S4.3), in the sense where (S4.4) implies (S4.3) but not vice versa. Furthermore, if a *white noise* is normally distributed, namely,

$$\varepsilon_t \sim N(0,\sigma_\varepsilon^2) \qquad (S4.5)$$

then the sequence $\{\varepsilon_t\}_{t=-\infty}^{\infty}$ is termed the *Gaussian white-noise sequence.*

Thus, the demand process given in (S4.1) is uncorrelated across the time, but not necessarily independent across the time. Inventory models in OR/MS literature have predominantly assumed the so-called *i.i.d.* (independent and identically distributed) demand, which can be characterized by (S4.1) with independent error term ε_t. In fact, the error term in an *i.i.d.* demand is usually referred as an *independent* normal white noise of (S4.5).

It is immediate to derive the mean, variance ($j = 0$), and autocovariances ($j \neq 0$) of the demand as:

$$E(d_t) = E(\mu) + E(\varepsilon_t) = \mu$$

$$\text{var}(d_t) = E(d_t - \mu)^2 = E(\varepsilon_t^2) = \sigma_\varepsilon^2 = \sigma^2$$

$$\text{cov}(d_t, d_{t-j}) = E(d_t - \mu)(d_{t-j} - \mu) = E(\mu + \varepsilon_t - \mu)(\mu + \varepsilon_{t-j} - \mu)$$
$$= E(\varepsilon_t \times \varepsilon_{t-j}) = 0 \,(\text{for all } j \neq 0).$$

Thus, the uncorrelated time-series as given in (S4.1) is automatically covariance-stationary.

Simulation characterization of uncorrelated time-series

Model verification by simulated sample residual

In this subsection, we illustrate a simulation-based method of evaluating the characteristics of the beer demand (given by Table S4.1) using an uncorrelated time-series model. As defined by Equation (S4.1), the error of an uncorrelated time-series, $d_t - \mu$, constitutes a pure white noise. If the white noise is normal (i.e., $\varepsilon_t \sim N(0,\sigma_\varepsilon^2)$), the time-series of (S4.1) is termed an uncorrelated Gaussian time-series process. For the sake of comparison, let us consider an uncorrelated Gaussian process with the same mean and variance as the weekly demand given in Example S4.1 (i.e., $\mu = 12,800$ and $\sigma^2 = 1,316^2$). Figure S4.2 shows a computer-simulated sample path of such a Gaussian process over 48 weeks.

An important use of simulated sample paths is to examine the model fitness by visual comparison of simulated sample paths. The sample paths in Figures S4.2 and S4.3 do not indicate that an uncorrelated time-series model is a fit for the weekly beer demand process, since the simulated path does not capture the "patterns" exhibited in weekly beer sales data. We can analyze the residuals by

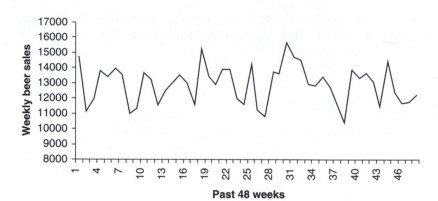

Figure S4.2 Uncorrelated time-series model for beer weekly demand.

Table S4.2 Sample residuals of beer sales under white-noise model

Week	$d_t - \mu$	Week	$d_t - \mu$	Week	$d_t - \mu$	Week	$d_t - \mu$
0	−300						
1	−1,473	13	−3,183	25	−505	37	1,064
2	−713	14	−2,842	26	1,644	38	310
3	813	15	−3,965	27	1,934	39	959
4	1,717	16	−3,145	28	3,633	40	−821
5	2,856	17	−2,449	29	1,707	41	−1,381
6	−327	18	−1,457	30	2,771	42	−2,419
7	−447	19	−1,312	31	189	43	−1,935
8	804	20	−1,180	32	662	44	−1,290
9	−564	21	−1,137	33	1,332	45	−811
10	−1,057	22	603	34	2,785	46	−850
11	−2,377	23	307	35	1,726	47	1,642
12	−3,392	24	13	36	598	48	−675

simulation to further clarify this "visual" result, which we briefly illustrate via the beer example. In this case, the residual is the remaining part in demand d_t with the *drift* excluded. If the weekly beer demand was an uncorrelated process as in (S4.1), then we can argue that the residual (i.e., the disturbance term), $\hat{e}_t = d_t - \mu$, must be a white noise $\varepsilon_t \sim N(0, \sigma^2)$ with $\sigma = 1{,}316$. Given $\mu = 12{,}800$, a table of sample residuals can be easily produced by subtracting $\mu = 12{,}800$ from each data entry in Table S4.1. The resulting sample residuals under a normal white-noise model are presented in Table S4.2, where d_t represents the same data entry as given in Table S4.1.

A plot of residuals given in Table S4.2 can then be produced, which should exhibit a sample path of white noise $N(0, 1316^2)$. Figure S4.3 contains the

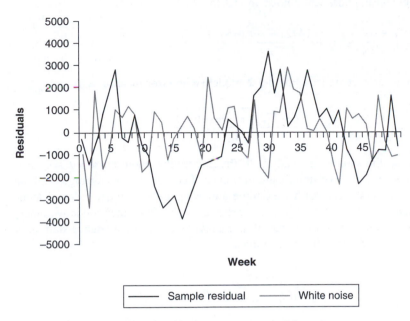

Figure S4.3 Sample paths of residuals versus normal white noise.

sample path of residuals given in Table S4.2, and also includes a simulated sample path of white noise $N(0,1316^2)$ for comparison.

As we can see from Figure S4.3, the sample white noise fluctuates around the zero line (i.e., horizontal axis) in a random fashion as expected, but the sample residual path indicates an apparent "meandering" pattern. Noting the difference between the two sample paths, we conclude that a white-noise time-series model is not a fit for the weekly beer demand process as given in Table S4.1.

The use of simulated sample paths described above can be applied to non-Gaussian time series (i.e., the error term is not normal). Given mean μ, variance $\sigma_\varepsilon^2 = \sigma^2$, and the white noise $\varepsilon_t \sim (0, \sigma_\varepsilon^2)$, sample paths of an uncorrelated demand process can be generated using a computer random number generator, or by general Monte Carlo simulation.

Statistical correlation of residuals under uncorrelated time-series model

Of course, nonsimulation-based statistical methods can be used for more accurate and rigorous data analysis. For example, we can compute sample mean and sample variance of the residuals, and compare them with the while noise $N(0,1316^2)$. These statistical measures can be easily computed from Table S4.2 as:

Sample mean under white-noise model for the beer sales data:

$$\bar{e} = \frac{e_1 + \cdots + e_{48}}{48} = \frac{(-1472) + \cdots + (-675)}{48} = -242$$

Sample variance under white-noise model (with error mean $\mu_\varepsilon = 0$):

$$S_e = \sqrt{\frac{e_1^2 + \cdots + e_{48}^2}{48}} = \sqrt{\frac{(-1472)^2 + \cdots + (-675)^2}{48}} = 1798.$$

Comparing the sample residuals with the underlying white noise ($\mu_\varepsilon = 0$ and $\sigma_\varepsilon = 1{,}316$), we observe significant differences between the two averages and the two variances. We can further examine and compare the higher order of auto-covariances γ_j for $j = 1, 2, \ldots$, as variance is the 0th order autocovariance. For comparison, we consider the jth *autocorrelation* of a covariance-stationary process, denoted and defined as follows:

$$\rho_j = \mathrm{corr}(d_t, d_{t-j}) = \frac{\mathrm{cov}(d_t, d_{t-j})}{\sqrt{\mathrm{var}(d_t)} \times \sqrt{\mathrm{var}(d_{t-j})}} = \frac{\gamma_j}{\sigma^2}.$$

When the sample data of size T are given without knowledge of probability distribution, sample *autocorrelation* can be alternatively considered:

$$\hat{\rho}_j = \frac{\dfrac{1}{T-j} \displaystyle\sum_{t=j+1}^{T} (d_t - \mu) \times (d_{t-j} - \mu)}{\sigma^2}.$$

Since white noise is uncorrelated, any non-zero lag correlation of white noise is zero, that is, $\rho_j = 0$ for $j \geq 1$ while $\rho_0 = 1$. Another simple but effective way of verifying whether a time-series model fits the sample data is to compare the auto-correlation of **sample residuals** with that of white noise. Figure S4.4 contains the sample autocorrelation of the sample residuals given in Table S4.2. As shown in Figure S4.4, sample residuals under an uncorrelated time-series model have exhibited significant correlation for lag 0 through lag 7.

The sample autocorrelation suggests that the residuals are **not** of white noise. In-depth statistical analysis, including a hypothesis test, is beyond the scope of this book, and therefore omitted. For practical data analysis, the readers may refer to Alwan (2000).

First-order moving average MA(1) process

Stationarity and correlation of MA(1) process

A moving average process contains correlation in the form of weighted sum of white noise $\{\varepsilon_t\}_{t=-\infty}^{\infty}$ where $\varepsilon_t \sim (0, \sigma_\varepsilon^2)$ for all t and $E(\varepsilon_t \varepsilon_\tau) = 0$ for any $t \neq \tau$.

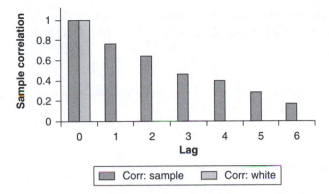

Figure S4.4 Autocorrelation of sample residuals.

A first-order moving average process, denoted as an MA(1), is constructed for all t as follows:

$$d_t - \mu = \varepsilon_t + \theta \varepsilon_{t-1} \tag{S4.6}$$

or

$$d_t = \mu + \varepsilon_t + \theta \varepsilon_{t-1}$$

where μ and θ are arbitrary constants. The term "moving average" reflects the fact that d_t in (S4.6) is constructed from a progressive weighted sum, akin to a moving average. Comparing to the uncorrelated model introduced in the previous section, an MA(1) process contains one extra term of the noise in the last period $t-1$ (i.e., the third term in the right-hand side of (S4.6)). That is, an uncorrelated time-series (S4.1) is special moving-average with zero lag (i.e., an MA(0) process). Next, we examine the mean and autocovariances of an MA(1) process, from which we will see that an MA(1) process is no longer uncorrelated. The expectation of d_t is given by

$$E(d_t) = \mu + E(\varepsilon_t) + \theta E(\varepsilon_{t-1}) = \mu.$$

Thus, the term $d_t - \mu$ gives the deviation from the mean. Rewriting (S4.6) equivalently as $d_t - \mu = \varepsilon_t + \theta \varepsilon_{t-1}$, we can see that an MA(1) process characterizes the following pattern in demand, namely, the current demand deviation is a weighted sum of the two most recent white-noise disturbances. The variance of d_t can be obtained as

$$\sigma^2 = \text{var}(d_t) = E\left(d_t - \mu\right)^2 = E\left(\varepsilon_t + \theta \varepsilon_{t-1}\right)^2$$
$$= E\left(\varepsilon_t^2 + 2\theta \varepsilon_t \varepsilon_{t-1} + \theta^2 \varepsilon_{t-1}^2\right)$$
$$= \sigma_\varepsilon^2 + 0 + \theta^2 \sigma_\varepsilon^2 = (1 + \theta^2)\sigma_\varepsilon^2.$$

Since $(1+\theta^2) \geq 0$, we can conclude that the variance of an MA(1) demand is no less than the variance of noise (i.e., $\text{var}(d_t) \geq \text{var}(\varepsilon_t)$). The first autocovariance is

$$
\begin{aligned}
\text{cov}(d_t, d_{t-1}) &= E(d_t - \mu)(d_{t-1} - \mu) \\
&= E(\varepsilon_t + \theta\varepsilon_{t-1})(\varepsilon_{t-1} + \theta\varepsilon_{t-2}) \\
&= E(\varepsilon_t\varepsilon_{t-1} + \theta\varepsilon_t\varepsilon_{t-2} + \theta\varepsilon_{t-1}^2 + \theta^2\varepsilon_{t-1}\varepsilon_{t-2}) \\
&= 0 + 0 + \theta\sigma_\varepsilon^2 + 0.
\end{aligned}
$$

All higher autocovariances are zero:

$$
\gamma_j = \text{cov}(d_t, d_{t-j}) = E(\varepsilon_t + \theta\varepsilon_{t-1})(\varepsilon_{t-j} + \theta\varepsilon_{t-j-1}) = 0 \quad (j \geq 2).
$$

Thus, an MA(1) process is **correlated**, as not all the autocovariances are zero. In fact, there is exactly one autocovariance, the first autocovariance that is non-zero. Since the mean and all the autocovariances are not functions of time for any value of θ, an MA(1) is covariance-stationary. The correlation of an MA(1) process can be then determined as:

$$
\rho_j = \frac{\gamma_j}{\sigma^2} =
\begin{cases}
\dfrac{\theta}{1+\theta^2} & j = 1 \\[2mm]
0 & j \geq 2
\end{cases}
$$

Simulation characterization of MA(1) process

Verification by simulated sample residual under MA(1) model

For sake of proposition, let us consider a Gaussian MA(1) process. Similarly, an MA process is said to be Gaussian if the error terms are normal (i.e., $\varepsilon_t \sim N(0, \sigma_\varepsilon^2)$ for all t). For comparison, we simulate sample paths of a Gaussian MA(1) process for some given value of θ with a fixed mean (e.g., $\mu = 12,800$). For each value of θ, the value of σ_ε is selected such that the MA(1) process has the same variance (e.g., $\sigma = 1,316$), that is,

$$
\text{var}(d_t) = (1+\theta^2)\sigma_\varepsilon^2 = \sigma^2.
$$

Figure S4.5 shows three simulated sample paths for $\theta = 0.2$, 0.5, and 0.8, respectively, each of which possesses the same mean and variance as that of Example S4.1, namely, $\mu = 12,800$ and $\sigma = 1,316$.

For example, as the sample path in Figure S4.5a is given with $\theta = 0.2$, the standard deviation of the white noise used in simulation is determined as

$$
\sigma_\varepsilon = \frac{\sigma}{\sqrt{1+\theta^2}} = \frac{1,316}{\sqrt{1+0.2^2}} = 1,290.
$$

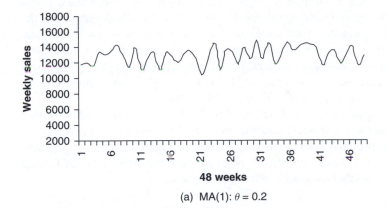

(a) MA(1): $\theta = 0.2$

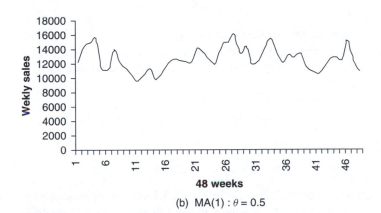

(b) MA(1) : $\theta = 0.5$

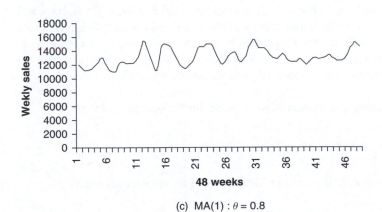

(c) MA(1) : $\theta = 0.8$

Figure S4.5 Simulated Gaussian MA(1) beer weekly sales.

Similarly, we can determine $\sigma_\varepsilon = 1{,}177$ for Figure S4.5(b) given $\theta = 0.5$, and $\sigma_\varepsilon = 1{,}028$ for Figure S4.5(c) given $\theta = 0.8$. With such, the time averages for the mean and the variance of each sample path shall approach $\mu = 12{,}800$ and $\sigma = 1{,}316$, respectively, of the original weekly beer demand. However, noticeable differences still exist when comparing with the original sample path of beer demand in Figure S4.1. In this case, an MA(1) process **does not** seem to characterize the beer demand process of Example S4.1 either.

We can also analyze the simulated residuals under an MA(1) model to further verify. To illustrate the residual analysis for an MA(1) model, let us consider the simulated sample path with $\theta = 0.5$ as shown in Figure S4.5(b). If the beer demand follows a Gaussian MA(1) process, then the MA(1) residual term $d_t - \mu - \theta \times \varepsilon_{t-1}$ would be a normal white noise, that is,

$$d_t - \mu - \theta \times \varepsilon_{t-1} \sim N(0, \sigma_\varepsilon^2), \text{ where } \sigma_\varepsilon = \frac{\sigma}{\sqrt{1+\theta^2}} = 1{,}177.$$

Assuming an initial sample residual value (e.g., $\varepsilon_0 = 0$), a series of sample MA(1) residuals can be computed from the sample data given in Table S4.1. For example, the first two weeks' sample residuals are computed as follows:

First week sample residual: $\varepsilon_1 = d_0 - \mu - \theta \times \varepsilon_0$

$$= 11{,}327 - 12{,}800 - (0.5) \times 0 = -1{,}4.$$

Second week sample residual:

$$\varepsilon_2 = d_1 - \mu - \theta \times \varepsilon_1 = 12{,}087 - 12{,}800 - (0.5)(-1{,}473) = 23.5.$$

Carrying out the iteration through the data in Table S4.1, all sample residuals can be computed. The sample path of residuals under a Gaussian MA(1) model is plotted in Figure S4.6.

The sample residuals in Figure S4.6 also exhibit some "meandering" trajectory, and **do not** appear to be a white-noise process as shown in Figure S4.3. We shall conclude that an MA(1) model **does not** represent the weekly beer demand of Example S4.1. For the residuals under a Gaussian MA(1) model, the sample residual mean and the sample residual variance are recorded from the simulation results as follows:

Sample residual mean under MA(1) model for the beer sales data:

$$\bar{e} = \frac{e_1 + \cdots + e_{48}}{48} = -173.$$

Sample residual variance under MA(1) model for the beer sales data:

$$S_e = \sqrt{\frac{e_1^2 + \cdots + e_{48}^2}{48}} = 1{,}425.$$

That is, the sample residuals do not possess the characteristics of a white noise.

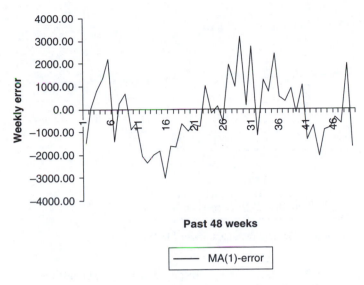

Past 48 weeks

$$\boxed{\quad\text{——}\quad \text{MA(1)-error}\quad}$$

Figure S4.6 Sample residuals under MA(1) model for beer sales.

Statistical correlation of residuals under MA(1) model

Now, let us consider statistical autocovariances of the sample residuals under the MA(1) model, and compare them with that of a white noise. Figure S4.7 contains the sample autocorrelation of the sample residuals as shown in Figure S4.6. We can see from Figure S4.7 that the sample residuals under the MA(1) model have exhibited significant correlation for lag 0 through lag 6.

Recall that the correlation of an MA(1) process is determined as:

$$\rho_j = \frac{\gamma_j}{\sigma^2} = \begin{cases} \dfrac{\theta}{1+\theta^2} & j=1 \\[2mm] 0 & j\geq 2 \end{cases}.$$

That is, the correlation of an MA(1) should be zero for any lag that is greater than 1. The sample autocorrelation shown in Figure S4.7 suggests that the MA(1) model does not fit with the weekly beer demand data. In practice, a more extensive simulation test on correlation should be conducted before making a final determination as to whether an acceptable fit exists or not.

First-order autoregressive AR(1) process

Stationarity and correlation of AR(1) process

A first-order autoregressive process, denoted as AR(1), is defined for all t by the following equation:

$$d_t = c + \phi d_{t-1} + \varepsilon_t \tag{S4.7}$$

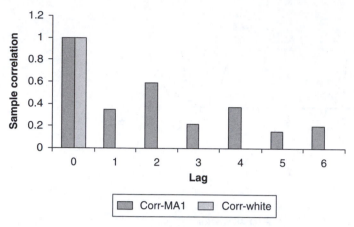

Figure S4.7 Autocorrelation of sample residuals under MA(1).

where $\varepsilon_t \sim (0, \sigma_\varepsilon^2)$ is a white noise, c is an arbitrary constant, and coefficient ϕ is confined to be within $|\phi| < 1$, as we will see as we proceed that an AR(1) process is covariance-stationary only if $|\phi| < 1$. First, let us assume that a covariance-stationary demand process can be indeed expressed as in (S4.7), with a stationary mean $\left(E(d_t) = E(d_{t-1})\right)$ and a stationary variance $\left(\mathrm{var}(d_t) = \mathrm{var}(d_{t-1})\right)$. Thus, we can obtain from (S4.7) that

$$E(d_t) = E\left(c + \phi d_{t-1} + \varepsilon_t\right)$$
$$= c + \phi \times E(d_{t-1}) + E(\varepsilon_t) \tag{S4.8}$$
$$= c + \phi \times E(d_{t-1}).$$

Since $E(d_t) = E(d_{t-1})$, we can obtain immediately the equality that connects the mean with the parameters c and ϕ as follows:

$$E(d_t) = \frac{c}{1 - \phi}. \tag{S4.9}$$

Equality (S4.9) shows that the AR(1) process is mean-stationary if $\phi < 1$, with a constant mean of $E(d_t) = \mu$ for all t. Using (S4.9), the AR(1) process of (S4.7) can be equivalently expressed as:

$$d_t - \mu = \phi(d_{t-1} - \mu) + \varepsilon_t. \tag{S4.10}$$

For the variance, we can write from (S4.8) that

$$\mathrm{var}(d_t) = \mathrm{var}\left(c + \phi d_{t-1} + \varepsilon_t\right) = \mathrm{var}\left(\phi d_{t-1} + \varepsilon_t\right)$$
$$= \mathrm{var}(\phi d_{t-1}) + \mathrm{var}(\varepsilon_t) + \mathrm{cov}(d_{t-1}, \varepsilon_t)$$
$$= \phi^2 \times \mathrm{var}(d_{t-1}) + \sigma_\varepsilon^2 + 0$$

Since $\mathrm{var}(d_t) = \mathrm{var}(d_{t-1})$, the equalities above lead to

$$\mathrm{var}(d_t) = \frac{\sigma_\varepsilon^2}{1-\phi^2}.$$

The equality above confirms that the AR(1) process is covariance-stationary if $|\phi|<1$, with a constant mean of $E(d_t)=\mu$ and a constant variance of $\mathrm{var}(d_t)=\sigma^2$ for all t. Now, let us consider the jth autocovariance of observations on d_t separated by j periods for any $j \geq 1$, defined and denoted as:

$$\mathrm{cov}(d_t, d_{t-j}) = E(d_t - \mu)(d_{t-j} - \mu) = \gamma_j.$$

Then we can derive using the expression (S4.10) for an AR(1) process that

$$\begin{aligned}
\mathrm{cov}(d_t, d_{t-j}) &= E(d_t - \mu)(d_{t-j} - \mu) = E\big(\phi(d_{t-1}-\mu)+\varepsilon_t\big)\big((d_{t-j}-\mu)\big) \\
&= E\big(\phi(d_{t-1}-\mu)(d_{t-j}-\mu)+(d_{t-j}-\mu)\varepsilon_t\big) \\
&= \phi E(d_{t-1}-\mu)(d_{t-j}-\mu)+0
\end{aligned} \qquad (\text{S4.11})$$

Note for the right-hand side of (S4.11) that

$$\text{For } j=1 : E(d_{t-1}-\mu)(d_{t-j}-\mu) = \mathrm{var}(d_{t-1}) = \sigma^2 = \gamma_0.$$

$$\text{For } j>1 : E(d_{t-1}-\mu)(d_{t-j}-\mu) = \mathrm{cov}(d_{t-1},d_{t-j}) = \gamma_{j-1}.$$

In combination, the equality (S4.11) can be written as:

$$\gamma_j = \mathrm{cov}(d_t, d_{t-j}) = \phi\,\mathrm{cov}(d_{t-1}, d_{t-j}) = \phi\gamma_{j-1}, (j \geq 1).$$

The equality above indeed verifies that all autocovariances of an AR(1) process are functions only of j (i.e., the number of periods separated from each other). By successive substitution, it is easy to see that the jth autocovariance $(j \geq 0)$ is connected with the variance as follows:

$$\gamma_j = \phi^j \gamma_0 = \phi^j \sigma^2 \qquad (\text{S4.12})$$

It is interesting to conclude that if $|\phi|<1$, an AR(1) process is autocovariance-stationary, with a non-zero autocovariance of any order j if $\phi \neq 0$. Also, the autocovariance decreases as j increases, specifically and precisely, that is,

$$\lim_{j\to\infty}\gamma_j = \lim_{j\to\infty}\phi^j \sigma^2 = 0$$

Thus, we can see that each observation of an AR(1) process is correlated with all the other observations. A higher value of $|\phi|$ results in a higher degree of correlation, and autocovariance γ_j will approach to zero "slower" as j increases.

Simulation characterization of AR(1) process

Verification by simulated sample residual under AR(1) model

Similarly, let us consider characterizing the beer demand with a Gaussian AR(1) model. An AR(1) process, $d_t = c + \phi d_{t-1} + \varepsilon_t$, is said to be Gaussian if the error terms are normal (i.e., $\varepsilon_t \sim N(0, \sigma_\varepsilon^2)$ for all t). For comparison, we simulate sample paths of a Gaussian AR(1) process for some given value of ϕ (e.g., $\phi = 0.35$ and 0.65), with a fixed mean and variance (e.g., $\mu = 12,800$ and $\sigma = 1,316$). That is, for each value of ϕ, the values of c and σ_ε^2 (error's variance) are selected so that

$$E(d_t) = \mu = \frac{c}{1-\phi} = 12,800, \text{and}$$

$$\mathrm{var}(d_t) = \sigma^2 = \frac{\sigma_\varepsilon^2}{1-\phi^2} = 1,316^2.$$

For example, for $\phi = 0.35$, we will have

$$c = \mu(1-\phi) = 12,800 \times (1-0.35) = 8,320$$

$$\sigma_\varepsilon^2 = \sigma^2 (1-\phi^2) = 1,316^2 \times (1-0.35^2) = 1,233^2$$

$$\sigma_\varepsilon = \sigma\sqrt{1-\phi^2} = 1,316\sqrt{1-0.35^2} = 1,233.$$

In theory, an AR(1) is originated back from infinite past, but in practice we need to take an initial value d_0 to facilitate the simulation of AR(1) sample paths. Given an initial value $d_0 = 12,500$ as in Table S4.1, Figure S4.8 shows the effect on the appearance of the AR(1) processes of varying the parameter ϕ with the same mean $\mu = 12,800$ and variance $\sigma^2 = 1,316^2$.

As the sample path in Figure S4.8(b) is most similar to that of beer demand, let us consider the simulated residuals for case 2 ($\phi = 0.65$). According to Equation (S4.7), the sample residual can be determined as

$$e_t = d_t - c - \phi d_{t-1}. \tag{S4.13}$$

Given $\phi = 0.65$, it is easy to compute the parameters:

$$c = \mu(1-\phi) = 12,800 \times (1-0.65) = 4,480$$

$$\sigma_\varepsilon^2 = \sigma^2 (1-\phi^2) = 1,316^2 \times (1-0.65^2) = 1,000^2$$

$$\sigma_\varepsilon = \sigma\sqrt{1-\phi^2} = 1,316\sqrt{1-0.65^2} = 1,000.$$

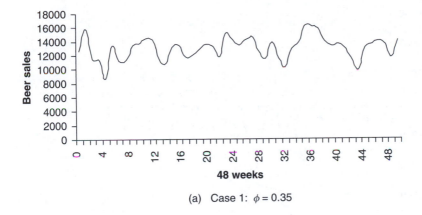

(a)   Case 1: $\phi = 0.35$

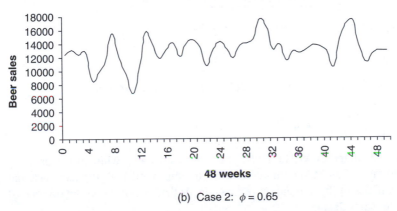

(b)   Case 2: $\phi = 0.65$

Figure S4.8 Simulated Gaussian AR(1) beer weekly sales: (a) case 1 and (b) case 2.

With an initial value $d_0 = 12,500$, the first sample residual is

$$e_1 = d_1 - c - \phi d_0 = 11,327 - 4,480 - 0.65 \times (12,500) = -1,278.$$

Then all the 48 sample residuals can be computed by continuing the iteration, and Figure S4.9 shows the residual sample path for AR(1) with $\phi = 0.65$.

Based on the simulation results, the sample mean and sample variance of the residuals are recorded as follows:

Sample mean under AR(1) model for the beer sales data:

$$\bar{e} = \frac{e_1 + \cdots + e_{48}}{48} = -90$$

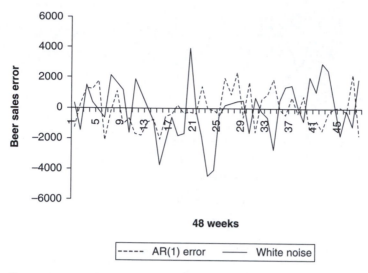

48 weeks

| ----- AR(1) error | ——— White noise |

Figure S4.9 Sample AR(1) residuals for beer sales.

Sample variance under AR(1) model (with error mean $\mu_\varepsilon = 0$):

$$S_e = \sqrt{\frac{e_1^2 + \cdots + e_{48}^2}{48}} = 1,175.$$

The residuals under an AR(1) model is the closest fit as a white noise, as compared with that of an MA(1) model or a white-noise model. Both visual test and
sample statistics of the simulation results concur that an AR(1) model offers a fit
for the beer sales data.

Statistical correlation of residuals under AR(1) model

Similarly, the goodness of fit by an AR(1) model can be tested by comparing
statistical autocovariances of the sample residuals under the AR(1) model with
that of a white noise. Sample correlations of residuals (as shown in Figure S4.9)
are computed and presented in Figure S4.10.

Relatively speaking, the AR(1) presents the closest fit with a white noise, in
terms of correlation. Of course, to validate the fit of the AR(1), we shall conduct
a more extensive simulation test by repeating the above simulation for an adequate number of independent simulation runs. That is, one can generate adequate
number of independent simulated sample AR(1) paths and sample residuals, and
then conduct simulation analysis of simulation outputs so as to verify the fit of
the suggested AR(1) model.

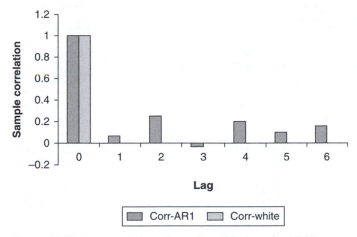

Figure S4.10 Autocorrelation of sample residuals under AR(1).

Plausibility of AR(1) model

The are two reasons why an AR(1) model is plausible, one theoretical and the other practical. The major theoretical advantage of an AR(1) model is its discrete feedback representation, which we can see from the AR(1) model formulation $d_t = c + \phi d_{t-1} + \varepsilon_t$. That is, the next realization d_t is only directly dependent on the current realized state d_{t-1} and the disturbance ε_t during period t, with fixed parameters c and ϕ. The major practical advantage of an AR(1) model is its flexible applicability; it is as shown in the vast volume of time-series research literature that one can represent a wide variety of process behaviors with AR models by varying the values of ϕ. When $\phi = 0$, we have an uncorrelated process with mean $\mu = c$ and variance σ_ε^2. For $-1 < \phi < 0$, the process is negatively correlated and will exhibit period-to-period oscillatory behavior. For $0 < \phi < 1$, the demand process will be positively correlated which is reflected by a wandering or meandering sequence of observations, as depicted in Figure S4.8.

The AR(1) model also has an advantage of computational simplicity in parameter estimation. Noting the linear structure of an AR model as given by (S4.7), with a given set of observation data the parameters c and ϕ can be estimated by simple linear regression. Let us illustrate the parameter estimation of an AR(1) model using the beer demand data of Table S4.1. According to the analysis of the data in Table S4.1 so far, let us select the AR(1) model to represent the weekly beer demand process. Starting with the initial data $d_0 = 12,500$, a set of 48 pairs of two consecutive data entries can be constructed, for example, $\{(d_t, d_{t-1}) : t = 1, 2, \ldots, 48\}$. For each pair of two consecutive data in Table S4.1, we run a linear regression, taking d_t as dependent variable on d_{t-1} as independent variable as follows:

$$d_t = a + b \times d_{t-1}.$$

Table S4.3 AR(1) model parameter estimation by linear regression

Week	d_t	d_{t-1}	Week	d_t	d_{t-1}	Week	d_t	d_{t-1}	Week	d_t	d_{t-1}
0	12,500										
1	11,327	12,500	13	9,617	9,408	25	12,295	12,813	37	13,864	13,398
2	12,087	11,327	14	9,958	9,617	26	14,444	12,295	38	13,110	13,864
3	13,613	12,087	15	8,835	9,958	27	14,734	14,444	39	13,759	13,110
4	14,527	13,613	16	9,655	8,835	28	16,433	14,734	40	11,979	13,759
5	15,656	14,527	17	10,351	9,655	29	14,507	16,433	41	11,419	11,979
6	12,473	15,656	18	11,343	10,351	30	15,571	14,507	42	10,381	11,419
7	12,353	12,473	19	11,488	11,343	31	12,989	15,571	43	10,865	10,381
8	13,604	12,353	20	11,620	11,488	32	13,462	12,989	44	11,510	10,865
9	12,236	13,604	21	11,663	11,620	33	14,132	13,462	45	11,989	11,510
10	11,743	12,236	22	13,403	11,663	34	15,585	14,132	46	11,950	11,989
11	10,423	11,743	23	13,107	13,403	35	14,526	15,585	47	14,442	11,950
12	9,408	10,423	24	12,813	13,107	36	13,398	14,526	48	12,125	14,442

The intercept a and the slope coefficient b constitute ordinary least-square (OLS) estimates of the AR(1) parameters c and ϕ. Table S4.3 shows the pair-wise data set listed for regression analysis. The outputs of regression are: $\hat{a} = 2,980$ (estimated intercept) and $\hat{\phi} = 0.76$. As the sample size increases both estimates should approach asymptotically to their respective true values of the parameters, c and ϕ.

Again we must point out that the parameter estimation can be considered only after a characterizing mode is correctly specified. The estimation method illustrated above is based on the assumption that the underlying demand process is correctly represented by an AR(1) model.

To close this section, we introduce another point of advantage of an AR(1) model, that is, an AR(1) model can be equivalently represented as an MA(∞) process in the following form:

$$MA(\infty)\ process: d_t = \mu + \varepsilon_t + \theta_1 \varepsilon_{t-1} + \theta_2 \varepsilon_{t-2} + \cdots$$

$$= \mu + \varepsilon_t + \sum_{j=1}^{\infty} \theta_j \varepsilon_{t-j}.$$

For a covariance-stationary AR(1) process, $d_t = c + \phi d_{t-1} + \varepsilon_t$, its mean is shown to be:

$$\mu = E(d_t) = \frac{c}{1-\phi}, or\ c = (1-\phi)\mu.$$

With the above equalities, we can then rewrite an AR(1) process as

$$d_t = c + \phi d_{t-1} + \varepsilon_t = (1-\phi)\mu + \phi d_{t-1} + \varepsilon_t$$

or

$$d_t = \mu + \phi(d_{t-1} - \mu) + \varepsilon_t, \text{ for all } t.$$

The above AR(1) expression applies to all t. Thus, for $t-1$ we have,

$$d_{t-1} = \mu + \phi(d_{t-2} - \mu) + \varepsilon_{t-1}.$$

Using the above equality for d_{t-1} in the original AR(1) process, we obtain

$$d_t = \mu + \phi\left(\mu + \phi(d_{t-2} - \mu) + \varepsilon_{t-1} - \mu\right) + \varepsilon_t$$
$$= \mu + \varepsilon_t + \phi\varepsilon_{t-1} + \phi^2(d_{t-2} - \mu).$$

By successive substitution with d_{t-j} for all $j \geq 2$, we can express an AR(1) process as follows:

$$d_t = \mu + \varepsilon_t + \phi\varepsilon_{t-1} + \phi^2\varepsilon_{t-2} + \cdots = \mu + \varepsilon_t + \sum_{j=1}^{\infty} \phi^j \varepsilon_{t-j}.$$

This can be viewed as an MA(∞) process with $\theta_j = \phi^j$ $(j = 1, 2, \ldots)$.

Mixed autoregressive moving average (ARMA) process

We have so far confined the discussion to the basic first-order time-series models. Although we will not discuss higher order models in this book, a quick overview of general time-series models can serve as a constructive summary of what we have learned thus far. An immediate extension to consider is the mixed autoregressive moving average (ARMA) models. A first-order mixed autoregressive moving average, denoted as ARMA(1,1), follows the equation:

$$d_t = c + \phi d_{t-1} + \varepsilon_t + \theta\varepsilon_{t-1} \tag{S4.14}$$

where c and θ are arbitrary constants, and $|\phi| < 1$. Clearly, an ARMA(1,1) is a direct combination of an AR(1) with an MA(1). It is easy to verify that for an ARMA(1,1) process:

$$\text{Mean of ARMA(1,1)} : E(d_t) = \frac{c}{1-\phi}$$

$$\text{Variance of ARMA(1,1)} : \text{var}(d_t) = \frac{1+\theta^2}{1-\phi^2}\sigma_\varepsilon^2.$$

Expanding to higher orders, we have qth-order moving average MA(q) and pth-order autoregressive AR(p) time-series processes, constructed as follows:

$$\text{MA}(q)\,\text{process} : d_t = \mu + \varepsilon_t + \theta_1\varepsilon_{t-1} + \theta_2\varepsilon_{t-2} + \cdots + \theta_q\varepsilon_{t-q}$$

$$\text{AR}(p)\,\text{process} : d_t = c + \phi_1 d_{t-1} + \phi_2 d_{t-2} + \cdots + \phi_p d_{t-p} + \varepsilon.$$

Or, an equivalent form for an AR(p) process:

$$d_t - \mu = \phi_1(d_{t-1} - \mu) + \cdots + \phi_p(d_{t-p} - \mu)$$

where $\mu = 1/(1 - \phi_1 - \phi_2 - \cdots - \phi_p)$.

Then an ARMA(p, q) process includes both AR(p) and MA(q) terms:

$$\text{ARMA}(p,q)\,\text{process}: d_t = c + \phi_1 d_{t-1} + \cdots + \phi_p d_{t-p} + \varepsilon_t + \theta_1 \varepsilon_{t-1}$$
$$+ \theta_2 \varepsilon_{t-2} + \cdots + \theta_q \varepsilon_{t-q}.$$

Or, an equivalent form for ARMA(p,q) process:

$$d_t - \mu = \phi_1(d_{t-1} - \mu) + \cdots + \phi_p(d_{t-p} - \mu) + \varepsilon_t + \theta_1 \varepsilon_{t-1} + \theta_2 \varepsilon_{t-2} + \cdots + \theta_q \varepsilon_{t-q}$$

where $\mu = 1/(1 - \phi_1 - \phi_2 - \cdots - \phi_p)$.

According to the modeling philosophy of Box and Jenkins (1976), the modeling of time-series processes shall use as few parameters as possible. This is because in practice analysts and managers must replace the true parameters (e.g., θ and ϕ) with estimates (e.g., $\hat{\theta}$ and $\hat{\phi}$) based on the data. The more parameters to estimate, the more room there is to go wrong. In light of such philosophy, we believe that the knowledge of basic first-order time models is sufficient for understanding necessary concepts and tools in the management of manufacturing and supply chains. Staying with the first-order time-series, we next introduce several nonstationary time-series models.

Nonstationary first-order time-series processes

First-order time-series with time trend

Many time-series encountered in practice are trended upward or downward over time, especially in economic and financial time-series. The specification of such time-series is a time-trend time-series model (Hamilton 1994). The time-trend model is constructed as a deterministic linear trend line imposed with an MA(0) (i.e., white noise), or with an MA(1):

$$d_t = a + bt + \varepsilon_t \,(\text{or } d_t = a + bt + \varepsilon_t + \theta \varepsilon_{t-1}),$$

where a and b are the intercept and slope coefficient of the trend line, and $\varepsilon_t \sim (0, \sigma_\varepsilon^2)$ is a white noise. It is easy to obtain for both trended MA(0) and MA(1) that:

Mean for both trended MA(0) and MA(1): $E(d_t) = a + bt$.

Variance of trended MA(0): $\text{var}(d_t) = E\big(d_t - E(d_t)\big)^2 = \text{var}(\varepsilon_t^2) = \sigma_\varepsilon^2$.

Variance of trended $MA(1)$: $\text{var}(d_t) = E(\varepsilon_t + \theta\varepsilon_{t-1})^2 = (1+\theta^2)\sigma_\varepsilon^2$.

Autocovariance of trended $MA(0)$ for $j \geq 1$: $\text{cov}(d_t, d_{t-j})$

$$= E\big(d_t - E(d_t)\big)\big(d_{t-j} - E(d_{t-j})\big) = E(\varepsilon_t)(\varepsilon_{t-j}) = 0.$$

Autocovariance of trended $MA(1)$ for $j \geq 1$: $\text{cov}(d_t, d_{t-j})$

$$= E\big(d_t - E(d_t)\big)\big(d_{t-j} - E(d_{t-j})\big)$$

$$= E\big(\varepsilon_t + \theta\varepsilon_{t-1}\big)\big(\varepsilon_{t-j} + \theta\varepsilon_{t-j-1}\big) = \begin{cases} \theta\sigma_\varepsilon^2 & \text{for } j = \pm 1 \\ 0, & \text{otherwise} \end{cases}.$$

Since the mean of a trended time-series is a function of time, it is nonstationary for the mean. Thus, the mean μ of the stationary $MA(0)$ or $MA(1)$ process is replaced by a linear function of time t. In other words, if one subtracts the trend line $a + bt$ from a trended time-series, the result is a stationary process. It is also interesting to note that both trended $MA(0)$ and $MA(1)$ are stationary for all the autocovariances. Figure S4.11 depicts a simulated sample path of a trended $MA(0)$ with the same Gaussian white noise as used for Figure S4.2.

The only predictable "pattern" in a trended time-series model is the mean that is a linear function of time t. Otherwise, what is left beside the mean is unpredictable white noise. Therefore, the specification for a trended process relies on the specification of the time-trend parameters a and b.

Autoregressive integrated moving average ARIMA(0,1,1) process

Recall that the mean and variance of an $AR(1)$ process are:

$$\text{Mean}: E(d_t) = \frac{c}{1-\phi}, \text{ and Variance}: \text{var}(d_t) = \frac{\sigma_\varepsilon^2}{1-\phi^2}.$$

Both mean and variance of an $AR(1)$ approach infinity as $\phi \to 1$. Thus, an $ARMA(1,1)$ process, which includes an $AR(1)$, becomes nonstationary if regressive coefficient $\phi = 1$. Setting $\phi = 1$ in an $ARMA(1,1)$ model produces an autoregressive *integrated* moving average **ARIMA(0,1,1)** process, expressed as:

$$d_t = c + d_{t-1} + \varepsilon_t + \theta\varepsilon_{t-1}, \text{where } \varepsilon_t \sim (0, \sigma_\varepsilon^2). \tag{S4.15}$$

The term "integrated" comes from the difference equation; taking first-order difference $\Delta d_t = d_t - d_{t-1}$, then d_t may be viewed as the integral over incremental time Δt from the lag-1 demand d_{t-1}. The first parameter (0) in the $ARIMA(0,1,1)$ notation refers to zero-order of autoregressive (not counting the item with $\phi = 1$), the second parameter (1) refers to the first-order of integration, and the third parameter (1) reflects the first-order of moving average. Simulated

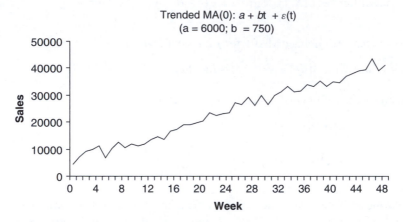

Figure S4.11 Simulated sample paths of trended MA(0) process.

sample paths of an ARIMA(0,1,1) with Gaussian white noise are illustrated in Figure S4.12. A higher order of ARIMA process may contain an AR(p), an I(d) (integral lags), and an MA(q), denoted ARIMA(p,d,q).

Taking a first-order difference of an ARIMA(0,1,1) as given in (S4.15) produces a stationary ARMA(0,1) (i.e., an MA(1)) process:

$$\Delta d_t = d_t - d_{t-1} = c + \varepsilon_t + \theta \varepsilon_{t-1}.$$

In short, the difference process Δd_t is of a stationary MA(1). Although a finite mean does not exist for an ARIMA(0,1,1) process, it does for the difference process Δd_t:

$$E(\Delta d_t) = E(d_t) - E(d_{t-1}) = E\big(c + \varepsilon_t + \theta \varepsilon_{t-1}\big) = c.$$

If there is a non-zero drift term $(c \neq 0)$, then it is obvious that $E(d_t) - E(d_{t-1}) \neq 0$ for all t. That is, not only is an ARIMA(0,1,1) nonstationary for the mean but also the means between d_t and d_{t-1} always differ by a constant c. Since Δd_t follows an MA(1) process, it is immediate to obtain its the variance as follows:

$$\mathrm{var}(\Delta d_t) = \mathrm{var}\big(c + \varepsilon_t + \theta \varepsilon_{t-1}\big) = (1 + \theta^2)\sigma_\varepsilon^2.$$

Prototype example: aggregation of time-series demand at Quick-Engine

When demand is drawn from multiple locations (e.g., the pistons needed by two Quick-Engine assembly plants as depicted in Figure S4.13), the supply of piston should be planned on basis of aggregated demand across the locations. Aggregation

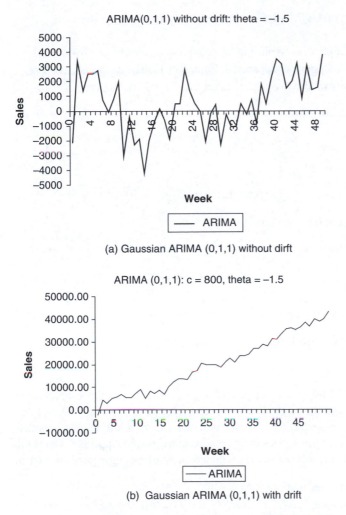

(a) Gaussian ARIMA (0,1,1) without dirft

(b) Gaussian ARIMA (0,1,1) with drift

Figure S4.12 Simulated sample paths of Gaussian ARIMA(0,1,1) processes: (a) Gaussian ARIMA(0,1,1) without drift and (b) Gaussian ARIMA(0,1,1) with drift.

of demand time-series in supply chains involves two typical situations: (1) merge of multiple demand streams and (2) sum of demands over a given number of periods (e.g., aggregation of demand over lead-time).

Sum of two MA(1) processes

We start with an example where the demand for pistons faced by a supplier is a sum of two MA(1) demand flows.

Example S4.2   MA(1) piston demand at Quick-Engine

The designated supplier is responsible for providing pistons for the two assembly plants at Quick-Engine, as depicted in Figure S4.13. The daily piston orders from the two plants follow two uncorrelated MA(1) processes, given as:

Piston orders from plant 1:

$$d_{1t} = \mu_1 + \varepsilon_{1t} + \theta\varepsilon_{1,(t-1)}, \varepsilon_{1t} \sim (0, \sigma_{\varepsilon 1}^2), \ \mu_1 = 1500, \ \sigma_{\varepsilon 1}^2 = 500^2, \ \theta = 0.5.$$

Piston orders from plant 2:

$$d_{2t} = \mu_2 + \varepsilon_{2t} + \theta^2 \varepsilon_{2,(t-1)}, \varepsilon_{2t} \sim (0, \sigma_{\varepsilon 2}^2), \mu_2 = 1500, \sigma_{\varepsilon 2}^2 = 500^2, \ \theta = 0.5.$$

Combined orders for supplier: $q_t = d_{1t} + d_{2t}$,

Question: Develop a time-series model for the combined piston order process q_t ?

We rewrite the combined piston order process as follows:

$$q_t = d_{1t} + d_{2t} = (\mu_1 + \mu_2) + (\varepsilon_{1t} + \varepsilon_{2t}) + \theta(\varepsilon_{1,(t-1)} + \varepsilon_{2,(t-1)})$$
$$= \tilde{\mu} + \tilde{\varepsilon}_t + \theta\tilde{\varepsilon}_{t-1}$$

where $\tilde{\mu} = \mu_1 + \mu_2 = 3,000$, $\tilde{\varepsilon}_t = \varepsilon_{1t} + \varepsilon_{2t}$, and $\tilde{\varepsilon}_{t-1} = \varepsilon_{1,(t-1)} + \varepsilon_{2,(t-1)}$. Since aggregated drift $\tilde{\mu}$ is a constant and the original two error terms are given (i.e., $\varepsilon_{1t} \sim (0, \sigma_{\varepsilon 1}^2)$ and $\varepsilon_{2t} \sim (0, \sigma_{\varepsilon 2}^2)$), the characterization of aggregated demand q_t is left only with modeling the aggregated error term $\tilde{\varepsilon}_t$. Deferring detailed derivation to Appendix S4B at the end of this chapter, we present below the characterization of the aggregated error term:

Aggregated error term: $\tilde{\varepsilon}_t \sim (0, \sigma_{\tilde{\varepsilon}}^2)$, where $\sigma_{\tilde{\varepsilon}}^2 = \sigma_{\varepsilon 1}^2 + \sigma_{\varepsilon 2}^2 = 2 \times (500^2)$.
Uncorrelated errors: $\text{cov}(\varepsilon_t, \varepsilon_{t-j}) = E(\varepsilon_t \times \varepsilon_{t-j}) = 0$, for all $j \geq 1$.

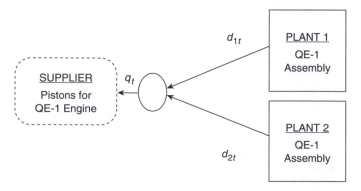

Figure S4.13 Sum of two MA(1) piston order flows.

Therefore, the aggregated order process q_t, which represents the sum of two MA(1) processes, exhibits another MA(1) process as follows (see Appendix S4B for details):

$$E(q_t) = \tilde{\mu} = \mu_1 + \mu_2 = 3,000$$

$$\text{var}(q_t) = (1 + \theta^2)\sigma_\varepsilon^2 = (1 + \theta^2)(\sigma_{\varepsilon 1}^2 + \sigma_{\varepsilon 2}^2)$$
$$= (1 + 0.25)(2 \times (500^2)) = (1 + 0.25)(2 \times (500^2))$$
$$= 790.57^2 = 625,000.$$

$$\text{cov}(q_t, q_{t-j}) = E(\varepsilon_t + \theta\varepsilon_{t-1})(\varepsilon_{t-j} + \theta\varepsilon_{t-j-1})$$
$$= \begin{cases} \theta\sigma_\varepsilon^2 = 0.5(2 \times (500^2)) = 500^2 & \text{for } j = \pm 1. \\ 0 & \text{otherwise} \end{cases}$$

Thus, the autocovariances are zero beyond lag 1, suggesting that the sum of two MA(1) processes represents another MA(1) process. Figure S4.14 shows simulated sample paths of the daily piston demands given in Example S4.2. Simulated sample paths of the aggregated piston demands are shown in Figure S4.14(a).

As shown in Figure S4.14(a), there are two simulated sample paths, one denoted "sim-q(t)" and the other "agg-q(t)". The sample path "sim-q(t)" is the sum of two 60-day sample paths independently generated by simulation, one from the MA(1) demand d_1 at plant 1, and the other from the MA(1) demand d_2 at plant 2. Specifically, the parameters used in the simulation are: $\mu_1 = \mu_2 = 1,500$, $\sigma_{\varepsilon 1}^2 = \sigma_{\varepsilon 2}^2 = 500^2$, and $\theta = 0.5$. The sample path "agg-q(t)" is directly generated by simulation from the aggregated demand $q_t = \tilde{\mu} + \tilde{\varepsilon}_t + \theta\tilde{\varepsilon}_{t-1}$ with $\tilde{\mu} = 3,000$ and $\tilde{\varepsilon}_t \sim (0, \sigma_{\tilde{\varepsilon}}^2)(\sigma_{\tilde{\varepsilon}}^2 = 2 \times (500^2))$. The two simulated sample paths are statistically indistinguishable. This confirms the theoretical result presented in Appendix S4B.

For comparison, two sample paths for MA(1) demands from plants 1 and 2 are presented in Figure S4.14(b). To further verify, one may consider residual analysis on the simulated aggregated demand, and examine if the residual of "agg-q(t)" exhibits white-noise behavior.

It turns out that the above result can be extended to the higher order moving average processes. In fact, it is mathematically proved that if two mutually uncorrelated moving average processes, $\text{MA}(q_1)$ and $\text{MA}(q_2)$, are added together, the result is a new moving average process $\text{MA}(q)$ whose order is the larger of q_1 and q_2:

$$\text{MA}(q_1) + \text{MA}(q_2) = \text{MA}(q), \text{where } q = \max\{q_1, q_2\}.$$

The detailed proof can be found in Hamilton (1994).

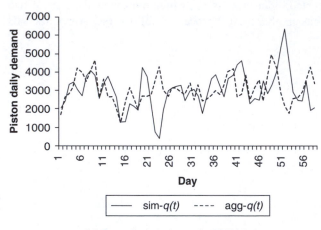

(a) Sum of two independent MA(1) processes

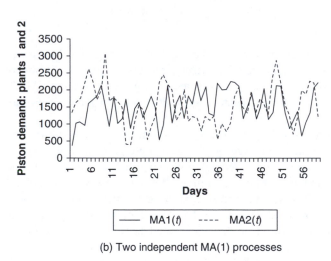

(b) Two independent MA(1) processes

Figure S4.14 Aggregated piston demand at plants 1 and 2: (a) sum of two independent MA(1) processes and (b) two independent MA(1) processes.

Sum of two AR(1) processes

Let us consider the same system in Example S4.2 except for the sum of two AR(1) processes, as restated below.

Example S4.3   AR(1) piston demand at Quick-Engine

Consider the same system as depicted in Figure S4.13. The daily piston orders from the two plants follow two independent AR(1) processes, given as:

Piston orders from plant 1:

$$d_{1t} = c_1 + \phi^I d_{1,(t-1)} + \varepsilon_{1t}, \varepsilon_{1t} \sim (0, \sigma_{\varepsilon1}^2),$$
$$|\phi^I| < 1, c_1 = 750, \sigma_{\varepsilon1}^2 = 500^2, \phi^I = 0.5.$$

Piston orders from plant 2:

$$d_{2t} = c_2 + \phi^{II} d_{2,(t-1)} + \varepsilon_{2t}, \varepsilon_{2t} \sim (0, \sigma_{\varepsilon2}^2),$$
$$|\phi^{II}| < 1, c_2 = 750, \sigma_{\varepsilon2}^2 = 500^2, \phi^{II} = 0.5.$$

With detailed derivation deferred to Appendix S4B at the end of this chapter, the result of adding two mutually uncorrelated AR(1) processes is a mixed second-order autoregressive first-order moving average process, that is,

$$AR(1) + AR(1) = ARMA(2,1).$$

Specifically, the resulting aggregated process is

$$q_t = d_{1t} + d_{2t} = \tilde{c} + \tilde{\phi}_1 q_{t-1} + \tilde{\phi}_2 q_{t-2} + \tilde{\varepsilon}_t + \tilde{\theta}\tilde{\varepsilon}_{t-} \qquad (S4.16)$$

where $\tilde{c} = (1-\phi^{II})c_1 + (1-\phi^I)c_2$, $\tilde{\phi}_1 = (\phi^I + \phi^{II})$, $\tilde{\phi}_2 = -\phi^I\phi^{II}$, and $\tilde{\varepsilon}_t = (0, \tilde{\sigma}_{\tilde{\varepsilon}}^2)$. However, the values of parameters $\tilde{\theta}$ and $\tilde{\sigma}_{\tilde{\varepsilon}}^2$ must be determined numerically from the following two equations (see Appendix S4B for more details):

$$\begin{cases} \left(1+\tilde{\theta}^2\right)\tilde{\sigma}_{\tilde{\varepsilon}}^2 = \left(1+(\phi^{II})^2\right)\sigma_{\varepsilon1}^2 + \left(1+(\phi^I)^2\right)\sigma_{\varepsilon2}^2 \\ \tilde{\theta}\tilde{\sigma}_{\tilde{\varepsilon}}^2 = -\phi^{II}\sigma_{\varepsilon1}^2 - \phi^I\sigma_{\varepsilon2}^2, \end{cases}$$

Using the data as given in Example S4.3, we can compute the right-hand sides of the simultaneous equations:

$$\begin{cases} \left(1+\tilde{\theta}^2\right)\tilde{\sigma}_{\tilde{\varepsilon}}^2 = 625,000 \\ \tilde{\theta}\tilde{\sigma}_{\tilde{\varepsilon}}^2 = -250,000 \end{cases}$$

For convenience, we write $\text{var}(\tilde{\varepsilon}_t) = \tilde{\sigma}_{\tilde{\varepsilon}}^2$, and then derive from the simultaneous equations

$$\text{var}(\tilde{\varepsilon}_t)^2 - 625,000\,\text{var}(\tilde{\varepsilon}_t) + 250,000^2 = 0.$$

Two values of $\text{var}(\tilde{\varepsilon}_t)$ can be found from the quadratic formula:

$$\text{var}(\tilde{\varepsilon}_t) = \frac{625,000 \pm \sqrt{625,000^2 - 4 \times 250,000^2}}{2} = 707^2 \text{ (or } 354^2\text{)}.$$

It is reasonable to consider the aggregated error with larger variance than the original error term. Since $\text{var}(\varepsilon_{1t}) = \text{var}(\varepsilon_{2t}) = 500^2$, we select $\tilde{\sigma}_{\tilde{\varepsilon}}^2 = \text{var}(\tilde{\varepsilon}_t) = 707^2$. Then we can obtain

$$\tilde{\theta} = \frac{-250,000}{707^2} = -0.5.$$

The aggregated piston demand, a sum of two AR(1) processes, can be now represented by an ARMA(2,1) as given in (S4.16), with $\tilde{\theta} = -0.5$ and $\tilde{\sigma}_{\tilde{\varepsilon}}^2 = 707^2$.

Aggregated first-order time-series process over lead-time

Let us consider aggregation of a first-order time-series process over a fixed lead-time. As reported in Alwan *et al.* (2002), the need for the aggregation arises in a wide range of inventory problems when the underlying demand process is of general ARMA time-series, such as an AR(1) process. We start with the piston inventory system under an AR(1) demand process, which is modified from Example 3.4 we studied in Chapter 3.

Example S4.4   AR(1) Piston demand over lead-time

Suppose that daily piston demand at Quick-Engine follows an AR(1) process as follows:

$$d_t = c + \phi d_{t-1} + \varepsilon_t = 320 + 0.68 \times d_{t-1} + \varepsilon_t$$

where $\varepsilon_t \sim (0, 24^2)$ for all t. The piston is provided by a local supplier, who requires a 3-day lead-time.

Question: What is the aggregated piston demand process over the 3-day lead-time?

It is easy to obtain the following characteristics of the given piston demand process:

$$E(d_t) = \frac{c}{1-\phi} = \frac{320}{1-0.68} = 1,000 \,(\text{pistons per day})$$

$$\text{var}(d_t) = \frac{\sigma_{\varepsilon}^2}{1-\phi^2} = \frac{24^2}{1-(0.68)^2} = 1,071 \approx 33^2.$$

Aggregated piston demand over the next lead-time period, denoted by D_{t+L}, is the amount of demand cumulated over the next L periods, that is, during the interval $[t+1, t+L]$. That is, for any given lead-time L, we consider the aggregated demand over different lead-time intervals, such as:

$$D_{t+L} = d_{t+1} + d_{t+2} + \cdots + d_{t+L}, \text{ for lead-time period } [t+1, t+L]$$

$$D_{t+2L} = d_{t+L+1} + d_{t+L+2} + \cdots + d_{t+L+L}, \text{ for lead-time period } [t+L+1, t+2L].$$

In general, we write

$$D_{t+kL} = d_{t+(k-1)L+1} + d_{t+(k-1)L+2} + \cdots + d_{t+kL} \tag{S4.17}$$

where the index k refers to the number of lead-time cycles (or lead-time periods). For a 3-day lead-time (i.e., $L=3$), we can write the demand over the next lead-time as

$$D_{t+L} = d_{t+1} + d_{t+2} + d_{t+3}.$$

Thus, the question in Example S4.4 is then to express D_{t+1}^L in the form of an ARMA model.

Aggregation of AR(1) process over lead-time L

For Example S4.4 with $L=3$, we can rewrite three AR(1) demand realizations over the lead-time as follows:

$$d_{t+1} = c + \phi d_t + \varepsilon_{t+1}$$

$$d_{t+2} = c + \phi d_{t+1} + \varepsilon_{t+2} = c + \phi(c + \phi d_t + \varepsilon_{t+1}) + \varepsilon_{t+2}$$

$$= c(1+\phi) + \phi^2 d_t + \phi\varepsilon_{t+1} + \varepsilon_{t+2} = c\sum_{j=1}^{2}\phi^{j-1} + \phi^2 d_t + \phi\varepsilon_{t+1} + \varepsilon_{t+2}$$

$$d_{t+3} = c + \phi d_{t+2} + \varepsilon_{t+3} = c + \phi(c(1+\phi) + \phi^2 d_t + \phi\varepsilon_{t+1} + \varepsilon_{t+2}) + \varepsilon_{t+3}$$

$$= c(1+\phi+\phi^2) + \phi^3 d_t + \phi^2\varepsilon_{t+1} + \phi\varepsilon_{t+2} + \varepsilon_{t+3}$$

$$= c\sum_{j=1}^{3}\phi^{j-1} + \phi^3 d_t + \phi^2\varepsilon_{t+1} + \phi\varepsilon_{t+2} + \phi_{t+3}.$$

Using $D_{t+L} = d_{t+1} + d_{t+2} + d_{t+3}$, we can derive the aggregated AR(1) demand over the three-period lead-time as:

$$D_{t+L} = d_{t+1} + d_{t+2} + d_{t+3} = c\left(1 + \sum_{j=1}^{2}\phi^{j-1} + \sum_{j=1}^{3}\phi^{j-1}\right) + (\phi+\phi^2+\phi^3)d_t$$

$$+ (1+\phi+\phi^2)\varepsilon_{t+1} + (1+\phi)\varepsilon_{t+2} + \varepsilon_{t+3} = C_L + \phi_L d_t + \tilde{\varepsilon}_{t+L}$$

where

$C_L = c\left(1 + \sum_{j=1}^{2}\phi^{j-1} + \sum_{j=1}^{3}\phi^{j-1}\right)$ is the combined constant term; $\phi_L = (\phi+\phi^2+\phi^3)$ is the combined lag coefficient; and $\tilde{\varepsilon}_{t+L} = (1+\phi+\phi^2)\varepsilon_{t+1} + (1+\phi)\varepsilon_{t+2} + \varepsilon_{t+3}$ is the combined error over the next lead-time period $[t+1, t+L]$. To clarify, we should note that the combined error $\tilde{\varepsilon}_{t+2L}$ represents the error terms incurred during another lead-time period $[t+L+1, t+2L]$, which is completely separate (i.e., nonoverlapped) with the first lead-time period.

Given $c = 320$, $\phi = 0.68$, and $\varepsilon_{t+i} \sim (0, 24^2)$ for $i = 1, 2, 3$), the parameters C_L and ϕ for Example S4.4 can be immediately computed. As to the combined error term $\tilde{\varepsilon}_{t+L}$, we shall formally examine its statistical characteristics, including $E(\tilde{\varepsilon}_{t+L})$, $\text{var}(\tilde{\varepsilon}_{t+L})$, and $\text{cov}(\tilde{\varepsilon}_{t+L}, \tilde{\varepsilon}_{t+kL})$ for all $k \geq 1$.

It is interesting to note that the aggregated lead-time demand D_{t+L} can be also characterized as an AR(1) process, if the combined error over lead-time is white, that is, $\tilde{\varepsilon}_{t+L} \sim (0, \sigma_{\varepsilon_L}^2)$ where $\sigma_{\varepsilon_L}^2 = \text{var}(\tilde{\varepsilon}_{t+L})$. With white error term $\varepsilon_{t+i} \sim (0, \sigma_\varepsilon^2)(i = 1, 2, 3)$, the following derivation easily confirms that the error term $\tilde{\varepsilon}_{t+L}$ is indeed a white noise:

$$
\begin{aligned}
E(\tilde{\varepsilon}_{t+L}) &= E\left((1+\phi+\phi^2)\varepsilon_{t+1} + (1+\phi)\varepsilon_{t+2} + \varepsilon_{t+3}\right) \\
&= (1+\phi+\phi^2)E(\varepsilon_{t+1}) + (1+\phi)E(\varepsilon_{t+2}) + E(\varepsilon_{t+3}) \\
&= (1+\phi+\phi^2) \times 0 + (1+\phi) \times 0 + 0 = 0
\end{aligned}
$$

$$
\begin{aligned}
\text{var}(\tilde{\varepsilon}_{t+L}) &= \text{var}\left((1+\phi+\phi^2)\varepsilon_{t+1} + (1+\phi)\varepsilon_{t+2} + \varepsilon_{t+3}\right) \\
&= (1+\phi+\phi^2)^2 \, \text{var}(\varepsilon_{t+1}) + (1+\phi)^2 \, \text{var}(\varepsilon_{t+2}) + \text{var}(\varepsilon_{t+3}) \\
&= \left((1+\phi+\phi^2)^2 + (1+\phi)^2 + 1\right)\sigma_\varepsilon^2 \\
&= \left((1+0.68+0.68^2)^2 + (1+0.68)^2 + 1\right) \times 24^2 = 4{,}845
\end{aligned}
$$

$$
\text{cov}(\tilde{\varepsilon}_{t+L}, \tilde{\varepsilon}_{t+kL}) = 0
$$

where $\text{cov}(\varepsilon_{t+i}, \varepsilon_{t+j}) = 0$ for any $i \neq j$ are assumed, and the combined error terms are defined as follows:

$$
\tilde{\varepsilon}_{t+L} = (1+\phi+\phi^2)\varepsilon_{t+1} + (1+\phi)\varepsilon_{t+2} + \varepsilon_{t+3}
$$

$$
\tilde{\varepsilon}_{t+kL} = (1+\phi+\phi^2)\varepsilon_{t+(k-1)L+1} + (1+\phi)\varepsilon_{t+(k-1)L+2} + \varepsilon_{t+kL}.
$$

Hence, with the above analysis we conclude that the aggregated AR(1) piston demand for Example S4.4 follows another AR(1) process with a set of parameters of C_L, ϕ_L, and $\sigma_{\varepsilon_L}^2 = \text{var}(\varepsilon_{t+1}^L)$. The above result for Example S4.4 can be easily extended to the general case. For any lead-time $L \geq 1$, the aggregated AR(1) process over the lead-time can be derived from expression (S4.17) as follows:

$$
\begin{aligned}
D_{t+L} &= d_{t+1} + d_{t+2} + \cdots + d_{t+L} = \sum_{i=1}^{L} d_{t+i} \\
&= c\sum_{i=1}^{L}\sum_{j=1}^{i} \phi^{j-1} + \sum_{j=1}^{L} \phi^j \times d_t + \sum_{i=1}^{L}\sum_{j=i}^{L} \phi^{L-j} \times \varepsilon_{t+i} \\
&= C_L + \phi_L \times d_t + \varepsilon_{t+1}^L
\end{aligned}
\tag{S4.18}
$$

where

$$
C_L = c\sum_{i=1}^{L}\sum_{j=1}^{i} \phi^{j-1} \text{ is the combined constant term,}
\tag{S4.19}
$$

$$\phi_L = \sum_{j=1}^{L} \phi^j \text{ is the combined lag coefficient, and} \tag{S4.20}$$

$$\varepsilon_{t+1}^L = \sum_{i=1}^{L} \sum_{j=i}^{L} \phi^{L-j} \times \varepsilon_{t+i} \text{ is the combined error term over lead-time } L. \tag{S4.21}$$

The combine error is white, that is, $\varepsilon_{t+1}^L \sim (0, \sigma_{\varepsilon_t}^2)$. Specifically, we have:

$$E(\varepsilon_{t+1}^L) = E\left(\sum_{i=1}^{L} \sum_{j=i}^{L} \phi^{L-j} \times \varepsilon_{t+i} \right) = 0, \text{ and}$$

$$\tag{S4.22}$$

$$\text{var}(\varepsilon_{t+1}^L) = \sigma_{\varepsilon_L}^2 = \sigma_\varepsilon^2 \sum_{i=1}^{L} \left(\sum_{j=i}^{L} \phi^{L-j} \right)^2.$$

It is easy to verify the following from the characteristics of an AR(1) process:

$$E(D_{t+L}) = \frac{C_L}{1 - \phi_L}, \text{ and var}(D_{t+L}) = \frac{\sigma_{\varepsilon_L}^2}{1 - (\phi_L)^2},$$

where parameters C_L, ϕ_L, and $\sigma_{\varepsilon_L}^2$ are as given in (S4.19)–(S4.22).

Simulation lab: Characterizing time-series demand processes

Assignment S4.1: Piston daily demand at Quick-Engine

Daily piston sales for the past 60 days at Quick-Engine are shown in Table S4.4. Suppose that the market condition has remained the same.

A Plot the 60-day sample path of daily piston sales. By visual inspection, identify if any time trend is exhibited from the sample path. Then, compute sample mean and sample variance based on the data given in Table S4.4. Hint: Given a set of samples: $\{d_1, d_2, \ldots, d_n\}$ with unknown theoretical mean $\mu = E(d_t)$, the sample mean and variance are defined as:

Sample mean: $\bar{d} = \dfrac{d_1 + \cdots + d_n}{n} = \dfrac{1}{n} \sum_{i=1}^{n} d_i$

Sample variance: $S^2 = \dfrac{(d_1 - \bar{d})^2 + \cdots + (d_n - \bar{d})}{n-1} = \dfrac{1}{n-1} \sum_{i=1}^{n} (d_i - \bar{d})^2$

Sample standard deviation: $S = \sqrt{\dfrac{1}{n-1} \sum_{i=1}^{n} (d_i - \bar{d})^2}$.

Table S4.4 Data for Assignment S4.1

Day	d_t	Day	d_t	Day	d_t
0	3,200				
1	3,108	21	2,980	41	3,082
2	2,926	22	2,810	42	3,231
3	3,035	23	2,533	43	3,287
4	3,018	24	2,398	44	3,152
5	2,974	25	2,576	45	2,926
6	2,907	26	2,730	46	2,914
7	3,072	27	2,833	47	2,829
8	3,128	28	2,904	48	3,006
9	3,129	29	2,947	49	2,872
10	2,929	30	2,818	50	2,991
11	3,062	31	2,915	51	3,091
12	3,076	32	2,904	52	3,364
13	3,019	33	2,866	53	3,613
14	2,917	34	2,694	54	3,367
15	2,650	35	2,823	55	3,153
16	2,597	36	2,964	56	2,982
17	2,689	37	3,055	57	2,893
18	2,655	38	3,009	58	3,031
19	2,645	39	2,910	59	2,741
20	3,045	40	3,061	60	2,777

B   Develop an MA(1) time-series model, using the sample mean and variance you obtained in A to determine model parameters. Then verify the
fitness of an MA(1) model for the piston data by analyzing the simulated
residuals.

C   Develop an AR(1) model for the piston sales data. Verify if the AR(1)
model is acceptable or not by similar analysis as you performed in B.

Assignment S4.2: Reorder point for brush contactor at Precision-Motor

(*This assignment involves the same situation as Assignment 3.3 except for
the demand.*) Jerry Schmidt, a material manager at the Precision-Motor
Company, needs to determine a "min" (i.e., reorder point) for brush contactors used in PM-x1, the best-selling precision motor at the moment. Each
PM-x1 requires two brush contactors, which are purchased from a single

supplier with a 3-week lead-time. After careful study of exhaustive sample data, Jerry has ascertained that the weekly demand on PM-x1 follows an AR(1) time-series with an unconditional mean of 979 and a lag-coefficient of 0.62 (the parameter ϕ). The company decides to establish the "min" so that an 85 percent in-stock probability over the lead-time can be achieved.

A Determine a reorder point for brush stock that will ensure an 85 percent service level.

B Simulate the reorder system under the reorder point you found in A above: Generate 40 samples of lead-time demand (not the weekly demand!) and then compute an average percent of in-stock over the 20 samples. (Hint: Compare each lead-time demand sample with the "min".)

Problems

Basic exercises

1 Daily piston sales for the past 60 days at Quick-Engine are shown in Table S4.5. Suppose that the market condition will remain the same.

    (a) Plot the 60-day sample path of daily piston sales. By visual inspection, identify if any time trend is exhibited from the sample path.

    (b) Then, compute sample mean and sample variance based on the data given in Table S4.4. Hint: Given a set of samples: $\{d_1, d_2, \ldots, d_n\}$ with unknown theoretical mean $\mu = E(d_t)$, the sample mean and variance are defined as:

$$\text{Sample mean: } \bar{d} = \frac{d_1 + \cdots + d_n}{n} = \frac{1}{n}\sum_{i=1}^{n} d_i$$

$$\text{Sample variance: } S^2 = \frac{(d_1 - \bar{d})^2 + \cdots + (d_n - \bar{d})^2}{n-1} = \frac{1}{n-1}\sum_{i=1}^{n}(d_i - \bar{d})^2$$

$$\text{Sample standard deviation: } S = \sqrt{\frac{1}{n-1}\sum_{i=1}^{n}(d_i - \bar{d})^2}.$$

    (c) Then, compute first-order (i.e., lag-1) sample autocovariance for the daily piston sales, using the given data. (Note: Sample variance is a zero-order (i.e., lag-0) autocovariance.)

2 Continue with the piston sales at Quick-Engine. After extensive study of past sales data, the management at Quick-Engine has concluded that the daily piston follows an AR(1) process: $d_t = c + \phi \times d_{t-1} + \varepsilon_t$, where ε_t denotes a white noise, i.e., $\varepsilon_t \sim (0, \sigma_\varepsilon^2)$. Help Quick-Engine to determine the best-fitting

Table S4.5 Data for Problem S4.1

Day	d_t	Day	d_t	Day	d_t
0	3,200				
1	3,108	21	2,980	41	3,082
2	2,926	22	2,810	42	3,231
3	3,035	23	2,533	43	3,287
4	3,018	24	2,398	44	3,152
5	2,974	25	2,576	45	2,926
6	2,907	26	2,730	46	2,914
7	3,072	27	2,833	47	2,829
8	3,128	28	2,904	48	3,006
9	3,129	29	2,947	49	2,872
10	2,929	30	2,818	50	2,991
11	3,062	31	2,915	51	3,091
12	3,076	32	2,904	52	3,364
13	3,019	33	2,866	53	3,613
14	2,917	34	2,694	54	3,367
15	2,650	35	2,823	55	3,153
16	2,597	36	2,964	56	2,982
17	2,689	37	3,055	57	2,893
18	2,655	38	3,009	58	3,031
19	2,645	39	2,910	59	2,741
20	3,045	40	3,061	60	2,777

parameter estimates, including c, ϕ, and σ_ε. Specifically, complete the following:

(a) Using the results you obtained in Problem 1, determine estimated parameters, c and ϕ, for the suggested AR(1) model that fits the piston sales data.
(b) Comparing to the given sales data, compute sample residuals of the proposed AR(1) model you just obtained.
(c) Obtain estimated variance of the sample residuals of the AR(1) model, which can be used as an estimate of error variance σ_ε^2.

Additional exercises

3   Daily beer sales (in thousands) for the past 60 days are shown in Table S4.6. Suppose that the market condition will remain the same.

Table S4.6 Data for Problem S4.3

Day	d(t) (000)	Day	d(t) (000)	Day	d(t) (000)
0	9.810				
1	11.624	21	4.317	41	10.892
2	8.623	22	5.555	42	11.267
3	8.045	23	8.624	43	11.554
4	7.566	24	6.482	44	9.591
5	7.663	25	8.812	45	10.147
6	6.013	26	9.335	46	11.307
7	8.481	27	8.220	47	9.109
8	10.094	28	10.182	48	9.589
9	8.364	29	9.451	49	11.317
10	9.924	30	12.019	50	11.796
11	8.158	31	10.572	51	10.138
12	11.960	32	12.439	52	8.596
13	9.381	33	10.030	53	8.294
14	8.261	34	10.022	54	8.545
15	8.762	35	11.916	55	6.328
16	7.052	36	11.808	56	7.082
17	9.402	37	12.461	57	7.333
18	10.019	38	13.245	58	9.864
19	8.577	39	13.641	59	10.949
20	6.007	40	13.582	60	10.262

(a) Plot the 60-day sample path of daily beer sales. By visual inspection, identify if any time trend is exhibited from the sample path.

(b) Determine a lag-1 time-series model that best fits the beer sales process.

Appendix S4A Stationarity and ergodicity

Stationarity

Intuitively speaking, a stationary demand process should exhibit a stable "flat" pattern of fluctuating around a consistent mean. Let $\{d_t\}_{t=-\infty}^{\infty}$ denote a time-series of incoming market demand (e.g., monthly demand with t as the monthly index). Suppose that each demand variable d_t has a definitive mean and autocovariance, which are defined, respectively, as follows:

$$\text{Mean}: E(d_t) = \mu_t, \text{for all } t$$

Autocovariance $(j\,\text{th}):\text{cov}(d_t,d_{t-j})=E(d_t-\mu_t)(d_{t-j}-\mu_{t-j})$

$$=\sigma_{jt}, \text{for all } t \text{ and any } j,$$

where the index j gives the number of time periods lagged from period t. The *variance* of d_t coincides with 0th autocovariance, that is,

Variance : $\text{var}(d_t)=E(d_t-\mu_t)^2=\sigma_t^2=\sigma_{0t}$.

Note that the mean and autocovariance can be related to the time index t. If the mean demand is a constant for all t (i.e., σ_{jt}), then the demand process is said to be stationary for the mean (or mean-stationary). Thus, the demand process for bottled beer in Example S4.1 is believed to be mean-stationary. A demand process $\{d_t\}_{t=-\infty}^{\infty}$ is said to be *covariance-stationary*, if neither the mean μ_t nor the autocovariances σ_{jt} depends on current time t, namely, for all t

$$E(d_t)=\mu$$

$$\text{cov}(d_t,d_{t-j})=E\big((d_t-\mu)(d_{t-j}-\mu)\big)=\sigma_{jt}=\gamma_j$$

with variance (i.e., for $j=0$) given by $\gamma_0=\sigma_{0t}=\sigma^2$ (a constant). It is important to note that the autocovariances of a covariance-stationary process are only a function of the time lags of j from any period t, regardless of the value of the time index t. Since the variance of weekly beer demand in Example S4.1 is a constant, thus the beer demand process is stationary for the variance. That is, the weekly demand has the same constant mean for any week. For Example S4.1, the constant mean is given as $E(d_t)=\mu=12{,}800$ and the variance of the weekly demand is given as $\text{var}(d_t)=\gamma_0=\sigma^2=1{,}316^2$.

Ergodicity

As noted earlier, the definitions of ensemble averages may seem a bit contrived, since usually all we can realistically have available is a single realization of a size T from the underlying process (e.g., $T=48$ in Example S4.1). In this case, an alternative choice of measure is concerned with time average, based on which we define ergodicity. Assuming the current time is $t=48$, then an immediate estimate of the height of the imaginary line is a **time average** for the demand mean, computed as follows:

$$\bar{d}_T=\frac{1}{T}\sum_{j=0}^{T-1}d_{t-j}=\sum_{j=0}^{T-1}d_{t-j}=12{,}558.$$

Then a covariance-stationary process is said to be ergodic for the mean (i.e., "very smooth" around the mean) if the limit of the time average exists and converges in probability (or with probability 1) to the ensemble average $E(d_t)=\mu$, which we express as:

Ergodic for the mean : $p\lim_{T\to\infty} \bar{d}_T = p\lim_{T\to\infty} \frac{1}{T} \sum_{j=0}^{T-1} d_{t-j}$

$$= E(d_t) = \mu = 12,800 \text{ (Example S4.1)},$$

where $p\lim$ is defined as follows:

$$\left(p\lim_{T\to\infty} \bar{d}_T = \mu \right) \equiv \Pr(\lim_{T\to\infty} \bar{d}_T = \mu) = 1.$$

Being ergodic for the mean, a process must be covariance-stationary, and its autoconvariances satisfy (see Hamilton 1994 for a detailed proof):

$$\sum_{j=}^{\infty} |\gamma_j| < \infty.$$

In words, the autocovariance γ_j of a mean-ergodic process quickly approaches zero as j (the lags) becomes large. Similarly, a time average for the variance can be computed from the given sample path as follows:

Time average for the variance: $\bar{\sigma}_T^2 = \dfrac{\sum_{t=1}^{T}(d_t - \mu)^2}{T} = 1,780^2.$

Or, sample time average: $\bar{\sigma}_T^2 = \dfrac{\sum_{t=1}^{T}(d_t - \bar{d}_T)^2}{T-1} = 1,782^2.$

Then, a covariance-stationary demand process is considered ergodic for the variance if

$$p\lim_{T\to\infty} \bar{\sigma}_T^2 = p\lim_{T\to\infty} \frac{\sum_{t=1}^{T}(d_t - \mu)^2}{T} = \sigma^2 = 1,316^2.$$

In terms of general autocovariances, we say the process is ergodic for the second moment if

$$p\lim_{T\to\infty} \frac{\sum_{t=j+1}^{T}(d_t - \mu) \times (d_{t-j} - \mu)}{T-j} = \gamma_j.$$

Although there are cases where a process is stationary but not ergodic, stationarity and ergodicity usually coexist with the same process for most applications. Let us confine our study herein to the ergodic stationary processes. Let $\{d_t\}_{t=-\infty}^{\infty}$ be a time-series of incoming market demand (e.g., monthly demand with t as the monthly index), with a known finite $\mu = E\{d_t\}$ and $\gamma_j = \text{cov}(d_t, d_{t-j})$ (note: $\gamma_0 = \sigma^2$). For example, we shall consider the weekly beer demand process of Example S4.1 to be covariance-stationary and ergodic for the second moment with $E(d_t) = 1,280$ and $\text{var}\{d_t\} = 1,316^2$. Given such, what remains in demand characterization is the dynamics of transitions over time (e.g., how weekly demands are correlated). For instance, a significant decrease in the sales of this week may be correlated with the demand in the next week.

Appendix S4B   Basic aggregated time-series processes

Sum of two uncorrelated MA(1) processes

Let d_{1t} and d_{2t} be two mutually uncorrelated MA(1) processes:

$$d_{1t} = \mu_1 + \varepsilon_{1t} + \theta \varepsilon_{1,(t-1)}, \varepsilon_{1t} \sim (0, \sigma_{\varepsilon 1}^2)$$

$$d_{2t} = \mu_2 + \varepsilon_{2t} + \theta \varepsilon_{2,(t-1)}, \varepsilon_{2t} \sim (0, \sigma_{\varepsilon 2}^2),$$

where ε_{1t} and ε_{2t} are uncorrelated with each other. We consider an aggregate process q_t that is the sum of d_{1t} and d_{2t}:

$$q_t = d_{1t} + d_{2t} = \tilde{\mu} + \tilde{\varepsilon}_t + \theta \tilde{\varepsilon}_{t-1},$$

where $\tilde{\mu} = \mu_1 + \mu_2$ and $\tilde{\varepsilon}_t = \varepsilon_{1t} + \varepsilon_{2t}$. It is easy to show that

$$E(\tilde{\varepsilon}_t) = E(\varepsilon_{1t}) + E(\varepsilon_{2t}) = 0 + 0 = 0$$

$$\text{var}(\tilde{\varepsilon}_t) = \text{var}(\varepsilon_{1t}) + \text{var}(\varepsilon_{2t}) = \sigma_{\varepsilon 1}^2 + \sigma_{\varepsilon 2}^2 = \sigma_{\varepsilon}^2$$

$$\text{cov}(\tilde{\varepsilon}_t, \tilde{\varepsilon}_{t-j}) = E(\varepsilon_{1t} + \varepsilon_{2t})(\varepsilon_{1,(t-j)} + \varepsilon_{2,(t-j)}) = 0, \text{for } j \geq 1.$$

This proves that $q_t = d_{1t} + d_{2t}$ follows an MA(1) with

$$E(q_t) = E(\tilde{\mu} + \tilde{\varepsilon}_t + \theta \tilde{\varepsilon}_{t-1}) = \tilde{\mu} = \mu_1 + \mu_2$$

$$\text{var}(q_t) = \text{var}(\tilde{\mu} + \tilde{\varepsilon}_t + \theta \tilde{\varepsilon}_{t-1}) = \text{var}(\tilde{\varepsilon}_t) + \text{var}(\theta \tilde{\varepsilon}_{t-1}) + 2 \text{cov}(\tilde{\varepsilon}_t, \theta \tilde{\varepsilon}_{t-1})$$
$$= (1+\theta^2)\sigma_{\tilde{\varepsilon}}^2 = (1+\theta^2)(\sigma_{\varepsilon 1}^2 + \sigma_{\varepsilon 2}^2)$$

$$\text{cov}(q_t, q_{t-j}) = E(\tilde{\varepsilon}_t + \theta \tilde{\varepsilon}_{t-1})(\tilde{\varepsilon}_{t-j} + \theta \tilde{\varepsilon}_{t-j-1})$$
$$= \begin{cases} \theta \sigma_{\tilde{\varepsilon}}^2 = \theta(\sigma_{\varepsilon 1}^2 + \sigma_{\varepsilon 2}^2) & \text{for } j = \pm 1 \\ 0 & \text{otherwise} \end{cases}.$$

Sum of two uncorrelated AR(1) processes

Let d_{1t} and d_{2t} be two mutually uncorrelated AR(1) processes:

$$d_{1t} = c_1 + \phi^{\mathrm{I}} d_{1,(t-1)} + \varepsilon_{1t}, \varepsilon_{1t} \sim (0, \sigma_{\varepsilon 1}^2)$$

$$d_{2t} = c_2 + \phi^{\mathrm{II}} d_{2,(t-1)} + \varepsilon_{2t}, \varepsilon_{2t} \sim (0, \sigma_{\varepsilon 2}^2)$$

It is then known for an AR(1) process that

$$E(d_{1t}) = \frac{c_1}{1 - \phi^{\mathrm{I}}} = \mu_1, \text{and } E(d_{2t}) = \frac{c_2}{1 - \phi^{\mathrm{II}}} = \mu_2.$$

First we show that the sum $q_t = d_{1t} + d_{2t}$ has the same characteristic lag-operator equation as an ARMA(2,1). A lag-operator, denoted by L, will increase the time lag by one when applied. For example, if we apply L to the aggregated demand q_t, the result will be the aggregated demand in period $t-1$, that is, $Lq_t = q_{t-1}$ (but except for a constant, e.g., $Lc_1 = c_1$).

The operator L can be repeatedly applied, for example,

$$L^2 q_t = L(Lq_t) = L(q_{t-1}) = q_{t-2}.$$

Similarly, for the original demands we can write

$$d_{1,(t-1)} = Ld_{1t}, d_{1,(t-2)} = L^2 d_{1t}, d_{2,(t-1)} = Ld_{2t}, \text{and } d_{2,(t-2)} = L^2 d_{2t}.$$

Then the two AR(1) processes can be expressed in term of lag-operator L as follows:

$$d_{1t} = c_1 + \phi^{\mathrm{I}} Ld_{1t} + \varepsilon_{1t}, \text{or} (1 - \phi^{\mathrm{I}} L)d_{1t} = c_1 + \varepsilon_{1t}$$

$$d_{2t} = c_2 + \phi^{\mathrm{II}} Ld_{2t} + \varepsilon_{2t}, \text{or} (1 - \phi^{\mathrm{II}} L)d_{2t} = c_2 + \varepsilon_{2t}.$$

Multiplying the first AR(1) equation by $(1 - \phi^{\mathrm{II}} L)$ and the second by $(1 - \phi^{\mathrm{I}} L)$ will yield the following:

$$(1 - \phi^{\mathrm{II}} L)(1 - \phi^{\mathrm{I}} L)d_{1t} = (1 - \phi^{\mathrm{II}} L)(c_1 + \varepsilon_{1t})$$

$$(1 - \phi^{\mathrm{I}} L)(1 - \phi^{\mathrm{II}} L)d_{2t} = (1 - \phi^{\mathrm{I}} L)(c_2 + \varepsilon_{2t}).$$

Then adding the two AR(1) processes and noting $q_t = d_{1t} + d_{2t}$, we obtain

$$(1 - \phi^{\mathrm{I}} L)(1 - \phi^{\mathrm{II}} L)q_t = (1 - \phi^{\mathrm{II}} L)\varepsilon_{1t} + (1 - \phi^{\mathrm{I}} L)\varepsilon_{2t}. \tag{AS4.1}$$

Note that each of the two terms on the right-hand side above represents an MA(1) process, that is,

$$(1-\phi^{\mathrm{II}}L)(c_1+\varepsilon_{1t})=(1-\phi^{\mathrm{II}})c_1+\varepsilon_{1t}-\phi^{\mathrm{II}}\varepsilon_{1,(t-1)}$$

$$(1-\phi^{\mathrm{I}}L)(c_2+\varepsilon_{2t})=(1-\phi^{\mathrm{I}})c_2+\varepsilon_{2t}-\phi^{\mathrm{I}}\varepsilon_{2,(t-1)}.$$

Thus, the right-hand side of the expression (AS4.1) is a sum of two MA(1) processes. It was shown earlier that the sum of two MA(1)s also has an MA(1) representation. Thus, we can write the left-hand-side as another MA(1) process:

$$(1-\phi^{\mathrm{II}}L)(c_1+\varepsilon_{1t})+(1-\phi^{\mathrm{I}}L)(c_2+\varepsilon_{2t})=\tilde{c}+(1+\tilde{\theta}L)\tilde{\varepsilon}_t, \qquad \text{(AS4.2)}$$

or equivalently,

$$\tilde{c}+\varepsilon_{1t}-\phi^{\mathrm{II}}\varepsilon_{1,t-1}+\varepsilon_{2t}+\phi^{\mathrm{I}}\varepsilon_{2,t-1}=\tilde{\varepsilon}_t+\tilde{\theta}\tilde{\varepsilon}_{t-1}$$

where $\tilde{\varepsilon}_t=(0,\tilde{\sigma}_{\tilde{\varepsilon}}^2)$, and $\tilde{c}=(1-\phi^{\mathrm{II}})c_1+(1-\phi^{\mathrm{I}})c_2$. We defer the derivation of parameters $\tilde{\sigma}_{\tilde{\varepsilon}}$ and $\tilde{\theta}$ to a later part in this proof. The right-hand side of (AS4.1) can be expanded and expressed in term of lag-operator L as follows:

$$(1-\phi^{\mathrm{II}}L)(1-\phi^{\mathrm{I}}L)q_t=\left(1-(\phi^{\mathrm{I}}+\phi^{\mathrm{II}})L+\phi^{\mathrm{I}}\phi^{\mathrm{II}}L^2\right)q_t$$

$$=(1-\tilde{\phi}_1L-\tilde{\phi}_2L^2)q_t=q_t-\tilde{\phi}_1q_{t-1}-\tilde{\phi}_2q_{t-2} \qquad \text{(AS4.3)}$$

where $\tilde{\phi}_1=(\phi^{\mathrm{I}}+\phi^{\mathrm{II}})$ and $\tilde{\phi}_2=-\phi^{\mathrm{I}}\phi^{\mathrm{II}}$. We can see that (AS4.3) has an AR(2) representation. Thus, we can write from (AS4.1) the aggregated process $q_t=d_{1t}+d_{2t}$ as follows:

$$q_t=\tilde{c}+\tilde{\phi}_1q_{t-1}+\tilde{\phi}_2q_{t-2}+\tilde{\varepsilon}_t+\tilde{\theta}\tilde{\varepsilon}_{t-1}. \qquad \text{(AS4.4)}$$

Clearly, the process represented by (AS4.4) is an ARMA(2,1), namely, a mix of AR(2) and MA(1) processes. Now, we derive the moving-average parameter $\tilde{\theta}$, which is determined such that the equality (AS4.2) holds for all autocovariances. Taking variance on both sides of (AS4.2) we obtain

$$\mathrm{var}\left(\varepsilon_{1t}-\phi^{\mathrm{II}}\varepsilon_{1,t-1}+\varepsilon_{2t}-\phi^{\mathrm{I}}\varepsilon_{2,t-1}\right)=\mathrm{var}\left(\tilde{\varepsilon}_t+\tilde{\theta}\tilde{\varepsilon}_{t-1}\right),$$

or

$$\left(1+(\phi^{\mathrm{II}})^2\right)\sigma_{\varepsilon1}^2+\left(1+(\phi^{\mathrm{I}})^2\right)\sigma_{\varepsilon2}^2=\left(1+\tilde{\theta}^2\right)\tilde{\sigma}_{\tilde{\varepsilon}}^2. \qquad \text{(AS4.5)}$$

Similarly for the first-order autocovariance ($j = 1$) of the right-hand side of (AS4.2), we can obtain

$$\text{cov}(\tilde{\varepsilon}_t + \tilde{\theta}\tilde{\varepsilon}_{t-1}, \tilde{\varepsilon}_{t-j} + \tilde{\theta}\tilde{\varepsilon}_{t-j-1}) = \tilde{\theta}\tilde{\sigma}_\varepsilon^2.$$

Letting equality (AS4.2) hold for the first-order autocovariance, we derive

$$-\phi^{II}\sigma_{\varepsilon 1}^2 - \phi^{I}\sigma_{\varepsilon 2}^2 = \tilde{\theta}\tilde{\sigma}_\varepsilon^2 \qquad (AS4.6)$$

Note that all the higher autocovariances of an MA(1) process are zero. The question is thus whether there always exist values of $\tilde{\theta}$ and $\tilde{\sigma}_\varepsilon^2$ so that equations (AS4.5) and (AS4.6) are satisfied simultaneously:

$$\begin{cases} \left(1 + \tilde{\theta}^2\right)\tilde{\sigma}_\varepsilon^2 = \left(1 + (\phi^{II})^2\right)\sigma_{\varepsilon 1}^2 + \left(1 + (\phi^{I})^2\right)\sigma_{\varepsilon 2}^2 \\ \tilde{\theta}\tilde{\sigma}_\varepsilon^2 = -\phi^{II}\sigma_{\varepsilon 1}^2 - \phi^{I}\sigma_{\varepsilon 2}^2 \end{cases}$$

It turns out that there always do. The values of the two parameters, however, cannot be analytically solved and therefore need to be attained numerically. The proof of the existence of the two values and the algorithm to determine the values are beyond the scope of this book, and therefore omitted. The readers may refer to Hamilton (1994) for more details of the proof and the algorithm.

Similar result can be obtained for the general case of adding two mutually uncorrelated AR processes. That is, adding $AR(q_1)$ and $AR(q_2)$ that are uncorrelated at all leads and lags produces an $ARMA(q_1 + q_2, \max\{q_1, q_2\})$ process, a mix of $(q_1 + q_2)$th-order AR and $\max\{q_1, q_2\}$th-order MA process.

Bibliography

Alwan, L. 2000. *Statistical Process Analysis*, Boston, MA: Irwin/McGraw Hill.

Alwan, L., J. Liu, and D.Q. Yao. 2002. "Stochastic Characterization of Upstream Demand Processes in a Supply Chain," *IIE Transactions* 34.

Box, George E.P., and Gwilym M. Jenkins. 1976. *Time-series Analysis: Forecasting and Control*, San Francisco, CA: Holden-Day.

Hamilton, J.D. 1994. *Time-series Analysis*, Princeton, NJ: Princeton University Press.

La Londe, B.J. 1998. "Supply Chain Evolution in Numbers," *Supply Chain Management Review* 2(1), 7–8.

Part II
Supply chain management

Sourcing and outsourcing

5 Supply chain economics and efficiency

Key items:

- Supply chain efficiency: the energy of Sun Zi that powers the flow of the supply chain
- Supply chain coordination and governance
- The sustainable supply chain

Thus far, supply chain efficiency, a key performance measure of supply chain management, has mainly been studied along the dimension of supply output, typically in terms of single-output inventory systems, such as the well-studied case of the newsvendor. However, the economics of productivity and efficiency are now coming to the forefront of the well-advanced field of efficiency studies. A classical economic efficiency (EE) model suited to econometric analysis is the well-known concept of the production frontier, which is defined as the optimal performance level of a production system. For the sake of clarity, production is broadly defined as the transformation of necessary inputs into desirable outputs by means of manufacturing and service technologies and operations. Production frontier analysis is the central element in the EE theory pioneered by Arrow *et al.* (1961) and McFadden (1963). Frontier analysis has predominantly been developed in relation to a construction of quantity-cost optimization based on the theory of the firm as a production function, where firms maximize profit through a cost-minimized choice of supply inputs. The construction of the production frontier is formulated according to a heuristic framework, as follows:

$$(\text{Growth})(\text{Production}) = \text{Production frontier}, \tag{5.1}$$

where the laws of production technology are characterized by a "production" function of regular (technical) input factors (e.g., capital, labor, and material), which is interacted and modulated with a "growth" function of irregular (non-technical) exogenous factors (e.g., time and environment). A production frontier specifies the output of a firm, an industry, or an entire economy as a function of all combinations of technical and nontechnical inputs.

According to the idea of the transaction cost efficiency of supply chain management (Williamson 2008), certain forms of transaction costs (e.g., the costs of governance and coordination), as opposed to the typical production costs (e.g., purchasing and inventory costs), can affect the allocative efficiency and governance efficiency of supply chain management. Regarding allocative efficiency, transaction cost theory asserts that transaction costs can be mitigated through the adoption of suitable exogenous organizational forms which may, in turn, reduce the costs of asymmetric information and, as a result, reduce allocative inefficiencies. With governance efficiency, on the other hand, other forms of transaction costs (e.g., costs of coordination and administrative control) serve as exogenous sources of operational inefficiencies, in addition to the endogenous information asymmetries. Although supply chain governance is largely absent in the mainstream supply chain models, the impact of transaction costs has been recognized by supply chain researchers. For example, Cachon and Lariviere (2005) found that, in the case of a revenue-sharing supply chain contract with an inventory cost structure, the administrative cost of implementing the revenue-sharing scheme, which is a form of transaction cost of governance, was a key (exogenous) factor limiting the practical adoption of the well-studied revenue-sharing contract. As far as can be ascertained from the literature, supply chain efficiency has mainly been studied along the lines of output-allocative efficiency (e.g., single-output inventory systems, such as the well-studied example of the newsvendor problem), with little consideration of input-allocative efficiency and essentially none of governance efficiency.

Back to basics: the economics of supply chain management

Theory of the firm as a production function

Once again, *manufacturing*, and **production** in general, involve the transformation of inputs of resources and materials into outputs of goods and services. All in all, the economics of production still comes down to the basic competitive-equilibrium structure of Arrow and Debreu (1954). Consumers are perfectly informed about, and have preferences for, a group of well-characterized available goods and the suppliers (producers) of the goods are sufficiently endowed with the necessary production-possibility sets (or technology-possibility sets). All of these economic agents, as they are termed in economics, are assumed to be price takers and to be engaged in a competitive organization. That is, the consumers maximize their welfare in terms of the *demand function*, $D(p)$, which relates the desirable demand quantity D to the market price p. The suppliers maximize the profits of their production possibilities in terms of the *supply function*, which

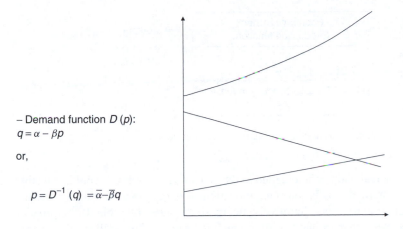

– Demand function $D(p)$:
$q = \alpha - \beta p$

or,

$p = D^{-1}(q) = \bar{\alpha} - \bar{\beta}q$

Figure 5.1 Examples: demand and cost functions.

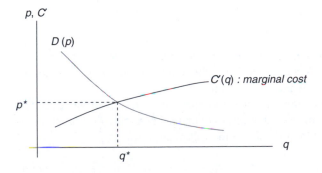

Figure 5.2 Economic equilibrium.

relates the quantity of goods available for supply to the cost of the inputs (i.e., the cost) incurred in producing the supply, typically expressed in the form of a cost function $C(q)$ where q signifies the quantity of supply produced. Figure 5.1 illustrates typical examples of the demand and cost functions.

A *competitive equilibrium* is a set of prices with associated demands and supplies of goods, denoted by the pair (p^*, q^*), such that the markets (one for each good) clear off (i.e., total demand does not exceed total supply). A key property of competitive equilibrium is that each good is sold at marginal cost, that is, $p^* = C'(q^*)$, where $C'(q^*)$ is the marginal cost incurred in producing the equilibrium quantity of supply, as depicted in Figure 5.2. In economics, this property is referred to as the Pareto optimality of competitive equilibrium, where a fully

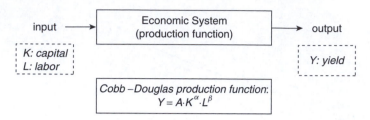

Figure 5.3 Economics of manufacturing (production function).

informed "social planner" (so-called in the economics literature) would be unable to find an alternative solution (i.e., allocation of goods) that would increase the welfare of all consumers. Intuitively, the reasoning goes like this. If the price of a good exceeds the marginal cost of producing the good, the supplier will increase their profit by expanding production. On the other hand, if the price of a good is less than its marginal cost, the supplier will contract out the production of the good, either partially or fully.

Production function

As to how supply is provided, an economist often examines production and cost using the so-called *production function*, which relates output supply to the required input demand, as depicted in Figure 5.3.

Let Y be the maximized output of an economic system directly driven by inputs of capital K and labor L, measured in physical units. The production function f is defined as a real-valued function, taking the following form:

$$Y = f(K, L). \tag{5.2}$$

Although, in this case, we consider capital K and labor L to be one-dimensional, they can be multidimensional in general, such as $K = (K_1, K_2, \ldots, K_m)$ for multiple investment inputs and $L = (L_1, L_2, \ldots, L_n)$ for multiple variable labor inputs.

An example of a specific production function is the Cobb–Douglas function:

$$Y = AK^\alpha L^\beta, \tag{5.3}$$

where $\alpha + \beta$ gives the degree of homogeneity, and A is a coefficient of technological impact. Specifically, a production function is said to be as follows:

- *Constant return to scale*, if $\alpha + \beta = 1$, which is termed *homogeneous of degree 1*.
- *Decreasing return to scale*, if $\alpha + \beta < 1$.
- *Increasing return to scale*, if $\alpha + \beta > 1$.

Let us consider the operational costs incurred in short-run production subject to a given production function. With any given desirable output level Q (e.g., annual demand), the firm must acquire the necessary inputs at minimum cost (fixed costs on capital and variable costs on labor). Let the cost be expressed as follows:

$$C = F + vQ$$

where C is the total cost of acquiring the inputs, F is a fixed cost directly associated with the capital input K in a production function, and v is the variable cost in dollars per unit of the output to be produced. Accordingly, the output level Q is governed by the production function, such that $Q = AK^{\alpha}L^{\beta}$. As operational costs are mostly concerned with short-run production under a given capital setup, the capital input K is considered fixed, as is the capital cost F. Short-run production involves seeking the minimum cost for obtaining sufficient supply to meet demand.

Creative destruction and economic growth

Economists have long recognized the impacts of science and technology on long-term economic growth. This has led to the economic theory that *technological change* is the most crucial element in economic growth. Retrospectively, it is fair to say that economic *growth theory* has largely evolved around some of Schumpeter's more controversial conjectures. In his influential work, the *Theory of Economic Development* (1912), Schumpeter theorized that

> the hallmark of capitalism was … the dynamic evolutionary growth, which depended primarily upon innovations: new consumer goods, new methods of production and transportation, new markets, and new forms of industrial organization.

Indeed, Schumpeter's theory of economic growth inspired the formulation of his enduring phrase *creative destruction*, first articulated in his masterpiece *Capitalism, Socialism, and Democracy* (1942). Here, technological change is said to lead to superior products and services while, at the same time, undermining the economic position of firms committed to old technologies. Schumpeter attributed the dramatic gains brought about by economic growth (e.g., increased net income per capita) to *technological progress*. He insisted that technological progress (later termed *technological change*) functioned as both an endogenous and an exogenous factor in driving the growth of the economy, stating that

> it is therefore quite wrong … to say … that capitalist enterprise was one, and technological progress a second, distinct factor in the observed development of output; they were essentially one and the same thing or … the former was the propelling force of the latter.

(Schumpeter 1942, p. 110)

Hence, *technological change* should not be treated in isolation from firms. In another, more radical conjecture, Schumpeter argued against mainstream Western economic thought, which extolled the virtues of competitive markets as the well-spring of prosperity. He claimed,

> In this respect, perfect competition is not only impossible, but (also) inferior, and has no title to being set up as a model of ideal efficiency. It is hence a mistake to base the theory of government regulation of industry on the principle that big business should be made to work as the respective industry would work in perfect competition.
>
> (Schumpeter 1942, p. 106)

Schumpeter's provocative conjectures gave rise to a series of vivid and long-lasting debates over a wide spectrum of economic issues. The following is a summary of the debated issues that are still relevant today:

* Equilibrium versus nonequilibrium economics. First, let us clarify the terms *formal* theorizing versus *appreciative* theorizing. Here, *formal* theorizing is based on deductive quantitative methods, such as optimization, as opposed to the inductive methods employed in *appreciative* theorizing. Formal economic theories are typically predicated on the ideal goal of the economy: steady-state equilibrium. However, Schumpeterian economists argue that equilibrium is only a transient state and that nonequilibrium processes are prevalent, as characterized by the notion of *creative destruction*.
* Exogenous versus endogenous factors. Earlier theories of economic growth (e.g., Solow 1957) measured technological change using exogenous variables. Here, a new technology is seen as an external source enabling firms to generate increased productivity. Economic growth theory then considered the role of endogenous variables in technology innovation (Romer 1990), such as the concept of human capital, which largely refers to the stock of technical knowledge. The rate of technological change has been shown to be immensely influenced by the ways in which individual firms invest in their human capital.

These ongoing debates gave rise to the so-called *economic growth theory*. Economists now view the total output of the economy as the result of the various inputs (e.g., labor and capital) into the productive process. Within this framework, growth theory focuses on the *formal* theorization of the relationship between technological change and economic growth while also taking inputs from *appreciative* theorization. The "old" growth models introduced in the late 1950s, include Solow's (1956) classic work, for which he received the Nobel Prize, and the works by Abramovitz (1956) and Kendrick (1956) among others. These models attributed whatever portion of the measured growth in output that could not be explained by the inputs to external technological change. More recently, the renewed interest in growth theory in the late 1980s led to the development of "new" growth models that differ from the "old" models by incorporating sources of endogenous growth (Romer 1990).

To quantify the impact of *technological change* on economic growth, an *aggregate production function* is then constructed as a time series, as follows:

$$Y(t) = A(t)f(K,L). \tag{5.4}$$

With the special case of *neutral* technological change, where the marginal impact of *technological change* is independent of the impact of K and L, the time-variant coefficient $A(t)$ gives the *cumulative* effect of technological change over time. In this quantified manner, the growth model (5.4) reveals important relationships between economic growth and technological change, which can be summarized as follows:

- *Diminishing return on capital*. The higher the level of K, the less capital contributes to increasing Y.
- *Zero long-term growth*. As a result of the diminishing return of capital, capital accumulation becomes more and more difficult, eventually leading to zero growth in the long run.
- *Technological change*. The accumulation of capital, as measured by capital per labor, is a direct consequence of technological change.

According to classical production theory, the production function must satisfy the so-called regularity conditions that require the production function to be nondecreasing and semicontinuous [e.g., see Diewert (1971) for a thorough and rigorous characterization of regularity conditions]. Noting the fact that the production function of a firm is never known in practice, it is suggested that the function be econometrically calibrated under regularity conditions and then estimated from empirical data using either a nonparametric method [e.g., data envelope analysis (DEA)] or a parametric method [e.g., stochastic frontier analysis (SFA)].

Profit maximization

Profit function

The profit of a firm is defined as total revenue (TR) minus the total costs (TC) incurred in generating an output supply level of y and using a set of input demands $x = (x_1, \ldots, x_n)$ given an output price p and an input cost $w = (w_1, \ldots, w_n)$, as follows:

$$\pi = \text{TR} - \text{TC} = py - wx'. \tag{5.5}$$

A profit-maximizing firm is to determine an output level $\tilde{y}$ and input mix $\tilde{x}$, to maximize profit under a certain production technology ($y = f(x)$), and with given input and output prices. The (output) supply function under profit maximization is denoted by

$$\tilde{y} = \tilde{y}(p, w).$$ (5.6)

The corresponding (input) demand function is then written as follows:

$$\tilde{x}_i = \tilde{x}_i(p, w), \quad i = 1, \ldots, n.$$ (5.7)

Then, the profit function of the profit-maximizing firm can be defined as the maximum profit as a function of particular input and output prices, in the following form:

$$\tilde{\pi}(p, w) = p\tilde{y}(p, w) - w\tilde{x}^t(p, w),$$ (5.8)

where $\tilde{x}(p, w) = (\tilde{x}_1(p, w), \ldots, \tilde{x}_n(p, w))$, and $w\tilde{x}^t(p, w) = \sum_{i=1}^{n} w_i \tilde{x}_i(p, w)$.

Hotelling's lemma

If the profit function $\tilde{\pi}(p, w)$ is differentiable, then the partial derivatives of the profit function provide the output supply and input demand equations, as follows:

$$\frac{\partial \tilde{\pi}(p, w)}{\partial p} = \tilde{y}(p, w)$$ (5.9)

$$\frac{\partial \tilde{\pi}(p, w)}{\partial w_i} = -\tilde{x}_i(p, w), \quad i = 1, \ldots, n.$$ (5.10)

Under the regularity conditions of the production function, the profit function, $\tilde{\pi}(p, w)$, has the following properties [see Beattie and Taylor (1985) for proofs]:

1. $\tilde{\pi}(p, w)$ is nonnegative for nonnegative prices, that is, $\tilde{\pi}(p, w) \geq 0$, for $p, w \geq 0$
2. $\tilde{\pi}(p, w)$ is nondecreasing in p
3. $\tilde{\pi}(p, w)$ is nonincreasing in w
4. $\tilde{\pi}(p, w)$ is homogeneous of degree one in all prices
5. $\partial \tilde{\pi}(p, w)/\partial p$ and $\partial \tilde{\pi}(p, w)/\partial w_i$ are homogeneous of degree zero in all prices
6. $\tilde{\pi}(p, w)$ is convex in all prices if the production function is strictly concave.

Cost minimization

When output supply is exogenously determined, input cost minimization for a given output level can be considered. Similarly, a cost function is defined as the minimum input cost of producing a particular output level y, with a given input price w, as follows:

$$\tilde{c}(y;w) = w\tilde{x}^t(y;w),\tag{5.11}$$

where $w\tilde{x}^t = \sum_{i=1}^{n} w_i\tilde{x}_i(y;w)$. Then, we have the following Shephard's lemma.

Shephard's lemma

If the cost function $\tilde{c}(y;p,w)$ is differentiable, then the partial derivatives of the cost function give the input demand equation, for a given output level y, as follows:

$$\frac{\partial\tilde{c}(p,w)}{\partial w_i} = \tilde{x}_i(y;w).\tag{5.12}$$

It is appropriate to mention that Hotelling's lemma and Shephard's lemma characterize the duality of production. Noting that a profit-maximizing firm is to determine input demand $\tilde{x}$, the cost function can provide an alternative way of obtaining the output supply and input demand functions. With the duality of production, the properties of the cost function are obtained as follows:

1. $\tilde{c}(y,w)$ is nonnegative for $w \geq 0$ and $y > 0$
2. $\tilde{c}(y,w)$ is nondecreasing in w
3. $\tilde{c}(y,w)$ is homogeneous of degree one in all input prices
4. $\partial\tilde{c}(p,w)/\partial w_i$ is homogeneous of degree zero in all prices
5. $\tilde{c}(y,w)$ is weakly concave in input prices if the production function is strictly quasi-concave

Total surplus and social welfare

The concept of a total surplus is one of the most important foundation blocks in the theory of industrial organization. With regard to supply capacity, we elaborate the idea of a total surplus in the context of a supply contract under perfect information, that is, the supplier and the consumer can access the same set of complete information. Under perfect information, an optimal supply contract $\{q^0,p^0\}$ satisfies the condition of competitive equilibrium, that is, $p^0 = C'(q^0)$, as illustrated in Figure 5.4.

Supplier surplus and consumer surplus

Suppose that the supplier starts fulfilling the contract, incurring a marginal cost (MC) of $C'(k)$ for producing the kth item $(k = 1,2,\ldots,q^0)$. As the contract value for each item produced is p^0, the surplus generated from producing an item k can

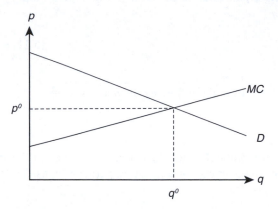

Figure 5.4 A supply contract under perfect information.

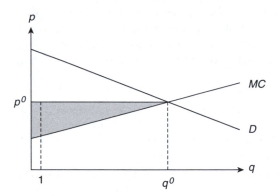

Figure 5.5 Total supplier surplus. (a) Consumer reservation value and (b) total consumer surplus.

be determined as $p^0 - C'(k) \geq 0$ for $k = 1, 2, \ldots, q^0$. Then, the total surplus for the supplier under the contract can be defined as follows:

$$\text{Supplier surplus} = \int_0^{q^0} \left(p^0 - C'(x) \right) dx = \text{the shaded area in Figure 5.5.}$$

The supplier surplus represents the total value the supplier can appreciate in fulfilling the contract.

Similarly on the consumer (buyer) side, the reservation value for the kth purchase can be determined from the demand curve as v_k, as depicted in Figure 5.6a,

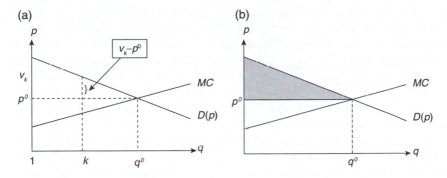

Figure 5.6 (a) Consumer reservation value and (b) total consumer surplus.

and a surplus of $v_k - p^0$ can be appreciated by the kth buyer. The total consumer surplus can be defined as follows:

$$\text{Consumer surplus} = \int_{p^0}^{\bar{p}} D(p)\mathrm{d}p = \text{the shaded area in Figure 5.6b.}$$

Outsourcing: transaction cost economics

In terms of industrial ordering and supply provision, the mainstream supply chain management works have thus far been underpinned by the science of choice approach, as opposed to the science of contract approach. However, the latter approach has recently been advanced by Williamson's much celebrated heuristic masterpieces "The Theory of the Firm as Governance Structure: From Choice to Contract" (2002) and "Outsourcing: Transaction Cost Economics and Supply Chain Management" (2008). According to Williamson (2002),

> Economics throughout the twentieth century has been developed predomi-
> nantly as a science of choice ... Choice has been developed in two parallel
> constructions: the theory of consumer behavior, in which consumers maxi-
> mize utility, and the theory of the firm as production function, in which
> firms maximize profit.

The science of choice approach treats the firm as a bilateral-monopoly (e.g., supplier-manufacturer) system that generates outputs using viable inputs and certain forms of technology, and focuses on the allocative efficiency of endogenous choices, mainly in terms of how changes in prices and the availability of resources influence quantities. In this case, the alternative choices are quantified using regular input factors under the theory of the firm as a production function. However, the science of choice as a lens for studying economic phenomena is seen by some as being preoccupied with optimization tools and, therefore, not always the most instructive approach (e.g., Buchanan 1975; Williamson 2002, 2008). In this regard, supply chain management research has followed a surprisingly similar analytical path, evolving as an intrinsic domain of the optimization-based disciplines of Operations Management and Management Science. On the other hand, the science of contract approach, which was developed in the mid-twentieth century by James Buchanan (1964, 1975), no longer describes the firm as a stand-alone black box. Rather, the firm is seen as a "sketched diagram," that is, as an organization with alternative modes of governance subject to the current technological environment. In contrast with the mechanical design and agent theories of the firm, the contract/governance approach associates firms with three attributes, namely, incentive intensity, administrative control, and contract law regime. These irregular (exogenous) factors are excluded from the models of the firm as a production function.

However, the science of contract was largely neglected until Williamson streamlined the approach in relation to the concept of transaction cost economics (TCE). With reference to a specific class of transactions, Williamson examines the contract/governance approach in the context of make-or-buy decisions about private ordering. For example, Commons (1932, p. 4) posed the fundamental question regarding the choice of input: "should a firm make an input itself, perhaps by acquiring a firm that makes the input, or should it purchase the input from another firm?" Accordingly, Williamson (2002, p. 175) noted that "the ultimate unit of activity … must contain in itself the three principles of conflict, mutuality, and order. This unit is a transaction." Asset specificity (which gives rise to bilateral dependency), uncertainty (which poses adaptive needs), and frequency are the three key attributes of transactions. Each of these attributes incurs different transaction cost consequences (highly nonlinear) under different modes and attributes (discrete) of the governance structure. For example, "the requisite mix of autonomous adaptations and coordinated adaptations vary among transactions. Specifically, the need for coordinated adaptations builds up as asset specificity deepens" (Williamson 2002). For easy reference, we recall Williamson's (2002) heuristic model, as illustrated in Figure 5.7, where k denotes asset specificity, and M, H, and X denote three modes of governance, namely, market, hierarchy, and hybrid, respectively.

Efficiency of supply chain management and logistics

Supply chain efficiency concerns an intrinsic measure of supply chain performance that consists of three dimensions, namely, operation, coordination, and governance. The operational efficiency of a supply chain is a well-studied branch of supply chain management that takes a science-of-choice approach to the management of supply chain operations (endogenous). As this performance measure is covered in mainstream supply chain management textbooks, this chapter focuses on the coordination and governance dimensions of supply chain efficiency. Supply chain coordination is predicated on attaining an incentive-induced equilibrium

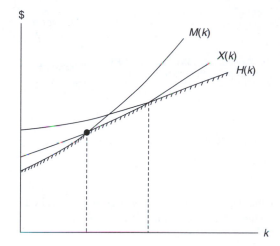

Figure 5.7 Cost of governance under transaction cost; $, cost of governance; *k*, assest specificity; *M*(*k*), markets mode of governance; *H(k)*, hierarchy mode of governance; *X*(*k*), hybrid mode of governance.

Source: Williamson 2002.

under a principal-agent type contract, with the underlying market as the ultimate source of revenue generation for the supply chain as a whole. On the other hand, supply chain governance refers to administrative activities and transactions under the supply contract terms.

Prototype example: container port performance benchmarking

Since the mid-1970s, most general cargo traditionally transported by the break-bulk method has been transported in containers. Since then, the container port industry has become a very important link in the international trade network. Consequently, with the change in cargo transport, supply chain logistics has evolved from being firm-focal (i.e., inbound and outbound goods, with the company as the center) to port-focal (i.e., inbound and outbound goods, with a port/airport as a center). Port logistics, which is broadly defined as the transportation logistics of a seaport, airport, and dry port, integrated with supply chain logistics has become the artery of international trade and global supply chain operations, especially for the contract-manufacturing-based retail business, such as Wal-mart, Ikea, and Target. A port-focal supply chain, especially of a Wal-mart type, involves a selective network of heterogeneous contract manufacturers (e.g., of different industries and products), together with the direct distribution network of a supermarket chain. In contrast, a firm-focal supply chain (e.g., a manufacturer–supplier, or manufacturer–distributor type) is homogeneous, in the sense that it consists of firms in the same industry with each firm serving a production function.

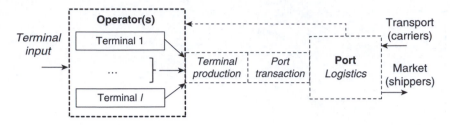

Figure 5.8 A port-operator logistics (POL) system.

Port-focal supply chain logistics

The logistics of a port-focal supply chain employing a port-operator logistics (POL) system and with the port as a governance structure is illustrated in Figure 5.8.

Port production

The production output of a port is measured in terms of volume of containers (i.e., TEUs, 20-foot equivalent units), and production input consists of regular "capital inputs," which are divided into the three categories of cargo-handling equipment, terminal infrastructure, and storage facilities (e.g., cargo-handling capacity, cargo-storage capacity, and fixed capital). In addition, port input includes several *individual characteristics* and environmental variables (i.e., degenerative inputs), such as the number of operators in port, the level of managerial coordination, gross domestic product (GDP), import, and export. That is, "capital inputs" are regular and endogenous in terms of port technology as a production function, while the individual characteristics are degenerative and exogenous in terms of the individual system heterogeneity of port production. In sum, a port production function is expressed in terms of output volume (y) as a function of regular input (x), as follows:

$$y = f(x) = A(\tau)g(x), \tag{5.13}$$

where $A(\tau)$ represents a growth/environment coefficient as a function of (exogenous) system parameters τ.

Efficiency measurement

This subsection presents a brief review of the classical productivity and efficiency theory, as a necessary methodological foundation for the efficiency analysis of supply chain management.

Production efficiency

The production efficiency (PE) of a firm, as a production function in terms of transforming inputs into desirable outputs using a certain manufacturing or service type of production technology, is broadly defined as a ratio of the measure of actual productivity (AP) measure to the relevant measure of frontier productivity (FP) measure, that is:

$$\text{Production efficiency (PE)} = \frac{\text{Actual productivity (AP)}}{\text{Frontier productivity (FP)}}.$$

According to the classical efficiency theory, PE is measured along two dimensions: (1) *technical efficiency* (TE), which measures a firm's performance in terms of maximizing output from a given set of inputs; and (2) *allocative efficiency*, which measures a firm's performance in terms of the allocation of inputs, outputs, and between the two, given certain prices and production technology. That is, the combination of the two component measures provides a measure of total *economic efficiency*, generically formulated as follows:

$$\text{Economic efficiency} = (\text{Allocative efficiency})(\text{Technical efficiency}).$$

The classical measurement of efficiency is gauged by two measurement constructions, namely, an input-based efficiency measurement, which is based on the selection of an effective input mix to produce a certain mix of outputs, and an output-based efficiency measurement, which is based on attaining effective output quantities using a given set of inputs.

Classical frontier efficiency analysis

Production frontier analysis

A classical EE model suited to econometric analysis is the well-known concept of the production frontier, which is defined as the optimal performance level of a production system. Production frontier analysis is the central element in EE theory, as pioneered by Arrow *et al.* (1961) and McFadden (1963). Frontier analysis has predominantly been developed in relation to a construction of quantity-cost optimization based on the theory of the firm as a production function, where firms maximize profit through a cost-minimized choice of supply input. The construction of the production frontier is formulated in the following heuristic framework:

$$(\text{Growth})(\text{Production}) = \text{Production frontier,}$$

where the laws of production technology are characterized by a production function of regular (technical) input factors (e.g., capital, labor, and material), which is interacted and modulated with a "growth" function of irregular (nontechnical) exogenous parameters. A production frontier specifies the output of a firm, an industry, or an entire economy as a function of all combinations of technical and nontechnical inputs.

To preserve the regularity conditions, the technical input factors must be "regular" in terms of: (1) homogeneity, that is, the production function is homogeneous with regard to the technical input factors as independent variables; and (2) cost linearity, that is, the total input cost can be completely measured as an inner product of the unit costs and quantities supplied. The production frontier of a cost-minimizing firm is defined as the functional output $\tilde{y} = Ag(\tilde{x})$, according to the theory of the firm as a production function, where A is the (exogenous) growth coefficient and $g(\tilde{x})$ represents the choice of cost-minimized inputs, $\tilde{x}$, which can be solved from the following cost-minimization problem, with given input prices (vector) w:

$$
\begin{cases}
\min\limits_{x} wx^{t} & = \sum_{i=1}^{n} w_i x_i \\
\text{s.t.} & x \in L(y) \equiv \{x : f(x) = Ag(x) \ge y, \quad \text{for } y \ge 0\}. \\
& \text{given: } y \ge 0, w \ge 0
\end{cases}
\tag{5.14}
$$

Input-allocative technical frontier efficiency

The input-allocative TE of the firm as a homogeneous function of the "regular" technical input can then be measured against its frontier $\tilde{y} = Ag(\tilde{x})$ as an optimal benchmark. Let $\hat{y}$ denote the actual production output of the firm with a frontier input $\tilde{x}$, with an inefficiency factor denoted by $\Delta \ge 0$, expressed in the following format:

$$
\hat{y} = f(\tilde{x}) e^{-\Delta} \le f(\tilde{x}). \tag{5.15}
$$

That is, the firm reaches the frontier $\tilde{y} = f(\tilde{x}) = Ag(x)$ only if it is efficient (i.e., $\Delta = 0$). Given the same cost-minimizing input $\tilde{x}$, the input-allocative technical frontier efficiency $\left(\text{TFE}_{\text{input}}\right)$ is calculated as:

$$
\text{TFE}_{\text{input}} = \frac{\hat{y}}{\tilde{y}} = e^{-\Delta}. \tag{5.16}
$$

Conversely, the technical inefficiency is given as $1 - e^{-\Delta}$.

Remarks: input- and output-based efficiency measures

We note the following remarks on the frontier efficiency measures we have defined:

1   As neither the production function nor the inefficiency term are ever known in practice, practical assessment of the frontier efficiency of a firm relies on the estimation of the firm's production (frontier) function, together with the inefficiency term, from sample data. The major methods for frontier function estimation, and thus efficiency assessment, include a nonparametrical approach (e.g., the DEA method) and a parametrical approach (e.g., the SFA method).

2   Input-allocative versus input-based efficiency measures. If input prices (w_i's) are known and $\tilde{x}$ can be determined from frontier model (5.14), then the $\text{TFE}_{\text{input}}$ given in (5.16) is of an input-allocative type. Otherwise, if the input prices are unknown, the technical frontier efficiency as given in (5.16) is an input-based type (as opposed to an input-allocative type), for which an input-based frontier output ($\tilde{y}$) can be calculated as the maximum outputs achievable for a given set of input combinations, without using the frontier model (5.14) which requires input prices.

3   In theory, production output y can have multiple dimensions. For example, a seaport may have two outputs, one of containers (y_1) and the other of bulk cargoes (y_2). In practice, the outputs are measured separately along each of the output dimensions. No particular composite measurement of multiple outputs has been practically adopted.

4   Output-allocative efficiency measures. Based on production duality, an output-allocative efficiency measure can be constructed in a similar manner as the revenue-maximizing output mix ($\tilde{y}$), subject to a given region of input constraint ($x \in X$) with respect to output prices and the production technology. Similarly, if the output prices are unknown, output-based efficiency can be measured based on the maximum output frontier achievable from a given set of input combinations, without using output prices.

5   The allocative efficiency measures above can be devised from either cost-minimization or revenue-minimization constructions, but not from a profit-maximization construction which requires both input and output prices.

Frontier efficiency assessment

As discussed earlier, the production function is never known in practice and the function and the derived efficiency measures need to be estimated from empirical data. In this section, two major econometrical frontier efficiency models, namely, SFA and DEA, are elaborated using a prototype example of global container port performance benchmarking.

Case study: container port performance benchmarking

Although the efficiency of container ports has attracted a great deal of attention from academic researchers and government policy analysts, a rigorous modeling framework for evaluating efficiency that can take the intrinsic characteristics of this industry into account is still lacking. Two alternative approaches have been employed to empirically assess the TE of container ports: nonparametric DEA and parametric SFA. However, two intrinsic characteristics of the port industry, the heterogeneous production technologies of individual ports and the time-varying nature of TE, have been generally ignored in these studies. In sum, several fundamental questions regarding the efficiency of port logistics, and therefore supply chain logistics, remain unanswered.

Individual ports face different natural conditions and business environments that are largely out of the control of port management. Given the same inputs, but under different external factors, the possible maximal outputs of any two ports are likely to differ. Such a difference in outputs should be interpreted as a result of technological heterogeneity, rather than efficiency differences, because both operators are in fact using their inputs in the best way possible. The DEA model cannot deal with the technological heterogeneity, and the heterogeneity has not been taken into account in the aforementioned SFA studies of port efficiency.

In sum, a container port is engaged in port production to generate the required container throughput in TEUs, using a certain production technology as a function of regular technical inputs and individual characteristics, as detailed in Table 5.1.

Data collection and analysis

The data used in this section cover operators from the world's top 100 container ports from 1997 to 2004 (as ranked in 2005). Restricted to container operators, the output can be reasonably measured as the number of TEUs handled in a year. This output measure is in standard use in the industry and has been used in most academic studies in the field. The capital inputs used to handle containers are classified into the following categories: cargo-handling equipment, terminal infrastructure, and storage facilities. For cargo-handling equipment, the capital inputs are further divided into two types: those at the quay side, such as the quay cranes and ship-shore cranes that load and discharge containers to and from ships; and those at the yard, such as forklifts and yard cranes, which move containers at the storage area. The terminal infrastructure is measured on the basis of the number of berths, the length of the quay line, and the terminal area. As for the storage facilities, the inputs are measured using the storage capacity of the port and the number of electric reefer points. The data on output and capital inputs are compiled from the *Containerization International Yearbooks 1997–2004* published by the Lloyd's MIU.

Unfortunately, it is difficult to collect credible data on the labor inputs of the terminal operators. However, labor inputs can be ignored if it can be assumed that the ratio between capital and labor inputs varies little across operators.

Finally, measures of port/terminal characteristics include water depth, the number of calling liners, and the number of operators, as well as proxies for possible missing inputs caused by technological heterogeneity at the port/terminal level. These variables are also compiled from the *Containerization International Yearbooks 1997–2004*, as illustrated in Table 5.1.

SFA model

For a cost-minimizing port $k(k = 1, 2, \ldots)$, a stochastic frontier (SF) model is constructed by taking the logarithm of the frontier production function given in (5.15), that is, $Y = \ln(\hat{y})$ with $\hat{y}$ given by (5.15), as follows:

$$Y^k = \alpha_k + BX^k - \Delta_k + \varepsilon_k, \quad k = 1, \ldots, m, \tag{5.17}$$

Table 5.1 Input and output statistics of global container ports

Variables	Mean	Standard deviation	Minimum	Maximum
A Terminal output				
TEU: container throughput in TEUs (000's)	936.4	1,741.7	4.6	20,600
B Terminal inputs				
1 Cargo-handling equipment:				
Cargo-handling capacity at quay in tonnage[a]	385.0	470.7	23.9	5,416.2
Cargo-handling capacity at yard in tonnage[b]	5,116.5	7,060.9	38.6	62,731.8
2 Terminal infrastructure:				
Number of berths	5.1	5.2	1	37
Length of quay line in meters	1,361.3	1,181.6	200	9,000
Terminal area in squared meters (000's)	604.9	844.6	7.7	8,092
3 Storage facilities:				
Storage capacity in number of TEUs (000's)	23.2	72.4	0.6	1,200
Number of electric reefer points	480.6	539.7	4	3,768
C Individual characteristics				
1 Terminal and port level:				
EDI (in fraction of total sample)	0.3			
Depth of water in meters	13.2	3.5	4.5	32.0
Number of liners calling at the terminal	16.2	14.5	1	114
Number of operators in port	3.7	2.6	1	10
Number of terminals in port	6.8	6.2	1	31
2 Operator group dummies (in fraction of total sample):				
Global carrier	0.09			
Global stevedore	0.15			
Other: do not belong to any of above groups	0.76			
3 Country characteristics:				
GDP in current US$ (billion)[c]	2,240	3,270	5.4	12,500
Goods exports in US$ (billion)[c]	271	249	0.4	972
Goods imports in US$ (billion)[c]	308	365	1.8	1,670
GDP per capita in current US$[c]	18,654.9	12,367.8	405	37,651
4 Continental distribution (in fraction of total sample):				
Asia	0.37			
Europe	0.27			
North America	0.17			
Latin America	0.06			
Oceania	0.09			

(Continued)

Table 5.1 (Continued)

Variables	Mean	Standard deviation	Minimum	Maximum
Africa	0.04			
Period	1997–2004			
Number of countries	39			
Number of ports	78			
Number of terminal operators	141			
Number of terminals	397			
Number of observations	597			

Source: Yan *et al.* 2009.

Notes
a An aggregate of (1) quay cranes and (2) ship-shore container gantries.
b An aggregate of (1) gantry cranes, (2) yard cranes, (3) yard gantries, (4) reachstackers, (5) yard tractors, (6) yard chassis trailers, (7) forklifts, (8) straddle carriers, (9) container lifters, and (10) mobile cranes.
c The country data can be found at the World Bank website: http://devdata.worldbank.org/dataonline/old-default.htm

where X^k represents the technical input mix used by port k, $\alpha_k = \ln(A_k)$ is the logarithm of the individual growth coefficient, $B = (B_1, \ldots, B_n)$ is a frontier slope vector, Δ_k is the nonnegative technical inefficient term, and ε_i is an error term which accounts for random measurement errors and other random factors. Thus, $\alpha_k + BX^k$ gives the logarithm of the technical frontier function of port k, that is:

$$\hat{y}^k = f(X^k) = A_k e^{BX^k} = e^{\alpha_k + BX^k}. \tag{5.18}$$

In terms of technical inefficiency (Δ_k) and random measurement error ε_k, which can only be measured statistically, the econometrical SF model (5.17) (see Aigner *et al.* 1977; Coelli *et al.* 1998), can be econometrically calibrated with the sample production data without the requiring information on input prices. Assuming a cost-minimization port as a production function, the TE of each port k can be estimated as follows:

$$\text{TFE}^k = \frac{f(X^k) e^{-\Delta_k}}{f(X^k)} = e^{-\Delta_k}. \tag{5.19}$$

A geometrical description of the SF model is illustrated in Figure 5.9.

Estimation of technical frontier efficiency

Assuming that each port k is cost minimizing with unknown input prices, the SF model is used to estimate the technical frontier $e^{\alpha_k + BX^k}$ in terms of the intercept coefficient α_k and the technical frontier slope vector B. Together with the technical inefficiency term Δ_k, all the coefficient terms of the SF model need to be estimated from the sample data of each port k.

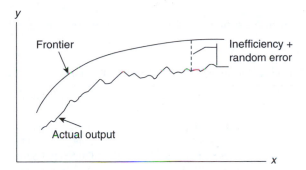

Figure 5.9 Stochastic frontier model: technical inefficiency.

To develop an estimation method of the SF model, we let $\hat{a}_k = \alpha_k - \Delta_k$, and rewrite the SF model in a reduced form as follows:

$$Y^k = \hat{a}_k + BX^k + \varepsilon_k. \tag{5.20}$$

Given a set of sample data in the format of (Y_t^k, X_t^k) for period t, for $t = 1, 2, \ldots, T$, the reduced SF model (5.20) can be estimated in terms of $\hat{a}_k = \alpha_k - \Delta_k$ and B. Now, the key to further assessing the TE (TFE^k) relies on differentiating the inefficiency term Δ_k from the intercept term α_k. To this end, we consider the individual technical characteristics of Table 5.1, denoted by vector τ^k for port k. Using the term $A(\tau)$, as defined in production frontier function (5.13), we construct a second-level estimation equation on the intercept term α_k of the SF model (5.17), as follows:

$$\alpha_k = \beta_k + \Theta\tau^k + v_k, \tag{5.21}$$

where β_k is an intercept term, Θ represents the slope vector of technical characteristics, τ^k is the vector of technical characteristics of port k (time, number of terminals, etc. as listed in category C of Table 5.1), and v_k is another error term. According to the SF model (5.17) and production frontier function (5.13), the inefficiency Δ_k is independent of technical characteristics τ^k. An econometrical SFA model can be constructed by combining the estimation systems of (5.17) and (5.21):

$$\begin{cases} Y_{kt} = \alpha_{kt} + BX_{kt} - \Delta_{kt} + \varepsilon_{kt} \\ \alpha_{kt} = \beta_{kt} + \Theta\tau_k + v_{kt} \\ k = 1, \ldots, m; \quad t = 1, \ldots, T \end{cases} \tag{5.22}$$

SFA case study: benchmarking of global container ports performance

In this section, we present the results of applying an SFA model for the case study of global container ports performance benchmarking, using the data set as highlighted in Table 5.1. The port production frontier is assumed to be of a Cobb–Douglas type.

The results of econometrical SFA estimation of port frontier are presented in Table 5.2.

Table 5.2 Posterior means and standard deviations of coefficients of SFA model

Variable	Heterogeneous model	Conventional model
1 Log inputs:		
Quay superstructure (β_1)	0.1815 (0.0725)	0.2142 (0.0581)
Yard equipment (β_2)	0.0200 (0.0361)	0.0527 (0.0315)
Berth number (β_3)	0.0953 (0.0509)	0.0290 (0.0576)
Quay length (β_4)	0.0802 (0.0507)	0.1228 (0.0589)
Terminal area (β_5)	0.0268 (0.0582)	0.0912 (0.0444)
Storage capacity (β_6)	0.0087 (0.0229)	−0.0406 (0.0274)
Reefer points (β_7)	0.1400 (0.0355)	0.2125 (0.0320)
2 Individual intercept:		
Constant (θ_0)	−0.7063 (0.3121)	0.8267 (0.3495)
2.1 Port characteristics		
Water depth (θ_1)	0.4184 (0.2770)	0.6644 (0.2626)
Ship calls (θ_2)	0.1322 (0.0369)	0.1550 (0.0399)
Number of operators (θ_3)	−0.0520 (0.0985)	−0.3789 (0.0761)
Number of terminals (θ_4)	−0.0219 (0.0886)	0.1992 (0.1039)
2.2 Country characteristics		
GDP (θ_5)	−0.3815 (0.0872)	0.2437 (0.0972)
Goods exports (θ_6)	0.0660 (0.1024)	−0.1715 (0.0719)
Goods imports (θ_7)	0.3088 (0.1114)	−0.0023 (0.0697)
GDP per capita (θ_8)	−0.7931 (0.2498)	−0.4889 (0.1123)
2.3 Operator group		
Carrier (θ_9)	0.3594 (0.2344)	0.3780 (0.1626)
Stevedore (θ_{10})	0.4538 (0.1874)	1.6053 (0.3623)
2.4 Time trend		
Time r_1	−0.0719 (0.0870)	−0.5350 (0.2197)
Time squared r_2	0.1031 (0.0430)	0.1553 (0.0996)
3 Variance of the constant σ_v^2	0.4437 (0.0650)	
4 Inefficiency parameters:		
Coefficient of constant (g_1)	−1.8584 (0.3797)	0.3517 (0.1554)
Coefficient of time (g_2)	−0.5967 (0.4785)	−0.4790 (0.1711)
Coefficient of time squared (g_3)	−1.1674 (0.2398)	−0.0812 (0.0913)
Coefficient of carrier (g_4)	−0.3961 (0.4313)	0.7357 (0.3945)
Coefficient of stevedore (g_5)	−1.0024 (1.0824)	−0.1368 (0.2601)
Variances (Σ_{11})	2.2743 (0.7468)	0.3327 (0.0838)
Variances (Σ_{22})	2.0274 (0.8271)	0.2680 (0.0688)
Variances (Σ_{33})	1.4244 (0.4569)	0.1736 (0.0386)
Variances (Σ_{44})	1.5650 (0.9784)	0.7158 (0.4536)
Variances (Σ_{55})	1.9605 (1.1155)	0.5996 (0.2482)
5 Other parameters:		
Variance of noise σ_ε^2	0.0321 (0.0029)	0.0371 (0.0034)

Note: Numbers in parentheses are the posterior standard deviations. All the input and output variables are normalized with respect to their sample means before taking log.

Port production frontier estimation

The first column of figures in Table 5.2 presents the estimation results by the basic SFA model (5.22). The second column presents the estimation results by a reduced SFA model, by not controlling the individual characteristics τ^k. The third column gives the estimation results by the model without controlling the unobservable individual heterogeneity (i.e., $v_k = 0$).

Efficiency benchmarking results by SFA

The estimation results of frontier efficiency are illustrated in Figure 5.10(a) for conventional SFA and in Figure 5.10(b) for heterogeneous SFA.

DEA model

Alternatively, the production frontier can be estimated by a nonparametrical method of DEA, which requires only a nonparametrical form of production function.

Basic DEA model

Consider that a constant-returns-to-scale (CRS) port k ($k = 1,\ldots,m$) produces an l-dimension output vector $y^k = (y_j^k)_{j=1}^l$, using an n-dimension input (vector) $x^k = (x_i^k)_{i=1}^n$. The basic DEA model is formulated as a mathematical programming problem. For each port k, find the weights $u^k = (u_j^k)_{j=1}^n$ and $v^k = (v_i^k)_{i=1}^n$ that solve the following linear program:

$$
\begin{cases}
\max\limits_{u^k,v^k} & u^k y^k = \sum\limits_{j=1}^l u_j^k y_j^k \\
\text{s.t.} & v^k x^k = 1 \\
& u^k y^j - v^k x^j \le 0, \quad j = 1,\ldots,m \\
& u^k, v^k \ge 0
\end{cases}
\tag{5.23}
$$

The optimal weights u^{k*} and v^{k*} will give the maximum ratio of $(u^{k*} y^k)/(v^{k*} x^k)$ (with $v^{k*} x^k = 1$), that is, the maximum ratio of all weighted outputs versus weighted inputs for port k. By duality of linear programming (LP), an equivalent *envelopment* form of DEA model (5.23) can be derived for a given port k, as follows:

$$
\begin{cases}
\min\limits_{\theta^k,\xi^k} & \theta^k \\
\text{s.t.} & Y\xi^k - y^k \ge 0 \\
& \theta^k x^k - X\xi^k \ge 0 \\
& \xi^k \ge 0
\end{cases}
\tag{5.24}
$$

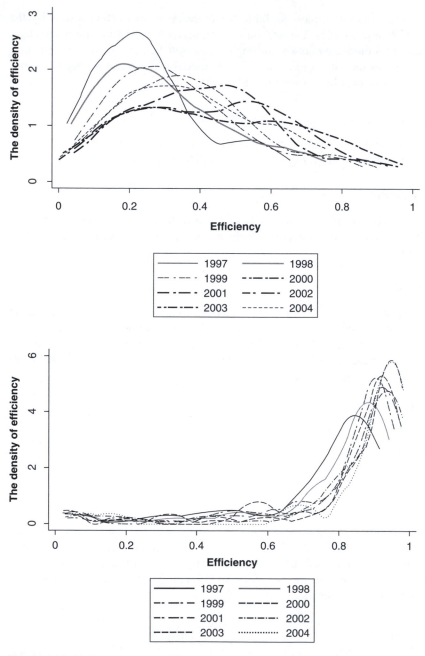

Figure 5.10 (a) Conventional stochastic frontier analysis model. (b) Heterogeneous stochastic frontier analysis model.

where θ^k is a scalar weight on the kth port and $\theta^k \leq 1$, $\xi^k = (\xi_m^k, \ldots, \xi_m^k)$ is an m-vector weight scaled across all the m ports, $Y = \left(y_i^j\right)_{lm}$ is an lm output (data) matrix observed from all the ports $(i = 1, \ldots, l; j = 1, \ldots, m)$, and $X = \left(x_i^j\right)_{nm}$ is an mn input (data) matrix observed from all the ports $(i = 1, \ldots, n; j = 1, \ldots, m)$. Given input data

X and output data Y, a set of optimal weights for port k, $(\hat{\theta}^k, \hat{\xi}^k)$, can be determined by solving the LP problem (5.24), and the minimized value of $\hat{\theta}^k$ by (5.24) will be the (technical) efficiency score for the kth port. If $\hat{\theta}^k = 1$, port k reaches its technical frontier and is technically efficient. This process can be repeated for all ports.

Remarks: The basic DEA uses deterministic linear optimization methods to construct a nonparametric piece-wise linear frontier, which can be estimated from empirical data on output and input. Although the piece-wise linear frontier estimation was first proposed by Farrel (1957), the formal method, which is termed DEA and was first developed by Charnes *et al.* (1978), is input based and assumes CRS.

The variable-returns-to-scale DEA model

The basic DEA model above assumes CRS, which is applicable when all ports (firms) operate at an optimal scale. However, a firm may not operate at optimal scale under variable-returns-to-scale (VRS) situations, where the sizes of ports are heterogeneous due to a number of factors, such as imperfect competition and constraints on finance. A VRS model can be modified from (5.23) by requiring an additional convexity constraint on the weights vector ξ for a given port k, that is:

$$1 \times \xi^k = \sum_{i=1}^{m} \xi_i^k = 1. \tag{5.25}$$

Then, the VRS DEA model can be constructed as follows:

$$\begin{cases} \min_{\theta^k, \xi^k} & \theta^k \\ \text{s.t.} & Y\xi^k - y^k \geq 0 \\ & \theta^k x^k - X\xi^k \geq 0 \cdot \\ & 1 \times \xi^k = 1 \\ & \xi^k \geq 0 \end{cases} \tag{5.26}$$

Note that the constraint (5.25) ensures that inefficient ports are only compared against ports of smaller size. For the CRS case, the convexity constraint (5.25) is not imposed, thus the ξ-weights will not be restricted to sum to one.

Cost minimization

If the input prices for port k, denoted by $w^k = w_1^k, \ldots, w_n^k$, are known, then the VRS DEA model (5.26) can be expanded to a cost-minimization DEA, given the data sets X and Y, as follows:

$$
\begin{cases}
\min\limits_{\hat{x}^k, \xi^k} & w^k \hat{x}^k = \sum\limits_{i=1}^{n} w_i^k \hat{x}_i^k \\
\text{s.t.} & Y\xi^k - y^k \geq 0 \\
& \hat{x}^k - X\xi^k \geq 0 \\
& 1 \times \xi^k = 1 \\
& \xi^k \geq 0
\end{cases}
\tag{5.27}
$$

The solution of the cost-minimization DEA (5.27) will determine the cost-minimizing input quantities for port k, denoted as $\hat{x}^{k*}$, given the output levels y^k. The cost efficiency (or EE) of port k can be calculated as follows:

$$
CE^k = \frac{\text{Minimized cost}}{\text{Observed cost}} = \frac{w^k \hat{x}^{k*}}{w^k x^k}.
\tag{5.28}
$$

With the TE obtained from CRS or VRS DEA, the allocative efficiency of port k can be calculated by

$$
AE^k = \frac{\text{Cost efficiency}}{\text{Technical efficiency}} = \frac{CE^k}{TE^k}.
\tag{5.29}
$$

Revenue maximization

If the output prices for port k, denoted by $p^k = p_1^k, \ldots, p_l^k$, are known, a revenue-maximization DEA problem can be similarly constructed, given the data sets X and Y, as follows:

$$
\begin{cases}
\min\limits_{\hat{y}^k, \xi^k} & p^k \hat{y}^k = \sum\limits_{i=1}^{l} p_i^k \hat{y}_i^k \\
\text{s.t.} & Y\xi^k - \hat{y}^k \geq 0 \\
& x^k - X\xi^k \geq 0 \\
& 1 \times \xi^k = 1 \\
& \xi^k \geq 0
\end{cases}
\tag{5.30}
$$

In this case, the EE of port k can be calculated using the revenue-maximizing output levels $\hat{y}^{k*}$ solved from (5.30), as follows:

$$EE^k = \frac{\text{Observed revenue}}{\text{Maximized revenue}} = \frac{p^k y^k}{p^k \hat{y}^{k*}}. \tag{5.31}$$

In sum, the DEA models use LP techniques to estimate the efficiency frontier from sample data on input demand and output supply. There are various types of algorithms and software packages that are particularly suited for DEA applications. However, the major limitation of the DEA method is its deterministic modeling framework, which excludes any possible measurement error and other forms of noise.

Bibliography

Abramovitz, M. 1956. "Resource and Output Trends in the United States Since 1870," *AER Papers and Proceedings*, 46, 5–23.

Aigner, A., C.A.K. Lovell, and P. Schmidt. 1977. "Formulation and Estimation of Stochastic Frontier Production Function Models," *Journal of Econometrics*, 86, 21–37.

Arrow, K.J. and G. Debreu. 1954. "Existence of an Equilibrium for a Competitive Economy," *Econometrica*, 22, 265–290.

Arrow, K.J., H.B. Cheney, B.S. Minhas, and R.W. Solow. 1961. "Capital-Labor Substitution and Economic Efficiency," *Review of Economics and Statistics*, 63, 225–250.

Beattie, B. and C. Taylor. 1985. *The Economics of Production*, New York: Wiley.

Buchanan, J.M. 1964. *Is Economics the Science of Choice? Roads to Freedom: Essays in Honour of Friedrick A. von Hayek*, London: Routledge and Kegan Paul, pp. 47–64.

Buchanan, J.M. 1975. "A Contractarian Paradigm for Applying Economics Theory," *American Economic Review*, 65, 225–230.

Cachon, G.P. and M. Lariviere. 2005. "Supply Chain Coordination with Revenue-Sharing Contracts: Strengths and Limitations," *Management Science*, 51(1), 30–44.

Charnes, A., W.W. Cooper, and E. Rhodes. 1978. "Measuring the Efficiency of Decision Making Units," *European Journal of Operational Research*, 2, 429–444.

Coelli, T., D.P. Rao, and G.E. Battese. 1998. *An Introduction to Efficiency and Productivity Analysis*, Cambridge: Cambridge University Press.

Commons, J. 1932. "The Problem of Correlating Laws, Economics and Ethics," *Wisconsin Law Review*, 3–26.

Diewert, W.E. 1971. "An Application of the Shephard Duality Theorem: A Generalized Leontief Production Function," *Journal of Political Economics*, 79(3), 481–507.

Farrel, M.J. 1957. "The Measurement of Productive Frontier," *Journal of the Royal Statistical Society, Series A,* CXX, Part 3, 253–290.

Goldratt, E. and J. Cox. 1992. *The Goal: Excellence in Manufacturing,* 2nd Edition, Corton-Hudson, NY: North River Press.

Kendrick, J.W. 1956. "Productivity Trends: Capital and Labor," *Review of Economics and Statistics*, 38, 248–257.

McFadden, D. 1963. "Constant Elasticity of Substitution Production Functions," *Review of Economic Studies*, 30, 73–83.

Romer, P. 1990. "Endogenous Technological Change, Part 2: The Problem of Development: A Conference of the Institute for the Study of Free Enterprise Systems," *The Journal of Political Economy*, 98(5), S71–S102.

Schumpeter, J.A. 1912/1934. *The Theory of Economic Development: An Inquiry into Profits, Capital, Credit, Interest, and the Business Cycle*, New Brunswick, NJ: Transaction.

Schumpeter, J.A. 1942. *Capitalism, Socialism and Democracy*, New York: Harper.

Solow, R.M. 1956. "A Contribution to the Theory of Economic Growth," *Quarterly Journal of Economics*, 70, 65–94.

Solow, R.M. 1957. "Technical Change and the Aggregate Production Function," *Review of Economics and Statistics*, 39(3), 312–320.

Williamson, O.E. 2002. "The Theory of the Firm as Governance Structure: From Choice to Contract," *Journal of Economic Perspectives,* 16(3), 171–195.

Williamson, O.E. 2008. "Outsourcing: Transaction Cost Economics and Supply Chain Management," *International Journal of Supply Chain Management*, 44(2), 1559–1576.

Yan, J., X. Sun, and J. Liu. 2009. "An Empirical Model to Assess Container Operators' Efficiencies and Efficiency Changes with Heterogeneous and Time-Variant Frontiers," *Transportation Research-B*, 43(1), 172–185.

6 Transportation and distribution

Key items:

- *Distribution in supply chain*
- *Transportation systems*
- *Distribution in manufacturer–distributor systems*
- *Distribution in warehouse-retailer systems*

Distribution in the supply chain

Without distribution, manufacturing would be purposeless. A distribution task comprises three highly dynamic elements: when, where, and how much is to be distributed. According to Sun Zi's winning-before-doing (WBD) principle, one must make sure to win with speed. His secret to winning with speed is through calculated quickness. In the business of distribution, this means that one must deliver the exact quantity on time. There are two approaches to quick wins in distribution: push and pull, as we have studied in Chapters 1 and 2. A push distribution system centers on "getting ready" by securing quantity in advance, whereas a pull distribution relies more on Just in Time (JIT) delivery. In reality, a successful distribution strategy must involve both push and pull systems, because distribution, by its nature, is a mixed network of both systems.

A transportation system constitutes physical links between stages (or points), whereas distribution is the driver of the links. By nature, transportation, and thus distribution, involve at least two stages in the supply chain: supplier–manufacturer and manufacturer–wholesaler distribution systems. As we have learned so far, each pair of linked stages form a seller–buyer chain, which in turn represents a bargaining situation as we studied in the previous chapter. In this sense, distribution in a supply chain engages a system of bargaining games. Two inevitable elements in distribution can thus be immediately identified: order fulfillment and the information network. Next, let us consider the distribution problem in a brewery supply chain.

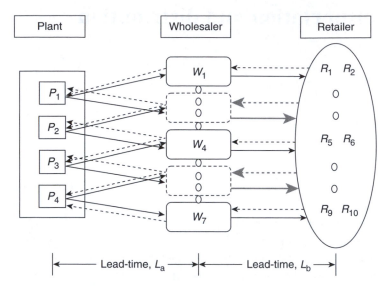

Figure 6.1 Distribution in brewery supply chain.

Prototype example: distribution at Mega Brewery

Consider the supply chain of bottled beer for the same market as in section "Warehouse cross-item value-stream balancing" (p. 317), with a weekly order cycle. The distribution in the supply chain involves Mega Brewery's (MB) four beer plants (denoted by P_1, P_2, P_3, P_4), seven authorized wholesalers (i.e., the buyers denoted by $W_1, \ldots, W_7$), and 10 retailers (denoted by $R_1, \ldots, R_{10}$). Suppose that a typical three-echelon distribution system is currently in operation, as illustrated in Figure 6.1. The dotted arrows in Figure 6.1 indicate the flow of order information and the solid arrows represent the flow of beer delivery.

Figure 6.1 shows that the distribution system currently in place requires that each of the ten retailers places orders through his or her designated group of wholesalers who are authorized to submit orders directly to some pre-allocated beer plants. The details of assignments of wholesalers and beer plants will be specified later in this section. Let L denote the order cycle, and thus for the weekly distribution system of bottled beer, we can write $L = 1$. Suppose that the lead-time for order fulfillment and delivery from a beer plant to a wholesaler is within 1 week (i.e., $L_a \leq 1$), and that the lead-time from a wholesaler to a retailer is also within one week (i.e., $L_b \leq 1$).

Beer production and transportation

Suppose that the weekly production capacity at plant P_i ($P_1, \ldots, P_4$), denoted by Q_i^P (in 1,000 cases per week), is currently scheduled as,

Table 6.1 Shipping cost from brewery plants to wholesalers ($ per 1,000 cases)

P	W						
	W_1	W_2	W_3	W_4	W_5	W_6	W_7
P_1	70	47	22	53	–	–	–
P_2	–	38	19	58	90	34	–
P_3	–	–	37	82	111	40	29
P_4	45	40	–	–	–	86	25

Production capacity in week t (1,000 cases per week):

$$Q_t^{P_1} = 40, Q_t^{P_2} = 35, Q_t^{P_3} = 37, Q_t^{P_4} = 42 \ \left(\text{Total}: 154,000 \text{ cases per week}\right) (6.1)$$

Each plant i produces and then delivers orders to an authorized group of whole-salers, with production cost of $500 per 1,000 cases and shipping cost data ($ per 1,000 cases) as given in Table 6.1. A cell with "—" in Table 6.1 indicates a non-designated pair of plant and wholesaler, and thus shipping is infeasible between the two. To simplify, we denote each cell by a pair (i, j) with plant i and whole-saler j, and the cost in cell (i, j) by C_{ij}.

For example, the unit shipping cost from plant 2 to wholesaler 5 is $C_{2,5} = 90$ ($ per 1,000 cases). The shipping associated with a nondesignated cell can be considered infinite (or very large). The shipping for cell $(1,6)$, for example, can be set to $C_{1,6} = \infty$ (or $C_{1,6} = M$, where M is so large that nobody could afford it).

The transportation costs from wholesaler to retailer are given in Table 6.2, with nondesignated pairs of wholesaler–retailer similarly indicated by "—".

The beer distribution problem at MB

The management at MB is currently examining two major aspects of its distribu-tion system: the operational aspect and the strategic aspect. The operational aspect of MB's distribution is mainly concerned with improving current routine distribution operations. Regarding the strategic aspect, MB is considering a recently submitted outsourcing proposal from Schneider Logistics, a major third-party logistical service company. Here are more details on both aspects of MB's beer distribution problems.

OPERATIONAL DISTRIBUTION PROBLEM

The beer produced at the four beer plants is to be distributed through the distribu-tion system, as shown in Figure 6.1, to meet total demand generated from the ten retailers. The current retail demand is stable, as given in Table 6.3.

Table 6.2 Shipping cost from wholesalers to retailers ($ per 1,000 cases)

W	R_1	R_2	R_3	R_4	R_5	R_6	R_7	R_8	R_9	R_{10}
W_1	3	21	31	44	60	33	17	–	–	–
W_2	–	54	45	60	27	9	14	39	–	–
W_3	–	–	32	15	25	11	34	56	44	37
W_4	22	37	25	35	42	23	27	45	–	–
W_5	14	32	–	–	–	41	47	33	17	29
W_6	–	–	42	27	33	28	51	24	21	19
W_7	33	–	–	8	20	22	35	17	30	41

Table 6.3 Retail demand data (in 1,000 cases per week)

D	R_1	R_2	R_3	R_4	R_5	R_6	R_7	R_8	R_9	R_{10}	Total
Demand	17	12	20	9	11	17	14	19	15	16	150

Table 6.3 shows that the total weekly retail demand is 150,000 cases, which are to be produced at the four beer plants with a combined weekly capacity of 154,000 cases of beer. Suppose that the total retail orders of 150,000 cases of bottled beer have been forwarded to the respective designated wholesalers, and that the wholesalers then combine (i.e., aggregate) the received retail orders and then submit in terms of wholesale orders to the respective designated beer plant(s).

The *beer distribution problem* at hand is to complete the following tasks with minimum total cost, including production and transportation costs:

1   Allocate the total production order of 150,000 cases of beer among the four beer plants, subject to the respective production capacity limits of the plants.
2   The brewer produces the allocated wholesale orders, and then delivers them to the respective wholesalers.
3   The wholesalers then deliver the beer to the respective retailers.

In fact, the beer distribution operations involve two basic distribution systems: *manufacturer–distributor* and *warehouse–retailer* distribution. In addition to the above routine distribution operations, the MB management is also exploring the following operational improvement initiatives:

1   Explore the benefit of adopting direct distribution with a *manufacturer–retailer* system, which has become more and more common in Internet-based supply chain operations, typically referred to as direct distribution (or online distribution). Note that current distribution involves more traditional distribution methods, namely, manufacturer–distributor and warehouse–retailer distribution. As we proceed with this chapter, we will study these three basic distribution systems.
2   Whether or not to remove the limits across designated distributor/retailer groups. That is, whether all of the "infeasible" cells in the cost tables should be "feasible," so there is no prohibited delivery route.

THIRD-PARTY LOGISTICS PROPOSAL

Under the proposed 5-year contract of third-party logistics, Schneider Logistics will directly receive from MB weekly orders of plant-to-retailer shipments. It will be responsible for complete weekly order fulfillment, including truck loading at MB's shipping docks, and delivery of beer directly to retailers. Further, it will submit a quarterly quotation of origin–destination transportation rates, as depicted in Table 6.4. Although the proposed pricing structure does not explicitly involve transitional shipments via wholesalers, the transportation costs related to wholesales may be reflected in the quarterly quotation. Under the third-party logistics proposal, whether or not to involve wholesalers in transportation is decided at Schneider's discretion. The quoted rate is fixed for the effective quarter, unless there are sudden drastic changes in the market condition. In this event, an emergent amendment can be applied.

In this way, MB will be able to base the weekly plan of beer production directly on retail demand, which the MB management believes will improve the accuracy of production planning and delivery.

Table 6.4 Sample: third-party quotation of transportation rates ($ per 1,000 cases)

P	R									
	R_1	R_2	R_3	R_4	R_5	R_6	R_7	R_8	R_9	R_{10}
P_1	71	41	53	54	76	113	77	52	75	92
P_2	59	94	55	76	117	59	94	89	62	37
P_3	42	37	52	45	85	107	64	96	64	87
P_4	63	64	49	38	92	86	95	57	60	71

However, there can be potential problems with the outsourcing agreement, which must be addressed before moving along with the proposal. The MB management has identified a list of issues to be examined and analyzed:

1   The issue that concerns the MB management the most is how to maintain MB's control over the priority and flexibility in distribution that has been developed in the past. For example, there have been "preferred" customers around whom some localized distribution capacity has been established, so as to make expedited deliveries.

2   Would there be sufficient potential cost savings under the origin–destination pricing, as depicted in Table 6.4, compared with the existing distribution system? If so, can such savings, if any, be routinely realized? That is, how can cost-minimizing shipping routes be determined and then implemented on a weekly basis?

3   How to incorporate the origin–destination shipments with both wholesale and retail orders? The MB management wants to continue receiving orders from wholesalers, except that the destination (i.e., retail sites) of each wholesale order must now be specified so that the ordered beer will be delivered directly to the retailers. At the same time, MB can now receive orders directly from selected retailers. How would such a change in the ordering process affect production planning?

This chapter is devoted to the methods and tools that are needed and useful for addressing the above distribution problems and beyond. As the methods and tools are developed in accordance with a strategic framework that underpins distribution systems, in the following subsection, we present two emerging strategic components in logistical distribution operation: push versus pull distribution systems and third-party logistics.

Push versus pull distribution systems

As suggested by Simchi-Levi *et al.* (2000), push and pull distribution systems stem from JIT manufacturing, but the mechanism of push and pull in JIT distribution differs from that of JIT manufacturing. Next, let us examine closely the recent movements in logistical distribution.

Push distribution system

Under **push** distribution strategy, goods are shipped to stocking points (e.g., warehouses) before the buyers of the goods are secured. Thus, the distribution decisions must be facilitated by a forecast of sort, either analytical or empirical, or even by some guesswork. For the example of the MB brewery supply chain (Figure 6.1), certain stock levels (or base stocks) are established in advance at the wholesalers based on a forecast of the weekly wholesale demand. Wholesale

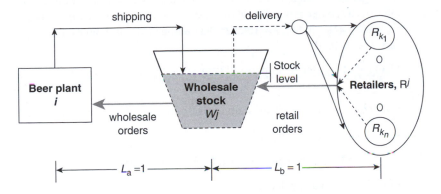

Figure 6.2 Demand aggregation in push distribution.

orders are issued weekly to replenish the wholesale stock. In essence, the beer plants produce to fill each wholesaler's stock, which in turn are utilized to satisfy the retail demand. Determining the wholesalers' stock levels is based on the forecast of aggregated retail demand. There is a 1-week lead-time; hence, each wholesaler must obtain a 1-week forecast of aggregated retail demand from which the wholesale stock level can be determined. Note that the wholesale demand at each wholesaler is an aggregation of the retail demand from the designated retailers, as depicted in Figure 6.2.

In Figure 6.2, the order cycle is assumed to be one period (e.g., 1 week). Thus, orders are submitted on a cycle-by-cycle basis, similar to the lot-for-lot ordering in MRP. Given that each lead-time is within one cycle, they are equal to one cycle (i.e., $L_a = L_b = 1$), reflecting the fact that the orders are fulfilled and delivered period by period (i.e., weekly in this case). Although **push** distribution stems from the term *push manufacturing*, the two are not exactly the same. The sense of "push" in distribution mainly lies in the interactions between the beer plant and the wholesaler, as the production is governed by the rule of filling up to the wholesale stock level. In contrast, the operation between the wholesaler and retailers is of the pull type in the sense that the delivery by the wholesaler is triggered by the retail orders (indicated by dotted arrows). For the exposition purpose, let us introduce the following notation associated with a distribution situation as depicted in Figure 6.2.

$\mathbf{W}^i$ = Index group of wholesalers authorized for plant i. For example, in the MB distribution, the authorized wholesaler group for plant 4 can be determined from Table 6.1 as $\mathbf{W}^4 = \{j : 1, 2, 6, 7\}$.

$\mathbf{P}^j$ = Index group of plants responsible for orders from wholesaler j. For example, in the MB distribution, the authorized plant group for wholesaler 5 can be determined from Table 6.1 as $\mathbf{P}^5 = \{i : 5 \in \mathbf{W}^i; i = 3, 4\}$.

$\mathbf{R}^j$ = Index group of retailers authorized for wholesaler j. For example, the authorized retailer group for wholesaler 5 can be determined from Table 6.2 as $\mathbf{R}^j$ ={k: index for retailer Rk authirized for wholesaler 5} = {k:1,2,6,7,8,9,10}.

$D_t^{R_k}$ = Demand at retailer R_k in period t (e.g., weekly retail demand).

$D_t^{Rj} = \sum_{k \in R^j} D_t^{R_k}$ = Sum of retail demand in period of the retailer group R^j authorized for wholesaler W_j.

$D_t^{W_j}$ = Aggregated retail demand in period t for wholesaler W_j.

S^{W_j} = Stock level at wholesaler W_j.

S^{R_k} = Stock level at retailer R_k.

If the retail demand is deterministic such as that given in Table 6.3, the wholesale stock level S^{W_j} can be set equal to the aggregated retail demand over lead-time L; that is,

$$S^{W_j} = \text{Wholesale stock level} = \sum_{t=1}^{L} D_t^{R^j}. \tag{6.2}$$

In the case of MB's beer distribution, the order cycle is 1 week (i.e., $L = L_a = L_b = 1$, as shown in Figure 6.2). In the general case where lead-times may be greater than 1, we can select $L = \max\{L_a, L_b\}$ and consider the effective lead-time between each of the two pairs to be the same L. Similarly, each retailer R_k in the retailer group R^j will also establish a retail stock level as the sum of retail demand over lead-time L:

$$S^{R_k} = \text{retail stock level} = \sum_{t=1}^{L} D_t^{R_k}. \tag{6.3}$$

In the case of MB's beer distribution, the wholesale stock level shall be set equal to aggregated retail demand over 1 week. With deterministic demand, the amount of total weekly demand (as given in Table 6.3) will be produced at the responsible beer plants and will then be delivered to the retailers for consumption via wholesalers. In this case, the wholesalers become pure transition and rerouting points. Then, the major decision is to allocate the production orders among responsible beer plants, because multiple plants can be responsible for a single retailer. Such push distribution can be modeled as a **transshipment** problem, an application of a **transportation** model as studied in the field of operations research (Hillier and Lieberman 2009). We will further discuss the modeling details of the transshipment problem as we proceed in this chapter. However, the solution methods and algorithms to the transportation problems require in-depth knowledge of linear programming, which should be prepared separately by studying the subjects of management science or operations research. Therefore, the details of solution algorithms will be omitted from this book, and reference to commercial solvers will be provided when appropriate.

When the demand is variable, there may well be the case where excess or insufficient stocks occur at the wholesale and the retail levels. When this occurs, the safety stock issue should be considered in a similar way as we studied it in Chapter 3. In short, a push distribution may consist of a mix of push and pull systems, with a push type occurring at upstream chains.

Push distribution can be distinguished from push manufacturing in the ways decisions are made. In push distribution, major decisions are concerned with from–to routes and the associated quantities. However, in push manufacturing, decisions are made in the form of planned order release (POR), as we studied in Chapter 2.

Pull distribution system

On the other hand, under **pull** distribution, goods are produced and shipped only when the buyers of the goods have already been identified at the retail level or lower. Parallel to pull manufacturing, two types of pull mechanism can also be identified in distribution systems: Kanban pull and point of sale (POS) pull. Orders in Kanban pull distribution are triggered by market demand, and then relayed upward, stage by stage, to the retailer, then the wholesaler, until orders reach the plant, as depicted in Figure 6.3. This type of order pull mechanism is similar to that seen in Kanban manufacturing. We shall note that there is not necessarily any Kanban used in conveying order information between stages.

In fact, MB's beer distribution illustrated in Figure 6.1 is of a Kanban pull type. That is, orders start at retailers, and are relayed to the wholesaler, which then trigger the beer production at the brewery plants. As the order cycle is 1 week long, each retailer needs to "commit" (or promise) to an order 1 week in advance.

To see this, let us take a quick look at the mechanism of a Kanban pull in distribution using the MB case as an example:

- Suppose that each stage has currently established a 1-week stock. Specifically, the plant has the input supply for 1 week of beer production, the wholesaler has an adequate stock of beer for 1-week aggregated retail demand, and each authorized retailer has an adequate stock of beer for his or her local consumption.
- A new order cycle starts with each retailer submitting a 1-week retail order that is to be delivered by the wholesaler within 1 week.
- The wholesaler immediately reacts to the retail orders by shipping the ordered beer, which will take 1 week to reach each of the retailers. At the same time, a wholesale order to replenish the wholesale stock will be immediately issued to the plant.
- The plant will then react to the wholesale order and will begin production. The wholesale order will be fulfilled and delivered to the wholesaler in 1 week.

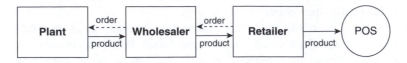

Figure 6.3 A Kanban pull distribution system.

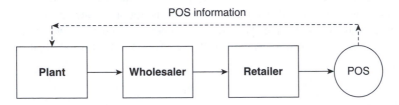

Figure 6.4 A POS pull distribution system.

In contrast, in POS pull distribution, POS information is directly transferred to the plant stage so as to initiate immediate production of replenishment goods, as illustrated in Figure 6.4. Compared to the Kanban pull distribution in Figure 6.3, the POS pull is directly communicated to the manufacturer (the plant in this case), without relaying the pull signal upward from the retailer, through the wholesaler, then to the manufacturer. Obviously, the idea behind the POS pull is to bypass the relay of external demand information through intermediate stages to avoid errors that may potentially occur during the interactions between stages. Think of this as eliminating the "middle man."

If there is no uncertainty in sales or in the distribution system, then both Kanban pull and POS pull systems would work equally well in terms of meeting the demand with the least possible cost. For example, if the demand process fluctuates significantly, one type of pull distribution may respond to the market better than the other, depending on the pattern of the fluctuation and how inventory stocks are managed at each stage.

Third-party logistics

Another notable strategic development in the field of logistical distribution is third-party logistics (Coyle *et al.* 2000).

Growing trend

Rapidly growing along with Internet technology is third-party logistics, which refers to the practice of contracting all or part of a firm's logistics function—especially distribution—to an outside company. As we know, specialized transportation services, such as trucking and warehousing, have long been outsourced to logistics companies. Then what is the difference between regular distribution services and third-party logistics? First, there is a difference between a third-party logistical firm and third-party logistics. A third-party carrier, such as Schneider Logistics™, typically provides transaction-based (e.g., by arm's length contract) transportation and shipping services. Such logistical services are provided for general purpose on relatively short terms and, therefore, they are of a highly specialized function to a wide range of industries. In contrast, third-party logistics entail a form of termed contract, or framework, between a shipper and a third-party carrier for a designated set of logistical functions. These functions may range from inbound logistics to transportation and delivery, and may even involve supply chain coordination. For example, Whirlpool Corporation has contracted, on a 5-year term, all of its inbound logistics to Ryder Dedicated Logistics. Under this kind of third-party logistics contract, Ryder is responsible for designing, managing, and operating all the inbound logistics for Whirlpool (Leahy *et al.* 1995).

The increasing use of third-party logistics can be attributed to information technology (IT) in general and Internet technology in particular. The reason for Internet use is twofold. Internet technology has eliminated location and boundary limitations for many large global companies. The logistics—especially the distribution systems—for global operations have become more and more sophisticated, and at the same time the expectations of them have become more and more demanding. For example, global delivery of medical equipment at GE Healthcare has evolved into a worldwide network spanning five continents. Technology advancements have reduced the expected delivery cycle time from more than a year in the non-IT age to less than 3 months. Today, firms such as 3M, GE, Eastman Kodak, and Sears, Roebuck and Co. have found that internal integration of distribution functions has become an insurmountable burden on themselves, and that performing logistics with internal resources leads to serious distraction from focusing on a company's core competencies. That is why many global firms have embarked on the practice of third-party logistics for various portions of their logistical operations.

Similarly to the provider side of third-party logistics, advances in IT have afforded an outside company's (especially a small-sized one) technological capability to perform boundary-spanning tasks for different firms. That is why the providers of third-party logistics come in all sizes, from small million-dollar firms to large multibillion-dollar multinationals. Major carrier-based providers of third-party logistics include Ryder Logistics, Schneider Logistics, Customized Transportation, and Menlo Logistics (Stock and Lambert 2001).

Advantages and limitations of third-party logistics

On the demand side, advantages to companies adopting third-party logistics include the following:

- Increasing the scope and quality of logistics service, by selecting highly competent and specialized third-party logistics providers.

- Focusing on firms' own core competencies and technological innovations.
- Maintaining flexibility in strategic distribution system design without major capital commitment.

However, the use of third-party logistics is not without its weaknesses. Long-term contracts with third-party logistics providers may result in loss of, or weakened control of, distribution decisions.

On the supply side, third-party logistics providers can accurately forecast and, therefore, plan workloads during the contract period. Thus, logistics providers can focus on perfecting their professional performance.

Basic transportation systems

Pull or push distribution systems must both involve transporting goods from suppliers to customers. A basic transportation problem is finding the most economically efficient means of transporting goods available at a given set of suppliers to designated destinations. The mathematical tool for obtaining solutions to the transportation problem is referred to as a transportation model, which is conventionally formulated in terms of cost-minimizing objectives.

Transportation costs and pricing

Transportation costs and pricing are determined on the concept of professional transportation service. Commercial transportation service, as a vital part of the worldwide economy, is governed by the economics between the buyer and the seller of the service. In terms of business logistics, the provider of transportation services is typically called a transportation *carrier*, and the buyer of such a service is called a *shipper*. Although the price must be mutually acceptable to both the shipper and the carrier, the factors influencing transportation costs and pricing mainly stem from the carrier's side, depending on technological capacity and economical conditions of the service provider(s). Therefore, it is common practice in the field of transportation that a shipper solicits quotes from carriers, and then selects carrier(s) accordingly.

Transportation carriers

Commercial transportation carriers can be classified as either for-hire (or third-party) carriers or self-owned (or internal) carriers. As indicated by recent field practice, there is an increasing trend in the use of for-hire carriers. In turn, for-hire carries can be grouped into three forms: common, contract, and exempt carriers.

COMMON CARRIERS

A common carrier offers transportation service to general shippers between designated points at published rates. A common carrier must be authorized by an appropriate federal regulatory agency to legally operate. They are required to provide their services to the general public on a nondiscriminative basis. For example, public air cargo transporters can serve any shipper as long as the commodities of shipment match with technical specifications.

CONTRACT CARRIERS

This is another form of the for-hire carrier who serves the shippers only on the basis of specific contractual agreements. Given that the service and the cost are specified in a contract, contract carriers can usually perform more effectively and, therefore, contract rates are typically lower than common carrier rates. Another reason for more effective performance by contract carriers is that the demand is known in advance via contract terms, unlike the case of common carrier service where demand in a public market is highly uncertain. This is why many common carriers have turned into contract carriage (Stock and Lambert 2001).

EXEMPT CARRIERS

An exempt carrier is given exempt status to transport certain products that require special exemptions. Such products include agricultural products and farm supplies, such as livestock, fish, poultry, and plants.

Carriers' pricing strategies

There are two basic pricing strategies used by carriers: cost-of-service pricing and value-of-service pricing.

COST-OF-SERVICE PRICING

Under this pricing strategy, a carrier establishes transportation rates based on incurred costs, including both fixed and variable costs, plus an appropriate profit margin. This pricing method requires accurate analysis of cost data, which can become complicated and difficult. For example, conversion of fixed cost to cost-per-unit rate often poses a problem of accurate forecast of shipment volume, which is highly uncertain in most situations.

In general, variable transportation costs constitute a major component in cost-of-service pricing. Variable transportation costs are dependent on two factors: distance and volume. The simplest distance-based costing is the cost-per-distance measure for each origin–destination pair. However, in reality the distance of the actual route may need to be considered. High-volume shipments by motor carriers are priced according to truckload (TL) rates, which are typically lower than the less-than-truckload (LTL) rate due to economies of scale.

VALUE-OF-SERVICE PRICING

Although this pricing approach has been given a number of different definitions, according to Coyle *et al.* (2000), the value-of-service pricing is dictated by the market value of the product. For example, high-value products are charged high prices for their transportation, and low-value goods are charged low prices. This point is somewhat reflected in the cost-of-service pricing as well, but not used as the guideline for pricing. It can be problematic when prices are simply based on the value of products, especially when the market is competitive. Shippers are usually not willing to pay higher prices based on the value of the product alone, when lower-priced alternatives are available. This is because lower transportation rates can be offered if other factors, such as the cost and efficiency of transportation, are taken into account. Therefore, value-of-service pricing is often criticized for ignoring other factors in transportation pricing.

Origin–destination transportation model

An origin–destination transportation system generally transports goods from m production sites (e.g., $P_i, i = 1, 2, \ldots, m$) to n consumption points (e.g., $R_k, k = 1, 2, \ldots, n$), such as the beer distribution system in Table 6.4. Production capacity in period t at each production site i is given as $Q_t^{P_i}$ (e.g., 1,000 cases per week), and the demand at each consumption point k is given as $D_t^{R_k}$ (e.g., 1,000 cases per week). Transportation cost between any pair of origin i and destination k is given in Table 6.4, denoted by C_{ik}. For example, shipping 1,000 cases of beer from plant 2 to retailer 6 can be determined from Table 6.4 as \$59 (i.e., $C_{2,6} = 59$).

The basic transportation model of this type of system is to determine the shipments between each origin–destination pair (i, k), such that the total transportation costs are minimized, while all the demands at the consumption points are met. A mathematical model for solving the transportation problem is termed a transportation model, which has two forms of representation: *tableau* format and *mathematical programming* format. Let us begin with tableau transportation modeling.

Transportation tableau

Let us develop a basic transportation model for the origin–destination beer distribution example shown in Table 6.4. There are four beer production plants, with their production capacities (in 1,000 cases per week) given as:

$$Q_t^{P_1} = 40, Q_t^{P_2} = 35, Q_t^{P_3} = 37, Q_t^{P_4} = 42; \text{total weekly capacity} = 154$$

There are 10 retail consumption points with weekly demand $D_t^{R_k}$ ($k = 1, 2, \ldots, 10$) for any given week t) as given in Table 6.3. Let

$$X_{ik} = \text{shipments} (1,000 \text{ cases}) \text{ from plant } i \text{ to retailer } k.$$

The variable X_{ik} ($i = 1, 2, 3, 4; k = 1, 2, \ldots, 10$) is termed the decision variable, and we have a total of $4 \times 10 = 40$ decision variables. A value taken in each decision variable X_{ik} indicates the shipment made from plant i to k. The **basic transportation problem** is then to determine a value for each of the decision variables, such that

Table 6.5 Transportation tableau for MB distribution problem

W	R										
	R_1	R_2	R_3	R_4	R_5	R_6	R_7	R_8	R_9	R_{10}	Q_t^{Pi}
P_1	71	41	53	54	76	113	77	52	75	92	40
P_2	59	94	55	76	117	59	94	89	62	37	35
P_3	42	37	52	45	85	107	64	96	64	87	37
P_4	63	64	49	38	92	86	95	57	60	71	42
$D_t^{R_k}$	17	12	20	9	11	17	14	19	15	16	

the total transportation costs are minimized. Each set of values for X_{ik}s is termed a **solution** to the transportation problem. Let us first examine the transportation tableau for the MB transportation model (Table 6.5).

In the transportation tableau of Table 6.5, each decision variable X_{ik} corresponds to a cell (i,k) in row i and column k, with the transportation cost C_{ik} in the upper-right corner of each cell (i,k), where the costs C_{ik} are the same as given in Table 6.4. For example, the transportation cost from plant 1 to retailer 1 (i.e., from P_1 to R_1) is given in Table 6.4 as \$71 per 1,000 cases; thus, a "71" appears in the upper-right corner of cell $(1,1)$ in the transportation tableau in Table 6.5.

Transportation solutions

Initially, every cell in the transportation tableau is blank (representing zero assignment by default), excluding the cost in the upper-right hand corner of each cell. A solution to the transportation problem can then be obtained by filling each cell with a number such that the sum across row i is less than or equal to plant Q_t^{Pi}, and the sum across each column k equals to the retail demand $D_t^{R_k}$. For example, Table 6.6 gives one of the solutions with blank cells representing zero assignment.

The bottom row of Table 6.6 gives demand $D_t^{R_k}$ for each retailer R_k ($k = 1, 2, \ldots, 10$). The far right column gives the weekly production capacity Q_t^{Pi} ($i = 1, 2, 3, 4$). Each number in italics in Table 6.6 gives a transportation assignment. For example, the number "17" in the upper-left corner cell $(1,1)$ gives an assignment of transporting 17,000 cases from plant 1 to retailer 1. Note that the sum of all assignments in row 1 (i.e., the row for P_1) must be no more than the weekly capacity of plant 1, which is indicated in the far right column as 40 (1,000 cases).

Let us take a look at the number "6" in cell $(2,6)$ (i.e., $X_{26} = 6$), which gives that 6,000 cases of beer are produced at plant 2, and shipped to retailer 6. Total weekly demand at retailer 6 is 17,000 cases. Thus, another 11,000 cases is to be

Table 6.6 A transportation tableau solution for MB distribution problem

P	R										Q_t^{Pi}
	R_1	R_2	R_3	R_4	R_5	R_6	R_7	R_8	R_9	R_{10}	
P_1	71	41	53	54	76	113	77	52	75	92	40
	17	*12*	*11*								
P_2	59	94	55	76	117	59	94	89	62	37	35
			9	*9*	*11*	*6*					
P_3	42	37	52	45	85	107	64	96	64	87	37
						11	*14*	*12*			
P_4	63	64	49	38	92	86	95	57	60	71	42
								7	*15*	*16*	
D_t^{Rk}	17	12	20	9	11	17	14	19	15	16	

produced at plant 3 and shipped to retailer 6. That is, the total sum across column 6 is 17,000 cases, which is equal to the total demand at retailer 6. In fact, the solution in Table 6.6 is generated by the **northwest-corner** method, which is a heuristic method used to obtain an initial solution. Here is an algorithmic description of the northwest-corner method for the initial transportation solution found in Table 6.6:

1. Given an unassigned transportation tableau, let row $i = 1$ and column $k = 1$. Let $\bar{D}_k$ be the unmet demand at retailer k, and $\bar{Q}_i$ be the remaining weekly capacity at plant i. Set $\bar{Q}_i = Q_t^{Pi}$ and $\bar{D}_k = D_t^{R_i}$.

2. For cell (i, k),

   - If $\bar{Q}_i > \bar{D}_k$, then
     $$X_{ik} \Leftarrow \bar{D}_k; \ \bar{Q}_i \Leftarrow \bar{Q}_i - X_{ik}; \ k \Leftarrow k+1; \ \bar{D}_k = D_t^{R_k}.$$

   - Else, if $\bar{Q}_i = \bar{D}_k$, then
     $$X_{ik} \Leftarrow \bar{D}_k; \ i \Leftarrow i+1; \ k \Leftarrow k+1; \ \bar{Q}_i = Q_t^{Pi}; \ \bar{D}_k = D_t^{R_k}.$$

   - Else, if $\bar{Q}_i < \bar{D}_k$, then
     $$X_{ik} \Leftarrow \bar{Q}_i; \ \bar{D}_k \Leftarrow \bar{D}_k - X_{ik}; \ i \Leftarrow i+1; \ \bar{Q}_i = Q_t^{Pi}.$$

3. If $i = 4$ and $k = 10$, then stop, and a solution is obtained; otherwise, go to step 2 and repeat.

In brief, a **transportation solution** to an m plant, n retailer transportation model is a complete set of nonnegative values assigned to each of the transportation decision variables (i.e., shipments), denoted by

$$\{X_{ik} \geq 0 : i = 1, 2, \ldots, m; k = 1, 2, \ldots, n\},$$

because only positive X_{ik} in a solution indicates shipments and the rest zero-valued decision variables (i.e., empty cells in the transportation tableau) incur no shipments. Therefore, it is natural to focus on the positive variables in a transportation solution. For this reason, the set of positive valued X_{ik}s in a transportation solution is termed the **basic solution**, while the set of rest zero-valued X_{ik}s is termed the **nonbasic solution**.

We can verify from Table 6.6 that the sum across each column k ($k = 1, 2, \ldots, 10$) is equal to the weekly demand $D_t^{R_k}$ of retailer R_k, while the sum across each row i ($i = 1, 2, 3, 4$) is no more than the capacity $Q_t^{P_i}$ of plant i. That is,

$$\sum_{k=1}^{10} X_{ik} \leq Q_t^{P_i} \ (i = 1, 2, 3, 4) \left(\text{supply constraints}\right) \tag{6.4}$$

$$\sum_{i=1}^{4} X_{ik} = D_t^{R_k} \ (k = 1, 2, \ldots, 10) \left(\text{demand constraints}\right) \tag{6.5}$$

$$X_{ik} \geq 0 (i = 1, 2, \ldots, m, k = 1, 2, \ldots, n).$$

An underlying assumption made by default in constraints (6.4) and (6.5) is that the total production capacity is adequate to meet the total demand. This assumption is indeed met in the MB distribution example, where total weekly capacity is 154,000 cases (as given in (6.1)) and the total weekly retail demand is 150,000 cases (as given in Table 6.3). Now, let us consider the total cost associated with a solution. It is easy to see that the cost of shipping X_{ik} (in 1,000 cases) beer from plant i to retailer k can be computed as $C_{ik} \times X_{ik}$. Ignoring the blank cells, the total cost associated with the solution in Table 6.6 can be computed as:

$$\textbf{Total cost} = C_{1,1} \times X_{1,1} + C_{1,2} \times X_{1,2} + \cdots + C_{4,10} \times X_{4,10}$$
$$= 71 \times (17) + 41 \times (12) + \cdots + 71 \times (16) = \$10,762$$

Therefore, we will say that the total transportation cost required for the solution given by Table 6.6 is $10,762. An **optimal solution** to a transportation problem is then defined as the solution that incurs the least total cost.

Linear programming transportation model

The transportation model for the MB distribution problem can then be stated as: obtain a solution that satisfies constraints (6.4) and (6.5), such that the associated total cost is minimized.

For all of the four plants and 10 retailers, the total transportation costs of a solution $\{X_{ij} : i = 1, 2, 3, 4; j = 1, 2, \ldots, 10\}$ can be computed by summing up the costs for all the origin–destination pairs, as follows:

$$\text{Total transportation costs} = \sum_{i=1}^{4} \sum_{k=1}^{10} C_{ik} X_{ik}.$$

A basic transportation model formulates an m origin, n destination transportation problem, such as the one depicted by Table 6.4, with a cost-minimizing **linear programming** (LP) format, which is generally presented as follows:

$$\min Z = \sum_{i=1}^{m} \sum_{k=1}^{n} C_{ik} X_{ik} \tag{6.6}$$

subject to

$$X_{i1} + X_{i2} + \cdots + X_{in} \leq Q_t^{P_i} \; (i = 1, 2, \ldots, m) \, (\text{supply constraints})$$

$$X_{1k} + X_{2k} + \cdots + X_{mk} = D_t^{R_{ji}} \; (k = 1, 2, \ldots, n) \, (\text{demand constraints})$$

$$X_{ik} \geq 0 \, (i = 1, 2, \ldots, m, k = 1, 2, \ldots, n).$$

Linear programming, a special branch of mathematical optimization (or mathematical programming), is an important subject in the field of operations research (also referred to as management science). As we can see from the LP transportation model in (6.6), mathematical optimization in general and LP in particular are concerned with seeking an optimal solution that will minimize objective cost (or maximize objective profit), subject to a given set of constraints.

Solution algorithms for transportation model

To obtain an optimal solution, it is necessary to develop (or construct) certain search procedure(s), termed solution algorithm(s). The scope of the solution search is obviously dependent on the number of origins and destinations. Intuitively, when the scope of search is relatively small, an optimal solution can be determined by exhaustive comparison of possible alternative route and shipping assignments. In most realistic distribution applications, the exhaustive search method would be ineffective or even infeasible due to size and complexity. We will also note that the tableau representation of transportation problems is typically suited for relatively small scopes, such as MB's beer distribution problem. If the number of beer plants and/or the number of retailers become large (e.g., in hundreds), it is only feasible to use the LP format (6.6).

The theory of mathematical optimization has long been recognized as the theoretical foundation of solution algorithms for transportation problems. Numerous commercial optimization software packages have been developed and are available in the marketplace, such as GAMS and LINDO. An optimization solution package, called "solver," is also included as a built-in component of Microsoft Excel. The details of mathematical optimization algorithms are covered in-depth in operations research and management science textbooks, and are thus omitted from this book.

Considering what is relevant to supply chain management, in this book we concentrate on modeling and formulating transportation and distribution problems, so that optimal solutions to these problems can be obtained by using proper commercial optimization software. As an illustration, let us formulate the MB transportation problem in an LP format that is compatible with the model input for LINDO (Table 6.7).

We will walk through a step-by-step LINDO solution for the MB transportation model in the Simulation lab at the end of this chapter. Similarly, the MB transportation problem can be represented in a modified tableau format and then solved using Microsoft Excel's Solver, which we will also study in the Simulation lab.

Without involving algorithmic details, let us conclude this section with a general solution framework, under which most transportation algorithms are constructed.

Table 6.7 MB beer transportation model with LINDO format

LINDO model for MB transportation problem

$$\min 71X_{101} + 41X_{102} + 53X_{103} + 54X_{104} + 76X_{105} + 113X_{106} + 77X_{107} + 52X_{108} + 75X_{109} + 92X_{110}$$

$$+59X_{201} + 94X_{202} + 55X_{203} + 76X_{204} + 117X_{205} + 59X_{206} + 94X_{207} + 89X_{208} + 62X_{209} + 37X_{110}$$

$$+42X_{301} + 37X_{302} + 52X_{303} + 45X_{304} + 85X_{305} + 107X_{306} + 64X_{307} + 96X_{308} + 64X_{309} + 87X_{310}$$

$$+63X_{401} + 64X_{402} + 49X_{403} + 38X_{404} + 92X_{405} + 86X_{406} + 95X_{407} + 57X_{408} + 60X_{409} + 71X_{410}$$

Subject to:

$$X_{101} + X_{102} + X_{103} + X_{105} + X_{106} + X_{107} + X_{108} + X_{109} + X_{110} \leq 40$$

$$X_{201} + X_{202} + X_{203} + X_{205} + X_{206} + X_{207} + X_{208} + X_{209} + X_{210} \leq 35$$

$$X_{301} + X_{302} + X_{303} + X_{305} + X_{306} + X_{307} + X_{308} + X_{309} + X_{310} \leq 37$$

$$X_{401} + X_{402} + X_{403} + X_{405} + X_{406} + X_{407} + X_{408} + X_{409} + X_{410} \leq 42$$

$$X_{101} + X_{201} + X_{301} + X_{401} \geq 17 \text{ (retailer 1 demand)}$$

$$X_{102} + X_{202} + X_{302} + X_{402} \geq 12 \text{ (retailer 2 demand)}$$

$$X_{103} + X_{203} + X_{303} + X_{403} \geq 20 \text{ (retailer 3 demand)}$$

$$X_{104} + X_{204} + X_{304} + X_{404} \geq 9 \text{ (retailer 4 demand)}$$

$$X_{105} + X_{205} + X_{305} + X_{405} \geq 11 \text{ (retailer 5 demand)}$$

$$X_{106} + X_{206} + X_{306} + X_{406} \geq 17 \text{ (retailer 6 demand)}$$

$$X_{107} + X_{207} + X_{307} + X_{407} \geq 14 \text{ (retailer 7 demand)}$$

$$X_{108} + X_{208} + X_{308} + X_{408} \geq 19 \text{ (retailer 8 demand)}$$

$$X_{109} + X_{209} + X_{309} + X_{409} \geq 15 \text{ (retailer 9 demand)}$$

$$X_{110} + X_{210} + X_{310} + X_{410} \geq 16 \text{ (retailer 10 demand)}$$

Transportation solution scheme:

1   Obtain an initial solution (e.g., by the northwest-corner method).
2   Evaluate current solution, and check if the current solution can be further improved in terms of reducing total cost. If not, then the current solution is optimal; otherwise, continue to the next step.
3   Generate a modified alternative solution with reduced total cost. Let the modified solution be the current solution to consider, and repeat step 2.

Distribution network decisions

Transshipment problems

A transshipment problem is an extension of a transportation problem when intermediate pass-through stages (e.g., warehouses and stocking points) are allowed between the origins and the destinations. For example, the existing distribution system at MB as shown in Figure 6.1 presents a transshipment problem. As shown in Figure 6.1, the wholesalers are termed transshipment nodes, which do not contain production capacity or incur direct demand consumption. In fact, MB's distribution system can be viewed as a mix of two transportation problems: plant–wholesaler as one and wholesaler–retailer as another.

Standard transshipment model

In general, a transshipment model allows shipments between any pair of origin (plant) i and transshipment node j (wholesaler), and between any pair of transshipment node j and destination (retailer) k. In the MB distribution case, however, each of the four beer plants is designated to a limited and different group of wholesalers as authorized transshipment nodes, and similarly each of the seven wholesalers is responsible for a limited and different group of retailers as authorized destinations. In this sense, the MB distribution system is a special transshipment problem. For the sake of exposition, let us consider a generalized version of MB distribution system, namely, removing the limits of designated groups such that it presents a standard transshipment problem with four origins, seven transshipment nodes, and ten destinations. The transportation costs in Tables 6.1 and 6.2 are also modified in Tables 6.8 and 6.9, respectively.

Compared with original cost data in Table 6.1, now there are no infeasible routes (i.e., forbidden cells "—") for the plant–wholesaler transportation. For convenience, we introduce the following decision variables for origin–transshipment transportation:

$X_{ij}^P \geq 0$: amount of shipment from origin (plant) i to transshipment node (wholesaler) j for $i = 1, 2, \ldots, m$ and $j = 1, 2, \ldots, J$.

For the MB distribution case, we have $m = 4$ and $J = 7$. The transshipment capacity at each wholesaler is assumed to be unlimited, and thus the origin–transshipment shipments are only limited by the supply capacity at each origin (plant).

Table 6.8 Modified plant–wholesaler shipping costs ($ per 1,000 cases)

P	W						
	W_1	W_2	W_3	W_4	W_5	W_6	W_7
P_1	70	47	22	53	83	76	46
P_2	51	38	19	58	90	34	39
P_3	42	45	37	82	111	40	29
P_4	45	40	42	64	97	86	25

Table 6.9 Modified wholesaler–retailer shipping costs ($ per 1,000 cases)

W	R									
	R_1	R_2	R_3	R_4	R_5	R_6	R_7	R_8	R_9	R_{10}
W_1	3	21	31	44	60	33	17	44	39	24
W_2	27	54	45	60	27	9	14	39	28	36
W_3	12	60	32	15	25	11	34	56	44	37
W_4	22	37	25	35	42	23	27	45	38	44
W_5	14	32	54	22	50	41	47	33	17	29
W_6	28	47	42	27	33	28	51	24	21	19
W_7	33	39	37	8	20	22	35	17	30	41

For MB's case, the total amount shipped from plant i should not exceed the capacity $Q_t^{P_i}$:

$$\text{Plant capacity constraints}: X_{i1}^P + X_{i2}^P + \cdots + X_{iJ}^P \le Q_t^{P_i} \ (i = 1, 2, \ldots, m) \qquad (6.7)$$

The total plant–wholesaler shipping costs can then be expressed as:

$$\sum_{i=1}^{m} \sum_{j=1}^{J} C_{ij} X_{ij}^P \qquad (6.8)$$

For MB distribution, costs C_{ij} are as given in Table 6.8 ($i = 1, 2, 3, 4, j = 1, 2, \ldots, 7$).

Comparing with the original wholesaler–retailer shipping costs in Table 6.2, there are no infeasible shipping routes for wholesaler–retailer transportation (Table 6.9). For transshipment–destination transportation, we introduce the following decision variables:

$X_{jk}^R \ge 0$: amount of shipment from transshipment node (wholesaler) j to destination k for $j = 1, 2, \ldots, J$ and $k = 1, 2, \ldots, n$.

For the MB distribution case, we have $n = 10$. Given that the transshipment capacity at wholesaler is unlimited, the amount shipped from wholesaler j to retailer k is only limited by the retailer demand $D_t^{R_k}$. That is,

$$\text{Retailer demand constraints}: X_{1k}^R + X_{2k}^R + \cdots + X_{Jk}^R$$
$$= D_t^{R_k}, \text{for } k = 1, 2, \ldots, n \qquad (6.9)$$

The total wholesaler–retailer shipping costs can then be expressed as:

$$\sum_{j=1}^{J}\sum_{k=1}^{n} C_{jk} X_{jk}^{R}.$$ (6.10)

Transshipment flow balance equations

We may notice that by far the constraints and total costs are the same as the standard transportation model, except for notational differences. Now, let us examine transshipment nodes, which, in fact, make the transshipment problem different. A pure transshipment node only reroutes and redistributes goods to retailers according to retail demand without limits; therefore, the aggregate flow into each transshipment node equals the aggregate flow out of it. The flow into each transshipment node j can be expressed as:

$$\sum_{i=1}^{m} X_{ij}^{P} = X_{1j}^{P} + X_{2j}^{P} + \cdots + X_{mj}^{P}.$$

The flow out of each transshipment node j can be expressed as:

$$\sum_{k=1}^{n} X_{jk}^{R} = X_{j1}^{R} + X_{j2}^{R} + \cdots + X_{jn}^{R}.$$

Thus, transshipment flow balance at each transshipment node j can be derived as:

$$\sum_{i=1}^{m} X_{ij}^{P} = \sum_{k=1}^{n} X_{jk}^{R}, \text{for all } j = 1, 2, \ldots, J.$$ (6.11)

LP formulation of transshipment problem

Note that a transshipment problem can be formulated as cost-minimizing LP model, similar to the transportation model given in (6.6). The objective cost function can be expressed as the sum of the costs given in (6.8) and (6.10), and the constraints included supply constraints (6.7), demand constraints (6.9), and transshipment balance constraints (6.11). Thus, an **LP transshipment model** can be constructed as:

$$\min Z = \sum_{i=1}^{m}\sum_{j=1}^{J} C_{ij} X_{ij}^{P} + \sum_{j=1}^{J}\sum_{k=1}^{n} C_{jk} X_{jk}^{R}$$ (6.12)

subject to

$$X_{i1}^{P} + X_{i2}^{P} + \cdots + X_{iJ}^{P} \leq Q_{t}^{P_i} \ (i = 1, 2, \ldots, m) \left(\text{supply constraints}\right)$$

$$X_{1k}^{R} + X_{2k}^{R} + \cdots + X_{Jk}^{R} = D_{t}^{R_k} \ (k = 1, 2, \ldots, n) \left(\text{demand constraints}\right)$$

$$\sum_{i=1}^{m} X_{ij}^{P} - \sum_{k=1}^{n} X_{jk}^{R} = 0 \,(j = 1, 2, \ldots, J) \left(\text{transshipment constraints}\right)$$

$$X_{ij}^P \geq 0 \, (i = 1, 2, \ldots, m, j = 1, 2, \ldots, J)$$

$$X_{jk}^R \geq 0 \, (j = 1, 2, \ldots, J, k = 1, 2, \ldots, n).$$

In principle, the LP transshipment model of (6.12) can be solved by general LP software, such as GAMS and LINDO, among others. However, the amount of computing time will be a major obstacle for large problems (i.e., the number of variables). In practice, it is an important issue to minimize the number of variables. For example, any prohibited (or infeasible) routes in a transshipment or transportation problem will result in reduced number of variables, as there will be no need for variables representing shipments on the infeasible routes. Note that the original MB transshipment problem has infeasible routes (i.e., cells) as shown with "—" in Tables 6.1 and 6.2.

LP transshipment model with infeasible routes

Let us construct an LP transshipment model for the MB distribution model as given by Tables 6.1 and 6.2. First, the transportation routes given in Table 6.1 are between plants and wholesalers (i.e., origin and transshipment); thus, the shipments assigned to these routes are represented by variables X_{ij}^P. Each shipment variable corresponding to an infeasible route marked with "—" can be simply removed. For example, route (i.e., cell) (2,1) is infeasible; therefore, $X_{2,1}^P$ is removed from the LP transshipment model. That is, the LP model will need one less decision variable. From Table 6.1, there are two infeasible cells in column 1, one in column 2, and so on, giving a total of ten infeasible cells; thus, ten decision variables can be removed from the LP model in (6.12). Specifically, the ten removed **plant–wholesaler** shipment variables are:

From plant 1: $X_{1,5}^P, X_{1,6}^P, X_{1,7}^P$ (prohibited)

From plant 2: $X_{2,1}^P, X_{2,7}^P$ (prohibited)

From plant 3: $X_{3,1}^P, X_{3,2}^P$ (prohibited)

From plant 4: $X_{4,3}^P, X_{4,4}^P, X_{4,5}^P$ (prohibited).

Similarly, from Table 6.2 the following 17 **wholesaler–retailer** shipment variables are no longer valid and, therefore, can be removed from the LP transshipment model of (6.12):

From wholesaler 1: $X_{1,8}^R, X_{1,9}^R, X_{1,10}^R$ (prohibited)

From wholesaler 2: $X_{2,1}^R, X_{2,9}^R, X_{2,10}^R$ (prohibited)

From wholesaler 3: $X_{3,1}^R, X_{3,2}^R$ (prohibited)

From wholesaler 4: $X_{4,9}^R, X_{4,10}^R$ (prohibited)

From wholesaler 5: $X_{5,3}^{R}, X_{5,4}^{R}, X_{5,5}^{R}$ (prohibited)

From wholesaler 6: $X_{6,1}^{R}, X_{6,2}^{R}$ (prohibited)

From wholesaler 7: $X_{7,2}^{R}, X_{7,3}^{R}$ (prohibited).

Hence, for the MB transshipment model a total of 27 shipment variables (10 plant–wholesaler and 17 wholesaler–retailer routes) are prohibited and thus removed from the LP transshipment model (6.12). In essence, MB's LP transshipment model can be considered as the model of (6.12) with the above 27 variables removed. However, in practice we need a generic LP formulation for the transshipment problem with prohibited routes. Next, we develop a general LP transshipment model with infeasible routes.

Recall that the index set of transshipment nodes that are designated (i.e., authorized) for each origin i is denoted by $\mathbf{W}^{i}$. For example, for plant 1 excluding the prohibited routes, the designated transshipment index set is:

$$\mathbf{W}^{1} = \{j : j = 1,2,3,4\} \,(\text{from plant}\,1).$$

With the index set $\mathbf{W}^{i}$, the designated supply constraints for each origin i can then be conveniently expressed as:

$$\sum_{j \in \mathbf{W}^{i}} X_{ij}^{P} \leq Q_{t}^{P_{i}}, i = 1,2,\ldots,m.$$

In addition, the index set of destinations that are designated for each transshipment node j is denoted by $\mathbf{R}^{j}$. In Table 6.2, for example, authorized retailers for wholesaler 2 is:

$$\mathbf{R}^{2} = \{k : k = 2,3,4,5,6,7,8\} \,(\text{from wholesaler}\,2).$$

Thus, the demand constraints in (6.12) can be modified to reflect designated shipping routes by using $\mathbf{R}^{j}$ as follows:

$$\sum_{k \in R^{j}} X_{jk}^{R} = D_{t}^{R^{j}}, j = 1,2,\ldots,J.$$

The flow balance equation for each transshipment node j can be derived similarly, excluding all the infeasible routes. For each transshipment node j, we denote all the indices of plants that are responsible by

$$\mathbf{P}^{j} = \left\{i : j \in \mathbf{W}^{i}\right\}.$$

The balance equation for transshipment node j can then be expressed as:

$$\sum_{i=\mathbf{P}^{j}}^{m} X_{ij}^{P} - \sum_{k=\mathbf{R}^{j}}^{n} X_{jk}^{R} = 0, j = 1,2,\ldots,J.$$

Thus, an **LP transshipment model with prohibited routes** can be modified from (6.12) as follows:

$$\min Z = \sum_{i=1}^{m} \sum_{j=\mathbf{W}^i} C_{ij} X_{ij}^P + \sum_{j=1}^{J} \sum_{k=\mathbf{R}^j} C_{jk} X_{jk}^R \qquad (6.13)$$

subject to

$$\sum_{j \in \mathbf{W}^i} X_{ij}^P \le Q_t^{P_i} \ (i = 1, 2, \ldots, m)(\text{supply constraints})$$

$$\sum_{k \in \mathbf{R}^j} X_{jk}^R = D_t^{R^j} \ (j = 1, 2, \ldots, J)(\text{demand constraints})$$

$$\sum_{i=\mathbf{P}^j}^{m} X_{ij}^P - \sum_{k=\mathbf{R}^j}^{n} X_{jk}^R = 0 \, (j = 1, 2, \ldots, J)(\text{transshipment constraints})$$

$$X_{ij}^P \ge 0 \, (i = 1, 2, \ldots, m, j = 1, 2, \ldots, J)$$

$$X_{jk}^R \ge 0 \, (j = 1, 2, \ldots, J, k = 1, 2, \ldots, n)$$

In reality, there can be further limitations and requirements imposed on transshipment problems. For example, all (or some) shipments must be made in integer amounts (e.g., in terms of number of containers). In this case, an integer (or mixed-integer) LP transshipment model can be constructed simply by requiring the corresponding shipment variables to be integers. The main body of the transshipment model, such as the one in (6.13), remains the same. If the shipments in the transshipment problem with prohibited routes must all be integers, then the model (6.13) will remain, except that all the shipment variables X_{ij}^P and X_{jk}^R are now limited to positive integers. In principle, the transshipment models of (6.12) and (6.13) are of LP formulation and, thus, can be solved by LP algorithms.

Cross-docking of transshipments

We shall note that the transportation and transshipment models we studied so far are concerned with the aggregate flow of shipments, without differentiating items within a shipment order. However, in reality each shipment order may contain a number of different items, and each wholesaler may have a different number of items moving through his or her warehouses. For example, a shipment order of bottled beer may contain a specific combination of regular beer, dark beer, and light beer. In general, let us denote the total number of different items being transshipped at wholesaler j by h_j, and denote the total set of items at wholesaler j by

$$\mathbf{I}^j = \left\{ I_j : \text{holding item index } I_j = 1, 2, \ldots, h_j \right\}.$$

In practice, there are two basic warehousing strategies: traditional strategy of itemized stocking and a recent strategy of cross-docking. Typically, a wholesaler warehouse under the itemized stocking strategy functions as itemized inventory holding and stocking points, where all incoming shipments are sorted and stored by different items without regards to the destinations of the transshipments. Cross-docking warehousing, which was made famous by Wal-Mart, is based on destinations of the goods. In a *cross-docking* system, wholesale warehouses mainly serve as inventory coordination points and not as inventory holding points. That is, as soon as incoming shipments arrive, they are not sorted and stored by different items. Instead, they are regrouped and cross-docked according to their destinations, so that goods spend much less time in storage at wholesale warehouses. Next, we elaborate both traditional and cross-docking transshipment operations using MB's beer distribution as an example.

Transshipment operations without cross-docking

First, let us consider wholesale transshipment operations without cross-docking at a wholesaler j in a transshipment system consisting of m plants and n retailers with a total of h_j items involved at the wholesaler j (Figure 6.5).

Figure 6.5 shows that each shipment order from plant i to wholesaler j, X_{ij}^P, consists of a certain combination of the five types of beer (i.e., items). As soon as incoming shipments arrive at the wholesale warehouse (e.g., by truck loads), they are sorted and then stored according to product or item types (e.g., five types of bottled beer in this case), without reference to where the incoming shipments are destined. In many cases, the destinations of incoming shipments are not specified yet when they arrive at the wholesaler. After all incoming shipments are stocked by item type at the wholesaler, outgoing shipments to each retailer k, denoted by TR_{jk} in Figure 6.5, are then scheduled and shipped. In terms of the transshipment

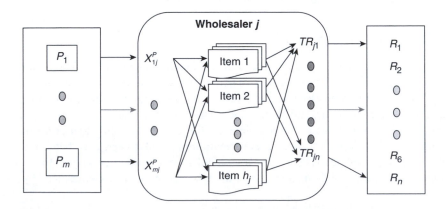

Figure 6.5 Wholesale warehouse operations without cross-docking.

model of (6.13), it holds that order picking for retailer k at wholesaler j should be in accordance to the shipments assigned from wholesaler j to retailer k; that is, $TR_{jk} = X_{jk}^R$.

Goods may stay at the wholesale warehouse for a significant amount of time before being shipped out (e.g., for days or even months). For the MB case of transshipment of bottled beer, according to each retailer's order, shipping trucks are scheduled and items are then picked and loaded onto the trucks at the shipping docks. In effect, the traditional warehouse function divides the original transshipment problems into three separate transportation/distribution problems, as listed below:

1   Plant–wholesaler shipments, X_{ij}^P, from plant i to wholesaler j ($i = 1,2,\ldots, m$, and $j = 1,2,\ldots,J$).
2   Retail order picking from warehouse stock $S_{I_j}^{W_j}$, where $S_{I_j}^{W_j}$ represents the stocks of item I_j held at wholesaler $j (I_j = 1,2,\ldots,h_j)$.
3   Shipping order release from wholesaler j to retailer k, TR_{jk} ($k = 1,2,\ldots,n$).

The major advantage of itemized warehousing is the ease of inventory management, and there are many computerized warehousing systems available on the market today. Itemized inventory stocking is especially useful when a wide range of different items are involved in transshipment warehouse operations. Another advantage of itemized warehousing is that the division into three subproblems can reduce the impact of demand variability, which we will further examine as we proceed to the next chapter.

Cross-docking transshipment

Cross-docking transshipment at a wholesaler j is destination-based warehousing, which Wal-Mart made famous. In a cross-docking system, incoming shipments are transferred to outgoing shipping docks that are destined to retailers, as depicted in Figure 6.6.

Figure 6.6 shows that itemized stocks are no longer needed in cross-docking transshipment. Instead, incoming goods are regrouped in terms of intended retail destinations directly, and are delivered to the retailers as quickly as possible. The cross-docking system has been shown to reduce inventory costs and increase inventory turnovers. However, a cross-docking system is much more difficult to manage, because it requires accurate coordination among wholesale centers, retailers, and suppliers.

In short, the cross-docking system is to warehousing by destination, what traditional wholesale distribution system is to warehousing by itemization.

Direct delivery channels

Direct delivery refers to shipping items directly from suppliers (e.g., plants) to retailers, typically adopted in a **direct-selling** system such as the one developed

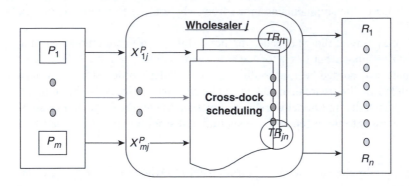

Figure 6.6 Cross-docking wholesale warehouse operations.

by Dell Computers. Internet technology has made direct selling a feasible option for many manufacturing firms that typically rely on distributor-based delivery. An increasing number of manufacturers have added, and some even totally switched to, the option of online direct selling. For example, Barnes and Noble has opened up online "bookstores" in addition to existing traditional bookstores, and Amazon.com solely operates online. Distribution under the direct delivery system occurs in basic ways, namely, third-party logistics and transshipment with mixed modes.

Direct delivery by third-party logistics

For a direct seller, distribution by third-party logistics can be viewed as a standard transportation problem of *m* origin and *n* destination, as depicted in Figure 6.7. The direct seller in Figure 6.7 receives orders online directly from customers (or retailers), and produces the ordered products at the *m* plants. The seller is responsible for allocating the production of received orders among the *m* plants, and then informing the contracted third party about the delivery schedule of the promised customer orders. This includes conveying the details of distribution and logistics of order delivery deferred under contract to the third logistical party. The delivery schedule that the seller will release to the third party mainly consists of the quantity to be picked up from each supplier (plant) and then what is to be shipped to each retailer.

For the sake of simplicity, we will present the seller's order delivery problem as a transportation model, just like MB's beer distribution as depicted in Table 6.4. The seller's delivery schedule, x_{ik} (for all plant *i* and retailer *k*), can be obtained by solving the transportation model for the seller's order delivery problem, and will then be released to the third party who will perform all the distribution and logistical tasks outlined in the delivery schedule. We must note that the distribution tasks faced by the third logistical party may differ drastically from that of the seller's (i.e., the wholesaler's as depicted in Figure 6.6).

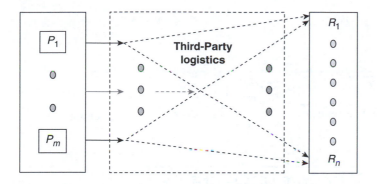

Figure 6.7 Cross-docking retail warehouse operations.

Example 6.1   Saturn–Ryder third-party delivery system

As widely reported in the mid-1990s (e.g., Davis 1995), the partnership between Ryder Logistics and the Saturn Division of General Motors has been regarded as a pioneering success in third-party delivery within the automobile industry. Through the Saturn–Ryder delivery partnership, Saturn is able to focus on the automobile manufacturing side of operations, under a build-to-order production scheme. In response to a time series of demand (e.g., promised quarterly customer orders), of which many come directly from customers online, Saturn initiates the order fulfillment process by placing EDI (electronic data exchange) orders for parts from over 300 different suppliers in the United States, Canada, and Mexico. At the same time, Saturn sends Ryder a copy of the EDI ordering information, plus a delivery schedule of finished vehicles. Ryder is responsible for picking up ordered parts from the suppliers, delivering parts to the Saturn assembly plants in Spring Hill, Tennessee, and delivering finished Saturn cars to the dealers that placed the original orders. The overall production system under the Saturn–Ryder partnership can be represented by an SOF (supply order fulfillment) system, as shown in Figure 6.8. In this SOF system, Saturn is responsible for production capacity and materials planning, while Ryder is charged with parts and finished products delivery.

For illustrative purposes, let us summarize Saturn's quarterly distribution planning process:

- Receive and process direct customer orders quarterly.
- Generate quarterly production and shipping schedules, from which quarterly MRP schedules are then derived. The key is the quarterly production planning, which is based on the following aspects of automobile manufacturing:

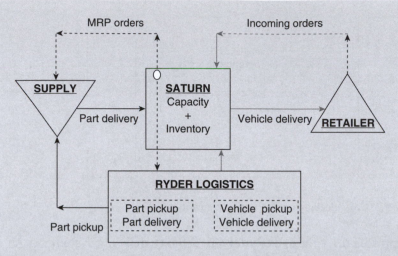

Figure 6.8 Saturn–Ryder SOF logistical partnership system.

- stocks of finished products;
- available capacity at the assembly plants (multiple assembly facilities at Saturn);
- current inventory status on parts and materials needed for assembly orders.
- Release EDI orders to authorized suppliers according to the quarterly MRP schedules, and inform Ryder of the released MRP schedules for part pickups.
- Notify Ryder of the final shipping schedules for vehicle delivery.

From the logistical partnership's point of view, Saturn is faced with a workload allocation problem, which is then taken as input for distribution planning by Ryder. In terms of modeling, Saturn's allocation problem can be modeled as two basic transportation models, whereas Ryder's distribution problem can be formulated as a complicated transshipment model. For example, given m suppliers, q assembly plants at Saturn, and n authorized dealers, Saturn's MRP schedules can be obtained from an m-supplier, q-plant transportation model with total production cost as the objective, and its delivery schedules can be obtained from another q-plant, n-dealer transportation model with total inventory cost as objective. On the other hand, the distribution and transportation planning for Ryder can be derived from solutions to an m-supplier, q-warehouse, and n-dealer transshipment model. We shall note that the solution of these kinds of large-scale transportation and transshipment models requires using very complicated decision-support software.

Integrated distribution with direct channels

Instead of completely "farming out" logistical tasks, a direct seller can engage itself in the distribution of goods under direct customer orders, so that distribution planning can be integrated with production planning and even post-sale service planning under unified control by the direct seller. In this case, the seller (e.g., Saturn) would need to acquire additional in-house capacity of transshipment that is otherwise assumed by the logistical third party (e.g., Ryder). This would translate to significant additional investments, both in equipment (e.g., trucks) and in IT (e.g., planning software). The following innovative forms of direct-channel distribution have emerged in modern supply chain operations:

- **Transferred channel assembly:** The manufacturer (factory) delegates certain assembly operations to authorized distributor(s) toward the end of a distribution channel. **Channel assembly** typically results from the so-called **postponement** of product differentiation under which assembling of certain customized features (or modules) is postponed as close to the point of sales as possible. For example, the power adaptor of an HP Inkjet printer is differentiated by regional markets (e.g., US 110-volt system versus European 220-volt system) and, therefore, the appropriate adaptor will be assembled to the main unit at the regional distributors. The transferred channel assembly can be performed either externally (by authorized distributors) or internally (by the company's own regional representatives).
- **Mass customization delivery:** A manufacturer produces the orders that are customized to individual customers' needs, and delivers directly to the customers. Mass customized delivery typically results from mass customization of the manufacturing process, as further described in Pine (1993) and Zipkin (2000).
- **Value-added retail:** A manufacturer authorizes retailers to provide customers with value-generating options, features, and services. For example, retailers of camcorders such as Best Buy can offer extended service plans to prospective customers.

Each form of direct-channel distribution calls for special delivery and transportation strategies that directly relate between suppliers and customers. All in all, the integrated distribution with direct channels can be formulated as a transshipment model with direct delivery channels, as depicted in Figure 6.9.

Warehousing and delivery systems

Warehousing has traditionally served a vital strategic role of storage and retrieval of materials and supplies, so as to attain the advantage of being "the first in field" as advised by Sun Zi. We can then relate that warehousing is an intrinsic aspect of WBD in business. In terms of national economics, manufacturers preserve the "being-ahead" advantage by producing an inventory of goods and selling from

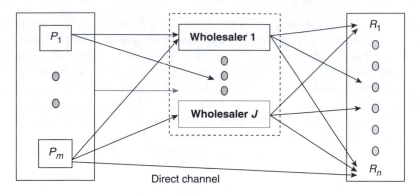

Figure 6.9 Transshipment with direct channels.

the inventory stored in the warehouse. The term *warehouse* is broadly defined as a wide spectrum of facilities and locations that provide warehousing, including the storage of ore and mine in open fields; the storage of finished goods in production facilities; and the storage of raw materials, supplies, and finished goods in transport. It is seemingly obvious that the advantage gained by warehousing would diminish as we enter the IT age. Surprisingly, the role of the warehouse has never been as vital as it is now in the world of e-business and supply chain operations. At the same time, business innovations have brought about drastic changes in warehousing, from inventory-based operations to value-added delivery. Nonetheless, warehousing is as necessary, if not more so, in modern supply chain operations. Here is a partial point of explanation. As IT has increased the speed of information flow in business transactions, the quickness of actual transactions has become more dependent on the speed of materials flow, which is the primary purpose of warehousing (i.e., the "being-ahead" advantage).

The importance of warehousing in our national economy is apparent and widely recognized. For example, in 1999, warehousing costs in the United States have amounted to $7.5 billion, or 0.81 percent of the GDP (see for more details Coyle *et al.* 2002; Delaney and Wilson 2000).

Basic warehouse operations

In terms of business functions and operations, the warehouse is a distribution factory and warehousing operation concerns the orderly execution of physical goods as well as informational storage and retrieval activities. Figure 6.10 shows a schematic layout of a typical warehouse, which consists of five areas: *inbound, storage and retrieval, picking and mixing, cross-docking,* and *outbound.* Each of the layout areas is clustered with a certain set of warehouse operations and activities (Figure 6.10). Across the areas are flows of physical materials and informational data, which are facilitated by warehouse equipment (e.g., conveyor) and its IT systems (e.g., computerized picking and sorting system).

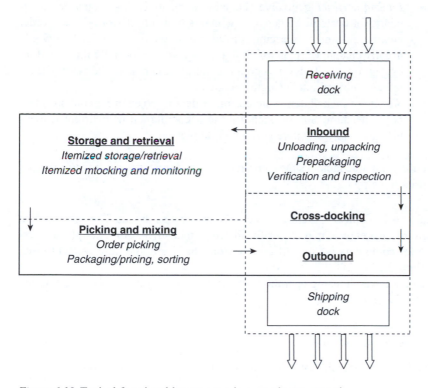

Figure 6.10 Typical functional layout areas in a warehouse operation.

The layout areas in Figure 6.10 are defined as:

Inbound area includes receiving dock and receiving/unloading area.

Storage and retrieval area is occupied by a system of storage/retrieval equipment, which is typically integrated with a computer, referred to as an automated storage/retrieval system (AS/RS).

Picking and mixing area is reserved for fulfilling outgoing orders. An outgoing delivery order (e.g., truckloads of supplies to a target store) contains a specific mix of different items with specific quantities. To fill such an order, the correct amount of items must be picked up at the right storage place, and then mixed together into a complete order package that can be shipped to the intended destination. The picking and mixing process typically contains three subprocesses:

- *Order picking* involves removing items from storage according to order requirements. It is the basic function a warehouse provides and is the basis of warehouse design.

- *Packaging/pricing* involves containerizing individual items or assortments for customized delivery, which is typically performed after order picking. Pricing or repricing is needed after picking, as price lists would usually change while items sit in the inventory, especially for short-life-cycle products. Today, it is common for picking tickets and price stickers to be combined into a single document.
- *Sorting* of picked items into custom orders when an order contains more than one item. Sorting includes the accumulation of distributed picks because many orders require multiple picks.

Outbound area includes the shipping dock, and spaces for unitizing activities prior to shipping.

Figure 6.10 depicts a common schematic warehouse layout. The actual layout design of a warehouse may differ for different industries. For example, a warehouse for computers is built differently from that for home-improvement products (Frazelle 2002).

We divide warehousing operations into two major categories: (1) *basic activities* and (2) *value-adding roles*.

Basic warehouse activities

A warehouse is typically intended for the following basic routine operations:

1   *Transfer*. This refers to activities involved in transferring goods. From reception and storage to retrieval and delivery, these activities are facilitated by special warehousing equipment and transport devices, such as case conveyors and pallet vehicles.
2   *Receiving*. Warehouse receiving consists of all the activities involved in the receipt of incoming shipments of materials and goods. Typical receiving activities include unloading, unpacking (unbundling), prepackaging, verification and inspection of received materials, and putaway (i.e., placing merchandise in storage). Note that not all activities are required at the same time. For example, unpacking and prepackaging are applied when products are received in bulk, and after unloading and unpacking, products can either be put away (in storage) or be cross-docked for shipping.
3   *Storage*. Most warehouse items are to be deposited and held at a designated space in the warehouse for a given period of time.
4   *Handling*. Warehouse material handling involves loading/unloading and transporting of items within a warehouse, forming warehouse material flows indicated by the arrows in Figure 6.10.
5   *Packaging*. Packaging or repackaging is required by several warehouse functions. For example, both receiving and product mixing may require packaging activities, as previously explained.

Emerging value-adding roles of warehousing

Along with the revolutionary changes brought about by computers and IT, innovative value-adding warehousing roles have emerged, which include the following:

1   *Consolidation*. This refers to activities of networking, especially online, which has consolidated once scattered customer orders and shipments into large, coordinated shipments resulting in significant transportation savings.

2   *Product mixing and assortment*. When placing orders, customers often bundle several items around a product line (e.g., a dozen of four-piston sets, a dozen of eight-valve kits). Therefore, warehouse order-filling involves mixing up items to the order specifications and sorting out groups (or families) of similar mixed items according to customer order patterns.

3   *Customer delivery service*. A recent warehousing trend leverages warehouse proximity to provide certain customers with increased delivery service. A service warehouse is strategically located to meet customer demands on time. Stocking decisions (i.e., what and how much to store) are critical to operating a service warehouse effectively. Given that customer demand is ever changing, cost-effective stocking decisions are extremely complicated and difficult.

4   *Value-adding distribution*. Another trend in supply chain management is to operate a warehouse as a *distribution factory*, where manufacturers delegate certain value-adding manufacturing tasks, such as channel assembly and channel maintenance, to qualified warehouse distributors and retailers. Value-adding distribution (namely, the distribution factory) is intended to produce to customer orders in a timely fashion by performing certain feature-dependent manufacturing tasks at stages that are closest to the ultimate customer demand.

Warehouse-delivery systems

All in all, the primary purpose of warehousing is to provide points of storage and retrieval for speedy customer delivery. The contents of warehouses include raw materials (e.g., the piston stocks of Example 3.5), WIP, and finished goods. Stocking decisions are vitally important and inevitably challenging in warehouse operations. As a distribution factory, the warehouse has been configured as building blocks in delivery network of finished goods to customers. According to Frazelle (2002), five typical configurations of the warehouse-delivery system can be observed in the current practice of supply chain operations: (1) *factory warehouse (or center)*; (2) *distribution warehouse (or center)*; (3) *fulfillment warehouse (or center)*; (4) *retail delivery warehouse*; and (5) *value-added service warehouse*. Figure 6.11 illustrates the logistical roles and deployments of the five warehouse-delivery systems. This chapter describes the operational processes and decision-making tools needed for managing these warehouse-delivery systems. From an operational point of view, key warehousing operations involve

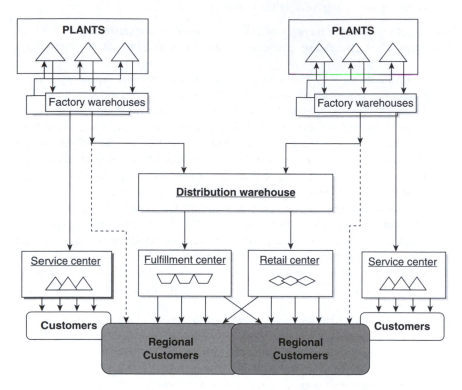

Figure 6.11 Logistical deployment of warehouse-delivery network.

storage and retrieval. First, we provide a summary of the functional configuration of these warehouse-delivery systems. In real-world warehousing, it is common to see a hybrid of multiple configurations combined into one warehouse-delivery system. Combinations of multiple warehouse-delivery systems then comprise a complex logistics network.

Factory warehouses perform inbound and outbound logistical functions required for factory operations, including storage and release of raw materials, staging and transferring of WIP, and docking and shipping of finished goods. The outbound factory warehouses can ship finished goods, parts, and accessories to distribution and service centers, and possibly directly to customers, as depicted by the dotted-line routes in Figure 6.11.

Distribution warehouses accumulate and consolidate goods from within a firm, or from several firms, so as to deliver shipments to customers, retailers, and other channel assemblers (i.e., fulfillment centers). Distribution warehouses can be either privately or publicly owned.

Fulfillment warehouses are consumer driven and are intended for receiving, picking, and shipping small orders for individual customers.

Retail warehouses are locally distributed for rapid response to customer demand. They are suited for frequent delivery (e.g., daily) of a limited range of items needed by regional customers.

Value-added service warehouses serve as a channel assembly and service facility where product customization and service activities are executed, including packaging, labeling, pricing, return processing, service calls, and channel maintenance service.

Warehousing operations management

We can see from the previous section that warehouse operations are related to the storage/retrieval activities that occur between inbound order receipt and outbound order delivery (Figure 6.10). The center of the storage and retrieval activities is the stocking decision; namely, the determination of how each line of items will be stocked, monitored, and replenished in a warehouse. In terms of Sun Zi's principle, the key is how to attain the advantage of being "the first in the field." Consistent with the two WBD principles, namely, win-with-speed and win-by-singularity, **WBD strategies** applicable to the field of warehousing can be outlined as follows:

- *Itemized stocking.* Warehouse stocks are itemized into families according to the patterns of demand (customer order), such that customer orders can be delivered Just in Time.
- *Balanced value stream.* Value-added warehouse operations are balanced, so that overall productivity is consistently maintained at the highest possible level. There are two major characteristics in the value-adding process concerned herein; that is, lead-times and order flows between stages of operations. In particular, lead-times associated with each stage of the value stream must be reduced and balanced.
- *Customized order delivery.* The bottom line is to satisfy customer needs with high-quality service in the most cost-effective fashion.

The implementation of the WBD strategies is, of course, by Sun Zi's well-known method of **five tactics** (TACBE): targeting, assessing, calculating, balancing, and executing, as described in Chapter 1. The rest of this chapter will be devoted to the above three WBD warehousing strategies. In the next subsection, we will begin with a study of itemized warehouse operations.

Prototype example: itemized warehouse stocking

Figure 6.10 in the previous section shows that warehouse storage and stocking are typically itemized, whereas warehouse order picking combines multiple items into delivery orders according to customer specifications. We are concerned here with how each line of items be stocked and replenished in the warehouse storage/retrieval system, which is referred to as *warehouse stocking*. In fact, warehouse stocking in a warehouse constitutes a specific type of repetitive inventory system: itemized inventory decisions on how much to stock and when to replenish. Similar to the inventory systems we studied in Chapter 3, such decisions must be based on the demand on each item and the lead time incurred for each item. On the other hand, *warehouse stocking* can be differentiated from the inventory systems we studied in Chapter 3 in two major aspects: (1) multiple streams of customer demand orders in the form of time series, consisting of mixed items and (2) demand on each item is aggregated from customer orders. Let us proceed by examining the interaction between customer demand and itemized demand in a typical warehouse operation.

Customer demand versus itemized demand in warehousing

Figure 6.10 illustrates that customer demand arrives at a warehouse in the form of time-series orders for delivery. Each customer delivery order is typically composed of a mix of items stocked in the storage/retrieval system of the warehouse. Arrival of a customer order will then trigger the order-picking process—the process of retrieving all the items with the correct quantity as specified in the customer order. The aggregation of the demand generated from order picking on each of the individual items is the itemized demand, which is expressed in the form of time series termed *pick order for the item*. Figure 6.12 illustrates the aggregation process of pick orders for each of the m items that are stocked in the storage/retrieval system of a warehouse.

We now explain the notations for the itemized warehouse stocking system shown in Figure 6.12. Consider a warehouse storage system stocking a total of m items, with each item indexed by index i for $i = 1, 2, \ldots, m$. The stocks of m items are intended to meet the delivery orders requested by n customer demand nodes, with each customer node indexed by index k for $k = 1, 2, \ldots, n$. Each customer (node) is distinguished with a specific pattern of demand orders. A customer order submitted in period t by customer k, denoted by S_t^k, specifies a specific "mix" of items in the warehouse to be "picked" (or retrieved) from the warehouse stocking system.

Specifically, each customer order S_t^k consists of an index set of the "mix" denoted by ξ^k, and order quantity for each item i included in the order mix, denoted by Q_{it}^k. Therefore, the ordering process of customer node k can be formally expressed as follows: $S_t^k = \{Q_{it}^k : i \in \xi^k\}$: customer order submitted by customer k in period t, where Q_{it}^k is the order quantity for item i that is specified in the index set of order mix, denoted by ξ_t^k. The mix index set $\xi^k = \{i_1^k, i_2^k, \ldots, i_{m_k}^k\} \subseteq \{1, 2, \ldots, m\}$ specifies the item indices that are included in the order mix. For example, $\xi^k = \{3, 5, 11, 17\}$ specifies a type-k mix of items indexed 3, 5, 11, and 17 in the customer order S_t^k.

In effect, each customer order will be split into itemized *pick orders* according to the item-mix. Customer orders accumulated over period t will generate aggregate pick orders for each item i over period t, denoted by d_{it} ($i = 1, 2, \ldots, m; t = 0, \pm1, \pm2 \ldots$). The

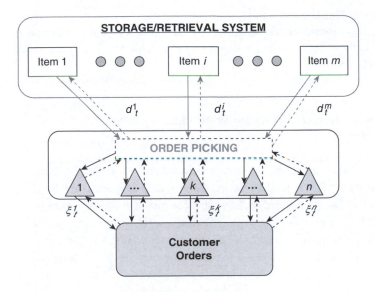

Figure 6.12 An itemized warehouse stocking system.

itemized order d_{it} is an aggregated time-series demand for the item i, triggered by time-series customer orders. We assume that current stationary market conditions are fundamentally maintained and thus the itemized time-series demand d_{it} preserves certain stationary characteristics of an ARMA process as studied in Chapter 4. Thus, we assume that each itemized time-series demand d^{it} follows a stationary ARMA model, which can be determined upon statistical study of itemized data of past observations as described in Chapter 4.

Stocks of itemized inventory are established and maintained at the warehouse, denoting the inventory stocking status for item i by x_{it}. Warehouse stocking decisions are mainly pertinent to how much to stock and when to replenish each of the items. There is a known lead time, denoted by L_i, for replenishing each item i. As such, warehouse stocking decisions are then based on the characteristics of itemized demand processes within a warehouse and itemized lead-time incurred from suppliers of the items. Next, we present time-series characteristics of itemized warehouse demand. Before we proceed, let us compile and introduce a list of proper notation for an itemized warehouse stocking system.

$I = \{1, 2, \ldots, m\}$: index set of all m items in the warehouse stocking system.
$K = \{1, 2, \ldots, n\}$: index set of all n customer demand nodes of the warehouse.
d_{it}: itemized aggregate demand for item i $(i \in I)$ in period t $(t = 0, \pm 1, \pm 2 \ldots)$. The itemized demand d_{it} is aggregated over the customer orders S_t^k across all customer nodes $k \in K$.
x_{it}: on-hand inventory position for item i at the beginning of period t. A negative stock position x_{it} indicates backordering.

L_i: lead-time to replenish stock item $i(i \in I)$.

$\mathbf{S}_t^k = \{Q_{i,t}^k : i \in \xi^k\}$: customer order submitted by customer $k(k \in K)$ in period t, where Q_{it}^k is the order quantity for item i that is specified in $\xi^k \subseteq I$, the index set of order mix.

Example 6.2   Itemized warehouse stocking system at Quick-Engine

Consider a private warehouse with two stocking lines of piston (i.e., two stocking items) for QE-1 stand-by generator at Quick-Engine, as depicted in Figure 6.13. The itemized daily demand for piston line 1 is given as $d_{1,t} \sim (210, 75^2)$, that is, $E(d_{1,t}) = \mu_1 = 210$ and $\text{var}(d_{1,t}) = \sigma_1^2 = 75^2$, while daily demand for piston line 2 is given as $d_{2,t} \sim (120, 45^2)$, that is, $E(d_{2,t}) = \mu_2 = 120$ and $\text{var}(d_{2,t}) = \sigma_2^2 = 45^2$. Suppose that the demands on the two lines are uncorrelated, that is, $\text{cov}(d_{1,t}, d_{2,t}) = 0$.

Both lines of pistons are supplied to the warehouse from a single supplier who requires a 1-week lead-time with five working days per week for piston line 1 and a 3-day lead-time for piston line 2 (i.e., $L_1 = 5$ and $L_2 = 3$). The warehouse operations cost data are determined as follows: purchase prices for pistons 1 and 2 are $60 and $75, respectively. Warehouse holding costs are 40 percent of purchase values. The costs of each unit of back-ordering for pistons 1 and 2 are $55 and $70, respectively. Setup costs for both items are negligible.

Question: The management at Quick-Engine is considering a proposal to develop an itemized continuous-reviewed one-bin (i.e., base-stock) stocking system for the two lines of pistons. The Q-E is to determine the base-stock levels for each of the two stocks, such that the expected total cost is minimized.

We defer the detailed analysis of Example 6.2 to separate sections later in this chapter, and will further study the example via simulation projects in the Simulation lab of this chapter. We continue the discussion on the WBD strategies: balanced value stream and customized order delivery. For the sake of exposition, we will refer to the context of Example 6.2.

Warehouse stocking policies

We know that a decision (or an action) is a realization enabled by an underlying policy. For example, a decision on order quantity (e.g., $Q = 1,000$) is determined

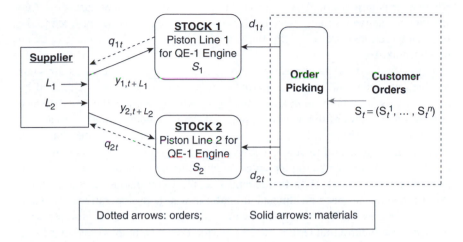

Figure 6.13 Two-item piston stocking system.

according to a pre-specified (R,Q) order policy (i.e., reorder-point, order-quantity policy). In the context of a warehouse storage of multi-items inventory, another distinction between decision and policy is that different stocking decisions for different items may be generated from the same stocking policy. It is common in warehousing that a single stocking policy, such as (s,S) (or min-max) policy, is applied to almost all the items across the entire warehouse. Stocking policies in warehousing are actually of the order-up-to type, comprising two major forms: (1) base-stock (or S) policy and (2) min-max (or (s,S)) policy.

Stocking policy

For the sake of exposition, we rephrase the definitions of these three stocking policies in the context of m uncorrelated items in a warehouse:

S_i **policy** (or base-stock policy): Orders are placed as soon as the stock of item i decreases below a prescribed order-up-to level S_i, so as to maintain total stock of item i at the level S_i.

(s_i,S_i) **policy** (or min-max policy): Whenever an inventory stock level for item $i (i = 1, 2, ..., m)$ is at or below a prescribed stock level s_i (also termed reorder level), place an order so that the total stock of item i is raised up to a prescribed level. $S_i (s_i \leq S_i)$, which is also termed order-up-to level.

Both S_i and (s_i, S_i) policies are referred to as order-up-to type. It can be argued that an S_i policy is a special case of (s_i, S_i) policy, if the reorder level in the S_i system is set just below the order-up-to level (or precisely expressed as $s_i = S_i - \delta$, where $\delta > 0$ is infinitesimal). As the analysis of warehousing under base-stock (S_i) stocking is relatively simple (which will become apparent when we proceed to the following sections), we will defer the details of the case with min-max stocking to Appendix A6.

We shall note that the implementation of a stocking policy requires a review mechanism, either continuous or periodic. A review mechanism is signified by the review cycle time for item i, denoted by τ_i, which specifies the time between consecutive reviews of the inventory status of item i. Under a time-series setting with time index $t = 0, \pm1, \pm2, \ldots$, a continuous review scheme stipulates that stock status be monitored and reviewed within every period (i.e., $\tau_i \le 1$). Each of the S_i and (s_i, S_i) policies can be implemented under either continuous review $(\tau_i < 1)$ or periodic review $(\tau_i > 1)$. With the advances in IT, a continuous review of time-series measures has become almost automatic in warehouse operations. As warehouse orders are indeed presented in the form of a time series, the stocking decisions are incurred under a period-by-period (i.e., continuous) review of system status.

Replenishment stocking decisions

Under a given stocking policy, decisions to replenish warehouse stocks for each item i can then be made dynamically, generating a time series of replenishing orders. Specifically, let us consider a replenishing order time series generated from each of the three stocking policies.

STOCKING DECISIONS UNDER BASE-STOCK POLICY

Under a continuous review, replenishment stocking decision $q_{i,t}$, denoting the order quantity for item i, is determined in a period-by-period manner. Recall that x_{it} denotes the on-hand inventory position for item i in period t. The stocking decision under a continuously reviewed base-stock S_i policy is determined period by period as follows:

$$q_{it} = (S_i - x_{it})^+ = \begin{cases} S_i - x_{it}, & \text{if } S_i - x_{it} > 0 \\ 0, & \text{otherwise} \end{cases} \qquad (6.14)$$

A practical modification of the above base-stock decision is a simple linear rule:

$$q_{it} = S_i - x_{it} \qquad (6.15)$$

With this modification, the stocking decision q_{it} may become negative, a rare but possible event in the real world. A negative stocking is typically interpreted as goods returned back to the supplier.

Note that the above two order-up-to types of stocking policies under stationary demand are typically independent of time t. For example, the policy parameter S_i in a base-stock policy for each item i is independent of time. For practical reasons, warehouse stocking policies in this chapter are confined to those of time invariant. However, we note that there are cases, such as when the itemized demand process is nonstationary (e.g., with time trend), where the viable stocking policies may be time variant. In this case, policy parameters (e.g., the order-up-to levels) can be adjusted period by period.

STOCKING DECISIONS UNDER MIN-MAX POLICY

The stocking decision q_{it} under an (s_i, S_i) policy can be determined as,

$$q_{it} = \begin{cases} S_i - x_{it}, & \text{if } x_{it} < s_i \\ 0, & \text{if } x_{it} \geq s_i \end{cases} \tag{6.16}$$

We can see from (6.16) that stocking decisions under an (s_i, S_i) policy corresponds to a reorder-point order-quantity (R_i, Q_i) system, connected via the following two equalities:

Reorder point : $R_i = s_i$ and Order quantity : $Q_i = S_i - s_i$.

Warehousing performance measures

It is critically important to select and implement the best stocking policy in warehouse stocking operations. Determination of a stocking policy can be viewed as the adaptive planning we have studied in previous chapters, in which a dynamic set of viable strategies (i.e., stocking policies) are dynamically evaluated using a prescribed set of performance measures. Similar to those used in typical inventory systems, the performance measures used in the selection of stocking policy are basically of two types: **operational cost** and **quality of service**. Given a performance measure, the determination of a stocking policy involves a two-step decision-making process:

1   Select a stocking policy that will yield the best performance under a certain performance measure. For three forms of stocking policies, we are confined to selecting S_i for base-stock policy, or selecting (s_i, S_i) for min-max policy.
2   Determine the values of the policy parameters that will yield the best performance measure. In the case of base-stock policy, we determine optimal order-up-to level S_i. In the case of (s_i, S_i) policy, we need to determine the optimal reorder level s_i and order-up-to level S_i.

Regarding the **optimal stocking policy**, it is obtained in inventory theory that:

If the itemized demands are i.i.d. with

$\text{cov}(d_{it}, d_{jt}) = 0, \text{for any } i \neq j,$

then,

- An S_i base-stock policy is optimal under a linear cost structure without step-wise setup cost. For example, a typical linear per-period cost associated with item i, denoted by TC_{it}, takes the following form:

$$TC_{it} = c_{p_i} \times q_{it} + c_{h_i} x_{it}$$

where c_{p_i} is the unit purchase cost of item i, and c_{h_i} is the unit cost for inventory holding of item i in period t.

- An (s_i, S_i) policy is optimal under a linear cost structure plus a stepwise setup cost (e.g., dollar-per-pick-order cost). In this case, the per-period cost can be expressed as follows:

$$TC_{it} = c_{s_i} \times 1_{q_{it} > 0} + c_{p_i} \times q_{it} + c_{h_i} x_{it}$$

where c_{s_i} represents setup cost per order, and $1_{q_{it} > 0}$ is an indicator function, taking a value of 1 if $q_{it} > 0$, otherwise $1_{q_{it} > 0} = 0$.

In what follows in this chapter, assuming that a stocking policy has been selected, we focus on determining the policy parameters (e.g., s_i and S_i) under a prescribed performance measure, either expected cost or quality of service.

The **operational cost** incurred in warehouse stocking includes typical inventory costs as studied in Chapter 3 (e.g., storage and setup costs), but is also affected by additional factors such as those related to order picking. According to Frazelle (2002), *order picking* is the most labor-intensive, and thus most costly, function in a warehouse, representing more than 50 percent of the warehouse operating costs as compared with other costs, such as shipping cost (around 15 percent), receiving cost (around 15 percent), and storage cost (around 20 percent). For example, according to a recent study 63 percent of operating costs in a typical warehouse in the United Kingdom can be attributed to order picking. The interrelations between itemized stocking and order picking are immediate. It is obvious that a higher order-picking cost will translate into a higher order-setup cost for itemized stocking. Along another dimension, itemized stocking levels will be affected by the number of itemized items incurred in the order picking. A more detailed itemization of the warehouse materials will result in a larger number of different stocks, which in turn will lead to lower stocking levels for individual items. It is easy to see that stocking level, of course, is directly connected with the inventory holding cost of the item.

The performance measures on **quality of service** relevant to warehouse stocking are formulated in regards to two major aspects: (1) *warehouse service level* and (2) *warehouse fill rate*.

Warehouse service level

The **service level** is defined as the probability of being adequately stocked for each item i during a certain time period. As shown in Chapter 3, the in-stock probability is equivalent to none out of stock during the lead time L_i for replenishment of item i, i.e.,

Warehouse service level under (s_i, S_i) policy:

$$\Pr\left(\text{in-stock during replenishment leadtime}\right) \equiv \Pr(D_t^{L_i} \leq s_i),$$

where $D_t^{L_i}$ represents aggregated demand for item i over lead-time L_i.

Warehouse service level under base-stock S_i policy:

$$\Pr\left(\text{in-stock during replenishment lead-time}\right) \equiv \Pr(D_t^{L_i} \leq S_i).$$

Warehouse fill rate

Another useful measure of warehouse performance is the **fill rate**, or the average proportion of item demand that can be met by warehouse stocks. Under stationary itemized demand, the fill rate (FR) of item i under continuous review $(\tau_i = 1)$ can be constructed as follows:

Warehouse FR on item i per period:

$$\text{FR}_i \equiv \frac{\text{expected onhand inventory}}{\text{expected demand}} = \frac{E\left(\min\{x_{it} + q_{i,t-L_i}, d_{i,t}\}\right)}{E(d_{i,t})}$$

where x_{it} represents the beginning inventory position for item t, and $q_{i,t-L_i}$ is the realized replenishment order with a lead-time L_i. Under periodic review $(\tau_i > 1)$, the fill rate can be constructed as follows:

FR on item i per order cycle:

$$\text{FR}_i \equiv \frac{\text{expected order fulfilled per cycle}}{\text{expected review cycle demand}} = \frac{E\left(\sum_{j=1}^{\tau_i} \min\{x_{i,t+j} + q_{i,t-L_i+j}, d_{t+j}\}\right)}{E\left(\sum_{j+1}^{\tau_i} d_{i,t+j}\right)}.$$

When appropriate, a long-term FR can also be used:

Long-term FR on item i:

$$\text{FR}_i \equiv \lim_{\tau_i \to \infty} \frac{E\left(\sum_{j=1}^{\tau_i} \min\{x_{i,t+j} + q_{i,t-L_i+j}, d_{t+j}\}\right)}{E\left(\sum_{j+1}^{\tau_i} d_{i,t+j}\right)}.$$

In the next section, we will study basic warehouse stocking decisions regarding when and how much to replenish the itemized warehouse stocks.

Winning-before-doing warehouse strategies and operations

By the WBD method of TACBE (see Chapter 1), an adaptive targeting and balancing process must be engaged in implementing and executing the threefold

WBD warehousing strategies: itemization, value-stream balancing, and customized delivery. This section is devoted to the study of operational characteristics of WBD warehousing strategies, with a focus on the balancing of itemized warehouse operations. For an already itemized stocking system, we derive and then analyze the dynamics of value-stream balancing and delivery associated with each of the items. As the analysis is applicable to all the items separately, we remove the item index "*i*" from the derivations in this section, without loss of correctness.

Warehouse operations with lead-time balancing

We can see from the analysis presented previously that warehouse operations after itemization are centered on warehouse stocking. Hence, let us focus our attention on the basic warehouse stocking systems.

As an illustration, let us next consider optimal stocking levels for piston lines 1 and 2 of Example 6.2. Each piston line $i(i = 1,2)$ can be treated as a two-stage SOF system, which we have studied in Chapter 2, depicted in Figure 6.14.

For reference, we summarize the notation in Figure 6.14 below:

$d_{i,t}$: Demand on item i in period t.

$x_{i,t}^{j}$: Beginning on-hand inventory on item i at stage j at beginning of period t.

$q_{i,t}^{j}$: Stage j outgoing order on item i released at the beginning of period t.

$y_{i,t}^{j}$: Outbound delivery on item i from stage j between the beginning of period $t-1$ and the beginning of period t.

Recall that the piston demands for piston lines 1 and 2, $d_{1,t}$ and $d_{2,t}$, are stationary with the following characteristics:

Line 1: $E(d_{1,t}) = \mu_1 = 210$, $\text{var}(d_{1,t}) = \sigma_1^2 = 75^2$;
Line 2: $E(d_{2,t}) = \mu_2 = 120$, $\text{var}(d_{2,t}) = \sigma_2^2 = 45^2$.

For simplicity, we assume both demands are normally distributed. The cost data for pistons 1 and 2 are given, respectively, as,

$c_{h_1} = 0.40 \times \$60 = \$24$ per unit held per period; $c_{b_1} = \$55$ per unit backlogged

$c_{h_2} = 0.40 \times \$75 = \$30$ per unit held per period; $c_{b_2} = \$72$ per unit backlogged

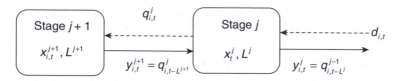

Figure 6.14 A two-stage segment of a supply chain as a LAGOF system.

Recall that the lead-times for lines 1 and 2 are $L_1 = 5$ and $L_2 = 3$ days (i.e., piston line 1 is the bottleneck item). According to the lead-time balancing procedure (see Chapter 5 for details), the Takt time (i.e., the bottleneck time) across the two piston lines can be determined as $\text{Takt} = \max\{L_1, L_2\} = 5$. Rescaling with Takt time, the balanced common cycle time becomes 1, written as $\tilde{L} = 1$. The aggregated cycle demands for the two lines can then be computed as:

$$\tilde{d}_{1,t} \sim (\tilde{\mu}_1, \tilde{\sigma}_1) : \tilde{\mu}_1 = 5\mu_1 = 1,050, \tilde{\sigma}_1^2 = 5\sigma_1^2 = 5 \times 75^2 = 28,125 = 168^2$$

$$\tilde{d}_{2,t} \sim (\tilde{\mu}_2, \tilde{\sigma}_2) : \tilde{\mu}_2 = 5\mu_2 = 600, \tilde{\sigma}_2^2 = 5\sigma_2^2 = 5 \times 45^2 = 10,125 = 101^2.$$

It is immediate to compute,

$$\Pr(Z_1 \le z_1) = \frac{c_{b_1}}{c_{h_1} + c_{b_1}} = 0.696, \text{ and } \Pr(Z_2 \le z_2) = \frac{c_{b_2}}{c_{h_2} + c_{b_2}} = 0.706$$

The safety stock factors can then be determined from the Standard Normal Table as,

$$z_1 = 0.514 \text{ and } z_2 = 0.541.$$

The optimal stocking levels for piston lines 1 and 2 can thus be determined as,

$$S_1^* = \tilde{\mu}_1 + z_1 \tilde{\sigma}_1 = 1,050 + 0.514 \times (168) = 1,136, \text{and}$$

$$S_2^* = \tilde{\mu}_2 + z_2 \tilde{\sigma}_2 = 600 + 0.541 \times (101) = 654.$$

Warehouse cross-item value-stream balancing

In the previous section, our study was confined to the stocking decisions within each item stocked in a warehouse. Now, we consider a warehouse stocking system as depicted in Figure 6.12, consisting of total m stock items needed for the delivery of orders from a total of n different customers. Although it is not possible to obtain a unified solution to this kind of multi-item stocking problem, recent findings in the practice of supply chain management have indicated a generically plausible method of *value-stream balancing*.

Procedure for value-stream balancing

A newly emerging method of value-stream balancing focuses on eliminating waste by balancing value-added processes throughout an entire firm and across a complete supply chain. From a methodological point of view, it is an extension of itemized value-stream balancing, as previously studied, to an aggregate level of operations management. In aggregate warehouse operations, value-stream balancing is involved with making multi-item, multistage storage/retrieval decisions. To this end, we outline the procedure for value-stream balancing of aggregate warehouse operations:

- Lead-time-based grouping: Group warehouse items that require similar lead-time into a warehouse stocking family (or cluster).
- Balance each family with a unified lead-time: Treat each family as one item, and apply the itemized balancing as described in the section on "Maritime cargo (p. 379)".
- ABC classification of each balanced warehouse item family: Apply 80-20 rule to each of the balanced families, according to the value-adding status within each family.
- Optimal stocking decisions: Determine optimal stocking policy and stocking levels for different classifications of items within each of the balanced families. A stocking policy, or performance target, is first established for each family, from which optimal stocking levels are determined for each item within the family.

We shall point out that the value-stream balancing characteristics described above correspond with Sun Zi's method of five tactics: targeting, assessing, calculating, balancing, and executing (TACBE). According to the TACBE method, the above procedure of value-stream balancing is then carried out dynamically; that is, the procedure will be applied (or reapplied) whenever degradation in performance is detected. Therefore, to detect the degradation, acquiring an effective online monitoring technology and devising an accurate diagnostic method are important. Further, the outcome and the method of transaction will not be the same each time when applying the TACBE method. Hence, it is as Sun Zi says:

> The way to win shall not be repeated, but let your methods be regulated by the infinite variety of circumstances. 故其战胜不复，而应形于无穷.
>
> *The Art of War*, Chapter 6, Verse 6.26. (500 BC, by Sun Zi)

Next, we apply the value-stream balancing method to warehouse stocking problems through an example of a multi-item inventory system.

Example 6.3   Multi-item warehouse stocking

Consider 20 mechanical parts that are stocked in a regional warehouse, with operational data given in Table 6.10. The itemized annual demands are assumed to be i.i.d. normal for all the items, and lead-times for replenishment are all given in weeks.

To focus on the illustration of the procedure of value-stream balancing, let us assume that these lead times cannot be further reduced. The holding cost for each item is computed as 22 percent of its value, as listed in Table 6.10. Suppose that we are to determine an optimal stocking level for each of the 20 items, assuming 52 working weeks per year.

Table 6.10 Selected 20 warehouse items in Example 6.3

Item index	Price ($/unit)	Annual demand		Lead-time (in weeks)	Holding cost	Backorder cost
		Mean	StDev			
1	22.50	26,000	5,817	1	4.95	12.00
2	28.00	470	61	2.5	6.16	6.50
3	17.50	2,500	283	2	3.85	13.50
4	7.50	40,000	2,534	1	1.65	4.00
5	44.50	6,500	1,494	1	9.79	11.33
6	61.00	22,000	1,829	2.5	13.42	14.17
7	31.00	12,500	1,551	2	6.82	8.83
8	13.20	78,000	8,025	1	2.90	2.00
9	128.00	1,400	80	3	28.16	4.33
10	249.95	30,000	6,931	1.5	54.99	18.00
11	77.50	2,400	481	2.5	17.05	5.67
12	6.75	7,000	1,539	1.5	1.49	4.50
13	2.50	5,500	1,093	1	0.55	5.00
14	38.90	57,500	13,507	3	8.56	3.17
15	77.00	6,500	724	3	16.94	3.67
16	62.25	8,000	1,557	2.5	13.70	4.83
17	8.50	12,500	1,583	2	1.87	2.67
18	7.75	60,000	3,000	1	1.71	5.33
19	12.30	5,000	401	2	2.71	2.17
20	40.50	1,200	223	3	8.91	7.00

Formation of a lead-time-based warehouse stocking family

To identify items with similar lead times, we sort the 20 items in ascending order by lead-times, as shown in Table 6.11. Based on commonality in lead time, three warehouse stocking families (groups) can be readily recognized by three ranges of lead-times: less than or equal to 1 week, more than 1 but no more than 2 weeks, and greater than or equal to 3 weeks.

Specifically, we define three stocking families, each with its upper-limit lead-time as the family's lead-time, as follows:

Family I: Item index set $\xi_I = \{1,4,5,8,13,18\}$, with family lead-time $L_I = 1$.
Family II: Item index set $\xi_{II} = \{10,12,3,7,17,19\}$, with family lead-time $L_{II} = 2$.
Family III: Item index set $\xi_{III} = \{2,6,11,16,9,14,15,20\}$, with family lead-time $L_{III} = 3$.

ABC classification within each stocking family

Each of the stocking family k (for $k = I, II, III$) can be treated as a multi-item inventory system as described in Chapter 3, and similarly, the items within each stocking family can be ABC classified according to the 80-20 rule also described in Chapter 3. Briefly, the items within each family are rearranged in descending

Table 6.11 Warehouse items sorted by lead-time

Item index	Price ($/unit)	Annual demand		Lead-time (in weeks)	Holding cost	Backorder cost
		Mean	StDev			
1	22.5	26,000	5,817	1	4.95	12.00
4	7.5	40,000	2,534	1	1.65	4.00
5	44.5	6,500	1,494	1	9.79	11.33
8	13.2	78,000	8,025	1	2.90	2.00
13	2.5	5,500	1,093	1	0.55	5.00
18	7.75	60,000	3,000	1	1.71	5.33
10	249.95	30,000	6,931	1.5	54.99	18.00
12	6.75	7,000	1,539	1.5	1.49	4.50
3	17.5	2,500	283	2	3.85	13.50
7	31	12,500	1,551	2	6.82	8.83
17	8.5	12,500	1,583	2	1.87	2.67
19	12.3	5,000	401	2	2.71	2.17
2	28	470	61	2.5	6.16	6.50
6	61	22,000	1,829	2.5	13.42	14.17
11	77.5	2,400	481	2.5	17.05	5.67
16	62.25	8,000	1,557	2.5	13.70	4.83
9	128	1,400	80	3	28.16	4.33
14	38.9	57,500	13,507	3	8.56	3.17
15	77	6,500	724	3	16.94	3.67
20	40.5	1,200	223	3	8.91	7.00

order of their annual values in transactions. It is suggested by the 80-20 rule that around 80 percent of the annual transaction values of each family should be contributed from around 20 percent of items in that family. By the theory of 80-20 rule, items in the top 20 percentile are classified as the most important class A items, and items in the bottom 50 percentile are classified as class C, leaving all the items in the middle as class B. Table 6.12 contains the results of an ABC classification as applied to stocking family I. As shown in Table 6.12, the A class of stocking family I includes three items indexed as 8, 1, and 18, which represent 78 percent of the annual value. The bottom C class consists of two items (numbers 5 and 13), representing only 11 percent of the total annual value of the family, while the single item B class (item number 4) represents 11 percent of the total value. The classification can be similarly applied to other families.

Different classifications are then devised with different monitoring policies (e.g., continuous versus periodical reviews), and stocking policies (e.g., base-stock versus min-max). For the purpose of illustration, we consider in Example 6.3 that continuous monitoring and base-stock policy are applied to all the ABC classes.

Optimal stocking levels by stocking family

With a fixed lead-time L_k for each stocking family k (for $k = I, II, III$), an optimal base-stock stocking level can be determined for each item $i_k \in \xi_k$. For example, for stocking family I, we apply the formulae to each item $i_1 \in \xi_1 = \{1, 4, 5, 13, 18, 8\}$.

Table 6.12 ABC classification of stocking family I of Example 6.3

Family I Item	Price ($/unit)	Annual demand		Item value	Cumulative value	Cumulative %	Class
		Mean	StDev				
8	13.2	78,000	8,025	1,029,600	1,029,600	0.38	
1	22.5	26,000	5,817	585,000	1,614,600	0.60	
18	7.75	60,000	3,000	465,000	2,079,600	0.78	A
4	7.5	40,000	2,534	300,000	2,379,600	0.89	B
5	44.5	6,500	1,494	289,250	2,668,850	0.99	
13	2.5	5,500	1,093	13,750	2,682,600	1.00	C

Let us consider an optimal stocking level for item number 13 in family I (i.e., $i_1 = 13$). With a 1-week lead-time for family (i.e., $L_1 = 1$) (assuming 52 working weeks per year), we compute the following for the lead-time demand for item $i_1 = 13$:

$$\mu^{i_1}_{L_1} = L_1 \times \mu_{i_1} = (1) \times \frac{5,500}{52} = 106 \,(\text{per week}); \text{and}$$

$$\sigma^{i_1}_{L_1} = \sqrt{L_1 \times (\sigma_{i_1})^2} = \sqrt{(1) \times \frac{(1,039)^2}{52}} = 152$$

where μ_{i_1} and σ_{i_1} are the mean and standard deviation of weekly demand for item i_1, respectively. The following calculations can be carried out:

$$F(z_{i_1}) = \frac{c_{b_i}}{c_{h_i} + c_{b_i}} = \frac{5}{0.55 + 5} = 0.9009$$

$$z_{i_1} = F^{-1} \left(\frac{c_{b_i}}{c_{h_i} + c_{b_i}} \right) = F^{-1}(0.9009) = 1.2867$$

$$S^*_{i_1} = \mu^{i_1}_{L_1} + z_{i_1} \times \sigma^{i_1}_{L_1} = 106 + (1.2867) \times (152) = 301.$$

The stocking levels can be similarly determined for other stocking families ($k = $ II, III), except for using the corresponding family lead time L_k in calculation of lead-time demand (in this case, $L_{II} = 2$ and $L_{III} = 3$). In summary, the base-stock level for i.i.d. item $i_k \in \xi_k$ in a stocking family k ($k = $ I, II, III) can be determined by the following formulae:

$$\mu^{i_k}_{L_k} = L_k \times \mu_{i_k}, \text{and} \, \sigma^{i_k}_{L_k} = \sqrt{L_k \times (\sigma_{i_k})^2}$$

$$F(z_{i_1}) = \frac{c_{b_i}}{c_{h_i} + c_{b_i}}, \text{and} \, z_{i_1} = F^{-1} \left(\frac{c_{b_i}}{c_{h_i} + c_{b_i}} \right)$$

$$S^*_{i_1} = \mu^{i_1}_{L_1} + z_{i_1} \times \sigma^{i_1}_{L_1}.$$

Table 6.13 Optimal stocking levels for Example 6.3

Item index	Annual demand		c_h	c_b	$F(S^*)$	z	S^*
	Mean	StDev					
1	26,000	5,817	4.95	12.00	0.7080	0.5474	942
4	40,000	2,534	1.65	4.00	0.7080	0.5474	962
5	6,500	1,494	9.79	11.33	0.5365	0.0917	144
8	78,000	8,025	2.90	2.00	0.4078	−0.2331	1,241
13	5,500	1,093	0.55	5.00	0.9009	1.2867	301
18	60,000	3,000	1.71	5.33	0.7578	0.6991	1,445
10	30,000	6,931	54.99	18.00	0.2466	−0.6852	222
12	7,000	1,539	1.49	4.50	0.7519	0.6804	475
3	2,500	283	3.85	13.50	0.7781	0.7658	139
7	12,500	1,551	6.82	8.83	0.5643	0.1619	530
17	12,500	1,583	1.87	2.67	0.5878	0.2219	550
19	5,000	401	2.71	2.17	0.4447	−0.1392	181
2	470	61	6.16	6.50	0.5134	0.0337	28
6	22,000	1,829	13.42	14.17	0.5135	0.0339	1,284
11	2,400	481	17.05	5.67	0.2494	−0.6762	60
16	8,000	1,557	13.70	4.83	0.2609	−0.6407	222
9	1,400	80	28.16	4.33	0.1334	−1.1106	59
14	57,500	13,507	8.56	3.17	0.2701	−0.6126	1,330
15	6,500	724	16.94	3.67	0.1779	−0.9233	214
20	1,200	223	8.91	7.00	0.4400	−0.1510	61

Table 6.13 contains optimal stocking levels determined for all the 20 items in Example 6.3.

Applicability of value-stream balancing method

From the previous section, we know that the value-stream balancing method is applicable to an S_i-LAGOF system when each itemized demand process is i.i.d. In this section, we examine the applicability of the method for a more realistic scenario under an S_i-LAGOF system, that is, when itemized demand is independent across the items, but is itemized autoregressively.

Value-stream balancing of itemized autoregressive S_i-LAGOF system

Suppose that itemized demand is independent across the items stocked in the warehouse, but each itemized demand itself is autoregressive (i.e., is correlated across time t), for example, following a stationary ARMA process. It can be verified that the method of value-stream balancing introduced in Subsection 6.5.1 is also applicable if each itemized demand follows a stationary ARMA model. Let us elaborate this claim through Example 6.3.

Consider the same 20 items in Example 6.3, except that the demand of each item follows an AR(1) process, expressed in the following form:

$$d_{i_k,t} = \mu_{i_k} + \phi_{i_k}(d_{i_k,t-1} - \mu_{i_k}) + \varepsilon_{i_k,t}, |\phi_{i_k}| < 1 \tag{6.26}$$

where $i_k \in \xi_k$ is an item in stocking family k, $\mu_{i_k} = E(d_{i_k,t})$ is the mean of the itemized demand, and $\varepsilon_{i_k,t} \sim (0, \sigma^2_{\varepsilon_{ik}})$ is a white noise incurred to item i_k. It is known that the demand of (6.26) is covariance-stationary, with a time-invariant variance determined as,

$$\sigma^2_{i_k} = \text{var}(d_{i_k,t}) = \frac{\sigma^2_{\varepsilon_{ik}}}{1 - \phi^2_{i_k}}.$$

The formulae in (6.24) and (6.25) only require lead-time demand possess time-invariant mean and variance, $\mu^{i_k}_{L_k}$ and $\left(\sigma^{i_k}_{L_k}\right)^2$, for each item $i_k \in \xi_k$ in each stocking family k. The lead-time demand, denoted by $d^{L_k}_{i_k,t}$, is an aggregate demand over the family lead-time L_k (i.e., sum of time series over the lead-time). Chapters 4 and 5 show that an aggregated stationary time series can be expressed as another stationary time series, usually in the form of an ARMA process. In this case, it can be claimed that lead-time demand $d^{L_k}_{i_k,t}$ is covariance-stationary, especially with constant mean and variance, that is,

$$E(d^{L_k}_{i_k,t}) = \mu^{i_k}_{L_k} = L_k \times \mu_{i_k}, \text{and var}(d^{L_k}_{i_k,t}) = (\sigma^{i_k}_{L_k})^2. \tag{6.27}$$

Note that the mean of autoregressive lead-time demand is computed the same way as in formula (6.23), but the variance must be computed differently (see Chapter 4 for details). Although the computation of variance of autoregressive lead-time demand may be complicated, in theory it can be obtained as a constant. Therefore, the value-stream balancing method is applicable to an itemized autoregressive S_i-LAGOF warehouse system.

Simulation lab: Transportation and distribution

Assignment 6.1: Solution of MB's origin–destination transportation model

Consider the cost data quoted in section "Prototype example: distribution at Mega Brewery" (p. 272) by Schneider Logistics for the distribution of MB's bottled beer, reprinted in Table 6.14. The capacity limits of the four plants are the same as given by Equation (6.1), and weekly demand data are as given in Table 6.3.

A   Develop a transportation model for the distribution of MB's bottled beer.
B   Use LINDO to find an optimal solution for MB's transportation problem.

Table 6.14 Data for Assignment 6.1 ($ per 1,000 cases)

W	R									
	R_1	R_2	R_3	R_4	R_5	R_6	R_7	R_8	R_9	R_{10}
P_1	71	41	53	54	76	113	77	52	75	92
P_2	59	94	55	76	117	59	94	89	62	37
P_3	42	37	52	45	85	107	64	96	64	87
P_4	63	64	49	38	92	86	95	57	60	71

Assignment 6.2: Solution of MB's transshipment model with prohibited routes

Consider the transshipment problem at MB, as depicted in Figure 6.1. The cost data are given in Tables 6.1 and 6.2.

A   Develop a transshipment model for the distribution of MB's bottled beer in which the prohibited routes as indicated in Tables 6.1 and 6.2 must be reflected properly.

B   Use LINDO to solve the transshipment model.

C   Compare the minimized total transshipment cost with the total cost obtained in Assignment 6.1.

Problems

Basic exercises

1   Consider the following transportation problem with costs (Table 6.15).

Table 6.15 Data for Problem 6.1

From \ To	X	Y	Z	Supply
A	50	100	100	110
B	200	300	200	160
C	100	200	300	150
Demand	140	200	80	

A   Find an initial solution by the Northwest Corner method.

B   Find an optimal solution by completing the rest of the computation.

2 A firm producing a single product has four plants and five customers. The four plants will produce 3,000, 5,000, 4,000, and 3,500 units per month, respectively. The five customers will buy 4,000, 3,500, 1,000, 4,000, and 3,000 units per month, respectively. The net profit associated with shipping one unit from plant i for sale to customer j is given by Table 6.16:

Table 6.16 Data for Problem 6.2

Plant	Customer				
	1	*2*	*3*	*4*	*5*
1	65	63	62	64	60
2	68	67	65	62	63
3	63	60	59	60	59
4	70	61	64	58	61

The management wishes to know the best monthly distribution from each of the plants to each of the customers to maximize profit.

A Develop a transportation tableau for the above problem.
B Find an initial solution using the Northwest Corner method.
C Solve for the optimal solution using LINDO.

3 A realtor plans to sell four plots of land and has received individual bids from each of five developers. Given the amount of capital required, these bids were made with the understanding that no developer would purchase more than one plot. The bids are shown in Table 6.17. The realtor wants to maximize total income from these bids. Solve this problem by the Hungarian method and compute the resulting total income (without use of computer).

Table 6.17 Data for Problem 6.3

Plot	Developer				
	1	*2*	*3*	*4*	*5*
A	16	15	25	19	20
B	19	17	24	15	25
C	15	15	18	0	16
D	19	0	15	17	18

4 A paper mill has paper plants in Augusta, Maine, and Tupper Lake, New York. Warehouse facilities are located in Albany, New York, and Portsmouth, New Hampshire. Distributors are located in Boston, New York, and Philadelphia. The plant capacities and distributor demands for the next month are as given in Table 6.18.

Table 6.18 Data for Problem 6.4

Plant	Capacity (units)	Distributor	Demand (units)
Augusta	300	Boston	150
Tupper Lake	100	New York	100
		Philadelphia	150

The unit transportation cost ($) for shipments from the two plants to the two warehouses and from the two warehouses to the three distributors are as in Table 6.19.

Table 6.19 Data for Problem 6.4

Plant	Warehouse	
	Albany	Portsmouth
Augusta	7	5
Tupper Lake	3	4

A   Draw the network representation of the paper mill's problem.
B   Formulate the paper mill's problem as an LP transshipment problem.
C   Solve the problem using LINDO, and attach a hard copy of the LINDO solution output without sensitivity analysis.

Appendix 6   Review: linear programming

Linear programming formulation

For convenience, we review the basics of LP in the context of beer production at MB. Let x_j be the weekly production quantity of beer product j, and c_j be the associated unit production cost ($j = 1, 2, \ldots, n$). Let b_i be the weekly production order for wholesaler i ($i = 1, 2, \ldots, m$). Then, the beer production problem objective is to produce a mix of n products to meet—with minimized costs—the demand such that it can be formulated as the following LP model:

$$\min z = c_1 x_1 + c_2 x_2 + \cdots + c_n x_n$$

subject to

$$a_{11} x_1 + a_{12} x_2 + \cdots + a_{1n} x_n \geq b_1$$

$$a_{21} x_1 + a_{22} x_2 + \cdots + a_{2n} x_n \geq b_2$$

$$a_{m1} x_1 + a_{m2} x_2 + \cdots + a_{mn} x_n \geq b_m$$

$$x_j \geq 0, \text{for } j = 1, 2, \ldots, n$$

where a_{ij} the coefficient of order mix of product j for wholesaler i. An LP problem can be easily presented as a maximization problem, when c_j $(j = 1, 2, \ldots, n)$ represents unit profit (instead of cost) and b_i $(i = 1, 2, \ldots, m)$ now represents limits of production resources. A standard form of LP with maximization is usually given as:

$$\max z = c_1 x_1 + c_2 x_2 + \cdots + c_n x_n$$

subject to

$$a_{11} x_1 + a_{12} x_2 + \cdots + a_{1n} x_n \le b_1$$

$$a_{21} x_1 + a_{22} x_2 + \cdots + a_{2n} x_n \le b_2$$

$$a_{m1} x_1 + a_{m2} x_2 + \cdots + a_{mn} x_n \le b_m$$

$$x_j \ge 0, \text{for } j = 1, 2, \ldots, n.$$

Applications of LP

A prototype LP problem: MB production planning

Mega Brewery produces two types of beer (bottled and canned) on a weekly schedule. Net profit for each case of bottled beer is $50, and $40 for canned beer. Each case of bottled beer requires one loads of labels, two loads of packing materials, and three shipping packs. A case of canned beer requires two packs of labels, one load of packing materials, and one shipping pack. The limits on total number of loads of labels and packing materials per week are 15 and 16, respectively. The minimum number of shipping packs per week is 12.

According to the result of a recent marketing research, it is required by the management that at least one case of canned beer should be produced for every two cases of bottled beer produced. How should MB plan the weekly production mix of bottled and canned beer, such that the weekly profit is maximized?

We formulate the MB's weekly production planning problem as an LP. Let

x_1: cases of bottled beer to produce weekly
x_2: cases of canned beer to produce weekly.

Then the LP for the MB production problem is:

$$\text{Maximize} \, 50 x_1 + 40 x_2$$

subject to

$$x_1 + 2 x_2 \le 15$$

$$2 x_1 + x_2 \le 16$$

$$3x_1 + x_2 \geq 12$$

$$x_1 - 2x_2 \leq 0$$

$$x_1, x_2 \geq 0.$$

Marketing research

Market Pro, Inc. (MPI) specializes in evaluating consumer reaction to new products and services. MPI is currently conducting a marketing research project regarding a newly marketed appliance product, which involves both day and evening interviews with households with and without children. According to the project contract, MPI must conduct 1,000 interviews under the following quota guidelines.

1　Interview at least 400 households with children.
2　Interview at least 400 households without children.
3　The total number of households interviewed during the evening must be at least equal to the number of day interviews.
4　At least 40 percent of the interviews for households with children must be conducted during the evening.
5　At least 50 percent of the interviews for households without children must be conducted during the evening.

Because the interviews for households with children take additional interview time and because evening interviewers are paid more than daytime interviewers, the cost varies with the type of interviews. The interview costs are estimated as in Table 6.20.

Table 6.20 Data for Appendix "Applications of LP"

Household	Interview cost ($)	
	Day	*Evening*
Children	20	25
No children	18	20

What is the interview plan (on household and time-of-day) that will satisfy the contract requirements at a minimum total interview cost?

Portfolio selection (financial application)

Welte Mutual Funds, Inc., has just obtained $100,000 by converting industrial bonds cash and is now looking for other investment opportunities for these funds.

According to professional financial analysis, the firm has decided that all new investments must be made in the oil industry, steel industry, or in government bonds. The firm has identified five investment opportunities and projected their annual rates of return, as shown in Table 6.21.

Management of Welte has imposed the following investment guidelines.

1 Neither industry (oil or steel) should receive more than $50,000.
2 Government bonds should be at least 25 percent of the steel industry investments.
3 The investment in Pacific Oil, the high-return but high-risk investment, cannot be more than 60 percent of the total oil industry investment (Table 6.21).

Table 6.21 Data for Appendix "Applications of LP"

Investment	Projected rate of return (%)
Atlantic oil	7.3
Pacific oil	10.3
Midwest steel	6.4
Huber steel	7.5
Government bonds	4.5

What portfolio recommendations—investments and amounts—should be made for the available $100,000?

Production planning with fixed cost

ChemPro produces three products: a fuel additive, a solvent base, and a carpet cleaning fluid (all measured in tons). Each product is a mix of two or three materials. One ton of fuel additive is a blend of 0.4 tons of material 1, and 0.6 tons of material 3. Each ton of solvent base requires 0.5 tons of material 1, 0.2 tons of material 2, and 0.3 tons of material 3. One ton of carpet cleaning fluid needs 0.6 tons of material 1, 0.1 tons of material 2, and 0.3 tons of material 3. ChemPro has 20 tons of material 1, 5 tons of material 2, and 21 tons of material 3. The profit contributions are $40 per ton for the fuel additive, $30 per ton for the solvent, and $50 per ton for the carpet cleaning fluid.

In addition, there are setup costs and maximum production quantity for each of the three products (Table 6.22).

Table 6.22 Data for Appendix "Applications of LP"

Product	Setup cost ($)	Maximum production (tons)
Fuel additive	200	50
Solvent base	50	25
Carpet cleaning fluid	400	40

How should ChemPro determine the production quantities for the upcoming planning period?

Solving LP models

Graphic solution for two-variable LP

Consider the MB model:

$$\text{Maximize } 50x_1 + 40x_2$$

subject to

(1) $x_1 + 2x_2 \leq 15$

(2) $2x_1 + x_2 \leq 16$

(3) $3x_1 + x_2 \geq 12$

(4) $x_1 - 2x_2 \leq 0$

$x_1, x_2 \geq 0.$

The set of constraints forms a feasible region, which can be presented graphically as in Figure 6.15. The constraints are numbered in Figure 6.15 for ease of

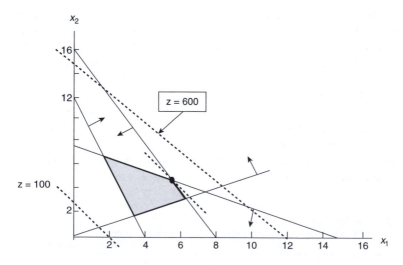

Figure 6.15 Example of graphic LP solution.

reference. Each constraint confines the feasible points to a half-plane. For example, the first constraint, $x_1 + 2x_2 \leq 15$, confines the feasible points to be on or below the boundary line, $x_1 + 2x_2 = 15$.

Now, we introduce the concept of a z-level objective line. Suppose that a target profit level of $z = 100$ is determined. Any production plan, denoted by (x_1, x_2), meeting the target z will satisfy the following equality:

$$z = 50x_1 + 40x_2 = 100$$

which is a line, shown as dotted line in Figure 6.15. For a higher value of z, the objective line will be parallel to the original line, but will be higher (i.e., above the original line).

Thus, an optimal solution can be determined by finding the intersection of the feasible region and the highest z level of the objective line. Such an intersection can be graphically identified to be the corner point, as shown in Figure 6.15. This corner is termed an optimal corner point, and the set of coordinates of the corner, denoted as s(x_1^*, x_2^*), is then called an optimal solution. Since the optimal corner is the intersection of the boundaries of constraints (1) and (2), the optimal solution can be determined by solving the system of two simultaneous equations, that is, $x_1 + 2x_2 = 15$ and $2x_1 + x_2 = 16$. The optimal solution can be determined as: $x_1^* = 17/3$, and $x_2^* = 14/3$, under which the maximum profit is

$$z^* = 50 \times \frac{17}{3} + 40 \times \frac{14}{3} = 470.$$

In summary, a two-variable LP can be solved graphically by: (1) drawing the feasible region according to the complete set of constraints; (2) drawing a z-level objective line; and (3) finding the intersection of the feasible region and the highest (or lowest) z-level objective line for a maximization (or minimization) LP problem.

Bibliography

Coyle, J.J., E.J. Bardi, and R.A. Novack. 2000. *Transportation*, Cincinnati, OH: South-Western.

Coyle, J., E. Bardi, and C.J. Langly. 2002. *Management of Business Logistics: A Supply Chain Perspective*. 7th Edition, Mason, OH: Thomson Learning.

Davis, D. 1995. "Third Party Deliver," *Manufacturing Systems*, 13, 66–68.

Delaney, R.V., and R. Wilson. 2000. *11th Annual State of Logistics Report*. St. Louis, MO: Cass Information Systems and Prologis.

Frazelle, E.H. 2002. *Supply Chain Strategy*. Chicago, IL: McGraw-Hill.

Hillier, F.S., and G.J. Lieberman. 2009. *Introduction to Operations Research*, 9th Edition, Chicago, IL: McGraw-Hill.

La Londe, B.J. 1998. "Supply Chain Evolution in Numbers," *Supply Chain Management Review*, 2(1), 7–8.

Leahy, S., P. Murphy, and R. Poist. 1995. "Determinants of Successful Logistical Relationships: A Third Party Provider Perspective," *Transportation Journal*, 35, 5–13.

Pine, J.B. II. 1993. *Mass Customization*. Boston, MA: Harvard Business School.

Simchi-Levi D., P. Kaminsky, and E. Simchi-Levi. 2000. *Designing and Managing Supply Chain: Concepts, Strategies, and Case Studies*, Burr Ridge, IL: Irwin/McGraw-Hill.

Stock, J.R., and D.M. Lambert. 2001. *Strategic Logistics Management*, Boston, MA: McGraw-Hill/Irwin.

Zipkin, P. 2000. *Foundation of Inventory Management*. Chicago, IL: McGraw-Hill.

7 Maintenance and contingent supply chains

Key items:

- *Maintenance and contingent supply chains*
  - *Maintenance services versus contingent-sale operations*
  - *Contingent services versus operations*
- *Maintenance and contingent-sale demand*
  - *Maintenance demand: service calls*
  - *Characterizing contingent-sale demand: Poisson arrivals*
- *Managing contingent-sale value-adding activities*
  - *Parts and accessories production*
- *Warranty services*

Maintenance and contingent supply chains

As opposed to a mainstream supply chain, which is intended for existing markets of typical consumer and manufacturing goods, a maintenance supply chain is intended to meet the contingent needs for contingent production supplies, such as maintenance, repair, and operation (MRO) materials and contingent-sale parts and accessories (P&A). As depicted in Figure 7.1, a maintenance supply chain coexists, as a necessary companion, with a regular supply chain, or even a network of supply chains. The concept of the maintenance supply chain has evolved and advanced as an interdisciplinary area of operations management and reliability theory. The study of the maintenance supply chain has recently expanded into the emerging field of the contingent supply chain, which includes the study of energy supply chains, healthcare supply chains, and humanitarian supply chains.

As shown in Figure 7.1, a maintenance supply chain provides contingent-sale services, mainly of two types, namely, MRO services and customer services. For the sake of exposition, the discussion of the contingent supply chain in this chapter is presented in the context of a maintenance supply chain, appended with generalized applications for other forms of contingent supply chains.

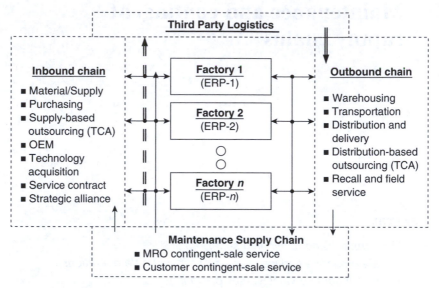

Figure 7.1 Maintenance supply chain versus regular supply chain.

Firm-focal maintenance supply chain management

In addition to maintaining the firm-focal supply chain, each firm must also maintain a maintenance supply chain to perform two necessary business functions: (1) MRO supplies for production maintenance; and (2) P&A for customer service, both of which are triggered by contingent sales.

Contingent-sale operations

Herein, contingent-sale operations are defined as consisting of two branches of activities: one overlaps with customer service in after-sales service operations, and the other branch goes beyond customer relationship management (CRM) and includes contingent-sale production activities, such as producing accessories and repair parts. In this chapter, we focus on contingent-sale supplier–customer interactions from a supply chain management perspective and consider the following aspects of contingent-sale operations:

- P&A supply chain operations: production planning, order release, and delivery of after-sale necessities, such as spare/repair P&A.
- Warranty-based service operations: the implementation and delivery of warranty services. Warranty operations also include the dynamic analysis and design (redesign) of warranty terms, according to technological advances, market structural changes, and customer feedback.

P&A supply chain operations are value-adding activities that mostly take place after sales and typically involve durable goods and technology-intensive products. The demand for P&A stems from the customer's need to maintain and improve the services rendered by the products they have acquired. As such, the demand for P&A is sporadic, low in volume, and widely spread in the product mix. For example, the P&A market associated with a particular automobile may involve hundreds of repair parts for different functions and different models of the car.

Warranty-based service operations are another set of value-adding activities that typically take place after the point of sale (POS). A warranty is, by definition, the contractual documentation of a time-constrained guarantee, established between the supplier and the consumer, which includes the responsibilities of the supplier (the maker) for correcting any legitimate problems with the item he or she has provided (Brennan 1994) Warranty policies are determined before POS and are specified as effective for a particular period of time or use after an item has been purchased. Warranty service operations are the activities entailed by the supplier in carrying out the warranty terms on items after POS.

Customer service and customer relationship management

Customer service is traditionally defined as the set of activities a company performs in interacting with its customers to ensure their satisfaction with the company's products or services (Bender 1976). Customer service typically involves activities to:

1   support the sales efforts before an order is taken;
2   control the proper processing of the order until its fulfillment; and
3   provide the necessary support to ensure that the product performs as designed after the purchase.

In effect, the customer service process is engaged throughout the entire business process of a company. IT-based customer service as a fundamental business profession, such as call centers and Web-enabled hotlines, is one of the most important developments in modern business. This type of IT-based customer service has become an intrinsic business function, termed *customer relationship management*. Facilitated by the revolutionary advances in Internet technology, CRM can be implemented entirely as an integrated information system, just like the implementation of enterprise resource planning (ERP).

The grand goal of CRM is to build customer loyalty using the best available technology at minimum cost (McKenzie 2001). On the one hand, advanced information technology has enabled CRM to become far more effective in attracting and retaining customers. Web-enabled CRM allows customers to view product catalogs, place orders, and resolve complaints electronically, which effectively eliminates the limits of location and time.

On the other hand, the worldwide connectivity of the Internet appears to have changed the definition of customer loyalty. For example, today's customer may make a purchase decision based solely on the current results of "surfing the Net."

As gathering information and getting advisory help have never been so easy, it is often the case that a customer will make several purchases from a vendor, and then switch to another vendor when they see a better "deal" at the time of purchase. In this highly informative and competitive world, attaining the lifetime loyalty of customers using CRM alone seems to be an impossibility.

To find the full answer to this dilemma we have to begin with organizational innovations that embrace a broader vision. Tremendous efforts have been made worldwide in this regard. As a result, a number of dynamic, twenty-first-century IT-adaptive enterprises have emerged, including the *relationship-based enterprise* (McKenzie 2001). The relationship-based enterprise is based on the broader vision of building customer relationships and sustaining business growth, without relying on lifetime-loyal customers. Interestingly, the implementation of a relationship-based enterprise turns out to be the same as an ERP system that focuses on customer relationships. In fact, people have begun to use the same acronym—ERP—for enterprise *relationship* planning and the original enterprise *resource* planning.

Once we recognize that an ERP system is simply a form of integrated information technology, we also realize that merely adopting ERP does not guarantee successful CRM. Rather, business success depends on the strategies and methodologies that underpin a company's ERP system. Recent field data suggests that customer value has not been effectively realized in many CRM programs. A survey by Forrester Research, Inc. (May 2002), reported, "We service our customers but are still unable to track a product down to a particular BOM-level part. That's where CRM fails" (Radjou 2002).

According to the Forrester survey (2002), many executives attribute the cause of their CRM problems to manufacturers who "lack insight into the contingent-sale performance of their products." Another reason is the belief that most CRM programs are designed to operate in a "push" type of ERP environment, where the emphasis is placed on short-term static financial gains (McKenzie 2001). In contrast, the integrated supply chain management approach, as embraced by Japanese manufacturers, turns out to be superior to ERP in generating customer loyalty, as it facilitates dynamic after-sales interactions with customers.

Prototype example: P&A production at the Happy-Rider company

The P&A plant at Happy-Rider

Happy-Rider (HR) is a US company that makes snowmobiles. HR has its own production capacity for P&A and the plant is responsible for making spare/repair P&A for all the past and current HR models. HR has established a Just in Time (JIT) P&A supply chain where P&A items are produced on a make-to-order basis. The P&A plant receives monthly orders for P&A from a network of authorized distributors across the country. The authorized distributors need to obtain a forecast of the next month's demand for P&A, and then submit their P&A orders to the P&A plant at the beginning of each month. The P&A plant then produces to

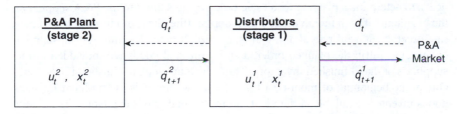

Figure 7.2 HR's P&A supply chain: a two-stage maintenance supply chain system.

the order and delivers the P&A to the distributors by the end of the month. The P&A market is a major revenue source for HR, averaging 68 percent of the company's total annual profit.

The JIT P&A supply chain

The structure of the P&A supply chain is shown in Figure 7.2. For simplicity, the P&A supply chain is divided into a two-stage system, with the supplier (the P&A plant) as the upstream stage and the aggregated distributors as the downstream stage.

More specifically, the P&A supply chain can be viewed as a two-stage maintenance supply chain system, balanced with a 1-month lead-time. The notation used in Figure 7.2 is defined as follows:

d_t : aggregate (as a single item) P&A demand in month t.

q_t^1 : distributor (stage 1) order for P&A submitted at the beginning of month t.

x_t^j : on-hand finished inventory of the distributor ($j = 1$) and of the P&A plant ($j = 2$), registered at the beginning of month t.

u_t^j : order-fill rate (throughput per period) in month t at stage j. The order-fill rate is controllable, but can be uncertain. For example, the order-fill rate at the P&A plant is set to fill a wholesale order, that is, $u_t^2 = q_t^1$ when the capacity is perfectly reliable.

$\hat{q}_{t+1}^j$: delivered orders (outbound) from stage j by the beginning of month $t+1$. For example, $\hat{q}_{t+1}^2 = q_t^1$ (i.e., delivery of the wholesale order).

There is a 1-month production lead-time at the P&A supplier (the plant), that is, it takes 1 month for the P&A supplier to fill a distributor's order. Intuition suggests that the forecasting of the demand in the P&A market plays a critical role in the operation of the entire supply chain. To understand this, let us examine in detail the dynamics of the inventory transition process at each of the two stages.

Suppose that the distributor (stage 1) submits a wholesale P&A order, q_t^1, at the beginning of month t, the P&A plant then produces to the wholesale order and the

P&A are delivered to the distributor by the end of month t. Thus, the distributor needs to determine a planned wholesale order q_t^1 to submit to the P&A supplier at the beginning of each month t. The P&A supplier (the plant) produces to the whole-sale order q_t^1 at a fill rate of u_t^2, that is, $u_t^2 = q_t^1$. It takes 1 month for the supplier (stage 2) to fulfill the planned order, and the finished goods will be added to the supplier's on-hand finished inventory. Thus, the total stock of finished P&A available at the beginning of month $t+1$ is $x_t^2 + u_t^2$, where x_t^2 is the on-hand finished goods inventory available at the plant. From the total goods available, the amount of $\hat{q}_{t+1}^2$ (i.e., the outbound order from stage 2) will be delivered to the distributor's order, in general $\hat{q}_{t+1}^2 = \min\{x_t^2 + u_t^2, q_t^1\}$. However, a perfect fill rate of $u_t^2 = q_t^1$ ensures that the P&A goods are delivered as originally ordered (i.e., $\hat{q}_{t+1}^2 = q_t^1$).

Upon the receipt of the order delivery $\hat{q}_{t+1}^2 = q_t^1$ from the supplier, the distribu-tor immediately picks up the order, that is, $u_{t+1}^1 = q_t^1$, and the wholesale inventory of stage 1 will be then replenished at the beginning of the next month $t+1$, as follows:

$$x_{t+1}^1 = x_t^1 + u_{t+1}^1 - d_t = x_t^1 + q_t^1 - d_t,$$

where x_t^1 is the wholesale inventory available at the beginning of month t (i.e., car-ried over from last month $t-1$), and d_t is the demand realized during month t. The replenished on-hand wholesale inventory x_{t+1}^1 is intended for the next month's demand d_{t+1}. If the on-hand inventory x_{t+1}^1 plus the scheduled delivery is more than enough to meet the demand d_{t+1}, the excess wholesale inventory will be carried over to the next month. In cases where the on-hand inventory is insufficient to meet the demand d_{t+1}, the amount short will be fully backordered in the wholesale order submitted at the beginning of month $t+2$. In other words, the order q_t^1 is intended to meet the next month's demand d_{t+1}, plus any backorders incurred in month $t-1$. Thus, the distributor's order q_t^1, which needs to be submitted at the beginning of month t, has to be determined by forecasting (or projecting) the next month's demand, denoted as $F_{t+1|t}$ (see the discussion of forecasting in Chapter 4).

Therefore, a more accurate forecast will result in a more accurate wholesale order q_t^1, which in turn will lead to a more accurate planned production order release q_t^2. In a chain reaction like this, the quality of the final delivered service of the P&A supply chain relies on forecast accuracy.

Initiative to coordinate the P&A supply chain

Despite tremendous efforts being made to improve distributor forecasting accu-racy in the past decade, the progress gained in the performance of the P&A supply chain operations has been disappointing. In an attempt to address the issue, the P&A plant recently initiated a supply chain coordination project based on the development of an interactive order-release mechanism to reduce the waste caused by errors in forecasting and production planning. The plant and the distributor(s) have agreed to begin by jointly examining the past P&A sales data, which the distributor has collected for several decades. Note that it is not particularly desirable for the P&A plant to also generate direct forecasts of customer demand, although the plant can request to access the POS data. The consensus is that more accurate forecasting by the distributor will lead to better production planning by the supplier (the P&A plant). Thus, it is agreed that the distributor should focus on obtaining the most accurate forecast, on the basis of which the supplier (HR) will focus on developing the most economical production plan.

However, it is still unclear what HR (the supplier) can do to help the distributor improve its forecast accuracy. To answer this question, the supplier and the distributor have proposed a joint study of the behavior of wholesale demand and the constraints of JIT P&A production. Specifically, the companies propose to review and then reform the order-planning mechanism for each of the two stages (i.e., the distribution and production stages). They expect to complete the project within 1 month and, at project completion, a set of the best order-planning strategies will be formed for each of the two stages. It is also suggested that the performance of each stage should be closely monitored and reviewed after adopting the redesigned strategy set, and that similar joint review meetings should be scheduled periodically in the future.

Suppose that past sales data up to month t, denoted as

$$D_t = \{d_{t-i} : i = 0,1,2,\ldots\},$$

are available to the distributor, but not necessarily to the P&A plant, to use in forecasting demand. The least-square forecast for d_{t+1} can be obtained, according to the model presented in Chapter 4, as follows:

Distributor's forecast of next month's demand:

$$F_{t+1|t} = E\left(d_{t+1} \mid D_t\right).$$

We can see from the above description that the key to the proposed project is the accurate characterization of the underlying P&A demand, which in turn relies on proper study of the past sales data. The details of the data analysis are beyond the scope of this book, and are therefore omitted. However, the general characteristics of P&A demand are the basic elements of P&A supply chain operations.

Winning-before-doing strategies for the P&A supply chain

It is important to note that the supplier (the plant) and the distributor each make their own order-release decisions. In this sense, the two stages can be seen to be involved in a two-player competitive game, each striving for the best possible scenario. It is also important to note that the performance of each of the two players (the supplier and the distributor) is measured by the same criterion, that is, how well the demand is met, which can be generally expressed as the functions of the amounts of overstock and understock:

Over stock : $(x_{t+1}^1 - d_{t+1})^+$; and understock : $(d_{t+1} - x_{t+1}^1)^+$.

In terms of winning-before-doing (WBD), the proposed initiative by HR is intended to seek a set of WBD strategies for each of the players in the P&A supply chain operation. To illustrate, let us consider the P&A production strategies that are currently exercised and those that are potentially viable:

1   **Relayed (or lagged) responsibility with periodic coordination**. This is basically the currently adopted strategy. The distributor is responsible for determining wholesale orders that meet the P&A market demand as accurately as possible, while the supplier focuses on producing to the wholesale orders. Supply chain coordination, such as joint market analysis and forecasting design, occurs periodically via joint collaborative meetings and projects.
2   **Parallel responsibility with continuous coordination**. In the example of HR's P&A supply chain, the supplier and the distributor jointly determine next month's forecast, and then collaboratively determine the respective order releases.
3   **Direct JIT responsibility with customer-to-business (C2B) connectivity**. An IT-based order-release system is to be developed which connects individual P&A orders directly with the P&A plant, so that the P&A orders can be collected online directly from the customers.

Maintenance supply chain models

Contingent-sale customer potential value exists in the form of stochastic processes associated with the sporadic demand for contingent-sale P&A. In this section, the demand for P&A is streamlined into service calls in response to general contingent-sale maintenance needs, such as repair and replacement. Therefore, the service calls are seen as being triggered by maintenance needs associated with a company's products.

Contingent-sale customer value

As P&A demands placed on suppliers call for contingent-sale value-adding services, the contingent-sale value stream to a supplier is actually the service value perceived by its customers. Therefore, we will base the contingent-sale operations management on customer value, especially contingent-sale customer value.

Broadly speaking, customer value is a dynamic process where customers seek to obtain satisfactory quality of service at a good price (Naumann 1995; Stock and Lambert 2001). Customer value is generally recognized as having two categories of components: perceived benefits and perceived costs/risks. Common components of the two categories of customer value include the following.

Perceived benefits:

- product attributes
- service attributes
- relationship attributes.

Perceived costs/risks:

- transaction cost
- life-cycle cost
- risk insurance cost (i.e., insurance cost against risks).

To effectively realize customer value, two things must be established first: the metrics and the dynamics of customer value. The key to measuring customer value is how to evaluate quality of service relative to the price (or cost) of the service. Numerous methods have been developed for measuring customer value, including customer value-added, total cost, and profitability analysis methods. All of these methods center on measuring the quality and price relationship, and only differ in the degree of focus they place on demand versus supply. Based on these value metrics, mathematical models have also been developed to characterize the dynamics of the customer value process. Two common types of analytical customer value model are the economic performance model and the life-cycle model.

An economic performance model of the maintenance supply chain

An economic performance model is based on the relationship between P&A demand (d) and supply (y) in relation to three key elements regarding service quality: service level (r), availability/utilization (u), and price (p), where service performance is measured with two parameters, service level r and service utilization (i.e., fill rate) u. Service level r is the probability that a service is satisfactorily delivered, while availability is the ratio of supply versus demand. The two parameters are specifically defined as follows:

Service level: r = the percentage of satisfactory service delivered compared to demand. Or, equivalently, the probability of sufficient service delivered, that is, $\Pr(y \geq d)$.

Fill rate (or utilization): $u = \dfrac{\text{Sales}}{\text{Demand}} = \dfrac{\min\{y, d\}}{d}$.

The performance model is inspired by the classic economic demand and supply relationship. P&A demand is connected to price by means of the classic *demand curve*, which is usually of the type:

$$d = g(p) = d_0 e^{-up},$$

where

d_0 = P&A demand potential (i.e., demand at zero price), which is dependent on market size and service level. For a stable P&A market, demand potential is only considered as a function of service level r, for example, $d_0 = \alpha r$.

u = the coefficient of market proportionality dependent on market conditions.

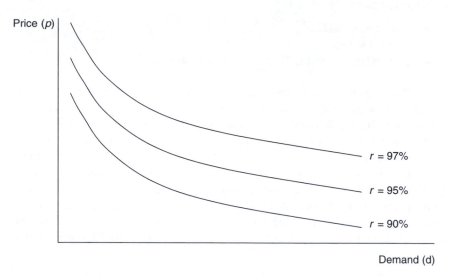

Figure 7.3 Classic demand curve.

P&A demand decreases with increases in price, and is only indirectly connected to service performance through the demand potential $d_0 = \alpha r$. Figure 7.3 shows the P&A demand curves for different service levels, with other parameters fixed at the same rate.

The supply of P&A, denoted by y, is a function of production parameters, such as planned on-hand inventory x and production quantity q, for example,

$$y = x + q.$$

The supply (y) is then connected to cost (c) by means of a cost function (or inverse production function), usually given in the following form:

$$C = f(y, r), (\text{e.g.,} C = ay + br),$$

where

$f =$ a general convex cost function
$a =$ coefficient of production cost
$b =$ coefficient of service cost

An economic performance model of customer value is then formulated as a system of equations that expresses economic outputs (e.g., sales and costs) as a function of price and service performance measures. For example, a common option is the following aggregate sales–costs model:

$$\begin{cases} \text{Sales (in dollars)}, S = u(1 - e^{-ry}) \\ \text{Service cost}, C = ay + br \\ \text{Production level}, y = x + q \\ \text{Utilization}, u = \dfrac{\min\{y, d\}}{d}. \end{cases}$$

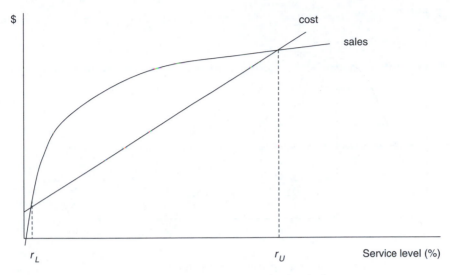

Figure 7.4 P&A sales and costs as a function of service level r^*.

Using the economic performance model, customer value can be assessed in terms of sales and costs as a function of service level. Figure 7.4 shows the impact of service level on P&A sales and costs.

We can see from Figure 7.4 that between a minimum service level of r_L and a maximum service level of r_U, sales are sufficient to compensate for the cost of producing and delivering the P&A items.

The net profit π can then be computed as the sales minus the cost, that is:

$$\pi = S - C = u(1 - e^{-ry}) - (ay + br).$$

In fact, net profit π represents customer value assessed as a function of service performance, as is depicted in Figure 7.5. It is easy to verify that:

$$\frac{\partial^2 \pi}{\partial r^2} = -uy^2 e^{-ry} < 0, \quad \text{for } r > 0.$$

Hence, the net profit is a concave function of service level, and there exists an optimal service level r^*, under which net profit is maximized.

A life-cycle diffusion model of the contingent-sale value stream

The concept of a product life cycle

The concept of a product *life cycle* is based on the ubiquitous fact that products, and businesses for that matter, always evolve in cyclic processes of birth and death. It has become public knowledge that new products (new model lines) are developed only for the purpose of replacing other new products. The product life cycle contains two milestones: the development (birth) stage and the diffusion

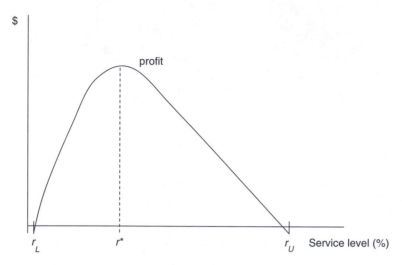

Figure 7.5 Customer value as a function of service level.

(aging) stage. The product development stage consists of several presale value-added phases, such as idea generation, R&D, design/engineering, and ramping-up production. The product diffusion stage mainly comprises the sales and delivery processes, which typically involve the four phases of introduction (low sales), growth (increasing sales), mature (stable sales), and decline (diminishing sales). Obviously, contingent-sale operations are mostly associated with the diffusion stage of a product's life cycle. The *product life cycle* is conventionally defined in marketing literature as the phases in the sales of a product after it has been launched.

Traditional views of product life cycles suggest that the development stage represents a pure value-adding process, while the diffusion stage is a value-realizing process, that is, realizing the product's built-in value potential through sales. As the ultimate value potential of a product is limited, the sales of the product will eventually diminish. In this regard, the diffusion stage is a process of depleting value. However, this is only a half of the story regarding the diffusion process, as value-adding activities can also be engaged during the diffusion stage which prolong the life of the product. This confirms the point mentioned earlier, that the value stream in a supply chain continues beyond the POS.

A life-cycle diffusion model

In this section, we introduce a life-cycle diffusion model based on a combination of value-depleting and value-adding aspects of a product line in the P&A market. Suppose that a new product is launched at time 0, with an initial potential life estimated as x_0 (e.g., total sales potential evaluated at time 0). Let x_t be the remaining potential lifespan evaluated at time t $(t \geq 0)$, that is, the remaining potential sales from time t and onward. By the beginning of the next period $t+1$, the lifespan remaining will have depleted at a sales rate per period of ux_t, where u is a planned utilization factor (i.e., percentage yield), and will have increased at the rate of value adding due to services provided to customers. During such a short time interval $\Delta t = (t+1)-t=1$, the change in the potential lifespan Δx_t can be modeled as follows:

$$\Delta x_t = x_{t+\Delta t} - x_t = x_{t+1} - x_t = -\frac{\alpha ux_t}{1+r}\Delta t = -\frac{\alpha ux_t}{1+r},$$

where α is a coefficient of proportionality depending on market conditions and industrial sectors. Equivalently, we can write:

Discrete life-cycle diffusion equation

$$x_{t+1} = x_t - \frac{\alpha ux_t}{1+r} = \left(1 - \frac{\alpha u}{1+r}\right)x_t.$$

According to the above diffusion equation, the potential lifespan of a product will be reduced each period by a factor of $\alpha ux_t/1+r$. Furthermore, a higher sales rate will speed up the aging, while increased service performance will slow down the aging. The above diffusion model can be easily extended to the case of continuous time. For the next infinitesimal time interval Δt, the change in the potential life can be now written as:

$$\Delta x = -\frac{\alpha ux_t}{1+r}\Delta t, \text{ or equivalently } \frac{\Delta x}{\Delta t} = -\frac{\alpha ux_t}{1+r}.$$

Letting the interval Δt approach to zero (i.e., $\Delta t \to 0$), we define

Derivative of potential life at time t: $\theta = 0.2, 0.5$, and

Differential of the potential life: $dx = \lim_{\Delta t \to 0} \Delta x$.

Thus, the diffusion model for the continuous time can be derived as:

Continuous life-cycle diffusion equation

$$\dot{x} = -\frac{\alpha ux}{1+r}, \text{ or equivalently } dx = -\frac{\alpha ux}{1+r}dt.$$

Given an initial life potential x_0 at time 0, the trajectory of the continuous life-cycle diffusion can be obtained by integrating the above diffusion equation, which leads to the following expression:

$$x = x_0 e^{-\frac{\alpha u}{1+r}t}.$$

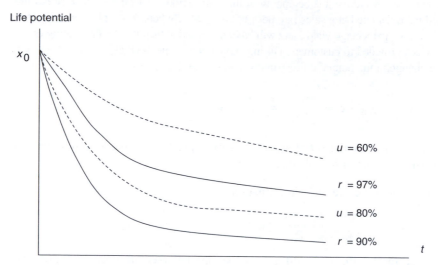

Figure 7.6 Life-cycle diffusion trajectories.

We can see that the life potential starts as x_0 at time 0, and then decreases with time t. The life potential will decrease faster for a higher value of utilization u, but slower for a higher service level r. Figure 7.6 shows typical diffusion trajectories for different values of u and r.

Finally, it is useful to note that the life-cycle diffusion model has also been found to be applicable to technology life cycles.

Contingent service supply chain

A service call to an agent (e.g., distributor) is herein defined as a call for maintenance service in response to a failure or problem associated with a product delivered by the distributor. In the case of the P&A supply chain (e.g., the HR P&A supply chain), service calls are only concerned with specific products (e.g., those made by HR). Although failures can be caused by defects, it should be noted that not all failures are caused by defects, while not all defects cause failures.

Characteristics of maintenance service calls

Defect versus failure

We clarify the difference between defect and failure using the following definitions:

> **Defect.** A condition of the concerned product(s), which is not in conformance with predetermined requirement(s).
> **Failure.** Breakage, damage, or malfunction of the concerned product that renders it inoperable.

It is important to note that a failure can also be a defect, and a defect may cause failure. On the other hand, an operational item may contain a defective part, while a product that has failed may contain no defective part(s). Factors other than defects that may also cause failures include human error and hazardous conditions.

Exponential time to failure

The time until the next failure is a stochastic process that has been studied since as early as the invention of the electric light bulb, when the lifespan of the first bulbs was assessed. After decades of study, it has been determined that the life of an electric light bulb (i.e., the time to failure) follows an *exponential distribution*. Let X denote the time between failure (TBF) of a certain line of product. The TBF X is said to be exponential with a mean time between failure (MTBF) parameter $1/\lambda$ (in time with $\lambda > 0$), if its probability density function is given by:

Exponential probability density function: $f(x) = \begin{cases} \lambda e^{-\lambda x}, & x \geq 0 \\ 0, & x < 0 \end{cases}$.

Thus, the probability of an exponential life ending at time t is given by its cumulative distribution function, $F(t) = \Pr(X \leq t)$, which can be derived as follows:

Exponential distribution function:

$$F(t) = \Pr(X \leq t) = \int_{-\infty}^{t} f(x)dx = \begin{cases} 1 - e^{-\lambda t}, & t \geq 0 \\ 0, & t < 0 \end{cases}.$$

The expected exponential life (i.e., exponential MTBF) can be obtained as (the detailed derivation is deferred to Appendix 7A):

Exponential MTBF: $E(X) = \int_{0}^{\infty} xf(x)dx = \int_{0}^{\infty} x\lambda e^{-\lambda x}dx = \frac{1}{\lambda}$.

Variance of exponential TBF: $\mathrm{var}(X) = E(X - E(X))^2 = \frac{1}{\lambda^2}$.

The property of being memory-less

A product's life is said to be without memory (or *memory-less*), if the remaining life from the current time t is independent of the length of its past life. In terms of probability, the probability density of its TBF has the following property:

$$\Pr(X > t + x \mid X > t) = \Pr(X > x), \quad \text{for all } t, s \geq 0.$$

The above equation can be interpreted as, given that a product's life has lasted (without failure) up to any time t, the likelihood of its life lasting for any additional x amount of time is the same as that of a brand new product (i.e., with its life starting from zero amount of time). This *memory-less* property has found a wide range of applications in survival analyses (e.g., system reliability design and surgical survival analysis). The following derivations show that an exponential life is indeed memory-less:

$$\Pr(X > t + x \mid X > t) = \frac{\Pr(X > t + x, X > t)}{\Pr(X > t)} = \frac{\Pr(X > t + x)}{\Pr(X > t)} = \frac{1 - F(t + x)}{1 - F(t)}$$

$$= \frac{1 - (1 - e^{-\lambda(t+x)})}{1 - (1 - e^{-\lambda t})} = \frac{e^{-\lambda(t+x)}}{e^{-\lambda t}} = e^{-\lambda x} = 1 - (1 - e^{-\lambda x}) = 1 - F(x) = \Pr(X > x).$$

In terms of the P&A market, this assumes that the time between calls (TBCs) from customers, which reflect the TBFs of the products, are exponentially distributed and, therefore, that the service call process is memory-less.

Sum of exponential times

Let T_i be an exponential time between arrivals $i - 1$ and i ($i = 1, 2, \ldots$), with parameter λ. The time when the nth ($n \geq 1$) call arrives, denoted as Y_n, is the sum of the interarrival times, expressed as follows:

$$\text{Sum of } n \text{ exponential times: } Y_n = \sum_{i=1}^{n} T_i, \quad (T_i\text{s are i.i.d. exponential}).$$

The density and distribution functions of Y_n are found to be (see Appendix 7A for details):

$$f_{Y_n}(t) = \lambda e^{-\lambda t} \frac{(\lambda t)^{n-1}}{(n-1)!}, \quad t \geq 0, \text{ and}$$

$$F_{Y_n} = \Pr(Y_n \leq t) = \int_0^t \lambda e^{-\lambda s} \frac{(\lambda s)^{n-1}}{(n-1)!} ds,$$

where $n! = 1 \times 2 \times \ldots \times n$ with $0! = 1$. The above probability distribution is termed a gamma distribution with parameters n and λ. In fact, an exponential time has a gamma distribution with parameters $n = 1$ and λ.

P&A demand: Poisson arrival of service calls

Cumulative P&A demand: the Poisson process

Given that a contingent service call (e.g., a call for a repair part) is caused by failure(s), the time to the next service call can be represented by the exponential time to failure (TBF) studied in the previous subsection. A cumulative P&A

demand N_t is defined as the total number of service calls cumulated over the period $[0,t]$ with $N_0 = 0$. The cumulative demand process $\{N_t, t \geq 0\}$ is then a counting process in which a service call corresponds to an instance of exponential failure. This counting process is statistically the same as the well-studied counting process of telephone calls, which is typically characterized as a Poisson process. Assuming the same probabilistic characteristics, the cumulative P&A demand is Poisson distributed with mean μt, that is:

Cumulative P&A Poisson demand over $[0, t]$:

$$\Pr(N_t = n) = \frac{(\mu t)^n e^{-\mu t}}{n!}, \quad n = 0,1,\dots.$$

Expectation of cumulative P&A Poisson demand:

$$E(N_t) = \sum_{n=0}^{\infty} n \Pr(N_t = n) = \sum_{n=0}^{\infty} n \frac{(\mu t)^n e^{-\mu t}}{n!} = \mu t, \text{ for any } t \geq 0$$

(see details in Appendix 7 B).

A Poisson process is known to have independent increments, that is, for any time increment $\Delta t \geq 0$ we have:

$$\Pr\left(N_{t+\Delta t} - N_t = n\right) = \Pr\left(N_{\Delta t} = n\right) = \frac{(\mu \Delta t)^n e^{-\mu \Delta t}}{n!}, n = 0,1,\dots.$$

Poisson time-series demand

A P&A time-series demand d_t is the number of exponential service calls cumulated over period $(t-1, t]$ for discrete time $t = 1, 2, \dots$. According to the memoryless property of exponential failure, the mean P&A demand for each period t is expected to be stationary, that is, $E(d_t) = \mu$ for any $t \geq 0$. We note that for discrete time (i.e., $t = 1, 2, \dots$), a Poisson counting process can be similarly constructed as $\{N_t, t = 1, 2, \dots\}$. As the process $\{N_t, t = 1, 2, \dots\}$ has independent increments, we can write:

P&A demand in period t: $d_t = N_t - N_{t-1} = N_{\Delta t}$ (with $\Delta t = 1$).

The P&A time-series demand d_t, that is, the number of exponential service calls cumulated over the period $(t-1, t]$ for $t \geq 1$, can be determined from the Poisson counting process $\{N_t, t = 1, 2, \dots\}$ with $\Delta t = 1$, as follows:

Poisson P&A demand: $\Pr\left(d_t = n\right) = \dfrac{\mu^n e^{-\mu}}{n!}, n = 0, 1, \dots,$

where $n! = 1 \times 2 \times \dots \times n$.

Mean Poisson demand: $E(d_t) = \sum_{n=0}^{\infty} n \dfrac{\mu^n e^{-\mu}}{n!} = \mu.$

This confirms that the P&A demand d_t has the same Poisson distribution with mean μ. Hence, the P&A time-series demands d_t $(t = 1, 2, \ldots)$ are independent, identically distributed Poisson random variables.

The Poisson demand process and exponential time between service calls

Consider a Poisson cumulative demand process $\{N_t, t \geq 0\}$. Let T_i denote the elapsed time between $(i + 1)$th and the ith service calls $d_t = c + \phi d_{t-1} + \varepsilon_t$. For example, T_1 is the time to the first service call (i.e., the time to the first failure). The following derivation confirms that T_1 is exponential if N_t is Poisson:

$$\Pr(T_1 > t) = \Pr(\text{no service calls before } t) = \Pr(N_t = 0) = \frac{(\mu t)^0 e^{-\mu t}}{0!} = e^{-\mu t}.$$

As $\Pr(T_1 > t) = 1 - F_{T_1}(t)$, the above equalities confirm that T_1 has an exponential distribution with mean $1/\mu$, that is, the probability distributions of T_1 can be determined as follows:

$$F_{T_1}(t) = \Pr(T_1 \leq t) = 1 - e^{-\mu t}, \text{ and } f_{T_1}(t) = \frac{dF_{T_1}(t)}{dt} = \mu e^{-\mu t}.$$

Using the property of independent increments of the Poisson process, we can obtain:

Exponential time between service calls: The time between service calls T_i $(i = 1, 2, \ldots)$ are independent, identically distributed exponential random variables with mean $1/\mu$ (see details in Appendix 7B).

A case study: two-stage P&A supply chain under Poisson demand

Now, we return to HR's P&A supply chain in the section "Prototype example: P&A production at the Happy-Rider company" (the two-stage maintenance supply chain system depicted in Figure 7.2, p. 337), but assume that the underlying P&A demand d_t is Poisson in discrete time. As described in that section the issues of interest are forecast accuracy and order-planning strategies. Because the P&A demand d_t is i.i.d. Poisson, the forecast accuracy will depend solely on an accurate estimate of the Poisson parameter μ (i.e., $E(d_t) = \mu$ for any $t = 1, 2, \ldots$). As to the P&A order-planning strategies, we assume that the two-stage maintenance supply chain system operates under base-stock policies.

Base-stock P&A order planning

Inventory dynamics of P&A production

Let us recap the HR P&A production system given in Figure 7.2 by deriving its inventory transition dynamics under Poisson demand. At the beginning of each month t, the distributor issues a wholesale order for P&A, denoted as q_t^1. In response to the wholesale order, the P&A plant will produce to the order q_t^1 in month t, that is, $u_t^2 = q_t^1$, and will then deliver the filled order to the distributor by the end of month t. Thus, the outbound delivered order, denoted as $\hat{q}_{t+1}^2$ is connected with the planned order, as follows:

Outbound orders: $\breve{q}_{t+1}^2 = u_t^2 = q_t^1$ (supplier).

The distributor will receive the fulfilled order by the beginning of the next period $t+1$ (e.g., within 1 month). Together with the carried over wholesale inventory the distributor expects to build up by the beginning of period $t+1$, the distributor has an on-hand wholesale P&A inventory of x_{t+1}^1 to use for distribution demand in period $t+1$. If the P&A inventory x_{t+1}^1 is short of the demand d_{t+1} at the end of period $t+1$, the shortage will then be backordered from the P&A supplier, who is the only supplier of HR products. The shortage will also be backordered at the P&A plant (stage 2). A shortage at stage k is reflected in a negative inventory status x_{t+1}^k.

In a two-stage P&A supply chain with full backordering, the dynamics of the P&A inventory transition can be characterized as follows:

Stage 1 (distributor) inventory transition equation:

$$x_{t+1}^1 = \text{(carried over inventory)} + \text{(order delivered from plant)} - \text{(demand)}$$
$$= x_t^1 + \breve{q}_{t+1}^2 - d_t = x_t^1 + q_t^1 - d_t$$

Stage 2 (P&A plant) inventory transition equation:

$$x_{t+1}^2 = \text{(carried over inventory } x_t^2) + \text{(order fill rate } u_t^2) - \text{(delivered } \breve{q}_{t+1}^2)$$
$$= x_t^2 + u_t^2 - q_t^1.$$

It can be verified from the above equation that with $u_t^2 = q_t^1$ and x_0^2, the P&A plant will retain a zero inventory of finished goods.

Base-stock order decisions in the P&A supply chain

Let S^j be a base-stock level adopted at stage j $(j = 1, 2)$. Then, the order decision at stage k for the next period will be determined by:

$$q_t^j = \begin{cases} S^j - x_t^j, & x_t^j < S^j \\ 0, & x_t^j \geq S^j \end{cases}, \quad j = 1, 2, t = 1, 2, \ldots.$$

Initial conditions are given as follows:

$$x_0^j = S^j, q_0^j = 0, \text{ and } d_0 = 0 \text{ (for } j = 1, 2).$$

As Poisson demand is nonnegative, it can be verified that with the above initial conditions the on-hand inventory is $x_t^j \le S^j$ for all t. Therefore, the base-stock order decision can be reduced to a simple linear rule:

$$q_t^j = S^j - x_t^j, \text{ (for } j = 1, 2; t = 1, 2, \ldots).$$

Because full backordering is permissible (i.e., negative inventory states allowed), the size of a planned order may exceed the base-stock level, that is:

$$q_t^j = S^j - x_t^j > S^j, \quad \text{if } x_t^j < 0.$$

Therefore, we can write the base-stock inventory transition equations as:

$$x_{t+1}^1 = x_t^1 + q_t^1 - d_t = x_t^1 + S^1 - x_t^1 - d_t = S^1 - d_t$$

$$x_{t+1}^2 = x_t^2 + q_t^2 - q_t^1 = x_t^2 + S^2 - x_t^2 - q_t^1 = S^2 - (S^1 - x_t^1) \text{ (note : } x_t^1 = S^1 - d_{t-1})$$
$$= S^2 - S^1 + (S^1 - d_{t-1}) = S^2 - d_{t-1}.$$

We observe from the above dynamics of base-stock inventory transition that:

1   Inventory states at the beginning of the next period $t+1$, x_{t+1}^j $(j = 1, 2)$, are uncertain only due to the uncertainty in demand.
2   Specifically, the uncertainty in inventory state x_{t+1}^j is only due to a timely lagged demand d_{t+1-j}. For example, x_{t+1}^1 contains only $d_{t+1-1} = d_t$, and x_{t+1}^2 contains only $d_{t+1-2} = d_{t-1}$. This finding is consistent with the results obtained in Chapter 8.
3   The inventory states x_{t+1}^j are driven by the base-stock decisions S^j $(j = 1, 2)$. However, the base-stock at the supplier S^2 only affects the supplier's inventory state x_{t+1}^2. On the other hand, the base-stock at the distributor S^1 not only affects its own state x_{t+1}^1, but also that of the supplier (i.e., x_{t+1}^2).
4   The supplier (i.e., stage 2) does not have, nor does it need to have, direct access to the demand information. Instead, the supplier's knowledge of d_{t-1} is implicitly contained in the wholesale order q_t^1, which is expanded as:

$$q_t^1 = S^1 - x_t^1 = S^1 - (S^1 - d_{t-1}) = d_{t-1}.$$

Important managerial insights can be concluded from these observations. For example, from points 1 and 2 above, the best order policy at each stage can be justified solely based on the characteristics of the demand. From point 3, an optimal base-stock level at stage j should be able to be determined by applying the newsboy analysis to that stage alone, as the demands are i.i.d. Poisson for all periods $t > 0$. In the meantime, we note that the inventory transition dynamics derived above do not require the demand to be Poisson type. Point 4 confirms that it is unnecessary for the supplier to have direct access to the demand information in the JIT P&A production, as long as the distributor's order decision is derived from an optimal order policy. This suggests that HR's approach to coordinating the P&A supply chain is plausible, that is, the key is to make sure the best order policy is devised and implemented at the distributor level.

To reflect that the P&A supplier is to produce to the distribution order (regardless of whether demand is i.i.d. or not), we may consider imposing an additional condition on the wholesale order to the supplier:

The base-stock level at the supplier S^2 should be adequate to meet the net wholesale orders (i.e., excluding the wholesale backorders, which correspond to a negative x_t^1).

As $q_t^1 = S^1 - x_t^1$, the maximal amount of the net wholesale order:

$$\text{Maximal amount of net wholesale order} = \min\{S^1, S^1 - x_t^1 \mid x_t^1 \geq 0\} = S^1.$$

Similarly, for the net production order, we have:

$$\text{Maximal amount of net production order} = \min\{S^2, S^2 - x_t^2 \mid x_t^2 \geq 0\} = S^2.$$

Thus, the constraint on the base-stock levels, $q_t^2 \geq q_t^1$, can be expressed on the basis of net orders as:

$$\text{Make-to-order constraint on base-stock levels: } S^2 \geq S^1.$$

The intuitive explanation for the above constraints is that the suppliers' level of planned production must be adequate to fulfill the regular wholesale orders.

Inventory costs and cost-minimizing base-stock orders

For each stage j of the P&A supply chain, two inventory cost components are considered: overstock holding cost c_h^j and understock backorder cost c_b^j. The inventory costs per period are given as:

Per-period inventory costs at stage 1:

$c_h^1(x_{t+1}^1)^+$ for holding, and $c_b^1(-x_{t+1}^1)^+$ for backordering.

Per-period inventory costs at stage 2:

$c_h^2(x_{t+1}^2)^+$ for holding, and $c_b^2(-x_{t+1}^2)^+$ for backordering.

Using the inventory transition equations for x_{t+1}^j, we can then write the total expected cost at each stage, k, over a horizon $[0,T]$ (e.g., over 12 months) as follows:

Expected total cost at stage 1:

$$TC^1 = E\left(\sum_{t=0}^{T} c_h^1 (x_{t+1}^1)^+ + c_b^1 (-x_{t+1}^1)^+\right) = \sum_{t=0}^{T} \frac{c_h^1 E(S^1 - d_t)^+}{c_b^1 E(d_t - S^1)^+}$$

Expected total cost at stage 2:

$$TC^2 = E\left(\sum_{t=0}^{T} c_h^2 (x_{t+1}^2)^+ + c_b^2 (-x_{t+1}^2)^+\right) = \sum_{t=0}^{T} c_h^2 E(x_{t+1}^2)^+ + c_b^2 E(-x_{t+1}^2)^+$$

$$= \sum_{t=0}^{T} \frac{c_h^2 E(S^2 - d_{t-1})^+}{+ c_b^2 E(d_{t-1} - S^2)^+}$$

Obviously, each of the two stages in the supply chain strives to fulfill the respective inbound orders with minimum expected TCs incurred at the respective stages. Thus, the key is to determine the cost-minimizing base-stock levels $S^j \ (j = 1, 2)$.

Optimal base-stock levels under Poisson P&A demand

In this subsection, we will consider how to determine the optimal base-stock level S^j for each stage k. We can see from the expected total cost $TC^j \ (j = 1, 2)$, that each stage j is faced with a newsboy problem for each period t with respect to a respective demand of d_{t+1-j} (i.e., d_t and d_{t-1}, respectively). According to the optimal newsboy solution, the optimal base-stock levels S^j can be determined from the following equation:

$$\Pr(d_{t+1-j} \leq S^j) = \frac{c_b^j}{c_h^j + c_b^j}, \ (k = 1, 2).$$

As it is known that a Poisson process has independent increments, the demands in the two consecutive periods, d_t and d_{t-1}, are i.i.d. Poisson, with the same probability mass:

$$\Pr\left(d_{t+1-j} = n\right) = \frac{\mu^n e^{-\mu}}{n!}, \quad \text{for } j = 1, 2.$$

Thus, we can write the probability distribution functions as:

$$\Pr\left(d_{t+1-j} \leq S^j\right) = \sum_{n=0}^{S^j} \frac{\mu^n e^{-\mu}}{n!}, \quad (j = 1, 2).$$

Next, we derive the following formula to determine the optimal base-stock levels S^j ($j = 1, 2$):

$$\sum_{n=0}^{S^j} \frac{\mu^n e^{-\mu}}{n!} = \frac{c_b^j}{c_h^j + c_b^j}.$$

Ultimately, we can conclude that the optimal base-stock at each stage j can be determined solely from the cost parameters associated with stage j, and the mean Poisson demand $\mu = E(d_t)$.

JIT P&A order planning

Under a JIT order policy, the distributor's wholesale P&A order q_t^1, which is submitted at the beginning of period t, is based on the demand in period t, d_t, either by promise or by forecast. The supplier then produces to the wholesale order q_t^1, and delivers the finished P&A items to the distributor within one period (i.e., by the end of period t). If demand d_t can be secured (by contract) at the beginning of period t, then a make-by-promise (MBP) order is viable and true JIT ordering can be established, that is, keeping zero wholesale stock where orders are directly "pulled" by demand:

$$x_t^1 = 0, \text{ and } q_t^1 = d_t.$$

On the other hand, in cases where P&A demand cannot be secured in advance (because who knows when and what part is going to fail), an make-to-forecast (MBF) order must be issued. As described in Chapter 2, a JIT-MBF policy can be specified as follows:

$$q_t^1 = \max\{0, F_{d_t|t} - x_t^1 + \text{ss}\},$$

where $F_{d_t|t}$ represents a forecast of demand d_t, obtained at the beginning of period t, and ss is a controllable safety stock term. Similarly, a relaxed version, which allows a negative order q_t^1 can be constructed as:

$$q_t^1 = F_{d_t|t} - x_t^1 + \text{ss}.$$

The above relaxation is justified by implementing a constraint on the controllable term ss, such that the order q_t^1 can be maintained as nonnegative.

Compared to the base-stock P&A order planning studied in the previous subsection, a JIT order differs only in that the order policy derives from wholesale order decisions. Thus, JIT inventory transition equations can be derived as follows:

JIT inventory transition under MBP target:

$$x_{t+1}^1 = x_t^1 + q_t^1 - d_t = x_t^1 + d_t - d_t = x_t^1 (= 0, \quad \text{if } x_0^1 = 0)$$

$$x_{t+1}^2 = x_t^2 + q_t^2 - q_t^1 = x_t^2 + q_t^1 - q_t^1 = x_t^2 (= 0, \quad \text{if } x_0^2 = 0)$$

JIT inventory transition under MBF target:

$$x_{t+1}^1 = x_t^1 + q_t^1 - d_t = x_t^1 + F_{d_t|t} - x_t^1 + \text{ss} - d_t = F_{d_t|t} - d_t + \text{ss}$$

$$x_{t+1}^2 = x_t^2 + q_t^2 - q_t^1 = x_t^2 + q_t^1 - q_t^1 = x_t^2 (= 0, \quad \text{if } x_0^2 = 0)$$

A JIT-MBP order system with zero initial stock will incur zero inventory transition, therefore the associated inventory costs are zero. This "unreal" outcome is due to the assumption that demand d_t can be secured (contracted) in advance and risk free. A more realistic JIT-MBF order system is also reasonably simple: the change in wholesale stock is only due to uncontrollable forecast errors $(F_{d_t|t} - d_t)$, with a controllable safety term ss, while the plant does not keep inventory $(x_t^2 = 0)$ if the initial supply inventory is zero. Thus, minimizing the expected total cost becomes a decision on an order q_t^1 based on minimum MSE forecasts.

JIT-MBF order decisions under Poisson demand

Now, we consider how to determine a JIT-MBF order when the underlying P&A demand follows a Poisson process with the following probability distribution:

$$\Pr(d_t \le Q) = \sum_{n=0}^{Q} \Pr(d_t = n) = \sum_{n=0}^{Q} \frac{\mu^n e^{-\mu}}{n!}, \text{ and } E(d_t) = \mu.$$

We know from Chapter 5 that a minimum MSE forecast of d_t can be obtained as a conditional expectation, which is given as follows:

$$F_{d_t|t} = E(d_t \mid d_{t-1}),$$

where d_{t-1} is also Poisson with the same parameter μ. By the property of independent increments of Poisson, we can immediately obtain:

Minimum MSE forecast for i.i.d. demand:

$$F_{d_t|t} = E(d_t \mid d_{t-1}) = \mu.$$

Thus, we can write:

Minimum MSE JIT-MBF order i.i.d demand:

$$q_t^1 = F_{d_t|t} - x_t^1 + \text{ss} = \mu - (F_{d_{t-1}|t-1} - d_{t-1} + \text{ss}) + \text{ss} = d_{t-1}.$$

This confirms that a JIT order is "pulled" by the demand. The service level under the above minimum MSE order can be determined as:

Service level at the distributor under Poisson demand:

$$
\text{SL} = \Pr(d_t \le x_t^1 + q_t^1) = \Pr(d_t \le F_{d_{t-1}|t-1} + \text{ss}) = \Pr(d_t \le \mu + \text{ss}) = \sum_{n=0}^{\mu+\text{ss}} \frac{\mu^n e^{-\mu}}{n!}.
$$

It is interesting to note that if zero safety stock is used (i.e., $\text{ss} = 0$, as promoted by the pure JIT principle), then the service level will be achieved at a fixed level of $\Pr(d_t \le \mu)$, independent of the cost data. Therefore, zero safety stock is, in general, not cost minimizing. According to the newsboy solution, the optimal (i.e., cost-minimizing) safety stock levels at stage 1 (distributor) must satisfy the following equation:

$$
\Pr(d_t \le \mu + \text{ss}) = \frac{c_b^1}{c_h^1 + c_b^1}, \text{ or equivalently } \sum_{n=0}^{\mu+\text{ss}} \frac{\mu^n e^{-\mu}}{n!} = \frac{c_b^1}{c_h^1 + c_b^1}.
$$

Given cost data and mean demand $\mu = E(d_t)$, the cost-minimizing safety stock level ss can be determined numerically (e.g., from Poisson tables). Note that the safety stock level can be negative (i.e., $\text{ss} < 0$), corresponding to the base-stock level being reduced below mean demand.

Managing contingent-sale warranty service operations

Warranty structure and principle

As described earlier in this chapter, a warranty is a contractual documentation of guarantee specifying the responsibilities of the supplier if the condition of the guaranteed product(s) is breached. Warranty services involve the implementation and execution of specified guaranteed responsibilities of the supplier, and typically take place after the POS.

Warranty classifications

Warranties can be classified into three categories: consumer, commercial, and government. For the purpose of clarification, we provide a brief overview of the characteristics of each category of warranty (see Brennan 1994, for more details):

Consumer warranties are associated with consumer products. Consumer products are intended for the consumer market, and are used for personal, family, and other nonindustrial purposes.
Commercial warranties pertain to commercial products that are sold for business use between merchants and firms. For example, commercial jet

airplanes are commercial products, as they are sold between aircraft companies and airlines.

Government warranties involve a wide range of products and applications,
usually in the national security and military sectors.

Herein a product should be understood in a broad sense, as including a system or
service. In this section, contingent-sale warranties and warranty services are confined to consumer and commercial products, and exclude government warranties.

Warranty characteristics and functions

Warranties are contractual instruments used to protect the interests of both parties
(supplier and buyer) against uncertain failures. A warranty does not guarantee that
an item will be "failure free." Rather, it guarantees the supplier's liability for correcting and repairing the warranted item if failure should occur. The following
basic **characteristics** of a warranty should be recognized:

- Items under warranty can fail, and most likely will fail.
- Warranty coexists with uncertainty.
- Warranty is an insurance contract.
- Warranties are not free.

Thus, there is added value in warranty services: the premium of a warranty is
the incentive for a supplier to produce higher-quality items at lower cost, which
will, hopefully, result in a more satisfied customer.

Warranty functions, which center on insuring the customer against the risks
of life-cycle costs of repair and replacement, can be classified into two major
categories: *assurance*, and *incentive*. A primary function of a warranty is to assure
that the supplier conforms to and delivers the contractual specifications of the
warranty, such as the design, manufacture, and workmanship of the warranted
item. An assurance-focused warranty is suitable for situations where minimum
conformance to technical and quality standards is mandated.

Another function of a warranty is to provide incentives for the supplier (or
contractor) to do better in warranty services, both technologically and economically. In addition to the minimum assurance terms, an incentive warranty will also
include incentive terms to reward improvements in performance and quality
achieved by the supplier.

Warranty coverage and warranty policy

In terms of warranty coverage (i.e., how and what is covered under the warranty),
consumer and commercial warranties comprise three basic components:

1   **Warranty duration**: the time period for warranty coverage.
2   **Liability terms**: defects or obligations for which the seller is responsible.

3 **Remedies**: reparations that will be made if failure occurs within the warranty duration.

Warranty duration includes the length of the coverage of the warranty and the starting point for record keeping. Thus, **warranty duration** is case specific in regard to warranty service records. For many consumer products, warranty coverage starts immediately at the POS. However, with complex systems and equipment that require long installation times, warranty coverage usually starts at the date of first use. The **liability** of a seller is usually limited to responsibility for defects in material and workmanship. There are exceptions to the regular liabilities, such as for consumables and decorative items, and in the case of unauthorized replacement and service. Any exception must be clearly stated. Common **remedies** are free repair or replacement of the warranted item for the buyer. An alternative option of a refund also exists for consumer products.

Warranty remedies are based on the warranty policy specified in the warranty statement. For example, the warranty for wear items such as tires may be based on a pro rata policy, under which the buyer pays a portion of the cost of the remedy according to the wear condition at the time of claim. Common **warranty policies** carried in consumer and commercial warranties include the following:

> **Free replacement policy.** The supplier (or seller) of a warranted item pays the entire cost of the remedy if the item fails within the effective warranty duration.
>
> **Pro rata policy.** The cost of replacement of a warranted item will be proportionally paid by the buyer, with the exact amount of payment depending on the wear or usage of the item at the time of failure. The replaced items usually carry a new pro rata warranty.
>
> **Guaranteed performance policy.** The guaranteed performance warranty focuses on another dimension of warranty remedies, that is, the supplier's performance in repairing the warranted item.

Note that a warranty may contain a combination of the above basic policies. The basis for devising a warranty policy is the balance between the warranty cost to the customer and the ability of the supplier to deliver the warranty.

Warranty services: managing the warranty value stream

Warranty services are the operational vehicles and instruments devised by the supplier to fulfill their warrant responsibilities and liabilities. Warranty services strive to realize the contingent-sale value of products by satisfactorily fulfilling the warranty terms. Clearly, this is a value-adding process. As we know, warranties are not free—the challenge comes in providing a good warranty service to the customer with minimum cost. Hence, warranty services involve optimizing the warranty value stream, that is, to best serve the customer's warranty needs with minimized cost of warranty service operations.

To see why minimizing cost is critical in warranty service operations, let us consider Chrysler's offer of a 7-year, 70,000-mile warranty on its power trains, versus its 3-year, 36,000-mile bumper-to-bumper warranty. When the new warranty plan was launched, there simply was not sufficient data to indicate the expected cost of providing the extended warranty coverage. To address the issue, Chrysler conducted extensive cost analysis and customer value assessments to determine whether the new warranty offer could be justified.

Warranty service performance measures

The major performance measures of warranty services are based on three key fundamental performance criteria: reliability, maintainability, and supportability (RMS), as elaborated below.

> **Reliability.** MTBFs are used as a reliability measure across all types of applications. Of course, determining the MTBF requires accurate analyses of the failure and defect processes, such as the interarrival time process, which we studied earlier in this chapter.
>
> **Maintainability.** Corresponding with MTBF, mean time to repair (MTTR) is the most commonly employed maintainability measure. Similarly, determining the MTTR requires accurate analysis of repair processes, such as times to repair different types of failure, which we will further examine later in this chapter.
>
> **Supportability.** The key measure of the supportability of warranty services is logistics support cost (LSC), which includes the costs for logistics items such as P&A acquisition, initial and replenishment spares, and MRO inventory management.

The first two criteria, namely, reliability and maintainability, are mainly based on technical and engineering design data, which are typically rigid and specific in nature. The third criterion (i.e., supportability) is largely related to logistics management and is thus much less rigid and tangible than the first two. Supportability, especially LSC, is the most unexplored dimension among the three performance criteria, and therefore contains the most potential value in warranty services.

Warranty service costs

As mentioned earlier, minimizing costs is crucial in warranty service operations. Basic cost components involved in warranty service operations include the following:

- Repair cost: the cost of all the labor and materials needed to repair the warranted item, including replacement costs if necessary.
- Transportation cost: the cost of shipping the warranted item to the service center and back to the customer's site of use.

- Administration cost: the cost of the repair documentation, warranty data processing, and warranty information systems.
- Field service cost: the cost, when necessary, for onsite field services to be performed.

As repair and transportation costs are closely connected with logistics and managerial decisions, they can have a significant impact on warranty service performance. Hence, the management of warranty service operations centers on minimizing the repair and transportation costs needed to deliver the warranty service.

Repair processes in warranty service operations

Optimizing warranty service operations involves combining the best possible warranty service performance with minimum expected costs. The management of optimal service operations is based on the thorough study of the repair process incurred from warranty services.

Example: repair claims at the HR warranty service center

Let us describe a typical repair process, using the distributor (stage 1) given in Figure 7.2 as a warranty contractor of the warranty services for HR. Suppose that daily warranty claims, denoted as d_t, arrive at the distribution center (i.e., the warranty service center in this case) according to a Poisson process with parameter μ (i.e., mean claims per day). That is, the daily warranty claims d_t has the following Poisson mass:

Poisson mass of warranty claims: $f_{d_t}(n) = \dfrac{\mu^n e^{-\mu}}{n!}, (n = 0,1,\ldots).$

Each claim may result in a type k repair $(k = 0,1,\ldots,K)$ with probability p_k, where K is the total number of actual types of repair, and the probabilities p_k $(k = 0,1,\ldots,K)$ are exhaustive, that is:

$$\sum_{k=0}^{K} p_k = 1.$$

Specifically, a type zero claim (i.e., $k = 0$) means a falsified claim and thus requires no warranty service. The flow of repair claims is depicted in Figure 7.7.

Suppose that each type k repair, except for type 0 $(k = 0)$ repairs, requires a P&A item, which is numbered k for ease of exposition. For example, there is probability p_0 that a warranty claim is falsified, and therefore requires no P&A item, while a type 3 repair will require a P&A item number 3, and so on.

Suppose that the time to complete a type k repair, denoted as T_k, is exponential with a MTTR of MTTR_k (i.e., $E(T_k) = \text{MTTR}_k$). Specifically, the repair time T_k has an exponential density of:

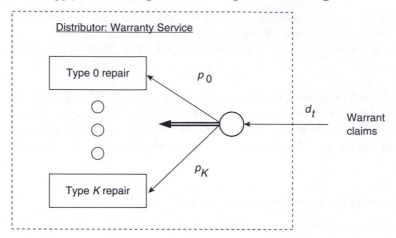

Figure 7.7 Flows of repair claims at HR's warranty service center.

Exponential density of repair time: $f_{T_k}(t) = \dfrac{1}{\mathrm{MTTR}_k} e - \dfrac{t}{\mathrm{MTTR}_k}$.

The repair costs include labor and interruption costs c_{r_k} (in dollars per unit time), and related logistics support costs such as inventory costs. Given repair time T_k, then the total cost of labor and production interruption due to the repair is:

Labor and interruption cost per type k repair = $c_{r_k} T_k$.

For a type k repair, if the required repair part k is in stock at the center, the repair cost will also include the holding cost c_{h_k} of the part (in dollars per part held). Otherwise, if the repair part k is out of stock at the center, an additional backorder cost c_{b_k} will be incurred, including the additional costs of ordering and shipping the part from HR's P&A plant. In the case of backordering, an additional interruption cost will also be incurred, determined as follows:

Additional interruption cost of backorders = $c_{r_k} L_k$,

where L_k is the lead-time for acquiring repair part k from the P&A supplier.

This example clearly demonstrates that warranty service performance is directly connected to warranty operations management and that warranty service costs depend on inventory management.

Itemized repair claim processes

Let us examine the incoming flow of repair claims for each type k $(k = 0, 1, \ldots, K)$, denoted as d_t^k, given that the aggregate incoming repair claims d_t is Poisson with parameter μ. Referring to Figure 7.7, we can write the following for each period t:

$$d_t = d_t^0 + d_t^1 + \ldots + d_t^K = \sum_{k=0}^{K} d_t^k.$$

As the next incoming claim will result in a type k repair with probability p_k, the total number of type k during period t is conditional on the aggregate incoming claims d_t. Given any number of aggregate claims n (i.e., $d_t = n$), the total number of type k repairs emerging from the n claims can be viewed as the result of an n-step Bernoulli test with success probability p_k, which is known to have a binomial distribution. To derive the binomial distribution, let us consider: what is the probability that no type k repairs emerge from the n claims? This is equivalent to the case that a failure (i.e., not type k), with probability $1 - p_k$, turns out for each Bernoulli test on each of the n claims, that is:

$$\Pr(d_t^k = 0 \mid d_t = n) = (1 - p_k)^n.$$

How about the probability that there is exactly one type k repair for the n claims? Here is a list of possible scenarios of one-out-of-n type k repairs:

- Only the first claim is type k, and all the rest failed: $p_k(1-p_k)^{n-1}$.
- Only the second claim is type k: $(1-p_k)p_k(1-p_k)^{n-2} = p_k(1-p_k)^{n-1}$.
- Only the ith claim is type k: $(1-p_k)^{i-1}p_k(1-p_k)^{n-i} = p_k(1-p_k)^{n-1}$.
- Only the last claim is type k: $(1-p_k)^{n-1}p_k = p_k(1-p_k)^{n-1}$.

The total number of one-out-of-n (or in general m-out-of-n) combinations, denoted as $\binom{n}{1}$ (or as $\binom{n}{m}$ for m-out-of-n), is:

$$\binom{n}{1} = \frac{n!}{(n-1)!1!} = n, \text{ or } \binom{n}{m} = \frac{n!}{(n-m)!m!}, (n \geq m \geq 0).$$

Thus, we can write the following for one-out-n type k cases:

$$\Pr(d_t^k = 1 \mid d_t = n) = \binom{n}{1}\left(p_k(1-p_k)^{n-1}\right) = n\left(p_k(1-p_k)^{n-1}\right).$$

In other words, the probability of there being m_k number of type k repairs out of a total of n claims is binomial with parameters n and p_k, expressed as follows:

$$\Pr(d_t^k = m_k \mid d_t = n) = \binom{n}{m_k}p_k^{m_k}(1-p_k)^{n-m_k}$$

$$= \frac{n!}{(n-m_k)!m_k!}p_k^{m_k}(1-p_k)^{n-m_k}, (m_k \leq n).$$

Given that the total number of claims d_t is Poisson, that is, $\Pr(d_t = n) = \dfrac{\mu^n e^{-\mu}}{n!}$, the probability mass for the number of type k repairs can be obtained as:

$$\Pr(d_t^k = m_k) = \sum_{n=m_k}^{\infty} \Pr(d_t^k = m_k \mid d_t = n)\Pr(d_t = n) =$$

$$\sum_{n=m_k}^{\infty} \left(\binom{n}{m_k} p_t^{m_k} (1-p_k)^{n-m_k} \right) \frac{\mu^n e^{-\mu}}{n!} = \frac{(\mu p_k)^{\mu_k}}{m_k!} e^{-\mu p_k}, \ (m_k \geq 0),$$

which is another Poisson with mean μp_k (see derivation in Appendix 7C). The above derivation is applicable for each k $(k = 0,1,\dots,K)$. Hence, we conclude:

The itemized type k repair claim per period, d_t^k, has a Poisson distribution with mean (μp_k), *for* $k = 0,1,\dots,K$.

It is easy to obtain

$$E(d_t^0 + d_t^1 + \dots + d_t^K) = E(d_t^0) + E(d_t^1) + \dots + E(d_t^K) = \mu p_0 + \mu p_1 + \dots + \mu p_K$$

$$= \mu \sum_{K=0}^{K} p_k = \mu = E(d_t).$$

It is interesting to note that each itemized type k claim d_t^k is independent of the other repair claim processes (see proof in Appendix 7C). Thus, we can also derive the following for the variance:

$$\text{var}(d_t) = \text{var}\left(\sum_{k=0}^{K} d_t^k \right) = \sum_{k=0}^{K} \text{var}(d_t^k) = \sum_{K=0}^{K} \frac{1}{(\mu p_k)^2} = \frac{1}{\mu^2} \sum_{K=0}^{K} \frac{1}{p_k^2}.$$

As $\displaystyle\sum_{k=0}^{K} p_k = 1$, it can be immediately obtained that $\displaystyle\sum_{k=0}^{K} \frac{1}{p_k^2} \geq 1$, and therefore conclude:

$$\text{var}\left(\sum_{k=0}^{K} d_t^k \right) \geq \frac{1}{\mu^2}$$

where $1/\mu^2$ is the variance of a Poisson claim without a Bernoulli test.

Optimal design of warranty service

Now, we consider the design of the supplier's warranty service, based on the thorough understanding of warranty repair processes as studied in the previous subsection. A key criterion in warranty service design is the cost-justified service level incurred in the warranty service operations. For example, the analysis of Chrysler's offer of a 7-year/70,000-mile warranty on power trains, versus a 3-year/36,000-mile bumper-to-bumper warranty, was mainly based on the cost-justified warranty service delivery. In other words, the key question to be answered is what is the minimum cost required to deliver the 7:70,000 warranty at a given (or guaranteed) service level.

Supportability-based design of warranty service

We know that warranty service costs are based on RMS. We also know that the costs related to reliability and maintainability are largely determined during the engineering design phase, and are too complicated to frequently change and redesign. Thus, contingent-sale warranty service costs are mainly affected by the factors of supportability, such as P&A production and inventory planning and control. In this section, we introduce a supportability-based method for warranty service design. Assuming that a complete database of warranty repair process is available (including technical and cost data), the supportability-based design method can be outlined as:

1   Establish a target minimum service level, $r_{\min}$, applicable to each type k repair service for all service types $k = 0, 1, \ldots, K$.

2   For each repair type $k = 0, 1, \ldots, K$, compute the cost-minimizing service level $\hat{r}_k$, using the newsboy formula:

$$\hat{r}_k = \Pr(d_t^k \leq \hat{S}_k) = \frac{c_{b_k}}{c_{h_k} + c_{b_k}}, \; k = 0, 1, \ldots, K,$$

where $\hat{S}_k$ is the cost-minimizing stock level for type k repair parts, c_{h_k} is the holding cost for type k repair parts, and c_{b_k} is the backorder cost for type k repair parts.

3   Identify and separate the repair types, for which the newsboy service levels do not meet the minimum service level. Specifically, let $K_<$ and $K_\geq$ be the set of below-minimum repair types and the set of the rest types, respectively, defined as follows:

$$K_< = \left\{ k \in \{0, 1, \ldots, K\} : \hat{r}_k < r_{\min} \right\}, \text{ and}$$

$$K_\geq = \left\{ k \in \{0, 1, \ldots, K\} : \hat{r}_k \geq r_{\min} \right\},$$

where $\hat{r}_k$ is as determined in step 2 above.

4   Determine the optimal repair base-stock level $\hat{S}_k$ for $k \in K_\geq$, using the newsboy formula and the type k claim process:

$$\hat{r}_k = \Pr(d_t^k \leq \hat{S}_k) = e^{-\mu p_k} \sum_{n=0}^{\hat{S}_k} \frac{(\mu p_k)^n}{n!},$$

where $\hat{r}_k$ is determined in step 2.

5   Determine $r_{\min}$, the adjusted repair base-stock level $\tilde{S}_k$ for $k \in K_<$, using the newsboy formula and the type k claim process:

$$r_{\min} = \Pr(d_t^k \leq \tilde{S}_k) = e^{-\mu p_k} \sum_{n=0}^{\tilde{S}_k} \frac{(\mu p_k)^n}{n!},$$

where $r_{\min}$ is determined in step 1 above.

6   Within a given warranty duration T, compute the expected total costs under $\hat{S}_k$ for each $k \in K_{\geq}$, and the total costs under $\tilde{S}_k$ for each $k \in K_{<}$, that is:

$$\mathrm{TC}_k = \sum_{t=0}^{T} c_{h_k} E(\hat{S}_k - d_t^k)^+ + c_{b_k} E(d_t^k - \hat{S}_k)^+, \quad \text{for } k \in K_{\geq}$$

$$\mathrm{TC}_k = \sum_{t=0}^{T} c_{h_k} E(\tilde{S}_k - d_t^k)^+ + c_{b_k} E(d_t^k - \tilde{S}_k)^+, \quad \text{for } k \in K_{<}$$

where T is the warranty duration.

7   Identify the set of repair types that have the top 20 percent highest expected total costs. Seek if reduction in cost data (e.g., c_{h_k} and c_{b_k}) can be achieved among the top 20 percent group, by redesigning and re-engineering reliability and maintainability. Repeat step 1 if a reduction in costs is indeed attainable. Otherwise, the current warranty service design is the most cost effective, and the expected total warranty service cost can be computed by summing up the total costs obtained in step 6 across all $k = 0, 1, \ldots, K$.

Simulation lab: Contingent-sale operations management

Assignment 7.1: HR's P&A supply chain operations with full backordering

Consider HR's JIT-MBF P&A supply chain in the section "Prototype example: P&A production at the Happy-Rider company" (p. 336), with detailed data as shown in Figure 7.8. Specifically, monthly P&A demand d_t is Poisson with mean $\mu = 12,000$ units per month. The P&A supply response time is 2 months ($a = 2$), and the delivery at the distributor is immediate ($b = 0$).

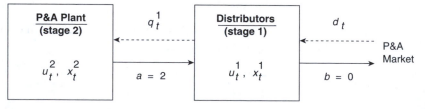

Figure 7.8 HR's P&A supply chain for Assignment 7.1.

Inventory transitions allow full backordering:

$$x_{t+1}^1 = x_t^1 + q_{t+1-a}^1 - d_t$$

$$x_{t+1}^2 = x_t^2 + q_t^2 - q_{t+1-a}^1$$

Suppose that the supply chain operates under a JIT-MBF schedule:

$$u_t^1 = q_t^1 = F_{d_{t+a}|t} - x_t^1 + \text{ss, and } u_t^2 = q_t^2 = q_t^1,$$

where $F_{d_{t+a}|t}$ is the forecast demand in period $t + a$. The cost data are given as follows:

Stage 1: holding $c_h^1 = \$5.00$ (per unit per month); backorder $c_b^1 = \$12.00$

Stage 2: holding $c_h^2 = \$15.00$ (per unit per month); backorder $c_b^2 = \$20.00$

A Using $q_t^1 = d_{t-1}$, simulate the transitions of order flow and inventory in the P&A supply chain for 1 year (i.e., $t = 1, 2, \ldots, 12$), assuming zero initial inventory, that is, $x_0^1 = x_0^2 = 0$. Simulate the system for ten independent simulation runs. For each simulation run, compute the monthly total costs at each stage, and the annual costs at each stage as well. Then, compute an average and a sample variance of the annual total costs at each stage over the ten runs.

B Repeat the simulation in item A above, but using different initial inventory values, and recommend the best initial inventory values, by comparing the simulated results on the costs. Note: The initial inventory values at the two stages may differ (i.e., $x_0^1 \neq x_0^2$).

C Now, use the MBF order policy $q_t^1 = \mu - x_t^1 + \text{ss}$, and determine the safety stock (ss) with the newsboy formula given in "Base-Stock P&A Order Planning." Using the determined ss, repeat the simulation as in item A. Compare the respective averages and the respective sample variances of annual costs obtained in items A and C. Report what you can observe from the comparison. (*Hint*: To use the newsboy formula given in the section "Base-stock P&A order planning" (p. 351), you need to balance the supply chain at response time a, such that the balanced lead-time at stage 2 is $\tilde{L}^2 = 1$.)

Assignment 7.2: HR's P&A supply chain operations with lost sales

Repeat Assignment 7.1, except that the inventory transitions do not allow full backorder, that is:

$$x_{t+1}^1 = \max\{x_t^1 + q_{t+1-a}^1 - d_t, 0\}$$

$$x_{t+1}^2 = \max\{x_t^2 + q_t^2 - q_{t+1-a}^1, 0\}.$$

A Compare the respective averages and respective sample variances of the annual costs between the two systems, that is, backordering versus lost-sales systems.

B Compare the average service levels incurred under the backorder versus lost-sales systems.

C Compare the average fill rates incurred under the backorder versus lost-sales systems. (*Hint*: Compute the per-period fill rate, and then average them over a year.)

Appendix 7A Exponential process

Characteristics and properties of exponential distribution

Let X be exponentially distributed with its probability density function given by

$$f(x) = \begin{cases} \lambda e^{-\lambda x}, & x \geq 0 \\ 0, & x < 0 \end{cases}.$$

Its expectation is given by definition as,

$$E(X) = \int_0^\infty xf(x)dx = \int_0^\infty x\lambda e^{-\lambda x}ds.$$

Note that the derivative of $e^{-\lambda x}$ is equal to $-\lambda e^{-\lambda x}$, that is,

$$\frac{d}{dx}\left(e^{-\lambda x}\right) = -\lambda e^{-\lambda x}.$$

Integrating by parts $(u = x, dv = \lambda e^{-\lambda x})$, we obtain the exponential MTBF as follows:

$$E(X) = -xe^{-\lambda x}\Big|_0^\infty + \int_0^\infty e^{-\lambda x}dx = 0 - \frac{1}{\lambda}e^{-\lambda x}\Big|_0^\infty = \frac{1}{\lambda}.$$

We can then derive the variance $\text{var}(X)$ as follows:

$$\text{var}(X) = E\left(X - E(X)\right)^2 = E\left(X^2\right) - \left(E(X)\right)^2 = E\left(X^2\right) - \frac{1}{\lambda^2}.$$

For the second moment of an exponential random variable, we have

$$E\left(X^2\right) = \int_0^\infty x^2 \lambda e^{-\lambda x} dx.$$

Integrating by parts twice (first $u = x^2, dv = \lambda e^{-\lambda x}$, and then $u = x, dv = e^{-\lambda x}$), we obtain

$$E\left(X^2\right) = -x^2 e^{-\lambda x}\Big|_0^\infty + \int_0^\infty 2x e^{-\lambda x} dx = -x^2 e^{-\lambda x}\Big|_0^\infty + 2\left(-\frac{x}{\lambda} e^{-\lambda x}\Big|_0^\infty + \frac{1}{\lambda}\int_0^\infty e^{-\lambda x} dx\right)$$

$$= 0 + 2\left(0 - \frac{1}{\lambda^2} e^{-\lambda x}\Big|_0^\infty\right) = \frac{2}{\lambda^2}.$$

Thus, we can write the variance as

$$\text{var}(X) = E\left(X^2\right) - \frac{1}{\lambda^2} = \frac{2}{\lambda^2} - \frac{1}{\lambda^2} = \frac{1}{\lambda^2}.$$

Sum of i.i.d. exponential times: gamma distribution

Denote a sum of exponential times as

$$Y_n = \sum_{i=1}^n T_i \ (T_i \text{s are i.i.d. exponential}).$$

First, we consider the distribution of $Y_2 = T_1 + T_2$ (i.e., $n = 2$), by writing out its distribution function as,

$$F_{Y_2}(t) = F_{T_1 + T_2}(t) = \Pr(T_1 + T_2 \le t) = E\left(\Pr\left(T_2 \le t - T_1 \mid T\right)\right) = \int_0^t F_{T_2}(t - s) f_{T_1}(s) ds$$

$$= \int_0^t \Pr(T_2 \le t - s) f_{Y_1}(s) ds = \int_0^t (1 - e^{-\lambda(t-s)}) \lambda e^{-\lambda s} ds = 1 - e^{-\lambda t} - \lambda t e^{-\lambda t}.$$

Hence, the density $f_{T_1 + T_2}(t)$ can be derived by differentiating the above, as follows:

$$f_{Y_2}(t) = f_{T_1 + T_2}(t) = \lambda^2 t e^{-\lambda t} = \lambda e^{-\lambda t} \frac{(\lambda t)^{n-1}}{(n-1)!} \ (\text{with } n = 2).$$

Now, we show by mathematical induction that the density $f_{Y_n}(t)$ is gamma with parameters n and λ. Assume that Y_{n-1} has gamma density with parameters $n-1$ and λ, that is,

$$f_{Y_{n-1}}(t) = f_{T_1+\ldots+T_{n-1}}(t) = \lambda e^{-\lambda t} \frac{(\lambda t)^{n-2}}{(n-2)!}.$$

Thus,

$$F_{T_1+\ldots+T_n}(t) = \Pr(Y_n \le t) = \Pr(T_1+\ldots+T_n \le t) = E\left(\Pr(T_n \le t - Y_{n-1} \mid Y_{n-1})\right)$$

$$= \int_0^t \Pr(T_n \le t - s) f_{Y_{n-1}}(s)\,ds = \int_0^t \left(1 - e^{-\lambda(t-s)}\right) f_{Y_{n-1}}(s)\,ds$$

$$= \int_0^t f_{Y_{n-1}}(s)\,ds - \int_0^t e^{-\lambda(t-s)} f_{Y_{n-1}}(s)\,ds$$

$$= F_{Y_{n-1}}(t) - \int_0^t e^{-\lambda(t-s)}\left(\lambda e^{-\lambda s}\frac{(\lambda s)^{n-2}}{(n-2)!}\right)ds$$

$$= F_{Y_{n-1}}(t) - e^{-\lambda t}\frac{(\lambda t)^{n-1}}{(n-1)!}.$$

Taking derivative with respect to t, we obtain the density of Y_n as follows:

$$f_{Y_n}(t) = \frac{dF_{Y_n}(t)}{dt} = f_{Y_{n-1}}(t) + \lambda e^{-\lambda t}\frac{(\lambda t)^{n-1}}{(n-1)!} - \lambda e^{-\lambda t}\frac{(\lambda t)^{n-2}}{(n-2)!} =$$

$$f_{Y_{n-1}}(t) + \lambda e^{-\lambda t}\frac{(\lambda t)^{n-1}}{(n-1)!} - f_{Y_{n-1}}(t) = \lambda e^{-\lambda t}\frac{(\lambda t)^{n-1}}{(n-1)!}.$$

The density above is, by definition, gamma with parameters n and λ. Hence, we conclude that the sum of n i.i.d. exponential times, Y_n, has gamma distribution with the parameters n and λ.

Appendix 7B Poisson process

Increment-stationary expectation

Let $\{N_t, t \ge 0\}$ be the Poisson counting process with parameter μt and $N_0 = 0$, that is,

$$\Pr(N_t = n) = \frac{(\mu t)^n e^{-\mu t}}{n!}, \quad n = 0,1,\ldots, \text{ for } t \ge 0.$$

The expected number of service calls over $[0,t]$ can be then derived as

$$E(N_t) = \sum_{n=0}^{\infty} n \frac{(\mu t)^n \mathrm{e}^{-\mu t}}{n!} = \sum_{n=1}^{\infty} \frac{(\mu t)^n \mathrm{e}^{-\mu t}}{(n-1)!} = (\mu t)\mathrm{e}^{-\mu t} \sum_{n=1}^{\infty} \frac{(\mu t)^{n-1}}{(n-1)!}$$

$$= (\mu t)\mathrm{e}^{-\mu t} \sum_{n=0}^{\infty} \frac{(\mu t)^k}{k!} = (\mu t)\mathrm{e}^{-\mu t}\mathrm{e}^{\mu t} \ (\text{note}: \sum_{n=0}^{\infty} \frac{(\mu t)^k}{k!} = \mathrm{e}^{-\mu t}) = \mu t.$$

Hence, the expected number of Poisson arrivals during time interval $[0,t]$ is a linear function of time increment t. Since a Poisson process has stationary increments, that is, for any $t_0 \geq 0$, the Poisson arrival process during period $[t_0, t_0+t]$ is identical to that in $[0,t]$:

$$\Pr(N_{t_0+t} - N_{t_0} = n) = \mathrm{e}^{-\mu t} \frac{(\mu t)^k}{k!}.$$

It then immediately follows that Poisson incremental arrival process, denoted as

$$\Delta N_{t_0+t} = N_{t_0+t} - N_{t_0},$$

is increment-stationary, that is,

$$E(N_{t_0+t} - N_{t_0}) = \mu(t_0+t-t_0) = \mu t.$$

Exponential time between Poisson arrivals

Given that the counting process $\{N_t, t \geq 0\}$ is Poisson with parameter μt, we have shown in the section "A life-cycle diffusion model of the contingent-sale value stream" (p. 343) that the time to the first arrival T_1 is exponential with its probability distribution given as follows:

$$F_{T_1}(t) = \Pr(T_1 \leq t) = 1 - \mathrm{e}^{-\mu t}.$$

Let T_2 be the time elapsed between the first and the second arrivals. It is then immediate to write for any $t \geq T_1$ the following:

$$\Pr(T_2 > t) = \Pr(N_t - N_{t-T_1} = 0) = \mathrm{e}^{-\mu t}.$$

Thus, we conclude that T_2 is also exponential with parameter μ, that is,

$$F_{T_2}(t) = \Pr(T_2 \leq t) = 1 - \mathrm{e}^{-\mu t}.$$

Appendix 7C Warranty repair claim process

Itemized binomial Poisson repair claim

Consider the probability of m_k number of type k repair claims per period, given a Poisson aggregate repair claim d_k with mean μ. For any $m_k \geq 0$, we write

$$\Pr(d_t^k = m_k) = \sum_{n=m_k}^{\infty} \Pr(d_t^k = m_k \mid d_t = n) \cdot \Pr(d_t = n)$$

$$= \sum_{n=m_k}^{\infty} \left(\binom{n}{m_k} p_t^{m_k} (1 - p_k)^{n - m_k} \right) \cdot \frac{\mu^n e^{-\mu}}{n!}$$

$$= \sum_{n=m_k}^{\infty} \frac{n!}{(n - m_k)! m_k!} p_t^{m_k} (1 - p_k)^{n - m_k} \cdot \frac{\mu^n e^{-\mu}}{n!}$$

$$= \frac{p_k^{m_k} \mu^{m_k}}{m_k!} \sum_{n=m_k}^{\infty} \frac{n!}{(n - m_k)!} (1 - p_k)^{n - m_k} \cdot \frac{\mu^{n - m_k} e^{-\mu}}{n!} \quad (\text{use: } \mu^n = \mu^{m_k} \mu^{n - m_k})$$

$$= e^{-\mu} \frac{(\mu p_k)^{m_k}}{m_k!} \sum_{n=m_k}^{\infty} \frac{n!}{(n - m_k)!} \cdot \frac{\left(\mu(1 - p_k) \right)^{n - m_k}}{n!}$$

$$= e^{-\mu} \frac{(\mu p_k)^{m_k}}{m_k!} \sum_{i=0}^{\infty} \frac{\left(\mu(1 - p_k) \right)^i}{i!} \quad (\text{let: } i = n - m_k)$$

$$= e^{-\mu} \frac{(\mu p_k)^{m_k}}{m_k!} e^{\mu(1 - p_k)}$$

$$= \frac{(\mu p_k)^{m_k}}{m_k!} e^{-\mu p_k}.$$

This confirms that type k repair claim d_t^k is Poisson with mean μp_k.

Independence between itemized repair claims

Suppose that an aggregate claim process d_t is given as

$$d_t = \sum_{i=0}^{K} d_t^i.$$

Let $\tilde{d}_t^k = d_t - d_t^k$ (i.e., excluding d_t^k from aggregate claim d_t) for any k ($k = 0, 1, \ldots, K$). Thus, a claim will be type k with probability p_k, or equivalently with probability $1 - p_k$ the claim will not be type k. It is easy to verify that d_t^k and $\tilde{d}_t^k$ are both Poisson with parameters as p_k and $1 - p_k$, respectively. Now, we are to prove that d_t^k is independent of $\tilde{d}_t^k$ for any k. It is equivalent to show the joint distribution factors, that is,

$$\Pr(d_t^k = m_k, \tilde{d}_t^k = n_k) = \Pr(d_t^k = m_k)\Pr(\tilde{d}_t^k = n_k), \text{ for any } m_k, n_k \geq 0.$$

Since d_t^k is binomial Poisson with parameter μp_k, we can write the joint probability as follows:

$$
\begin{aligned}
\Pr(d_t^k = m_k, \tilde{d}_t^k = n_k) &= \binom{m_k + n_k}{m_k} p_k^{m_k} (1 - p_k)^{n_k} \Pr(d_t = m_k + n_k) \\
&= \binom{m_k + n_k}{m_k} p_k^{m_k} (1 - p_k)^{n_k} \frac{\mu^{m_k + n_k}}{(m_k + n_k)!} e^{-\mu} \\
&= \frac{(m_k + n_k)!}{m_k! n_k!} p_k^{m_k} (1 - p_k)^{n_k} \frac{\mu^{m_k + n_k}}{(m_k + n_k)!} e^{-\mu} \\
&= \frac{(\mu p_k)^{m_k}}{m_k!} e^{-\mu p_k} \frac{\left(\mu(1 - p_k)\right)^{n_k}}{n_k!} e^{-\mu(1 - p_k)} \\
&= \Pr(d_t^k = m_k)\Pr(\tilde{d}_t^k = n_k).
\end{aligned}
$$

Hence, we conclude that type k claim d_t^k is independent of other type of claims for any k $(k = 0, 1, \ldots, K)$.

Bibliography

Bender, P. 1976. *Design and Operation of Customer Service Systems*, New York: AMACOM (a division of the American Management Association).

Brennan, J.T. 1994. *Warranties: Planning, Analysis, and Implementation*, New York: McGraw-Hill.

McKenzie, R. 2001. *The Relationship-Based Enterprise*, New York: McGraw-Hill.

Naumann, E. 1995. *Creating Customer Value: The Path to Competitive Advantage*, Cincinnati, OH: Thompson Executive Press.

Radjou, N. 2002. "The Collaborative Product Life Cycle," *The TechStrategy™ Report*, May, Cambridge, MA: Forrester Research.

Stock, J.R. and D.M. Lambert. 2001. *Strategic Logistic Management*, New York: McGraw-Hill.

Part III
Integrated supply chain and transport logistics

Integration of all-mode supply chain logistics

8   Maritime logistics

Key items:

- *Maritime trade: cargo flows and shipping logistics*
- *Maritime economics*
- *Ship chartering*

Basics of maritime logistics

Maritime logistics is the backbone of international trade. Transporting by sea is the cheapest and most cost-effective means of transport besides being the most environmentally friendly. That is why shipping is the prime method of carrying commodities, especially bulk commodities over long distances, where all or some elements of sea passage are necessary.

The cargo volume covered by maritime logistics has been growing for many years and is expected to continue to do so in the coming years. Maritime logistics is a unique mode of logistics and possesses particular features. In particular, it covers a wide spectrum of operations with special characteristics: from tramp to liner, from deep-sea to short-sea, from ocean-going to inland waterway. This chapter starts with maritime trade and ships and then discusses chartering and its strategies.

Maritime trade flows

Demand for shipping is a derived demand. This means that shipping has no reason to exist on its own. Shipping exists to meet the needs of international and national trade. As such, the factors that influence the demand for sea transport are the same as those that influence the global economy. This chapter gives an overview of some of the aspects of maritime logistics and their relationship to supply chain and transport logistics.

Table 8.1 World maritime trade in 2007

	Crude oil	Oil products	Iron ore	Coal	Grain	Others	World total
Millions of tons	1,888	535	799	798	332	3,220	7,572
Billions of ton-miles	9,685	2,755	4,790	3,750	1,857	10,095	32,932
Average transport distance (miles)	5,130	5,150	5,995	4,699	5,593	3,135	4,349

Source: *Fearnleys Reviews 2007*, p. 48.

Table 8.2 Development of international maritime trade 1970–2008 (millions of tons loaded)

Year	Tanker cargo	Dry cargo	Five main dry bulks[a]	World total
1970	1,442	1,124	448	2,566
1980	1,871	1,838	796	3,704
1990	1,755	2,253	968	4,008
2000	2,163	3,821	1,288	5,983
2001	2,177	3,844	1,331	6,020
2002	2,146	3,981	1,352	6,127
2003	2,223	4,257	1,475	6,480
2004	2,318	4,528	1,587	6,846
2005	2,422	4,687	1,701	7,109
2006	2,648	4,897	1,888	7,545
2007	2,705	5,177	2,013	7,882
2008	2,749	5,419	2,097	8,168
Average growth rate of 1970–2008[b]	1.7%	4.2%	4.1%	3.1%

Sources: UNCTAD, *2009 Review of Maritime Transport,* Table 3.

Notes
a   Five main dry bulks are: iron ore, coal, grain, bauxite and alumina, and phosphate.
b   Average growth = (value in 2008/value in 1970) ^ (1/38).
Units: millions of tons loaded.

   Maritime trade was estimated to be more than 7,500 million tons in 2007 (Table 8.1). This means an increase of approximately 4,000 million tons since 1987. The major commodities include iron ore, coal, and grain but there has been an increase in the transport of all other commodities. The average transport distance for commodities in international shipping is approximately 4,300 nautical miles (×1.85 = 8,000 km) while the major bulk commodities have average transport distance of 5,000 nautical miles.
   Table 8.2 shows that since 1970, there has been a growth in international trade of 3.1 percent annually, although there has been some fluctuation year to year.

Dry cargo trade has seen an increase of 4.2 percent growth rate between 1970 and 2008, which is higher than tanker cargo trade.

Maritime cargo

A brief introduction to various types of cargo is given. The cargo type has implications on the operating costs of ships. The cargo types can be categorized as general cargo, containers, pallets, and bulk cargoes.

- *General cargo* is also called break bulk cargo, and consists of a variety of commodities carried by the traditional cargo liners. Today most of these commodities are carried by container vessels or Roll On Roll Off (RORO) ships. However, traditional handling of cargo between ship and shore is still quite common in many countries where traditional ships are still used in shipping lines.
- *Containers* have taken over a large part of the traditional break bulk market. The largest part of the international liner fleet now consists of container or RORO ships. Back in the 1960s, attempts were made to introduce pallet-based overseas liner services. However, these attempts failed as the customers preferred their cargo to be carried in containers. Today most shipping operators rely on the standard ISO containers, either 20-ft or 40-ft long.
- *Pallets* are generally used in coastal or short-sea shipping, as well as in road and rail transport.
- *Bulk cargoes* vary in specific weight and thus in stowage factor (i.e., relationship between volume and weight of the cargo). Loading and discharging of bulk cargoes can be carried out by means of grabs, pneumatic suction equipment, elevators, conveyors, or from silos. Experience shows that the handling performance during discharge decreases as the discharge progresses and less cargo is left in the ship.

Ships

A number of different types of ships are available in international shipping. The trend has been toward specialization, making an individual ship more suited for specific cargo. This normally results in more efficient operations, but on the other hand, it makes ships less flexible and more dependent on a particular trade.

Cargo ships can be divided mainly into tankers, dry bulk carriers (or bulk carriers), general cargo ships (or cargo ships), and container ships.

The size of ships is measured in different ways, but transport capacity is also dependent on performance at sea as well as in ports. The size of ships can be given in weight tons and volume (Table 8.3). The four most popular measures of ship size are:

1   **Displacement**. The weight of the water displaced by the ship in the fully loaded condition, that is, the actual weight of the ship including cargo, bunkers, and so on. Displacement is given in weight tons.

Table 8.3 The size of ships can be measured by weight and by volume

Measurement by weight	Measurement by volume
Displacement	Net tonnage
Light displacement	Registered tonnage
Deadweight tonnage	Grain capacity

Table 8.4 Size of ships

Dry bulk carriers		Tankers	
Handysize	20,000–34,999 dwt	Aframax	50,000–99,999 dwt
Handymax	35,000–49,999 dwt	Suezmax	100,000–149,999 dwt
Panamax	50,000–79,999 dwt	Very large crude-oil carrier (VLCC)	150,000–299,999 dwt
Capesize	80,000+ dwt	Ultra large crude-oil carrier (ULCC)	300,000+ dwt

Source: Lloyd's Register.

2   **Deadweight (DWT)**. The total weight the ship can carry when immersed to a particular loadline (normally summer loadline), that is, cargo, bunkers, fresh water, stores, crew, or, the difference between the loaded and light displacement of a ship. DWT is given in weight tons.

3   **Gross tonnage (GT)**. The total volume of all enclosed spaces within a ship. GT is the measured volume in cubic meters.

4   **Net tonnage (NT)**. The total volume of enclosed spaces within a ship available for cargo. NT is the measured volume in cubic meters.

The GT is normally used as a basis for determining the size of the crew of the vessel, except for the size of the engine crew which is based on the output of the main engine, its degree of automation, and so on. Canal and port charges are also normally charged according to the GT. The DWT, or volume of the cargo holds, is a particularly interesting quantity for a charterer, when considering a ship. However, the actual volume of cargo holds is especially important for transporting cargo of low specific weight, that is, not utilizing the DWT capacity. The charter rates are normally related to the DWT of the ships, in terms of $ per deadweight tons (dwt). The volume is measured in cubic meters and is given as bale capacity or grain capacity. Bale capacity is the total cubic capacity of the ship's hold for the carriage of solid cargo which is not able to fill the spaces between the ship's frames. When cargo is free-flowing and is capable of filling these spaces, the cubic capacity is known as grain capacity. Four groups of bulk carriers and tankers are listed in Table 8.4.

Tramp shipping

Tramp shipping is a speculative business since it is very difficult to anticipate freight rates. The ships are free to trade where they can, carrying whatever cargoes they can. The nature of tramp shipping implies efficiency, since there are no direct controls over this sector of shipping.

The cargoes in tramp shipping are often coal, ores, grain, bauxite, fertilizers, sulfur, timber, steel, pig iron, cars, cotton, wool, salt, sugar, minerals, concentrates, and so on. These are low-value, large-volume cargoes in most cases. The ships used vary from the small 2,000 dwt to the largest afloat of around 500,000 dwt. The unit of productivity for the ships is ton-mile (tons of cargo moved per nautical mile).

Tramp shipping is important to world trade for the following reasons:

- It provides shipping space for all commodities whose annual movement cannot be predicted with certainty and which cannot be carried on liners.
- It transports tonnage requirements in respect of those commodities where the bulk of traffic is lifted by integrated fleets.
- It provides liner services with a reserve of shipping space to deal with seasonal or other flushes of cargoes.
- It offers shippers lower rates than they could get under the liner system where individual cargo tonnage is sufficient to compose full loads.
- It provides good, readily available shipping to meet international needs.

In the short run, the spot market of tramp shipping is the closest that it is possible to get to an economist's view of a perfect market. No individual can influence price or freight rates in the spot market. The spot market represents the balance of supply and demand, and freight rates in different parts of the world are equalized through exchanges. The market matches demand for shipping spaces and the supply of the same on the spot. The bargaining between the buyer and seller of shipping space results in the cost efficiency in bulk trades. Neither side is large enough to influence the freight rates. The freight rates agreed are a reflection of the equilibrium of supply and demand of shipping in the spot market. In bulk shipping, there exists an economic output (e.g., speed) of ships against freight rates (see Figure 8.1)

By adjusting the output (e.g., speed), shipowners maximize profits and reduce costs, being then able to stay longer in the market before reaching the point of laying the ship. The fluctuation of freight rates in the spot market indicates the efficiency of the shipping market. Freight rates are adjusting according to the changes in the supply and demand of shipping space. For instance, fuel price (an external factor) influences freight rates, and the response from shipowners to reduced freight rates is to reduce speed, as long as demand remains constant (Figure 8.1).

Demand also shows efficiency in relation to freight rates. It is seen that there is an inverse relationship between demand and freight rates. As freight rates rise, shippers look for closer cargo sources to reduce ton-miles freight costs. For example, when oil was being shipped around the Cape of Good Hope to Europe and America, shippers looked for cargo sources in Africa to reduce the distance over which the cargo was shipped.

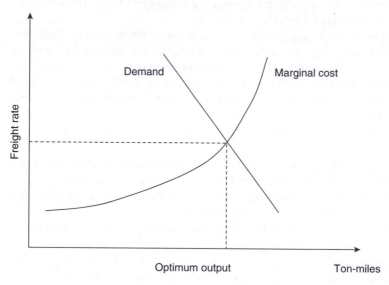

Figure 8.1 Economic speed versus freight rate.

Another aspect of short-run efficiency is the movement of ships that operate on the margins of different sectors from one sector to another. For example, product tankers move from clean oil trades to the chemical trades, and vice versa, depending on the market opportunities.

Ship chartering

The freight market is like any other freely competitive market. There are a number of buyers and a number of sellers, none of whom actually have any impact upon the market as individuals. The 'commodity' for sale is shipping space on ships or access to ships by shippers/cargo owners.

In the freight market, the shipowner wants to sell shipping space and the cargo owner wants to buy it. Both want the best possible deal from their points of view. Bargaining takes place until they both accept that they have the best deal possible, under the circumstances. Most often the services of a broker are used. The function of a broker is to bring the two parties together in matching cargoes with suitable ships. He or she plays a crucial role in bringing negotiations to a successful conclusion. To take place in the bargaining, some knowledge of the market and the parameters of operations are expected from both parties. In particular, this knowledge must include:

- the main trade(s) that their business is involved in;
- the geographical area within which they trade;
- the ports involved and the sailing time between these ports;
- the seasonality of various trades;

- the characteristics of various cargoes that their business is involved in;
- the abbreviations and jargon of the charter market.

In addition, they must know the characteristics as well as the common names of the different types of ships that are involved in the trades. Central to the successful execution of a charterparty is the role of the ship's master. Negotiations during the process of chartering follow a protocol. The parties negotiating the charter need to be aware of the elements of this protocol.

The important underlying thread that runs through all this discussion on chartering is that the shipowner really needs to know his cost of operations, under different conditions, as he negotiates a charter. Shipping cycles typically comprise some years of low profits followed by a few years of good earning. This makes it necessary for the shipowner to operate as cheaply as possibly, while keeping up his quality of output. He needs to have a good idea of his expenses (like manning, provisions, maintenance, repairs, insurance, etc.) but for expenses outside his control, he can get information from various sources, including Lloyd's List and the Baltic and International Maritime Council (BIMCO).

Chartering versus purchase

A time chartering is a contract whereby the shipowner (the lessor) of an asset (a ship) grants to anther party (the lessee) the exclusive right to the use of the asset for an agreed period, in return for the periodic payment of rent. Time chartering should not be confused with hire purchase, which also features periodic payments from the charterer to the shipowner. The key difference between the two is that hire purchase agreements are essentially a deferred payment mechanism for the charterer eventually to own the ship. This could be a five-year period for a ship, since the intention is to own the ship from the outset. It is this ownership feature that distinguishes hire purchase from chartering.

A time chartering is a contract between a shipowner (lessor) and charterer (lessee) such that the charterer:

- selects the ship specifications;
- makes specified payments to the shipowner for an obligatory period;
- is granted exclusive use of the ship for that period;
- does not own the ship at any time during the charter period.

The charterer could be a bank or specialist company (e.g., ship pool), or it could be a company set up by high-tax-paying investors seeking capital allowances to offset against their income, thereby reducing their tax payments. The charterer will normally be a cargo trader.

The advantages of chartering to the charterer are:

- volume discounts for ship purchase can be passed on to the charterer (particularly attractive to smaller charterers);
- the conservation of a charterer's working capital and credit capital;

- the provision of up to 100 percent of finance, with no deposits or pre-payment (up to 33 percent of the cost of the ship paid in advance to shipbuilders, or 15 percent of the cost required by banks to be paid by the charterer as a condition of loan finance;
- shifting the obsolescence risk of ship to shipowner (short-term charter);
- no ship trading experience needed;
- the possibility of excluding charter finance from the balance sheet.

Possible disadvantages could be:

- a higher cost than, say, debt finance for purchase;
- the profit from eventual sale of the ship going to the shipowner (as title owner);
- higher gearing than, say, purchase with equity finance;
- ship specification not tailor-made for charterer (short-term charter).

Ship chartering is clearly advantageous for shipbuilders and shipowners, since it increases opportunities for business. The documentation for chartering is usually simpler than for ship financing. The greatest disadvantage is the risk that insufficient care will be taken of the ship.

Bareboat chartering—financing

Bareboat chartering accounts for around 30 percent of new ship financing for the world. The chartering period can be between 10 and 30 years but is more likely for a period of at least 15 years. It is noncancelable, or cancelable only with a major penalty. The shipowner expects to gain a normal profit on the ship from one charterer, without being involved in, or necessarily having an understanding of, the charterer's business. The charterer is likely to have a purchase option at the end of the time chartering terms, at fair market value, for a percentage of the cost, or for a normal (very low) price.

The normal risks and benefits of ownership are the responsibility of the charterer, although they are not the legal owner of the ship at any time during the bareboat charter period (title may or may not be eventually transferred to the charterer). The bareboat charter period is for the major part of the ship's life. It follows that the charterer is responsible for repairs, maintenance, and insurance of the ship, but that the risk of obsolescence lies with the shipowner. The charterer does not consider the residual value of the ship at the end of the charter period important, and does not need to be technically knowledgeable about the ship or shipping business.

The shipowner may demand that the charterer pay a specified amount of the hire on the first day of the charter payment.

Time chartering—operating

Although the dividing line between time chartering and bareboat chartering has recently become more blurred, the key features of time chartering are:

- It allows charterers to respond rapidly to changes in market conditions.
- It is of shorter term, usually one to several years, or an average of 3 years, and can be returned to the shipowner at relatively short notice and without major penalty.
- The charterer cannot choose the ship specification (except for good customers or first users of ship).
- The charterer gains the use of a ship without the obligation to pay off its full cost. The shipowner is usually responsible for the maintenance of the ship.
- The shipowner expects to profit from either selling or chartering the ship.

The ship's residual value is important to the shipowner, and is a key factor in determining the chartering hire that can be offered. The cost of fixing a ship with another charterer also needs to be considered in rate negotiations, given the ship may be fixed with at least three different charterers over the ship's lifetime. Time charter hires vary quite significantly over the economic cycle, with the shipowner often accepting a short-term drop in monthly hire to avoid remarketing or even laying-up the ship.

Time charter may have a purchase option for the charterer to buy the ship at the end of the time charter term, sometimes at a fair market value and sometimes at a stated price. There will almost definitely be an option for the charterer to extend the charter for a further or several charter period(s).

The shipowner assumes the risks of ship obsolescence and needs to know the ship and shipping business (and ensure that maintenance and overhaul is carried out to high standards). There are specialist ship management firms that take care of the technical management of time charter for the shipowners. They can also deal with the commercial side of the business (hire collection, contracts, etc.) as well as remarketing, fixing, and sales. With the increasing trend of separation of ownership and ship operation, ship management firms have an assured future.

The redelivery condition of the ship is very important to a shipowner, since he or she will wish to fix it with another charterer with the minimum of delay. For example, if a ship has been delivered to a charterer, the charterer would be expected to redeliver the ship in a similar condition at the end of the charter period. A fund, or maintenance reserve, is usually established for the major overhauls, which the charterer will contribute to, and out of which any such maintenance and repairs needed, will be paid. For better risk-controlled charterers, these maintenance and repairs would be dealt with at the end of the charter period.

The charterer will have to comply with seaworthiness directives and service bulletins that are issued by the regulatory authorities (flag states, port states, classification societies) or shipbuilders. Ship charterers have usually signed contracts for most of the ships that they will take delivery of over the next 2 years, but after that the orders are more speculative. Many charterers in the United States and Europe have had to rely on chartering to obtain Asian ships.

Shipping pools

Shipping pools are currently used in almost all segments of the tramp shipping market including the products tanker business, the chemical tanker business, the

LPG business, the bulk carrier business, and the crude tanker business. A shipping pool acts as a single entity in the allocation of its vessels to meet the various contracts that it has entered into. The ships are generally managed and fixed by an external company, each owner-member being paid a proportion of the profits. A shipping pool behaves like a big shipowner, and the pool tonnages are used to fulfill contracts of affreightment and time charter commitments. By pooling tonnages, the shipowners have been able to enjoy economies of scale, reduce their ballast legs, reduce idle time, and enjoy higher load factors. Small shipowners or owners of old ships can then maintain their business in the shipping market with reliable income and relatively lower risks.

Sale and charterback

Sale and charterback occurs when sellers who own ships decide to realize the capital value of the ship, but at the same time continue to operate it. This may be because they have cash flow problems, but it may also be for the following reasons:

- to meet capital requirements for new ships or investment;
- to realize the current value of a ship that is likely to be retired in a few year's time, especially when the market price of the ship will probably declined significantly over that period.

The typical duration for such deals is 3–5 years. The other party involved (i.e., the buyer) is likely to be a bank, which will structure the charter to gain tax benefits. The risk to the bank is relatively low, first because the duration is short and second because the seller will probably be a good credit risk shipowner, perhaps one that is already known to the bank.

Shipbroking

When a shipowner looks to place the services of a ship on the spot market, he or she looks for cargo that suits the size of his or her ship. The ship must be fixed on time, estimating closely when the ship will be available for the next fixture, while maintaining some flexibility.

An area is then chosen in which the ship will work, keeping in mind seasonal fluctuations in demand for various commodities like grain, coal, and so on. Industry requirements, it must be remembered, are not controlled by season.

When the shipowner has all of this worked out, a shipbroker is contacted. The shipbroker tries to match the shipowner's requirements with what is available among the cargoes that are seeking ships to move them. The shipbroker makes his recommendations and the shipowner makes his calculations (i.e., voyage estimation) to decide which of the voyages offered is most profitable. He will then start offering on various cargoes, specifying the details of his ships. The bargaining for freight rate begins. The shipowner wants to earn maximum freight

Table 8.5 Cost allocation of ship chartering

	Voyage charter	Volume COV	Time charter	Shipping pool	Bareboat charter
Voyage cost	S	S	C	C	C
Running cost	S	S	S	S	C
Capital cost	S	S	S	S	S

Notes: Voyage cost = cargo cost + ship cost.
S = shipowner.
C = charterer.
COV – contract of affreightment.

while the cargo owner wants the cheapest service possible. The shipbroker tries to match the two.

When an agreement is reached, the ship is fixed. The shipbroker then draws up a charterparty. The shipowner must make sure the shipment of cargo is performed according to the clauses in the charterparty. He works out his bunker (fuel) plan, voyage instructions to the master of the ship, instructions to the agents in various relevant ports and makes sure the ship is properly supplied. The shipbroker assists in passing messages to the charterers, passing accounts in time and collecting freight.

Table 8.5 illustrates the cost allocation of different ways of using ships. The shipowner wants to fix on voyage or time charter, depending on the market reports he has and his own experience of the market. Typically, if the market is strengthening, he will wish to fix on voyage charter but if the ship is difficult to fix or the market is expected to weaken, he will seek time charters. On time charter, the shipowner's calculations become easier because he usually does not pay fuel or port charges as these costs lie with the charterer. He is also not subject to risks like strikes, disasters, and so forth. Time charter is usually a safe option for a shipowner inexperienced in the cargo market.

Maritime economics

Shipping costs

The study of shipping costs is an important part of the study of maritime logistics. Not only is it important to understand the role of costs in maritime logistics, but maritime logistics becomes easier to understand through a study of the costs involved.

Costs in maritime logistics can be viewed from two sides: the cost of providing the service, and the cost of buying the service. The focus is on the former. The maritime logistics market is cyclical in nature, with periods of rich and poor earning following each other. The successful managing of these periods to leave a profit in the long term determines the success of the organization.

The financial strength accumulated by the shipping companies in a time of healthy profit making needs to carry it through the lean times. Those that can do this, and invest money in units of production, including ships, in the time when the market is going through a downturn, stand to make good profits when the market picks up again. Those who are unable to survive the downturn, go out of business, either temporarily or permanently.

The costs for operating can be divided into

- capital costs;
- running costs (daily operation costs);
- voyage costs (voyage-dependent operation costs).

All these costs will be affected by choosing a ship with a higher sailing speed. The building costs will go up due to more expensive machinery thus affecting capital costs. The maintenance and lubricant oil consumption will normally be higher, and the bunker costs will also increase. On the other hand, the greater number of round voyages will increase the total carrying capacity and hence the potential earning capacity of the transport service.

The capital costs depend for a large part on the shipbuilding price of the ship. Normally the capital costs can be divided into two parts: the payment for borrowed money and the capital depreciation of the vessel. Factors which will influence the capital costs can be summarized as follows:

- the investment costs, that is, shipbuilding or second-hand price of the ship, including shipbrokers commission, costs related to the delivery of the ship, and so on;
- the financial structure of the shipbuilding, that is, the relationship between liability (borrowed money) and equity;
- the interest rate paid on borrowed money;
- the economic life of the ship;
- tax regulations which may influence the rate of depreciation.

The operating costs are defined as costs purely related to the operational aspects of the ship. The operating costs only comprise fixed costs (running costs) whereas the variable costs depend on the actual sailing of the ship (voyage costs).

The daily running costs consist of the following items:

- crew costs determined by type of vessel, level of automation, nationality of the crew, flag of registration, relieve schedule;
- maintenance and repairs;
- stores, supplies, and lubricating oil;
- insurance costs;
- management overhead, including administration.

Some flag states specify the manning requirements in great detail, while other flag states leave it entirely up to the shipowners. The nationality of the crew members also affects the crew costs as wage levels show great variation.

The voyage costs consist of bunker costs, port costs, and canal dues. The fuel consumption of a ship is determined by the size of the ship, hull shape, the laden condition, speed, weather, type and output of the main engine, and the type and quality of the fuel. Bunker is the term used for fuel used in ships. The bunker costs on a voyage depend on the consumption at sea, the consumption during the stay in port, as well as the price of bunker.

During the last 25 years, there have been considerable fluctuations in the price of bunker, being directly dependent on oil prices. With bunker one of the largest cost items in shipping operations, fuel economy has become more important. Previously steam turbines were quite common as propulsive machinery for large ships, particular very large crude-oil carriers (VLCCs) and up to 1979, a large proportion of tankers were turbine powered. Steam turbines, however, have a specific fuel consumption which is 10–15 percent higher than for diesel engines.

The fuel consumption is dependent on the actual output of the engine in any operating condition. The difference in consumption between laden and ballast conditions varies with the individual ship. As a rule of thumb, the consumption per hour for a given ship will increase by the cubic of sailing speed.

Port charges make up an important item of the voyage costs. The port charges cover aspects of port operations such as:

- port agency fees (handling of paperwork in connection with the call);
- harbor dues (use of harbor, quays, mooring, or buoys);
- pilotage;
- tugboats and mooring crew.

The port charges are different for the same ship calling at different ports and also the composition of the charges may be different. Port charges are normally dependent on the GT of the vessel, and in some cases, also on the amount of cargo being loaded and discharged.

Canal dues have to be paid when the ship passes through a toll-based canal. Examples are the Panama Canal, the Suez Canal, the Kieler Canal, and the St. Lawrence Seaway. The canal dues are charged based on the GT of the vessel and the laden condition. Alternative routes to the canal, for sample, sailing around the Cape of Good Hope in the case of the Suez Canal, are also taken into account.

Cargo handling costs depend on:

- type of commodity (oil, chemicals, grain, forest products, container, etc.);
- quantity of cargo;
- type of ship;
- terminal and port characteristics;
- individual charges in the different ports.

The loading and discharging are normally carried out by independent stevedoring companies, or by the exporter or importer of the cargo. The costs of cargo handling can vary considerably from port to port.

Economic ship size

The total transport quantity of a shipping operation in a year is expressed by:

$$Q_T = Q_a N_v,$$
(8.1)

where

Q_T = total quantity carried per year
Q_a = average quantity per round voyage
N_v = number of voyages per year.

The transport capacity of a cargo ship for an individual voyage is dependent on the DWT, volume of holds, the stowage factor (the shape of cargo holds), and type of cargo carried. For pallet carriers, it is normally not possible to utilize more than 65–70 percent of the actual volume of the cargo holds, thus the pallet capacity is an important factor.

The number of voyages (from discharging to discharging), depending on the time taken per voyage and the length of the time period considered, is expressed by Equation (8.2):

$$N_v = \frac{T_a}{T_v},$$
(8.2)

where

N_v = number of voyages
T_a = annual time available for shipping operation
T_v = time taken per round voyage.

The time taken per voyage can be expressed by Equation (8.3):

Voyage time = sea time + port time (working) + port time (idle).

$$T_v = \frac{D_v}{V_s} + \frac{2Q}{V_c} + T_p,$$
(8.3)

where

T_v = time taken per round voyage
D_v = total distance of round voyage
V_s = average sailing speed of the ship
Q = cargo transported in tons (indicated by the ship capacity)
V_c = average cargo handling speed in port, for example, tons loaded (discharged) per hour; each unit of cargo is handled twice, loading and discharging
T_p = idle time in ports.

Thus the productivity of a ship in a given service will, to a considerable degree, depend on productivity in the ports. For large container ships, for example, it is important that the ports are being worked around the clock. The sailing speed of the ship is also an important factor when determining the number of round voyages per year. However, the possible income of extra voyages must be compared with the extra costs involved by increasing the speed of the vessel.

On short voyages, the port time makes up a much larger part of the time per round voyage than for longer voyages. Thus the efficiency in port is more important for the productivity of a ship on shorter than on longer voyages.

There are trade-offs between the transport frequency, Equation (8.2), and the round-voyage time, Equation (8.3). The components of the round voyage are sea time and port time. The sea time depends on the ship's sailing speed V_s and the distance between ports D_v. The port time depends on the cargo handling speed V_c and the amount of cargo transported Q, plus the idle time in ports T_p. The idle time in ports covers additional time that ships may also need for maneuvering, mooring, and paperwork, thus increasing the port turnaround time not accounted for by cargo handling. In a congested port, the ship may also have to queue for port facilities or wait for cargo.

It should be noticed that the port time has a double effect compared to the sea time. This is due to the loading and discharging in each port that amplifies that impact of loading speed changes on the round voyage frequency, especially on shorter voyages. The maximum annual operating time, T_a, is 365×24 h, but in practice it is reduced by the number of days the ship is out of service for repair, maintenance, or other reasons.

The model of Equations (8.2) and (8.3) together can be used to compare the impact of alternative investments in cargo handling and ship propulsion on the economies of speed of ships. It also supports the decision to assign different ships to alternative routes. Two investments in cargo handling V_c and ship propulsion V_s may be compared by analyzing hypothetical cases in tramp shipping. A suitable measure of performance is the reduction of round voyage time and the resulting increase of the number of annual round voyages.

In order to achieve a given number of round voyages during a time period or to arrive at specific times at the destination, choosing the right sailing speed is an important decision. The costs per year may be determined by Equation (8.4).

$$\text{Total costs} = \text{capital costs} + \text{running costs} + \text{voyage costs}, \qquad (8.4)$$

$$C_{\text{total}} = C_{\text{capital}} + C_{\text{running}} + C_{\text{voyage}},$$

where

$$\text{Voyage costs} = \text{ship costs} + \text{cargo costs} + \text{canal dues} + \text{port charges},$$

$$C_{\text{voyage}} = C_{\text{ship}} + C_{\text{cargo}} + C_{\text{canal}} + C_{\text{port}},$$

in which

> Cargo costs = quantity of cargo handled (in tons)
>
> $\times$ cargo handling rate $(\$/\text{ton})$,

$$C_{\text{cargo}} = 2QH_c,$$

Ships costs = voyage time $\times$ bunker price,

$$C_{\text{ship}} = T_v B_p.$$

Jansson and Shneerson (1987) found that the ship construction costs rise with ship size according to the two-third power rule and the running cost is constant, regardless of ship size:

$$C_{\text{capital}} = \alpha Q^{\frac{2}{3}}.$$

Finally,

$$C_{\text{total}} = \alpha Q^{\frac{2}{3}} + C_{\text{running}} + \left(\frac{D_v}{V_s} + \frac{2Q}{V_c} + T_p \right) B_p + 2QH_c + C_{\text{canal}} + C_{\text{port}},$$

$$C_{\text{total}} = \alpha Q^{\frac{2}{3}} + \beta Q + \gamma.$$

There exist economies of scale of ship size, when only costs are considered. However, there is an economic ship size, if the income is meanwhile considered. The total income per year may be expressed as Equation (8.5):

Total income = quantity $\times$ freight rate + demurrage,   (8.5)

$$I_c = QF_r + D.$$

The most economic quantity is the quantity that will give the largest profit, when cost and income variation for potential speeds of vessels are taken into account:

$$I_c - C_{\text{total}} = -\alpha Q^{\frac{2}{3}} + (F_r - \beta)Q + (D - \gamma).$$

The economic ship size Q is approximately

$$Q \approx \frac{8\alpha^3}{27(F_r - \beta)^3}.$$

For a transport service, it is also important to remember that there may be sudden changes in the total costs of a transport service if an extra vessel is required to fulfill the demands of the transport users. Alternatively an increase in speed may be necessary in order to be able to maintain an acceptable frequency, even if this speed is higher than the most economic one for the ship concerned. The total result for the whole operation, however, may be different from comparing the results of individual ships. This may be due to sudden changes in capital and running costs by introducing an extra ship in order to maintain the required frequency of transport service.

The economic speed for a ship in a given service, depends on a number of factors such as:

- sailing distance
- transport quantity
- required frequency
- required departure and arrival time in ports
- time in port in comparison to time at sea.

Increase in speed for a given ship requires a higher engine output. Generally speaking the power requirements are proportional to the cubic of sailing speed. An increase in speed from 15 to 16 knots (+7 percent) will require an increase in output of $(16/15)^3 = 1.21$ (+21 percent). This will also give an increase in bunker consumption of 21 percent. If the original output of a given ship was 5,000 horsepower (hp), the new speed will require an output of $(5,000 \times 1.21 =)$ 6,100 hp. With a bunker consumption of 100 g/hp/h, this will increase the bunker consumption by $[100 \times (6,100 - 5,000) =]$ 110 kg/h or 2.6 ton/day. At a bunker price of \$100, the voyage costs will increase by \$2,600 per day. The bunker costs will thus play an important part in deciding on the most economic speed in a transport service. Low bunker prices will make it more profitable to increase the speed. As the sailing time is reduced, the extra costs per nautical mile will increase by $(16/15)^2 = 1.14$ (+14 percent).

Strategies in ship chartering

This section is mainly based on theories developed by Porter (1985) and Wijnolst and Wergeland (1997). Figure 8.2 shows that the shipping market is not homogeneous but can be divided according to specialization (or differentiation) and economies of scale. Specialization results in the development of different cargo handling systems and requires to varying degrees, access to quays, cargo-handling equipment, storage capacity, and so on. Economies of scale exist where the volume of cargo throughput is large. The scale economies are frequently the driving force for large companies. Figure 8.3 illustrates the features of shipping segments and competitive advantages in different segments.

Ship acquisition strategy

Figures 8.4 and 8.5 examine the strength of the shipping operation for an individual shipowning company in terms of fleet renewal and employment risk strategy, models which were developed by Arrow Research (Sadler 2007).

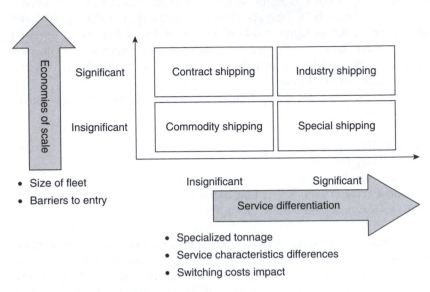

- Specialized tonnage
- Service characteristics differences
- Switching costs impact

Figure 8.2 Shipping segments—dimensions.

Source: Wijnolst and Wergeland (1997), p. 300.

Contract shipping	**Industry shipping**
• Few suppliers	• Few suppliers
• Economies of scale in fleet	• Economies of scale in fleet
• Fairly homogenous service	• Specialized service
• Liquid second-hand market	• Difficult second-hand market
• Close customer relations	• Tailor-made customer products
Commodity shipping	**Special shipping**
• Many suppliers	• Few suppliers
• No economies of scale	• No economies of scale
• Homogeneous service	• Specialized services
• Liquid second-hand market	• Difficult second-hand market
• Little customer contact	• Direct customer contact

Figure 8.3 Shipping segments—characteristics.

Figure 8.4 illustrates the size and age and the fleet as factors in company ship-building plans and scrapping in a given period so as to determine how the profile of the fleet is likely to change over the period by presenting changes to average age. The solid and empty circles represent the size and age of a fleet today and in the future, respectively. The circle pairs for each company are connected with a line to create a fleet development path, interpreted to provide an effective health check, with regard to a company's success in managing the aging process of its

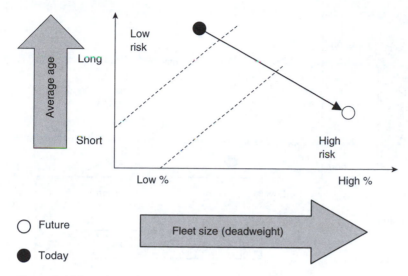

Figure 8.4 Fleet size and age trajectory.

fleet. The most positive trajectory would be one that heads to the bottom right hand corner of the chart (a big and youthful fleet). The least positive trajectory would be one that heads vertically up and is produced by a company without shipbuildings and with no scrapping. In this case, average age will simply increase in the study period. There is unlikely to be a trajectory heading toward the bottom right, which means that no fleet is getting bigger and younger, which would demand significant fleet acquisition and/or selling a block of older tonnage. Usually, a company builds in growth, and the fleet average age growth is moderated. A young fleet is important for attracting good quality charterers, retaining investors and securing credit.

Ship employment strategy

Figure 8.5 looks at the percentage of tonnage in a study period and the average charter duration over the period in order to illustrate risk position. The chart in Figure 8.5 plots the percentage of vessels on time charter employment (bottom axis) against average time charter duration (left-hand axis) for a shipowning company. The size of the circle provides a third dimension to the chart by taking into account the composition of the operating fleet for each shipowner. Companies appearing in the bottom left corner of the chart have low period/short duration and are considered high risk (low-guaranteed income), while companies appearing top right have high period/long duration and are considered low risk (high-guaranteed income). The company best placed to survive a downturn might be expected to come from the latter group. The former group may show a dramatic profit occasionally. Rather like a low average age, shipowners tend to grow if

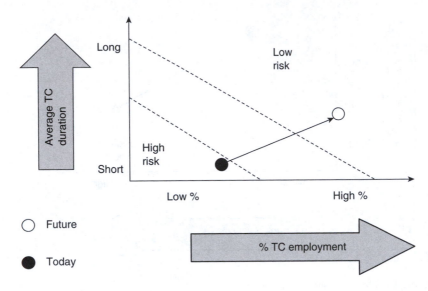

Figure 8.5 Employment risk analysis.

they can show significant long-term period employment. A company with a high percentage of period but relatively low average duration finds itself with a bridge coming down in the middle of the danger zone. However, the issue of ship employment risk is not as simple as measuring the strength of period. The volatility of the spot market may provide the greatest earnings potential.

Summary

This chapter has given an overview of some of the aspects of maritime logistics as a component of supply chain and transport logistics. The aim has been to highlight special characteristics in the maritime logistics sector. The existing literature on logistics mostly considers maritime operations as "cost centers," bearing in mind that the purpose of logistics is largely to provide the required transport services at minimum transport cost. From the point of view of the maritime sector, the independent shipping companies consider maritime logistics as "profit centers." This brings a new perspective to supply chain and transport logistics.

Remarks and acknowledgments

This chapter is prepared from materials from the subject *Ship Chartering Strategies* for *Master of Science in International Shipping and Transport Logistics*, Department of Logistics and Maritime Studies, The Hong Kong Polytechnic University. I would like to acknowledge the patience of the editor,

Professor John J. Liu who has waited calmly for this contribution to his book and provided admirable comments, suggestions, and criticisms.

Bibliography

Gorton, L., P. Hillenuius, R. Ihre, and A. Sandevarn. 2004. *Shipbroking and Chartering Practice*, 6th Edition, London: Informa.

Evans, J.J. and P.B. Marlow. 1990. *Quantitative Methods in Maritime Economics*, 2nd Edition, Coulsdon, Surrey: Fairplay.

Fearnleys. 2008. *Fearnleys Reviews 2007*, Oslo: Fearnleys.

ISL. 2007. *Shipping Statistics Yearbook*, Bremen: Institute of Shipping Economics and Logistics.

Jansson, J.O. and D. Shneerson. 1987. *Liner Shipping Economics*, London: Chapman and Hall.

Porter, M.E. 1985. *Competitive Advantage*, New York: Free Press.

Sadler, I. 2007. *Storm Preparation*. Stamford, CT: Marine Money (www.marinemoney.com).

Stopford, M. 2009. *Maritime Economics*, 3rd Edition, London: Routledge.

UNCTAD. 2009. *Review of Maritime Transport, 2009*. Geneva: United Nations Conference on Trade and Development.

Wijnolst, N. and T. Wergeland. 1997. *Shipping*, Delft, the Netherlands: Delft University Press.

9 Global ports and logistics facilitation

Contemporary issues and challenges

Key items:

- Port as a key component in logistics facilitation
- Implications on port management and governance
- Implications on the port community

As suggested at the beginning of this book, the efficiency of logistics, or timely provision of supply, is vital for any business to succeed within this increasingly competitive world. In this chapter, we focus on ports—a vital component in deciding the efficiency of logistics nowadays due to its role acting as the nodal point between different transportation modes, especially given that more than 90 percent of the cargoes are currently moved by ships (Ng and Liu 2010). We will discuss how the development of global supply chains has reshaped the role of ports nowadays, their evolution, and reform and restructuring in management and governance. This chapter is structured as follows. After illustrating the background, we will introduce the restructuring of the container liner industries and the development of multimodal supply chains. This is followed by the role of ports in facilitating global supply chains, as well as how such development affects a port's evolution, the composition of the port community, and the challenges ahead.

Background

Containerization has changed not only the contents, structure, and interactions of the geography of maritime transport. Several factors have helped to shape recent global container shipping, including the growth of trade, the emergence of new markets, the emergence of new carriers, and supply chain logistics. The growth of trade and the rise of new markets had increased the demands for container services, which in turn had led to the emergence of new carriers and the extension of logistics services. Further control over the logistics chain implies enormous capital investment and multimodal integration, which led to the restructuring of the industry (Brooks 2000).

Changes in technological improvements and international trade patterns since the 1980s had led to a shift in economic philosophy. With globalization and the rise of multinational corporations, the global economy has entered a period emphasizing greater variety, customer-oriented business strategies, fitting individual demands, and better product quality. To succeed under such an environment, producers have to achieve a more changeable business attitude. Indeed, to keep pace with the development of other economic sectors, the shipping industry has sought to further rationalize its organizational structure, resulting in the increase in ship sizes and service frequency (Martin and Thomas 2001; Notteboom and Winkelmans 2001). For example, container liner services provided by the top 20 shipping lines increased from little more than 400 in the late 1980s to nearly 600 in the late 1990s. Some scholars go even further and argue that the implications of the global economy on global container shipping has already shifted from demand-pull to supply-led strategies, and cargoes followed ships rather than the other way round (Chilcote 1988; Cullinane and Khanna 2000). With the assistance of the economies of scale in ship size and increasingly easy accessibility to advanced technology, shipping lines adjust their development strategies based on their own future perceptions. Nowadays, the deployment of mega-sized containerships is a common practice among major shipping lines, of which virtually all possess a fleet with ships with more than 10,000 TEUs loading capacity.

Another implication of technological and economic development within the shipping industry is the rise of maritime logistics. As mentioned earlier in this book, logistics is the process of planning, implementing, and controlling the efficient and effective flow of raw materials, inventory, finished goods, services, and related information from the point of origin to point of consumption for the purpose of responding to customer requirement (Coyle *et al.* 1999). Supply chain management encompasses coordination and collaboration with channel participants, that is, suppliers and customers, and the organization itself, which includes all the logistic activities with the primary goal to maximize consumption satisfaction and to minimize a firm's costs. The international transportation system, which plays an important role in reducing transit time and cost, has been widely considered by decision-makers, as exemplified by various shipping lines expanding businesses through vertical integration such as: acquiring dedicated terminals, for example, COSCO in Hong Kong, Hanjin in Osaka, Gwangyang and Kaohsiung, and so on; operating inland transportation, like Maersk operating the European Rail Shuttle (ERS) connecting Rotterdam and the rest of Europe; and setting up subsidiary branches in providing logistical advice and services, for example, APL, OOCL, NYK (operate as APL Logistics, OOCL Logistics and NYK Logistics, respectively); and so on. Hence, ports have gradually been integrated into a worldwide network of intermodal supply chains (see Figure 9.1).

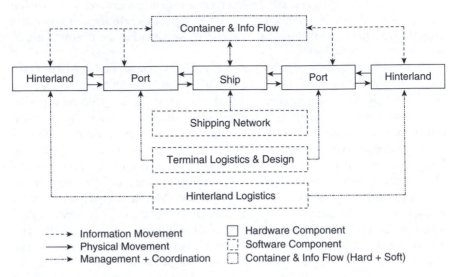

Figure 9.1 Maritime logistics and intermodal supply chains.

Ports as a key component in logistics facilitation

As a crucial part of the international transportation systems, ports are not solely an independent and natural area for the transfer of physical goods, but also a systematic element of a multimodal logistical supply chain. Thus, the role of ports within this system is becoming particularly important due to their role in the coordination of materials and information flows. Minimizing costs, and reliable cargo handling are becoming crucial as a functional part of global logistics and supply chain management. Increasingly demanding customers push service providers hard to provide speedy, Just in Time services at reasonable prices. This may require shipping lines to carry cargo with a much more flexible schedule and needing more ports to cope with it. In the European Union, for example, in the promotion of short sea shipping (SSS), ports complement the objective of SSS promotion in the context of European transport network planning, as the quality of nodes is critical for the cohesion, integration, and intermodality of various transport networks within the European Union (Nijkamp *et al.* 1994). Thus, the success of the logistics entities largely depends on the efficiency of ports acting as the integrating and coordinating nodes between different components (Bichou and Gray 2004; Miyashita 2004).

Integration means the extent which separates stakeholders from working together in a cooperative and collaborative manner in achieving mutually acceptable outcomes, commonly termed the "optimal solution" (Carbone and Martino 2003). Theoretically, while larger ships enable ship operators to become better off in terms of unit cost through economies of scale, the reality is that ships with larger capacity are obliged to tackle additional challenges. Large

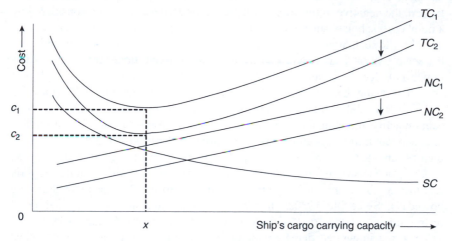

Figure 9.2 Relationship between ship's cargo-carrying capacity and transport cost.

ships are often harder to handle due to more demanding requests in financial resources, time, and physical limits, for example, navigation channels along rivers and canals, ports' berthing drafts, and cargo-handling facilities. Thus, the optimal ship size should not just be decided by the cost of operating the ship at open sea, but also by the negative externalities that the ship's physical size could impose on other components along the logistical supply chain (Jansson and Shneerson 1982). Indeed, larger ships, usually accompanied with deeper water draft, are often restricted by the physical restrictions imposed by the port conditions. This causes changes in the proportions of products received from various sources, and such requirements can pose a problem to traders and stop certain ships proceeding to where demands are present (Kendall 1972). This largely explains why deep-sea ship operators often impose substantial pressure to port operators to improve their intra- and superstructures so that they can economically benefit from deploying larger ships (Notteboom and Winkelmans 2001; Heaver 2002). Such a relationship can be found in Figure 9.2.

In Figure 9.2, *TC* is the total cost of freight transportation, *SC* is the ship-related cost, and *NC* is other nonship-related costs incurred during the shipping process, including those at ports/terminals. When both ship- and nonship-related costs are included in the analysis, it results in a U-shaped cost curve. Initially, given a ship's carrying capacity, say x, the optimal point (i.e., the lowest possible transport cost) would be c_1. However, with better coordination, for example, higher cargo-stevedoring efficiency in terminals, *NC* would decrease, thus resulting in an overall decrease in the total system costs along the supply chain, moving the optimal point to c_2. This implies that, while shipping lines invest heavily in their fleets, the commitments from ports become even greater because only improvements in port efficiency can reduce the overall transport costs (both monetary and nonmonetary), thus improving the quality of the supply chain (Slack 1998). Indeed, the negative implications of larger ships on ports has been considered by a number of scholars since the 1970s. They question how many ports can practically handle such large amount of containers and thus the economic feasibility of the scale economy approach. Large ships cannot waste time in calling at additional ports for more cargoes due to high capital costs, as well as the high port costs for serving them (Gilman 1980; Chilcote 1988; Notteboom 2002; Panayides and Cullinane 2002). Since the development of large high-speed ships is deemed economically impractical in the foreseeable future (World Bank 2007), it implies that service frequency and turnaround time of large containerships have to increase and decrease, respectively, while port calls have to be reduced. As noted by Chilcote (1988), before containerization, ships usually called at a dozen ports within a region within a liner service, compared to usually not more than five nowadays. Since the 1980s, shipping networks have also experienced rapid restructuring toward a trunk-and-feeder system (see Figures 9.3 and 9.4).

Thus, the integrated demands for ports to achieve the logistical goals have brought forward the port logistics concept. Under such a mechanism, the port operation process should be integrated into the multimodal supply chain based on efficient physical cargo flows and common strategic goals, as well as innovative organizational relationships. Physical flows consist of the port entry, stevedoring, transit, storage, and linkage systems, while information flow relates to all relevant operational information concerning the physical cargo flows. Each subsystem is interconnected in accordance with the cargo flow within the port logistics concept. Moreover, ports within the system can provide additional value-added services. These do not only include basic logistical functions, for example, cargo loading, warehousing, and so on, but also include those which can facilitate (and accelerate) integration; for example, quality control, repackaging, assembly, re-export, and so on. In short, a port logistics system plays an intermediary role of connecting the whole logistical process. Apart from their traditional role as a sea–land interface, port areas can also serve as ideal locations where different stakeholders can meet and interact.

Another implication of contemporary technological and economic development of liner shipping is that it has considerably enhanced the bargaining power of users against port service suppliers. With improved transport networks through technological innovation, shipping has become more footloose in choosing ports-of-call, and the traditional understanding that ports possess certain natural hinterlands and thus are not concerned about losing customers is becoming obsolescent. Hence, ports have gradually become the "servants" of their users where increasing borderless trade, especially in developed regions like Western Europe, would break down discrete natural hinterlands and be replaced by common ones (Hayuth and Hilling 1992; McCalla 1999). Such a development would have an influential impact on the port's competitive position. Nowadays, shipping lines have immense power in controlling the fate of different ports, especially since ports have increasingly become an important component within the global logistics chains (Heaver 2002). Indeed, the radical changes in the ports-of-call have

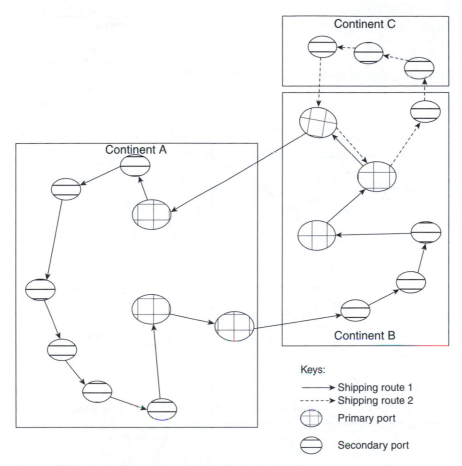

Figure 9.3 Typical shipping network before containerization.

contributed to the growing similarities between shipping lines, leading to the phenomenon that while winners win more, losers lose even more (Slack 2003). Moreover, when conducting business, most ports negotiate with users independently and thus liners' bargaining power is enhanced through better information and playing the same "threatening game" to different ports (World Bank 2007). Under the development of economies of scale within the shipping industries, shipping lines also have few choices but to pressurize ports because the increased earning capacities of their ships cannot materialize if containers are not handled efficiently (Stubbs *et al.* 1984).

Thus, competition between ports has intensified, as described by Slack (1993), being "pawns in the game" of a global transportation system. With changing demands circumstances, the traditional philosophy in port management becomes obsolescent especially since the traditional objective that a port should act as the

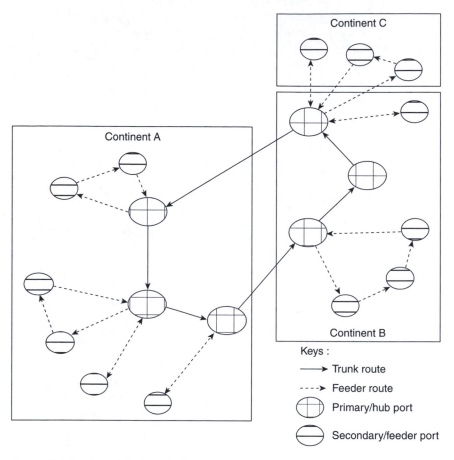

Figure 9.4 Trunk-and-feeder shipping network.

base to control its hinterland market during the colonial period (World Bank 2007) has long gone. Increasing intensity in port competition is especially significant in Western Europe where the emergence of a single market has exerted pressures on national and regional governments to give up protective measures, such as state aid, to their respective ports (Hinz 1996). Not to be left out, major ports are forced to continuously improve their facilities and services and attract potential customers to use their services (Meersman and Van de Voorde 1998). The market shares of ports are no longer guaranteed and the global actions of shipping lines have often led to hardship (McCalla 1999). As Heaver (1993) and Slack *et al.* (1996) have noted, specially designed ports for cargo handling, in particular container handling, intensified the competitive environments for port services as containerization represented capital intensive activities, and thus substantial financial burden, to port authorities around the world. Also, the scale economy approach adopted by shipping lines requires high load factors, and thus the demand for quality services on ports is becoming more intensified than ever (Slack 1998). Such developments have transformed port operation to a much more complicated industry with particular complex functions (Robinson 2002) and contemporary port development has been dictated by shipping development rather than the other way round. It did not take long after the container revolution for the labor-intensive landscape of ports to be replaced by expensive cranes and ancillary container-moving vehicles dedicated for container-stevedoring, while many ports have relocated themselves away from the city core to the more peripheral sites on more cheaply available land.

Of course, even after such expensive commitments, there is no guarantee that ships will visit. From the port's perspective, better facilities and more space are required to accommodate these bigger ships, which would ultimately increase fixed and operational costs substantially, leading to the question of how ports should charge these ships reasonably, so as to sustain the port's competitiveness, while still being able to cover the investment costs. For example, port infrastructures were often built far ahead of existing demands simply in the fear that they would fall behind if they did not do so (Haralambides 2000). In such cases, ports will be trapped into vicious cycles of creating wasteful overcapacities due to panic and unnecessary speculation. Thus, various scholars urged for the introduction of market principles in future development so as to diminish such potential dangers (Psaraftis 1998; Van Ham 1998). Similarly, Powell (2001) has emphasized that long-term planning can pay dividends only if investments do not exceed the benefits derived from it. However, the loyalty of port customers cannot be taken for granted, not only because of deficiencies in port service but also due to rearrangements in shipping networks and new partnerships or shipping alliances (cf. Notteboom 2002; Ng 2009).

Hence, similar to shipping lines, ports face the dilemma that heavy investments are required to remain competitive but adequate traffic is not guaranteed. Indeed, contemporary port operation is a highly speculative lottery game and investments in expensive, dedicated facilities usually bear significant risks, not only to small, peripheral ports but also to the large and established ones (Hayuth and Hilling 1992; Slack *et al.* 1996). It is important for decision-makers to evaluate their development plans carefully and needless duplication of facilities should be avoided as much as possible (Rimmer 1998). Indeed, development within the shipping industries has added substantial pressure on ports to operate on increasingly thinner profit margins due to increased competition and heavy capital investment requirements (Psaraftis 1998). In order to enhance port competitiveness, decision-makers are forced to change their focus from the traditional issue of whether the port possesses the ability to handle a certain amount of cargo effectively to whether the port possesses the ability to attract potential customers. Such changes pose significant implications for the methods used in assessing port performance because this is where "port choice" has been put into question (Ng 2009). As long as users are offered options to choose from, rather than measuring physical output, port performance within a competitive market should be assessed through evaluating the economic cost, that is, the ability of a port in attracting potential customers to use it and fighting off competitors.

To sustain competitiveness, ports must ensure that the increase in operation cost for liners does not lead to significant increases in the values of goods being transported (Gubbins 1988). Sensible investments could be achieved with the availability of objective port demand forecasting instruments. Peters (2001) emphasized the vital role of objectivity in avoiding over-/understated future demands so that ports would not have to tackle serious congestion, nor waste substantial amounts of money by leaving expensive infra- and superstructures laid idle for too long. Nevertheless, the degree of reliability and objectivity of assessment instruments was often doubtful.[1] Ports often needed to convince customers that they had bright prospects but at the same time ensuring that port projects looked appealing enough to generate adequate funds to proceed, thus often causing exaggerated forecasts and inferences (Huybrechts *et al.* 2002). This was not helped by the increasing difficulty in making realistic forecasts due to the increase in common hinterlands, transhipment traffic and the existence of hub hopping, where the number of competing ports grew so rapidly that ships could shift their calls with minimal costs (World Bank 2007). This complemented the view of Bennathan and Walters (1979) who argued that if competition existed between transhipment ports within the same region, transhipment demand of liners would tend to be elastic.

All these indicate that port projects can be highly risky and successful managers must be able to make good decisions through a shrewd and creative trade-off between providing more capacities and thus higher quality services (which could possibly attract more businesses) without creating overcapacity to meet future market demands at the same time. In this situation, instead of just monetary cost, quality of service is likely to play a more pivotal role in the competitive positions of ports (Slack 1985; Clark *et al.* 2001; Ng 2009). Later, Slack (1998) further strengthens this view and argues that rather than physical innovation, organizational arrangement becomes even more important to meet the new circumstances. In fact, such a requirement was recognized as early as the 1970s. Using the competition between Singapore and Hong Kong as an example, due to an increase in port size, as well as investment costs in facility construction, the proportion of fixed costs becomes more significant and this inhibits the effectiveness of cost leadership, thus implying greater emphasis on service quality differentials (Bennathan and Walters 1979). Although some scholars (for instance, Brooks 2000) attempted to play down the importance of port service quality by claiming that customers would find it increasingly difficult to distinguish between port services as infrastructure and equipment become more standardized, the increasing importance of service quality in deciding port competitiveness seems to be generally accepted within the shipping community.

To tackle these challenges, port management has to be more responsive to customer needs because new developments in the global economy and shipping ensure that the physical layouts of ports are not necessarily in line with user requirements (Juhel 2001). Such requirements partly explain the increasing privatization of port operations in different parts of the world. For example, container-stevedoring responsibility in most North European ports is now undertaken by the private sector, while most of the ports in this region are operating under the landlord or fully privatized port formula, mainly through the involvement of multinational port operators (cf. Baird 2002; Heaver 2002; Ng 2009).

Implications for port management and governance

As a strategically important component of global logistics and supply chains, the demands for ports become greater and more complicated, and port operators are confronted with various challenges. Indeed, the need of integrating different components within the system while at the same time sustaining a high efficiency level is not easy for ports. A typical example can be found in the European Union. According to a report released by the European Commission, 12 of the 22 identified bottlenecks along its SSS-included multimodal supply chains[2] had been directly related to port conditions, for example, poor infrastructures, congestion, inefficient connections with the interior part of the EU, and so on (European Commission 2006).

When certain exogenous circumstances like those mentioned above started to change, the operation environment also changed, thus causing substantial pressure, no matter functional, political, or social (Oliver 1992), to the original institutional setting. In the case of ports, for example, the changing environment had ensured that ports, often characterized by bureaucracy in their pre-containerized stage (World Bank 2007), found it difficult, if not impossible, to tackle the new pressure effectively, causing unsatisfactory outcomes, for example, inefficiency, lack of competitiveness, and so on. It is such an external contingency change of circumstances that has triggered most institutional changes. Indeed, the changing environment has meant that the concept of port has had to be changed from a simple sea–land interface to a freight distribution logistics center, mobilized by rapidly changing political and economic systems (Aldridge 1999). At this time, ports are faced with the following options: either to drop out or to establish new management structure and operation practice, based on (in)formal evaluation of different reform approaches. Throughout the past decades, most contemporary ports have undertaken such reforms, with many of them gradually moving away from direct public management to increasing private participation, resulting in more perplexing hybrid organizational port entities (Cullinane and Song 2001; Brooks and Cullinane 2007) aiming to address inefficiency, derive economic benefits through competition, minimize the negative influences of bureaucracy, reduce demands from public sector investments, enhance management skills, and adopt more efficient port labor organization. Nearly all reforms share common goals—to enable the port to refit within the changed environment—thus leading to satisfactory outcomes again, and such attempts have been well documented, for example, Heaver (1995); Cass (1998); Notteboom and Winkelmans (2001); Wang *et al.* (2004), Ng and Pallis (2010), and so on (see Figures 9.5 and 9.6 and Table 9.1 for further details).

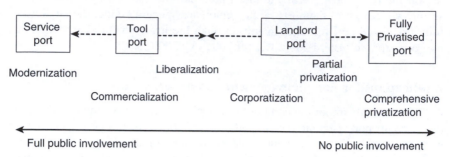

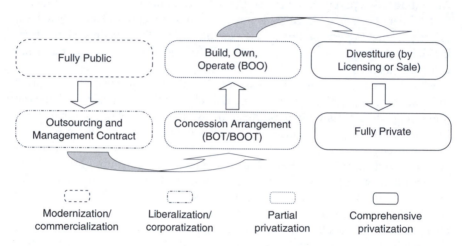

Figure 9.5 Major port reform models and reform approaches.

Figure 9.6 Major tools of port management reforms.

Table 9.1 The role of the public sector in different port models

Port model	Port authority owns infrastructures	Port authority owns superstructures	Port authority provides commercial services
Service	✓	✓	✓
Tool	✓	✓	✗
Landlord	✓	✗	✗
Fully privatized	✗	✗	✗

Source: World Bank (2007).

Implications for the port community

The changing role of ports within the supply chain since containerization also meant a change within the port community. Before the 1960s, ports had been the

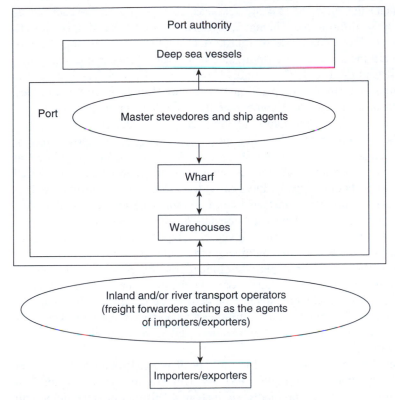

Figure 9.7 Precontainerization port community and cargo flows.

Source: Redrawn from Ng (2002).

economic and cultural centers of particular regions serving various functions, many of which were extremely important for the local economies. Indeed, ports were not only sites for taxes and revenues, but also industrial plants, communication nodes, and central market places. Cargo-handling technology was relatively simple and ports required pools of nonskilled labor for "break-bulk" freight handling, thus offering substantial employment opportunities (Figure 9.7). Within this community, little communication or coordination existed between stakeholders. Hence, throughout the transportation chain, cargoes had to pass through several agents and companies. Moreover, due to such fragile community structure, the role of the port authority as an "authority"—in terms of coordination and regulation—was extremely important. Together with the lack of inter-port competition (the so-called natural hinterland) and the fact that ports were traditionally only acting as "entry-doors" of continents (World Bank 2007), the significance of stability and sustainability within the ports often overrode efficiency. Indeed, before containerization, the loading rate per day was only 10–15 mt.

A berth with an annual throughput of 150,000 mt was regarded as efficient, thus ensuring that ships often had to wait for at least 10 days to complete each stevedoring process (Martin and Thomas 2001). Also, ports were simply sites to transfer goods from one mode of transport to another by providing the link between maritime and inland transport, and the interface between different transport infrastructures. The port's traditional role has been viewed as a place that handles ships and cargo with operational efficiency (Robinson 2002), and they contributed to economic development of the hinterland through carrying out functions of accommodating ships and other transport modes efficiently.

Nevertheless, under the changing circumstances outlined above, freight transportation is most efficient only if cargoes can move along the supply chain with minimum interruption. As mentioned earlier, containerization has altered the nature of ports dramatically. Physically, it has led to the significant reduction of labor requirements. Instead of large amount of workers at the piers waiting for work, the port landscape consists of multimillion dollar container cranes and ancillary container-moving vehicles. Due to the need for large areas of flat spaces to accommodate containers and machines, modern ports tend to relocate from the city center to peripheral locations. Moreover, the changes are not only restricted to physical alternations like the presence of large machines, automated facilities, and larger space. The nature of the industry also changed, with a new term "terminal" being introduced to ports, emphasizing the comprehensive and integrated activities that have taken place in the ports since containerization.[3]

Such developments have altered the nature of ports, leading to the rise of new port communities (see Figure 9.8). As demands for efficiency and fast handling of containers in ports increase, instead of distinct organizations with each doing their own works in traditional ports, a unified organization that can integrate and manage most of the activities of modern port operations is encouraged and some organizations have been merged. For example, the tasks of wharf-fingers and master stevedores were merged under a unified operation by terminal operators, while shipping lines took on the responsibilities of ship agents. On the other hand, freight forwarders took up the responsibilities of shippers, while warehousing was transferred from the port authority to terminal operators.

Such development ensures that the port authority does not necessarily dominate the community. Indeed, such a community may not even need an "authority," potentially reducing the need for regulations and port authority's coordination (Martin and Thomas 2001). This implies that the system has to be reformed in order for a port to sustain competitiveness and survive in this dynamic world. Given that such reform attempts to bridge the gap between changing environment and obsolescent port structure and strategy, can a particular reform approach really achieve the objective of refitting the changed environment, thus leading to a satisfactory outcome again? It is possible that the new system and strategies will find it difficult to solve the problems and fit in with the changing environment, especially since reform often means an increasing number of actors involved in port

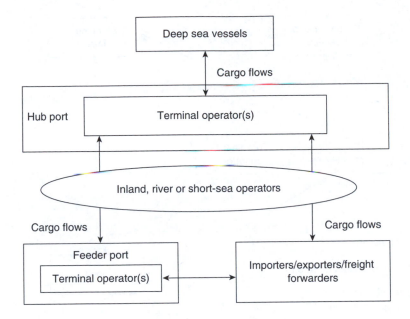

Figure 9.8 Postcontainerization port community and cargo flows.

Source: Redrawn from Ng (2002).

operation and management. The system may thus emerge in a more perplexing functional relationship within the hybrid organizational entities (Ng and Pallis 2010) leading to greater difficulty in managing the new structure. This has been noted in a number of works, for example, Baltazar and Brooks (2001), Notteboom and Winkelmans (2001), Wang and Slack (2000), Wang *et al.* (2004), Brooks and Cullinane (2007), and so on (see Figure 9.9 for further information).

Even within port reform itself, given the realistic situation within different countries, notably diversity in political tradition, institutions, and systems (Ng and Pallis 2007), will a similar solution, when applied to different cases, lead to the same outcome? In other words, can the same solution be generically applied to different ports around the world? With the potential pitfalls of increasing governance complexity, is there a so-called best reform practice that can fit to the new circumstance and be globally applicable, or does the choice of appropriate reform approach actually depend on the regional or local circumstances? Moreover, given port reform often emphasizes the improvement of efficiency, can the post-reform setting really ensure the competitiveness of ports, especially in view of the intensified port competition mentioned earlier? Last but not least, given the increasing importance of security and environmental concern in global logistics (cf. Ng and Liu 2010; Ng and Song 2010), can a restructured port address these new issues nowadays? All these are critical issues which require further investigation.

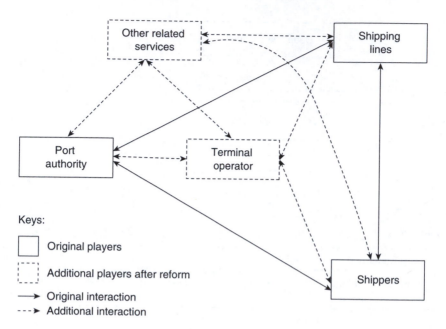

Keys:

☐ Original players

⌐⌐⌐ Additional players after reform

──→ Original interaction

---→ Additional interaction

Figure 9.9 Additional complexity in port after management reform.

Conclusions

This chapter discusses how the restructuring of the shipping industry has affected port development, as well as the port's increasingly important role acting as a facilitation point in the development of efficient global supply chains. As illustrated in the analysis above, the smoothness of cargo flows along the supply chains is highly dependent on whether ports can act as an effective intersection point between ships and other transport modes, where their efficiency and performance would be pivotal in deciding the level of optimization of the maritime logistical system. In turn, this implies it is necessary for contemporary ports to be competitive and customer oriented in terms of management and operation.

It is important to note that this process is not without its challenges, especially what exactly optimization should be; that is, the relative importance of different attributes in benchmarking the quality of supply chains. Port managers, when making strategic decisions, also need to address various challenges when attempting to fulfill a port's role as the nodal points along the supply chain, notably extra investment costs, reduction in flexibility (higher switching costs), longer and more complicated decision-making processes, potential organizational complexity, and different management culture, and so on. Last but not least, this chapter provides a suitable platform for further investigation into port evolution and development.

Notes

1 Of course, mismatch between port demand and supply always exists. Generally speaking, ports usually regard 80 percent of the utilization rate of theoretical capacity as the realistic target. However, it seems that most ports still tend to overestimate the demands of users, possibly as a strategy to justify the funding of proposed projects, marketing purpose to customers, and minimizing congestion in the future.
2 Here country-specific bottlenecks had been excluded.
3 The terms "port" and "terminal" have to be handled with care. For example, Hong Kong has ten container terminals (including the River Trade Terminal in Tuen Mun), where the port authority is usually responsible for the whole port. On the other hand, terminal operators may be responsible for the operations of the whole port (like the British port of Felixstowe operated by HPH) or may run one or more terminal(s) in a port (like Hong Kong). For further details, see Ng (2002).

Bibliography

Aldridge, H.E. 1999. *Organisations Evolving,* London: Sage.
Baird, A.J. 2002. "The Economics of Container Transhipment in Northern Europe," *International Journal of Maritime Economics,* 4(3), 249–280.
Baltazar, R. and M.R. Brooks. 2001. "The Governance of Port Devolution: A Tale of Two Countries," *Proceedings of the 9th World Conference on Transport Research*, Seoul, South Korea.
Bennathan, E. and A.A. Walters. 1979. *Port Pricing and Investment Policy for Developing Countries*, Oxford: Oxford University Press.
Bichou, K. and R. Gray. 2004. "A Logistics and Supply Chain Management Approach to Port Performance Measurement," *Maritime Policy and Management,* 31(1), 47–67.
Brooks, M. 2000. *Sea Change in Liner Shipping: Regulation and Managerial Decision-Making in a Global Industry*, Oxford: Pergamon.
Brooks, M.R. and K. Cullinane (eds.). 2007. *Devolution, Port Governance and Port Performance,* London: Elsevier.
Carbone, V. and M. Martino. 2003. "The Changing Role of Ports in Supply-Chain Management: An Empirical Analysis," *Maritime Policy and Management,* 30(4), 305–320.
Cass, S. 1998. *World Port Privatisation: Finance, Funding and Ownership: A Cargo Systems Report*, London: IIR.
Chilcote, P.W. 1988. "The Containerization Story: Meeting the Competition in Trade," in M.J. Hershman (ed.) *Urban Ports and Harbour Management*, London: Taylor & Francis. pp. 125–146.
Clark, X., D. Dollar, and A. Micco. 2001. "Maritime Transport Costs and Port Efficiency," Washington, DC: World Bank Group. pp. 1–38.
Coyle, J.J., E.J. Bardi, and R.A. Novack. 1999. *Transportation*, Cincinnati, OH: South-Western College Publishing.
Cullinane, K. and M. Khanna. 2000. "Economies of Scale in Large Container Ships," *Journal of Transport Economics and Policy,* 33(2), 185–208.
Cullinane, K. and D.W. Song. 2002. "Port Privatization Policy and Practice," *Transport Reviews,* 22, 55–75.
European Commission. 2006. *Mid-Term Review of the Programme for the Promotion of Short Sea Shipping,* Brussels: European Commission [COM (2006) 380 final].
Gilman, S. 1980. "A Critique for the Super-Port Idea," *Maritime Policy and Management,* 7(2), 1.

Gubbins, E.J. 1988. *Managing Transport Operations*. London: Kogan Page.

Haralambides, H.E. 2000. "A Second Scenario on the Future of the Hub-and-Spoke System in Liner Shipping," Paper submitted to *Latin Ports and Shipping 2000 Conference*, Lloyd's List, November 14–16, Miami, FL.

Hayuth, Y. and D. Hilling. 1992. "Technological Change and Seaport Development," in B. Hoyle and D. Pinder (eds.) *European Port Cities in Transition*, London: Belhaven. pp. 4–58.

Heaver, T.D. 1993. "Shipping and the Market for Port Services," in G. Blauwens, G. De Brabander, and E. Van de Voorde (eds.) *The Dynamics of a Harbour*, Kapellen: Uitgeverij Pelckmans. pp. 227–248.

Heaver, T.D. 1995. "The Implications of Increased Competition Among Ports for Port Policy and Management," *Maritime Policy and Management,* 22(2), 125–133.

Heaver, T.D. 2002. "The Evolving Roles of Shipping Lines in International Logistics," *International Journal of Maritime Economics,* 4(3), 210–230.

Hinz, C. 1996. "Prospects for a European Ports Policy: A German View," *Maritime Policy and Management,* 23(4), 337–340.

Huybrechts, M., H. Meersman, E. Van de Voorde, E. Van Hooydonk, A. Verbeke, and W. Winkelmans. 2002. *Port Competitiveness: An Economic and Legal Analysis of the Factors Determining the Competitiveness of Seaports*, Antwerp: De Boeck.

Jansson, J.O. and D. Shneerson. 1982. "The Optimal Ship Size," *Journal of Transport Economics and Policy,* 16(3), 217–238.

Juhel, M.H. 2001. "Globalization, Privatisation and Restructuring of Ports," *International Journal of Maritime Economics,* 3, 139–174.

Kendall, P.M.H. 1972. "A Theory of Optimum Ship Size," *Journal of Transport Economics and Policy,* 1(2), 128–146.

McCalla, R.J. 1999. "Global Change, Local Pain: Intermodal Seaport Terminals and Their Service Areas," *Journal of Transport Geography,* 7(4), 247–254.

Martin, J. and B.J. Thomas. 2001. "The Container Terminal Community," *Maritime Policy and Management,* 28(3), 279–292.

Meersman, H. and E. Van de Voorde. 1998. "Coping With Port Competition in Europe: A State of the Art," in G. Sciutto and C.A. Brebbia (eds.) *Marine Engineering and Ports,* Southampton: WIT Press. pp. 281–290.

Miyashita, K. 2004. "The Logistics Strategy of Japanese Ports: The Case of Kobe and Osaka," in T.W. Lee and K. Cullinane (eds.) *World Shipping and Port Development*, New York: Palgrave Macmillan. pp. 181–198.

Ng, A.K.Y. 2002. *Port Operation, Reform and Governance in China: A Case Study,* MPhil thesis, The University of Hong Kong, Hong Kong.

Ng, A.K.Y. 2009. *Port Competition: The Case of North Europe,* Saarbrucken: VDM Verlag.

Ng, A.K.Y. and J.J. Liu. 2010. "The Port and Maritime Industries in the Post-2008 World," *Research in Transportation Economics,* 27(1), 1–3.

Ng, A.K.Y. and A.A. Pallis. 2007. "Reforming Port Governance: The Role of Political Culture," *Proceedings of the IAME Conference 2007*, Athens, Greece, July 4–6.

Ng, A.K.Y. and A.A. Pallis. 2010. "Port Governance Reforms in Diversified Institutional Frameworks: Generic Solutions, Implementation Asymmetries," *Environment and Planning A*, 42(9), 2147–2167.

Ng, A.K.Y. and S. Song. 2010. "The Environmental Impacts of Pollutants Generated by Routine Shipping Operations on Ports," *Ocean and Coastal Management,* 53(5–6), 301–311.

Nijkamp, P., J.M. Vleugel, R. Maggi, and I. Masser. 1994. *Missing Transport Networks in Europe,* Aldershot: Avebury.

Notteboom, T.E. 2002. "Consolidation and Contestability in the European Container Handling Industry," *Maritime Policy and Management,* 29(3), 257–269.

Notteboom, T.E. and W. Winkelmans. 2001. "Structural Changes in Logistics: How Will Port Authorities Face the Challenge?" *Maritime Policy and Management,* 28(1), 71–89.

Oliver, C. 1992. "The Antecedents of Deinstitutionalization," *Organisation Studies,* 13(4), 563–588.

Panayides, P.M. and K. Cullinane. 2002. "Competitive Advantage in Liner Shipping: A Review and Research Agenda," *International Journal of Maritime Economics,* 4, 189–209.

Peters, H.J.F. 2001. "Developments in Global Sea Trade and Container Shipping Markets: Their Effects on the Port Industry and Private Sector Involvement." *Maritime Economics and Logistics,* 3(1), 3–26.

Powell, T. 2001. *The Principles of Transport Economics,* London: PTRC Education and Research Services.

Psaraftis, H.N. 1998. "Strategies for Mediterranean Port Development," in G. Sciutto and C.A. Brebbia (eds.) *Maritime Engineering and Ports,* Southampton WIT Press. pp. 255–262.

Rimmer, P.J. 1998. "Ocean Liner Shipping Services: Corporate Restructuring and Port Selection/Competition," *Asia Pacific Viewpoint,* 39(2), 193–208.

Robinson, R. 2002. "Ports as Elements in Value-Driven Chain Systems: The New Paradigm," *Maritime Policy and Management,* 29(3), 241–255.

Slack, B. 1985. "Containerization, Inter-Port Competition and Port Selection," *Maritime Policy and Management,* 12(4), 293–303.

Slack, B. 1993. "Pawns in the Game: Ports in a Global Transportation System," *Growth and Change,* 24, 579–588.

Slack, B. 1998. "Intermodal Transportation," in B. Hoyle and R. Knowles (eds.) *Modern Transport Geography,* 2nd Edition, New York: John Wiley & Sons.

Slack, B. 2003. "The Global Imperatives of Container Shipping," in D. Pinder and B. Slack (eds.) *Shipping and Ports in the Twenty-First Century,* London: Routledge.

Slack, B., C. Comtois, and G. Sletmo. 1996. "Shipping Lines as Agents of Change in the Port Industry," *Maritime Policy and Management,* 23(3), 289–300.

Stubbs, P.C., W.J. Tyson, and M.Q. Dalvi. 1984. *Transport Economics,* London: George Allen & Unwin.

Van Ham, J.C. 1998. "Changing Public Port Management in the Hamburg–Le Havre Range," in G. Sciutto and C.A. Brebbia (eds.) *Maritime Engineering and Ports,* Southampton: WIT Press. pp. 13–21.

Wang, J.J. and B. Slack. 2000. "The Evolution of a Regional Container Port System: The Pearl River Delta," *Journal of Transport Geography,* 8, 263–276.

Wang, J.J., A.K.Y. Ng, and D. Olivier. 2004. "Port Governance in China: A Review of Policies in an Era of Internationalising Port Management Practices," *Transport Policy,* 11(3), 237–250.

World Bank. 2007. *World Bank Port Reform Tool Kit,* 2nd Edition, Washington, DC: World Bank Group Transport Division.

10 Information technology in supply chain management and transportation logistics

Key items:

- *Supply chain management and information systems (ISs)*
- *Strategic use of ISs*
- *IT infrastructure for a global supply chain*
- *Applications of ISs*
- *Customer relationship management (CRM) systems*
- *Enterprise resource planning (ERP)*
- *Supplier management systems (SMSs)*

Background

Information Technology (IT) has become an important enabler of today's global supply chain, and it not only facilitates the management of information flow along the supply chain, but also enhances the planning of product flow and cash flow.

Companies are complicated systems, facing tremendous challenges in managing tons of information. For example, the retailer giant, Wal-Mart, is keen in visualizing the status of products along the supply chain (Roberti 2005). Using advanced IT, such as radio frequency identification (RFID), Wal-Mart attempts to closely monitor the products moving from suppliers to retail stores. Accordingly, Wal-Mart needs to transmit and update real-time product information for more than 3 million items per week. Without an extensive use of IT, it would be impossible for Wal-Mart to process such a large volume of data for supply chain management.

Why is information visualization so important to companies such as Wal-Mart? How can Wal-Mart manage tons of information? How does IT relate to today's business and supply chain management? Why do successful big companies, such as Wal-Mart, keep investing in innovative IT and information systems (ISs) in their business? In this chapter, we are going to seek answers to these questions.

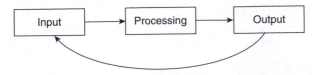

Figure 10.1 Three components of ISs.

IT and ISs

Information technology, in general, refers to the technology of information processing, which includes three aspects: storage, computation, and transmission. Storage is to keep information in a media for future access. Computation is to execute calculations from input data to generate output. Transmission is to transfer information from one location to another for data sharing. From this perspective, many ancient inventions in history, such as papers, abacuses, and pigeons, were IT for storage, computation, and transmission. They are comparable to modern technology, such as hard-disks, processors, and fiber-cables, but the latter are much more efficient than the former in terms of costs and performance.

From a system perspective, *information systems* consist of three components as shown in Figure 10.1: input, processing, and output, where inputs are put into a processing component which generates outputs, and then, outputs are used as feedbacks to adjust the inputs, forming an iterative process. For example, a demand forecasting system usually receives two kinds of inputs: the historical sales information, and the future market indicators such as seasonality. Based on the input, it calculates and generates the predication of future demand. According to the output, the manager may adjust the market indicators as a feedback to the system to enhance further predictions.

Based on the definitions of IT and IS above, what ITs and ISs need to be adopted if companies, such as Wal-Mart, plan to build RFID applications for supply chain management? At the 104 Wal-Mart stores and 36 Sam's Clubs, RFID readers are installed between the back room and the retail room to trace cases of goods shipping in and out automatically (Roberti 2005). The readers serve as the backbone for data transmission, and, together with other hardware and software, constitute an IS. The inputs of this IS consist of signals sent from the RFID tags attached in the cases, the processing module is in the RFID readers to capture signals and to update the status of the cases, and the output is generated and transferred to update the new status of the cases in databases of the stores. The RFID itself belongs to IT, to send, capture, and process signals, and to trace goods. Such a tracking function is fundamentally important in global supply chain management, because accurate information about goods is critical in enhancing the logistics management and production scheduling. Moreover, to build the whole RFID project for Wal-Mart, it requires hardware including

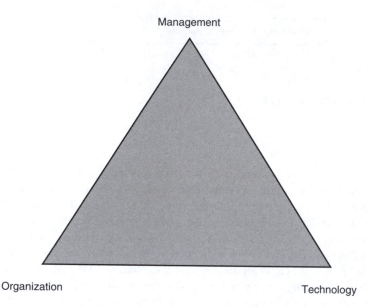

Management

Organization

Technology

Figure 10.2 Three dimensions of ISs.

RFID tags and readers, software including database management systems, data processing systems, and data analysis systems, and networking facilities including wireless routers, and so on.

As we have seen, Figure 10.1 illustrates an IS from a system point of view and a technical perspective. However, managers who use an IS to operate business are more interested in managerial perspectives of the IS, such as how the IS can enhance competitive advantages of a business, and how the IS affects organizations of a company. This, together with the technical perspective, leads to a three-dimensional definition of IS, which includes an organization dimension, a management dimension, and a technology dimension, and can be plotted in a triangle as shown in Figure 10.2.

As shown in Figure 10.2, in addition to technology, ISs also relate to organization and management. Utilizing ISs to help a company's logistics and supply chain management should involve participation of different departments in a company, and coordination of different companies along a supply chain. For example, when introducing RFID technology to stores, Wal-Mart needs to understand the difficulties in changing staff, operations, and resource allocations in Wal-Mart as well as in stores and other external partners. With this understanding, Wal-Mart is then able to encourage their partners to share product information, and to gain benefit from the sharing.

In a company, the management's objective is to generate profits out of many complicated situations. Mangers need to develop strategies, formulate action plans, and guide an execution of the plan to solve problems. Today, ISs have become critical resources to a company, and must be well managed to bring sufficient returns. As we have seen, the aim of the RFID project in Wal-Mart is to improve the efficiency of logistics operations. However, when traditional barcodes are replaced by RFID tags, staff need to be retrained to understand how to use RFID technologies, and inventory management needs to be reviewed more frequently to harness the benefit of visualizing real-time inventory data. Therefore, it is important to manage the change well when adopting new IT for business.

In a summary, IT is a fundamental infrastructure of an IS, which, as an important resource to a company, needs to be well managed. Accordingly, building an IS for business is a process of changes, and is not only about IT, but also related to management and organization issues and impacts.

Supply chain management and ISs

When looking at the history of supply chain management and IT, both of them share some similarities. In 1960s, a transistor-based computer appeared, but was only able to process simple routine calculations. In the same period, SAP R1 (Monk *et al.* 2006), a simple accounting system, was developed to automate the generation of accounting routinely, and industry was talking about establishing efficient assemble lines to assign every task as a routine job.

In the 1970s and 1980s, an integrated circuit-based computer was invented. It was faster and smaller, and able to compute more complicated analyses, such as to play chess against a human. In the same period, SAP R2, a comprehensive enterprise system was developed, with more complicated functions to support planning and scheduling (Monk *et al.* 2006). The industry was talking about improving decision making as well.

In the 1990s, the network was established. Through the network, individual computers were able to exchange information and to collaborate for high-performance computation. In this period, SAP R3 was developed to allow the enterprise system to be distributed in different locations and to be connected through the network (Monk *et al.* 2006). The industry at that time proposed the idea of a supply chain, which was about integrating the decisions for suppliers and demanders as well as other participants of a supply chain.

In the twenty-first century, globalization is changing world economy. The American economy and other advanced industrial economies in Europe and Asia have increasingly depended on imports and exports. Today, Wal-Mart has over 3,800 stores in the United States (Zook and Graham 2006). More than 50 percent of Americans live within five miles (that is about a 10-min drive) from their closest Wal-Mart store. About 98 percent of products in Wal-Mart are imported from places such as China, Mexico, and Vietnam. Foreign trade, including both exports and imports, accounts for more than 25 percent of the goods and services produced in the United States. Such a percentage is even higher in countries such as Japan and Germany. Due to globalization there are no barriers or borders any more. Companies can do business in every part of the world. The world is changing and actually becoming flat.

It is also in the twenty-first century that the Internet emerges, allowing an international communications system, which has significantly reduced the costs of operating business on a global scale, to be built. Through the Internet, customers can shop for almost everything almost anywhere from the global marketplace. They can obtain price and quality information in real time. Companies can reduce costs significantly by finding low-cost suppliers and outsourcing production facilities in other countries. Manufactures today, such as Dell, can sell products directly to customers through the Internet, and duplicate their business models in multiple countries without having to redesign their expensive IS infrastructure. Such changes point to a trend of a digital supply chain, in which relationships and transactions among customers, suppliers, and employees are digitally connected and supported. A digital supply chain has no barriers of space and time. Companies and individuals can do business everywhere to their best potential. For example, American customers can order Dell computers online from Dell's website, which will trigger the production of computers in Dell's factories in China, the purchase of components in the Philippines, and the shipment of the final products, as well as other logistics activities around the world.

In summary, on the one hand, with the development of IT, ISs are able to form an international communication system, to facilitate the development of globalization. On the other hand, the development of globalization drives the development of ISs, which further drives the development of IT.

Strategic use of ISs

IT has become a necessity for doing global business today, mainly because it can help companies achieve the following strategic goals.

Operations management efficiency: One of the most fundamental features of IT is the power of computations, data storage, and data transmissions. Equipped with IT, an IS is often used to automate the data processing, to enhance efficiency of operations management. For example, in the 1960s, reservation management at the Hilton hotels was manually processed at a call center. Surprisingly, such a manual system could achieve a very high service level. Customers could get confirmation within three minutes. However, there was a very big problem in such a manual system: the scalability. When the market went large, the cost of expanding the manual system was high, while the cost of expanding an IS was significantly lower. This explains why most hotels today, no matter how small or how big, use ISs to handle reservation requests, as well as other data processing and queries.

Cooperation effectiveness: With the appearance of the Internet, business today can achieve its reach of suppliers and customers in the optimum way. Information is shared among different companies as well as among different departments of a company. For example, Wal-Mart has built an IS, called

Retail-Link, which digitally links its suppliers to every one of Wal-Mart's 5,289 stores worldwide. As soon as a customer purchases an item, the supplier will be noted to ship a replacement off the shelf. It allows Wal-Mart to establish the most efficient supermarket chain in the retailing industry. Without the IS, it would be impossible for Wal-Mart to manage 17,400 suppliers in 80 countries.

Innovative business models: A business model describes how a company produces, delivers, and sells products or services to generate profit. IT, especially the Internet, has expanded a company's supply chain to reach customers. From that, numerous innovative business models have appeared. For example, Amazon, the world number one book retailer today, sells millions of books to customers online, while 20 percent of its sales are for books that do not appear in off-line book stores.

Sustainable competitive advantages: Changes breed opportunities. As IT keeps progressing, new opportunities always appear to companies. A company, who can take advantage of IT to improve its supply chain management, will gain sustainable competitive advantages against competitors, because IT itself is a platform for innovative applications to enhance operations efficiency and decision making. For example, since Dell foresaw the increasing populations of Internet users, its online direct sales model, which is able to offer customers low-price computers, has brought them competitive advantage for 10 years.

Flexible organization structure: With IT, the structure of a supply chain can be much more flexible than before. For example, the RFID systems built in Wal-Mart' stores allow suppliers to observe sales data directly through the ISs, and adjust their production and inventories to respond to market changes in real time. This can help in reducing the operational costs of Wal-Mart's supply chain.

Managing new business assets: IT today has become one of the most important capitals in a company, accounting for more than 50 percent of the capital-goods dollars spent in the United States (Laudon and Laudon 2010). It becomes as important as traditional assets, such as people, money, and machines. The success of a business today will well depend on how it makes IT investment decisions.

Developing solid business fundamentals: IT is not only an enabler of today's business, but also a fundamental infrastructure. When seeking for suppliers in Asia, international retailers, such as Metro, often evaluate candidates by not only cost and quality issues, but also IT facilities, such as access of the Internet, database management systems, IT skills of the staff, and so on. This is because without these facilities, it would be very difficult for the international companies to collaborate with their Asian partners.

IT infrastructure for a global supply chain

Equipped with IT, an IS is able to enhance various business processes of a company, helping to save costs and increase revenues. A *business process* is a set of

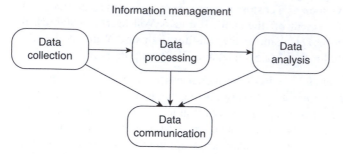

Figure 10.3 Four basic aspects of managing business information.

related tasks that companies develop to produce business outputs. It is determined by the way a company organizes its workflows, the methods it uses to accomplish tasks, and the way it coordinates its activities among employees, customers, and suppliers. An IS herein enhances business processes by either increasing the efficiency of existing processes, or enabling new processes to transform the business, or both. Therefore, managing an IS is not only about technology, but also related to understanding business processes, managing changes in business processes, and generating values for companies.

As summarized in Figure 10.3, there are four basic categories of IT infrastructures for enhancing business processes of a company, including data collection, data processing, data analysis, and data communication.

Information collection infrastructure

A successful IS for supply chain and logistics management relies on a database which supports high-quality collection and storage of business data. A database is a group of data. When opening your laptop, there will be many files. Each file stores your personal data, company data, contact data of your customers, and so on. From this perspective, every file constitutes a special database, in which data entities are stored sequentially. For example, if Wal-Mart wants to store the information of their products with RFID tags, it is very natural to store the information into a file in which each data entry consists of attributes, such as product ID, product description, RFID tag ID, locations of the RFID tag, and so on, as shown in Figure 10.4.

However, using sequential files to store data has its drawbacks. If one record appears in multiple files, problems of data redundancy and inconsistency will occur. For example, if the warehouse management system and transportation system use two different files that both store information about products and RFID tags, it not only requires more space to store the redundant information, but also makes it difficult to update data when changes occur. Suppose a product batch of lights arrive at a warehouse, the location of the RFID tags will be updated in the

Product ID	Product Description	RFID ID	RFID Location	RFID Timestamp
P0001	Lights	R0100	Hong Kong Airport	12:00:00, 01/01/2008
P0002	Books	R0101	Shen Zheng Factory	12:00:00, 31/12/2007

Figure 10.4 A sample file of data entries for products and RFID information.

file associated with the warehouse system, but not in the file associated with the logistics system.

To resolve the data redundancy and inconsistency problems, a more complicated database management system is often needed, which will centralize the data management and provide a standard way for the application to access data, modify data, and manage data. The database management system is an interface between application programs and physical data files, to separate the two views of data. As shown in Figure 10.5, one is called a logical view, which defines how data are perceived by end users, and the other is called a physical view, which determines how data are organized in the physical storage media of an IS.

One typical architecture of database management systems commonly used in today's ISs for supply chain management is the *relational database*. In the relational database, all data are represented by two-dimensional tables called relations, to relate data with attributes in the same table as well as to relate data across different tables that have the same attributes. Figure 10.5 consists of two tables, one for RFID tags and the other for products. The common data element "RFID ID" represents a relationship between products and RFID tags, that is, the products with Product ID are tagged by RFID with RFID ID. Based on such tables, we can have basic operations to manipulate data, such as selection, join, and projection, as well as other operations that are usually a mixture of these three basics. Oracle, IBM DB2, MySQL, and Microsoft SQL Server are the major vendors of relational database management systems.

In addition to a well-designed database, a company has to further ensure that the data in databases are accurate and reliable, and contain the information it needs, which is often referred to as data quality. Maintaining a database with high-quality data is very important in today's business world. The quality of decision making in a company depends very much on the quality of data in its databases. If data are inaccurate or inconsistent with other sources of information, it can create serious operational and financial problems.

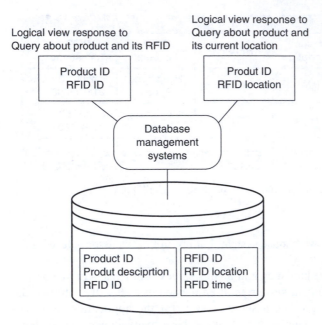

Figure 10.5 Two views of a sample database system.

Inaccurate and low-quality data cost US businesses $600 billion every year (Eckerson 2002).

To ensure high-quality business data, a company can either conduct a data quality audit, or do data cleaning exercises. A data quality audit involves a structured survey in the company on the accuracy and the completeness of the data in its current IS. Data cleansing consists of activities for detecting and correcting data in a database that are incorrect, incomplete, inconsistent, improperly formatted, or redundant.

Finally, the business data stored in a database management system are either manually input, or from other ISs. For example, the product-tracking system is one of the most widely used tools to monitor operations of supply chains and collect business data in real time. It is built based on ITs such as GPS, RFID, Smart Card, and so on. For example, Wal-Mart uses RFID to visualize the supply chain, based on a set of hardware to capture signals from tags, and a set of software to store data transferred from the tags (Roberti 2005).

Data processing infrastructure

With business data available in a database, an IS can be built to automate operational processes in each stage of the supply chain. The functions of an IS can be described, from a functional perspective, to facilitate after-sale services, sales and marketing, manufacturing and logistics, finance and accounting, procurement, and human resource management.

After-sale service systems: Today, more and more companies compete for after-sale services to customers. The mission of service is to increase the loyalty of customers. Therefore, more and more companies establish websites to allow customers to find contacts for help, useful information in FAQ, and other customized services. For example, most courier service providers such as FedEx allow customers to track their goods online, which is a typical IS for after-sale service in the logistics industry.

Sales and marketing systems: The mission of marketing is to identify the customers and their demands. That of sales is to sell products or services to the customer. Since both are so closely related, their information requirements are similar. For this reason, most ISs for supply chain management combine functions for sales and marketing. The input of the sales and marketing systems is sales data, such as tractions records, product recodes, and so on. Through this system, various sales reports, such as a summary of sales in different locations, can be generated automatically, and this can be accessed by managers and staffs of sales, and by marketing departments for future planning.

Manufacturing and logistics systems: After sales and marketing departments sell a product or service, the company has to produce it and ship it to customers. The manufacturing and logistics ISs facilitate this process, by controlling machines as well as supporting decisions for production and transportation planning. For example, an IS is often used to help managers decide where the manufacturing plants will be located, how many raw materials will be needed and ordered, and how to produce and deliver products on a daily basis. Such systems can facilitate information sharing and coordinate different participants of the supply chain. The most commonly used manufacturing and logistics system is an order management system. It allows merchandisers to process daily orders, trace the orders, fulfill the orders, and deliver the orders.

Finance and accounting systems: Finance and accounting systems are widely used in companies. They were implemented in the first generation of management ISs in the early 1970s. These systems allow companies to monitor their financial conditions, such as how much money will be available for future expansion, when will be the next time to receive payment, and so on. Information from different sources is first integrated in the finance and accounting systems, and is then passed to other systems for further processing for different purposes within a company.

Procurement systems: Procurement systems aim to streamline the procurement processes by automation and to get competitive purchasing rates from suppliers by conducting online auctions. For example, Philips Electronics has developed a freight procurement system to purchase transportation services from major transportation service providers, such as DHL and FedEx, at the beginning of every year. Such a system can reduce the period of the purchasing cycle as well as saving total purchasing costs.

Human resources systems: With human resources ISs, companies can get people with the right skills and the right experiences to do the right job. The system achieves the personal information of existing employees and job applicants. Based on these data, the system can generate reports for the evaluation of the performance of employees, the positions for next hiring, the current organizational structure of the company, and which job applicants the company should invite for further interview. For example, many companies, such as Google, release job openings on their websites, and applicants can simply submit applications through email. It connects the company and their future employees much more closely than before.

Data analysis infrastructure

The power of computations in ISs not only supports the automation of supply chain management, but also provides decision supports. Business intelligence is a set of applications and technologies that form a data analysis infrastructure to analyze business data and information, and to support decisions for companies.

Since the supply chain management involves a large volume of real-time business data, companies today are strongly urged to use business intelligence systems to analyze these data and support decisions in their business. Business intelligence has been scored as the number one IT that most CEO would like to invest in and implement (EXP 2009). For example, by having real-time product information obtained from RFID, Wal-Mart expected a saving of $287 million by reducing lost sales, because these real-time data can be analyzed by a business intelligence system to monitor changes in the market, and to improve forecasting and inventory management, which will eventually generate significant profits.

The maturity of business intelligence can be measured in four levels: statistical analysis, forecasting, predictive models, and optimizations.

Statistical analysis monitors the company performance, and illustrates what is happening in your company. For example, to evaluate performance of a supply chain, a company needs to define key supply chain indicators, such as inventory levels, turnover rates, transportation costs, sales volume, and so on. An IS can be used to streamline a process to monitor these indicators. For example, statistics analysis has been widely used in sales and marketing systems, which basically generate sales reports consisting of sales statistics.

Since companies collect huge amount of data, how to define the statistics for interest and how to calculate the statistics on demand are very important. Online analytical processing (OLAP) serves this purpose. OLAP treats the business data as data entries with multiple attributes, and calculate statistics based on queries with restrictions on attributes. It creates multidimensional views of data in a database, which enables users to view and analyze large volumes of data in different ways, and to obtain online answers to *ad hoc* questions in a very short time. For example, by queries through OLAP, users can quickly know the aggregated sales volume in different regions and for different products.

Forecasting analysis reveals the business trends from statistics. The basic tools are charts and regression analysis. It extracts data from a database and plots statistics and trends. For example, suppose you are a production manager. What kinds of data will you want to review at the end of every month? It can be monthly production volume, the production plan for next month, as well as their trends. An IS is often used to facilitate such a function for production managers, and includes producing trend charts about the production plan. These charts can help managers see the large picture about the current production status and see what is going to be produced in the near future.

Predictive models reveal the hidden knowledge behind statistics. Typical technologies include data clustering, decision tree analysis, and so on, and are based on a large amount of computation. Data clustering technology plots the data entries with multiple attributes and groups them into clusters according to the distance between them. For example, you can plot your customers based on their attributes, such as ages, identities, locations, and so on, and find that they naturally form groups. Customers within the same groups usually have similar tastes in products, which will help you develop your marketing campaign. The decision tree analysis reveals a set of logic rules behind phenomena. For example, a marketing manager of a commercial bank will be interested in what kinds of customers are going to be interested in new life insurance plans. From the historical sales data on similar insurance plans, a set of rules can be generated in the form of a tree to project who will be interested in the plan. An example of a decision tree is shown in Figure 10.6.

Optimization suggests how to operate your business in the best way. Traditionally, to use optimization technology, it usually requires managers with help from optimization professionals to formulate their problems into mathematical forms, which can then be passed to optimization solvers to solve. Typical commercial optimization solvers include the ILOG/CPLEX, GAMS, LINGO, and so on. For example, suppose the logistics manager wants to plan a route for his vehicles to pick up and deliver cargoes so as to minimize the total transportation time. Such a vehicle-routing problem can be formulated as a mathematical programming model, and can be solved by ILOG optimization solver. In addition to using a general optimization solver, some companies develop an IS for solving particularly problems, such as vehicle-routing problems, which are more user-friendly for the managers to use. These specialized an ISs are sometimes web based, allowing customers to submit instances of their problems online, and to receive solutions from the system upon payment by the customers. By clicking and dragging tasks, the manager can easily define the problem instance and run the solver.

Today it is a common practice for companies to use an IS to collect and store large volumes of data about their business and customers. However, it is rare and challenging for companies to turn data into useful information and effective decision supports. With improved business intelligence technology, companies will be able to create new opportunities to connect their business with customers and suppliers, by extracting information more easily and more precisely

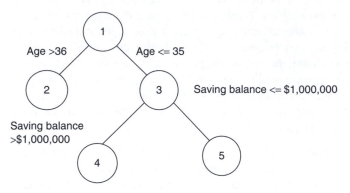

Figure 10.6 A sample decision tree obtained from data-mining.

from their database. Companies, who are more successful in using data analysis and optimization techniques to reach customers and suppliers through the supply chain, will achieve more sustainable competitive advantage in today's business world.

Data communications infrastructure

The data communication infrastructure of an IS for supply chain management is mainly based on networks, which are formed by connecting computers and other computational devices for information and data sharing. With resources and information shared, networks are able to increase productivity. For example, Wal-Mart has used RFID-based systems to share sales information at stores with suppliers so that suppliers are able to adjust production and inventory planning quickly in response to changes in customers' requirements, and therefore increase productivity. Networks play an important role in today's global supply chain. About $769 billion is spent in the United States on telecommunications equipment and services, and the spending keeps increasing every year.

The technology of computer networks and telecommunications can benefit the business in the following six aspects. The first is to decrease transaction costs, because networks dramatically reduce the cost of communication, which allows companies to buy and sell products in a much cheaper manner. The second is to decrease agency costs, because with networks, companies can monitor employee performance and market changes in a much cheaper manner. The third is to increase agility of a company's business and organization, because with networks, the company has an integrated system to control the business which is more responsive to any changes in the market. The fourth is to enhance the quality of management decisions, because networks allow companies to share information in real time, so that decisions can be made more accurately based on such timely information. The fifth is to remove geographical barriers, because with networks, companies can reach suppliers and customers even in other continents. The last is to remove temporal barriers, because with computer networks companies are able to control business and manufacturing 7 days a week.

The success of Dell's business in the personal computer (PC) market provides a good illustration of the benefit of networks. In September 1999, there was an earthquake in Taiwan. As most suppliers of PC components were located in Taiwan, this earthquake resulted in a delay of shipments of PC components to the United States for several weeks. A lot of PC manufacturers, such as Apple, Compaq, and so on, suffered from this delay, while Dell was an exception. At that time, Dell already had a very advanced networking infrastructure. They were able to get data on the earthquake early, to change prices of its PC configurations overnight, and thus allow sales representatives to adjust prices in real time. By shifting demands, Dell avoided market loss (Lee 2004). Its networking facility reduced operational costs for Dell, including the transaction costs for selling products to customers all over the world, and the agency costs for monitoring inventory. It also increased the agility of Dell's response to the change of suppliers quickly. It also provided real-time data for sales representatives to adjust prices based on the inventories shown in the system. It removed geographical barriers and temporal barriers for Dell to do business all over the world.

A computer network consists of two or more computers that are connected. A simple desktop computer connects to the network by a network interface card (NIC). To share network resources, such as printers, and to route communications on a local area network (LAN), it requires a special software system, called network operating system (NOS), which is usually running in a server computer for all the applications on LAN. Besides NOS, it also requires hardware, such as hubs and switches, to help route communication on the LAN to the right computing device. Figure 10.7 illustrates the basic components of networking. When two or more LANs are connected to each other, it requires a router to guarantee data communication to the correct network device.

It is interesting to see that the network infrastructure is similar to a supply chain or a supply network. The only difference is that the objects transferred in the network are data, while the objects transferred in the supply chain are mainly the physical products. One may also notice that supply chain management is not only about managing physical goods, but also managing cash, service, and information, which are closely related to computer networks. Accordingly, many useful applications based on the network infrastructure have been invented for logistics and supply chain management. Among them, we are going to look at three typical applications: Internet applications, electronic data interchange (EDI) networks, and RFID.

Internet applications are mainly based on client/server computing. Servers are computers processing computation tasks, while clients are interfaces to the users. Networks connect clients and servers. For example, when customers buy books on Amazon, they browse the websites through their laptops which serve as clients. Requests for information retrieval and book transactions are transferred through the Internet to remote database and transaction servers, which extract

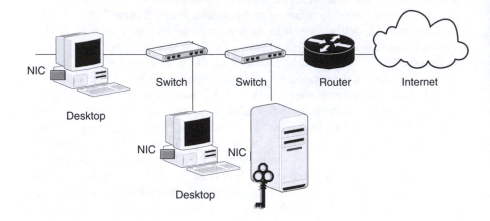

Figure 10.7 Basic components of networking: NIC, server, router, and switch.

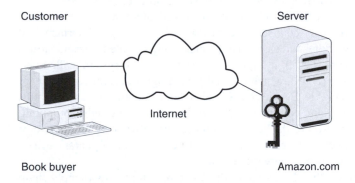

Figure 10.8 A client/server model for Internet applications.

information from the database and process the transactions. Figure 10.8 shows this simple client/server model of online book purchasing.

The major benefits of client/server model are to separate the heavy-loaded computational tasks away from the weak-loaded interactions with users, which allows suppliers and demanders to trade online and form a digital market called *e-commerce*.

In e-commerce, companies are able to trade through the Internet rather than in the physical world. For example, Dell adopts their direct sale model to do business in *e-commerce*. Through Dell's web portal, customers can easily customize computer components online for their own interests, and trigger the whole production and delivery process. Internet technology has significantly reduced the operational costs of order management and customizations. The computer networks can also enhance the procurement activities of a company. For example, MS Market is an Internet application

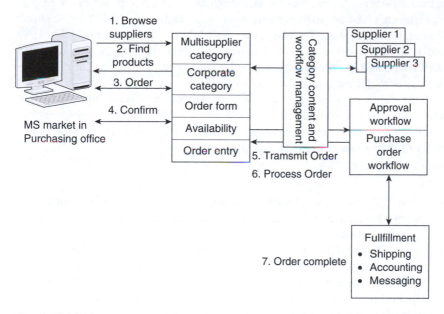

Figure 10.9 Using Internet and MS Market to automate the procurement process.

which facilitates the internal purchasing process in a company. As shown in Figure 10.9, the purchasing officers can use MS Market to share information among internal buyers and external suppliers through the Internet, and can also streamline the purchasing procedure to reduce transaction costs.

Trading in a digital market can reduce the operations and logistics costs dramatically. It also reduces marginal costs that are spent in providing customized products and services to your partners in the supply chain. This has led to the appearance of many new businesses. For example, presentation consulting companies have become very hot in the United States today. Their job is to make professional presentations for customers. It requires innovative ideas as well as image processing skills. The former are usually accomplished in the United States, while the latter are outsourced to Asia for the low labor costs. Unlike the manufacturing industry, the logistics cost for outsourcing image processing is almost zero as the Internet is used to transfer the digital images back and forth. Without the Internet, such an outsourcing strategy is impossible. The Internet itself is an important facility for companies in forming and managing their global supply chain.

EDI networks connect application systems to transfer business data from one organization to another in a structured data format (in terms of standards and specifications). The data transmission is through a transmission medium, which can be a value-added network (VAN) or the Internet. EDI was proposed in the United States and Europe in 1960s, and started to be popular in the 1980s. In 1991, it was reported that EDI helped General Motors save $250 per car, and helped IBM save $6 million. In Asia, both the Hong Kong and the Singapore Governments started EDI projects in 1980s. During 1986–1987, Singapore Government started the TradeNet project, and the system was launched in 1989, and fully implemented in 1991. Through TradeNet, the Singapore Government has saved $60 million transaction costs by automating the trading for companies in Singapore (Bower and Konsynski 1995).

EDI requires a standard format of documents for transactions through the network. For example, to transmit a purchasing order, the document should include a three-digit numeric code (850) to indicate the purchasing order, followed by data in heading areas, detail areas, and summary areas. To transfer the document, the EDI transactions usually consist of seven steps:

- Step 1: Application software—The originating enterprise application (such as an ERP package) prepares an electronic business document in company-specific format.
- Step 2: Translation software—Translates outgoing messages so that they are in standard message format. It precludes the need for an organization to reprogram its application so that it can communicate with each trading partner's application, translates software and performs administrative, audit, and control functions, logs incoming and outgoing messages, and routes messages to and from the appropriate business software.
- Step 3: Communications network—Routes EDI messages to VAN mailbox. There are two options. One is to use a proprietary network where the trading parties contribute to the development of a proprietary network and purchase hardware, software, and telecom infrastructure to enable the network. The other is to use EDI service bureaus which act as an intermediary between a large hub company and its suppliers.
- Step 4: A VAN serves as the electronic postman. Provides a communications capability for organizations who do not want to purchase their own communications infrastructure, to log the EDI message, translate the message to required communications protocol, translate the message to required EDI standard, encrypt and authenticate the message, check for message integrity (completeness and authorization) and route to the appropriate destination party's mailbox. Typical VANs include Advantis (IBM), Inovis, GEIS, and so on. Companies can also use the public Internet to communicate but security is a major concern.
- Step 5: Communications network—Picks up EDI messages from mailbox.
- Step 6: Translation software—Decodes messages from a particular EDI standard to business document format and performs audit and control functions.
- Step 7: Application software—destination application software processes incoming document.

Today using a VAN is still the most popular procedure in EDI applications. The VAN basically acts as a regional post office that collects and dispatches the EDI

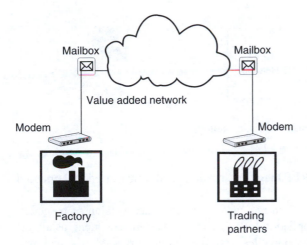

Figure 10.10 EDI networks.

documents as depicted in Figure 10.10. VANs also provide a number of additional services, for example, retransmitting documents, providing third-party audit information, acting as a gateway for different transmission methods, and handling telecommunications support. However, with increasing use of the Internet, some smaller companies that cannot afford the cost of EDI are using Internet services offered by vendors, such as Amazon, as a way to allow product ordering and shipment tracking to communicate with traditional EDI networks. This emerging technology is so-called Web EDI.

RFID is a wireless communication device that facilitates the tracing of goods that move along the supply chain. There are three components of RFID technology, as shown in Figure 10.11. The first component is the RFID tags, which are attached to the objects to be traced, and send and receive signals to and from the readers. The second component is the RFID readers, which keep communicating with the tags through antenna. Signals received by the readers are then passed to remote computer servers through the network. The last component is the computer networks, which serve as the backbone for the communication between the RFID reader and remote servers. The network can be a cable network and/or a wireless network.

A typical application of RFID in supply chain management is to trace and visualize product flows in a supply chain. For example, suppose products are moving from a factory, through a distribution center, to retail stores. It is very important for the manufacturers, logistics service providers, and customers to know the exact status of the products. For this purpose, RFID tags can be attached to every piece of product. Readers can be installed in the factory, the distribution center, and the stores. When products are moving in and out, their exact status can be automatically captured by the

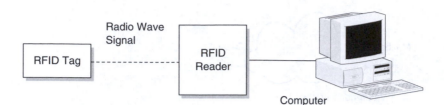

Figure 10.11 Three components of RFID technology.

communication between RFID tags and readers, and transmitted and updated through the network.

The RFID technology is often regarded as an upgraded version of barcodes, which have been widely applied in today's supply chain management, as almost every product has a barcode. Barcodes were first adopted by K-Mart, which was the number one retailer in the United States in the 1980s. When using barcodes, one needs to first attach a paper tag to each product with a code representing the information associated with the product. To access the information contained in a barcode tag, one needs to use a barcode scanner to scan the tag, and the code printed on the tag can be read and passed to the computer for being further processed.

Compared with barcodes, the RFID technology has the following advantages. Generally speaking, RFID is more convenient to use. Reading RFID is faster than reading barcodes. Barcodes can only be read individually, while a set of RFID tags can be read simultaneously. Barcodes cannot be read if they are dirty or damage, while RFID tags are more robust and can even be integrated into packaging materials to avoid the impact of a dirty environment. Second, RFID can save laboring costs, because RFID tags and readers can communicate with each other without the aid of humans, while barcodes are usually processed by people. Third, information stored at RFID is more responsive to changes and has larger capacity for storage than the barcode tags. Due to this feature, RFID tags can be used to monitor any change in the product or the environment when integrated into circuits.

However, RFID has its own drawbacks. First, the technology itself is not mature yet, and it is difficult for readers and tags to communicate when metals and liquids are around, because these can interfere with the signals sent by tags and readers. A lot of research is being conducted to resolve the interference problems for RFID technology. Second, the price of RFID tags is still high, mainly because the production cost is still high and the production scale is still low. The price of 1,000 tags is about $0.5–$1.0/each, and the price of 100,000 is about $0.35–$0.85/each. However, as shown in Figure 10.12, tags prices continue to decrease as the demand increases and the technology improves.

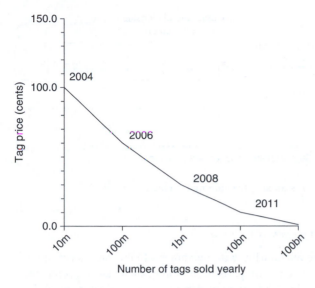

Figure 10.12 Tag prices drop as demand increases and technology improves for RFID.

Despite the drawbacks, many companies are seeking ways to apply RFID technology in logistics and supply chain management. For example, Wal-Mart plans to install RFID readers in every retails store to trace their products. They are targeting for significant cost savings from this RFID project. Where will these savings come from? They will mainly come from the easy access of real-time product information, which allows companies to adjust their planning and operations according to *ad hoc* market changes. Giordano, one of the largest clothing stores in Hong Kong, plans to install RFID in their retail store to track the move of products so that they can understand customer behavior in choosing clothing. This helps them to understand the market, because not only can they see what the exact sales figures are, but can also see how much clothing has been tried but not sold. In Hong Kong airport, every piece of luggage has an RFID tag attached, which helps improve the operational efficiency at the airport. In Esquel, one of the largest cloth manufacturers in China, the RFID tags are attached to the bags of cotton to improve the transportation efficiency, and attached to cloths to monitor the status of production.

Applications of ISs

In the following, we are going to discuss three typical applications of ISs for supply chain management, defined by their roles in the supply chain management, including customer relationship management (CRM) systems, enterprise resource planning (ERP) systems, and supply chain management systems as shown in Figure 10.13.

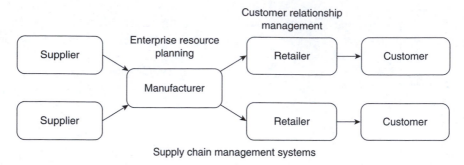

Figure 10.13 Three types of ISs for supply chain management.

Customer relationship management systems

CRM aims to enhance the relationship with customers. In customer-centric business, it is easy for customers to do comparison shopping, and to switch companies. for Customer relationships have become a company's most valued asset and are very important in supply chain management. Companies should form their business strategy so as to find and retain the most profitable customers possible, and use ISs to manage their customer relationships. The meaning of customer relationship has two aspects. One is about providing the company with a single and complete view of every customer at every touch point and across every channel. For example, most sales managers archive customers' contact details as their potential sales targets. The other aspect is about providing the customer with a single and complete view of the company and its extended channels. For example, Dell provides customers a single online platform to configure and order their PC online.

CRM uses IT to create a cross-functional enterprise system that mainly integrates and automates the following customer-serving processes to manage the customer relationships:

- Contact and account management: to help sales, marketing, and service staffs organize relevant data about every contact with prospects and customers together with their life-cycle events. Data are captured through events related to customers, such as email, fax, websites, and so on.
- Sales: to provide sales representatives with the tools and data to manage their sales activities. The most common data are about account status and history of customers. It allows sales representatives in different departments or locations to share information about customers.
- Marketing and fulfillment: to help automate tasks of marketing campaigns, such as qualifying leads for targeted marketing, scheduling and tracking mails, managing responses, and so on.
- Customer service and support: to provide real-time access for customer service representatives to the same database that is managed by sales and marketing.

Using web-based systems, customers can also access personalized information by themselves. For example, Dell allows customers to configure computers to specify technical or nontechnical problems in the online customer support system.

- Retention and loyalty programs: the primary objective of CRM is to identify, reward, and market the most loyal and profitable customers, and evaluate targeted marketing and relationship programs. Retention and loyalty programs are very important to the company, because it has been reported that selling to a new customer costs much more than selling to older customers.

The goals of CRM systems are to optimize revenue, profitability, customer satisfaction, and customer retention, which leads to three phases of the CRM process in a CRM system: acquiring, enhancing, and retaining. First, to help acquire new customers, CRM software supports superior contact management, sales prospecting, selling, direct marketing, and fulfillment. It helps customers perceive the value of a superior product offered by an outstanding company. Besides physical mails, many companies today will send emails frequently to their customers to promote new services or products. Second, to enhance the relationships with customers, an account management tool and a customer service and support tool of CRM software can help keep customers satisfied. A sales force automation tool and a direct marketing and fulfillment tool of CRM software can help companies to cross-sell and up-sell products or services to customers. It makes customers perceive the convenience of one-stop shopping at attractive prices. Finally, to retain customers, a database management and analysis tool of CRM software can help a company identify and reward the most loyal and profitable customers. It makes customers perceive the value of a rewarding personalized business relationship with the company.

With the development of IT, CRM systems are evolving. Below are four typical new CRM systems:

1   Operational CRM: to support customer interaction with greater convenience through a variety of channels; synchronizes customer interactions consistently across all channels, and makes the company easier to do business with.
2   Analytical CRM: to extract in-depth customer history, preferences, and profitability from databases. Such information is used to predict values and the behavior of customers, to improve demand forecasting, and to help tailor information and offers to customer needs.
3   Collaborative CRM: to ease the collaboration with customers, suppliers, and partners, and to improve efficiency and integration throughout the supply chain. It provides greater responsiveness to customer needs through outside sourcing of products and services. In this perspective, the CRM system is a part of the supply chain management system.
4   Portal-based CRM: to provide users with tools and information that fit their needs. It empowers employees to respond to customer demands more quickly, helps representatives become truly customer-faced, and provides instant access to all internal and external customer information.

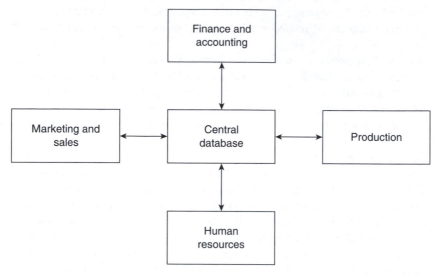

Figure 10.14 Modules of an ERP system.

Enterprise resource planning

ERP is a cross-functional enterprise backbone that integrates and automates processes within manufacturing, logistics, distribution, accounting, finance, and human resources. It is an integrated suite of software modules, supports basic internal business processes, and facilitates business, supplier, and customer information flows. Figure 10.14 illustrates the architecture of an ERP system. It has interdependent software modules with a common central database that supports basic internal business processes, and enables data to be used by multiple functions and business processes for precise organizational coordination and control.

The fundamental aim of the ERP software is to automate the operational process of a company. Consider the example of an order management process for a sales person to create a sale order, fill in details of each order line, submit the order for financial approval, get payment from the customer, and deliver the product to the customer. Without the ISs, the process above will be accompanied by lots of manual processes and paper work, which can lead to delays and human errors. Since most ERP systems have an order management module, the order management process can be well facilitated and processed electronically (see Figure 10.15).

There are many ERP software vendors, such as SAP, Oracle, Compiere, and so on. Among them, SAP is the largest one. Today, SAP has more than 41,000 customers worldwide. The early products of SAP are developed from SAP R/1, SAP R/2, to SAP R/3 with different hardware and software infrastructure. SAP R/1 and SAP R/2 were developed in the 1960s and were only accountant software in mainframe computers. SAP R/3 extended functions by introducing production planning

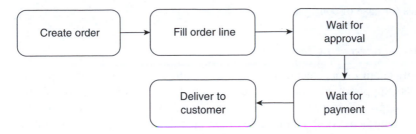

Figure 10.15 The process of order management in ERP.

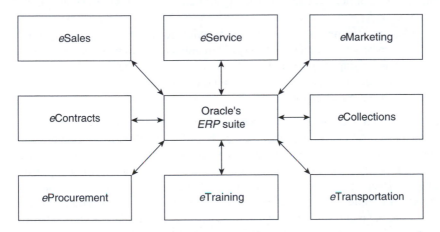

Figure 10.16 Oracle ERP software package (suite).

modules, sales and distribution modules, quality management modules, and so on. The infrastructure of SAP R/3 changed to a network system with client/server model. Later SAP changed the name of its product SAP R/3 to MySAP ERP, to emphasize that it was a customized software, to MySAP.com to pursue Internet bubbles, to SAP Business One to emphasize that it is an integration of different business modules and flexible enough for customizations, and finally to SAP ERP.

The history of SAP illustrates the development and trends of ERP software. The ERP systems are evolving from a single accounting module to a more flexible, web-enabled, interenterprise software suite (see Figure 10.16). For flexibility, SAP R/1 and SAP R/2 are only accounting systems for mainframe computers. SAP R/3 extends the functions to other business functions by using a client/server framework. SAP R/3 is more flexible than SAP R/2, regarding functions and architecture. Today ERP systems support web technology by using Internet or Intranet to communicate. In some ERP systems (e.g., SAP), there is also a module called supply chain management. Basically ERP vendors today try to extend the system to interenterprise and allow communications (or data sharing) among different ERP systems. ERP software today, such as Oracle E-Business Suite, is often released as a software package (suite), which integrates various functional modules for ease of configurations.

Supplier management systems

In supply chain management, collaborations with suppliers are very important concepts. Suppliers and manufacturers should share information so that the overall supply chain costs can be reduced by avoiding so-called bull-whip effects. Manufacturers should be able to maintain good relationships with their suppliers, so that strategic alliances can be formed and efficient sourcing processes can be achieved. Manufacturers should also be able to monitor the performance of suppliers so that they can be sure about the product/service quality and status.

Supplier management systems (SMSs) provide such a collaborative platform for manufacturers and suppliers, and enable manufacturers to manage the transactions and relationships of the suppliers. The major activities that relate to suppliers' management include supplier account management, procurement management, and information exchange management.

Supplier account management is to manage the account information about suppliers, such as contacts, locations, services provided, and so on. Basic functions of supplier account management are similar to the customer account management systems. It is important for a company to have accurate contacts with its suppliers during transactions and sourcing processes. Moreover, since suppliers that the company is trading with are usually enterprises, they usually have unique rules in production, payment, shipping, and so on. Therefore it is important to maintain a master database of supplier information in an SMS, so that merchants of the manufacturers can easily access the information about suppliers they are contacting. For example, the catalog in SAP Supplier Relationship Management (SAP SRM) enables effective master data management through: (1) master data consolidation, which is to perform data cleansing and de-duplication; (2) master data synchronization, which is to synchronize master data information automatically; (3) centralized master data management, which is to create and update master data and conduct ongoing data quality checks; (4) product content management, which is to facilitate loading, aggregating, and searching product data and supporting online publishing; and (5) global data synchronization, which is to exchange item data with retailers.

Procurement management is to manage a sourcing process to purchase materials, products, or services from suppliers. The procurement process usually has four stages: (1) request for information (RFI) to collect procurement requirements from internal departments; (2) request for quotation (RFQ) to get price quotations from suppliers; (3) negotiation to bargain the price with suppliers and make decision on picking suppliers; and (4) contracting and execution to purchase from suppliers and pay. Without the help of ISs, a lot of staff need to be involved in the process to manually collect and process the information. When the types of the products to be purchased have many variations, it will be impossible for the company to have a strong and detailed agreement with suppliers, due to the lack of resources to prepare information and data. For this reason, more and more big companies today use procurement management systems to support the purchase of raw material or services. For example, Philips Electronics developed a transportation procurement system in 2003, which allowed them to invite transportation service providers, such as DHL, FedEx, to bid shipping rates online (Lim *et al.* 2006). SAP SRM provides procurement management modules for companies to execute operational activities in the following areas: (1) requisitioning, which is to create requisitions automatically, or allow users to create them manually; (2) order management, which is to assign suppliers to the orders, validate restrictions, and perform order generation and tracking; (3) receiving—to capture the process of receiving goods and services, and to prepare for follow-on processes such as automated financial settlement; (4) financial settlement—to handle financial transactions and make financial settlement more efficient by using automation tools.

Information exchange management aims to facilitate information sharing between participants in a supply chain. For example, SAP SRM supports the company in linking suppliers to the purchasing processes via the SAP Supplier Network or through the suppliers' portal. With SAP SRM, a company can automate numerous business processes and documents sharing in the following areas: (1) document exchange—to exchange documents in various formats across different systems both internally and externally; (2) supplier portal management—to provide suppliers direct access to their customers' information in SAP and non-SAP enterprise systems; (3) supplier collaboration—to facilitate collaborations with suppliers throughout the product life cycle, and to support the integrated planning and operations with suppliers of all sizes.

Simulation lab: IS plan for enhancing supply chain performance

You work for a professional IT consulting firm. You have to work closely with your team members to produce a report that offers a proposal pertinent to the use of ISs to improve the supply chain performance of a client. Aspects of the following two questions may help the progress of your project.

1   The current situation (including strategies, organizations, operations, and existing IS/IT practices of the firm and its competitors):

- What is the business strategy of the firm? How does it perform? What are the major competitors?
- What is the supply chain of the firm? How does it perform? What are the special characteristics of the firm's supply chain?

- What is the current IS/IT strategy of the firm? What services are offered by the IS/IT? How does IS/IT facilitate the operations and decision making of the firm? Is the IS/IT strategy consistent with the corporate strategy? What is the contribution of IS/IT to the corporate goal? Has the IS/IT strategy brought competitive advantage to the firm? What is the current investments in IS/IT?
- What are the IS/IT strategies of major competitors?
- What is the current organizations of the firm, the IS/IT department, and the supply chain management department? Does it support the business strategy and the existing IS/IT practices in the firm?
- Has the firm embarked on any IS/IT project? If so, what were the cost and the benefit of such a project? If not, what stopped the firm introducing new IS/IT?
- What is the current performance of the supply chain, with respect to internal operational performance, customer satisfaction, and quality of products from suppliers, and so on?
- What are the problems in the firm's operations and management that need to be improved? What are the causes and the effects of these problems? What is the current practice of the company regarding these problems? Can IS/IT help in solving these problems better? Why?

2   The proposed IS plan (including issues related to technology, management, and organizations):

- Which management problems are you going to solve?
- What will be the new IS strategy?
- What types of systems can the firm afford? Which of the emerging technologies are related to helping the firm?
- What types of IS/IT are you looking for? What services and functions does this new system provide, with respect to the tasks concerning internal operations, and interactions with customers, suppliers, and other external business partners?
- Who will use the new systems? How will the users interact with the system? What kinds of skills should users have to fully utilize the service of the new systems?
- What is the benefit of using this new system, especially for the supply chain management? How can the benefit before the deployment of the system be estimated? How can the benefit after the deployment of the system be evaluated?
- Are there any IS/IT products on the market that can be adopted or customized to implement your new IS strategy? If so, what analysis

will be performed to select them? If not, what is your strategy to develop the system?

- What factors have been taken into consideration in the decision making?
- What is your implementation plan for the new IS strategy? What will be the organization of the project team? What are the possible changes in the company's organization and supply chain operations? What are your suggestions for managing these changes?

You are requested to form a group, and to prepare a presentation to the senior managers of your client company, and submit a consulting report.

Problems

Read the article, titled "The Art, Science and Software Behind Placing Coca-Cola Products on Store Shelves" (Wailgum 2009), and answer all five questions.

Question 1

1   Describe the decision-making process for Coca-Cola to place products on retailers' shelves. What is the business value of this decision-making process?
2   What problems did Coca-Cola Enterprise (CCE) face with its placement of products on retailers' shelves? How did they affect decision making and business performance?

Question 2

1   What did the CCE do to remedy those problems that you identified in Question 1? How did the solution perform?
2   Please explain why JDA's software can enhance the decision making of the CCE?

Question 3

1   If you were Luisa, what requirements would you request from JDA to demonstrate the capability of their software before purchase? Why?

Question 4

1   After the JDA's software was implemented, what additional efforts did Coca-Cola make to guarantee the gain of benefits from the software?
2   Why did Coca-Cola make such efforts?

Question 5

1　Did the system proposed in your project contain a decision support module? If yes, please describe it. If no, please suggest one.
2　If you are the supply chain manager of Coca-Cola, what application of ISs would you suggest be implemented next in Coca-Cola? Why?

Bibliography

Bower, M. and B. Konsynski. 1995. "Singapore TradeNet: A Tale of One City," *Harvard Business School Case,* No. 9191009.

Eckerson, W.W. 2002. *Data Quality and the Bottom Line: Achieving Business Success Through a Commitment to High Quality Data*, Chatsworth, CA: The Data Warehousing Institute.

Gartner EXP. 2009. *Meeting the Challenge: The 2009 C10 Agenda*, CT, Gartner Inc.

Laudon, K.C. and J.P. Laudon. 2010. "The Role of Information Systems in Business Today," in E. Svenden (ed.) *Management Information Systems: Managing the Digital Firm*, 11th Edition, pp. 35–45. Upper Saddle River, NJ: Pearson Education.

Lee, H.L. 2004. "The Triple-A Supply Chain," *Harvard Business Review,* 82, 102–113.

Lim, A., Z. Xu, B. Cheang, H.W. Kit, and S. Au-yeung. 2006. "TPBOSCourier: A Transportation Procurement System (for the Procurement of Courier Services)," *Proceedings of the 18th Conference on Innovative Applications of Artificial Intelligence*, Menlo Park, CA: AAAI Press. pp. 1712–1719.

Monk, E.F., B.J. Wagner, and J.J. Brady. 2006. "The Development of Enterprise Resource Planning Systems," in A. von Roseberg (ed.) *Concepts in Enterprise Resource Planning*, Boston, MA: Thomson Course Technology. pp. 17–46.

Roberti, M. 2005. "Wal-Mart Begins RFID Process Changes," *RFID Journal Online.* Available HTTP: www.rfidjournal.com/article/view/1385.

Wailgum, T. 2009. "The Art, Science and Software Behind Placing Coca-Cola Products on Store Shelves," *CIO Online.* Available HTTP: http://www.cio.com/article/print/487339.

Zook, M. and M. Graham. 2006. "Wal-Mart Nation: Mapping the Reach of a Retail Colossus," in S.D. Brunn (ed.) *Wal-Mart World*, London: Routledge. pp. 15–25.

11 Aviation logistics management

Key items:

- *Aviation logistics in a supply chain*
- *Production and cost of aviation services*
- *Aviation demand*
- *Revenue management in aviation logistics*
- *Regulation for international aviation logistics*

On 17 December 1903, the Wright brothers took off from Kitty Hawk, North Carolina on the first ever manned flight. Just one hundred years on, air transportation is now a pillar industry worldwide. Boeing (2006) estimated that the commercial aviation sector contributes up to 8 percent of the global economy as measured in gross GDP. In terms of weight, air transport accounted for only 1 percent of international trade during the period 1985–2005. However, in terms of value, it accounted for 34 percent of all exported goods and services. Historical patterns have shown that the growth rate of air cargo is usually twice that of the overall economy. That is, if the world economy grows at 3 percent per year, then the growth rate of the aviation logistics industry will be around 6 percent. Clearly, aviation logistics is now an important growth engine of the global economy.

In its early days, air transport was mainly used for the shipment of urgent, high-value products. With the growing use of intermodal transportation and logistics services, aviation is now managed in the context of a supply chain network. In this chapter, we first review the service characteristics of air transport and their implications for supply chain management. We then study the essential attributes

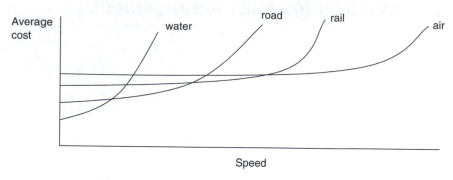

Figure 11.1 Diseconomies of speed.

of aviation logistics in terms of production and demand analysis. This is followed by a discussion of aviation pricing and yield management fundamentals. We conclude the chapter with a brief review of air transport regulations, and in particular the various air freedoms needed to provide international services.

Aviation logistics in a supply chain

In this section, we first review the service characteristics of air transport, and then analyze how aviation logistics management can offer the best value in the context of supply chain management.

Service characteristics of air transport

As one would expect, the main advantage of air transport is its speed. Every transport mode has its inherent optimal speed. Although technology improvements such as high-speed rail and jet boats are constantly increasing the speed limit of other modes of transport, the costs of such speed gains often offset the benefits. This is referred to as diseconomies of speed (for a particular transport mode). As shown in Figure 11.1, the average costs of each transport mode remain fairly stable within a given speed interval, but then increase exponentially when a certain threshold is passed.

Air transport is extensively used for high-value, time-sensitive, or perishable shipments due to its service advantages over other shipping modes, which can be summarized as follows.

- **Fast:** The inherent speed advantage of aviation makes it ideal for express shipments or for the transportation of perishable products such as documents, medical drugs, blood samples, flowers, live stock, and seafood.
- **Secure:** Over the years, aviation has become the safest mode of transportation. The safety standards of cargo screening, ground handling, and flight operations are well established and tightly regulated by governments and

international organizations. This has made air transport the preferred shipping option for valuable goods such as jewelry, bank notes, electronics, and semiconductors.

- **Reliable:** As air transport is usually used for high-value goods, most countries and logistics companies have developed superior infrastructure to support the high service standards commonly demanded in the air transport industry. Many countries give preferred customs clearance treatments to products shipped by air. The punctuality of aviation operations also tends to be superior to that of other shipping modes. In the United States, a flight is classified as "on-time" only if the departure or arrival time is within 15 minutes of the scheduled time. Such service standards are rarely matched by other shipping modes.

These high service standards nevertheless often come at a cost. Until recently, air transport was regarded as the most expensive shipping mode. However, this perception is not always valid. A common feature of most transport modes is economies of distance traveled, whereby the average cost of moving a shipment over a certain distance declines as the travel distance increases. This is because the almost fixed costs of warehousing, loading and unloading, and aircraft landing and take-off charges can be allocated to a longer distance traveled. The effect of economies of distance traveled is particularly evident with air transport. Lifting a fully loaded aircraft to cruise latitude requires substantial energy, which implies a large amount of fuel. However, modern jet aircrafts are very fuel efficient at cruising altitude, when they need only moderate thrust to maintain a smooth and steady flight. When the travel distance is sufficiently long the operation cost of moving a passenger or cargo by air may be lower than the shipping cost using the most efficient car or truck. Over time, technological progress, productivity growth, and competition have forced down the price and average shipping costs of air transport. Indeed, Boeing has estimated that the world air freight yield for the period of 1985–2003 dropped by 2.4 percent annually.

As stated, the premium service offered by air transport makes it a desirable shipping mode for high-value goods, for which logistics-related expenses only constitute a small proportion of the final delivered price. Trade experts have found that when modeling shipping and trade demands, it is very useful to measure shipping costs in *ad valorem* terms, that is, in terms of the cost of shipping $1 of goods between the origin and destination. The *ad valorem* price can be calculated as

$$Ad\,valorem\,\text{price} = \frac{\text{Shipping cost}}{\text{Value of goods}}. \tag{11.1}$$

The intuition is clear. Logistics demands can be segmented with respect to the value and time sensitivity of shipments. The final mode choice for each market segment must be made based on a trade-off between service quality requirements and logistic costs, or the "relative cost," which is best measured by the *ad valorem* price. This has important implications for firms who are considering providing advanced logistics services, in that the absolute cost or price of these services is not a good indicator of service feasibility or profitability. The more important question is whether such firms are offering the right service to the right customer.

Of course, the inherent cost structure of air transport limits its usage for the shipment of bulk goods. However, in some cases it could be the only choice if other factors are also considered. For example, in December 2002, six subway cars were shipped by air from Germany to Guangzhou, China. The rail cars were originally planned to be shipped by sea, but the German manufacturers encountered a production delay. To meet the subway operation deadline, the company decided to hire the largest aircraft in the world, the AN-124, to ship the first batch of cars. Was this simply a case of poor planning, or does it reflect some general logistics principle? To answer this question, we need to consider the bigger picture of aviation logistics.

Aviation logistics in supply chain management

With the trends of globalization and trade liberalization, the production, distribution, and consumption of goods are all conducted within a large spatial network backed by increasingly complex supply chains. Taking aircraft manufacturing as an example, a Boeing 777 aircraft contains about 132,500 major component parts that are produced by more than 500 suppliers. Airlines have the option of choosing their own engines, onboard entertainment equipment, and even seat color. Molex, a leading electrical switch and connector producer, has over 100,000 product lines. It has 55 factories in 18 countries and 27 R&D centers in 15 countries. Such complexity in production planning introduces major logistics challenges. On a strategic level, several conflicting factors need to be considered by a supply chain manager of operations in multiple locations.

- **Holding cost:** As we learnt in previous chapters, maintaining a large inventory can be both expensive and risky. With an annual interest rate of 8 percent, the pure financial cost of an inventory worth $100 million is about $22,000 per day, exclusive of other expenses such as warehousing, packaging, and inspection. When the market is very dynamic, having a large inventory is risky. On April 16th, 2001, Cisco announced that it would scrap around $2.5 billion of surplus raw materials in one of the largest inventory write-offs in history. Clearly, for expensive and time-sensitive products such as computers and semiconductors, it is extremely expensive to maintain a large inventory. For many telecom equipment vendors, inventory unsold within 1 year will automatically be written off.
- **Stock out penalty cost:** To reduce inventory costs, many firms have introduced "Just in Time" (JIT) systems. By making deliveries just before they are needed, firms can maintain a small inventory and thus reduce their holding costs and material wastage. However, maintaining a lean inventory means a

greater risk of stock out. The overall production process may be forced to stop if certain key components are temporarily out of stock. In 1999, several chip-makers in Taiwan had to shut down for days because of a major earthquake. The production glitch spread globally as numerous downstream firms relied on these chip-makers as original equipment manufacturers (OEMs). With a small inventory buffer, a moderate delay or disruption to one supplier can cause significant loss to the supply chain as a whole.

- **Transportation cost:** With rapid and reliable transportation services, a manager can reduce the transit time and thus respond to demand or supply shocks quickly. This allows firms to reduce both their inventory level and the stock out penalty. However, fast shipping services, such as air cargo and high speed rail, often involve higher transportation costs. When holding costs and stock out costs are high, or equivalently when the value of time is high, the costs associated with high-speed shipping can be more easily justified. The increasing value of time has played an important role in changing modern logistics services. Hummels (2006) found that aviation services are increasingly used for long-distance shipments, whereas marine cargo is shipped over shorter distances.[1]

To balance these conflicting factors, companies now aim to build an efficient but flexible logistics network. One strategy is to utilize a multimodal system. For example, a company can plan for transportation by using relatively cheap shipping methods, such as marine, rail, or truck. Fast but expensive transportation, such as air cargo, may be used as a contingency only when there is an unexpected delay or substantial risk of stock out. Firms following this strategy often choose to locate their distribution centers near a logistics hub with a well-developed multimodal infrastructure. This is one of the major factors that makes the Netherlands an ideal location for European distribution centers. The Netherlands has the world's leading marine ports (Rotterdam and Amsterdam) and aviation hub (Amsterdam Schiphol airport). It accounts for about half of all European inland river shipping, and has extensive rail and road connections to destinations throughout Europe. These advantages explain why more than 56 percent of European distribution centers owned by US and Asian firms are located in the Netherlands (Oum and Park 2004). Aviation logistics has much greater value when it is used in the context of a supply chain or multimode transportation system.

The aviation logistics industry profile

Many different types of firms and government agents are involved in offering aviation logistics services. They can be broadly classified into the following categories.

Airports

Airports provide essential services to the aviation industry. The main functions offered include: aircraft landing and take-off; the loading and unloading of

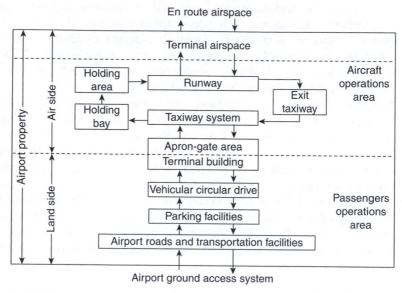

Figure 11.2 Components of an airport.

Source: Wells and Young (2004).

passengers and cargo; various ground services such as fuelling, de-icing, and aircraft checks and maintenance; aircraft parking; and traffic control. Many airports also directly own and operate cargo terminals and logistics service businesses. These subsidiaries provide services such as (airport) warehousing, shipment build-up (for pallets), airway bill data handling, customs clearance, ground transportation, the handling of dangerous goods, and security screening, etc.

The airport area and related services can be divided into those offered land side and those offered air side. Land side services refer to any activities conducted in the (passenger or cargo) terminal buildings, ground transportation, parking within the airports, and other road and transportation facilities (such as light rail lines linking terminals) within the airport area. Air side services refer to facilities that are directly linked to aircraft landing and take-off, such as traffic control in the airport terminal airspace, taxi and runway control and maintenance, and safety and emergency related services such as fire services and security control. Figure 11.2 shows a (rough) breakdown of the various airports facilities.

Historically, all airports were government invested and operated. In recent years, there has been a global trend to privatize and commercialize airports so that they can operate as ordinary business. Most airports in the United States and Canada have been set up as not-for-profit airport authorities that operate and control airports outside of the government budget. In New Zealand and Australia, some airports have been fully privatized and are owned by (or sometimes leased to) private companies. In other countries, airports have been commercialized and

Figure 11.3 Air cargo using belly space versus cargo freighter.

Source: China.com.

are listed on stock exchanges, but with the government remaining as either a major or a minor shareholder. Regardless of their ownership structure, most airports are subject to some sorts of price regulation, and need government approval to change the service prices that they charge.

Carriers (airlines)

Two types of airlines offer aviation logistics services. Most airlines are so-called passenger cargo combi-carriers. These airlines mainly focus on passenger travel, but also utilize the extra capacity in the aircraft belly to carry air cargo. As the same belly space is used for passenger luggage, these passenger airlines usually provide simple airport-to-airport services for small shipments. In some cases, the airlines simply lease out extra capacity to freight forwarders or integrators.

Another group of carriers are the so-called all-freight carriers. They use aircrafts that are configured especially for air cargo, and provide many value-added services, such as door-to-door transportation, warehousing, inventory control, packaging, shipment tracking, and customs clearance. Many such airlines are subsidiaries of passenger airlines, and can thus share certain functions and costs with passenger operations, such as aircraft maintenance and pilot training (Figure 11.3).

Freight forwarders and third-party logistics firms

Rather than selling services directly to end users (shippers), airlines usually provide services to freight forwarders and third-party logistics (3PL) firms. These firms work as agents for the shippers and carriers: they receive the orders from shippers, and then either pass them to airlines for a commission, or handle the orders by themselves using aircraft space purchased or leased from carriers. With the substantial growth in aviation logistics, freight forwarders and 3PLs are becoming increasingly powerful. They provide many value-added logistics services across large networks. In some cases, manufacturers outsource their whole logistics function to such firms.

Integrators

A few large companies such as FedEx, UPS, DHL, and TNT offer comprehensive logistics services. Many of them started as courier service providers for the door-to-door delivery of small packages and documents. With the growing demand for aviation logistics services from medium-sized and large businesses, they now provide very comprehensive and sophisticated logistics solutions. In addition to their own aircraft fleets, these companies also operate extensive distribution networks worldwide, which include multimodal transport systems, distribution centers, IT facilities, and consulting services.

Governments

Governments have always played an important role in the aviation logistics industry. Except in the United States, airlines in most countries started off being government owned and operated. Although the majority of airlines in the world have now been privatized, governments still perform important functions and services, such as air traffic control, bilateral service negotiation, safety checks and regulation, customs clearance, and investment in related public infrastructure. Many of these services are covered by government budgets. However, there has been a trend of switching to a user-pay system without government subsidy. This will surely affect costs and pricing in the aviation logistics sector.

Production and cost analysis of aviation services

To understand the dynamics of the aviation logistics market, it is necessary to know the production details and cost of providing aviation services. In a market free of regulation, the market structure ultimately depends on the value of each firm's service for consumers (the demand side of the market) and firms' cost structures (production, or the supply side of the market). In this subsection, we first briefly review the definitions of the production and cost functions. We then study and compare three important concepts: economies of scale, economies of scope, and economies of density.

Production function

Firms have costs because they employ factors of production such as labor, machinery, and energy. They use factors as inputs into a production process that may be represented as a production function. For example, if there were just two inputs, capital (K) and labor (L), we might write $y = f(K, L)$, where y is the total output. In general, if there are many inputs, denoted as x_1, x_2, and x_3, then a

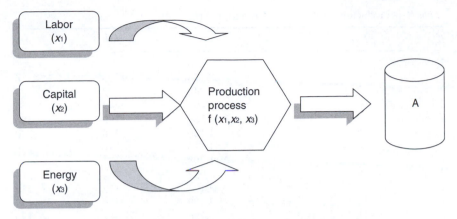

Figure 11.4 Production process with multiple inputs and a single output.

production function can be specified as $y = f(x_1, x_2, x_3)$. A production function specifies the maximum amount of output that can be produced from any specified set of inputs, given the existing technology.

We use Figure 11.4 to emphasize that even the production of a single output requires multiple inputs. After the decision about how much to produce, the company needs to find out the best way to produce, including the best combination (ratios) of each input. In reality, the production process is far more complex than this, as virtually no firm produces a single output and a firm's production scale is affected by market fluctuations and interfirm competition. For now, let us examine the simplest case whereby a firm uses two inputs (capital K and labor L) to produce one output (y) with technology represented by the production function $y = f(K, L)$. If we fix the amount of capital used ($K^* = 2$) but gradually increase the amount of labor, then we will observe the production pattern given in Table 11.1.

Table 11.1 shows that when capital is fixed, initially each additional unit of labor produces more output (increasing marginal product). Such efficiency gain reaches its maximum when five or six units of labor are used (at which point MP_L, the marginal product of labor, reaches its maximum of 316), while the corresponding values of AP_L, the average product of labor, are 220 and 236 respectively. If we continue to increase the labor usage, then the marginal product of labor declines, which is referred to as *diminishing marginal product*. In extreme cases, the marginal product can be negative (if too many people are assigned to one task, you may end up doing nothing!). In the case in the foregoing table, we observe different marginal returns of labor. In particular, the returns on labor are

(i) *Increasing*: from 0 to 5 units of labor.
(ii) *Decreasing*: from 6 units upwards.
(iii) *Negative*: at 11 units and (probably) higher.

Table 11.1 Production function with fixed capital ($K^* = 2$)

K^*	L	ΔL	y	MP_L	AP_L
2	0	—	0	—	—
2	1	1	76	76	76
2	2	1	248	172	124
2	3	1	492	244	164
2	4	1	784	292	196
2	5	1	1,100	316	220
2	6	1	1,416	316	236
2	7	1	1,708	292	244
2	8	1	1,952	244	244
2	9	1	2,124	172	236
2	10	1	2,200	76	220
2	11	1	2,156	-44	196

Rather than increasing the amount of one input (labor L in the foregoing example) while holding the other input (capital L) fixed, we have the option of increasing all of the inputs by the same factor. For example, we could double all of the inputs at the same time. There is a possibility (but not always) that we will obtain twice the output. This is called *Constant Returns to Scale*. Mathematically, it is represented as

$$f(2K, 2L) = 2f(K, L).$$ (11.2)

In general, if we scale all of the inputs by λ, then constant returns to scale imply that we would obtain λ times as much output, or mathematically

$$f(\lambda K, \lambda L) = \lambda f(K, L).$$ (11.3)

If we produce proportionally more output when we increase all of the inputs by a factor of λ, then we have *Increasing Returns to Scale*, which is also frequently referred to as *Economies of Scale*. Mathematically, when $\lambda > 1$, we have

$$f(\lambda K, \lambda L) > \lambda f(K, L).$$ (11.4)

Similarly, we have *Decreasing Returns to Scale* if mathematically, when $\lambda > 1$, we have

$$f(\lambda K, \lambda L) < \lambda f(K, L).$$ (11.5)

Understanding returns to scale is important for any industry. If there are significant increasing returns to scale, then it is more efficient to allow only a few large firms to produce rather than having many small companies in the market. That was what many policy-makers believed until major deregulations. Governments artificially created entry barriers and regulations in the hope that a few large firms would serve the entire market efficiently. Although North American and European countries have now abolished such regulations, airlines in some other countries are still constrained in various ways. For example, an airline may have to seek approval from the government before it is allowed to serve a market or city. In certain cases, an airline is not even allowed to change the price it charges without filing a report with the regulator.

A production function defines the maximum amount of output that can be produced given certain inputs. In real life, it is often more convenient to define efficiency as the ability to produce a certain amount of output at a minimum cost. This is the definition of the cost function.

Cost function

In the foregoing example, imagine that the prices for labor and capital are w_L and w_K, and we wish to find out the most efficient (cheapest) way to produce a given output. Mathematically, this involves defining a cost function, as follows:

$$C(w_L, w_K, y) = \min w_L L + w_k \times K, \text{such that } f(L, K) \geq y \qquad (11.6)$$

where $f(L, K)$ is the production function that we have already defined. With given prices of inputs, a cost function is defined as the minimum cost necessary to achieve the desired level of output. From Equation (11.6), it is already clear that the production function and cost function are closely related. With some regularity conditions, it can be shown that cost functions are the "duel" of production functions, and it is equivalent to study either a production function or a cost function.[2] Many researchers, however, have found it more convenient to study cost functions, as they give monetary values.

So far, we have assumed that a firm can always use the optimal combination of inputs to minimize production costs. In reality, it is usually difficult to change inputs in the short run. To model this situation, we use the following definitions.

> **Fixed costs (FC):** Costs that do not change with output level. Whereas most costs vary in the long run, many important costs cannot be changed quickly. In the case of aviation, these include the runway, terminal, and number of pilots hired.
> **Variable costs (VC(Q)):** Costs that change with output level, such as fuel, loading and unloading charges, and landing and take-off fees. In the long run (almost) all costs are variable.

The classification of fixed cost and variable cost depends greatly on production technology and a firm's planning and arrangements. For example, it is well known that aviation logistics firms usually face fluctuating human resource requirements. An example of the manpower needed for an air cargo terminal is described in Figure 11.5. The vertical axis represents the manpower demand

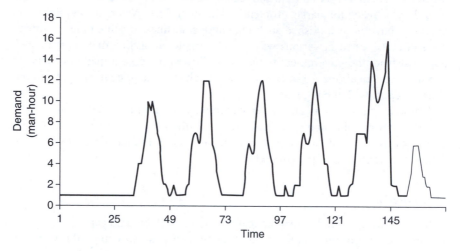

Figure 11.5 Manpower demand profile for an airport terminal over a week.

Source: Yan *et al.* (2006).

measured by man hours and the horizontal axis represents the time measured in hours throughout the week, starting from Sunday morning. As the figure shows, no manpower is needed from Sunday to Monday morning. However, the demand fluctuates during the day, as the arrival of shipments is stochastic (random). Nevertheless, the manpower demands from Monday to Thursday are similar, except that there is a peak demand on Friday. This is due to the fact that many shippers try to beat the Friday deadline so that cargo can be shipped out in the weekend and reach its destination by the following Monday. If the time horizon is by year, then we would probably also observe some seasonal fluctuations. The peak demand in North America is usually observed in November and early December, as many shipments need to be made for Thanksgiving and Christmas. With stochastic demand, a logistics firm has many options in planning its operations. If it decides to rely on its own staff and long-term employment contracts, then its labor cost may be classified as a fixed cost. However, if the firm decides to outsource cargo handling to other firms and make payments proportional to the cargo volume, then the cost becomes variable. Hence, even the same type of input can be classified as either variable or fixed.

When using the cost function, we also use different terms for the various returns to scale. They refer to the same supply pattern as those used for the production function, but from the point of view of cost.

- *Economies of Scale* (or Increasing Returns to Scale) exist whenever the long-run average total cost declines as output increases.
- *Diseconomies of Scale* (or Decreasing Returns to Scale) exist whenever the long-run average total cost increases as output increases.

Economies of density and hub-and-spoke networks

Just before the airline deregulation in 1978 in the United States, some experts expected that small airlines would soon reach bankruptcy because they could not exploit scale economies as effectively as their larger competitors. Were firms allowed to compete freely, these experts argued, only the large and efficient airlines would survive. However, this prediction did not materialize. Instead, two unexpected changes took place in the aviation industry. First, small airlines continued to compete actively in many markets, rather than going bankrupt. Second, many airlines switched to so-called hub-and-spoke networks. These developments have prompted researchers to pay more attention to the effects of airline networks. Unlike most other industries, the production of transportation and logistics services are fulfilled over a spatial network. Network configuration thus has an important influence on a carrier's cost structure and productivity.

Caves *et al.* (1984) identified two types of cost reduction effects: economies of traffic density and economies of scale. Economies of density are also called returns to density. They refer to the efficiency gains achieved when a firm increases its output within a given network, such as carrying more traffic within a network of a constant size.[3] Economies of scale refer to the efficiency gains made when a firm achieves output growth with a proportional increase in network size, such as carrying more traffic by expanding its network. Formally, returns to density are defined as

$$RTD = \frac{1}{\varepsilon_y}, \tag{11.7}$$

where ε_y is the elasticity of total cost with respect to output. Returns to scale are defined as

$$RTS = \frac{1}{\varepsilon_y + \varepsilon_p}. \tag{11.8}$$

where ε_y is the elasticity of total cost with respect to network size as measured by the number of points served. Caves *et al.* (1984) and other studies on the airline industry, such as that of Gillen *et al.* (1990), have found few instances of returns to scale but a significant occurrence of returns to density. That is, an airline cannot lower its average costs by carrying more traffic over a larger network. However, if the output growth is achieved mainly by carrying more traffic over an existing network, then the average cost can be significantly reduced. Traffic density has a direct and more significant impact on an airline's average cost compared to the effects of total output volume and network coverage.

Air transport and logistics productions involve three types of basic operations: (1) support activities, including marketing and sales, accounting, finance and insurance, advertisement, and IT support; (2) terminal operations, such as loading and unloading, warehousing, security check, packing; and (3) line haul operations,

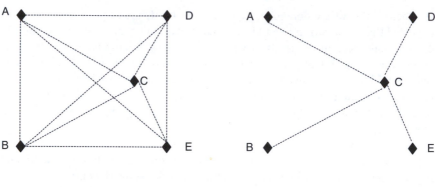

Fully connected network

Hub-and-spoke network

Figure 11.6 Fully connected network versus hub-and-spoke network.

such as landing and take-off, and movements from origin to destination. Adding one more destination to a firm's network usually involves fixed costs associated with support activities and terminal operations. Carrying more traffic over the same network allows a firm to fully utilize its existing facilities and operations, and thus achieve greater efficiency and lower average costs. Although small airlines have a lower total output, they can achieve high traffic density by focusing on several major routes. As there are limited economies of scale but significant economies of density in the aviation logistics industry, small firms can achieve a level of efficiency comparable to that of large competitors by focusing on certain niche markets rather than serving a national or global network.

One method of increasing traffic density, and thus saving costs, is to utilize a so-called hub-and-spoke network. Consider a firm that has a network choice of serving five destinations, as in Figure 11.6. One configuration is to use a fully connected network in which any two destinations are linked with a direct service. Alternatively, the firm can utilize a hub-and-spoke network in which traffic between two (spoke) nodes can be served by an itinerary that connects to a central point (hub).

Compared with fully connected networks, hub-and-spoke networks allow a carrier to serve the same number of nodes with a much simpler network and higher traffic density. To serve N destinations, a fully connected network requires $N(N–1)/2$ connections or links, whereas a hub-and-spoke network only needs $(N − 1)$ connections. This, of course, greatly simplifies a carrier's operation and thus may reduce its costs. In addition, by routing the traffic between two nodes via a hub, traffic density can be increased, which further reduces the operation costs. In the network depicted above, if the transport demand between any two points (A–B, A–C, A–D, A–E, B–C, B–D, B–E, C–D, C–E, D–E) is 100, then a fully connected network can achieve a traffic density of 100 on each route. The hub-and-spoke network, however, can achieve an average traffic density of 400. This is because the route A–C, for example, not only carries traffic along A–C, but also routes traffic between A–B, A–D, and A–E. The significantly increased traffic density allows an operator to use larger, more efficient aircraft. It also enables a company to offer more frequent flights between the nodes and hub, and thus more frequent (connection) services between any two nodes.

Routing traffic between two spoke nodes via a hub, rather than offering a direct flight, does involve some extra time and costs, such as loading and unloading costs, connection time, allowance for congestion at the hub airport, and extra cruise time. However, a hub-and-spoke network simplifies the operational complexity and increases traffic density and flight frequency. It has been extensively used since deregulation. Today, aviation logistics companies mostly base their operations on hub-and-spoke networks and then complement the network with direct services between a few major nodes. Similar network configurations have also been used for local road distribution. Logistics firms often set up a distribution center within a region in which all shipments are first sorted before they are distributed locally or shipped to another city. The network configurations for international services are usually more complex, as most governments still have regulations restricting route entry and operational capacity. These restrictions prevent operators from optimizing their network operations as a free market would otherwise allow. Many countries are moving forward to fully liberalize the aviation market across borders. This objective is often achieved by implementing "open skies" agreements, which are discussed in the section on aviation regulation.

Economies of scope in aviation production

Virtually no logistics firms provide one single product or service. Taking Hong Kong Air Cargo Terminals (HACTL) as an example, the firm provides services including physical cargo handling, shipping documents preparation, ramp services, customs clearances, consolidation, security screening, shipping unit release, ground transportation, pickup and delivery and even air cargo handling training. FedEx started with simple air courier services. Now it offers hundreds, if not thousands, of services, from document printing via Kinko to total logistics solutions for corporations. There are many factors that lead firms to offer multiple services. On the demand side, many customers prefer to purchase all of the services that they need from just a few suppliers that they trust. On the supply side, a firm's expertise and resource endowment often make it cheaper to produce a group of services together. This is referred to as *economies of scope*. For example, if a cargo terminal can handle Q_1 units of express cargo and Q_2 units of regular air freight at a cost given by $C(Q_1,Q_2)$, then economies of scope occur if we have

$$C(Q_1,Q_2) < C(Q_1,0) + C(0,Q_2). \tag{11.9}$$

This means that it is more efficient to build one cargo terminal to handle both kinds of freight. However, if there are *diseconomies of scale*, or $C(Q_1,Q_2) > C(Q_1,0)+C(0,Q_2)$, then the airport should plan two terminals dedicated to express cargo and regular freight, respectively.

Table 11.2 Major air freight carriers in 2005

Airline	Region	FTK[a] million	Pax/cargo
1 Fedex	North America	14,579	No
2 Korean Air	Asia Pacific	8,264	Yes
3 Lufthansa	Europe	8,040	Yes
4 UPS	North America	7,353	No
5 Singapore Airlines	Asia Pacific	7,143	Yes
6 Cathay Pacific	Asia Pacific	5,876	Yes
7 China Airlines	Asia Pacific	5,642	Yes
8 Atlas Air	North America	5,536	No
9 Eva Air	Asia Pacific	5,477	Yes
10 Air France	Europe	5,388	Yes
33 Air Canada	North America	1,367	Yes

Source: Air Cargo World Online, airlines' websites.

Note
a   Freight ton Kilometers.

It is generally believed that there are sufficient economies of scope for airlines to produce both passenger services and cargo services. Both operations require common infrastructure and support, such as aircraft maintenance, airport ground services, staffing and pilots. Moreover, one can produce the two services with the same aircraft. Most aircraft are configured such that passengers occupy the upper deck whereas the belly space is used for luggage and air cargo. Due to such economies of scope, many freight service providers are also passenger carriers. Among the top ten air freight carriers in 2005, seven carried both passengers and air freight (Table 11.2).

Historically, passenger revenue was far more significant than cargo. However, with the trends of globalization and trade liberalization, air cargo services worldwide have been growing at approximately twice the rate of passenger services. Many airlines have expanded their freight operations considerably. As shown in Table 11.3, some of the major airlines in the world had raised their cargo revenue share to well above 20 percent as early as in 2002. This trend reversed a bit during the 2008–2009 financial crisis. Since early 2010, the revenue share of cargo services has continued to grow steadily. In the foreseeable future, air cargo will continue to outperform passenger business in most markets.

There are many sources of economies of scope. One source is the sharing of common fixed costs when expensive facilities are used to produce multiple outputs. For example, cargo operations and passenger operations share runway capacity, air traffic control, and ground services. However, whereas passenger flights usually depart and arrive at convenient times, air freighters may use the airport around the clock. This enables the expensive runway capacity to be better utilized. Mathematically, we may assume that the cost function for producing the two outputs together is

$$C(Q_1, Q_2) = F + \mathrm{mc}_1 \times Q_1 + \mathrm{mc}_2 \times Q_2, \tag{11.10}$$

Table 11.3 Cargo revenue share for the top 10 mixed passenger/cargo airlines, 2002

Airline	Cargo (%)	Passenger (%)	Passenger + cargo (%)
EVA Air	43	50	93
China Airlines	39	55	94
Lan Chile	36	55	91
Asiana	29	62	91
Korean Air	29	59	88
Cathay Pacific	28	68	96
Singapore Airlines	24	65	88
China Eastern	19	77	95
Emirates	17	68	84
Thai Airways	16	79	95
Average	*28*	*50*	*95*

where F is the fixed cost and mc_1 and mc_2 are the constant marginal costs of producing outputs Q_1 and Q_2. The cost of producing them separately requires the duplication of fixed costs, and the total cost is therefore

$$C(Q_1, 0) + C(0, Q_2) = F + mc_1 \times Q_1 + F + mc_2 \times Q_2. \qquad (11.11)$$

The natural question that arises here is why, if there are economies of scope between passenger operations and cargo operations, there is increasing demand for air freighters (aircraft designed to ship cargo only). An important factor is that passenger travel demand can be very different from air freight demand. Most passengers make round trips, which creates symmetrical demand to and from a destination. However, cargo traffic is usually one way, which creates unbalanced demand for the front haul and back haul. This requires aviation logistics managers to devise a different operations plan.

Take the cell phone supply chain in East Asia as an example. Japan has the leading electronics technology in the region, and can produce sophisticated semi-conductors efficiently with its established capital and knowledge base. Many South Korean telecom firms, however, have accumulated expertise in efficiently designing and producing cell phone modules. Chinese firms, utilizing the abundant labor supply in the country, offer far more cost-effective final assembly. We thus observe a circular flow of cargo traffic: Japanese semiconductors are shipped to South Korea, where they are made into IC chips and cell phone modules. These components are then shipped to mainland China, where they are assembled together with locally produced batteries and keyboards. The final products are packaged and delivered to Japan for distribution to end users. To handle this kind of traffic flow, it is apparently more efficient to have an airline flow from Japan → South Korea → China → Japan, rather than to plan three round-trip operations between the three countries, as in a typical passenger market (Figure 11.7).[4]

To accommodate one-way cargo traffic, airlines now increasingly utilize all-cargo aircraft (freighters) to serve markets in which the shipping demands are

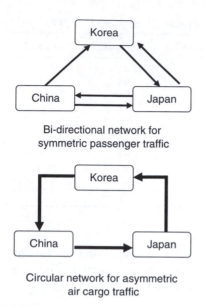

Figure 11.7 Sample air freight flow of electronics products in East Asia.

sufficiently high. Accordingly, the network or operational routes are usually circular, rather than linear.[5]

Estimation of a cost function for air carriers[6] (for advanced readers)

Understanding cost structure is important both for a firm's daily operations and for its long-term strategies, such as production plans, price setting, and product line design. Regulators also need detailed cost analyses to make decisions on public policy and regulations (e.g., price control, entry conditions, antitrust in merger and acquisition cases, investigating predatory pricing complaints). Most companies routinely conduct cost analyses using accounting information. The financial department first compiles information on the accounting costs related to a service (e.g., express cargo), with which they predict the implications of changes in output for the total cost. However, this approach suffers from several problems. First, it fails to recognize the substitution effects between different inputs. As we have explained, a firm utilizes multiple inputs in production. If the price of one input (e.g., labor) increases sharply, then the firm will try to use other inputs (e.g., capital or machines) more extensively to substitute for the expensive input. Such information is not clearly revealed in accounting data. Second, the accounting approach has great trouble in assigning common costs to each individual service. Where the same aircraft carries passengers and luggage, express cargo, ordinary cargo, regular mail, and leased containers, it is difficult to determine how the operation costs of a flight should be allocated to each of these services. Finally, the accounting approach does not distinguish fixed costs from variable costs. Rather, the costs related to fixed assets are usually treated as depreciation, and the relationship between outputs and inputs is not clearly outlined. Thus, although the accounting approach is extensively used in day-to-day operations, the estimation of a cost function is more useful for long-term planning, industry studies, and policy evaluation.

In estimating a cost function, a similar but more general specification to Equation (11.6) is

$$C = C(w, y),$$ (11.12)

where w is a vector of input prices (for labor, fuel, capital inputs such as fleet, ground handling and cargo terminal equipment, energy, outsourcing costs, landing and parking charges at airports, finance and insurance charges, and maintenance costs), and y is a vector of outputs (express cargo, normal air freight, courier services, leased containers, air mail, and other value-added services such as warehousing and ground delivery services).

As an air carrier may experience increasing, constant, or decreasing returns to scale, it is better to use a flexible specification of the functional form for the cost function, which allows the cost function to be U-shaped. Translog multiproduct cost functions are quite often used. It is a second-order approximation of any unknown cost function around the mean, which may be specified as

$$\ln C = \beta_0 + \sum \beta_i \ln y_i + \sum \gamma_j \ln w_j + \sum\sum \delta_{ij} \ln w_j \ln y_i$$
$$+ \frac{1}{2}\sum\sum \varepsilon_{ik} \ln y_i \ln y_k + \frac{1}{2}\sum\sum \phi_{jl} \ln w_j w_l.$$ (11.13)

This specification involves the estimation of many parameters (vectors of β_i, γ_j, δ_{ij}, ε_{ik}, ϕ_{jl}), which may be challenging when there is only limited data for the carriers under investigation. It is thus usual practice to jointly estimate this function with the following cost share equations, which can be derived using Shephard's lemma.

$$S_j = \frac{\partial \ln C}{\partial \ln w_j} = \gamma_j + \sum \delta_{ij} \ln y_i + \sum \phi_{jl} \ln w_l.$$ (11.14)

With the specifications in Equations (11.13) and (11.14), it is possible to statistically estimate all of these parameters using (usually aggregate) data for air carriers or any logistics service provider. In the econometric estimation, the following restrictions are often imposed so that all of the cost shares add up to 1 and when all of the input prices increase in identical proportion, the total cost increases by the same proportion.[7]

$$\sum \gamma_j = 1, \sum\sum \delta_{ij} = 0, \sum\sum \phi_{jl} = 0.$$ (11.15)

Other problems also arise in estimating the cost functions for air carriers. First, a carrier can potentially be regarded as providing many different types of services. For example, a domestic cargo service between Osaka and Tokyo may be different from an international cargo service between Tokyo and Los Angeles. If this is the case, then a medium-sized carrier may be providing hundreds of outputs, and there will be too many parameters to estimate. A firm's outputs are instead usually aggregated into certain common output measures, such as available ton kilometers (ATK, which indicates the total capacity supplied by a carrier) or revenue ton kilometers (RTK, which indicates the actual capacity used or sold by the carrier). As described earlier, the cost of producing the same outputs may differ depending on an airline's network structure, traffic density, and average flight stage distance. It is thus necessary to control for such factors in estimating the cost function. Such a cost function is often referred to as a "hedonic cost function." For example, Gillen *et al.* (1990) studied the following hedonic cost function using panel data on several airlines:

$$
\ln C(F, N, y, W) = \beta_0 + \sum f_k D_k + \alpha_p \ln N + \sum \beta_i \ln y_i + \gamma_j \ln w_j
$$
$$
+ \frac{1}{2} \sum \sum \varepsilon_{ik} \ln y_i \ln y_k + \frac{1}{2} \sum \sum \delta_{jl} \ln y_i \ln y_k
$$
$$
+ \frac{1}{2} \sum \sum \phi_{jl} \ln y_i \ln w_j + \frac{1}{2} \sum c_{pi} \ln N \ln y_i
$$
$$
+ \frac{1}{2} \sum e_j \ln N \ln w_j + \frac{1}{2} c_{pp} (\ln N)^2
$$

where C is the total cost, D_k are dummy variables for each airline, and N is the number of cities (nodes) served by an airline, which captures the network size effects. More control variables, such as average stage length and quality of services, can be added to the specification. This not only allows the analyst to control for more factors, but also requires more data, as it introduces more coefficients to estimate.

The assumption in most cost function estimations is that firms seek to minimize their costs. However, often an analyst can only obtain data for a relatively short period, usually a couple of years. Major aviation equipment such as aircraft and cargo terminal machinery, however, can be used for up to 20 years. That is, for the short period during which the analyst accumulates data, certain fixed costs do not change, which contradicts the assumption that the cost function is the result of the management's efforts to minimize costs. In the aviation logistics industry, this is overcome by estimating a variable cost function when data over a long period cannot be obtained.

Aviation demand

While transport and logistics demands have been extensively investigated in general, aviation demand possesses some special features. In this section, we review some essential topics related to aviation demand analysis.

Determinants of aviation logistics demand

There are two ways to model aviation demand. The "macro" way is to study the determinants of aviation logistics demand using economic models. These models allow the estimation of the "average" demand during a certain period, and the evaluation of the demand impacts of various social and economic changes. These models include classic demand function estimation, discrete choice models, and gravity models. Alternatively, the "micro" way is to use operational models to simulate the random arrival of booking requests for a particular flight. For example, Gamma distribution and Poisson distribution are frequently used in operations planning for logistics services. Either way, it is first necessary to identify the factors that affect the potential and realized demand. Oum and Thretheway (1990) identified the following important factors.

- **Price:** When the price of aviation logistics is lowered, it becomes a more affordable alternative to other shipping modes, such as rail and road. Thus, a reduction in price leads to a growth in demand.
- **Economic growth and income effects:** Logistics services are important inputs to various economic activities. Economic growth requires more movement of industrial goods, such as semiconductors, computers, and sophisticated machinery. The income growth accompanying economic growth leads to increased shipments of expensive consumption goods, such as seafood, luxury apparel, and watches.
- **Frequency of service:** Shippers usually have different time preferences over a week or even over a day. Some shippers need to transfer the unfinished goods to another factory for further processing in the middle of the week. Others may prefer to ship the finished goods on Thursdays so that they can be for sale on the shelves by the weekend. Depending on the production schedule, the same manufacturer may need to make multiple shipments separately in the morning and afternoon. The difference between a shipper's desired departure time and the most preferred available departure time is called the "schedule delay." When the frequency of service increases, shippers have a greater choice of departure time, and thus experience less schedule delay. This leads to an increase in service quality, and thus an increase in demand.
- **Timing of service:** The demand for air transport services fluctuates. Most shippers prefer to either make deliveries early in the morning or late in the afternoon. These popular times usually face a higher demand, and are thus referred to as "peak" hours. All other things being equal, a cargo flight and logistics operations during peak hours will attract more services.
- **Safety:** Aviation logistics is usually safer than other modes of transport. However, as cargo shipped by air is usually of high value, a good safety record is important in maintaining business and customers.
- **Distance:** Distance has a mixed impact on aviation logistics demand. In general, the longer the shipping distance involved, the less the shipping

demand due to the increased transportation costs involved. However, longer distances reduce the substitution effects of other shipping modes, such as rail and truck. The "net" effects depend on the market and goods to be shipped.

- **Technology progress:** Technology progress also increases aviation logistics demand. In the early days, flight operation was greatly subject to weather conditions. This made aviation a risky and unreliable mode of transport. When jets were first introduced, there was a noticeable increase in demand. The reduction in the transcontinental flying time from ten to five hours made air travel a far more efficient and valuable shipping mode. Fuel efficiency is of increasing importance to both carriers and shippers in recent years due to the sharp increase in fuel prices. Today, other shipping technologies, such as cooling devices for perishable products and package tracking technology such as radio frequency identification (RFID), have contributed to demand growth for aviation logistics services.

To quantify the impacts of such demand determinants, it is best to estimate the demand functions that control these variables. However, this involves rich data and a relatively complex estimation procedure. In practical analysis, elasticity is extensively used as a simple substitute.

Transport demand elasticity

Elasticity is a measure of responsiveness, or the percentage change in one variable in response to a 1-percent change in another. In the case of demand, the own-price elasticity of demand is the percentage change in quantity demanded in response to a 1-percent change in its price. The own-price elasticity of demand is expected to be negative, that is, a price increase decreases the quantity demanded. Demand is said to be "price-elastic" if the absolute value of the own-price elasticity is greater than unity, that is, when a price change elicits a more than proportionate change in the quantity demanded. A "price-inelastic" demand has a less than proportionate response in the quantity demanded to a price change, that is, it has an elasticity of between 0 and -1. Once one has estimated the demand function $Q = Q(P)$, where Q is the demand and P is the price, the own-price elasticity can be calculated as

$$\varepsilon = \frac{\Delta Q\%}{\Delta P\%} = \frac{dQ}{dP}\frac{P}{Q}.$$

(11.17)

The own-price elasticity is distinguished from the cross-price elasticity. The latter is the percentage change in quantity demanded for, say, air freight in response to a percentage change in the price of another service such as trucking. For substitutable goods and services, the cross-price elasticity is positive. If two products are unrelated to each other in the minds of consumers, then the cross-price elasticity demand is zero, whereas for complementary goods and services the cross-price elasticity is negative. The cross-price elasticity for aviation logistics and other shipping modes depends on the actual market considered. Aviation logistics is inherently intermodal in the sense that air freight needs to be moved by truck to and from airports. However, trucking can be a substitutable shipping method for air freight over short to medium distances, which means that trucking can be both a complementary and a substitute service to air freight.

Another elasticity concept is income elasticity. This refers to the percentage change in quantity demanded with respect to a 1-percent change in income, all other variables, including prices, being held constant. If consumption increases more than proportionately with income (an income elasticity of greater than one), then the good is considered to be a "luxury" or "superior" good (e.g., a luxury cruise). Air transport is a superior good in that its income elasticity is usually estimated to be within the range of 1–3, with passenger income elasticity in the lower range while cargo income elasticity is in the upper range. For example, the US Department of Transportation estimated the income elasticity of air transport to be 1.74. The UK Department for Transport used a value of 1.5 for income elasticity. In their sensitivity tests, the value of 1.0 was used as the lower value for low "market maturity," while a value of 2.0 was used for high "market maturity." Gillen *et al.* (2003) surveyed 14 studies, and found the median income elasticity value of 1.39, with most estimates ranging between 0.5 and 2.5.

The dependence of air transport on overall economy provides an important and relatively convenient instrument for demand forecasting. As a matter of fact, income elasticity has been incorporated in virtually all forecast models used by major organizations:

- **Boeing:** Boeing has published an annual *Current Market Outlook* (CMO) since 1964. CMO offers a 20-year forecast for the worldwide aviation market involving jet aircraft with 30 seats or more. Traffic forecaster applies GDP to a top-down traffic model, which found that on average, air travel approximates to 1 percent of GDP over time. The Boeing forecasts also recognize that as trade rises as a share of GDP, air travel rises as well. In particular, Boeing (2008) attributes about two-thirds of traffic growth to GDP growth, and the rest to other factors such as increasing trade, lower costs, and improved services. These overall forecasts are combined with other modeling techniques to deliver detailed forecasts for major markets in the world.

- **Airbus:** Airbus offers its own version of the 20-year forecast, the Global Market Forecast (GMF). The forecast model also utilizes GDP-trend regression for traffic forecasting, with other factors such as trade, unemployment rate, inflation, and disposable income controlled in Airbus' econometric analysis. Statistical tests are conducted so that the model that best fits the historical traffic is selected for use. For market segments where classical econometric models are not sufficient, GMF uses "hybrid models" to take into account the effects of other factors such as the presence of low cost carriers, fuel price, growth of emerging economies, and intermodal competition between air and other transport modes.

Table 11.4 Past air traffic growth by key markets (in billion RPKs[a]), 2000–2007

	2000	2001	2002	2003	2004	2005	2006	2007	% Per year
				(billion RPK)					
Intra-Asia Pacific[a]	465.1	483.4	527.4	507.0	623.0	683.1	726.2	783.0	7.7
Domestic China	76.7	86.9	101.5	106.9	143.8	163.8	182.4	209.5	15.4
Intra-Europe	440.1	449.3	453.8	474.7	521.2	561.9	593.3	630.6	5.3
Intra-North America	857.5	812.8	783.5	828.3	927.7	972.3	977.4	1,016.6	2.5
Asia Pacific[b]– Europe	225.7	219.4	219.9	210.3	251.2	277.5	300.1	306.6	4.5
Asia Pacific[b]–N. America	235.5	220.6	211.4	180.6	218.9	234.4	239.6	251.4	0.9
Europe–N. America	420.0	373.8	346.0	349.5	375.7	390.7	403.4	418.2	−0.1
Europe–North America (IATA data)	n.a.	n.a.	n.a.	n.a.	n.a.	434.9	457.9	482.2	5.25 (2005–2007)
World total	**3,381**	**3,290**	**3,279**	**3,304**	**3,754**	**4,026**	**4,234**	**4,513**	4.2

Source: Boeing CMO 2008.

Notes
a Revenue passenger kilometers.
b Asia Pacific includes Australia and New Zealand.

- **ICAO:** ICAO (2007) utilizes a GDP trend model with the consideration of air traffic price, in terms of yields, to predict air traffic. In its forecast up to 2025, the overall income elasticity for air transport is estimated to be 1.27. That is, ceteris paribus, a 1-percent increase in GDP will lead to a 1.27-percent increase in air travel. ICAO further assumed that the world economy will grow at an average annual rate of 3.5 percent during 2005–2025, leading to a predicted growth rate for global air traffic of about 4.5 percent a year.

These income elasticity estimates are consistent with the traffic growth rates observed in key markets. As evidenced in Table 11.4, regions with strong economic growth, such as the intra-Asia Pacific region or Chinese domestic market, had experienced strong traffic growth during recent years.

A higher than unity income elasticity implies that the growth in aviation logistics is more volatile than the growth of the general economy. The air transport industry usually grows faster than the overall economy, but is worse hit when there is an economic recession. The industry is also subject to evident economic cycles. Oum *et al.* (2005) studied the before-tax profit margin of ten major North American airlines, and found that it was clearly correlated with the trend in the overall economy as shown in Figure 11.8.

It is thus important for aviation logistics firms to have a disciplined expansion plan when there is strong demand growth. Capital investments such as aircraft, cargo terminals, ground service equipment, and distribution centers can last for more than 20 years. Any attempt to accommodate all traffic demand in good years could lead to a serious financial burden when the economy slows down.

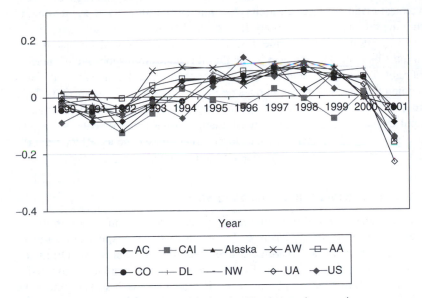

Figure 11.8 Before-tax profit margin of major North American carriers.

Nature of derived demand of transport and logistics

Elasticities are useful for demand forecasting at "macro" level. For example, if the income elasticity is two, then obviously the aviation logistics industry will grow at a rate of about 8 percent a year if the overall economy increases at a rate of 4 percent. However, one should be cautious in using price elasticity for "micro" demand forecasting of a particular market or product. Unlike other consumer goods, demand for shipping and logistics is derived from the consumption of other goods. Shipments are needed only when there is consumption demand for the goods at the destination. Consumers are sensitive to the *delivered price*, rather than the shipping costs.

Consider the following example. If the demand for laptop computers at the destination market can be specified as $Q = 5,000 - P$, where Q is the quantity of laptops delivered and P is the delivered price, then the delivered price P is the sum of the Free Onboard Price (FOB) price P_0 at origin market and the shipping cost P_s. When $P_0 = 3,000$, $P_s = 100$, then the demand for delivered laptops, which is also the demand for shipping services, is calculated as $Q = 5,000 - 3,000 - 100 = 1,900$. If laptop manufacturers can reduce the FOB price to $P_0 = 2,000$ and the logistics company increases the shipping costs to $P_s = 300$, then the demand for laptops becomes $Q = 5,000 - 2,000 - 300 = 2,700$. In this case, the logistics company has managed to increase the price by 200 percent while obtaining more shipping demand. This of course does not imply that the own-price elasticity is positive. One should always bear in mind that demand for shipping and logistics services is derived demand, and one must thus study the demand for the delivered goods to correctly forecast the shipping demand.

The nature of derived demand for freight also introduces considerable complexity in the estimation of price elasticity. As Oum *et al.* (2007) have pointed out, to measure the ordinary price elasticity for freight demand, the freight demand system must be estimated at the same time as the shippers' output decisions, that is, output must be treated as endogenous so that it changes in response to changes in freight rates. Ignoring the endogeneity of shippers' output decisions is equivalent to assuming that changes in freight rates do not affect shippers' output levels. This, in turn, is equivalent to ignoring the secondary effect of a freight rate change on the input demand caused by an induced change in the level or scale of outputs. Because many freight demand models do not treat this secondary effect properly, care must be taken in interpreting price elasticity estimates.

Revenue management in aviation logistics

The idea and techniques of revenue management were first introduced in the air transport sector for passenger business. In the late 1940s, in response to competition from charter carriers, US trunk airlines established coach fares. Originally offered only on special all-coach flights, these airlines eventually adopted a mixed cabin with first class and more densely allocated coach seats on the same aircraft. Later, the same types of seats were allocated to different fare classes to maximize the revenue of a flight. Such efforts gradually evolved over time into a full revenue management system that incorporates various modules such as demand forecasting, capacity planning, price discrimination, dynamic capacity allocation, and loyalty program integration.

In general, revenue management systems refer to a group of methods for maximizing revenue in industries (1) that deal with perishable goods or services that do not allow any inventory (once a flight takes off, the extra capacity on that flight can never be sold); (2) in which there is a possibility of price discrimination for goods jointly produced (the same flight can be used for different types of air freight with varying degrees of service quality, such as express cargo and ordinary cargo; and (3) for which demand forecasting is possible (although the actual amount of cargo for a particular flight cannot be precisely predicted, one can forecast demand patterns with a reasonable degree of accuracy). Today, revenue management applications are extensively used in industries such as cargo and logistics, cinemas, hotels, cruises, trucking services, and maritime shipping. Very sophisticated mathematical and control models have been developed over the years. It is impossible to give a detailed explanation of these in a short chapter. Thus, in this section we only describe the fundamentals of revenue management in the context of aviation logistics.[8]

In the following sections, we consider a very simple case of revenue management that involves only two types of air freight: express and ordinary. For the same amount of weight, express cargo brings more revenue than ordinary freight. *Ceteris paribus*, a carrier prefers to carry more express cargo. However, reserving too much capacity for express cargo will be costly, as the capacity utilization rate, which is usually measured by load factor,[9] will be reduced. A cargo carrier should

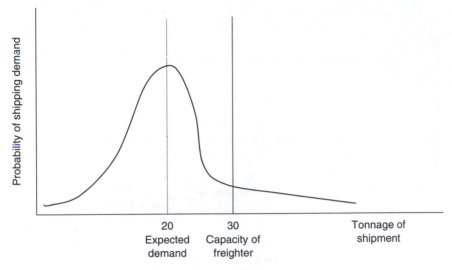

Figure 11.9 Total shipping demand of a cargo flight.

thus reserve optimal capacity for express cargo so that express cargo will be carried most of the time, and sell the unused capacity to ordinary cargo at a discount. This process usually involves the following steps.

I   Determine the capacity of a flight

Logistics firms need to plan their capacity well in advance. In reality, fleet and capacity planning is a very complex task involving overall demand forecasting, competition evaluation, and fleet operation planning for an airline's overall network. In our example, we simplify this step by assuming that a cargo freighter with a capacity of 30 tons is used.[10]

II   Forecast the demand for express cargo

The next step is to forecast the demand for express cargo. With historical data and some forecasting skills, it is possible to determine the expected shipping demand and variance for express cargo. The demand forecast can further be presented as a probability density function that reflects the nature of stochastic demand and the inherent variability in forecasting. For the market considered in our example, we assume the expected shipping volume per day to be 20 tons, as shown in Figure 11.9.

III   Determine the spill rate for express cargo

Given a cargo flight's capacity and demand forecast, the carrier needs to determine the capacity to be allocated to express cargo. This is equivalent to choosing a probability level at which express cargo can be fully accommodated. For

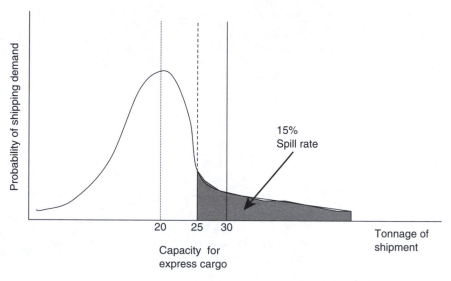

Figure 11.10 Determination of the spill rate.

example, the airline may decide that 85 percent of the time express cargo will be fully served. This means that the area under the density curve to the right of such reserved capacity equals 15 percent. That is, 15 percent of the time, some shipping requests for express cargo will be rejected due to lack of allocated capacity. This probability is referred to as the "spill" rate, and can also be used as a service quality indicator for express cargo. In our example, a 15 percent spill rate requires a reservation of 25 tons for express cargo on this flight (Figure 11.10).

VI Time-dependent demand and dynamic pricing

After reserving sufficient capacity for express cargo to achieve the expected spill rate, the remaining part, which in this case is an extra capacity of five tons, can be allocated to ordinary freight. This is a one-off static solution. As the demands for both types of freight are stochastic, it is necessary to dynamically adjust the initial capacity allocation to improve the load factor. For example, on days when there are insufficient shipments of express cargo, an operations manager can release more capacity to accommodate ordinary freight at a price discount.

Such dynamic capacity allocation again requires careful planning and monitoring. Shipping requests are time dependent, that is, they do not arrive at the same time. Express cargo is usually very urgent, and thus cannot be planned well in advance. Most express booking requests arrive just before the departure time. Shippers are usually able to plan better for ordinary air freight, as booking requests are usually made earlier. As shown in Figure 11.11, if a manager accepts booking requests on a first-come-first-served basis, then he or she is likely to run

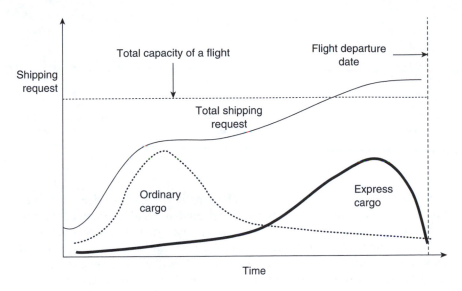

Figure 11.11 Time-dependent demand.[a]

Note:
[a]This graph can be derived from a booking curve used in revenue management. A very similar graph was first proposed in the 2006 POLYU lecture note by Dr. Keith Mason. A detailed interpretation of similar curves as real-time demand forecasting is provided in Dr. Michael Li's BT202 lecture notes of 2010.

out of capacity before the departure time. Capacity will then be occupied by cheap ordinary freights, forcing the manager to reject high-paying express cargo.

Static capacity allocation and dynamic adjustments should be used jointly. After the initial capacity allocation, firms should monitor the booking requests accumulated and compare them to "booking curves" identified using historical data. Only when the booking requests received clearly deviate from the normal historical pattern is a dynamic adjustment triggered. In this circumstance, early booking requests for ordinary freight may have to be rejected to ensure the reservation of sufficient capacity for high-yield express cargo. Not all of the rejected shipping requests will end up as sales losses. Some less urgent shipments can be diverted to the next flight, although the remaining proportion must be passed to competitors. If the amount of rejected shipments over a given period is sizable, then there is a need to supply more capacity to this market by using a larger aircraft or by adding more flights. Otherwise, customer satisfaction will be reduced in the long run, and competitors will find it potentially more profitable to enter the market.

The foregoing example is much simplified. In reality, a carrier needs to consider shipping demand on a multileg route, or even over a network. Further, logistics service providers usually provide a range of services, rather than express

Figure 11.12 First freedom.

and ordinary cargo only. The capacity to be supplied for each service needs to be planned and allocated far in advance so that preparations can be arranged in terms of flight rights, airport slots, crew allocation, and ground service operations. Ultimately, the pricing and capacity allocation decisions of a carrier also depend heavily on the strategy of its competitors. All of these factors make revenue management systems very complex in practice. Major logistics firms invest millions of dollars a year to improve their revenue management.

Regulation for international aviation logistics

A significant proportion of aviation logistics involves cross-border or international shipments. However, unlike in domestic markets,[11] airlines offering international services require special permission to serve certain destinations. Such rights are referred as "freedoms of the air," and are specified in bilateral service agreements (BSAs) signed by the governments of the origin and destination cities. BSAs are essential treaties between countries that have complete and exclusive sovereignty over the airspace above their territory as specified by the 1944 Chicago Convention. We will use a Japanese carrier as an example to demonstrate the main air freedoms.[12]

- **First freedom of the air:** the right or privilege granted by one State to another State or States to fly across its territory without landing (Figure 11.12).

Governments now routinely grant the first freedom to foreign carriers. For example, if a Japanese carrier wants to fly from a city in its home country, say Tokyo, to a destination in the Netherlands, say Amsterdam, then it needs to fly over Russian air space. The carrier thus needs to obtain the first freedom from Russia for this flight.

- **Second freedom of the air:** the right or privilege granted by one State to another State or States to land in its territory for non-traffic purposes (Figure 11.13).

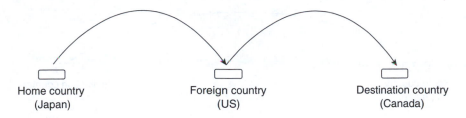

Figure 11.13 Second freedom.

The second freedom allows a carrier to make a technical stop in a foreign country on its way to the final destination (another foreign country) without loading or unloading. Historically, the second freedom was important because most aircraft had a relatively short flight range, and needed to refuel for long-distance flights. For example, many Asian carriers obtained the second freedom from the United States for their cross-Pacific flights as their flights needed to make a stop in Hawaii (Honolulu airport) to refuel before landing in other American destinations, such as Canada, Mexico, or Chile. With technological progress aircraft now can fly to almost any destination non-stop. This freedom therefore has become decreasing of importance in recent years.

- **Third freedom of the air:** the right or privilege granted by one State to another State to put down, in the territory of the first State, traffic coming from the home State of the carrier.
- **Fourth freedom of the air:** the right or privilege granted by one State to another State to take on, in the territory of the first State, traffic destined for the home State of the carrier (Figure 11.14).

The third and fourth freedoms are the essential basic freedoms for international travel. The third freedom allows an airline to carry traffic from its home country to a foreign country, whereas the fourth permits an airline to carry traffic from a foreign country to its home country. For example, a Japanese airlines needs to obtain the third and fourth freedoms from the United States to provide services between Japan and the United States.

- **Fifth freedom of the air:** the right or privilege granted by one State to another State to put down and to take on, in the territory of the first State, traffic coming from or destined for a third State (Figure 11.15).

The fifth freedom allows a carrier to operate a flight in the form of home country ⇔ first foreign country ⇔ second foreign country. This right is important to cargo carriers, as normally a cargo flight makes multiple stops before returning

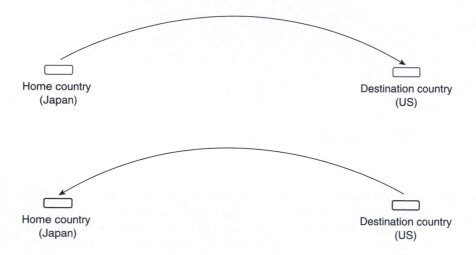

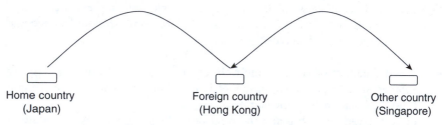

Figure 11.14 Third and fourth freedoms.

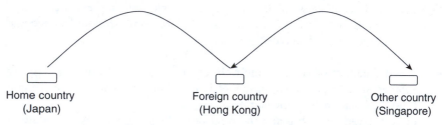

Figure 11.15 Fifth freedom.

to the city of origin. For example, if a Japanese airline wishes to operate a flight from Japan ⇔ Hong Kong ⇔ Singapore and to carry traffic between Japan and Hong Kong, Hong Kong and Singapore, and Japan and Singapore, then it needs to obtain the fifth freedom from Hong Kong in addition to the third and fourth freedoms. The carrier also needs to obtain the same rights from Singapore for such a flight.

- **Sixth freedom of the air:** the right or privilege to transport, via the home State of the carrier, traffic moving between two other States (Figure 11.16).

The sixth freedom allows an airline to provide traffic between two foreign countries via a hub in its home country. If a Japanese carrier wants to offer the flight Hong Kong ⇔ Japan ⇔ United States, then to carry traffic from Hong Kong to and from the United States, it needs to obtain the sixth freedom from Hong Kong in addition to the third and fourth freedoms. The carrier also needs to obtain the

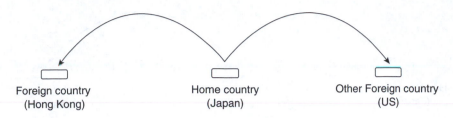

Foreign country
(Hong Kong)

Home country
(Japan)

Other Foreign country
(US)

Figure 11.16 Sixth freedom.

same set of freedoms from the United States. Without the sixth freedom, an airline cannot officially provide services between two foreign countries (from Hong Kong to and from the United States in this case). However, the carrier can always use the third and fourth freedoms from the two countries to bring shipments to the home country first, and then provide a connecting flight to the final destination (the Japanese carrier can fly Hong Kong cargo to Japan first, then sell the shipping service from Japan to the United States using the third freedom from the United States). The sixth freedom is thus not usually strictly monitored.

- **Seventh freedom of the air:** the right or privilege granted by one State to another State to transport traffic between the territory of the granting State and any third State with no requirement to include in such operation any point in the territory of the recipient State, that is, the service need not connect to or be an extension of any service to or from the home State of the carrier (Figure 11.17).

If a Japanese carrier wants to operate a flight between the United States and Mexico without initiating the flight in Japan, then it needs to obtain the seventh freedom from the United States and Mexico. This freedom enables an airline to establish a hub in a foreign country. The country granting the seventh freedom is essentially allowing a foreign carrier to compete directly with its own air carriers in its international markets. Consequently, few seventh freedoms have been awarded in the world, although in the 2005 Open Sky Agreement between Canada and the United States, the seventh freedom was granted to cargo flights.

- **Eighth freedom of the air:** the right or privilege to transport cabotage traffic between two points in the territory of the granting State in a service that originates or terminates in the home country of the foreign carrier or (in connection with the so-called seventh freedom of the air) outside the territory of the granting State (also known as "consecutive cabotage") (Figure 11.18).

The eighth freedom allows a carrier to compete in the domestic markets of a foreign country. For example, if a Japanese carrier were awarded the eighth freedom in addition to the third and fourth freedoms by the United States, then it

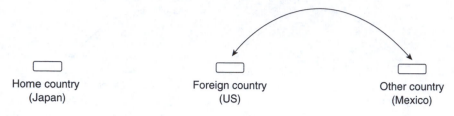

Figure 11.17 Seventh freedom.

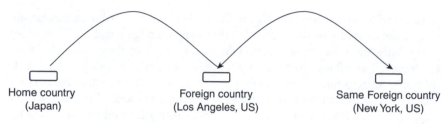

Figure 11.18 Eighth freedom.

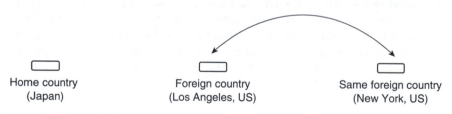

Figure 11.19 Ninth freedom.

could operate a flight such as Tokyo ⇔ Los Angeles ⇔ New York. In this case, the United States would not only have opened up its international market, but also its own domestic market. In reality, this freedom is rarely awarded except in the EU states.

- **Ninth freedom of the air:** the right or privilege to transport cabotage traffic in the granting State as a service performed entirely within the territory of the granting State (also known as "stand-alone" cabotage) (Figure 11.19).

Problems

1   A consultant studied the transport demand pattern between two cities, where the dominant transport modes are trucking and air. He found that when the price of trucking was reduced by 10 percent, trucking traffic increased by 12 percent. At the same time, air traffic volume decreased by 7 percent.

(a) Can we claim that the demand of trucking services is "elastic" to its own price?

(b) Other things unchanged, if the price of trucking increases by 5 percent, how would the air traffic change? Please write out the calculation process.

2 A business analyst wants to measure the efficiency and productivity of ABC Airlines, which provide both passenger and cargo services. He compiled the cargo service revenue and the total number of staffs employed during 2007 and 2008 as below:

ABC Airlines	2008	2007
Cargo revenue (US$ million)	5,804	4,952
Staff number	12,428	12,142
Cargo revenue per staff (US$ million)	0.467	0.408

He found that on average, in 2007 each employee generated $0.408 million cargo revenue, while in 2008 each employee generated $0.467 million cargo revenue. Based on this calculation, the analyst concluded that the airline improved its efficiency significantly in 2008. Apparently, the analyst has based his conclusion on wrong analysis. List at least two mistakes the analyst has made during his study.

3 "Hub-and-spoke" networks have been extensively used by airlines. What are the benefits of using hub-and-spoke networks? Are there any negative effects?

4 EasyExpress is a start-up airline to be based in the Philippines. The airline plans to provide services on the Manila–Dubai–London–Manchester route, flying passengers between the four cities.

(a) What are the freedoms that EasyExpress need to acquire from Dubai (the United Arab Emirates)?

(b) What are the freedoms EasyExpress need to acquire from the UK Government?

5 Martin owns a crystal gifts factory in Vietnam, and sells most of the products to large department stores in the United States. He uses air cargo for distribution extensively. Over time, he noticed that although regular air cargo service is cheaper, the freight forwarder often could not secure sufficient container space for him. However, he can almost always reserve cargo space at any time if he orders express cargo services. In some cases, he noticed that just before flight departure time there was still unused express cargo space. However, he still could not get regular air cargo space. He didn't understand why airlines would risk wasting capacity rather than sell it at a discount. His freight forwarder told him that this is mainly due to the fact that airlines use yield management to maximize revenue, and the air transport demand is time dependent. Martin is even more confused now. Please give a clear and concise explanation

about the meaning of time-dependent demand for air transport, and why this would affect airlines' pricing strategy.

6   Many airlines do overbooking. That is, for a particular flight, an airline may sell more tickets than the number of seats available on the aircraft. Why do airlines overbook their flights? What are the possible positive effects and negative effects of such practice?

7   A consultant collected the following data for American Airlines and Air Canada.

Year 2001	American Airlines	Air Canada
Revenue ton-km (RTK) (000)	18,514,241	7,779,111
Available ton-km (ATK) (000)	37,274,169	13,513,917
Total operating costs (US$'000)	16,490,609	5,489,829
Total operating revenue (US$'000)	15,638,794	5,252,416
Number of employees	92,485	42,301

(a) With the above data, calculate the load factors for American Airlines and Air Canada in 2001.

(b) On average, each employee of American Airlines produced 403,029 ATK, while each employee in Air Canada only produced 319,470 ATK. Based on such information, the consultant concludes that there is clear evidence that overall American Airlines is more efficient than Air Canada. Do you agree with him? Why?

8   One MBA student analyzed the market demand for express cargo services. He found that the three main determining factors for express cargo service demand (Q) are the price (P, in US$), overall economy (GDP, in billion dollars) and delivery time (time, in days). He estimated the demand function as follow:

$$\ln Q = 500 - 0.51 \ln P + 2 \ln \text{GDP} - 3 \ln \text{time}$$

(a) Based on the demand function estimated, what is the income elasticity of express cargo services?

(b) The student concluded that consumers are more sensitive to service quality (measured by delivery time) than price. Do you agree? Why?

(c) Due to the recent financial crisis, the IMF predicted that next year the GDP will shrink by 3 percent. If there will be no change in price and service quality, how would the market demand change?

Notes

1 Hummels (2006) found that worldwide ocean shipped cargo traveled an average of 2,919 miles in 2004, down from 3,543 miles in 1975. In contrast, air shipped cargo traveled an average of 3,383 miles in 2004, up from 2,600 in 1975.

2 The detailed proof is beyond the scope of this chapter. Interested readers should refer to intermediate-level economics textbooks. A much referred to result is that cost

minimization requires the marginal rate of substitution between any two inputs to be equal to the ratio of their prices. In the example we use, this implies that at the optimal, we have

$$\frac{\partial f / \partial K}{\partial f / \partial L} = \frac{w_K}{w_L}.$$

3　The word "scale" as defined in the previous chapters refers to the size of a firm's outputs. For transport and logistics services, outputs are often measured in RTK or ATK. Network size can be either measured by the number of points (nodes) served or the number of routes (origin–destination pairs, or OD pairs) in a network. Clearly, the number of routes is a more precise measurement of network size. However, as the number of nodes is easier to obtain for carriers in practice, most empirical studies have used the number of nodes in their analysis. Traffic density is calculated by dividing a firm's output by its network size.

4　Such an ideal operation requires airlines to obtain certain international air freedoms from the three countries. We discuss this issue in the section on regulation (pp. 474–478).

5　For example, one cargo route served by Air New Zealand has the following routing: Auckland–Melbourne–Shanghai–Frankfurt–Chicago–Auckland.

6　This section relies extensively on the studies of Gillen *et al.* (1990), Oum and Yu (1998), Oum *et al.* (2003), and Oum *et al.* (2005).

7　A couple of articles have pointed out that when estimations are made using aggregated data, such restrictions may not hold. However, a detailed discussion of this issue is well beyond the scope of this chapter.

8　The methodologies introduced in this section are reported in Li and Oum (2000), and Kraft *et al.* (1986).

9　The load factor is calculated by dividing the actual shipment weight by the available capacity.

10　This is again a simplification. The actual capacity of an aircraft is characterized by its maximum take-off weight and maximum landing weight. Over a shorter distance, an aircraft can carry less fuel so that more cargo can be loaded.

11　Historically, even for domestic markets, an airline needed the regulator's approval to conduct business in a particular city or airport pair. Since the late 1970s, most countries have deregulated their domestic markets to allow free market entry and free pricing. Only in a small number of developing countries do airlines still need government approval to serve certain destinations.

12　ICAO characterizes all "freedoms" beyond the fifth as "so-called" because only the first five "freedoms" have been officially recognized as such by international treaty. The definition used in this chapter is mainly based on the *ICAO Manual on the Regulation of International Air Transport*.

Bibliography

Airbus. 2007. *Global Market Forecast 2007–2026*.

Boeing (Boeing Commercial Aircrafts). 2006. *Current Market Outlook 2006–2025*.

Boeing (Boeing Commercial Aircrafts). 2008. "Review of Boeing commercial airplanes long-term airplane market forecast methodology and airlines' underlying requirement for economic profits," public distribution version.

Caves, D.W., L.R. Christensen, and M.W. Tretheway. 1984. "Economies of density versus economies of scale: why trunk and local service costs differ," *Rand Journal of Economics*, 15:471–489.

Gillen, D.W., T.H. Oum, and M.W. Tretheway. 1990. "Airline cost structure and policy implications: a multi-product approach for Canadian airlines," *Journal of Transport Economics and Policy*, 24(1):9–34.

Gillen, D.W., W.G. Morrison, and C. Stewart. 2003. *Air Travel Demand Elasticities: Concepts, Issues and Measurement*. Final Report, Department of Finance, Canada.

Hummels, D. 2006. "Global trends in trade and transportation," *ECMT-OECD Paper presented in the 17th International Symposium on Theory and Practice in Transport Economics and Policy*, Berlin, 25–27 October.

ICAO. 2007. *Outlook for Air Transport to the Year 2025*, International Civil Aviation Organization, Montreal.

Kraft, D.J.H., T.H. Oum, and M.W. Tretheway. 1986. "Airline seat management," *Logistics and Transportation Review*, 22(2):115–130.

Li, Z.F. and T.H. Oum. 2000. "Airline passenger spill analysis—beyond the normal demand," *European Journal of Operations Research*, 125(1):206–217.

Oum, T.H., and J.H. Park. 2004. "Multinational firms' location preference for regional distribution centers: focus on the Northeast Asian region," *Transportation Research E: Logistics and Transportation Review*, 40:101–121.

Oum, T.H. and M.W. Tretheway. 1990. "Airline hub and spoke system," *Journal of Transportation Research Forum*, 30:380–393.

Oum, T.H., and C. Yu. 1998. "Cost competitiveness of major airlines: an international comparison," *Transportation Research A: Policy and Practices*, 32(6):407–422.

Oum, T.H., C. Yu, and X. Fu. 2003. "A comparative analysis of productivity performance of the world's major airports: summary report of the ATRS Global Airport Benchmarking Research Report–2002," *Journal of Air Transport Management*, 9(5):285–298.

Oum, T.H., X. Fu, and C. Yu. 2005. "New evidences on airline efficiency and yields: a comparative analysis of major North American air carriers and its implications," *Transport Policy*, 12:153–164.

Oum, T.H., W.G. Waters, and X. Fu. 2007. "Transport demand elasticities", in D. Henser (ed.) *Handbook of Transport Modelling*, 2nd Edition, Elsevier.

Tretheway, M.W. and T.H. Oum. 1992. *Airline Economics: Foundations for Strategy and Policy*, Centre for Transportation Studies, The University of British Columbia.

Wells, A. and S.B. Young. 2004. *Airport Planning & Management,* 5th Edition, New York: McGraw-Hill Professional.

Yan, S., C.H. Chen, and C.K. Chen. 2006. "Long-term manpower supply planning for air cargo terminals," *Journal of Air Transport Management*, 12:175–181.

12 Environmental logistics

Overview *As the world economy goes global, supply chain operations go boundary-crossing: across firms, across countries, and across markets. The environmental impacts of such operations not only cross the physical boundary, but also penetrate into the future. The well-being of the future generation will be affected by present business practices, where the logistics manager can play a significant role.*

Logistics has been facilitating the movement of people and commodities, both domestically and internationally, ever since the advent of barter economy. From the "silk road" in the eighteenth century to the globalized economy today, logistics has helped to make efficient use of raw materials and commercial products to satisfy the ever-increasing needs and wants of the growing population, thus improving the global economy and quality of life in different places around the world. The increasingly competitive market and the technological development in management and information science in modern society have rigorously increased the efficiency of the logistics system, which in turn enabled higher economic development.

Looking into the future, human beings are increasingly aware of the "shadow price" of the tremendous economic growth—the serious environmental problems that come with this growth. Entering the twenty-first century, we are facing the biggest challenges from population explosion, global warming, environmental degradation, increasing solid, toxic and hazardous wastes, and resource scarcity (Figure 12.1). According to the US National Academy of Sciences and the Royal Society of London (Brundtland 1987), if the population grows as predicted and our life patterns remain unchanged, existing science and technology may not be able to stop the environmental degradation on the earth. Increasingly, individuals, businesses and governments worldwide have recognized and responded to these environmental challenges by demanding "green" products in the market, being a responsible business, and setting more stringent pollution regulations.

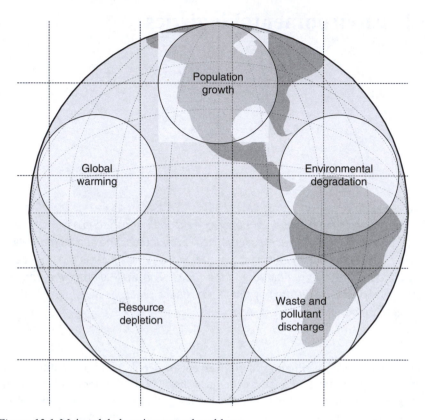

Figure 12.1 Major global environmental problems.

Logistics management is a critical area for proactive environmental management due to its cross-functional and integrative nature, and its numerous interactions with the environment. All business operations take place within the limits of the environment. The natural environment is both the source of resource inputs and the waste sink for all the activities from bringing in raw materials to delivering the final consumer products and after-sale services (Figure 12.2) (Wu and Dunn 1994). A healthy and productive environment and ecosystem are the foundation for continuous economic activities. If we can take good care of the environment and ecosystem in our logistics planning, we can continue to obtain resources from the environment and continue to use the assimilative capacity of the natural environment to solve our waste problem. Otherwise, we will break the foundation for resource generation and waste reception, and make further economic activities impossible.

Environmental logistics, a new topic with increasing popularity, has emerged to be an inevitable direction in logistics development. As an important step in sustainable development, environmental logistics addresses the environmental

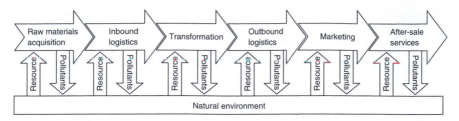

Figure 12.2 Interactions of logistics activities with the environment.

problems in the logistics process from two perspectives. First, from the perspective of business operation, a successful business should be able to cater for the increasing consumer preferences for environment-friendly products, create a public image of being a socially responsible corporative citizen, and pursue economic benefits observing the sustainable development objectives of society. Second, from the perspective of the public environmental governance, the regulatory bodies should understand the incentives and limitations for private businesses to increase their environmental performance, so as to identify the important logistic activities that need to be regulated by laws and regulations.

This chapter presents environmental issues in the logistics process and examines what measures can be taken to achieve environmental sustainability in logistics, from both the perspective of business operation and that of the public. First, it introduces the relationship among logistics, economic development, and the environment. Then it presents the current status of environmental management in logistics, including the major environmental problems and existing practices of environmental management in logistics. Important motivations for business managers to increase their firms' environmental performance are presented next. Because most of the environmental management initiatives of private businesses do not fully cover the full spectrum of environmental externalities, it also introduces the concept of externality and theory on optimal pollution control. As the key for optimal pollution management is to understand the value of environmental resources, the concept of economic value for environmental resources is also introduced. Last, the chapter outlines some of the most important international agreements that have impacts on the logistics activities of different industries.

The role of logistics in economic development and the environment

We introduce the concept of environmental logistics through the analysis of the role of logistics in global economic development, and its relationship with the environment. Efficient logistics management is essential to satisfy the ever-increasing needs and wants of human beings with limited resources. As a service industry in modern society, its growth depends on the economic development at

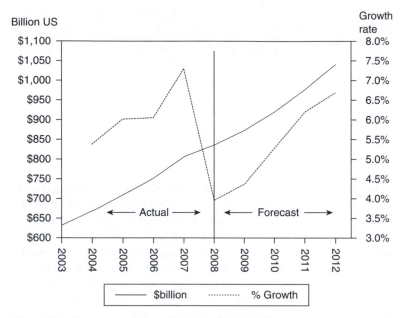

Figure 12.3 The market value of global logistics and its growth rate.

local, regional, and international levels. By servicing economic development, the logistics industry itself also constitutes a large part of economic growth world-wide. According to the report by Datamonitor (2008), the market value of global logistics has been growing around 6.2 percent per year from $633 billion in 2003, to $804 billion in 2007 (Figure 12.3). Due to the impact of the global financial crisis in 2008, Datamonitor forecast that the growth would slow down. However, the market value could reach $1,040 billion in 2012.

Economic development and logistics activity benefit from the environment both as the source of natural resources, and as the sink for waste and pollution. In addition to the interactions of the logistics activities with the environment as illustrated in Figure 12.2, all economic activities that support the global econ-omy will have certain impacts on the environment. The interaction of the logis-tics activities, economic growth, and environmental health are illustrated in Figure 12.4.

Logistics activities, economic development, and the environment are interde-pendent. Logistic activities such as transportation, inventory, warehousing, order processing, and purchasing have served global economic development. On the other hand, high economic development gives much impetus for innovation in logistics planning and development. As found in Rodrigues *et al.* (2005), devel-oped countries and regions can enjoy huge GDP with less logistics expenditure than developing countries. Take the United States as an example. The logistics expenditure decreased from 10.5 percent of total GDP in 1997 to 10.1 percent in

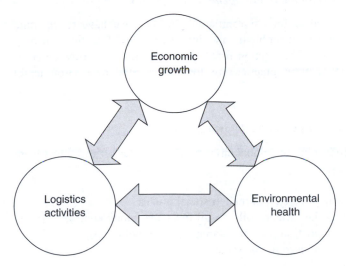

Figure 12.4 Relationship among logistics activities, economic development, and environmental health.

2000, and further down to 9.3 percent in 2002. In China, however, this number increased from 16.9 percent in 1997 to 17.7 percent in 2000 and 17.9 percent in 2002.

Undoubtedly, a healthy and productive environment is the foundation for economic growth. Without taking resources from Mother Nature, the world economic development would come to a standstill. However, economic development in human history has been following a way that impairs and even destroys environmental health through pollution, resource overexploitation, and waste disposal (Hardin 1968). As the World Commission on Environment and Development suggests, "if the current pattern of economic development is not changed, then the environment will not be able to support the continuous existence of our human being in this planet" (Brundtland 1987).

In curbing the current trend of environmental degradation, logistics managers play a very important role both internally and externally. Internally, they can reduce the adverse environmental stress imposed by the logistics activities. Externally, they can optimize the way resources are used in logistics activities through a systematic approach, including green purchasing, technical advancement in transportation, socially responsible business development, and increasing environmental awareness through customer relation management. However, as logistics managers are working in a competitive business environment where the nature of operation is to pursue economic benefits, it is impossible for them to consider all the environmental impacts in their decision making. Thus, we advocate the concept of environmental logistics, which addresses the environmental impacts not only from the private operator's perspective, but also from the perspective of our society.

Current status of environmental management in logistics

To understand the rationale for environmental logistics, we have to examine current global environmental problems and investigate how logistics can help to address such problems. This section first presents the major worldwide environmental issues and current practices in logistics related to environmental management.

Major environmental concerns in the logistics process

As stated in the introduction, the global environment is under serious threat from the following sources:

- population growth, poverty, and related social issues;
- resource depletion (i.e., water, soils, fossil fuels, and biodiversity);
- environmental degradation (i.e., air, water, and land pollution);
- solid waste; toxic and hazardous waste;
- global warming;
- ozone depletion.

Innovative planning in logistics supports population growth and poverty reduction, the major environmental problem in the list, through making efficient use of the scarce resources, and bringing resources in the less developed areas to the market. The negative impact of these logistic activities, however, is the over-exploitation of natural resources in the developing countries, such as the shrinking of the tropical rainforest, deforestation and desertification, which make further economic development more difficult. This is a worldwide problem of modern society, which requires the concerted effort of private business, governments, and international society.

In supporting global population growth and poverty reduction, the physical movement of goods and raw materials using air, land, and sea transportation requires the use of fossil fuel as the energy source. This creates environmental problems in two aspects. First, the fossil fuel is a nonrenewable energy resource: one gallon used today will reduce the available resources by one gallon for the future generation. In 2007, transportation accounted for 28.4 percent of US energy consumption (Golicic *et al.* 2010). Second, the emission from the use of fossil fuel in transportation creates local air pollution problems and leads to global environmental problems such as global warming and reduction in biodiversity. It is well known that emission of greenhouse gases (GHGs) is the major cause of irreversible accumulation of CO_2 in the atmosphere, the major cause for the rising of the earth temperature. According to Golicic *et al.* (2010), the emission from transportation activities in the United States accounted for 33.6 percent of the CO_2 emissions. Localized environmental problems include air quality degradation and the high incidence of respiratory disease. Indirect local environmental problems include habitat loss due to global warming, sea level rise, and deforestation because of acid rain. Although there is new development in alternative energy sources such as biodiesel oil, a complete ban on the use of fossil fuel is neither economical nor possible. Alternatively, better planning in transportation activities and technology development in vehicle engines is preferred as they can increase energy efficiency, reduce exhaustion, and help to mitigate global environmental problems and local air quality.

Another major environmental concern is the introduction of nonnative species, which has both positive effects on the global economy, as well as negative ones on the biodiversity of the ecological system. Some nonnative species transported inadvertently as a hitch-hiker have caused serious impacts on the local biological ecosystem. They are called invasive species because of their adverse impact. One important pathway for the invasive species is the use of ballast water in the shipping activity. To help stabilize the vessel, ballast water (with local organisms) is loaded in one port and discharged into the water body at other ports. Each year, about 10 billion tones of ballast water are transported around the world. This practice can bring huge amount of nonlocal organisms to coastal waters and ports.

Waste generated from the packaging material and the product at the end of the life cycle can create major environmental problems if not properly recycled or disposed of. Paper, cardboards, glass, plastic bags, and electronic devices may be reused or recycled if the value created can cover the cost of recycling. However, the cost of some of these recycling activities may be too high for private business. In this case, public initiatives may be necessary to prevent the insufficient provision of waste recycling services.

Many of these environment-friendly activities already exist in today's business environment. The next section introduces current practices in the environmental logistics for business operation, and discusses the limitations and possible problems in these practices.

Existing practices in environmental logistics

Many of the management practices that firms have adopted to improve environmental performance in their operations and their products/services are through logistics management. Gonzalez-Benito and Gonzalez-Benito (2006) summarized eight representative environmental logistics practices through four main logistics components—supply/purchasing, transportation, warehousing and distribution, and reverse logistics and waste management (Figure 12.5). The central activities in these eight areas are green purchasing, green transportation, life cycle assessment, and reducing the impact at the end of the product life cycle, which are introduced below.

Environmentally preferable purchasing (green procurement)

Obtaining inputs is the first step in any logistics planning for manufacturing consumer goods, providing customer services or organizing office supplies for a firm. Therefore, it is the first consideration of the logistics manager if the

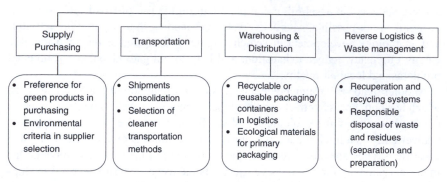

Figure 12.5 Environmental concerns from four major logistics components.

objective of the firms is to reduce the negative impact of their products or services on the environment.

Every product/service has certain undesirable environmental impacts because it consumes materials and creates waste at some point of the logistics process, including transportation, manufacturing, and storage. Environmental Preferable Purchasing (EPP) involves the purchase of products and services that have less negative environmental impact. It shifts the focus of pollution reduction from the production side to the consumption side. This is especially useful when the purchaser has a dominating market power in determining which product or service to choose from. When the purchaser has market power (e.g., as the purchasing manager in a big multinational corporation or governmental department), the supplier has to meet the environmental requirements specified by the consumers. EPP also promotes the use of goods and services that respond to basic human needs and bring a better quality of life, while minimizing the use of natural resources, toxic materials, and emissions of waste and pollutants over the life cycle, so as not to jeopardize the basic needs of future generations.

As with any purchase, EPP also involves decisions on what and where to purchase. However, in EPP, the purchase decision is guided by the desire to purchase goods and services that have less impact on the environment, in addition to the general requirement on the goods and services to be purchased. For example, the first guiding principle for EPP is "Environment + Price + Performance" which specifies that environmental considerations should become part of the general purchasing practice, consistent with such traditional factors as product safety, price, performance, and availability. In establishing the green office initiatives, the United Nations encourages the use of "4 Rs": (1) rethink the requirements to reduce environmental impacts; (2) reduce material consumption; (3) recycle materials/waste; and (4) reduce energy consumption. These 4 Rs link the purchasing decision with possible environmental impacts at every logistic component of the production life cycle. Specifically, the decision on what to purchase involves evaluating products based on a series of factors such as quality, function, design

Table 12.1 Environmental criteria for the CP approach in making purchasing decisions

Prevention	Does the product avoid waste from the start?
Precaution	Does the product reduce or eliminate toxic materials or harmful emissions to the air and water?
Integration	Will the use of the product create a problem elsewhere? Are there other "costs" that might follow from the purchase of the product that I should be aware of?
Participation	Does the product result from sufficient research or information? Is there any effort to make product information readily available?
Productivity	Does the product satisfy my practical requirements without adding to my future costs during its use? Will it give me value for money?

and price, and a variety of environmental criteria (Table 12.1) reflected in the Cleaner Production (CP) approach.

A clean product that meets the above criteria has three basic properties (Figure 12.6). First, it should save resources. Fewer virgin materials and nonrenewable energy resources should be used in both the production process and the life cycle of the products. Second, it should generate less pollution. The product should use fewer toxic substances and nondegradable materials, and have fewer harmful air and water emissions in both the production and the consumption processes. With the global effort in reducing CO_2 emissions, this consideration has become increasingly important in the clean product evaluation. Finally, the product should be less wasteful. It should generate less waste in the product life cycle, and the product itself should be recyclable, reusable and/or durable.

An example for assessing green products is shown in Figure 12.7 (Matsushita Group 2007). In this example, three main criteria for green products are prevention of global warming, effective utilization of resources, and nonuse of PVC resin. These criteria are consistent with the properties of green products shown in Figure 12.6.

Recycled products are not the synonym for green products, as they may not have the properties shown in Figure 12.6. For example, a recycled product may be manufactured with wasteful methods (i.e., it may not lead to resource savings). A recycled product can contain toxic or nondegradable materials, or it can consume higher nonrenewable energy resources than other products with the same function. Furthermore, an environment-friendly product may take longer to manufacture, especially when the parts are generated in the recycling process. To make the recycled products stand out in the market place, and to promote environment-friendly products, the International Organization of Standardization (ISO) advocated the environmental label or "Ecolabel" to educate consumers with their purchase decision, motivate, and assist the industry in marketing environmentally acceptable products.

According to ISO 14020 (2000), Ecolabel is defined as "a claim about the environmental aspects of a product (in) the form of a statement, symbol or

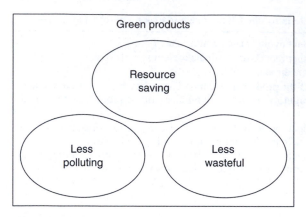

Figure 12.6 Properties of green products.

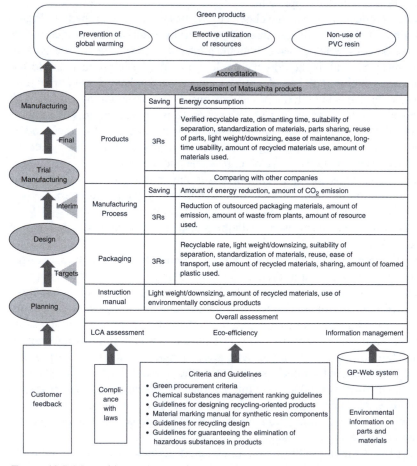

Figure 12.7 Matsushita's green product assessment system.

graphic on a product or package label, in product literature, in technical bulletins, in advertising or in publicity, among other things.". Owing to increasing environmental awareness, ecolabeling has emerged out of a global concern among governments, and the private and public sectors to protect the environment. A number of environmental labeling programs have emerged worldwide. According to USEPA (1998), there are three types of environmental labeling programs—positive, negative, and neutral. Positive labeling programs certify that the labeled products possess one or more environmentally preferable attributes. Typically, a logo is used to distinguish the product from other products that are less environment-friendly. Examples of such logos include Blue Angel of Germany, Eco-logo from Canada, and Green Seal from the United States. Negative ones warn consumers the potential harmful or hazardous ingredients contained in the labeled products. Most common ones are pesticide labels and the warnings on cigarettes. Neutral ones simply summarize environmental information about products and consumers have to understand, interpret, and use such information in making purchasing decisions. Examples include the nutrition label and the energy guide on most processed food. This different labeling system helps differentiate products in today's market place with increasing environmental awareness.

Environmental labeling is still considered as a work-in-progress. Its importance on purchasing activity is growing with the increasing coverage of green products.

Sustainable transportation

A sustainable transport system, as defined by Black (2010) through a review of the sustainability issues in the transport sector, is the transport system that provides transport and mobility with renewable fuels while minimizing emissions detrimental to the local and global environment and preventing needless fatalities, injuries, and congestion. This definition suggests the direction for the ideal practice in transportation. From the business operation's point of view, sustainable transportation is not only a requirement for its stakeholders, but also a means to increase its market competitiveness through better publicity, and a way to reduce cost in energy consumption.

The current mode of logistics operation conflicts with the goal of environmental management in the transportation sector. For example, the increased specialization and international sourcing heightened the demand for physical transportation of goods, while the increasing demand of customers for Just in Time (JIT) delivery, zero inventory, and no lead-time require more frequent and speedy shipment.

A survey on the environmental management practice for the Fortune 500 companies found that the current practices in addressing environmental impacts of transportation could be grouped into three levels, based on the scope of the sustainability demonstrated in the supply chain (Golicic *et al.* 2010):

Establishing a foundation: This is the entry level for environmental management of a firm. At this level, firms have developed goals and metrics to measure and limit the environmental impact from transportation activity, cooperated with the key companies in the supply chain to limit such impacts, and recognized potential benefits in the activity. The survey revealed that 44 firms in the Fortune 500 companies have established the foundation.

Changing internal practices: The second level is to change internal practice to reduce transportation emissions. Specifically, it includes managing the firm's vehicles to reduce emissions, educating the employees, and reinforcing a corporate culture of environmental awareness. The survey found that only 28 firms moved into the second level.

Impact supply chain practices: At this level, firms try to reduce greenhouse gas emissions from freight transportation in the supply chain through technological or operational tactics. This includes using more rail than trucking, biodiesel fuel, more energy efficient tires, and better vehicle utilization or efficient routing.

The three current levels of practices are relatively feasible, and often can result in both better environmental performance and financial results. However, to reach the ultimate goal of sustainable transportation requires closer cooperation with the partners in the supply chain. In addition, it will be increasingly difficult to make a tradeoff between the social impacts of sustainable transport and business performance, especially when these two sides have different directions.

Waste reduction, recycle, and reuse (3R)

Waste reduction, recycle, and reuse are the fundamental activities in environmental logistics due to the relative significance of waste in global environmental problems and the important role of logistics management in addressing these problems. These three terms appear similar, are sometimes used interchangeably, and each of them has its own focus. Although all three activities are to reduce waste, reuse emphasizes more using the product again with or without the re-production process, while recycle is to reuse the material after the re-production process. Waste paper, for example, can be sent back to the paper mill for paper production. Most packaging boxes can just be reused to pack the same product, if they are shipped back to the manufacturer. Waste reduction, on the other hand, focuses on reducing the waste generation rate through better technology in the production process. All these activities contribute to reducing the final waste that will otherwise end up at the waste disposal site.

Waste exists in all three physical forms—gas, liquid, and solid. Examples of waste in gaseous form include the exhaustion from burning fossil fuels, which are necessary to enable the current transportation activity, and emissions from industrial activities. There are not many recycling and reusing activities from air emissions due to the technical difficulties in recapturing the waste. Current practices in reducing air emissions from the transportation sector include the use of new engines with more complete and efficient combustion, technology development in increasing energy efficiency, and research and development in alternative and cleaner energy sources. The increase in oil price will increase the benefits of these activities, and make the transportation system more environment-friendly.

Waste water discharge is a major environmental concern in surface water when its discharging rate is higher than the assimilation capacity of the receptacle, because it can result in permanent and irreversible ecological changes in the water body. When the waste water discharge is close to the population center, it even poses serious health impacts to the local community. Most common water pollution problems in transportation activities are the accidental and operational oil pollution discharged from shipping activities—the most important component in global logistics. Accidental oil pollution is mainly from tanker transportation activities. Although the probability is low, once it has occurred, it has a detrimental impact on the local marine environment. New tankers used for oil transportation are required to have a "double hull", to reduce the risk of accidental oil spill. Operational oil pollution comes from the discharge of oil–water mixtures in the engine room. This source of oil pollution can be prevented by requiring ships to install oil–water separation facilities in their engine rooms and collect them in oil reception facilities for concentrated treatment. Major ports in the world are required to have waste oil reception facilities to treat oil residuals.

Solid waste comes from different varieties of used products, end-of-lifecycle (ELC) products, packaging materials, which may mix with different types of material such as plastics, paper, glasses, metals, organics, tires, used oils, and even hazardous materials. Their reuse and recycling may present sizable economic benefits and motivate the business to make use of them in the new products. International car manufacturers such as Volkswagen and BMW use reverse logistics[1] to make use of the parts in used products. Xerox and Canon also reuse many used parts in their products. The most common one is the ink cartridges in their copy machines. These recycling activities have brought them additional economic benefits in addition to the social benefits in waste reduction.

There are three common logistic activities involved in 3R (Matsushita Group 2007), including recapturing, primary processing, and packaging and transportation, regardless of the different target products:

1   *Recapturing*: Recapturing includes getting the used/ELC products from the customer's location to the collection center, and then shipping to the recycling/reusing/remanufacturing plant. The collection center could be the distribution center in the forward supply chain, or an exclusive collection center for recycling. Recapturing may include collection, transportation, and warehousing activities.

2   *Primary processing*: Depending on the nature of the used/ELC products, primary processing may be necessary before the transportation process. It

includes breaking down the products into parts according to their nature, form and condition, cleaning, and grouping. Parts that are not recyclable can be disposed of locally to save transportation cost.

3   *Packaging and transportation*: The reusable parts (or even the whole used products) need to be transported to the remanufacturing plant. To save transportation cost, the transportation can be performed by the back-trip vehicles used for the forward logistics activities.

Greater challenges exist in recapturing, processing, and transporting domestic waste to the recycling center, due to the nature of the wastes, spatial location of the waste sites, and the mixture of the recyclable with the nonrecyclables. The general procedure for waste reduction in domestic waste control is:

1   collecting waste materials from the recycling bins and delivering them to the recycling entity,
2   processing recyclables to create secondary raw materials,
3   using secondary materials to make new products, and
4   returning products to the new market place.

The degree of waste reduction in private business operations depends on the benefit/profit obtained from these recycling activities. However, the economic incentive alone cannot guarantee that the level of waste reduction will be socially optimal. This is the place where public incentive and policy may come into play.

Product life cycle assessment (LCA)

As shown in Figure 12.2, during the whole process from getting the raw materials for the production process to the final stage of after-sale service of the product, there are a number of interactions between the logistics activities and the natural environment. To identify the total environmental impact of a product, it is necessary to examine all the inputs and outputs throughout the life cycle of that process, from its birth (product design, raw material extraction, material production, part production, and assembly, warehousing, transportation), through its use (energy requirement, waste generation when using the product), and final disposal (recyclability, biodegradable, reusable).

Life cycle assessment (LCA) is a tool for evaluating the environmental effects of a product or process over the entire period of its life cycle, from raw material acquisition to disposal. The term LCA was first used to describe holistic environmental assessments in the late 1980s (SAIC 2006). The main motives for adopting LCA in business operations include increasingly tougher environmental regulations, growing awareness about the nature of many global environmental problems such as ozone depletion and climate change, increasing pressure from local environmental problems such as municipal waste disposal, and consumers'

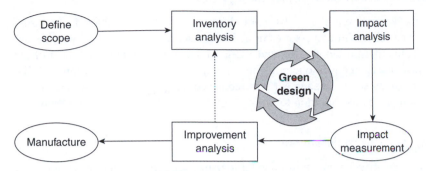

Figure 12.8 Three components in LCA.

increasing demand for information about the environmental impacts of products. To meet the challenges, LCA has to identify and quantify the energy and material used and the waste released to the environment, assessing their environmental impacts and evaluating opportunities for improvement.

The LCA is carried out in three separate but integrated stages or components (Figure 12.8). These stages overlap and build on each other in the development of a complete LCA. The first stage of a life cycle analysis is *inventory analysis*. In an inventory analysis, the goal is to examine all the inputs and outputs in a product's life cycle, beginning with what the product is composed of, where those materials come from, and where they go, and the inputs and outputs related to those component materials during their lifetime. It is also necessary to include the inputs and outputs during the product's use, such as whether or not the product uses electricity. The purpose of inventory analysis is to quantify what comes in and what goes out, including the energy and material associated with material extraction, product manufacture and assembly, distribution, use, and disposal and the resulting environmental emissions.

The next stage of a life cycle analysis is the *impact analysis*, in which the environmental impacts identified in the previous stage are enumerated, such as the environmental impacts of generating energy for the processes and the hazardous waste emitted in the manufacturing process. It involves using both qualitative and quantitative methods to identify and measure the impact on the environment.

The major purpose of the analysis is to evaluate, once the inputs and outputs are quantified, how the product affects the environment throughout its life cycle. After having calculated the general environmental impact, the next step is to conduct an improvement analysis to determine how the environmental impact of the product can be reduced by using an alternative production method. For example, conservation of energy or water in the manufacturing process will reduce the environmental impact of that process. Substituting a less hazardous chemical for a more toxic one would also reduce the impact. The change is then incorporated in the inventory analysis to recalculate its total environmental impact.

Controversies in environmental logistics

While advocating environment-friendly logistics activities to reduce the pollution and waste inputs through a series of activities such as environmental purchasing, sustainable transportation, 3Rs, and LCA, we have to recognize that most of the logistics management is operating in a competitive business environment. The purpose of logistics management is to reduce cost, especially the cost in the transportation process, in addition to timing, flexibility, and customer satisfaction.

1 Private versus public interest

The first controversy in environmental logistics, as in many other environmental management activities, is the difference between private interest and public requirements on the level of recycling activities, such as the difference in the expected level of waste reduction or pollution abatement between society and private business. Operating in a competitive market, private business would only conduct environmental management if the benefits from these recycling activities covered the costs. For example, a private firm will recycle and reuse if the benefit is greater than the cost required. Many of the small- and medium-sized enterprises, due to the limitation on operating scale, cannot effectively reduce the cost in recycling and reusing activities.

2 Global logistics planning versus local environmental degradation

Global logistics is exploring every possibility to reduce the cost of final consumer products, from raw material purchase to the delivery of final products. Although such logistics practices can increase customer satisfaction, they could create serious problems for the environment where the price of environmental resources is low, and the environmental regulations on preserving the natural resources are not strictly enforced. The overexploitation of forest resources in developing countries in the past decade has caused deforestation, even desertification, which imposes a serious threat to local biodiversity. Tougher environmental regulations in developed countries make factories relocate to developing countries, which creates serious local environmental problems.

Global logistics is supported by an efficient transportation system that has used a hub-and-spoke network in distribution and collection activities for all modes of transportation in the past 20 years. It has reduced costs and improved efficiency through the consolidation of freight and passengers at hubs. There are criticisms for this practice because the concentrated transportation activity at the small number of hubs exacerbates local environmental problems such as noise and air pollution and traffic congestion.

Technology development in transportation facilities expands the margin of economy of scale, which requires further expansion of transportation infrastructures to accommodate the new changes in transportation facilities. For example, container vessels are becoming increasingly bigger, which requires container ports to have longer berth length, deeper accessing channels and improved land

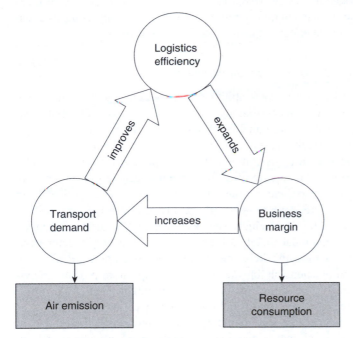

Figure 12.9 Environmental vicious circle of logistics.

access. These new requirements create local environmental problems on the hub port by increasing the pressure on land use, affecting coastal habitats, and elevating the air pollution level due to increased truck traffic.

3 Increase in logistics efficiency versus increase in air pollution from transportation activities

Innovative logistics management reduces cost and time in the transportation process, which makes possible door-to-door (DTD) transportation services using JIT delivery. This improvement in logistics efficiency expands the demand for transportation activities, making business operations previously impossible feasible. It could also form a vicious circle for the environment (Figure 12.9), as presented in Brewer *et al.* (2001).

Pursuing efficiency in logistics requires faster transportation modes such as air transportation and trucking rather than rail and water transportation, which also creates a controversy between logistics and environmental management, because trains and ships are more environment-friendly than trucks and airplanes in terms of energy efficiency and air emission per ton-mile of cargoes.

Practices in improving logistics efficiency, such as lean supply chain and JIT, attempt to increase the flow rate for raw materials and products, and reduce the waste or nonvalue-added time and activities. The central point of all these practices is in inventory reduction, which decreases the inventory cost for private businesses, but increases demand in transportation activities, thus increasing air emissions and bringing a greater environmental burden on society.

Business motivations for environmental management

Businesses succeed because of their ability to satisfy consumers' needs in the changing environment. With increasing awareness of global environmental problems and the importance of sustainable development, increasing numbers of people realize that the traditional pattern for economic development with high energy consumption and waste generation not only impairs environmental health today, but also sacrifices the opportunities for our future generations to develop. Customers prefer to use more environment-friendly products and services from companies that have a better environmental image, in addition to the conventional set of attributes required for the products, such as price, quality, and functionality. Governments and international society are also using increasingly stricter environmental rules to regulate the behavior of business operations. Facing the changed environment, responsible businesses try to adopt more proactive environmental management measures, including green purchasing, LCA, waste reduction through recycling and reuse, and pollution prevention.

Operating in a competitive environment, private businesses first have to achieve their business goal, that is, to generate the expected rate of return from the stakeholders, without which the business cannot be sustained. Realizing that irresponsible business activities such as excessive pollution and damaging the local environment will result in negative publicity and low earnings, stakeholder groups and operation managers are now more willing to improve the social image of their business through emphasizing social responsibility. Furthermore, with the promotion of many international standards such as ISO 9000 and ISO 14001, together with consumers' preference for green products and firms' practice in clean production, business operations tend to adopt the international environmental standard to improve its reputation as a responsible business and increase market competitiveness.

Financial incentives

Financial performance is one of the major indicators for business success, and is also the fundamental incentive of business operations. Many of the environmental management activities initiated by private business, such as waste reduction, recycle, and reuse, are driven by this incentive. Many firms around the world have obtained remarkable economic benefits from these activities. According to Hauser and Lund (2003), 52 percent of 256 surveyed firms took remanufacturing as their main business operation, and the average sales per employee in year 2000 amounted to $223,702. The range of sales, employment, and sales per employee for the surveyed firms are listed in Table 12.2. This table shows that the larger the scale of the operation, the higher the output per employee. This reveals that the

Table 12.2 Sales and employment statistics for remanufacturing firms in 2000

Annual sales range ($)	Firms	Total sales (US$)	Total employees	Sales per employee ($)
All ranges	256	1,591,192,172	7,113	223,702
0–99,999	21	1,077,000	29	37,723
100,000–499,999	75	19,291,653	339	56,992
500,000–999,999	36	22,981,559	254	90,657
1,000,000–1,999,999	42	55,931,346	602	92,986
2,000,000–4,999,999	41	117,850,677	909	129,649
5,000,000–9,999,999	19	117,098,937	720	162,637
10,000,000–24,999,999	12	166,000,000	768	216,146
≥25,000,000	10	1,090,961,000	3,494	312,238

remanufacturing business in the United Sttaes exhibits economy of scale, which is a very important factor in the recycling business.

The decision-making process for a private business to recycle is explained next. For private businesses, the decision for recycling is based on whether the benefit of recycling is larger than its costs. The benefits of remanufacturing, for example, are the cost savings in producing a product containing used parts, compared with producing the same product with all new parts. It is the difference between purchasing raw materials, manufacturing from scratch, and buying recycled materials for remanufacturing with used parts. For illustration purposes, the average/marginal benefit of recycling is assumed constant and the same across all the firms in the market that produce the same product.

The costs of recycling include collecting, transporting, cleaning, and all other activities involved in the whole process. For small- and medium-sized firm, the number of recyclable products is small. Thus, the average/marginal cost of recycling is large. The relationship between the benefit and cost of recycling is shown in Figure 12.10, where B stands for the constant average/marginal benefit obtained from recycling, and $C(q)$ is the average/marginal cost of recycling. Due to the economy of scale in recycling, $C(q)$ decreases with the quantity recycled. The solid line portion of $C(q)$ stands for small businesses, while the dotted line portion stands for the larger ones.

For small businesses, the potential maximum recyclable quantity is q_1, which is equal to the total amount of products sold in the market. At this quantity, the average recycling cost is higher than the benefit. If a firm recycles its products, it will lose money. Therefore, the firm will not recycle its products at the end of the life cycle: the economic incentive alone is not enough to motivate the private business to recycle its products.

However, for large firms, the economic incentive alone may motivate the recycling activity. For example, if the total potential recyclable products is q_2, because of the economy of scale in recycling, the average/marginal cost of recycling $C(q_2)$,

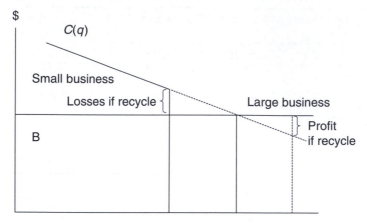

Figure 12.10 Recycling quantity and size of the firm.

can be lower than the marginal benefit B. There will be positive profit from the recycling activity. In fact, as long as the scale of the recycling activity is larger than q^*, the recycling activity can support the operation by itself. Therefore, a private firm will be motivated to recycle if the scale of operation is large enough.

Better corporative social image

In addition to financial incentives, private businesses are also motivated to improve their social image by accommodating the changing requirements from consumers, the community, government, and the market, and their expectations on the ethical responsibility of a business. For example, to achieve business goals and objectives, a firm must respond to increasing consumer demand for green products, comply with ever-tightening environmental regulations, and implement environmentally responsible plans as a good corporate citizen.

Carter and Jennings (2002) summarized that good corporate citizens should observe the Corporate Social Responsibility (CSR), or corporate social performance, which consists of four hierarchically related duties:

1 Economic responsibilities: to transact business and provide needed products and services in a market economy.
2 Legal responsibilities: to obey laws which represent a form of "codified ethics".
3 Ethical responsibilities: to transact business in a manner expected and regarded by society as being fair and reasonable, even though it is not legally required.
4 Voluntary/discretionary or philanthropic responsibilities: to conduct activities which are more guided by business's discretion than actual responsibilities or expectations.

Many CSR standards have been developed that require firms to comply with the reporting standards and procedures. These standards include Global Reporting Initiative's Sustainability Reporting Guidelines, Green Globe Certification/ Standards, ISO 14000 Environmental Management Standard, to list just a few that are on the environmental management side. By claiming compliance to these standards, a firm can demonstrate good business citizenship, and win social recognition both locally and globally, which will also bring the following tangible and intangible benefits to the business operation:

1 Customers' trust: consumers, business purchasers, and government organizations will have a clearer picture about the environmental performance of the firm, allowing the firm to be in a better competitive condition, and in a better position to access new markets.
2 Employees' loyalty: people are more likely to join and stay in a firm if it has a good reputation on environmental management, which includes workplace environment.
3 Accountability: a better environmental management strategy will reduce the risk of environmental accidents.
4 Brand differentiation: being certified by international standards on environmental performance can give a firm a unique market advantage that enables it to stand out from its competitors and to build up the loyalty of its customers.

However, many such attributes of being a CSR firm cannot be built overnight. On the other hand, once built, they will have significant long-term benefits for the success of the business operation. Orlitzky *et al* (2003) studied the relationship between corporate social/environmental performance (CSP) and corporate financial performance (CFP), and concluded that CSR and environmental responsibility are likely to pay off, and that there is a definite and positive relationship between CSP and CFP.

As logistics is the interface between business operations and the environment, it plays a central role in improving environmental performance of a firm. Specifically, in deciding how and where resources are obtained, logistics managers must understand the impact of their decisions on the environment. For example, in deciding where to purchase raw timber for producing furniture, the logistics manager should understand that excessive extraction of forest resources could destroy the local environment and lead to deforestation. Therefore, they should avoid purchasing from forests that have been heavily harvested. As it is increasingly evident that maintaining a good corporate image on being environment-friendly is critical for the success of the business, the logistics manager needs to identify environmentally relevant logistics activities and make environmentally responsible logistics decisions.

Having explored the incentives for businesses to invest in environmental management, we have to recognize the limitations for private business operations: they cannot accommodate much public interest in protecting the environment that cannot improve the business operation. To further improve the environmental performance and ensure sustainable development of the economy, it is necessary to establish public policies to regulate environmental practices in the logistics operation.

Public policies for environmental management in logistics operations

As stated in the overview, environmental logistics is not only about what logistics managers can do to improve environmental performance in the private industry, it should also include what the public should do to improve environmental performance in logistics operations. With effective environmental practices, firms will not only improve their own environmental performance, but will also benefit society by providing a clean, healthy, and productive environment for the public. On the other hand, irresponsible business operations generate negative environmental impacts, which in turn harm both the business operation and the public.

Private businesses, due to the scale of their operation and limited resources, may have limited capacity in dealing with environmental problems within their operation. Take recycling–remanufacturing as an example. For small firms, the cost in recapturing their ELC products and making them reusable may be too high because of the lack of economy-of-scale. If the recycling cost is higher than the cost savings obtained using the recycled parts or materials, they would rather purchase virgin materials for their production process. A study in assessing the motive for product recovery in engine remanufacturing (Seitz 2007) found that even in the automotive industry where the production size is large, the cost of recovering the used car/parts is still too high, and the supply of used engines (the core parts) is not stable. According to Seitz (2007), the automotive industry adopts reverse logistics and remanufacturing not for the financial incentive, but for its operational reasons—this is the only possible way to satisfy consumers' needs to rebuild and repair their vehicles within a short time period.

Regardless of the environmental performance of a private firm, if there is any waste discharge or emission to the environment, the firm will generate externality: the cost to the public, either in the form of damage, or the cost to clean up the polluted environment and restoration (like oil spill incidents). The impact of one individual's production (or consumption) decisions on the well-being of other individuals is called externality.

Environmental externality

Environmental externality exists when the uses of the environmental resources/ services from one individual affect the well-being of others in the same environment. If the external effect benefits the third party, this effect is a positive externality. If it generates cost to the third party, it is negative externality. As positive externality is not a concern in environmental logistics, in this chapter the term externality is exclusively used for negative externality.

Many different kinds of externalities are generated from almost every logistics activity, ranging from acquiring raw materials for production purposes, manufacturing, storing, and distributing, to finally delivering the products to the end user. Air emission from the transportation process, waste water from the manufacturing process, and the solid waste from the consumption of the final products are some of the inevitable "by-products" associated with these economic activities that brought sellers profits and consumers satisfaction. However, the degraded air quality, polluted environment, and the waste are left to the public to deal with.

Currently, there is no market for the environmental resources such as clean air and water, and a healthy and productive ecosystem. As such, there is no price tag on the use of such resources. Consequently, the cost to the environment is not fully reflected in the production decisions of private businesses. This will result in inefficiencies in resource utilization and the generation of environmental externalities. For example, the packaging material for a music CD (Textbox 12.1) creates environmental externalities for society.

Textbox 12.1 Environmental externality from the production and consumption of a music CD

Music compact disks (CDs) were sold in two boxes. The outer box was a 6-by-12-inch card box (long box) and the inside one a 5-by-5½-inch clear plastic jewel box. When consumers bought the music CD, they usually kept the CD in the jewel box, and threw the outer box away. This part of the packaging usually ended up at the municipal waste treatment facilities.

The costs associated with waste disposal were external to the producer, seller, and consumers of the music CD. The individual consumer did not pay the waste disposal cost specific to the long box in the trash bin. The producer was not charged by the number of long boxes in the disposal site that had its name on them. The cost was actually picked up by society—the municipal waste disposal site run by the government using tax money.

According to music company executives, there were two reasons for using the long box. First, the large size helped to discourage shoplifting. Second, the size of the long box just fit the existing display rack designed for 12-by-12-inch record album. There would have been an additional cost for the retailer to design special racks just for jewel box size CDs.

The use of the long box lasted for about a decade from 1982, until the environmental movement made both the industry and public aware of how their decisions adversely affected the environment. After April 1993, the whole industry started to use just the jewel box for music CDs.

The problem associated with environmental externality can be illustrated using Figure 12.11. In the figure, the MB line stands for the demand for music CDs at different levels, which is society's willingness to pay for one box of CDs, assuming all CDs are treated the same for simplicity. The MPC (marginal private cost)

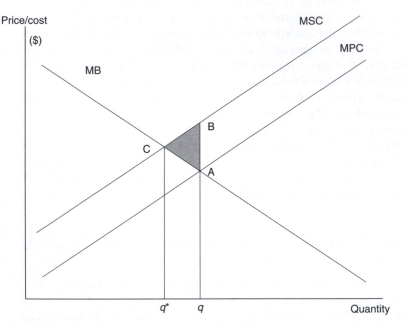

Figure 12.11 Illustration of environmental externality.

line stands for the cost to the music CD provider for producing one CD at different production levels.

When deciding on how many CDs to produce, the music CD producer will select the number of units (q) that makes the marginal benefit (MB) equal to the marginal cost (MPC) (at point A). Any production level other than q is not optimal from the producer's point of view. The producer can always increase the production to earn more profit if its output is less than q. On the other hand, it is not profitable to produce more than q, as the production cost is higher than what the consumers are willing to pay (WTP).

As neither the producer nor the consumer of the music CD pays for the waste disposal cost for the packaging material (long box), society has to pay for this part of the cost for each unit sold in the market. The MSC line in the figure stands for the Marginal Social Cost for the music CD box, which is the sum of the MPC and the disposal cost for each unit of CD. From society's point of view, the optimal level of production should be the one that makes the MSC equal to the MB, that is, point C on the graph.

As shown in the figure, the private optimal production level (q) is higher than the social optimal output (q^*), because the private production decision does not include the waste disposal cost—externality. If the music CD provider still decides to put q units into the market, there will be net social welfare losses for each unit between q^* and q, as the social cost (the private product cost and the disposal cost) is higher than the benefit (the consumers' willingness to pay) for that unit.

The net losses generated from the private production and consumption decision, defined as Dead Weight Losses (DWL), are the social welfare losses because of the externality. In this case, the invisible hand alone cannot guarantee the maximum efficiency in resource allocation. The private business will not automatically reduce its production to the socially optimal level. Therefore, some kind of public policy or government intervention is necessary, to tackle the problem.

Public policy toward reducing externality

Economic activities involve the production of waste residuals, in either energy or mass forms, and it is not possible to convert these residuals completely into useful forms through an economic process. The complete recycling of waste is neither possible nor economic. These waste residuals can become damaging pollutants if their flows into environmental sinks exceed the carrying capacity of these environmental media. These environmental externalities will have adverse impacts on people and economic activities. Today's and the future's economic development will be hindered by environmental externality.

There are different types of policy instruments for reducing environmental externalities and making best use of environmental resources. Some use the regulatory power of the government, while others harness the power of the free market. Regulatory measures, also called "command-and-control" measures, stipulate the maximum quantity of environmental externality (emission, waste, etc.) a firm can generate. Examples of market measures include tax, subsidy schemes, and marketable permits. These approaches modify the private production/consumption behavior by changing the price system. In the next section, some general properties for environmental policies are introduced, followed by a description of the policy instruments.

General properties for environmental policies

From an economics point of view, any environmental policy should meet two basic criteria. First, the total quantity of environmental externality to be reduced should be economically efficient. In other words, environmental externality should be maintained at the level where the cost to reduce an additional unit of externality should be equal to the damage of that unit of externality. Second, environmental externality should be reduced with minimum cost.

The first criterion explains the determination of efficient quantity (the level of externality to reduce), which is illustrated in Figure 12.12. The horizontal axis stands for the quantity of environmental externality generated in each time period. The downward sloping curve, named marginal abatement cost, stands for the cost to reduce one unit of the externality at different externality levels. The abatement cost decreases with the increase in the level of externality. For example, when the level of air pollution is high, the cost to improve air quality is relatively low compared with the cost to improve air quality when the air is already very clean. The quantity where marginal abatement cost is zero, that is, q, stands

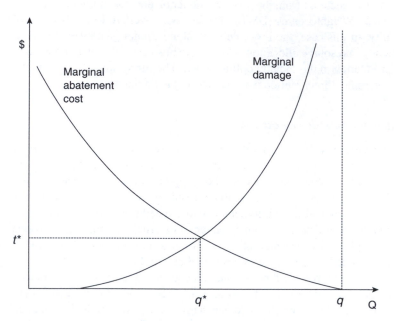

Figure 12.12 Determination of efficient pollution target.

for an uncontrolled level of externality. The upward sloping curve is the marginal damage of the externality. The marginal damage of the externality will increase with an increase of the externality level. Take air pollution as an example. When the air is clean, the health impact of air pollution is lower than that when the air is highly polluted.

To determine the optimal quantity of externality to abate, it is necessary to examine the relative position between marginal abatement cost and marginal damage. If the cost to reduce one unit of externality is higher than its damage (on the left of q^*), it is better not to reduce that unit, and let the externality grow. On the other hand, if the damage caused by one unit of externality is higher than the cost to reduce it (on the right of q^*), then it is better to spend money in reducing the externality, than to suffer from the damage of externality. Thus it is obvious that the economically efficient level of externality is q^*, and the optimal externality abatement is $q - q^*$.

After the abatement quantity is determined, the second criterion prescribes how to attain the environmental management target. There are many ways to meet this criterion, depending on the nature of the problem (see Figure 12.13 for illustration).

Assume that there are two firms in a region that produce a total of 90 units of emission. Firm A emits 40 units and firm B emits 50 units. The government wishes to reduce the air emission level from 90 units per period (the uncontrolled level) to 50 units per period. Firm A has lower marginal cost of abatement than

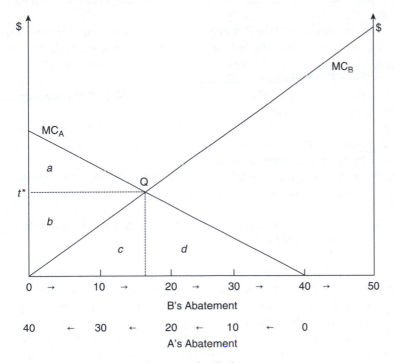

Figure 12.13 Least cost allocation of pollution quota.

firm B, due to the technology used in the transportation process. The relationship of the marginal cost of abatement for these two firms is shown in Figure 12.13.

The horizontal axis stands for the abatement quantity for A and B with different directions. From left to right, the abatement quantity for firm B increases, while from right to left is the abatement for firm A. As firm A only generates 40 units of emission, the maximum abatement for A is only 40.

At the left-most side of the horizontal axes, firm A has to abate all of the 40 units, and firm B continues to generate the 50 units. Moving away from that point means that firm A reduces one less unit, and firm B reduces one more unit. At any point left of Q, where the marginal cost of abatement for the two firms crosses, it is always better to let firm B reduce the unit, because B has lower marginal cost at that region. One the other hand, it is always better to let A abate to save the total abatement cost for that unit. Therefore, the best allocation of the abatement unit is at Q, where the marginal costs of the two firms are equal. At this point, the total abatement cost (the area $c + d$) is much less than the total cost if all the abatement is done by firm A (area $a + b + c + d$).

As stated before, there are many policy instruments that can be used to attain the goal of reducing environmental externality. To evaluate the property of each instrument, a number of criteria can be used, including:

1   Dependability: To what extent can the instrument be relied upon to achieve the goal?
2   Information requirements: How much information does the instrument require that the control authority has, and what are the costs of acquiring it?
3   Enforceability: How much monitoring is required for the instrument to be effective, and can compliance be enforced?
4   Long-run effects: Does the influence of the instrument strengthen, weaken, or remain constant over time?
5   Dynamic efficiency: Does the instrument create a continual incentive to improve products or production processes in ways that reduce the extent of externality for the given value of output?
6   Flexibility: Is the instrument capable of being adapted quickly and cheaply as new information arises, as conditions change, or as desired targets are altered?
7   Equity: What implications does the use of an instrument have for the distribution of income or wealth?

These criteria have different priorities for different nature of pollutants and from the perspective of different agents. For example, environmental policies addressing transportation of dangerous cargoes must make dependability a high priority criterion. Individual firms may prefer policy instruments that have higher dynamic efficiency, as this is consistent with the objective of business operation. Public agencies, on the other hand, may consider equity of the instrument more, to balance the interest from different sectors of the community. Therefore, in adopting individual policy instruments, it is necessary to consider the nature of the specific pollution generating industry, and the objectives of the policy making entity.

Government direct control methods

The most direct method in reducing environmental externality is for the government to announce directly the total amount of pollution to be reduced, and allocate this total amount to each of the firms who generate this pollutant. This method, often called a "command-and-control" instrument, is the most prevalent method of pollution control, whose success depends on the efficiency of the monitoring program, and the penalties for noncompliance. The most challenging part in allocating the quantity is that it is very difficult for the authority to know the marginal pollution abatement cost of every individual firm. Most of the time, the initial allocation is most likely not related to the marginal abatement cost of individual firms, due to the lack of information. In this case, the total pollution abatement target can be achieved, but not with the minimum cost.

Most of such direct control methods specify the environmental target in terms of the maximum permitted concentrations of pollutions in environmental media. Waste water discharge pollution management programs, for example, often require the effluent to meet some prescribed standards, before it can be discharged into the receiving water.

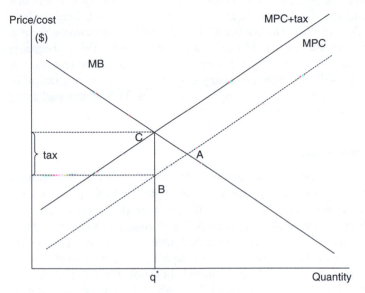

Figure 12.14 Tax policy for environmental externality.

Another variety of the command-and-control approach involves specifying required devices or technologies used in the production process or the pollution treatment process. Examples include the regulatory requirement to install catalytic converters in vehicle exhaust systems; maximum permitted lead content in engine fuels; the use of oil–water separation system in ocean-going vessels. Such measures are dependable, but not cost efficient as there is no incentive for the polluter to use other available least cost measures.

Tax on environmental externality

It is believed that market measures can achieve the best result in environmental management among all other environmental policies (Khanna and Anton 2002). These market measures give private firms incentives to adjust their production level through internalizing the externalities in the firm production process.

Let us continue to use the externality problem for the disposal of music CD packaging material as an example, to illustrate how to use market measures to improve efficiency in environmental management. If the government stipulates a tax policy that requires the music CD provider to pay tax for every unit of CD sold in the market, and the tax is set to the disposal cost for the music CD packaging material. In this case, in deciding how many CDs to produce, the music CD provider will equate the MPC + tax with the consumer's demand curve (in Figure 12.14).

It can be seen from the music CD example that the design of the tax rate is very important for the tax policy to be effective. First, the tax rate should be uniform, which means that the tax rate should be the same for the same type of CD that has the same long box. In other words, every producer who wants to keep the long box has to pay the same tax. This will make the externality control cost effective. Second, the level of the tax should equate the external cost. Third, the tax is imposed on externality, not on output. If a music CD provider eliminates the use of long boxes, this will not create externality and there will not be any tax for it. This can enable the private firm to use more environment-friendly packaging material for the music CD provider.

Tradable pollution permits

Another very flexible market mechanism in environmental pollution control is the tradable pollution permits. Using the same example outlined in the section "Government direct control method" (where the government wants to reduce the total emission from 90 units to 50 units), if the pollution quota (or abatement require-ment) is freely tradable in the market, the market trade of the permits (quota) will lead to efficient allocation of the permits (quota) regardless of the initial allocation.

For example, assuming that an arbitrary initial allocation of abatement requires firm A to reduce 30 units of pollution, and B to reduce 10 units of pollution, as shown by P1 line in Figure 12.15. The marginal cost of A is much higher than that of B. In this case, A is willing to purchase one permit from B so as to abate one unit less, as long as the payment required for obtaining the permit is less than its marginal cost. On the other hand, B is willing to accept the payment for abating one more unit of pollution, as long as the payment obtained from A is higher than the abatement cost for that unit. Therefore, if the initial allocation is P1, the abate-ment requirements for two firms will move toward the right by autonomous trade.

If the initial allocation is at P2 where B is required to abate 30 units and A is required to abate 10 units, firm B will have the incentive to purchase quotas from A, as long as the price of the quota is less than its marginal cost. Firm A is willing to be paid to abate more, as long as the payment obtained is higher than the abate-ment cost. As a result, the P2 line will move leftward with the process of trading.

When the marginal costs of the two firms are equal, there will be no incentive for either firm to make further trade. The equilibrium allocation of pollution permits is efficient, as illustrated in the section "Government direct control methods."

Compared with the tax policy, the tradable pollution permits are more depend-able, even when the cost function of individual firms is unknown. The distribu-tion issue of the tradable permits mostly depends on the way of initial allocation. Both the tax policy and the tradable pollution permits are flexible and dynami-cally efficient.

Value of environmental resources

Evaluation of environmental resources holds a central position in any environ-mental management decision-making process, including managing environmental

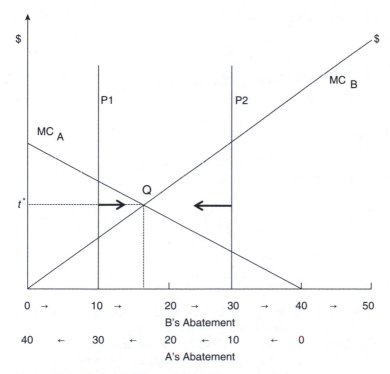

Figure 12.15 Illustration for tradable pollution permits.

externalities in the logistics process. When the public authority decides on an air-emission reduction amount, it has to balance the value of clean air to people, against the cost to achieve the target. Government policy on pollution tax, for example, has to be decided based on the cost of such pollution to the people, and this is also of value to the environment.

Unfortunately, most environment resources do not have a market where the prices of them can be revealed. For example, there is no market for clean air and water, two of the most important inputs to almost all economic activities. A very small number of environmental resources do have market prices, but their prices do not necessarily represent their social value. The market value of forest products, for example, only represents the use value as timber. It does not take into account the value of forests in regulating local and global environmental conditions.

The value of an environmental resource, as shown in Figure 12.16, includes intrinsic value and use value. Intrinsic value comes from the ethical consideration that resource has its own right of existence, which is not subject to economic analysis because it is independent of human use. The use value is the value derived from actual or potential future consumption of goods or services, which includes current use value, option value, quasi-option value, and existence value.

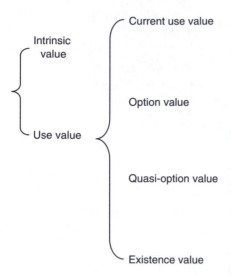

Figure 12.16 Value of environmental resources.

- *Current use value*: The utility gained by an individual from the consumption of goods or services, or vicariously from the consumption by others (e.g., parents may obtain utility from their children's consumption).
- *Option value*: The value for having an option to goods or services for which future demand is uncertain. It is an addition to the utility that may arise if the goods are actually consumed. When there is no uncertainty about future use, the option value is zero.
- *Quasi-option value*: The utility gain obtained by not taking irreversible decisions, and so by maintaining options for future use of some resources. If the decision is reversible, there will be no gain to defer the decision, because it can always be reversed at a later stage.
- *Existence value*: Human preferences for the existence of resources as such, not related to any application of the resources.

These four basic categories make up the total economic value of environmental resources. Valuation of the total economic value presents a big challenge in the decision-making process for projects that have significant negative impacts on environmental resources. The principle of economic valuation of environmental resources is based on the utility theory, a systematic theoretical framework describing an individual's level of satisfaction with different levels and combinations of consumption (Hanley *et al.* 1997). People prefer to live in a better environment. The quality of the environment is actually like goods/services that contribute to the satisfaction of an individual. People are WTP for an improvement in environmental quality; if the environmental quality is degraded, some compensation (willingness to accept, WTA) is necessary for them to maintain the same level of satisfaction. These two measures (WTP and WTA) provide the foundation for the economic evaluation of environmental resources. Different methods have been developed by environmental economists to estimate the economic value of different environmental goods or services. These have proven to be successful in helping logistics managers to decide the optimal level of environmental protection activities (Perman *et al.* 1996, pp. 264–265).

International laws, conventions, and standards on logistics environmental management

With the increasing trends in globalization, most environmental externalities generated from business logistics activities are having a much wider impact area, which has aroused intensive concern from the international society. Many international agreements have been developed to regulate business operations, including purchase of raw materials, transportation, and disposal of final waste. Next is a summary of key international environmental agreements that have impacts on logistics activities.

- Convention on the International Trade in Endangered Species of Wild Fauna and Flora (CITES)

This is one of the earliest international environmental agreements, with the main objective of controlling the trade of endangered species, their parts as well as products derived from them. It was drawn up in 1973 and entered into force in 1975. The affected sectors include agriculture, fishery, forestry, and pharmaceuticals industries.

- United Nations Convention on the Law of the Sea (UNCLOS)

In addition to the main objectives of providing ground rules for international relations with respect to the sea and ocean, UNCLOS has also established a comprehensive legal mechanism to prevent, reduce, and control marine pollution, which has significant impacts on offshore mining, maritime transportation, and waste treatment and disposal. Many activities in this legal mechanism are implemented by special technical organizations such as the International Maritime Organization (IMO).

- Vienna Convention on Substances that Deplete the Stratospheric Ozone Layer, with Montreal Protocol

This convention aims to control chemical gases that adversely affect the stratospheric ozone layer. Most of the chemicals in this category are used as cooling agents in many kinds of air conditioning devices. It has impact on logistics activities in the production of air conditioning equipment, as well as the transportation sectors that employ air conditioning.

- Basel Convention on the Control of Transboundary Movement of Hazardous Wastes and Their Disposal

The purpose of this convention is to minimize the generation of hazardous waste, and to prohibit the export of hazardous waste to countries that refuse to import them. This convention has significant implications on firms which generate hazardous waste and logistics companies which deal with storage and transport hazardous waste.

- Convention on Biological Diversity

The objective of the convention is to conserve biological diversity and sustainable use of its components, and to ensure fair and equitable sharing of the benefits arising from the use of genetic resources. It also has provisions for genetically modified organisms from the biotech industry that might have an adverse impact on biological diversity.

- Framework Convention on Climate Change (FCCC)

The objective of this convention is to initiate international cooperation in alleviating the global climate change by reducing greenhouse gas emission. The important consideration for the logistics industry is to reduce the consumption of fuel, increase fuel efficiency, and reduce CO_2 emissions.

- Rotterdam Convention on the Prior Informed Consent (PIC) Procedure for Certain Hazardous Chemicals and Pesticides in International Trade

This convention aims to protect human health and the environment by requiring export countries to show the contents of hazardous chemicals and pesticides in exporting commodities, so that import countries can decide whether or not to import them.

- Cartagena Protocol on Biosafety (Protocol to the Convention on Biological Diversity)

This protocol to the convention on biological diversity focuses on minimizing the risks associated with living modified organisms (LMOs)—living organisms that possess a new combination of genetic material produced by modern biotechnology. It involves the production processes of pharmaceutical and canned food companies in purchasing decisions and the transportation sector.

- International Standard on Environmental Management (ISO 14000)

Developed by the International Organization of Standardization, this is a collection of international specifications and guidelines for implementing environmental management systems. It includes guidelines for environmental auditing, environmental labeling, environmental performance evaluation, and life cycle analysis.

Summary

This chapter promotes the concept of environmental logistics, which is a systematic process to address the environmental problems generated from economic activities, from not only the perspective of private businesses, but also that of governments (at local and international level). Due to the central position of the logistics manager in the business operation, and the intensive interactions of logistics activities with the environment, environmental logistics will gain increasing popularity with increasing environmental awareness of the general public, and ever-heightening environmental challenges and environmental stress faced by human beings. Business logistics and the environment will be closely interlinked for continuation of today's economic development and for future generations.

Note

1 Reverse logistics is defined as the process of planning, implementing, and controlling the efficient, cost-effective flow of raw materials, in-process inventory, finished goods, and related information from the point of consumption to the point of origin for the purpose of recapturing or creating value or proper disposal. (Rogers and Tibben-Lembke 1999).

Bibliography

Black, W.R. 2010. *Sustainable Transportation—Problems and Solutions,* New York: The Guilford Press.

Brewer, A.M., K.J. Button, and D.A. Hensher. 2001. *The Handbook of Logistics and Supply-Chain Management.* London: Pergamon/Elsevier.

Brundtland, G.H. (ed.) 1987. *Our Common Future: The World Commission on Environment and Development.* New York: Oxford University Press.

Carter, C.R. and M.M. Jennings. 2002. "Logistics Social Responsibility: An Integrative Framework," *Journal of Business Logistics,* 23(1): 145–180.

Datamonitor. 2008. *Logistics Industry Profile: Global.* [Online] Available at: www.datamonitor.com [Accessed 3 December 2010].

Golicic, S.L., C.N. Boerstler, and L.M. Ellram. 2010. "'Greening' Transportation in the Supply Chain," *MITSloan Management Review,* 51(2): 46–55.

Gonzalez-Benito, J. and O. Gonzalez-Benito. 2006. "The Role of Stakeholder Pressure and Managerial Values in the Implementation of Environmental Logistics Practices," *International Journal of Production Research,* 44(7): 1353–1373.

Hanley, N., J.F. Shogren, and B. White. 1997. *Environmental Economics in Theory and Practice.* New York: Oxford University Press.

Hardin, G., 1968. "The Tragedy of the Commons," *Science,* 162: 1243–1248.

Hauser, W. and R.T. Lund. 2003. *The Remanufacturing Industry: Anatomy of a Giant.* Boston, MA: Boston University.

ISO-14020, 2000. *Environmental Labels and Declarations—General Principles.* [Online] Available at: http://www.iso.org/iso/catalogue_detail?csnumber=34425 [Accessed 5 December 2010].

Khanna, M. and W.R.Q. Anton. 2002. "Corporate Environmental Management: Regulatory and Market-Based Incentives," *Land Economics,* 78(4): 539–558.

Matsushita Group. 2007. *Matsushita Group Environmental Data Book 2007.* [Online] Available at: http://www.panasonic.net/eco/env_data/back_number/pdf/edb06e.pdf [Accessed 3 December 2010].

Murphy, P.P., R.F. Poist, and C.D. Braunschweig. 1996. "Green Logistics: Comparative Views of Environmental Progressives, Moderates and Conservatives," *Journal of Business Logistics,* 17, 191–211.

Orlitzky, M., F.L. Schmidt, and S.L. Rynes. 2003. "Corporate Social and Financial Performance: A Meta-Analysis," *Organization Studies*, 24, 403–441.

Perman, R., Y. Ma, and J. McGilvray. 1996. *Natural Resource & Environmental Economics*. London: Longman.

Rodrigues, A.M., D.J. Bowersox, and R.J. Calantone. 2005. "Estimation of Global and National Logistics Expenditures: 2002 Data Update," *Journal of Business Logistics*, 26, 1–15.

Rogers, D. and R. Tibben-Lembke. 1999. "Reverse Logistics: Strategies et Techniques," *Logistique & Management*, 7, 15–26.

SAIC. 2006. *Life Cycle Assessment: Principles and Practice*. McLean, VA: Scientific Application International Corporation.

Sarkis, J. and J.C. Janes. 2001. "An Empirical Evaluation of Environmental Efficiencies and Firms Performance: Pollution Prevention Versus End-of-Pipe Practice," *European Journal of Operational Research*, 135, 102–113.

Seitz, M.A. 2007. "A Critical Assessment of Motives for Product Recovery: The Case of Engine Remanufacturing," *Journal of Cleaner Production*, 15, 1147–1157.

USEPA. 1998. *Environmental Labeling Issues, Policies, and Practices Worldwide*. [Online] Available at: http://www.epa.gov/epp/pubs/wwlabel3.pdf [Accessed 5 December 2010].

Wu, H.-J. and S.C. Dunn. 1994. "Environmentally Responsible Logistics Systems," *International Journal of Physical Distribution & Logistics Management*, 25, 20–38.

Index